Leadership Perspectives

Leadership Perspectives

Edited by

Alan Hooper

The Centre for Leadership Studies, University of Exeter, UK

ASHGATE

Published by
Ashgate Publishing Limited
Gower House
Croft Road
Aldershot
Hampshire GU11 3HR
England

Ashgate Publishing Company
Suite 420
101 Cherry Street
Burlington, VT 05401-4405
USA

Ashgate website: http://www.ashgate.com

British Library Cataloguing in Publication Data
Leadership perspectives
 1. Leaderhship
 I. Hooper, Alan, 1941–
 658.4'092
 L EA
Library of Congress Control Number: 2006928397

ISBN: 0 7546 2612 1
ISBN: 978-0-7546-2612-1

Printed in Great Britain by TJ International Ltd, Padstow, Cornwall

Contents

PART III POWER AND LEADERSHIP

PART IV LEADERSHIP, IDENTITY AND DIFFERENCE

PART V   IMAGINATION

PART VI SPIRITUALITY IN ORGANIZATIONS

Acknowledgements

The editors and publishers wish to thank the following for permission to use copyright material.

Blackwell Publishing for the essays: Bertrand Russell (1986), 'The Forms of Power', in Steven Lukes (ed.), *Power: A Radical Review*, Basingstoke: Palgrave Macmillan, pp. 19–27; John Kenneth Galbraith (1986), 'Power and Organization', in Steven Lukes (ed.), *Power: A Radical Review*, Basingstoke: Palgrave Macmillan, pp. 211–28; Robert Dahl (1986), 'Power as the Control of Behavior', in Steven Lukes (ed.), *Power: A Radical Review*, Basingstoke: Palgrave Macmillan, pp. 37–58; Willa Bruce and John Novinson (1999), 'Spirituality in Public Service: A Dialogue', *Public Administration Review*, **59**, pp. 163–69.

Copyright Clearance for the essay: Jeffrey Pfeffer (1977), 'The Ambiguity of Leadership', *Academy of Management Review*, **2**, pp. 104–12. Copyright © 1977 Academy of Management.

Elsevier for the essays: Chi-Sum Wong and Kenneth S. Law (2002), 'The Effects of Leader and Follower Emotional Intelligence on Performance and Attitude: An Exploratory Study', *Leadership Quarterly*, **13**, pp. 243–74. Copyright © 2002 Elsevier Science Inc.; John Antonakis and Leanne Atwater (2002), 'Leader Distance: A Review and a Proposed Theory', *Leadership Quarterly*, **13**, pp. 673–704. Copyright © 2002 Elsevier Science Inc.

Harvard Business School Publishing Corporation for the essays: John P. Kotter (1990), 'What Leaders Really Do', *Harvard Business Review*, **90**, pp. 103–11. Copyright © 1990 Harvard Business School Publishing Corporation. All rights reserved; Michael Maccoby (2004), 'Narcissistic Leaders: The Incredible Pros, the Inevitable Cons', *Harvard Business Review*, January, pp. 1–9 [Original pp. 92–101]. Copyright © 2004 Harvard Business School Publishing Corporation. All rights reserved; Jonathan Gosling and Henry Mintzberg (2003), 'The Five Minds of a Manager', *Harvard Business Review*, November, pp. 1–9 [Original pp. 54–63]. Copyright © 2003 Harvard Business School Publishing Corporation. All rights reserved; Robert Tannenbaum and Warren H. Schmidt (1973), 'How to Choose a Leadership Pattern', *Harvard Business Review*, May–June, pp. 3–12. Copyright © 1973 Harvard Business School Publishing Corporation. All rights reserved; Daniel Goleman (2000), 'Leadership that Gets Results', *Harvard Business Review*, March–April, pp. 79–90. Copyright © 2000 Harvard Business School Publishing Corporation. All rights reserved; Jay A. Conger (1998), 'The Necessary Art of Persuasion', *Harvard Business Review*, May–June, pp. 84–95. Copyright © 1998 Harvard Business School Publishing Corporation. All rights reserved; James Waldroop and Timothy Butler (1996), 'The Executive as Coach', *Harvard Business Review*, November–December, pp. 111–17. Copyright © 1998 Harvard Business School Publishing Corporation. All rights reserved; Holly Weeks (2001), 'Taking the Stress Out of Stressful Conversations', *Harvard*

Introduction

Leadership is such a vast subject that it is quite daunting when a publisher asks you to produce a book containing the best published essays on this topic. However, it is easier to accept this challenge with the help of associates, and I am greatly indebted to the work of my colleagues at or associated with the Centre for Leadership Studies, University of Exeter, for their assistance in editing this collection. This has been very much a team effort that is, after all, an essential part of leadership. The members of the editorial team were: Group Captain Dan Archer, Professor Peter Case, Professor Jonathan Gosling, Professor Alan Hooper, Mr Pat Lyons, Mr David Pearce, Doctor John Potter and Doctor Martin Wood. The team was most ably supported by Mrs Tricia Doherty.

The purpose of this publication is to meet a need of all those who have an interest in leadership, be they students at business schools, academic researchers, leadership consultants or practical leaders. I have acted in all these capacities, and one of the recurring issues has been what are the key writings on leadership – and where do I find them? Well, at last, we have a collection of 33 essays and book chapters in one volume.

When the editorial team sat down to consider the publication we agreed on two guiding principles, and also acknowledged an overriding practical consideration. First, we agreed that we would only consider essays from peer-reviewed journals and self-contained book chapters. This guaranteed that the selection had already been subjected to a rigorous process of peer review and editing. Second, after much discussion, we agreed on six core themes. These six core themes emerged out of a series of detailed and fascinating discussions representing the diverse views of the editorial team. It was agreed that, where possible, each theme should contain some five essays ranging from key classic texts on the original root of the ideas through to recent essays on interpretation and application. This would provide the reader with a full range of essays on a particular theme in one volume – something that has not been done before.

After much deliberation, we decided to divide the volume into six parts covering the following themes:

- Understanding Leadership
- Relationships
- Power and Leadership
- Leadership, Identity and Difference
- Imagination
- Spirituality in Organizations

Whilst these themes offer a wide view on leadership, and were chosen specifically to cover a broad spectrum, such an approach cannot claim to produce a definitive list of essays. Turning now to the format of the book, we decided to write separate introductions for each of the six core themes. These explain the thinking behind the selection of the various essays for each theme and also provide a guide to their key points. It is suggested that the reader cast their eye over these before reading the essays in the relevant parts.

As has been mentioned above, this volume does not claim to provide a definitive set of readings. However, it is hoped that this publication will satisfy the need that has been identified and thus make it much easier for people to access some of the best published writing on leadership.

A final thought. The renewed interest in the topic of leadership in the past few years has led to an explosion in published works on this intriguing topic. This has led to a dynamic that both refers back to some of the classic essays and also embraces new approaches and ideas. 'Leadership' is thus a 'living' topic that embraces an international population including the academic researcher, the business student and the practical leader. It is therefore hoped that this publication is the first of a series of collected essays on leadership.

Notes on the Editorial Team

Group Captain Dan Archer is a graduate of the University of Exeter's Centre for Leadership Studies MA programme. His specific area of interest lies in the leadership of change and the role of leadership within organizational culture and development, as well as the concept of facilitated leadership exchanges. He has wide experience in leadership development, having been an instructor on Initial Officer Training, and also commander of the Airmen's Command Squadron.

Peter Case was Professor of Leadership and Organizational Studies at the Centre for Leadership Studies, University of Exeter, from 2003 until 2005. He is a sociologist by training and his research interests revolve around the manner in which humans pursue strategies of self-defeat in the organizations they co-create and the means by which such strategies are rationalized. He contributes regularly to management education workshops throughout Europe, and is a chair of the International Standing Conference on Organizational Symbolism. He joined the University of the West of England, Bristol Business School, as Professor of Organization Studies, in September 2005.

Jonathan Gosling is Director of the Centre for Leadership Studies and Head of Executive Education School of Business and Economics at the University of Exeter. He has designed and directed development programmes for many companies, focusing in particular on international and rapidly changing businesses. His current research looks at how leadership can foster continuity through tough transitions. Jonathan was co-founder of the International Masters Program in Practicing Management (IMPM), a collaboration of business schools around the world.

Alan Hooper is the founder and first Director of the Centre for Leadership Studies, University of Exeter. He is also a visiting Professor at British Business School. Formerly a colonel in the Royal Marines, Alan has broad leadership experience at the strategic level and consults widely on leadership and change management with a particular focus on helping people realize their leadership potential. He is the author of four books.

Pat Lyons is Chief Executive of Europa Academy and Human Resource Director of Glencullen Holdings. With a background in Human Resource, Marketing and Commercial Management, his career has encompassed senior positions within several multinational organizations. An experienced leadership development professional, he has a proven track record in creating and delivering high-value and effective business solutions for clients, especially within leadership, team and personal effectiveness projects. He has worked in Europe and Africa with a range of private and public sector organizations, including the University of Exeter, the Open University Business School and the Irish Management Institute. His professional and research interests lie in the areas of leadership, emotion in organizations and team development.

David Pearce is an independent coach and facilitator in management and leadership development. He assisted in the founding of Ashridge Consulting, and has been an associate tutor, consultant, coach and facilitator at Ashridge Management College for 25 years. David worked on the creation of a senior management leadership programme at GEC, utilizing action learning principles. This work was captured in the book *More than Management Development, Action Learning at GEC*, edited by David Casey and David Pearce (ANCOM, 1977).

Dr John Potter is a Chartered Psychologist with a PhD in Leadership. His current work is in management development with a particular interest in leadership, corporate culture and teamwork. John specializes in training and development programmes involving the whole workforce and promoting their commitment to the corporate vision and mission. He is joint author, with Alan Hooper, of *Intelligent Leadership* (Random House, 2000).

Dr Martin Wood is a former Programme Director for the Masters Degree in Leadership Studies at the Centre for Leadership Studies, University of Exeter. His research interests include process metaphysics and post-structural approaches to organization theory. In January 2005 he joined the Department of Management Studies at the University of York as a Senior Lecturer in Social Theory and Organization. He has published in top international organization studies, social science and applied health care journals and has also authored significant reports aimed at influencing national practice in the UK National Health Service.

Part I
Understanding Leadership

Introduction to Part I

Understanding Leadership

Alan Hooper

'Leadership' is a word that is used frequently in our everyday lives, and yet there appears to be little common understanding about what it really means. For instance, when we talk about 'leadership' are we referring to the qualities of a particular leader? Are we reflecting on the difference between leadership and management? Or are we talking about the leadership issues in an organization? This lack of clarity about the word 'leadership' is not solely due to the richness of the English language, it is also affected by the changing nature of leadership (such as the shift from autocracy to empowerment), by the constant change of the environment in which leadership operates and also by our growing comprehension about the different aspects of this illusive topic.

A significant contribution to our growing understanding about leadership has been made by Chris Argyris. In his excellent essay, 'Teaching Smart People How to Learn' (1991), he revealed that the dilemma for companies was the fact that it was the smartest people who found it the hardest to learn. As there are a lot of smart people at the top of organizations, it is therefore hardly surprising that 'understanding' leadership has been difficult. It has also not been helped by the fact that leadership has often been associated with doing – taking decisions and action – rather than with thoughtful reflection. This tendency towards 'single-loop' as opposed to 'double-loop' learning (Argyris, 1991, p.100) has led to the perception that there are not many thoughtful leaders. This perception is not true (consider Mahatma Gandhi and Nelson Mandela), but the myth persists.

Thankfully, much has been written in the last few years to enable us to gain a better understanding of the nature of leadership. The five essays in Part I explore this topic by examining the difference between leadership and management; managerial mindsets; narcissism; organizational totalitarianism; and the learning organization.

In the first essay John Kotter points out that leadership and management are both distinctive and complementary systems – and that not everyone can be good at both. Kotter's distinction between the two is that '[m]anagement is about coping with complexity' whereas 'Leadership, by contrast, is about coping with change' (p. 8). He then goes on to discuss in some detail the different processes between leadership and management (for example, setting a direction versus planning and budgeting; motivating people versus controlling and problem-solving). His major contribution is the explanation of the distinctive leadership and management roles in practical terms, reinforced with appropriate case studies. This, in turn, shows why it is difficult to be good at both. However, Kotter points out (p. 13) that the best companies have an ability to develop outstanding 'leader-managers' by introducing significant challenges early in their careers, and providing continual growth opportunities as these individuals progress up the managerial ladder.

In Chapter 4 Jonathan Gosling and Henry Mintzberg agree with Kotter that management is complicated and also stress that 'the separation of management from leadership is dangerous' (p. 41). Their significant contribution to the understanding of leadership is their finding that in order to focus not only on what needs to be done, but also on how they have to think, managers need various 'mindsets'. They stress the need for both action *and* reflection, which involves five perspectives:

- Managing self: the reflective mind-set
- Managing organisations: the analytic mind-set
- Managing context: the worldly mind-set
- Managing relationships: the collaborative mind-set
- Managing change: the action mind-set (p. 42).

This essay takes the thinking a step further than Kotter in that it addresses the difficult areas of leadership and management and acknowledges the complexity. In particular, Gosling and Mintzberg challenge some of the accepted conventions ('the problem for many managers today … is not a lack of analysis but too much of it – at least, too much conventional analysis' (p. 45)); point out the realities ('[t]his is a world made up of edges and boundaries, like a patchwork' (p. 46)); and indicate how to achieve success by 'moving towards a more engaging style. Engaging managers listen more than they talk' (p. 47). Their recipe for success in the action mindset 'is to mobilize energy around those things that need changing, while being careful to maintain the rest' (p. 48). The problem is that, as sound as this advice is, those people who oppose change tend to maintain the status quo with a persistent and annoying stubbornness.

However, Gosling and Mintzberg stress the need to consider the five mindsets as a whole and point out that '[e]ffective organizations tailor handsome results out of the woven mindsets of their managers' (p. 49).

This poetic language is in contrast to the world of the superstar CEOs. In Chapter 3 Michael Maccoby explores the characteristics of narcissistic leaders who are egotistical and self-promoting, with larger-than-life personalities. Throughout history such individuals have shaped the destiny of countries and organizations through their vision and their ability to inspire people. These are the leaders that people talk about. They fascinate us because it is difficult to understand why they are so effective, especially as many seem to lack empathy. It is in helping us to understand narcissistic leaders that Maccoby's work is so useful, especially because such individuals can be dangerous for organizations.

Maccoby provides three reasons why business leaders have higher profiles today: first, the fact that nowadays business plays a bigger role in our lives; second, the enormous changes in the business world, which call for more visionary leadership; and, third, the change in the personality of strategic leaders at the top (pp. 31–32). He goes on to explain that there are two types of narcissism: 'productive' and 'non-productive', and then considers their strengths and weaknesses.

The strengths are well understood (for example, great vision and an ability to attract followers) but the weaknesses are less so, and are therefore worth exploring because these can be the root cause of failure. Maccoby identifies these as being sensitive to criticism, being poor listeners, lacking empathy, distaste for mentoring and an intense desire to compete (pp.

35–37). These characteristics could be considered to be typical of many individualistic leaders which, in excess, could lead to self-destruction.

Maccoby's essay includes some useful advice for how such leaders can avoid the traps, and how others can best work with them. Given the energy which surrounds such individuals and the significant impact they can have on organizations, for good or ill, it is easy to see why the *Harvard Business Review* included this essay in both its *Best of HBR in 2000* and *Inside the Mind of the Leader* edition in 2004.

Narcissism also features in Howard Schwartz's essay (Chapter 2). Here, the emphasis switches to the organization, and Schwartz's thesis is based on the premise that 'the perfect organization' does not exist, but because people fail to accept that fact, many organizations delude themselves, which is both dangerous and non-productive. Such organizations tend to live out the narcissistic fantasies of those in power (p. 17). An extreme example of this was the Nazi party where officials wielded power 'even over their nominal superiors through their capacity for denunciation' (p. 23).

Such self-delusion can lead to those at or near the top of the hierarchy being perceived as representing 'the organizational ideal'. The fantasy is played out through 'passivity and slavishness, shamefulness, cynicism, loneliness' (p. 17). All of this can have a real impact on output because 'in the totalitarian organization, productive work comes to be less important than the maintenance of narcissistic fantasy' (p. 28). There are many organizations with these characteristics, and Schwartz helps us to understand why this is so.

The final essay in Part I has made a major contribution to our understanding of the 'learning organization.' At the beginning of his essay, Peter Senge points out that 'superior performance depends on superior learning' (p. 51), and that this develops effectively within an organization which is not only inquisitive, but also generates and adapts its learning, constantly adjusting to the changing environment. This dynamism requires leadership, but a different type to that of the past in which the emphasis has been on '*heroes* – great men (and occasionally women) who rise to the fore in times of crisis' (p. 52–53). In contrast, leadership in learning organizations requires a more subtle and adaptive approach.

Senge then explains that the key to a learning organization is leadership – and this starts with the creative tension between the vision and current reality (p. 53). This requires leaders to adopt the critical roles of designer, teacher and steward. These three roles are explained in detail, as are the skills and tools required to achieve the appropriate kind of leadership. In this essay, Senge brings together very effectively the essential thinking of the late 1980s and early 1990s, which has since become the cornerstone of effective leadership (namely, leader as teacher and steward, building a shared vision, systems thinking, coaching and so on). It is significant that the organizations that have managed change best in the last decade (such as BP, GE and the British military) are those that have become true 'learning organizations'. The key is proper empowerment which is well summarized at the end of the essay in the words of Lao Tsu:

> The great leader is he who the people say 'We did it ourselves.' (p. 66)

This section on 'Understanding Leadership' is not all-embracing (that would be impossible), but the five selected essays give us an insight into key aspects of leadership and thus enable us to have a better understanding of this complicated, illusive and fascinating subject.

Reference

Argyris, Chris (1991), 'Teaching Smart People How to Learn', *Harvard Business Review*, May–June, pp. 99–109.

[1]

Good management controls complexity;
effective leadership produces useful change.

What Leaders Really Do

by John P. Kotter

Leadership is different from management, but not for the reasons most people think. Leadership isn't mystical and mysterious. It has nothing to do with having "charisma" or other exotic personality traits. It is not the province of a chosen few. Nor is leadership necessarily better than management or a replacement for it.

Rather, leadership and management are two distinctive and complementary systems of action. Each has its own function and characteristic activities. Both are necessary for success in an increasingly complex and volatile business environment.

Most U.S. corporations today are overmanaged and underled. They need to develop their capacity to exercise leadership. Successful corporations don't wait for leaders to come along. They actively seek out peo-

John P. Kotter is professor of organizational behavior at the Harvard Business School and the author of The General Managers *(Free Press, 1982),* Power and Influence *(Free Press, 1985), and* The Leadership Factor *(Free Press, 1988). His most recent book is* A Force for Change: How Leadership Differs from Management *(Free Press, 1990).*

ple with leadership potential and expose them to career experiences designed to develop that potential. Indeed, with careful selection, nurturing, and encouragement, dozens of people can play important leadership roles in a business organization.

> Leadership complements
> management;
> it doesn't replace it.

But while improving their ability to lead, companies should remember that strong leadership with weak management is no better, and is sometimes actually worse, than the reverse. The real challenge is to combine strong leadership and strong management and use each to balance the other.

Of course, not everyone can be good at both leading and managing. Some people have the capacity to become excellent managers but not strong leaders. Others have great leadership potential but, for a variety of reasons, have great difficulty becoming strong managers. Smart companies value both kinds of people and work hard to make them a part of the team.

But when it comes to preparing people for executive jobs, such companies rightly ignore the recent literature that says people cannot manage *and* lead. They try to develop leader-managers. Once companies understand the fundamental difference between leadership and management, they can begin to groom their top people to provide both.

The Difference Between Management and Leadership

Management is about coping with complexity. Its practices and procedures are largely a response to one of the most significant developments of the twentieth century: the emergence of large organizations. Without good management, complex enterprises tend to become chaotic in ways that threaten their very existence. Good management brings a degree of order and consistency to key dimensions like the quality and profitability of products.

Leadership, by contrast, is about coping with change. Part of the reason it has become so important in recent years is that the business world has become more competitive and more volatile. Faster technological change, greater international competition, the deregulation of markets, overcapacity in capital-intensive industries, an unstable oil cartel, raiders with junk bonds, and the changing demographics of the work force are among the many factors that have contributed to this shift. The net result is that doing what was done yesterday, or doing it 5% better, is no longer a formula for success. Major changes are more and more necessary to survive and compete effectively in this new environment. More change always demands more leadership.

Consider a simple military analogy: a peacetime army can usually survive with good administration and management up and down the hierarchy, coupled with good leadership concentrated at the very top. A wartime army, however, needs competent leadership at all levels. No one yet has figured out how to manage people effectively into battle; they must be *led*.

These different functions – coping with complexity and coping with change – shape the characteristic activities of management and leadership. Each system of action involves deciding what needs to be done, creating networks of people and relationships that can accomplish an agenda, and then trying to ensure that those people actually do the job. But each accomplishes these three tasks in different ways.

Companies manage complexity first by *planning and budgeting* – setting targets or goals for the future (typically for the next month or year), establishing detailed steps for achieving those targets, and then allocating resources to accomplish those plans. By contrast, leading an organization to constructive change begins by *setting a direction* – developing a vision of the future (often the distant future) along with strategies for producing the changes needed to achieve that vision.

Management develops the capacity to achieve its plan by *organizing and staffing* – creating an organizational structure and set of jobs for accomplishing plan requirements, staffing the jobs with qualified individuals, communicating the plan to those people, delegating responsibility for carrying out the plan, and devising systems to monitor implementation. The equivalent leadership activity, however, is *aligning people*. This means communicating the new direction to those who can create coalitions that understand the vision and are committed to its achievement.

Finally, management ensures plan accomplishment by *controlling and problem solving* – monitoring results versus the plan in some detail, both formally and informally, by means of reports, meetings, and other tools; identifying deviations; and then planning and organizing to solve the problems. But for leadership, achieving a vision requires *motivating and inspiring* – keeping people moving in the right direction, despite major obstacles to change, by appealing to basic but often untapped human needs, values, and emotions.

A closer examination of each of these activities will help clarify the skills leaders need.

Setting a Direction vs. Planning and Budgeting

Since the function of leadership is to produce change, setting the direction of that change is fundamental to leadership.

Setting direction is never the same as planning or even long-term planning, although people often confuse the two. Planning is a management process, deductive in nature and designed to produce orderly results, not change. Setting a direction is more inductive. Leaders gather a broad range of data and look for patterns, relationships, and linkages that help explain things. What's more, the direction-setting aspect of leadership does not produce plans; it creates vision and strategies. These describe a business, technology, or corporate culture in terms of what it should become over the long term and articulate a feasible way of achieving this goal.

Most discussions of vision have a tendency to degenerate into the mystical. The implication is that a vision is something mysterious that mere mortals, even talented ones, could never hope to have. But developing good business direction isn't magic. It is a tough, sometimes exhausting process of gathering and analyzing information. People who articulate such visions aren't magicians but broadbased strategic thinkers who are willing to take risks.

Nor do visions and strategies have to be brilliantly innovative; in fact, some of the best are not. Effective business visions regularly have an almost mundane quality, usually consisting of ideas that are already well known. The particular combination or patterning of the ideas may be new, but sometimes even that is not the case.

For example, when CEO Jan Carlzon articulated his vision to make Scandinavian Airline Systems (SAS) the best airline in the world for the frequent business traveler, he was not saying anything that everyone in the airline industry didn't already know. Business travelers fly more consistently than other market segments and are generally willing to pay higher fares. Thus focusing on business customers offers an airline the possibility of high margins, steady business, and considerable growth. But in an industry known more for bureaucracy than vision, no company had ever put these simple ideas together and dedicated itself to implementing them. SAS did, and it worked.

What's crucial about a vision is not its originality but how well it serves the interests of important constituencies – customers, stockholders, employees – and how easily it can be translated into a realistic competitive strategy. Bad visions tend to ignore the legitimate needs and rights of important constituencies – favoring, say, employees over customers or stockholders. Or they are strategically unsound. When a company that has never been better than a weak competitor in an industry suddenly starts talking about becoming number one, that is a pipe dream, not a vision.

One of the most frequent mistakes that overmanaged and underled corporations make is to embrace "long-term planning" as a panacea for their lack of direction and inability to adapt to an increasingly competitive and dynamic business environment. But such an approach misinterprets the nature of direction setting and can never work.

Long-term planning is always time consuming. Whenever something unexpected happens, plans have to be redone. In a dynamic business environment, the unexpected often becomes the norm, and long-term planning can become an extraordinarily burdensome activity. This is why most successful corporations limit the time frame of their planning activities. Indeed, some even consider "long-term planning" a contradiction in terms.

In a company without direction, even short-term planning can become a black hole capable of absorbing an infinite amount of time and energy. With no vision and strategy to provide constraints around the planning process or to guide it, every eventuality deserves a plan. Under these circumstances, contingency planning can go on forever, draining time and attention from far more essential activities, yet without ever providing the clear sense of direction that a company desperately needs. After awhile, managers inevitably become cynical about all this, and the planning process can degenerate into a highly politicized game.

Planning works best not as a substitute for direction setting but as a complement to it. A competent planning process serves as a useful reality check on direction-setting activities. Likewise, a competent direction-setting process provides a focus in which planning can then be realistically carried out. It helps clarify what kind of planning is essential and what kind is irrelevant.

Aligning People vs. Organizing and Staffing

A central feature of modern organizations is interdependence, where no one has complete autonomy, where most employees are tied to many others by their work, technology, management systems, and hierarchy. These linkages present a special challenge when organizations attempt to change. Unless many individuals line up and move together in the same direction, people will tend to fall all over one another. To executives who are overeducated in management and undereducated in leadership, the idea of getting people moving in the same direction appears to be an organizational problem. What executives need to do, however, is not organize people but align them.

Managers "organize" to create human systems that can implement plans as precisely and efficiently as possible. Typically, this requires a number of potentially complex decisions. A company must choose a structure of jobs and reporting relationships, staff it with individuals suited to the jobs, provide training for those who need it, communicate plans to the work force, and decide how much authority to delegate and to whom. Economic incentives also need to be constructed to accomplish the

Setting Direction: Lou Gerstner at American Express

When Lou Gerstner became president of the Travel Related Services (TRS) arm at American Express in 1979, the unit was facing one of its biggest challenges in AmEx's 130-year history. Hundreds of banks were offering or planning to introduce credit cards through Visa and MasterCard that would compete with the American Express card. And more than two dozen financial service firms were coming into the traveler's checks business. In a mature marketplace, this increase in competition usually reduces margins and prohibits growth.

But that was not how Gerstner saw the business. Before joining American Express, he had spent five years as a consultant to TRS, analyzing the money-losing travel division and the increasingly competitive card operation. Gerstner and his team asked fundamental questions about the economics, market, and competition and developed a deep understanding of the business. In the process, he began to craft a vision of TRS that looked nothing like a 130-year-old company in a mature industry.

Gerstner thought TRS had the potential to become a dynamic and growing enterprise, despite the onslaught of Visa and MasterCard competition from thousands of banks. The key was to focus on the global marketplace and, specifically, on the relatively affluent customer American Express had been traditionally serving with top-of-the-line products. By further segmenting this market, aggressively developing a broad range of new products and services, and investing to increase productivity and to lower costs, TRS could provide the best service possible to customers who had enough discretionary income to buy many more services from TRS than they had in the past.

Within a week of his appointment, Gerstner brought together the people running the card organization and questioned all the principles by which they conducted their business. In particular, he challenged two widely shared beliefs – that the division should have only one product, the green card, and that this product was limited in potential for growth and innovation.

Gerstner also moved quickly to develop a more entrepreneurial culture, to hire and train people who would thrive in it, and to clearly communicate to them the overall direction. He and other top managers rewarded intelligent risk taking. To make entrepreneurship easier, they discouraged unnecessary bureaucracy. They also upgraded hiring standards and created the TRS Graduate Management Program, which offered high-potential young people special training, an enriched set of experiences, and an unusual degree of exposure to people in top management. To encourage risk taking among all TRS employees, Gerstner also established something called the Great Performers program to recognize and reward truly exceptional customer service, a central tenet in the organization's vision.

These initiatives led quickly to new markets, products, and services. TRS expanded its overseas presence dramatically. By 1988, AmEx cards were issued in 29 currencies (as opposed to only 11 a decade earlier). The unit also focused aggressively on two market segments that had historically received little attention: college students and women. In 1981, TRS combined its card and travel-service capabilities to offer corporate clients a unified system to monitor and control travel expenses. And by 1988, AmEx had grown to become the fifth largest direct-mail merchant in the United States.

Other new products and services included 90-day insurance on all purchases made with the AmEx card, a Platinum American Express card, and a revolving credit card known as Optima. In 1988, the company also switched to image-processing technology for billing, producing a more convenient monthly statement for customers and reducing billing costs by 25%.

As a result of these innovations, TRS's net income increased a phenomenal 500% between 1978 and 1987 – a compounded annual rate of about 18%. The business outperformed many so-called high-tech/high-growth companies. With a 1988 return on equity of 28%, it also outperformed most low-growth but high-profit businesses.

plan, as well as systems to monitor its implementation. These organizational judgments are much like architectural decisions. It's a question of fit within a particular context.

Aligning is different. It is more of a communications challenge than a design problem. First, aligning invariably involves talking to many more individuals than organizing does. The target population can involve not only a manager's subordinates but also bosses, peers, staff in other parts of the organization, as well as suppliers, governmental officials, or even customers. Anyone who can help implement the vision and strategies or who can block implementation is relevant.

Trying to get people to comprehend a vision of an alternative future is also a communications challenge of a completely different magnitude from organizing them to fulfill a short-term plan. It's much like the difference between a football quarterback attempting to describe to his team the next two or three plays versus his trying to explain to them a totally new approach to the game to be used in the second half of the season.

Whether delivered with many words or a few carefully chosen symbols, such messages are not necessarily accepted just because they are understood. Another big challenge in leadership efforts is credibility – getting people to believe the message. Many things contribute to credibility: the track record of the person delivering the message, the content of the message itself, the communicator's reputation for integrity and trustworthiness, and the consistency between words and deeds.

Finally, aligning leads to empowerment in a way that organizing rarely does. One of the reasons some organizations have difficulty adjusting to rapid changes in markets or technology is that so many people in those companies feel relatively powerless. They have learned from experience that even if they correctly perceive important external changes and

> Management controls people by pushing them in the right direction; leadership motivates them by satisfying basic human needs.

then initiate appropriate actions, they are vulnerable to someone higher up who does not like what they have done. Reprimands can take many different forms: "That's against policy" or "We can't afford it" or "Shut up and do as you're told."

Alignment helps overcome this problem by empowering people in at least two ways. First, when a clear sense of direction has been communicated throughout an organization, lower level employees can initiate actions without the same degree of vulnerability. As long as their behavior is consistent with the vision, superiors will have more difficulty reprimanding them. Second, because everyone is aiming at the same target, the probability is less that one person's initiative will be stalled when it comes into conflict with someone else's.

Motivating People vs. Controlling and Problem Solving

Since change is the function of leadership, being able to generate highly energized behavior is important for coping with the inevitable barriers to change. Just as direction setting identifies an appropriate path for movement and just as effective alignment gets people moving down that path, successful motivation ensures that they will have the energy to overcome obstacles.

According to the logic of management, control mechanisms compare system behavior with the plan and take action when a deviation is detected. In a well-managed factory, for example, this means the planning process establishes sensible quality targets, the organizing process builds an organization that can achieve those targets, and a control process makes sure that quality lapses are spotted immediately, not in 30 or 60 days, and corrected.

For some of the same reasons that control is so central to management, highly motivated or inspired behavior is almost irrelevant. Managerial processes must be as close as possible to fail-safe and risk-free. That means they cannot be dependent on the unusual or hard to obtain. The whole purpose of systems and structures is to help normal people who behave in normal ways to complete routine jobs successfully, day after day. It's not exciting or glamorous. But that's management.

Leadership is different. Achieving grand visions always requires an occasional burst of energy. Motivation and inspiration energize people, not by pushing them in the right direction as control mechanisms do but by satisfying basic human needs for achievement, a sense of belonging, recognition, self-esteem, a feeling of control over one's life, and the ability to live up to one's ideals. Such feelings touch us deeply and elicit a powerful response.

Good leaders motivate people in a variety of ways. First, they always articulate the organization's vision

Aligning People: Chuck Trowbridge and Bob Crandall at Eastman Kodak

Eastman Kodak entered the copy business in the early 1970s, concentrating on technically sophisticated machines that sold, on average, for about $60,000 each. Over the next decade, this business grew to nearly $1 billion in revenues. But costs were high, profits were hard to find, and problems were nearly everywhere. In 1984, Kodak had to write off $40 million in inventory.

Most people at the company knew there were problems, but they couldn't agree on how to solve them. So, in his first two months as general manager of the new copy products group, established in 1984, Chuck Trowbridge met with nearly every key person inside his group, as well as with people elsewhere at Kodak who could be important to the copier business. An especially crucial area was the engineering and manufacturing organization, headed by Bob Crandall.

Trowbridge and Crandall's vision for engineering and manufacturing was simple: to become a world-class manufacturing operation and to create a less bureaucratic and more decentralized organization. Still, this message was difficult to convey because it was such a radical departure from previous communications, not only in the copy products group but throughout most of Kodak. So Crandall set up dozens of vehicles to emphasize the new direction and align people to it: weekly meetings with his own 12 direct reports; monthly "copy product forums" in which a different employee from each of his departments would meet with him as a group; quarterly meetings with all 100 of his supervisors to discuss recent improvements and new projects to achieve still better results; and quarterly "State of the Department" meetings, where his managers met with everybody in their own departments.

Once a month, Crandall and all those who reported to him would also meet with 80 to 100 people from some area of his organization to discuss anything they wanted. To align his biggest supplier—the

Kodak Apparatus Division, which supplied one-third of the parts used in design and manufacturing—he and his managers met with the top management of that group over lunch every Thursday. More recently, he has created a format called "business meetings," where his managers meet with 12 to 20 people on a specific topic, such as inventory or master scheduling. The goal is to get all of his 1,500 employees in at least one of these focused business meetings each year.

Trowbridge and Crandall also enlisted written communication in their cause. A four- to eight-page "Copy Products Journal" was sent to employees once a month. A program called "Dialog Letters" gave employees the opportunity to anonymously ask questions of Crandall and his top managers and be guaranteed a reply. But the most visible, and powerful, form of written communication were the charts. In a main hallway near the cafeteria, these huge charts vividly reported the quality, cost, and delivery results for each product, measured against difficult targets. A hundred smaller versions of these charts were scattered throughout the manufacturing area, reporting quality levels and costs for specific work groups.

Results of this intensive alignment process began to appear within six months and still more after a year. These successes made the message more credible and helped get more people on board. Between 1984 and 1988, quality on one of the main product lines increased nearly one-hundredfold. Defects per unit went from 30 to 0.3. Over a three-year period, costs on another product line went down nearly 24%. Deliveries on schedule increased from 82% in 1985 to 95% in 1987. Inventory levels dropped by over 50% between 1984 and 1988, even though the volume of products was increasing. And productivity, measured in units per manufacturing employee, more than doubled between 1985 and 1988.

in a manner that stresses the values of the audience they are addressing. This makes the work important to those individuals. Leaders also regularly involve people in deciding how to achieve the organization's vision (or the part most relevant to a particular individual). This gives people a sense of control. Another important motivational technique is to support employee efforts to realize the vision by providing coaching, feedback, and role modeling, thereby helping people grow professionally and enhancing their self-esteem. Finally, good leaders recognize and reward success, which not only gives people a sense of accomplishment but also makes them feel like they belong to an organization that cares about them. When all this is done, the work itself becomes intrinsically motivating.

The more that change characterizes the business environment, the more that leaders must motivate people to provide leadership as well. When this works, it tends to reproduce leadership across the entire organization, with people occupying multiple leadership roles throughout the hierarchy. This is highly valuable, because coping with change in any complex business demands initiatives from a multitude of people. Nothing less will work.

Of course, leadership from many sources does not necessarily converge. To the contrary, it can easily conflict. For multiple leadership roles to work together, people's actions must be carefully coordinated by mechanisms that differ from those coordinating traditional management roles.

Strong networks of informal relationships – the kind found in companies with healthy cultures – help coordinate leadership activities in much the same way that formal structure coordinates managerial activities. The key difference is that informal networks can deal with the greater demands for coordination associated with nonroutine activities and change. The multitude of communication channels and the trust among the individuals connected by

> Despite leadership's growing importance, the on-the-job experiences of most people undermine their ability to lead.

those channels allow for an ongoing process of accommodation and adaptation. When conflicts arise among roles, those same relationships help resolve the conflicts. Perhaps most important, this process of dialogue and accommodation can produce visions that are linked and compatible instead of remote and competitive. All this requires a great deal more communication than is needed to coordinate managerial roles, but unlike formal structure, strong informal networks can handle it.

Of course, informal relations of some sort exist in all corporations. But too often these networks are either very weak – some people are well connected but most are not – or they are highly fragmented – a strong network exists inside the marketing group and inside R&D but not across the two departments. Such networks do not support multiple leadership initiatives well. In fact, extensive informal networks are so important that if they do not exist, creating them has to be the focus of activity early in a major leadership initiative.

Creating a Culture of Leadership

Despite the increasing importance of leadership to business success, the on-the-job experiences of most people actually seem to undermine the development of attributes needed for leadership. Nevertheless, some companies have consistently demonstrated an ability to develop people into outstanding leader-managers. Recruiting people with leadership potential is only the first step. Equally important is managing their career patterns. Individuals who are effective in large leadership roles often share a number of career experiences.

Perhaps the most typical and most important is significant challenge early in a career. Leaders almost always have had opportunities during their twenties and thirties to actually try to lead, to take a risk, and to learn from both triumphs and failures. Such learning seems essential in developing a wide range of leadership skills and perspectives. It also teaches people something about both the difficulty of leadership and its potential for producing change.

Later in their careers, something equally important happens that has to do with broadening. People who provide effective leadership in important jobs always have a chance, before they get into those jobs, to grow beyond the narrow base that characterizes most managerial careers. This is usually the result of lateral career moves or of early promotions to unusually broad job assignments. Sometimes other vehicles help, like special task-force assignments or a lengthy general management course. Whatever the case, the breadth of knowledge developed in this way seems to be helpful in all aspects of leadership. So does the network of relationships that is often acquired both inside and outside the company. When

Motivating People: Richard Nicolosi at Procter & Gamble

For about 20 years since its founding in 1956, Procter & Gamble's paper products division had experienced little competition for its high-quality, reasonably priced, and well-marketed consumer goods. By the late 1970s, however, the market position of the division had changed. New competitive thrusts hurt P&G badly. For example, industry analysts estimate that the company's market share for disposable diapers fell from 75% in the mid-1970s to 52% in 1984.

That year, Richard Nicolosi came to paper products as the associate general manager, after three years in P&G's smaller and faster moving soft-drink business. He found a heavily bureaucratic and centralized organization that was overly preoccupied with internal functional goals and projects. Almost all information about customers came through highly quantitative market research. The technical people were rewarded for cost savings, the commercial people focused on volume and share, and the two groups were nearly at war with each other.

During the late summer of 1984, top management announced that Nicolosi would become the head of paper products in October, and by August he was unofficially running the division. Immediately he began to stress the need for the division to become more

creative and market driven, instead of just trying to be a low-cost producer. "I had to make it very clear," Nicolosi later reported, "that the rules of the game had changed."

The new direction included a much greater stress on teamwork and multiple leadership roles. Nicolosi pushed a strategy of using groups to manage the division and its specific products. In October, he and his team designated themselves as the paper division "board" and began meeting first monthly and then weekly. In November, they established "category teams" to manage their major brand groups (like diapers, tissues, towels) and started pushing responsibility down to these teams. "Shun the incremental," Nicolosi stressed, "and go for the leap."

In December, Nicolosi selectively involved himself in more detail in certain activities. He met with the advertising agency and got to know key creative people. He asked the marketing manager of diapers to report directly to him, eliminating a layer in the hierarchy. He talked more to the people who were working on new product-development projects.

In January 1985, the board announced a new organizational structure that included not only category teams but also new-brand business teams. By the spring, the board was ready to plan an important motivational event to communicate the new paper products vision to as many people as possible. On June 4, 1985, all the Cincinnati-based personnel in paper plus sales district managers and paper plant managers—several thousand people in all—met in the local Masonic Temple. Nicolosi and other board members described their vision of an organization where "each of us is a leader." The event was videotaped, and an edited version was sent to all sales offices and plants for everyone to see.

All these activities helped create an entrepreneurial environment where large numbers of people were motivated to realize the new vision. Most innovations came from people dealing with new products. Ultra Pampers, first introduced in February 1985, took the market share of the entire Pampers product line from 40% to 58% and profitability from break-even to positive. And within only a few months of the introduction of Luvs Delux in May 1987, market share for the overall brand grew by 150%.

Other employee initiatives were oriented more toward a functional area, and some came from the bottom of the hierarchy. In the spring of 1986, a few of the division's secretaries, feeling empowered by the new culture, developed a Secretaries Network. This association established subcommittees on training, on rewards and recognition, and on the "secretary of the future." Echoing the sentiments of many of her peers, one paper products secretary said: "I don't see why we too can't contribute to the division's new direction."

By the end of 1988, revenues at the paper products division were up 40% over a four-year period. Profits were up 66%. And this happened despite the fact that the competition continued to get tougher.

LEADERS

enough people get opportunities like this, the relationships that are built also help create the strong informal networks needed to support multiple leadership initiatives.

> One way to develop leadership is to create challenging opportunities for young employees.

Corporations that do a better-than-average job of developing leaders put an emphasis on creating challenging opportunities for relatively young employees. In many businesses, decentralization is the key. By definition, it pushes responsibility lower in an organization and in the process creates more challenging jobs at lower levels. Johnson & Johnson, 3M, Hewlett-Packard, General Electric, and many other well-known companies have used that approach quite successfully. Some of those same companies also create as many small units as possible so there are a lot of challenging lower level general management jobs available.

Sometimes these businesses develop additional challenging opportunities by stressing growth through new products or services. Over the years, 3M has had a policy that at least 25% of its revenue should come from products introduced within the last five years. That encourages small new ventures, which in turn offer hundreds of opportunities to test and stretch young people with leadership potential.

Such practices can, almost by themselves, prepare people for small- and medium-sized leadership jobs. But developing people for important leadership positions requires more work on the part of senior executives, often over a long period of time. That work begins with efforts to spot people with great leadership potential early in their careers and to identify what will be needed to stretch and develop them.

Again, there is nothing magic about this process. The methods successful companies use are surprisingly straightforward. They go out of their way to make young employees and people at lower levels in their organizations visible to senior management. Senior managers then judge for themselves who has potential and what the development needs of those people are. Executives also discuss their tentative conclusions among themselves to draw more accurate judgments.

Armed with a clear sense of who has considerable leadership potential and what skills they need to develop, executives in these companies then spend time planning for that development. Sometimes that is done as part of a formal succession planning or high-potential development process; often it is more informal. In either case, the key ingredient appears to be an intelligent assessment of what feasible development opportunities fit each candidate's needs.

> Institutionalizing a leadership-centered culture is the ultimate act of leadership.

To encourage managers to participate in these activities, well-led businesses tend to recognize and reward people who successfully develop leaders. This is rarely done as part of a formal compensation or bonus formula, simply because it is so difficult to measure such achievements with precision. But it does become a factor in decisions about promotion, especially to the most senior levels, and that seems to make a big difference. When told that future promotions will depend to some degree on their ability to nurture leaders, even people who say that leadership cannot be developed somehow find ways to do it.

Such strategies help create a corporate culture where people value strong leadership and strive to create it. Just as we need more people to provide leadership in the complex organizations that dominate our world today, we also need more people to develop the cultures that will create that leadership. Institutionalizing a leadership-centered culture is the ultimate act of leadership. ⊍

[2]

On the Psychodynamics of Organizational Totalitarianism

Howard S. Schwartz

Oakland University

A theory of organizational totalitarianism is developed, based on Freud's concept of narcissism and his theory of the "ego ideal" (1921/ 1955, 1914/1957) Klein's (1948) theory of "splitting" and Shorris' (1981) thinking concerning the totalitarian aspects of the corporation. The idea of a perfect organization, referred to here as the "organization ideal," is a symbol that represents the return to narcissism—to being the center of a loving world. Since the return to narcissism is impossible, committed participants in the totalitarian organization maintain a belief in the organization ideal by believing that its attainment is achieved by progress through the organization's hierarchy. This requires commitment to the belief that individuals more advanced in the hierarchy represent the organization ideal. This turns organizational process into the living out of the narcissistic fantasies of those in power. Consequences of this are passivity and slavishness, shamefulness, cynicism, loneliness and the loss of the psychological gains that could otherwise come from socially useful work. The problems of American industry may be partly due to totalitarian processes and present attempts at management through culture may be a further stage of the disease.

Understandably, discussions of totalitarianism tend to focus upon its more dramatic manifestations. An unfortunate consequence of this is that it has led us to miss aspects of totalitarianism which pervade our own times and culture and which may be, if not equally destructive, at least sufficiently destructive to require study and criticism. An exception is the work of Earl Shorris (1981) on totalitarian aspects of corporate life.

Shorris defines totalitarianism as the process of defining people's happiness for them. The element that makes this process noxious is that the definer of hap-

Versions of this paper have been presented at the Conference on Critical Approaches to Organizational Theory, Baruch College, City University of New York, September 5-7, 1985; and at "Cultural Engineering—The evidence for and against," Standing Conference on Organizational Symbolism, University of Quebec at Montreal, June 25-27, 1986. The author wishes to thank Katherine Schwartz, Harry Levinson, Chris Argyris, Howell Baum, Abraham Korman, Lizabeth Barclay, David Doane and the reviewers of the *Journal of Management* for important help in revising the manuscript.

Address all correspondence to Howard S. Schwartz, School of Business Administration, Oakland University, Rochester, MI 48063.

piness is not the person whose happiness is being defined. This has the effect of taking the sense of the direction of the individual's life away from the determination of the individual and ceding it to another. But it is the process of giving the sense of direction to our lives, even if only in thought, that constitutes our moral autonomy. For Shorris, who in this respect echoes George Herbert Mead's (1934) distinction between the "I" and the "me," the human being stands apart from any symbol. It is this standing apartness that constitutes one's self-consciousness, that is the source of one's specific identity. To cause a person to collapse into a symbol one has projected for him or her is to cause the self-consciousness to become, not the essence of that person's identity, but something alien to it—to separate the person from him or herself.

This is the source of the fundamental psychodynamic of totalitarianism. It alienates people from themselves and gives them over to others. Whatever victories may ensue from this must be pyrrhic. Whatever happiness is to be attained here is not the happiness of the individual. Indeed, it is not happiness at all. It is the drama of happiness attaching to the role that the person plays in a play that is written and directed by others.

We gain insight into the underlying psychodynamics of this process by exploring the connection between Shorris' view and Freud's theory of narcissism and the psychology of the ego ideal.

Narcissism and the Ego Ideal

For Freud (1914/1957) the infant starts off in the congenial state of being at the center of a loving world. It is thus the perfect combination of agency and communion, subjectivity and objectivity, activity and passivity, freedom and determinateness, yang and yin. Freud refers to this happy synthesis as "narcissism."

But the world is, alas, not a loving place and we are not the center of it. No one in it loves us quite as much as we need to be loved. And if, as life goes on, they are to love us at all we must love them in return—to give up, in a word, the centrality that the love of others was an instrument for preserving. Further, even if I gain the love of a few individuals, what good does it do me? My real problem is with the world. And they cannot protect me from it any more than I can protect them. For the world can do very well without me. It did without me before I was and it will do without me after I am not. In the end, by virtue of the laws of biology if by nothing else, I get rubbed out. To be sure, I can make some contribution to the world. Perhaps, in some sense, that will live after me. But what is it that lives after me? Obviously, whatever it is, it is not me. Now, the world is precisely the arrangement that, among other things, this shall happen. Why should I love that? If I don't, what ground is there for my making any contribution to the world at all? Ultimately, the story of human life is this: the world does not care about me unless I become someone I am not. But if I become someone I am not, who does it care about that should make any difference to me?

What I have just outlined is an existential interpretation of what Melanie Klein (1948) called the "depressive position." You can understand why. But my purpose in this was not to depress anybody, but rather to show what it is that much of the psychology of social institutions is organized against.

For Klein, the depression of the depressive position is often defended against by adopting an earlier stage of development called the "paranoid-schizoid position." The characteristic psychology here is determined by what she calls "splitting," which is a lack of integration of the good aspects of the world with the bad aspects, and a denial of the ultimate reality of the bad aspects. In one way or another, we attribute the cause of our anxiety to a person, or a place, or a time, or a group, or a social arrangement, or a part of ourselves, and direct our aggression at this "bad" stuff. We hold before us the image of a perfect "good" world that will be our world when the bad stuff is gotten rid of or gotten away from. This good world represents for us the possibility of a return to narcissism, to a world in which annihilation is not a problem, a world in which it is perfectly all right to do whatever we want to do, a world which has us as its reason for being, a world free of anxiety. Stories of the goodness of the good world and stories of the roots of our anxiety represent culture for us. The function of culture, that is to say, is to give content and direction, to render sensible, our longings to return to narcissism and to avoid the evil arising from our mortality (Becker, 1971, 1973).

In Freudian terms, the representation that we make to ourselves of the good world is termed the "ego-ideal," and it is this toward which we are driven by our anxiety over our finitude, by our rejection of whatever it is about ourselves that is vulnerable and finite. Because this is our spontaneous self, it is always the case that the motivation toward the ego ideal involves the rejection (in Freudian terms, the *repression*) of our spontaneity. Thus, we experience the pursuit of the ego ideal as an obligation—as something that we ought to attempt, not a natural extension of what we are. The recognition that we are not what we are supposed to be, that we are playing a role rather than being the role which we are playing, is the experience of shame. Another consequence is that we never get to be the ego ideal. The ego ideal represents us as we believe we would be if we could get rid of what causes our anxiety. But what causes our anxiety is what is most specifically ourself. While we are alive we can never get rid of it—the reason being that it is our very life.

As Freud (1921/1955) pointed out, the ego ideal may be formed in any of a number of ways. Of particular interest to us is the case in which an abstraction, a "leading idea," has taken the place of a leader, and in which that abstraction is the idea of the organization itself. In this case, we may recognize the committed organizational participant as a person whose ego ideal is the organization. Thus, for the committed organizational participant, the organization represents a project for the return to narcissism.

In understanding how this is possible, we must realize that to talk about the organization as ego ideal is not to refer to the actual organization but to the committed person's *idea* of the organization, which may have little relation to the person's experience with the actual organization. It is what the committed organizational participant holds out as what the organization is supposed to be and would be except for the effect of "bad" aspects of the world, and what he or she accepts as an obligation to help bring about. This is clearly an ideal organization. Indeed, giving it an appropriate name, the idea of the organization serving the function of the ego ideal will be referred to as the *organization ideal*. Now, how does the organization ideal serve as an ego ideal and what are the consequences of this?

The Ego Ideal and the Organization Ideal

In the first place the organization ideal represents power. Denhardt (1981) has noted how deeply the concept of control is built into our concept of the organization. In psychoanalytic terms, the organization ideal serves as a "reaction formation" that covers over and represses the anxiety-evoking idea of our finitude, vulnerability, and mortality (Schwartz, 1985).

Second, the organization ideal is a scenario of love as well and offers the possibility of a return to centrality in a loving world. For by taking the organization as ego ideal, the individual takes as well the possibility of a boundary-dispelling relationship to others who have done so as well. Both love and centrality are possible in this scenario, because each of the individuals who have taken the organization as their ego ideal assumes that the others have also redefined themselves as the organization and therefore as essentially the same and having the same interest. Conflict is defined away, therefore, and along with it all social anxiety within the organization. Indeed, what we have here is a perfect analog for Freud's reference to the tale of Narcissus, who falls in love with his own image in a pond. Here, the other organizational participants would ideally provide a mirror for the focal participant and reflect his love for himself.

Third, a related point ties the intra-psychic processes involved to the normative structure of the organization. We have seen that individuals, by defining themselves in terms of the organization, put themselves into an interesting relationship with others who have done the same. On the one hand this is a relationship of idealized love that would not interfere with narcissism. On the other hand, it is a relationship of mutual responsibility because it is up to each to uphold the organization ideal for all the others. It becomes not only a matter of the fulfillment of mutual personal principle but the direct object of moral sanction—the threat of the loss of love—by ideally loved others. This gives a moral force to the maintenance of the definition of oneself and one's relations as the organization ideal.

Fourth, and perhaps most comprehensively, defining oneself as the organization removes from consideration a problem that in a way contributed most powerfully to the anxiety which the participant was trying to allay. As noted before, the self-conscious self, the spontaneous self, Mead's (1934) "I," though it is on the one hand what is most intimately myself, is also the cause of my greatest ontological trouble. For it can never be fully represented by a symbol (Mead's "me"), and therefore cannot become part of the enacted world, but always stands aside from my enactments and says of them, "that is not me, that is not me." Defining myself as the organization ideal solves this problem for me. Having defined myself in terms of the organization as an ethical standard, I have a basis upon which I can reject my spontaneous self-consciousness as an obstacle to my self and to my obligations. It becomes an impulse for me to negate: a source of shame and guilt. What I cannot deny phenomenologicaly, I can repudiate morally. To be sure, I can only do that by rejecting that part of me that is most uniquely myself. But after all, it was precisely the fact that I have a spontaneous self that got me into trouble in the first place.

An example: When interviewed, Wheeler Stanley (Terkel, 1974) was the youngest general supervisor in a Ford assembly plant. From an impoverished background, he had come, through Ford, to a position of status in the world and felt that he was in line for more. His ambitions lay within the company hierarchy and his conscious concerns were company concerns. His ego ideal was the organization ideal. But listen to the way this conversation evolved:

> I've got a great feeling for Ford because it's been good to me....My son, he's only six years old and I've taken him through the plant....And that's all he talks about: "I'm going to work for Ford, too." And I say, "Oh, no you ain't." And my wife will shut me up and she'll say, "Why not?" Then I think to myself, "Why not? It's been good to me." (p. 185)

What we see here was an underlying resentment at Ford, which was not acceptable to his moral consciousness. He reported an occasion when the veneer slipped and the thought was blurted out. But then it was repudiated as unworthy and the veneer of the company man was put back in place. "[Ford] has been good to me," replaced and covered over the apparent spontaneous opposite thought: "Ford has been bad to me."

Fifth, the repudiation of the spontaneous self leaves open a possibility of a redefinition of the self that is wholly in accordance with the organization ideal. This is a redefinition of the "wants" of the individual. In terms of the organization ideal, the participant undertakes to "want" to do what the organization needs doing. Thus, the polarity of subject and object, activity and passivity, is projected to be overcome.

The picture of the organization as organization ideal will be familiar to all teachers of organizational behavior. This is an organization in which everyone knows what they are doing, in which there is no conflict or coercion, in which communication is open and direct, in which people want to do what needs to be done, in which every member is solely concerned with and works diligently to promote the common good. The picture is of an organization that has never existed and never will. But somehow or other our students regard it as of the utmost importance for them to be able to believe in it.

Indeed, the picture of the organization as ego-ideal is familiar and important not only to the naive, but to the presumably sophisticated as well. The idea of the model organization as the integration of individual spontaneity and organizational necessity is after all, in one form or another, at the heart of many normative theories of organization, and the attainment of the organization ideal is a large part of the promise made by practitioners of organization development.

Often, as with Argyris (1957), organization development efforts are aimed at encouraging what Maslow (1970) called "self-actualization" through work. But notice here that an important shift takes place away from Maslow's concept. Instead of saying that self-actualization means: "Be healthy and then you may trust your impulses," (p. 179) these thinkers seem to say it means: "Want what the organization wants you to want, and then you may do what you want."

To this point, we have considered the nature of the organization ideal and its relation to the individual who adopts it as his or her ego ideal. But though the organizational processes so characterized may show resemblances to totalitarianism, they show resemblances to social processes which are, arguably, not only more benign, but often even positive, such as idealistic movements for social change. Indeed, arguably, we have moved broadly to reveal the psychodynamic underpinnings of social organization generally, or at least to the extent that people put their faith in it. If we have found that it involves repression and de-centering of the self, we have said no more than what Freud said in *Civilization and its Discontents* (1930/1961). And if the impossibility of attaining the ego ideal leads almost inevitably to disillusionment, it is at least arguable that disillusionment is a necessary element of adult development and growth (Levinson, 1978). In order to show how the processes we have described lead to totalitarianism, it will be necessary to show how they tend to degenerate in the context of organizational power.

Hierarchy and Ontological Differentiation

Because the organization ideal represents the return to narcissism, and because the return to narcissism can never be achieved, there must be some way of accounting for the failure of the return to narcissism while still remaining true to the idea of the organization ideal.

For the committed organizational participant, there are two available reasons why narcissism has not returned—why I still feel threatened, why everybody doesn't love me, why I am not doing what I want, and so on. One possibility is that the anxiety is due to "bad" forces, external or internal, that are threatening the organization. Once the forces can be given an identity, it is possible to struggle against them. The community of strugglers can be conceived as wholly good, because all the anxiety can be attributed to the enemy. Under the circumstances, a quite satisfying degree of localized collective narcissism can be achieved. This apparently represents the dynamic of the cohesiveness of many totalitarian organizations and cults. One might even see in it the root of the cohesiveness and high morale of work organizations that can reasonably identify some external threat or of parts of work organizations that can attribute the organization's problems to other parts of the same organization.

Organization against an enemy is certainly a tool used by totalitarian work organizations to increase their control. Thus, the president of a major auto manufacturing company referred to the Japanese as "the enemy" in an address to Oakland University students. He made it manifest that this climate of warfare was very much a part of the cultural process underlying his organization's "quality of working life" program. Certainly threat from an enemy increases the level of dependency on the organization and therefore the need to believe that the organization is the organization ideal. But the threat of an outside enemy is difficult to sustain, within a business organization, and mobilizing against an internal enemy tends to have an adverse impact on coordination and communication. Hence, totalitarian corporate organization tends to be more characterized by the other way of accounting for the failure of the return to narcissism.

This other way involves what I shall call the process of *ontological differentiation*. In this alternative the attribution of the cause of anxiety is made to the self and experienced as shame—shame for oneself and for the parts of the organization with which one is associated. Because the organization is understood as the organization ideal, and because one and one's associates fall short of this ideal, these have evidently not been fully integrated into the organization. This shame is experienced by contrast to others who are believed to be what they are supposed to be—who are more integrated with the organization ideal and presumably do not have the deficiency in their identity that one is ashamed of. This contrast is ontological differentiation.

In the classic bureaucratic organization, ontological differentiation takes the structural form of vertical differentiation, or hierarchy. As Arendt (1966) and Shorris (1982) note, what I am calling ontological differentiation does not always correspond precisely with the organizational pyramid. Arendt, for example, compares the totalitarian organization to an onion, in which one goes deeper and deeper, rather than higher and higher.[1] Thus, the Nazi party, for example, contained ideological fanatics at all levels of the state apparatus, trusted to wield power even over their nominal superiors through their capacity for denunciation. Nonetheless, as Shorris notes, the pyramid and the onion intersect at the point which is both highest and deepest. In traditional organizational terms, this is the top of the organization. For the purposes of this paper, the dimensions of vertical differentiation and depth will be taken to be combined in the organization's hierarchy.

In the traditional view, hierarchy serves a variety of managerial functions, such as coordination, control, and the like. Although there is certainly some truth to this view, it cannot provide fully for a phenomenology of hierarchy—for the simple fact that hierarchy represents not only a differentiation of function and task, but a moral differentiation as well (Parsons, 1940/1954). Thus, the organizational ladder is conceived as a sort of "great chain of Being." It represents, in a word, a structured adaptation to the idea that organizational participation does not amount to a return to narcissism, while retaining the idea of the organization as organization ideal, and therefore permitting the idea of the return to narcissism as a possibility.

Thus, it is easy to suppose that more status in the organization's hierarchy will represent a greater degree of attainment of the organization ideal, and therefore progress in the return to narcissism. On the one hand, the organization's actions will be more the result of my actions and its deliberations will include my thoughts. On the other hand, by definition, my actions and thoughts will be the appropriate actions and thoughts with regard to the organization.[2] The problem is that if I am going to hold the belief that progress in the hierarchy will mean progress in the attainment of the organization ideal for me, I am committed to the belief that it represents such progress for others as well.

Ontological differentiation is the vehicle through which social structure be-

---

[1]Note the connection between this depth dimension and Schein's (1980) concept of organizational "centrality."

[2]For a further discussion of the psychodynamics of hierarchy, see Schwartz (in press).

comes totalitarian. For at this point it becomes possible for some to use their ontological stature, and the power that goes with it, to impose their own narcissistic fantasies upon others as the organization ideal—in Shorris' terms, for some to define the happiness of others. The point is that the top of the organization is not merely an abstract position, but has a population and a history of action. Locating the return to narcissism at the head of the organization means more than establishing a direction toward the ego ideal. It involves establishing certain definite others, with their own way of looking at the world and at themselves, and with their own history of actions, as already ideal. It involves, in other words, acquiescing to the narcissism of some specific others as one's own moral obligation, collectively enforceable by all others who have done so and with whom one defines oneself as ideally in community. It legitimizes the use of coercion, on the part of the powerful, to cause the less powerful to act out a drama whose theme is the perfection of the powerful. And it does so in such a way that the powerful can feel self-righteous about this coercion—as if they were performing a service or committing a sacrifice.

Totalitarianism and Ontological Differentiation

The human consequences of ontological differentiation can be explored in any of a number of ways. One way is through consideration of the ways in which people's defenses work. It has become a commonplace of cognitive psychology that persons see the world in ways that are systematically biased. Weiner, et al. (1971), for example, note a self-enhancing bias that consists of seeing oneself responsible for positive outcomes and others responsible for negative outcomes. The self-enhancement that this bias promotes is the attributional correlate of narcissism.

Now, consider the vicissitudes of this bias in the structure we have described. Here, because the head of the organization serves as the specification of the organization ideal and hence as the definer of reality, we may expect that the reality so defined will have the leader's self-enhancing bias built into it. In terms of maintaining the stability of the organization ideal, this is necessary, but consider the consequences for the subordinate. The subordinate has to see the world in a way that enhances, not his or her own self-image, but the self-image of the leader. The self-enhancing bias which operates within the subordinate must be abandoned and overruled in favor of the self-enhancing bias of the leader. But whereas the self-enhancing bias of the leader arises naturally and almost automatically in the mind of the leader, approximating the leader's self-enhancing bias on the part of the subordinate must be tortuous, contrived, painful, and self-destructive. And yet the organization ideal demands just that. It demands, in a word, that in the name of the common good, the individual must not only deny his or her own natural tendencies toward self-enhancement and even self-protection, but morally condemn them. Moreover, informal pressure on the part of other participants and even legitimized formal coercion on the part of authorities may be used to enforce this self-abasement. This, it seems to me, is the source of the slavishness and passivity Shorris, for example, finds so common in totalitarianism.

What has been said with regard to cognitive bias could have been said as well in terms of the theory of retrospective sense-making (Weick, 1979). Here, a distinction would be noted between the leader, whose retrospective justifications would be taken as valid, and followers, who would have to adapt to the retrospective sense of the leader while being subject to having the sense of their own actions determined for them by the leader. Alternatively, the differentiation could have been drawn in terms of Argyris and Schon's (1974) distinction between espoused theories and theories-in-use. In this case, the espoused theories of the leader would have to be taken by followers as being the leader's theory-in-use, while the followers' theory-in-use would always be available to be held up by the leader as differing from the acceptable espoused theories—espoused theories which, as has been noted, must be publicly declared as guiding the behavior of the leader.

A related feature of totalitarian life is uncertainty regarding the appropriate. If the definition of the appropriate is based retrospectively on the actions and words of the leader, the subordinate must be in constant uncertainty as to what actions will correspond to the leader's whims. If the rationale of the leader's whims is not comprehended, the result must be not only uncertainty with regard to appropriate action, but uncertainty over one's own moral worth, because one's own perceptions, instincts and analyses cannot be relied upon as grounds for moral judgment, and because actions which turn out later to be deviations from the leader's position are condemnable. This is liable to be all the more so to the extent that the subordinate maintains the organization ideal and therefore cannot blame what are seen as inadequacies on the organization, but rather has to accept him or herself as the source of the blame. The result of this must be a more or less permanent state of shamefulness.

The alternative here is cynicism. Remember that the leader is defined as the ideal, rather than having that capacity in reality. The wisdom of the leader's actions and thoughts are limited in just the same way that the rest of ours are. Accordingly, rationality cannot be used as a guide to action on the part of the subordinate. Rather, the particular irrationality that the leader manifests must be the criterion. But a person's specific irrationality, we may suppose, is an outgrowth of that particular person's personality. Although it may come naturally to him or her, it must seem to others, if they understand it at all, as some sort of systematic quirkiness. Understanding this quirkiness, the subordinate may well be able to anticipate the leader's judgments and use this knowledge as a way of "playing the game." The problem is that this can only be achieved through giving up idealization of the organization ideal while, at the same time, one's actions conform to it and one's sense of value, such as it is, is structured by the attainment of it. This is cynicism.

Another feature of totalitarianism is the isolation of people from one another. This isolation is related to a similar dynamic. The organization ideal is held in place not only by the subordinates' own need to do what he or she feels ought to be done, but by sanctions issuing from ideally loved others. This means that deviations from them threaten the meaning structures of others whose love is needed to maintain one's own meaning structure. There is something not only unnatural but positively impossible about becoming someone else. But this is obligatory. The result is that the person one really is not only is unacceptable to oneself, but is unacceptable in social company, which is in turn composed of persons who are each unacceptable in social company for the same reasons. The result is that social interaction takes place not between persons, but between performances. Roles utter words at other roles. And if at any time any one of them said, as each of them somehow knows, "this is a bunch of nonsense," that person would become a pariah because he or she would bring out in all these people the anxiety that motivated the performance in the first place and maintains it at all times. Thus, each of these persons must live in more or less complete isolation and be terribly lonely.

An example may be useful to illustrate some of these processes. Some colleagues were doing consulting work for a corporation in our area that was getting ready to open a new plant. A distinguished professor, call him D, well known for his organization development work, was to give a presentation to the "design team," made up of middle managers recruited from the rest of the corporation, to help them in designing a compensation system for the new plant. I wangled an invitation.

The presentation turned out to be mostly a summary of D's widely published work, spiced with anecdotes about the utopian bliss in the factories he had installed. As the day went on, I shifted my interest from D's presentation to the response of the design team. I eavesdropped on their informal conversations and watched their body language. Particularly suggestive was the way they responded when it appeared that their leader was going to ask them a question. They looked for all the world like unprepared schoolchildren trying to make themselves inconspicuous so the teacher would not notice them.

It became increasingly clear to me that this was the first time the members of the "design team" had ever been exposed to systematic thinking about compensation systems. Aside from various idiosyncratic attitudes toward certain aspects of what D was saying, none of them had any thoughts on the matter at all. Moreover, they appeared to know that they were in over their heads. Behind a certain bluster in their facade, I thought I could detect shamefacedness and panic. Evidently, this was not unique to this particular subject. A colleague who had been sitting in on the meetings where they "designed" other "behavioral systems" reported that, despite tremendous time investment, very little progress was ever made. From my colleague's account, it appeared that the meetings were consumed by dependency reactions.

These team members had apparently been recruited into what they thought was a fast track position in a new direction the corporation was taking. Elements of the corporate personnel and training staffs, led by a guru who was officially a "consultant," had managed to persuade the corporate hierarchy to give them wide ranging control over the design of the new plant, which would employ a new culture, based upon a team concept. So, naturally, a team was recruited to do the design work, with the guru acting as "facilitator." Something magical was supposed to happen when a number of people got together in a room. They were each supposed to contribute themselves and the synergism of their cooperation would add up to a whole that was greater than the parts.

But, as it turned out, it was not themselves that they were contributing at all. What they had to do, instead, once they were committed, was to figure out what the guru thought the selves were that they were supposed to be, contribute those, and hope for the best. For their future was out of their own hands and in the hands of the guru. The best the group could do (the hidden agenda, really) was simply to take D's package and adopt it. But they would not be able to admit that they were doing this, because they were supposed to be the "design team" and to fit D's "recommendations" into their own conceptual framework. For the same reason, they couldn't even admit that the "facilitator" was in fact running the show. For the show that the guru was running was one in which they were autonomous, self-determining agents.

The point is that it was the guru's fantasy that was being enacted here. We can imagine that he saw himself as the shepherd loved by his flock, the Lone Ranger who makes factories and travels on, the Taoist sage who moves others without moving himself, perhaps even the revolutionary in the pin-striped suit. There is no place in any of these for the design team members as the persons that they were. Their function was to be absorbed into the guru's fantasy. Even the promise of the fast track, by which they were enticed, must have been felt as shameful in the fantasy they undertook to enact. No self-serving fantasy can fit into an organization designed around somebody else's narcissism. To be sure, one could come back and say that no narcissistic fantasy has a place in an organization— even the guru's. But that would be naive. For what we mean when we conceive an organization as being what it is supposed to be is an organization ideal; and an organization ideal is a narcissistic fantasy. The only question is who ultimately gets to be the narcissist.

In this case none of them got to be the narcissist. Not even the guru. The company did not build the plant. All of the design team members were laid off. I don't know where the guru is. He is probably pursuing his dream someplace else. And he has another line in his resume.

Finally, perhaps the most poignant loss suffered by participants in organizations of this sort is the loss of the sense of worth and human connectedness that could otherwise come from work. For organizations of this sort do not exist to do useful work. They do work in order to exist. And because their existence is the fiction of their organization ideal, we may say that everything that goes on within them finds its meaning in connection with maintaining this fiction.

One of my students invited me after class one night to have a drink. One drink turned to many and I soon was involved in a heart-crushing story of the crippling of a soul that bore upon many of the points I have described here. He was employed by a large corporation in a unit whose function had almost ceased to exist. Yet his supervisor spent all his time trying to expand his empire by hiring more people. What my student did all day, when he did anything at all, was to play up to the vanity of his supervisor and tell him and others how important the supervisor and the department were. He had to do this because he hated it there and wanted a transfer, which politically required the blessing of the supervisor. The heart of the dilemma turned out to be that the more he was successful at building up the supervisor's image, the more the supervisor refused to permit him to transfer, because the department was, according to the drama, already short on personnel. I asked him why he hated this so much; what he would do if he could do whatever he wanted to at work. He said : "I'm an engineer. All I want to do is build cars."

Concluding Reflections

This last observation, that totalitarianism may deprive organizational participants of the opportunity to do useful work, suggests that there is a practical dimension to this issue. It appears that, in the totalitarian organization, productive work comes to be less important than the maintenance of narcissistic fantasy. This cannot help but have an impact on the productivity of the entire enterprise. For totalitarianism represents a turning away from reality. And to the extent that organizations need to deal with real environments, even if this only means that they need to deal with narcissism projects that are not represented by the organization's own organization ideal, such turning away from reality must have serious consequences for the organization's effectiveness.

Indeed, it is tempting to speculate that part of the trouble in which American industry now finds itself may be due to the totalitarian processes that have been going on within it. If this is so, it is further tempting to speculate that current efforts to renew American industry by changing organizational culture may not be a cure, but rather a further development of the disease. In this view, the movement toward cultural management might be a case of escalating commitment to a mistaken course of action (Staw, 1980). Specifically, in this case we may be witnessing the attempt to replace reality by pretense, carried through on a redoubled scale, raised from unconsciousness to consciousness, and becoming not a sideshow that characterizes the dark side of organizational life, but the main organizational act (Schwartz, 1986).

Finally, a word should be said about the scope of the problem we are talking about. Is it possible to redesign organizations to avoid it? We might consider this question by examining an alternative proposed by Culbert and McDonough (1980). They make much of the idea that individuals in organizations should develop and maintain an alignment of their own personal values, interests, and skills with what they perceive to be the task requirements of the job. In our terms this would mean maintaining one's own ego ideal. But this ego ideal is embedded in an organization ideal in which all participants do their work within the context of their own self-serving alignments (recognizing that others are doing so as well) and in which all contributions within this context are adequately valued—the narcissistic synthesis of self and other again. But how much is adequate? My own reasoning concerning the ego ideal suggests that no valuation of an individual's alignment can be permanently satisfying, which would lead the individual to seek to have his or her alignment increasingly valued. But the capacity to frame organizational meaning to enhance the appreciation of one's alignment is Culbert and McDonough's definition of power. Thus, the self-serving alignments of the more powerful are valued and have legitimacy whereas the self-serving alignments of the less powerful are devalued and lack legitimacy—and back we are with ontological differentiation again.

It appears that the problem goes deeper than Culbert and McDonough imagined. I suggest it lies with our tendency to assign responsibility for the fulfillment of the ego ideal, the return to narcissism, to a social process—a tendency that arguably is becoming increasingly pronounced among us (Lasch, 1979). For the problems that the narcissistic defense is a defense against are existential problems—finitude, vulnerability, mortality—and social processes can deal only with the problems of the collective. They can deal with the problems of the individual only as an abstraction. But it is just the fact that the individual is not an abstraction, but a flesh-and-blood human being, that gives rise to existential problems in the first place. Thus, the attempt to assign the fulfillment of the ego ideal to social process has an illusion at its core—the illusion that the individual is the abstraction. I suggest that when we weave illusion so deeply into our social life that in order to maintain that social life we have to conceal from ourselves the fact that the illusion is an illusion, the result is, inevitably, totalitarianism.

References

Argyris, C. (1957). *Personality and organization: The conflict between the system and the individual*. New York: Harper and Row.

Argyris, C. & Schon, D.A. (1974). *Theory in practice*. San Francisco: Jossey-Bass.

Arendt, H. (1966). *The origins of totalitarianism*. New York: Harcourt, Brace and World.

Becker, E. (1971). *The birth and death of meaning*. (2nd. ed.). New York: Free Press.

Becker, E. (1973). *The denial of death*. New York: Free Press.

Culbert, S.A. and McDonough, J.J. (1980). *The invisible war: Pursuing self-interests at work*. New York: Wiley, 1980.

Denhardt, R.D. (1981). *In the shadow of organization*. Lawrence, Kansas: The Regents Press of Kansas.

Freud, S. (1961). *Civilization and its discontents*. (Standard edition, Volume 21). London: Hogarth Press. (Original work published 1930)

Freud, S. (1955). *Group psychology and the analysis of the ego*. (Standard edition, Volume 18). London: Hogarth Press. (Original work published 1921)

Freud, S. (1957). *On narcissism: An introduction*. (Standard edition, Volume 14). London: Hogarth Press. (Original work published 1914)

Klein, M. (1948). *Contributions to psychoanalysis: 1921-1945*. London: Hogarth Press.

Lasch, C. (1979). *The culture of narcissism: American life in an age of diminishing expectations*. New York: Warner.

Levison, D.J. (1978). *The seasons of a man's life*. New York: Knopf.

Maslow, A. H. (1970). *Motivation and personality*. (2nd. ed.). New York: Harper and Row.

Mead, G.H. (1934). *Mind, self and society*. Chicago: University of Chicago Press.

Parsons, T. (1954). An analytical approach to the theory of social stratification. In *Essays in sociological theory* (rev. ed.). New York: Free Press. (Original work published 1940)

Schein, E.H. (1980). *Organizational psychology*. (3rd. ed.). Englewood Cliffs, N.J.: Prentice-Hall.

Schwartz, H.S. (1983). Maslow and the hierarchical enactment of organizational reality, *Human Relations, 36* (10), 933-956.

Schwartz, H.S. (1985). The usefulness of myth and the myth of usefulness: A dilemma for the applied organizational scientist. *Journal of Management, 11* (1), 31-42.

Schwartz, H.S. (1986, June). *Totalitarianism and cultural engineering*. Paper presented at Standing Conference on Organizational Symbolism, Montreal.

Schwartz, H.S. (in press). Rousseau's *Discourse on Inequality* revisited: Psychology of work at the public-esteem stage of Maslow's hierarchy. *International Journal of Management*.

Shorris, E. (1981). *The oppressed middle: Politics of middle management/scenes from corporate life*. Garden City, New York: Anchor Press/Doubleday.

Staw, B.M. (1980). Rationality and justification in organizational life. In B.M. Staw & L.L. Cummings (Eds.), *Research in Organizational Behavior* (Vol. 2). (pp. 45-80). Greenwich, CT: JAI Press.

Terkel, S. (1974). *Working*. New York: Pantheon.

Weick, K.E. (1979). *The social psychology of organizing* (2nd. ed.). Reading, Mass.: Addison-Wesley.

Weiner, B., Frieze, I., Kulka, A., Reed, L., Rest, S., & Rosenbaum, R.M. (1971). *Perceiving the causes of success and failure*. Morristown, N.J.: General Learning Press.

Howard S. Schwartz is an Associate Professor of Organizational Behavior in the School of Business Administration at Oakland University.

[3]

Narcissistic Leaders
The Incredible Pros, the Inevitable Cons

by Michael Maccoby

When Michael Maccoby wrote this article, which was first published in early 2000, the business world was still under the spell of the Internet and its revolutionary promise. It was a time, Maccoby wrote, that called for larger-than-life leaders who could see the big picture and paint a compelling portrait of a dramatically different future. And that, he argued, was one reason we saw the emergence of the superstar CEOs—the grandiose, actively self-promoting, and genuinely narcissistic leaders who dominated the covers of business magazines at that time. Skilled orators and creative strategists, narcissists have vision and a great ability to attract and inspire followers.

The times have changed, and we've learned a lot about the dangers of overreliance on big personalities, but that doesn't mean narcissism can't be a useful leadership trait. There's certainly a dark side to narcissism—narcissists, Freud told us, are emotionally isolated and highly distrustful. They're usually poor listeners and lack empathy. Perceived threats can trigger rage. The challenge today—as Maccoby understood it to be four years ago—is to take advantage of their strengths while tempering their weaknesses.

There's something new and daring about the CEOs who are transforming today's industries. Just compare them with the executives who ran large companies in the 1950s through the 1980s. Those executives shunned the press and had their comments carefully crafted by corporate PR departments. But today's CEOs—superstars such as Bill Gates, Andy Grove, Steve Jobs, Jeff Bezos, and Jack Welch—hire their own publicists, write books, grant spontaneous interviews, and actively promote their personal philosophies. Their faces adorn the covers of magazines like *BusinessWeek*, *Time*, and the *Economist*. What's more, the world's business personalities are increasingly seen as the makers and shapers of our public and personal agendas. They advise schools on what kids should learn and lawmakers on how to invest the public's money. We look to them for thoughts on everything from the future of e-commerce to hot places to vacation.

There are many reasons today's business leaders have higher profiles than ever before. One is that business plays a much bigger role in our lives than it used to, and its leaders are more often in the limelight. Another is that the business world is experiencing enormous changes that call for visionary and charismatic leadership. But my 25 years of consulting both as a psychoanalyst in private practice and as an adviser to top managers suggest a third reason—namely, a pronounced change in the personality of the strategic leaders at the top. As an anthropologist, I try to understand people in the context in which they operate, and as a psychoanalyst, I tend to see them through a distinctly Freudian lens. Given what I know, I believe that the larger-than-life leaders we are seeing today closely resemble the personality type that Sigmund Freud dubbed narcissistic. "People of this type impress others as being 'personalities,'" he wrote, describing one of the psychological types that clearly fall within the range of normality. "They are especially suited to act as a support for others, to take on the role of leaders, and to give a fresh stimulus to cultural development or damage the established state of affairs."

Throughout history, narcissists have always emerged to inspire people and to shape the future. When military, religious, and political arenas dominated society, it was figures such as Napoléon Bonaparte, Mahatma Gandhi, and Franklin Delano Roosevelt who determined the social agenda. But from time to time, when business became the engine of social change, it, too, generated its share of narcissistic leaders. That was true at the beginning of this century, when men like Andrew Carnegie, John D. Rockefeller, Thomas Edison, and Henry Ford exploited new technologies and restructured American industry. And I think it is true again today.

But Freud recognized that there is a dark side to narcissism. Narcissists, he pointed out, are emotionally isolated and highly distrustful. Perceived threats can trigger rage. Achievements can feed feelings of grandiosity. That's why Freud thought narcissists were the hardest personality types to analyze. Consider how an executive at Oracle describes his narcissistic CEO Larry Ellison: "The difference between God and Larry is that God does not believe he is Larry." That observation is amusing, but it is also troubling. Not surprisingly, most people think of narcissists in a primarily negative way. After all, Freud named the type after the mythical figure Narcissus, who died because of

his pathological preoccupation with himself.

Yet narcissism can be extraordinarily useful—even necessary. Freud shifted his views about narcissism over time and recognized that we are all somewhat narcissistic. More recently, psychoanalyst Heinz Kohut built on Freud's theories and developed methods of treating narcissists. Of course, only professional clinicians are trained to tell if narcissism is normal or pathological. In this article, I discuss the differences between productive and unproductive narcissism but do not explore the extreme pathology of borderline conditions and psychosis.

Leaders such as Jack Welch and George Soros are examples of productive narcissists. They are gifted and creative strategists who see the big picture and find meaning in the risky challenge of changing the world and leaving behind a legacy. Indeed, one reason we look to productive narcissists in times of great transition is that they have the audacity to push through the massive transformations that society periodically undertakes. Productive narcissists are not only risk takers willing to get the job done but also charmers who can convert the masses with their rhetoric. The danger is that narcissism can turn unproductive when, lacking self-knowledge and restraining anchors, narcissists become unrealistic dreamers. They nurture grand schemes and harbor the illusion that only circumstances or enemies block their success. This tendency toward grandiosity and distrust is the Achilles' heel of narcissists. Because of it, even brilliant narcissists can come under suspicion for self-involvement, unpredictability, and—in extreme cases—paranoia.

It's easy to see why narcissistic leadership doesn't always mean successful leadership. Consider the case of Volvo's Pehr Gyllenhammar. He had a dream that appealed to a broad international audience—a plan to revolutionize the industrial workplace by replacing the dehumanizing assembly line caricatured in Charlie Chaplin's *Modern Times*. His wildly popular vision called for team-based craftsmanship. Model factories were built and publicized to international acclaim. But his success in pushing through these dramatic changes also sowed the seeds for his downfall. Gyllenhammar started to feel that he could ignore the concerns of his operational managers. He pursued chancy and expensive business deals,

Michael Maccoby is an anthropologist and a psychoanalyst He is also the founder and president of the Maccoby Group, a management consultancy in Washington, DC, and was formerly director of the Program on Technology, Public Policy, and Human Development at Harvard University's Kennedy School of Government in Cambridge, Massachusetts. This article was the basis for the book *The Productive Narcissist: The Promise and Peril of Visionary Leadership* (Broadway Books, 2003).

which he publicized on television and in the press. On one level, you can ascribe Gyllenhammar's falling out of touch with his workforce simply to faulty strategy. But it is also possible to attribute it to his narcissistic personality. His overestimation of himself led him to believe that others would want him to be the czar of a multinational enterprise. In turn, these fantasies led him to pursue a merger with Renault, which was tremendously unpopular with Swedish employees. Because Gyllenhammar was deaf to complaints about Renault, Swedish managers were forced to take their case public. In the end, shareholders aggressively rejected Gyllenhammar's plan, leaving him with no option but to resign.

Given the large number of narcissists at the helm of corporations today, the challenge facing organizations is to ensure that such leaders do not self-destruct or lead the company to disaster. That can take some doing because it is very hard for narcissists to work through their issues—and virtually impossible for them to do it alone. Narcissists need colleagues and even therapists if they hope to break free from their limitations. But because of their extreme independence and self-protectiveness, it is very difficult to get near them. Kohut maintained that a therapist would have to demonstrate an extraordinarily profound empathic understanding and sympathy for the narcissist's feelings in order to gain his trust. On top of that, narcissists must recognize that they can benefit from such help. For their part, employees must learn how to recognize—and work around—narcissistic bosses. To help them in this endeavor, let's first take a closer look at Freud's theory of personality types.

Three Main Personality Types

While Freud recognized that there are an almost infinite variety of personalities, he identified three main types: erotic, obsessive, and narcissistic. Most of us have elements of all three. We are all, for example, somewhat narcissistic. If that were not so, we would not be able to survive or assert our needs. The point is, one of the dynamic tendencies usually dominates the others, making each of us react differently to success and failure.

Freud's definitions of personality types differed over time. When talking about the erotic personality type, however, Freud generally did not mean a sexual personality but rather one

Productive narcissists have the audacity to push through the massive transformations that society periodically undertakes.

for whom loving and above all being loved is most important. This type of individual is dependent on those people they fear will stop loving them. Many erotics are teachers, nurses, and social workers. At their most productive, they are developers of the young as well as enablers and helpers at work. As managers, they are caring and supportive, but they avoid conflict and make people dependent on them. They are, according to Freud, outer-directed people.

Obsessives, in contrast, are inner-directed. They are self-reliant and conscientious. They create and maintain order and make the most effective operational managers. They look constantly for ways to help people listen better, resolve conflict, and find win-win opportunities. They buy self-improvement books such as Stephen Covey's *The 7 Habits of Highly Effective People*. Obsessives are also ruled by a strict conscience—they like to focus on continuous improvement at work because it fits in with their sense of moral improvement. As entrepreneurs, obsessives start businesses that express their values, but they lack the vision, daring, and charisma it takes to turn a good idea into a great one. The best obsessives set high standards and communicate very effectively. They make sure that instructions are followed and costs are kept within budget. The most productive are great mentors and team players. The unproductive and the uncooperative become narrow experts and rule-bound bureaucrats.

Narcissists, the third type, are independent and not easily impressed. They are innovators, driven in business to gain power and glory. Productive narcissists are experts in their industries, but they go beyond it. They also pose the critical questions. They want to learn everything about everything that affects the company and its products. Unlike erotics, they want to be admired, not loved. And unlike obsessives, they are not troubled by a punishing superego, so they are able to aggressively pursue their goals. Of all the personality types, narcissists run the greatest risk of isolating themselves at the moment of success. And because of their independence and aggressiveness, they are constantly looking out for enemies, sometimes degenerating into paranoia when they are under extreme stress. (For more on personality types, see the sidebar "Fromm's Fourth Personality Type.")

Strengths of the Narcissistic Leader

When it comes to leadership, personality type can be instructive. Erotic personalities generally make poor managers—they need too much approval. Obsessives make better leaders—they are your operational managers: critical and cautious. But it is narcissists who come closest to our collective image of great leaders. There are two reasons for this: they have compelling, even gripping, visions for companies, and they have an ability to attract followers.

Great Vision. I once asked a group of managers to define a leader. "A person with vision" was a typical response. Productive narcissists understand the vision thing particularly well, because they are by nature people who see the big picture. They are not analyzers who can break up big questions into manageable problems; they aren't number crunchers either (these are usually the obsessives). Nor do they try to extrapolate to understand the future—they attempt to create it. To paraphrase George Bernard Shaw, some people see things, and they say "why?"; narcissists dream things that never were and say, "Why not?"

Consider the difference between Bob Allen, a productive obsessive, and Mike Armstrong, a productive narcissist. In 1997, Allen tried to expand AT&T to reestablish the end-to-end ser-

vice of the Bell System by reselling local service from the regional Bell operating companies (RBOCs). Although this was a worthwhile endeavor for shareholders and customers, it was hardly earth-shattering. By contrast, through a strategy of combining voice, telecommunications, and Internet access by high-speed broadband telecommunication over cable, Mike Armstrong has "created a new space with his name on it," as one of his colleagues puts it. Armstrong is betting that his costly strategy will beat out the RBOC's less expensive solution of digital subscriber lines over copper wire. This example illustrates the different approaches of obsessives and narcissists. The risk Armstrong took is one that few obsessives would feel comfortable taking. His vision is galvanizing AT&T. Who but a narcissistic leader could achieve such a thing? As Napoléon—a classic narcissist—once remarked, "Revolutions are ideal times for soldiers with a lot of wit—and the courage to act."

As in the days of the French Revolution, the world is now changing in astounding ways; narcissists have opportunities they would never have in ordinary times. In short, today's narcissistic leaders have the chance to change the very rules of the game. Consider Robert B. Shapiro, CEO of Monsanto. Shapiro described his vision of genetically modifying crops as "the single most successful introduction of technology in the history of agriculture, including the plow" (*New York Times*, August 5, 1999). This is certainly a huge claim—there are still many questions about the safety and public acceptance of genetically engineered fruits and vegetables. But industries like agriculture are desperate for radical change. If Shapiro's gamble is successful, the industry will be transformed in the image of Monsanto. That's why he can get away with painting a picture of Monsanto as a highly profitable "life sciences" company—despite the fact that Monsanto's stock has fallen 12% from 1998 to the end of the third quarter of 1999. (During the same period, the S&P was up 41%.) Unlike Armstrong and Shapiro, it was enough for Bob Allen to win against his competitors in a game measured primarily by the stock market. But narcissistic leaders are after something more. They want—and need—to leave behind a legacy.

Scores of Followers. Narcissists have vi-

Fromm's Fourth Personality Type

Not long after Freud described his three personality types in 1931, psychoanalyst Erich Fromm proposed a fourth personality type, which has become particularly prevalent in today's service economy. Fromm called this type the "marketing personality," and it is exemplified by the lead character in Woody Allen's movie *Zelig*, a man so governed by his need to be valued that he becomes exactly like the people he happens to be around.

Marketing personalities are more detached than erotics and so are less likely to cement close ties. They are also less driven by conscience than obsessives. Instead, they are motivated by a radar-like anxiety that permeates everything they do. Because they are so eager to

please and to alleviate this anxiety, marketing personalities excel at selling themselves to others.

Unproductive marketing types lack direction and the ability to commit themselves to people or projects. But when productive, marketing types are good at facilitating teams and keeping the focus on adding value as defined by customers and colleagues. Like obsessives, marketing personalities are avid consumers of self-help books. Like narcissists, they are not wedded to the past. But marketing types generally make poor leaders in times of crisis. They lack the daring needed to innovate and are too responsive to current, rather than future, customer demands.

sion—but that's not enough. People in mental hospitals also have visions. The simplest definition of a leader is someone whom other people follow. Indeed, narcissists are especially gifted in attracting followers, and more often than not, they do so through language. Narcissists believe that words can move mountains and that inspiring speeches can change people. Narcissistic leaders are often skillful orators, and this is one of the talents that makes them so charismatic. Indeed, anyone who has seen narcissists perform can attest to their personal magnetism and their ability to stir enthusiasm among audiences.

Yet this charismatic gift is more of a two-way affair than most people think. Although it is not always obvious, narcissistic leaders are quite dependent on their followers—they need affirmation, and preferably adulation. Think of Winston Churchill's wartime broadcasts or J.F.K.'s "Ask not what your country can do for you" inaugural address. The adulation that follows from such speeches bolsters the self-confidence and conviction of the speakers. But if no one responds, the narcissist usually becomes insecure, overly shrill, and insistent—just as Ross Perot did.

Even when people respond positively to a narcissist, there are dangers. That's because charisma is a double-edged sword—it fosters both closeness and isolation. As he becomes increasingly self-assured, the narcissist becomes more spontaneous. He feels free of constraints. Ideas flow. He thinks he's invincible. This energy and confidence further inspire his followers. But the very adulation that the narcissist demands can have a corrosive effect. As he expands, he listens even less to words of caution and advice. After all, he has been right before, when others had their doubts. Rather than try to persuade those who disagree with him, he feels justified in ignoring them—creating further isolation. The result is sometimes flagrant risk taking that can lead to catastrophe. In the political realm, there is no clearer example of this than Bill Clinton.

Weaknesses of the Narcissistic Leader

Despite the warm feelings their charisma can evoke, narcissists are typically not comfortable with their own emotions. They listen only for the kind of information they seek. They don't learn easily from others. They don't like

to teach but prefer to indoctrinate and make speeches. They dominate meetings with subordinates. The result for the organization is greater internal competitiveness at a time when everyone is already under as much pressure as they can possibly stand. Perhaps the main problem is that the narcissist's faults tend to become even more pronounced as he becomes more successful.

Sensitive to Criticism. Because they are extraordinarily sensitive, narcissistic leaders shun emotions as a whole. Indeed, perhaps one of the greatest paradoxes in this age of teamwork and partnering is that the best corporate leader in the contemporary world is the type of person who is emotionally isolated. Narcissistic leaders typically keep others at arm's length. They can put up a wall of defense as thick as the Pentagon. And given their difficulty with knowing or acknowledging their own feelings, they are uncomfortable with other people expressing theirs—especially their negative feelings.

Indeed, even productive narcissists are extremely sensitive to criticism or slights, which feel to them like knives threatening their self-image and their confidence in their visions. Narcissists are almost unimaginably thin-skinned. Like the fairy-tale princess who slept on many mattresses and yet knew she was sleeping on a pea, narcissists—even powerful CEOs—bruise easily. This is one explanation why narcissistic leaders do not want to know what people think of them unless it is causing them a real problem. They cannot tolerate dissent. In fact, they can be extremely abrasive with employees who doubt them or with subordinates who are tough enough to fight back. Steve Jobs, for example, publicly humiliates subordinates. Thus, although narcissistic leaders often say that they want teamwork, what that means in practice is that they want a group of yes-men. As the more independent-minded players leave or are pushed out, succession becomes a particular problem.

Poor Listeners. One serious consequence of this oversensitivity to criticism is that narcissistic leaders often do not listen when they feel threatened or attacked. Consider the response of one narcissistic CEO I had worked with for three years who asked me to interview his immediate team and report back to him on what they were thinking. He invited me to his summer home to discuss what I had found. "So what do they think of me?" he asked with seeming nonchalance. "They think you are very creative and courageous," I told him, "but they also feel that you don't listen." "Excuse me, what did you say?" he shot back at once, pretending not to hear. His response was humorous, but it was also tragic.

In a very real way, this CEO could not hear my criticism because it was too painful to tolerate. Some narcissists are so defensive that they go so far as to make a virtue of the fact that they don't listen. As another CEO bluntly put it, "I didn't get here by listening to people!" Indeed, on one occasion when this CEO proposed a daring strategy, none of his subordinates believed it would work. His subsequent success strengthened his conviction that he had nothing to learn about strategy from his lieutenants. But success is no excuse for narcissistic leaders not to listen.

Lack of Empathy. Best-selling business writers today have taken up the slogan of "emotional competencies"—the belief that successful leadership requires a strongly developed sense of empathy. But although they crave empathy from others, productive narcissists are not noted for being particularly empathetic themselves. Indeed, lack of empathy is a characteristic shortcoming of some of the most charismatic and successful narcissists, including Bill Gates and Andy Grove. Of course, leaders do need to communicate persuasively. But a lack of empathy did not prevent some of history's greatest narcissistic leaders from knowing how to communicate—and inspire. Neither Churchill, de Gaulle, Stalin, nor Mao Tse-tung were empathetic. And yet they inspired people because of their passion and their conviction at a time when people longed for certainty.

In fact, in times of radical change, lack of empathy can actually be a strength. A narcissist finds it easier than other personality types to buy and sell companies, to close and move facilities, and to lay off employees—decisions that inevitably make many people angry and sad. But narcissistic leaders typically have few regrets. As one CEO says, "If I listened to my employees' needs and demands, they would eat me alive."

Given this lack of empathy, it's hardly surprising that narcissistic leaders don't score particularly well on evaluations of their interpersonal style. What's more, neither 360-degree

Narcissistic leaders often say that they want teamwork. What that means in practice is that they want a group of yesmen.

evaluations of their management style nor workshops in listening will make them more empathic. Narcissists don't want to change—and as long as they are successful, they don't think they have to. They may see the need for operational managers to get touchy-feely training, but that's not for them.

There is a kind of emotional intelligence associated with narcissists, but it's more street smarts than empathy. Narcissistic leaders are acutely aware of whether or not people are with them wholeheartedly. They know whom they can use. They can be brutally exploitative. That's why, even though narcissists undoubtedly have "star quality," they are often unlikable. They easily stir up people against them, and it is only in tumultuous times, when their gifts are desperately needed, that people are willing to tolerate narcissists as leaders.

Distaste for Mentoring. Lack of empathy and extreme independence make it difficult for narcissists to mentor and be mentored. Generally speaking, narcissistic leaders set very little store by mentoring. They seldom mentor others, and when they do they typically want their protégés to be pale reflections of themselves. Even those narcissists like Jack Welch who are held up as strong mentors are usually more interested in instructing than in coaching.

Narcissists certainly don't credit mentoring or educational programs for their own development as leaders. A few narcissistic leaders such as Bill Gates may find a friend or consultant—for instance, Warren Buffet, a superproductive obsessive—whom they can trust to be their guide and confidant. But most narcissists prefer "mentors" they can control. A 32-year-old marketing vice president, a narcissist with CEO potential, told me that she had rejected her boss as a mentor. As she put it, "First of all, I want to keep the relationship at a distance. I don't want to be influenced by emotions. Second, there are things I don't want him to know. I'd rather hire an outside consultant to be my coach." Although narcissistic leaders appear to be at ease with others, they find intimacy—which is a prerequisite for mentoring—to be difficult. Younger narcissists will establish peer relations with authority rather than seek a parentlike mentoring relationship. They want results and are willing to take chances arguing with authority.

An Intense Desire to Compete. Narcissistic leaders are relentless and ruthless in their pursuit of victory. Games are not games but tests of their survival skills. Of course, all successful managers want to win, but narcissists are not restrained by conscience. Organizations led by narcissists are generally characterized by intense internal competition. Their passion to win is marked by both the promise of glory and the primitive danger of extinction. It is a potent brew that energizes companies, creating a sense of urgency, but it can also be dangerous. These leaders see everything as a threat. As Andy Grove puts it, brilliantly articulating the narcissist's fear, distrust, and aggression, "Only the paranoid survive." The concern, of course, is that the narcissist finds enemies that aren't there—even among his colleagues.

Avoiding the Traps

There is very little business literature that tells narcissistic leaders how to avoid the pitfalls. There are two reasons for this. First, relatively few narcissistic leaders are interested in looking inward. And second, psychoanalysts don't usually get close enough to them, especially in the workplace, to write about them. (The noted psychoanalyst Harry Levinson is an exception.) As a result, advice on leadership focuses on obsessives, which explains why so much of it is about creating teamwork and being more receptive to subordinates. But as we've already seen, this literature is of little interest to narcissists, nor is it likely to help subordinates understand their narcissistic leaders. The absence of managerial literature on narcissistic leaders doesn't mean that it is impossible to devise strategies for dealing with narcissism. In the course of a long career counseling CEOs, I have identified three basic ways in which productive narcissists can avoid the traps of their own personality.

Find a trusted sidekick. Many narcissists can develop a close relationship with one person, a sidekick who acts as an anchor, keeping the narcissistic partner grounded. However, given that narcissistic leaders trust only their own insights and view of reality, the sidekick has to understand the narcissistic leader and what he is trying to achieve. The narcissist must feel that this person, or in some cases persons, is practically an extension of himself. The sidekick must also be sensitive enough to manage the relationship. Don Quixote is a classic example of a narcissist who was out of touch with reality but who was constantly saved from disaster by his squire Sancho Panza. Not surprisingly, many narcissistic leaders rely heavily on their spouses, the people they are closest to. But dependence on spouses can be risky, because they may further isolate the narcissistic leader from his company by supporting his grandiosity and feeding his paranoia. I once knew a CEO in this kind of relationship with his spouse. He took to accusing loyal subordinates of plotting against him just because they ventured a few criticisms of his ideas.

It is much better for a narcissistic leader to choose a colleague as his sidekick. Good sidekicks are able to point out the operational requirements of the narcissistic leader's vision and keep him rooted in reality. The best sidekicks are usually productive obsessives. Gyllenhammar, for instance, was most effective at Volvo when he had an obsessive COO, Håkan Frisinger, to focus on improving quality and cost, as well as an obsessive HR director, Berth

The Rise and Fall of a Narcissist

The story of Jan Carlzon, the former CEO of the Scandinavian airline SAS, is an almost textbook example of how a narcissist's weaknesses can cut short a brilliant career. In the 1980s, Carlzon's vision of SAS as the businessperson's airline was widely acclaimed in the business press; management guru Tom Peters described him as a model leader. In 1989, when I first met Carlzon and his management team, he compared the ideal organization to the Brazilian soccer team—in principle, there would be no fixed roles, only innovative plays. I asked the members of the management team if they agreed with this vision of an empowered front line. One vice president, a former pilot, answered no. " I still believe that the best organization is the military," he said. I then asked Carlzon for his reaction to that remark. "Well," he replied, "that may be true, if your goal is to shoot your customers."

That rejoinder was both witty and dismissive; clearly, Carlzon was not engaging in a serious dialogue with his subordinates. Nor was he listening to other advisers. Carlzon ignored the issue of high costs, even when many observers pointed out that SAS could not compete without improving productivity. He threw money at expensive acquisitions of hotels and made an unnecessary investment in Continental Airlines just months before it declared bankruptcy.

Carlzon's story perfectly corroborates the often-recorded tendency of narcissists to become overly expansive—and hence isolated—at the very pinnacle of their success. Seduced by the flattery he received in the international press, Carlzon's self-image became so enormously inflated that his feet left the ground. And given his vulnerability to grandiosity, he was propelled by a need to expand his organization rather than develop it. In due course, as Carlzon led the company deeper and deeper into losses, he was fired. Now he is a venture capitalist helping budding companies. And SAS has lost its glitter.

Jönsson, to implement his vision. Similarly, Bill Gates can think about the future from the stratosphere because Steve Ballmer, a tough obsessive president, keeps the show on the road. At Oracle, CEO Larry Ellison can afford to miss key meetings and spend time on his boat contemplating a future without PCs because he has a productive obsessive COO in Ray Lane to run the company for him. But the job of sidekick entails more than just executing the leader's ideas. The sidekick also has to get his leader to accept new ideas. To do this, he must be able to show the leader how the new ideas fit with his views and serve his interests. (For more on dealing with narcissistic bosses, see the sidebar "Working for a Narcissist.")

Indoctrinate the organization. The narcissistic CEO wants all his subordinates to think the way he does about the business. Productive narcissists—people who often have a dash of the obsessive personality—are good at converting people to their point of view. One of the most successful at this is GE's Jack Welch. Welch uses toughness to build a corporate culture and to implement a daring business strat-

egy, including the buying and selling of scores of companies. Unlike other narcissistic leaders such as Gates, Grove, and Ellison, who have transformed industries with new products, Welch was able to transform his industry by focusing on execution and pushing companies to the limits of quality and efficiency, bumping up revenues and wringing out costs. In order to do so, Welch hammers out a huge corporate culture in his own image—a culture that provides impressive rewards for senior managers and shareholders.

Welch's approach to culture building is widely misunderstood. Many observers, notably Noel Tichy in *The Leadership Engine*, argue that Welch forms his company's leadership culture through teaching. But Welch's "teaching" involves a personal ideology that he indoctrinates into GE managers through speeches, memos, and confrontations. Rather than create a dialogue, Welch makes pronouncements (either be the number one or two company in your market or get out), and he institutes programs (such as Six Sigma quality) that become the GE party line. Welch's strategy has been extremely effective. GE managers must either internalize his vision, or they must leave. Clearly, this is incentive learning with a vengeance. I would even go so far as to call Welch's teaching brainwashing. But Welch does have the rare insight and know-how to achieve what all narcissistic business leaders are trying to do—namely, get the organization to identify with them, to think the way they do, and to become the living embodiment of their companies.

Get into analysis. Narcissists are often more interested in controlling others than in knowing and disciplining themselves. That's why, with very few exceptions, even productive narcissists do not want to explore their personalities with the help of insight therapies such as psychoanalysis. Yet since Heinz Kohut, there has been a radical shift in psychoanalytic thinking about what can be done to help narcissists work through their rage, alienation, and grandiosity. Indeed, if they can be persuaded to undergo therapy, narcissistic leaders can use tools such as psychoanalysis to overcome vital character flaws.

Consider the case of one exceptional narcissistic CEO who asked me to help him understand why he so often lost his temper with subordinates. He lived far from my home city, and

Working for a Narcissist

Dealing with a narcissistic boss isn't easy. You have to be prepared to look for another job if your boss becomes too narcissistic to let you disagree with him. But remember that the company is typically betting on *his* vision of the future—not yours. Here are a few tips on how to survive in the short term:

Always empathize with your boss's feelings, but don't expect any empathy back. Look elsewhere for your own self-esteem. Understand that behind his display of infallibility, there hides a deep vulnerability. Praise his achievements and reinforce his best impulses, but don't be shamelessly sycophantic. An intelligent narcissist can see through flatterers and prefers independent people who truly appreciate him. Show that you will protect his image, inside and outside the company. But be careful if he asks for an honest evaluation. What he wants is information that will help him solve a problem about his image. He will resent any honesty that threatens his in-

flated self-image and will likely retaliate.

Give your boss ideas, but always let him take the credit for them. Find out what he thinks before presenting your views. If you believe he is wrong, show how a different approach would be in his best interest. Take his paranoid views seriously, don't brush them aside—they often reveal sharp intuitions. Disagree only when you can demonstrate how he will benefit from a different point of view.

Hone your time-management skills. Narcissistic leaders often give subordinates many more orders than they can possibly execute. Ignore the requests he makes that don't make sense. Forget about them. He will. But be careful: carve out free time for yourself only when you know there's a lull in the boss's schedule. Narcissistic leaders feel free to call you at any hour of the day or night. Make yourself available, or be prepared to get out.

so the therapy was sporadic and very unortho-dox. Yet he kept a journal of his dreams, which we interpreted together either by phone or when we met. Our analysis uncovered painful feelings of being unappreciated that went back to his inability to impress a cold father. He came to realize that he demanded an unrea-sonable amount of praise and that when he felt unappreciated by his subordinates, he be-came furious. Once he understood that, he was able to recognize his narcissism and even laugh about it. In the middle of our work, he even announced to his top team that I was psy-choanalyzing him and asked them what they thought of that. After a pregnant pause, one executive vice president piped up, "Whatever you're doing, you should keep doing it, be-cause you don't get so angry anymore." In-stead of being trapped by narcissistic rage, this CEO was learning how to express his concerns constructively.

Leaders who can work on themselves in that way tend to be the most productive nar-cissists. In addition to being self-reflective, they are also likely to be open, likable, and good-hu-mored. Productive narcissists have perspec-tive; they are able to detach themselves and laugh at their irrational needs. Although seri-ous about achieving their goals, they are also playful. As leaders, they are aware of being performers. A sense of humor helps them maintain enough perspective and humility to keep on learning.

The Best and Worst of Times

As I have pointed out, narcissists thrive in cha-otic times. In more tranquil times and places, however, even the most brilliant narcissist will seem out of place. In his short story *The Cur-few Tolls*, Stephen Vincent Benét speculates on what would have happened to Napoléon if he had been born some 30 years earlier. Re-tired in prerevolutionary France, Napoléon is depicted as a lonely artillery major boasting to a vacationing British general about how he could have beaten the English in India. The point, of course, is that a visionary born in the wrong time can seem like a pompous buffoon.

Historically, narcissists in large corporations have been confined to sales positions, where they use their persuasiveness and imagination to best effect. In settled times, the problematic side of the narcissistic personality usually con-spires to keep narcissists in their place, and

More and more large corporations are getting into bed with narcissists. They are finding that there is no substitute for narcissistic leaders in an age of innovation.

they can typically rise to top management po-sitions only by starting their own companies or by leaving to lead upstarts. Consider Joe Nac-chio, formerly in charge of both the business and consumer divisions of AT&T. Nacchio was a supersalesman and a popular leader in the mid-1990s. But his desire to create a new net-work for business customers was thwarted by colleagues who found him abrasive, self-pro-moting, and ruthlessly ambitious.

Two years ago, Nacchio left AT&T to be-come CEO of Qwest, a company that is creat-ing a long-distance fiber-optic cable network. Nacchio had the credibility—and charisma—to sell Qwest's initial public offering to finan-cial markets and gain a high valuation. Within a short space of time, he turned Qwest into an attractive target for the RBOCs, which were looking to move into long-distance telephony and Internet services. Such a sale would have given Qwest's owners a handsome profit on their investment. But Nacchio wanted more. He wanted to expand—to compete with AT&T—and for that he needed local service. Rather than sell Qwest, he chose to make a bid himself for local telephone operator U.S. West, using Qwest's highly valued stock to finance the deal. The market voted on this display of expansiveness with its feet—Qwest's stock price fell 40% between last June, when he made the deal, and the end of the third quar-ter of 1999. (The S&P index dropped 5.7% dur-ing the same period.)

Like other narcissists, Nacchio likes risk—and sometimes ignores the costs. But with the dramatic discontinuities going on in the world today, more and more large corporations are getting into bed with narcissists. They are find-ing that there is no substitute for narcissistic leaders in an age of innovation. Companies need leaders who do not try to anticipate the future so much as create it. But narcissistic leaders—even the most productive of them—can self-destruct and lead their organizations terribly astray. For companies whose narcissis-tic leaders recognize their limitations, these will be the best of times. For other companies, these could turn out to be the worst. ⛉

[4]

The Five Minds of a Manager

by Jonathan Gosling and Henry Mintzberg

The chief executive of a major Canadian company complained recently that he can't get his engineers to think like managers. It's a common complaint, but behind it lies an uncommonly important question: What does it mean to think like a manager?

Sadly, little attention has been paid to that question in recent years. Most of us have become so enamored of "leadership" that "management" has been pushed into the background. Nobody aspires to being a good manager anymore; everybody wants to be a great leader. But the separation of management from leadership is dangerous. Just as management without leadership encourages an uninspired style, which deadens activities, leadership without management encourages a disconnected style, which promotes hubris. And we all know the destructive power of hubris in organizations. So let's get back to plain old management.

The problem, of course, is that plain old management is complicated and confusing. Be global, managers are told, and be local. Collab-

orate, and compete. Change, perpetually, and maintain order. Make the numbers while nurturing your people. How is anyone supposed to reconcile all this? The fact is, no one can. To be effective, managers need to face the juxtapositions in order to arrive at a deep integration of these seemingly contradictory concerns. That means they must focus not only on what they have to accomplish but also on how they have to think. Managers need various "mind-sets."

Helping managers appreciate that was the challenge we set for ourselves in the mid-1990s when we began to develop a new master's program for practicing managers. We knew we could not rely on the usual structure of MBA education, which divides the management world into the discrete business functions of marketing, finance, accounting, and so on. Our intention was to educate managers who were coming out of these narrow silos; why push them back in? We needed a new structure that encouraged synthesis rather than separation. What we came up with—a structure based on the five aspects of the managerial mind—has proved not only powerful in the classroom but insightful in practice, as we hope to demonstrate in this article. We'll first explain how we came up with the five managerial mind-sets, then we'll discuss each in some depth before concluding with the case for interweaving the five.

The Five Managerial Mind-Sets

The International Federation of Red Cross and Red Crescent Societies, headquartered in Geneva, has a management development concern. It worries that it may be drifting too far toward a fast-action culture. It knows that it must act quickly in responding to disasters everywhere—earthquakes and wars, floods and famines—but it also sees the need to engage in the slower, more delicate task of building a capacity for action that is careful, thoughtful, and tailored to local conditions and needs.

Many business organizations face a similar problem—they know how to execute, but they are not so adept at stepping back to reflect on their situations. Others face the opposite predicament: They get so mired in thinking about their problems that they can't get things done fast enough. We all know bureaucracies that are great at planning and organizing but slow to respond to market forces, just as we're all acquainted with the nimble companies that react to every stimulus, but sloppily, and have to be constantly fixing things. And then, of course, there are those that suffer from both afflictions—for example, firms whose marketing departments are absorbed with grand positioning statements while their sales forces chase every possible deal.

Those two aspects establish the bounds of management: Everything that every effective manager does is sandwiched between *action* on the ground and *reflection* in the abstract. Action without reflection is thoughtless; reflection without action is passive. Every manager has to find a way to combine these two mind-sets—to function at the point where reflective thinking meets practical doing.

But action and reflection about what? One obvious answer is: about *collaboration,* about getting things done cooperatively with other people—in negotiations, for example, where a manager cannot act alone. Another answer is that action, reflection, and collaboration have to be rooted in a deep appreciation of reality

in all its facets. We call this mind-set *worldly,* which the *Oxford English Dictionary* defines as "experienced in life, sophisticated, practical." Finally, action, reflection, and collaboration, as well as worldliness, must subscribe to a certain rationality or logic; they rely on an *analytic* mind-set, too.

So we have five sets of the managerial mind, five ways in which managers interpret and deal with the world around them. Each has a dominant subject, or target, of its own. For reflection, the subject is the *self*; there can be no insight without self-knowledge. Collaboration takes the subject beyond the self, into the manager's network of *relationships*. Analysis goes a step beyond that, to the *organization;* organizations depend on the systematic decomposition of activities, and that's what analysis is all about. Beyond the organization lies what we consider the subject of the worldly mind-set, namely *context*—the worlds around the organization. Finally, the action mind-set pulls everything together through the process of *change*—in self, relationships, organization, and context.

The practice of managing, then, involves five perspectives, which correspond to the five modules of our program:

- Managing self: the reflective mind-set
- Managing organizations: the analytic mind-set
- Managing context: the worldly mind-set
- Managing relationships: the collaborative mind-set
- Managing change: the action mind-set

If you are a manager, this is your world!

Let us make clear several characteristics of this set of sets. First, we make no claim that our framework is either scientific or comprehensive. It simply has proved useful in our work with managers, including in our master's program. (For more on the program, see the sidebar "Mind-Sets for Management Development.") Second, we ask you to consider each of these managerial mind-sets as an attitude, a frame of mind that opens new vistas. Unless you get into a reflective frame of mind, for example, you cannot open yourself to new ideas. You might not even notice such ideas in the first place without a worldly frame of mind. And, of course, you cannot appreciate the buzz, the vistas, and the opportunities of actions unless you engage in them.

Third, a word on our word "mind-sets." We

Jonathan Gosling is the director of the Centre for Leadership Studies at the University of Exeter in Exeter, England. **Henry Mintzberg** is the Cleghorn Professor of Management Studies at McGill University in Montreal and the author of the forthcoming book *Managers Not MBAs* from Berrett-Koehler.

do not use it to *set* any manager's mind. All of us have had more than enough of that. Rather, we use the word in the spirit of a fortune one of us happened to pull out of a Chinese cookie recently: "Get your mind set. Confidence will lead you on." We ask you to get your mind set around five key ideas. Then, not just confidence but coherence can lead you on. Think, too, of these mind-sets as mind-*sights*—perspectives. But be aware that, improperly used, they can also be *mine sites*. Too much of any of them—obsessive analyzing or compulsive collaborating, for instance—and the mind-set can blow up in your face.

MANAGING SELF:
The Reflective Mind-Set

Managers who are sent off to development courses these days often find themselves being welcomed to "boot camp." This is no country club, they are warned; you'll have to work hard. But this is wrongheaded. While managers certainly don't need a country club atmosphere for development, neither do they need boot camp. Most managers we know already live boot camp every day. Besides, in real boot camps, soldiers learn to march and obey, not to stop and think. These days, what managers desperately need is to stop and think, to step back and reflect thoughtfully on their experiences. Indeed, in his book *Rules for Radicals*, Saul Alinsky makes the interesting point that events, or "happenings," become experience only after they have been reflected upon thoughtfully: "Most people do not accumulate a body of experience. Most people go through life undergoing a series of happenings, which pass through their systems undigested. Happenings become experiences when they are digested, when they are reflected on, related to general patterns, and synthesized."

Unless the meaning is understood, managing is mindless. Hence we take reflection to be that space suspended between experience and explanation, where the mind makes the connections. Imagine yourself in a meeting when someone suddenly erupts with a personal rant. You're tempted to ignore or dismiss the outburst—you've heard, after all, that the person is having problems at home. But why not use it to reflect on your own reaction—whether em-

Mind-Sets for Management Development

In 1996, when we founded the International Masters Program in Practicing Management with colleagues from around the world, we developed the managerial mind-sets as a new way to structure management education and development. Managers are sent to the IMPM by their companies, preferably in groups of four or five. They stay on the job, coming into our classrooms for five modules of two weeks each, one for each of the mind-sets, over a period of 16 months.

We open with a module on the reflective mind-set. The module is located at Lancaster University in the reflective atmosphere of northern England—the nearby hills and lakes inspire reflection on the purpose of life and work. Then it is on to McGill University in Montreal, where the grid-like regularity of the city reflects the energy and order of the analytic mind-set. The worldly mind-set on context comes alive at the Indian Institute of Management in Bangalore, where new technologies jostle ancient traditions on the crowded streets. Then comes the collabora-

tive mind-set, hosted by faculty in Japan, where collaboration has been the key to managerial innovations, and Korea, where alliances and partnerships have become the basis for business growth. Last is the action mind-set module, located at Insead in France, where emerging trends from around the world convert into lessons for managerial action.

So our locations not only teach the mind-sets but also encourage the participating managers to live them. And so have we, in the very conception of the program.

Our approach to management development is fundamentally reflective. We believe managers need to step back from the pressures of their jobs and reflect thoughtfully on their experiences. We as faculty members bring concepts; the participants bring experience. Learning occurs where these meet—in individual heads, small groups, and all together. Our 50-50 rule says that half the classroom time should be turned over to the participants, *on their agendas*.

The program is fully collaborative all around. There is no lead school; much of the organizational responsibility is distributed. Likewise, the faculty's relationship with the participants is collaborative. And faculty members work closely with the participating companies, which over the past eight years have included Alcan, BT, EDF Group and Gaz de France, Fujitsu, the International Red Cross Federation, LG, Lufthansa, Matsushita, Motorola, Royal Bank of Canada, and Zeneca.

We think of our setting as being especially worldly, because the participating managers and faculty host their colleagues at home, in their own cultures, and are guests abroad. We also believe that the program's reflective orientation allows us to probe into analysis more deeply than in regular education and work.

Finally, our own purpose is action: We seek fundamental change in management education worldwide—to help change business schools into true schools of management.

These days, what managers desperately need is to stop and think—to step back and reflect thoughtfully on their experiences.

barrassment, anger, or frustration—and so recognize some comparable feelings in yourself? Your own reaction now becomes a learning experience for you: You have opened a space for imagination, between your experience and your explanation. It can make all the difference.

Organizations may not need "mirror people," who see in everything only reflections of their own behavior. But neither do they need "window people," who cannot see beyond the images in front of them. They need managers who see both ways—in a sense, ones who look out the window at dawn, to see through their own reflections to the awakening world outside. "Reflect" in Latin means to refold, which suggests that attention turns inward so that it can be turned outward. This means going beyond introspection. It means looking in so that you can better see out in order to perceive a familiar thing in a different way—a product as a service, maybe, or a customer as a partner. Does that not describe the thinking of the really successful managers, the Andy Groves of the world? Compare such people with the Messiers and Lays, who dazzle with great mergers and grand strategies before burning out their companies.

Likewise, reflective managers are able to see behind in order to look ahead. Successful "visions" are not immaculately conceived; they are painted, stroke by stroke, out of the experiences of the past. Reflective managers, in other words, have a healthy respect for history—not just the grand history of deals and disasters but also the everyday history of all the little actions that make organizations work. Consider in this regard Kofi Annan's deep personal understanding of the United Nations, a comprehension that has been the source of his ability to help move that complex body to a different and better place. You must appreciate the past if you wish to use the present to get to a better future.

MANAGING ORGANIZATIONS:
The Analytical Mind-Set
Literally, analysis means to "let loose" (from the Greek *ana,* meaning "up" and *lyein,* meaning "loosen"). Analysis loosens up complex phenomena by breaking them into component parts—by decomposing them.

Analysis happens everywhere—in context (industry analysis), with relationships (360-degree assessments), and so on. But it is especially related to organization. You simply can't get organized without analysis, especially in a large company. Good analysis provides a language for organizing; it allows people to share an understanding of what is driving their efforts; it provides measures for performance. And organizational structure itself is fundamentally analytic—it is a means of decomposition to establish the *division* of labor. Just look at any organization chart, with all the boxes neatly lined up.

Picture the modern manager in an office in a tall building, looking down on the grid of the city below and across at the offices of companies in other buildings. From this perspective, the manager does not see individual people so much as systems of organization, power, and communication. Turning around, that manager is surrounded by the plush paraphernalia of his or her own company, the fruits of many people's tireless work on structures and systems and techniques. All of this represents analysis in the conventional sense: order and decomposition. How is such a manager to escape the analytic mind-set?

We prefer a different question: How is the manager to get truly inside the analytic mind-set, beyond the superficialities of obvious analysis, into the essential meanings of structures and systems? The key to analyzing effectively, in our view, is to get beyond conventional approaches in order to appreciate how analysis works and what effect it has on the organization.

Consider three related tasks, one simple, one complicated, one complex. Building a pleasure boat can be relatively straightforward—it's about such things as the ratio of displacement to length. Building an aircraft carrier is far more complicated, involving coordination of all kinds of subsystems and supply networks. Yet even here the component parts can be readily understood and the necessary behaviors made rather predictable. But a decision on whether or not to deploy that aircraft carrier can be truly complex: Who is to say with any certainty what is the right thing to do, or even what is the best thing under the circumstances?

Making that kind of complex decision means standing above shallow analysis and easy technique—just running the numbers—and going deeper into the analytic mind-set.

You have to take into account soft data, including the values underlying such choices. Deep analysis does not seek to simplify complex decisions, but to sustain the complexity while maintaining the organization's capacity to take action. That was the great power of Winston Churchill's rhetoric during World War II. His simple expressions captured the complexity that was Great Britain and the war in which it was engaged.

We have come across examples of deep analysis from managers participating in our own program who were being forced into obvious decisions by shallow analyses: Close the plant, speed up a slow project. After studying the analytic mind-set during the second module of our program, they went back to their jobs and probed more deeply. They analyzed the analyses of others—where these people were coming from, what data and assumptions they were using. They dug out other sorts of information that didn't make it into the conventional analyses and found limitations in the techniques used. Most important, they recognized biases in their own thinking. As a result, they saw things differently, encouraged others to change course, and helped resolve problems. Was this analysis or reflection? It was reflective analysis.

The problem for many managers today, as well as the business schools that train them, is not a lack of analysis but too much of it—at least, too much conventional analysis. This is exemplified by that popular metaphor in finance of the tennis player who watches the scoreboard while missing the ball (much like the marketer who studies the crowd while missing the sale). The trick in the analytic mind-set is to appreciate scores and crowds while watching the ball.

MANAGING CONTEXT:
The Worldly Mind-Set
We live on a globe that from a distance looks pretty uniform. "Globalization" sees the world from a distance, assuming and encouraging a certain homogeneity of behavior. Is that what we want from our managers?

A closer look reveals something rather different. Far from being uniform, this world is made up of all kinds of worlds. Should we not, then, be encouraging our managers to be more worldly, more experienced in life, in both sophisticated *and* practical ways? In other words,

should we not be getting into worlds beyond our own—into other people's circumstances, habits, cultures—so that we can better know our own world? To paraphrase T.S. Eliot's famous words, should we not explore ceaselessly in order to return home and know the place for the first time? That to us is the worldly mind-set.

Being worldly does not require global coverage, just as global coverage does not a worldly mind-set make. Indeed, global coverage does not even ensure a global perspective, given that the managers of so many "global" companies are rooted in the culture of the headquarters' country. But there are companies that seem to be reasonably global as well as worldly—a Shell, perhaps. Shell has, of course, long covered the globe. But because of social pressures, including a headquarters that has always had to work across two cultures (Dutch and British), it has struck us in personal contacts as rather worldly. By this we mean that the company tailors and blends its parts across the world, socially and environmentally as well as economically. It must find and extract oil without violating the rights of the people under whose territories the oil sits, and it has to refine and sell that oil in ways that are respectful of the local environment. That may seem clear enough today, but think about what companies like Shell went through to get there.

We conclude from this that while global managers may spend a lot of time in the air, and not just literally, they become worldly when their feet are planted firmly on the ground of eclectic experience. That means getting out of their offices, beyond the towers, to spend time where products are produced, customers served, and environments threatened. (For a comparison of the global and the worldly worldviews, see the exhibit "From Global to Worldly.")

Of course, shifting from a global to a worldly perspective is not easy. In James Clavell's novel *Shogun*, a Japanese woman tells her British lover, who is perplexed by the strange world of seventeenth-century Japan into which he has fallen, "It's all so simple, Anjin-san. Just change your concept of the world." Just!

But maybe it's not quite as hard as it seems. One way to begin (as in the novel) is through immersion in a strange context: Get into some-

Be global, managers are told, and be local. Change and maintain order. How is anyone supposed to reconcile all this? The fact is, no one can.

one else's world as a mirror to your own. That is why we hold our program's module on the worldly mind-set in India: For all but the Indian managers, India is not just another world, but, in a sense, otherworldly. Being there, especially among fellow managers from Indian companies, takes the non-Indian participants past the nice abstractions of economic, political, and social differences, down onto the streets, where these differences come alive.

"How can you possibly drive in this traffic?" an American marketing manager from Lufthansa, shaken up during her ride from the airport, asked an Indian professor. He replied, "I just join the flow." Learning can begin! That is not chaos on the streets of India, but another kind of logic. When you realize it, you have become that much more worldly.

We ask the participants in our program, after they go back to work between sessions, to write reflection papers on what they've learned at the modules. After the India module, a Russian manager from the Red Cross,

with his own share of third-world experiences, wrote about seeing a pile of tires with a huge black cross on it: "Black Cross: The Clinic for Tires" read the sign. He was struck by a symbol so familiar to him used in such a radically different context. He wrote: "Once again India [has reminded me] how interdependent, similar, and different at the same time are our worlds." This is the worldly mind-set in action: seeing differently out to reflect differently in. We might say that the worldly mind-set puts the reflective one into context.

In our view, to manage context is to manage on the edges, between the organization and the various worlds that surround it—cultures, industries, companies. What Ray Raphael has written about "Edges," in his book by that title, is germane to every manager:

> Many of the most interesting things, say the biologists, happen on the Edges—on the interface between the woods and the field, the land and the sea. There, living organisms encounter dynamic conditions that give rise to untold variety....
>
> Variety, perhaps, but there is tension as well. The flora of the meadows, for example, as they approach the woodlands, find themselves coping with increasingly unfavorable conditions: the sunlight they need might be lacking, and the soil no longer feels right. There is also the problem of competition with alien species of trees and shrubs. The Edges, in short, might abound with life, but each living form must fight for its own.

No wonder managers must be worldly. They have to mediate those wide zones where organization meets context—not just, for example, "customers" acting in "markets," however "differentiated," but all those particular people in particular places buying and using products in their own particular ways.

From Global to Worldly

By getting out of their offices and appreciating what the world looks like from the places where products are made and customers are served, managers can become truly worldly instead of merely global. The worldly perspective acknowledges that life on this globe is made up of all kinds of worlds.

The Global View	The Worldly View
What matters is generalizations about markets, values, and management practices.	What matters is attention paid to particular responses to specific conditions.
Local consequences are of less importance than overall economic performance. Global companies are not really responsible for local consequences.	Local consequences are a key indicator of performance, which has to add social as well as economic value. Companies are responsible for the local consequences of their actions.
Traveling around the world, we see a blur of differences.	Landing in different places, we join a plurality of worldviews.
The world is converging toward a common culture.	This is a world made up of edges and boundaries, like a patchwork.

MANAGING RELATIONSHIPS:
The Collaborative Mind-Set

It need hardly be said that managing is about working with people—not just as bosses and subordinates but, more important, as colleagues and partners. Yet despite all the rhetoric about collaboration, in the West, at least, we often take a narrow view. Thanks to the influence of economic theory, we see people as independent actors, detachable human "resources" or "assets" that can be moved around, bought and sold, combined, and "downsized." That is *not* the collaborative mind-set.

In fact, our own original definition of the collaborative mind-set got a jolt when our Japanese colleagues began to design the program's fourth module. It had been called Managing People. But they pointed out that a truly collaborative mind-set does not involve managing *people* so much as the *relationships* among people, in teams and projects as well as across divisions and alliances. Getting into a truly collaborative mind-set means getting beyond empowerment—a word implying that the people who know the work best must somehow receive the blessing of their managers to do it—and into commitment. It also means getting away from the currently popular heroic style of managing and moving toward a more engaging style.

Engaging managers listen more than they talk; they get out of their offices to see and feel more than they remain in them to sit and figure. By being worldly themselves, they foster collaboration among others. And they do less controlling, thus allowing other people to be in greater control of their own work. If "I deem, so that you do" is the implicit motto of the heroic manager, then for the engaging manager it is "We dream, so that we do." Our Japanese colleagues call this "leadership in the background"—it lets as many ordinary people as possible lead. (For a comparison of heroic and engaging management, see the exhibit "Two Ways to Manage.")

When John Kotter was asked if the members of the Harvard Business School class of 1974, whose careers he followed in his book *The New Rules*, were team players, he replied, "I think it fair to say that these people want to create the team and lead it to some glory as opposed to being a member of a team that's being driven by somebody else." That is not the collaborative mind-set. Having to run the team may be necessary at times—although we suspect it's needed far less often than most people think—but it hardly represents a collaborative point of view, nor does it foster teamwork. Leaders don't *do* most of the things that their organizations get done; they do not even make them get done. Rather, they help to establish the structures, conditions, and attitudes through which things get done. And that requires a collaborative mind-set.

We talk a great deal about networks these days, as well as teams, task forces, alliances, and knowledge work. Yet we still picture managers on "top." Well, then, picture yourself on top of a network, looking down on it. That puts you *out* of it; how can you possibly manage its relationships that way? To be in a collaborative mind-set means to be inside, involved, to manage *throughout*. But it has a more profound meaning, too—to get management beyond managers, to distribute it so that responsibility flows naturally to whoever can take the initiative and pull things together. Think of self-managing teams, of skunk works; indeed, think of who "manages" the World Wide Web.

Managing Change:
The Action Mind-Set
Imagine your organization as a chariot pulled by wild horses. (That may be easy for you to do!) These horses represent the emotions, aspirations, and motives of all the people in the organization. Holding a steady course requires just as much skill as steering around to a new direction.

Philosophers from Plato to Vivekenanda have used this metaphor to describe the need to harness emotional energy; it works well for management, too. An action mind-set, especially at senior levels, is not about whipping the horses into a frenzy, careening hither and yon. It is about developing a sensitive awareness of the terrain and of what the team is capable of doing in it and thereby helping to set and maintain direction, coaxing everyone along.

Action, and especially change, need no introduction, of course. Everybody today understands them and the need for them. That's the problem.

There is now an overwhelming emphasis on action at the expense of reflection. The Red Cross Federation is unusual, not in experiencing this problem, but in being aware of it. In addition, people are obsessed with change these days. We are told, relentlessly, that we live in times of great upheaval, that everything is changing, so we had better be in a constant state of alert. Change or else.

Well, then, look around. What do you see that has changed recently? Your clothing? (Your grandparents wore cotton and wool; they too buttoned buttons.) Your car? (It uses the basic technology of the Model T.) The

If you picture yourself on top of a network, looking down on it, then you are out of it. How can you possibly manage its relationships that way?

airplane you're flying in? (That technology is newer: the first commercial jet aircraft took flight in 1952.) Your telephone? (That changed—about ten years ago. Unless, of course, you are not using a cellular phone.)

Our point is not that nothing is changing. No, something is always changing. Right now it is information technology. But many other things are not changing at all—and these we don't notice (like buttons). We tend to focus on what is changing and conclude that every-

thing is. That is hardly a reflective mind-set, and it is detrimental as well to the action mind-set. We have to sober up to the reality that change is not pervasive, and that the phenomenon of change is not new. If the reflective mind-set has to respect history, then the action mind-set could use a little humility.

Change has no meaning without continuity. There is a name for everything changing all the time: anarchy. No one wants to live with that, certainly no organization that wishes to survive. Businesses are judged by the products they sell and the services they render, not the changes they make. So change cannot be managed without continuity. Accordingly, the trick in the action mind-set is to mobilize energy around those things that need changing, while being careful to maintain the rest. And make no mistake about it, managing continuity is no easier than managing change. Remember those wild horses.

The dominant view of managing change is Cartesian: Action results from deliberate strategies, carefully planned, that unfold as systematically managed sequences of decisions. That is the analytic mind-set, not the action one. Monsanto went into genetically engineered agriculture with that approach, with its strategy all worked out in advance. With control of seed varieties and certain pesticides and fertilizers, it could bring an entire ecosystem to the market. And it had the research capacity and presence worldwide to do it. So it set about a series of brilliantly conceived acquisitions and effectively positioned the company to be the Microsoft of agribusiness. But the farmers and consumers weren't there—they were more enthusiastic about continuity at that point—and the plan collapsed.

Change, to be successful, cannot follow some mechanistic schedule of steps, of formulation followed by implementation. Action and reflection have to blend in a natural flow. And that has to include collaboration. Satish Kumar, the director of the Schumacher Institute in the United Kingdom, put it nicely in the title of his latest book, *You Are Therefore I Am: A Declaration of Dependence.* We had better be reflectively collaborative, as well as analytically worldly, if we wish to accomplish effective change.

Of course, energized action is necessary too, but that doesn't mean being hyperactive or fiddling around endlessly with structure. It means

Two Ways to Manage

Heroic management (based on self)	Engaging management (based on collaboration)
Managers are important people, separate from those who develop products and deliver services.	Managers are important to the extent that they help other people do the important work of developing products and delivering services.
The higher "up" these managers go, the more important they become. At the "top," the chief executive is the corporation.	An organization is an interacting network, not a vertical hierarchy. Effective leaders work throughout; they do not sit on top.
Down the hierarchy comes the strategy—clear, deliberate, and bold—emanating from the chief, who makes the dramatic moves. Everyone else "implements."	Out of the network emerge strategies, as engaged people solve little problems that grow into big initiatives.
Implementation is the problem because, while the chief embraces change, most others resist it. That is why outsiders must be favored over insiders.	Implementation is the problem because it cannot be separated from formulation. That is why committed insiders are necessary to come up with the key changes.
To manage is to make decisions and allocate resources—including human resources. Managing thus means analyzing, often calculating, based on facts from reports.	To manage is to bring out the positive energy that exists naturally within people. Managing thus means inspiring and engaging, based on judgment that is rooted in context.
Rewards for increasing performance go to the leaders. What matters is what's measured—shareholder value, in particular.	Rewards for making the organization a better place go to everyone. Human values, many of which cannot be measured, matter.
Leadership is thrust upon those who thrust their will upon others.	Leadership is a sacred trust earned through the respect of others.

remaining curious, alert, experimental. Changing is a learning process, and so is maintaining course. We may think of stasis as the norm and change as driven, but it doesn't have to be that way. Active members of an organization may resist change imposed on them because they understand that the change would be dysfunctional. And they in turn may engage in "silent change" of their own, continually re-creating operations for better performance.

Weaving the Mind-Sets Together

Clearly, these five mind-sets do not represent hard-and-fast categories. We need distinct labels for them, but they obviously overlap, and they are more than mere words. They are more than metaphors too, but a metaphor can help us understand how they come together.

Imagine the mind-sets as threads and the manager as weaver. Effective performance means weaving each mind-set over and under the others to create a fine, sturdy cloth. You analyze, then you act. But that does not work as expected, so you reflect. You act some more, then find yourself blocked, realizing that you cannot do it alone. You have to collaborate. But to do that, you have to get into the world of others. Then more analysis follows, to articulate the new insights. Now you act again—and so it goes, as the cloth of your effort forms.

But one piece of cloth is not enough. An organization is a collective entity that achieves common purpose when the cloths of its various managers are sewn together into useful garments—when the organization's managers collaborate to combine their reflective actions in analytic, worldly ways.

We have been emphasizing the need for all managers to get deeply into all five mind-sets. But many managers naturally tilt to one or another, depending on their situations and personal inclinations. Some people are more reflective than others, some more action oriented, some more analytic, and so on. Finance and marketing have their share of calculating managers (lots of analysis), salespeople can sometimes be a little too worldly, those from HR a little too enthusiastic about collaboration. So the weaving often has to be collaborative, too, like the sewing, as managers come to understand one another and combine their strengths.

Companies have been quite concerned about seamlessness in recent years. Yet we all appreciate seams that are nicely sewn, just as we appreciate mind-sets that are nicely combined. Effective organizations tailor handsome results out of the woven mind-sets of their managers.   ▽

[5]

The Leader's New Work:
Building Learning Organizations

Peter M. Senge   *MIT Sloan School of Management*

OVER THE PAST two years, business academics and senior managers have begun talking about the notion of the learning organization. Ray Stata of Analog Devices put the idea succinctly in these pages last spring: "The rate at which organizations learn may become the only sustainable source of competitive advantage." And in late May of this year, at an MIT-sponsored conference entitled "Transforming Organizations," two questions arose again and again: *How can we build organizations in which continuous learning occurs?* and, *What kind of person can best lead the learning organization?* This article, based on Senge's recently published book, *The Fifth Discipline: The Art and Practice of the Learning Organization*, begins to chart this new territory, describing new roles, skills, and tools for leaders who wish to develop learning organizations.

Sloan
Management
Review

7

Fall 1990

HUMAN BEINGS are designed for learning. No one has to teach an infant to walk, or talk, or master the spatial relationships needed to stack eight building blocks that don't topple. Children come fully equipped with an insatiable drive to explore and experiment. Unfortunately, the primary institutions of our society are oriented predominantly toward controlling rather than learning, rewarding individuals for performing for others rather than for cultivating their natural curiosity and impulse to learn. The young child entering school discovers quickly that the name of the game is getting the right answer and avoiding mistakes—a mandate no less compelling to the aspiring manager.

"Our prevailing system of management has destroyed our people," writes W. Edwards Deming, leader in the quality movement.[1] "People are born with intrinsic motivation, self-esteem, dignity, curiosity to learn, joy in learning. The forces of destruction begin with toddlers—a prize for the best Halloween costume, grades in school, gold stars, and on up through the university. On the job, people, teams, divisions are ranked—reward for the one at the top, punishment at the bottom. MBO, quotas, incentive pay, business plans, put together separately, division by division, cause further loss, unknown and unknowable."

Peter M. Senge is Director of the Systems Thinking and Organizational Learning program at the MIT Sloan School of Management.

Ironically, by focusing on performing for someone else's approval, corporations create the very conditions that predestine them to mediocre performance. Over the long run, superior performance depends on superior learning. A Shell study showed that, according to former planning director Arie de Geus, "a full one-third of the Fortune '500' industrials listed in 1970 had vanished by 1983."[2] Today, the average lifetime of the largest industrial enterprises is probably less than *half* the average lifetime of a person in an industrial society. On the other hand, de Geus and his colleagues at Shell also found a small number of companies that survived for seventy-five years or longer. Interestingly, the key to their survival was the ability to run "experiments in the margin," to continually explore new business and organizational opportunities that create potential new sources of growth.

If anything, the need for understanding how organizations learn and accelerating that learning is greater today than ever before. The old days when a Henry Ford, Alfred Sloan, or Tom Watson *learned for the organization* are gone. In an increasingly dynamic, interdependent, and unpredictable world, it is simply no longer possible for anyone to "figure it all out at the top." The old model, "the top thinks and the local acts," must now give way to integrating thinking and acting at all levels. While the challenge is great, so is the potential payoff. "The person who figures out how to harness the collective genius of the people in his or her organization," according to former Citibank CEO Walter Wriston, "is going to blow the competition away."

Adaptive Learning and Generative Learning

The prevailing view of learning organizations emphasizes increased adaptability. Given the accelerating pace of change, or so the standard view goes, "the most successful corporation of the 1990s," according to *Fortune* magazine, "will be something called a learning organization, a consummately adaptive enterprise."[3] As the Shell study shows, examples of traditional authoritarian bureaucracies that responded too slowly to survive in changing business environments are legion.

But increasing adaptiveness is only the first stage in moving toward learning organizations. The impulse to learn in children goes deeper than desires to respond and adapt more effectively to environmental change. The impulse to learn, at its heart, is an impulse to be generative, to expand our capability. This is why leading corporations are focusing on *generative* learning, which is about creating, as well as *adaptive* learning, which is about coping.[4]

The total quality movement in Japan illustrates the evolution from adaptive to generative learning. With its emphasis on continuous experimentation and feedback, the total quality movement has been the first wave in building learning organizations. But Japanese firms' view of serving the customer has evolved. In the early years of total quality, the focus was on "fitness to standard," making a product reliably so that it would do what its designers intended it to do and what the firm told its customers it would do. Then came a focus on "fitness to need," understanding better what the customer wanted and then providing products that reliably met those needs. Today, leading edge firms seek to understand and meet the "latent need" of the customer—what customers might truly value but have never experienced or would never think to ask for. As one Detroit executive commented recently, "You could never produce the Mazda Miata solely from market research. It required a leap of imagination to see what the customer *might* want."[5]

Generative learning, unlike adaptive learning, re-

quires new ways of looking at the world, whether in understanding customers or in understanding how to better manage a business. For years, U.S. manufacturers sought competitive advantage in aggressive controls on inventories, incentives against overproduction, and rigid adherence to production forecasts. Despite these incentives, their performance was eventually eclipsed by Japanese firms who saw the challenges of manufacturing differently. They realized that eliminating delays in the production process was the key to reducing instability and improving cost, productivity, and service. They worked to build networks of relationships with trusted suppliers and to redesign physical production processes so as to reduce delays in materials procurement, production set up, and in-process inventory—a much higher-leverage approach to improving both cost and customer loyalty.

As Boston Consulting Group's George Stalk has observed, the Japanese saw the significance of delays because they saw the process of order entry, production scheduling, materials procurement, production, and distribution *as an integrated system*. "What distorts the system so badly is time," observed Stalk—the multiple delays between events and responses. "These distortions reverberate throughout the system, producing disruptions, waste, and inefficiency."[6] Generative learning requires seeing the systems that control events. When we fail to grasp the systemic source of problems, we are left to "push on" symptoms rather than eliminate underlying causes. The best we can ever do is adaptive learning.

The Leader's New Work

"I talk with people all over the country about learning organizations, and the response is always very positive," says William O'Brien, CEO of the Hanover Insurance companies. "If this type of organization is so widely preferred, why don't people create such organizations? I think the answer is leadership. People have no real comprehension of the type of commitment it requires to build such an organization."[7]

Our traditional view of leaders—as special people who set the direction, make the key decisions, and energize the troops—is deeply rooted in an individualistic and nonsystemic worldview. Especially in the West, leaders are *heroes*—great men (and occasionally women) who rise to the fore in times of crisis. So long as such myths prevail, they reinforce a focus on short-term events and charismatic heroes rather than on systemic forces and collective learning.

Leadership in learning organizations centers on subtler and ultimately more important work. In a learning organization, leaders' roles differ dramatically from that of the charismatic decision maker. Leaders are designers, teachers, and stewards. These roles require new skills: the ability to build shared vision, to bring to the surface and challenge prevailing mental models, and to foster more systemic patterns of thinking. In short, leaders in learning organizations are responsible for *building organizations* where people are continually expanding their capabilities to shape their future—that is, leaders are responsible for learning.

Creative Tension: The Integrating Principle

Leadership in a learning organization starts with the principle of creative tension.[8] Creative tension comes from seeing clearly where we want to be, our "vision," and telling the truth about where we are, our "current reality." The gap between the two generates a natural tension (see Figure 1).

Creative tension can be resolved in two basic

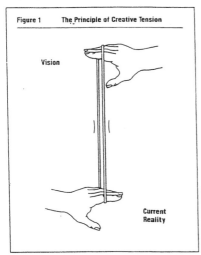

Figure 1   The Principle of Creative Tension

Vision

Current Reality

ways: by raising current reality toward the vision, or by lowering the vision toward current reality. Individuals, groups, and organizations who learn how to work with creative tension learn how to use the energy it generates to move reality more reliably toward their visions.

The principle of creative tension has long been recognized by leaders. Martin Luther King, Jr., once said, "Just as Socrates felt that it was necessary to create a tension in the mind, so that individuals could rise from the bondage of myths and half truths . . . so must we . . . create the kind of tension in society that will help men rise from the dark depths of prejudice and racism."[9]

Without vision there is no creative tension. Creative tension cannot be generated from current reality alone. All the analysis in the world will never generate a vision. Many who are otherwise qualified to lead fail to do so because they try to substitute analysis for vision. They believe that, if only people understood current reality, they would surely feel the motivation to change. They are then disappointed to discover that people "resist" the personal and organizational changes that must be made to alter reality. What they never grasp is that the natural energy for changing reality comes from holding a picture of what might be that is more important to people than what is.

But creative tension cannot be generated from vision alone; it demands an accurate picture of current reality as well. Just as King had a dream, so too did he continually strive to "dramatize the shameful conditions" of racism and prejudice so that they could no longer be ignored. Vision without an understanding of current reality will more likely foster cynicism than creativity. The principle of creative tension teaches that *an accurate picture of current reality is just as important as a compelling picture of a desired future.*

Leading through creative tension is different than solving problems. In problem solving, the energy for change comes from attempting to get away from an aspect of current reality that is undesirable. With creative tension, the energy for change comes from the vision, from what we want to create, juxtaposed with current reality. While the distinction may seem small, the consequences are not. Many people and organizations find themselves motivated to change only when their problems are bad enough to cause them to change. This works for a while, but the change process runs out of steam as soon

Sloan
Management
Review

9

Fall 1990

as the problems driving the change become less pressing. With problem solving, the motivation for change is extrinsic. With creative tension, the motivation is intrinsic. This distinction mirrors the distinction between adaptive and generative learning.

New Roles

The traditional authoritarian image of the leader as "the boss calling the shots" has been recognized as oversimplified and inadequate for some time. According to Edgar Schein, "Leadership is intertwined with culture formation." Building an organization's culture and shaping its evolution is the "unique and essential function" of leadership.[10] In a learning organization, the critical roles of leadership—designer, teacher, and steward—have antecedents in the ways leaders have contributed to building organizations in the past. But each role takes on new meaning in the learning organization and, as will be seen in the following sections, demands new skills and tools.

Leader as Designer

Imagine that your organization is an ocean liner and that you are "the leader." What is your role?

I have asked this question of groups of managers many times. The most common answer, not surprisingly, is "the captain." Others say, "The navigator, setting the direction." Still others say, "The helmsman, actually controlling the direction," or, "The engineer down there stoking the fire, providing energy," or, "The social director, making sure everybody's enrolled, involved, and communicating." While these are legitimate leadership roles, there is another which, in many ways, eclipses them all in importance. Yet rarely does anyone mention it.

The neglected leadership role is the *designer* of the ship. No one has a more sweeping influence than the designer. What good does it do for the captain to say, "Turn starboard 30 degrees," when the designer has built a rudder that will only turn to port, or which takes six hours to turn to starboard? It's fruitless to be the leader in an organization that is poorly designed.

The functions of design, or what some have called "social architecture," are rarely visible; they take place behind the scenes. The consequences that appear today are the result of work done long in the past, and work today will show its benefits far in the future. Those who aspire to lead out of a desire

to control, or gain fame, or simply to be at the center of the action, will find little to attract them to the quiet design work of leadership.

But what, specifically, is involved in organizational design? "Organization design is widely misconstrued as moving around boxes and lines," says Hanover's O'Brien. "The first task of organization design concerns designing the governing ideas of purpose, vision, and core values by which people will live." Few acts of leadership have a more enduring impact on an organization than building a foundation of purpose and core values.

In 1982, Johnson & Johnson found itself facing a corporate nightmare when bottles of its best-selling Tylenol were tampered with, resulting in several deaths. The corporation's immediate response was to pull all Tylenol off the shelves of retail outlets. Thirty-one million capsules were destroyed, even though they were tested and found safe. Although the immediate cost was significant, no other action was possible given the firm's credo. Authored almost forty years earlier by president Robert Wood Johnson, Johnson & Johnson's credo states that permanent success is possible only when modern industry realizes that:

• service to its customers comes first;
• service to its employees and management comes second;
• service to the community comes third; and
• service to its stockholders, last.

Such statements might seem like motherhood and apple pie to those who have not seen the way a clear sense of purpose and values can affect key business decisions. Johnson & Johnson's crisis management in this case was based on that credo. It was simple, it was right, and it worked.

If governing ideas constitute the first design task of leadership, the second design task involves the policies, strategies, and structures that translate guiding ideas into business decisions. Leadership theorist Philip Selznick calls policy and structure the "institutional embodiment of purpose."[11] "Policy making (the rules that guide decisions) ought to be separated from decision making," says Jay Forrester.[12] "Otherwise, short-term pressures will usurp time from policy creation."

Traditionally, writers like Selznick and Forrester have tended to see policy making and implementation as the work of a small number of senior managers. But that view is changing. Both the dynamic business environment and the mandate of the learning organization to engage people at all levels now make it clear that this second design task is more subtle. Henry Mintzberg has argued that strategy is less a rational plan arrived at in the abstract and implemented throughout the organization than an "emergent phenomenon." Successful organizations "craft strategy" according to Mintzberg, as they continually learn about shifting business conditions and balance what is desired and what is possible.[13] The key is not getting the right strategy but fostering strategic thinking. "The choice of individual action is only part of . . . the policymaker's need," according to Mason and Mitroff.[14] "More important is the need to achieve insight into the nature of the complexity and to formulate concepts and world views for coping with it."

Behind appropriate policies, strategies, and structures are effective learning processes; their creation is the third key design responsibility in learning organizations. This does not absolve senior managers of their strategic responsibilities. Actually, it deepens and extends those responsibilities. Now, they are not only responsible for ensuring that an organization have well-developed strategies and policies, but also for ensuring that processes exist whereby these are continually improved.

In the early 1970s, Shell was the weakest of the big seven oil companies. Today, Shell and Exxon are arguably the strongest, both in size and financial health. Shell's ascendance began with frustration. Around 1971 members of Shell's "Group Planning" in London began to foresee dramatic change and unpredictability in world oil markets. However, it proved impossible to persuade managers that the stable world of steady growth in oil demand and supply they had known for twenty years was about to change. Despite brilliant analysis and artful presentation, Shell's planners realized, in the words of Pierre Wack, that they "had failed to change behavior in much of the Shell organization."[15] Progress would probably have ended there, had the frustration not given way to a radically new view of corporate planning.

As they pondered this failure, the planners' view of their basic task shifted: "We no longer saw our task as producing a documented view of the future business environment five or ten years ahead. Our real target was the microcosm (the 'mental model') of our decision makers." Only when the planners reconceptualized their basic task as fostering learning rather than devising plans did their insights begin to have an impact. The initial tool used was "scenario analysis," through which planners encouraged operating managers to think through how they would manage in the future under different possible scenarios. It mattered not that the managers believed the planners' scenarios absolutely, only that they became engaged in ferreting out the implications. In this way, Shell's planners conditioned managers to be mentally prepared for a shift from low prices to high prices and from stability to instability. The results were significant. When OPEC became a reality, Shell quickly responded by increasing local operating company control (to enhance maneuverability in the new political environment), building buffer stocks, and accelerating development of non-OPEC sources — actions that its competitors took much more slowly or not at all.

Somewhat inadvertently, Shell planners had discovered the leverage of designing institutional learning processes, whereby, in the words of former planning director de Geus, "Management teams change their shared mental models of their company, their markets, and their competitors."[16] Since then, "planning as learning" has become a byword at Shell, and Group Planning has continually sought out new learning tools that can be integrated into the planning process. Some of these are described below.

Leader as Teacher

"The first responsibility of a leader," writes retired Herman Miller CEO Max de Pree, "is to define reality."[17] Much of the leverage leaders can actually exert lies in helping people achieve more accurate, more insightful, and more *empowering* views of reality.

Leader as teacher does *not* mean leader as authoritarian expert whose job it is to teach people the "correct" view of reality. Rather, it is about helping everyone in the organization, oneself included, to gain more insightful views of current reality. This is in line with a popular emerging view of leaders as coaches, guides, or facilitators.[18] In learning organizations, this teaching role is developed further by virtue of explicit attention to people's mental models and by the influence of the systems perspective.

The role of leader as teacher starts with bringing to the surface people's mental models of important issues. No one carries an organization, a market, or a state of technology in his or her head.

Sloan
Management
Review

11

Fall 1990

What we carry in our heads are assumptions. These mental pictures of how the world works have a significant influence on how we perceive problems and opportunities, identify courses of action, and make choices.

One reason that mental models are so deeply entrenched is that they are largely tacit. Ian Mitroff, in his study of General Motors, argues that an assumption that prevailed for years was that, in the United States, "Cars are status symbols. Styling is therefore more important than quality."[19] The Detroit automakers didn't say, "We have a *mental model* that all people care about is styling." Few actual managers would even say publicly that all people care about is styling. So long as the view remained unexpressed, there was little possibility of challenging its validity or forming more accurate assumptions.

But working with mental models goes beyond revealing hidden assumptions. "Reality," as perceived by most people in most organizations, means pressures that must be borne, crises that must be reacted to, and limitations that must be accepted. Leaders as teachers help people *restructure their views of reality* to see beyond the superficial conditions and events into the underlying causes of problems—and therefore to see new possibilities for shaping the future.

Specifically, leaders can influence people to view reality at three distinct levels: events, patterns of behavior, and systemic structure.

Systemic Structure
(Generative)
↓
Patterns of Behavior
(Responsive)
↓
Events
(Reactive)

The key question becomes *where do leaders predominantly focus their own and their organization's attention?*

Contemporary society focuses predominantly on events. The media reinforces this perspective, with almost exclusive attention to short-term, dramatic events. This focus leads naturally to explaining what happens in terms of those events: "The Dow Jones average went up sixteen points because high fourth-quarter profits were announced yesterday."

Pattern-of-behavior explanations are rarer, in contemporary culture, than event explanations, but

they do occur. "Trend analysis" is an example of seeing patterns of behavior. A good editorial that interprets a set of current events in the context of long-term historical changes is another example. Systemic, structural explanations go even further by addressing the question, "What causes the patterns of behavior?"

In some sense, all three levels of explanation are equally true. But their usefulness is quite different. Event explanations—who did what to whom—doom their holders to a reactive stance toward change. Pattern-of-behavior explanations focus on identifying long-term trends and assessing their implications. They at least suggest how, over time, we can respond to shifting conditions. Structural explanations are the most powerful. Only they address the underlying causes of behavior at a level such that patterns of behavior can be changed.

By and large, leaders of our current institutions focus their attention on events and patterns of behavior, and, under their influence, their organizations do likewise. That is why contemporary organizations are predominantly reactive, or at best responsive—rarely generative. On the other hand, leaders in learning organizations pay attention to all three levels, but focus especially on systemic structure; largely by example, they teach people throughout the organization to do likewise.

Leader as Steward

This is the subtlest role of leadership. Unlike the roles of designer and teacher, it is almost solely a matter of attitude. It is an attitude critical to learning organizations.

While stewardship has long been recognized as an aspect of leadership, its source is still not widely understood. I believe Robert Greenleaf came closest to explaining real stewardship, in his seminal book *Servant Leadership*.[20] There, Greenleaf argues that "The servant leader *is* servant first. . . . It begins with the natural feeling that one wants to serve, to serve *first*. This conscious choice brings one to aspire to lead. That person is sharply different from one who is leader first, perhaps because of the need to assuage an unusual power drive or to acquire material possessions."

Leaders' sense of stewardship operates on two levels: stewardship for the people they lead and stewardship for the larger purpose or mission that underlies the enterprise. The first type arises from a keen appreciation of the impact one's leadership can have on others. People can suffer economically, emotionally, and spiritually under inept leadership. If anything, people in a learning organization are more vulnerable because of their commitment and sense of shared ownership. Appreciating this naturally instills a sense of responsibility in leaders. The second type of stewardship arises from a leader's sense of personal purpose and commitment to the organization's larger mission. People's natural impulse to learn is unleashed when they are engaged in an endeavor they consider worthy of their fullest commitment. Or, as Lawrence Miller puts it, "Achieving return on equity does not, as a goal, mobilize the most noble forces of our soul."[21]

Leaders engaged in building learning organizations naturally feel part of a larger purpose that goes beyond their organization. They are part of changing the way businesses operate, not from a vague philanthropic urge, but from a conviction that their efforts will produce more productive organizations, capable of achieving higher levels of organizational success and personal satisfaction than more traditional organizations. Their sense of stewardship was succinctly captured by George Bernard Shaw when he said,

> This is the true joy in life, the being used for a purpose you consider a mighty one, the being a force of nature rather than a feverish, selfish clod of ailments and grievances complaining that the world will not devote itself to making you happy.

New Skills

New leadership roles require new leadership skills. These skills can only be developed, in my judgment, through a lifelong commitment. It is not enough for one or two individuals to develop these skills. They must be distributed widely throughout the organization. This is one reason that understanding the *disciplines* of a learning organization is so important. These disciplines embody the principles and practices that can widely foster leadership development.

Three critical areas of skills (disciplines) are building shared vision, surfacing and challenging mental models, and engaging in systems thinking.[22]

Building Shared Vision

How do individual visions come together to create shared visions? A useful metaphor is the hologram, the three-dimensional image created by interacting light sources.

If you cut a photograph in half, each half shows only part of the whole image. But if you divide a hologram, each part, no matter how small, shows the whole image intact. Likewise, when a group of people come to share a vision for an organization, each person sees an individual picture of the organization at its best. Each shares responsibility for the whole, not just for one piece. But the component pieces of the hologram are not identical. Each represents the whole image from a different point of view. It's something like poking holes in a window shade; each hole offers a unique angle for viewing the whole image. So, too, is each individual's vision unique.

When you add up the pieces of a hologram, something interesting happens. The image becomes more intense, more lifelike. When more people come to share a vision, the vision becomes more real in the sense of a mental reality that people can truly imagine achieving. They now have partners, co-creators; the vision no longer rests on their shoulders alone. Early on, when they are nurturing an individual vision, people may say it is "my vision." But, as the shared vision develops, it becomes both "my vision" and "our vision."

The skills involved in building shared vision include the following:

• **Encouraging Personal Vision.** Shared visions emerge from personal visions. It is not that people only care about their own self-interest—in fact, people's values usually include dimensions that concern family, organization, community, and even the world. Rather, it is that people's capacity for caring is *personal*.

• **Communicating and Asking for Support.** Leaders must be willing to continually share their own vision, rather than being the official representative of the corporate vision. They also must be prepared to ask, "Is this vision worthy of your commitment?" This can be difficult for a person used to setting goals and presuming compliance.

• **Visioning as an Ongoing Process.** Building shared vision is a never-ending process. At any one point there will be a particular image of the future that is predominant, but that image will evolve. Today, too many managers want to dispense with the "vision business" by going off and writing the Official Vision Statement. Such statements almost always lack the vitality, freshness, and excitement

Sloan
Management
Review

13

Fall 1990

of a genuine vision that comes from people asking, "What do we really want to achieve?"

• Blending Extrinsic and Intrinsic Visions. Many energizing visions are extrinsic—that is, they focus on achieving something relative to an outsider, such as a competitor. But a goal that is limited to defeating an opponent can, once the vision is achieved, easily become a defensive posture. In contrast, intrinsic goals like creating a new type of product, taking an established product to a new level, or setting a new standard for customer satisfaction can call forth a new level of creativity and innovation. Intrinsic and extrinsic visions need to coexist; a vision solely predicated on defeating an adversary will eventually weaken an organization.

• Distinguishing Positive from Negative Visions. Many organizations only truly pull together when their survival is threatened. Similarly, most social movements aim at eliminating what people don't want: for example, anti-drugs, anti-smoking, or anti-nuclear arms movements. Negative visions carry a subtle message of powerlessness: people will only pull together when there is sufficient threat. Negative visions also tend to be short term. Two fundamental sources of energy can motivate organizations: fear and aspiration. Fear, the energy source behind negative visions, can produce extraordinary changes in short periods, but aspiration endures as a continuing source of learning and growth.

Surfacing and Testing Mental Models

Many of the best ideas in organizations never get put into practice. One reason is that new insights and initiatives often conflict with established mental models. The leadership task of challenging assumptions without invoking defensiveness requires reflection and inquiry skills possessed by few leaders in traditional controlling organizations.[23]

• Seeing Leaps of Abstraction. Our minds literally move at lightning speed. Ironically, this often slows our learning, because we leap to generalizations so quickly that we never think to test them. We then confuse our generalizations with the observable data upon which they are based, treating the generalizations *as if they were data.* The frustrated sales rep reports to the home office that "customers don't really care about quality, price is what matters," when what actually happened was that three consecutive large customers refused to place an order unless a larger discount was offered. The sales rep treats her generalization, "customers care

only about price," as if it were absolute fact rather than an assumption (very likely an assumption reflecting her own views of customers and the market). This thwarts future learning because she starts to focus on how to offer attractive discounts rather than probing behind the customers' statements. For example, the customers may have been so disgruntled with the firm's delivery or customer service that they are unwilling to purchase again without larger discounts.

• Balancing Inquiry and Advocacy. Most managers are skilled at articulating their views and presenting them persuasively. While important, advocacy skills can become counterproductive as managers rise in responsibility and confront increasingly complex issues that require collaborative learning among different, equally knowledgeable people. Leaders in learning organizations need to have both inquiry *and* advocacy skills.[24]

Specifically, when advocating a view, they need to be able to:

—explain the reasoning and data that led to their view;

—encourage others to test their view (e.g., Do you see gaps in my reasoning? Do you disagree with the data upon which my view is based?); and

—encourage others to provide different views (e.g., Do you have either different data, different conclusions, or both?).

When inquiring into another's views, they need to:

—actively seek to understand the other's view, rather than simply restating their own view and how it differs from the other's view; and

—make their attributions about the other and the other's view explicit (e.g., Based on your statement that . . . ; I am assuming that you believe . . . ; Am I representing your views fairly?).

If they reach an impasse (others no longer appear open to inquiry), they need to:

—ask what data or logic might unfreeze the impasse, or if an experiment (or some other inquiry) might be designed to provide new information.

• Distinguishing Espoused Theory from Theory in Use. We all like to think that we hold certain views, but often our actions reveal deeper views. For example, I may proclaim that people are trustworthy, but never lend friends money and jealously guard my possessions. Obviously, my deeper mental model (my theory in use), differs from my espoused theory. Recognizing gaps between espoused views and theories in use (which often requires the help of others) can be pivotal to deeper learning.

• **Recognizing and Defusing Defensive Routines.** As one CEO in our research program puts it, "Nobody ever talks about an issue at the 8:00 business meeting exactly the same way they talk about it at home that evening or over drinks at the end of the day." The reason is what Chris Argyris calls "defensive routines," entrenched habits used to protect ourselves from the embarrassment and threat that come with exposing our thinking. For most of us, such defenses began to build early in life in response to pressures to have the right answers in school or at home. Organizations add new levels of performance anxiety and thereby amplify and exacerbate this defensiveness. Ironically, this makes it even more difficult to expose hidden mental models, and thereby lessens learning.

The first challenge is to recognize defensive routines, then to inquire into their operation. Those who are best at revealing and defusing defensive routines operate with a high degree of self-disclosure regarding their own defensiveness (e.g., I notice that I am feeling uneasy about how this conversation is going. Perhaps I don't understand it or it is threatening to me in ways I don't yet see. Can you help me see this better?)

Systems Thinking

We all know that leaders should help people see the big picture. But the actual skills whereby leaders are supposed to achieve this are not well understood. In my experience, successful leaders often are "systems thinkers" to a considerable extent. They focus less on day-to-day events and more on underlying trends and forces of change. But they do this almost completely intuitively. The consequence is that they are often unable to explain their intuitions to others and feel frustrated that others cannot see the world the way they do.

One of the most significant developments in management science today is the gradual coalescence of managerial systems thinking as a field of study and practice. This field suggests some key skills for future leaders:

• **Seeing Interrelationships, Not Things, and Processes, Not Snapshots.** Most of us have been conditioned throughout our lives to focus on things and to see the world in static images. This leads us to linear explanations of systemic phenomenon. For instance, in an arms race each party is con-

vinced that the other is *the cause* of problems. They react to each new move as an isolated event, not as part of a process. So long as they fail to see the interrelationships of these actions, they are trapped.

• **Moving beyond Blame.** We tend to blame each other or outside circumstances for our problems. But it is poorly designed systems, not incompetent or unmotivated individuals, that cause most organizational problems. Systems thinking shows us that there is no outside – that you and the cause of your problems are part of a single system.

• **Distinguishing Detail Complexity from Dynamic Complexity.** Some types of complexity are more important strategically than others. Detail complexity arises when there are many variables. Dynamic complexity arises when cause and effect are distant in time and space, and when the consequences over time of interventions are subtle and not obvious to many participants in the system. The leverage in most management situations lies in understanding dynamic complexity, not detail complexity.

• **Focusing on Areas of High Leverage.** Some have called systems thinking the "new dismal science" because it teaches that most obvious solutions don't work – at best, they improve matters in the short run, only to make things worse in the long run. But there is another side to the story. Systems thinking also shows that small, well-focused actions can produce significant, enduring improvements, if they are in the right place. Systems thinkers refer to this idea as the principle of "leverage." Tackling a difficult problem is often a matter of seeing where the high leverage lies, where a change – with a minimum of effort – would lead to lasting, significant improvement.

• **Avoiding Symptomatic Solutions.** The pressures to intervene in management systems that are going awry can be overwhelming. Unfortunately, given the linear thinking that predominates in most organizations, interventions usually focus on symptomatic fixes, not underlying causes. This results in only temporary relief, and it tends to create still more pressures later on for further, low-leverage intervention. If leaders acquiesce to these pressures, they can be sucked into an endless spiral of increasing intervention. Sometimes the most difficult leadership acts are to refrain from intervening through popular quick fixes and to keep the pressure on everyone to identify more enduring solutions.

While leaders who can articulate systemic ex-

Sloan
Management
Review

15

Fall 1990

Learning
Organizations

16

Senge

planations are rare, those who *can* will leave their stamp on an organization. One person who had this gift was Bill Gore, the founder and long-time CEO of W.L. Gore and Associates (makers of Gore-Tex and other synthetic fiber products). Bill Gore was adept at telling stories that showed how the organization's core values of freedom and individual responsibility required particular operating policies. He was proud of his egalitarian organization, in which there were (and still are) no "employees," only "associates," all of whom own shares in the company and participate in its management. At one talk, he explained the company's policy of controlled growth: "Our limitation is not financial resources. Our limitation is the rate at which we can bring in new associates. Our experience has been that if we try to bring in more than a 25 percent per year increase, we begin to bog down. Twenty-five percent per year growth is a real limitation; you can do much better than that with an authoritarian organization." As Gore tells the story, one of the associates, Esther Baum, went home after this talk and reported the limitation to her husband. As it happened, he was an astronomer and mathematician at Lowell Observatory. He said, "That's a very interesting figure." He took out a pencil and paper and calculated and said, "Do you realize that in only fifty-seven and a half years, everyone in the world will be working for Gore?"

Through this story, Gore explains the systemic rationale behind a key policy, limited growth rate—a policy that undoubtedly caused a lot of stress in the organization. He suggests that, at larger rates of growth, the adverse effects of attempting to integrate too many new people too rapidly would begin to dominate. (This is the "limits to growth" systems archetype explained below.) The story also reaffirms the organization's commitment to creating a unique environment for its associates and illustrates the types of sacrifices that the firm is prepared to make in order to remain true to its vision. The last part of the story shows that, despite the self-imposed limit, the company is still very much a growth company.

The consequences of leaders who lack systems thinking skills can be devastating. Many charismatic leaders manage almost exclusively at the level of events. They deal in visions and in crises, and little in between. Under their leadership, an organization hurtles from crisis to crisis. Eventually, the worldview of people in the organization becomes dominated by events and reactiveness. Many, es-

pecially those who are deeply committed, become burned out. Eventually, cynicism comes to pervade the organization. People have no control over their time, let alone their destiny.

Similar problems arise with the "visionary strategist," the leader with vision who sees both patterns of change and events. This leader is better prepared to manage change: He or she can explain strategies in terms of emerging trends, and thereby foster a climate that is less reactive. But such leaders still impart a responsive orientation rather than a generative one.

Many talented leaders have rich, highly systemic intuitions but cannot explain those intuitions to others. Ironically, they often end up being authoritarian leaders, even if they don't want to, because only they see the decisions that need to be made. They are unable to conceptualize their strategic insights so that these can become public knowledge, open to challenge and further improvement.

New Tools

Developing the skills described above requires new tools—tools that will enhance leaders' conceptual abilities and foster communication and collaborative inquiry. What follows is a sampling of tools starting to find use in learning organizations.

Systems Archetypes

One of the insights of the budding, managerial systems-thinking field is that certain types of systemic structures recur again and again. Countless systems grow for a period, then encounter problems and cease to grow (or even collapse) well before they have reached intrinsic limits to growth. Many other systems get locked in runaway vicious spirals where every actor has to run faster and faster to stay in the same place. Still others lure individual actors into doing what seems right locally, yet which eventually causes suffering for all.[25]

Some of the system archetypes that have the broadest relevance include:

• **Balancing Process with Delay.** In this archetype, decision makers fail to appreciate the time delays involved as they move toward a goal. As a result, they overshoot the goal and may even produce recurring cycles. Classic example: Real estate developers who keep starting new projects until the market has gone soft, by which time an eventual glut is guaranteed by the properties still under construction.

• **Limits to Growth.** A reinforcing cycle of growth grinds to a halt, and may even reverse itself, as limits are approached. The limits can be resource constraints, or external or internal responses to growth. Classic examples: Product life cycles that peak prematurely due to poor quality or service, the growth and decline of communication in a management team, and the spread of a new movement.

• **Shifting the Burden.** A short-term "solution" is used to correct a problem, with seemingly happy immediate results. As this correction is used more and more, fundamental long-term corrective measures are used less. Over time, the mechanisms of the fundamental solution may atrophy or become disabled, leading to even greater reliance on the symptomatic solution. Classic example: Using corporate human resource staff to solve local personnel problems, thereby keeping managers from developing their own interpersonal skills.

• **Eroding Goals.** When all else fails, lower your standards. This is like "shifting the burden," except that the short-term solution involves letting a fundamental goal, such as quality standards or employee morale standards, atrophy. Classic example: A company that responds to delivery problems by continually upping its quoted delivery times.

• **Escalation.** Two people or two organizations, who each see their welfare as depending on a relative advantage over the other, continually react to the other's advances. Whenever one side gets ahead, the other is threatened, leading it to act more aggressively to reestablish its advantage, which threatens the first, and so on. Classic examples: Arms race, gang warfare, price wars.

• **Tragedy of the Commons.**[26] Individuals keep intensifying their use of a commonly available but limited resource until all individuals start to experience severely diminishing returns. Classic examples: Sheepherders who keep increasing their flocks until they overgraze the common pasture; divisions in a firm that share a common salesforce and compete for the use of sales reps by upping their sales targets, until the salesforce burns out from overextension.

• **Growth and Underinvestment.** Rapid growth approaches a limit that could be eliminated or pushed into the future, but only by aggressive investment in physical and human capacity. Eroding goals or standards cause investment that is too weak, or too slow, and customers get increasingly unhappy, slowing demand growth and thereby making the needed investment (apparently) unnecessary or impossible. Classic example: Countless once-successful growth firms that allowed product or service quality to erode, and were unable to generate enough revenues to invest in remedies.

The Archetype template is a specific tool that is helping managers identify archetypes operating in their own strategic areas (see Figure 2).[27] The template shows the basic structural form of the archetype but lets managers fill in the variables of their own situation. For example, the shifting the burden template involves two balancing processes ("B") that compete for control of a problem symptom. The upper, symptomatic solution provides a short-term fix that will make the problem symptom go away for a while. The lower, fundamental solution provides a more enduring solution. The side effect feedback ("R") around the outside of the diagram identifies unintended exacerbating effects of the symptomatic solution, which, over time, make it more and more difficult to invoke the fundamental solution.

Several years ago, a team of managers from a leading consumer goods producer used the shifting the burden archetype in a revealing way. The problem they focused on was financial stress, which

Sloan
Management
Review

17

Fall 1990

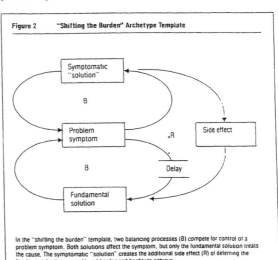

Figure 2   "Shifting the Burden" Archetype Template

In the "shifting the burden" template, two balancing processes (B) compete for control of a problem symptom. Both solutions affect the symptom, but only the fundamental solution treats the cause. The symptomatic "solution" creates the additional side effect (R) of deferring the fundamental solution, making it harder and harder to achieve.

Learning
Organizations

18

Senge

could be dealt with in two different ways: by running marketing promotions (the symptomatic solution) or by product innovation (the fundamental solution). Marketing promotions were fast. The company was expert in their design and implementation. The results were highly predictable. Product innovation was slow and much less predictable, and the company had a history over the past ten years of product-innovation mismanagement. Yet only through innovation could they retain a leadership position in their industry, which had slid over the past ten to twenty years. What the managers saw clearly was that the more skillful they became at promotions, the more they shifted the burden away from product innovation. But what really struck home was when one member identified the unintended side effect: the last three CEOs had all come from advertising function, which had become the politically dominant function in the corporation, thereby institutionalizing the symptomatic solution. Unless the political values shifted back toward product and process innovation, the managers realized, the firm's decline would accelerate—which is just the shift that has happened over the past several years.

Charting Strategic Dilemmas

Management teams typically come unglued when confronted with core dilemmas. A classic example was the way U.S. manufacturers faced the low cost–high quality choice. For years, most assumed that it was necessary to choose between the two. Not surprisingly, given the short-term pressures perceived by most managements, the prevailing choice was low cost. Firms that chose high quality usually perceived themselves as aiming exclusively for a high quality, high price market niche. The consequences of this perceived either-or choice have been disastrous, even fatal, as U.S. manufacturers have encountered increasing international competition from firms that have chosen to consistently improve quality *and* cost.

In a recent book, Charles Hampden-Turner presented a variety of tools for helping management teams confront strategic dilemmas creatively.[28] He summarizes the process in seven steps:

- **Eliciting the Dilemmas.** Identifying the opposed values that form the "horns" of the dilemma, for example, cost as opposed to quality, or local initiative as opposed to central coordination and control. Hampden-Turner suggests that humor can

be a distinct asset in this process since "the admission that dilemmas even exist tends to be difficult for some companies."

- **Mapping.** Locating the opposing values as two axes and helping managers identify where they see themselves, or their organization, along the axes.
- **Processing.** Getting rid of nouns to describe the axes of the dilemma. Present participles formed by adding "ing" convert rigid nouns into processes that imply movement. For example, central control versus local control becomes "strengthening national office" and "growing local initiatives." This loosens the bond of implied opposition between the two values. For example, it becomes possible to think of "strengthening national services from which local branches can benefit."
- **Framing/Contextualizing.** Further softening the adversarial structure among different values by letting "each side in turn be the frame or context for the other." This shifting of the implicit "figure-ground" relationship undermines any implicit attempts to hold one value as intrinsically superior to the other, and thereby to become mentally closed to creative strategies for continuous improvement of both.
- **Sequencing.** Breaking the hold of static thinking. Very often, values like low cost and high quality appear to be in opposition because we think in terms of a point in time, not in terms of an ongoing process. For example, a strategy of investing in new process technology and developing a new production-floor culture of worker responsibility may take time and money in the near term, yet reap significant long-term financial rewards.
- **Waving/Cycling.** Sometimes the strategic path toward improving both values involves cycles where both values will get "worse" for a time. Yet, at a deeper level, learning is occurring that will cause the next cycle to be at a higher plateau for both values.
- **Synergizing.** Achieving synergy where significant improvement is occurring along all axes of all relevant dilemmas. (This is the ultimate goal, of course.) Synergy, as Hampden-Turner points out, is a uniquely systemic notion, coming from the Greek *syn-ergo* or "work together."

"The Left-Hand Column": Surfacing Mental Models

The idea that mental models can dominate business decisions and that these models are often tacit and even contradictory to what people espouse can be very threatening to managers who pride themselves on rationality and judicious decision making. It is important to have tools to help managers discover for themselves how their mental models operate to undermine their own intentions.

One tool that has worked consistently to help managers see their own mental models in action is the "left-hand column" exercise developed by Chris Argyris and his colleagues. This tool is especially helpful in showing how we leap from data to generalization without testing the validity of our generalizations.

When working with managers, I start this exercise by selecting a specific situation in which I am interacting with other people in a way that is not working, that is not producing the learning that is needed. I write out a sample of the exchange, with the script on the right-hand side of the page. On the left-hand side, I write what I am thinking but not saying at each stage in the exchange (see sidebar).

The left-hand column exercise not only brings hidden assumptions to the surface, it shows how they influence behavior. In the example, I make two key assumptions about Bill: he lacks confidence and he lacks initiative. Neither may be literally true, but both are evident in my internal dialogue, and both influence the way I handle the situation. Believing that he lacks confidence, I skirt the fact that I've heard the presentation was a bomb. I'm afraid that if I say it directly, he will lose what little confidence he has, or he will see me as unsupportive. So I bring up the subject of the presentation obliquely. When I ask Bill what we should do next, he gives no specific course of action. Believing he lacks initiative, I take this as evidence of his laziness; he is content to do nothing when action is definitely required. I conclude that I will have to manufacture some form of pressure to motivate him, or else I will simply have to take matters into my own hands.

The exercise reveals the elaborate webs of assumptions we weave, within which we become our own victims. Rather than dealing directly with my assumptions about Bill and the situation, we talk around the subject. The reasons for my avoidance are self-evident: I assume that if I raised my doubts, I would provoke a defensive reaction that would only make matters worse. But the price of avoiding the issue is high. Instead of determining how to move forward to resolve our problems, we end our exchange with no clear course of action. My

assumptions about Bill's limitations have been reinforced. I resort to a manipulative strategy to move things forward.

The exercise not only reveals the need for skills in surfacing assumptions, but that we are the ones most in need of help. There is no one right way to handle difficult situations like my exchange with Bill, but any productive strategy revolves around a high level of self-disclosure and willingness to have my views challenged. I need to recognize my own leaps of abstraction regarding Bill, share the events

---

The Left-Hand Column: An Exercise

Imagine my exchange with a colleague, Bill, after he made a big presentation to our boss on a project we are doing together. I had to miss the presentation, but I've heard that it was poorly received.
Me: How did the presentation go?
Bill: Well, I don't know. It's really too early to say. Besides, we're breaking new ground here.
Me: Well, what do you think we should do? I believe that the issues you were raising are important.
Bill: I'm not so sure. Let's just wait and see what happens.
Me: You may be right, but I think we may need to do more than just wait.

Now, here is what the exchange looks like with my "left-hand column":

What I'm Thinking	What Is Said
Everyone says the presentation was a bomb.	*Me:* How did the presentation go?
Does he really not know how bad it was? Or is he not willing to face up to it?	*Bill:* Well, I don't know. It's too early to say. Besides, we're breaking new ground here.
	Me: Well, what do you think we should do? I believe that the issues you were raising are important.
He really is afraid to see the truth. If he only had more confidence, he could probably learn from a situation like this.	*Bill:* I'm not so sure. Let's just wait and see what happens.
I can't believe he doesn't realize how disastrous that presentation was to our moving ahead.	*Me:* You may be right, but I think we may need to do more than just wait.
I've got to find some way to light a fire under the guy.	

Learning at Hanover Insurance

Hanover Insurance has gone from the bottom of the property and liability industry to a position among the top 25 percent of U.S. insurance companies over the past twenty years, largely through the efforts of CEO William O'Brien and his predecessor, Jack Adam. The following comments are excerpted from a series of interviews Senge conducted with O'Brien as background for his book.

Senge: Why do you think there is so much change occurring in management and organizations today? Is it primarily because of increased competitive pressures?

O'Brien: That's a factor, but not the most significant factor. The ferment in management will continue until we find models that are more congruent with human nature.

One of the great insights of modern psychology is the hierarchy of human needs. As Maslow expressed this idea, the most basic needs are food and shelter. Then comes belonging. Once these three basic needs are satisfied, people begin to aspire toward self-respect and esteem, and toward self-actualization—the fourth- and fifth-order needs.

Our traditional hierarchical organizations are designed to provide for the first three levels, but not the fourth and fifth. These first three levels are now widely available to members of industrial society, but our organizations do not offer people sufficient opportunities for growth.

Senge: How would you assess Hanover's progress to date?

O'Brien: We have been on a long journey away from a traditional hierarchical culture. The journey began with everyone understanding some guiding ideas about purpose, vision, and values as a basis for participative management. This is a better way to begin building a participative culture than by simply "letting people in on decision making." Before there can be meaningful participation, people must share certain values and pictures about where we are trying to go. We discovered that people have a real need to feel that

they're part of an enobling mission. But developing shared visions and values is not the end, only the beginning.

Next we had to get beyond mechanical, linear thinking. The essence of our jobs as managers is to deal with "divergent" problems—problems that have no simple answer. "Convergent" problems—problems that have a "right" answer—should be solved locally. Yet we are deeply conditioned to see the world in terms of convergent problems. Most managers try to force-fit simplistic solutions and undermine the potential for learning when divergent problems arise. Since everyone handles the linear issues fairly well, companies that learn how to handle divergent issues will have a great advantage.

The next basic stage in our progression was coming to understand inquiry and advocacy. We learned that real openness is rooted in people's ability to continually inquire into their own thinking. This requires exposing yourself to being wrong—not something that most managers are rewarded for. But learning is very difficult if you cannot look for errors or incompleteness in your own ideas.

What all this builds to is the capability throughout an organization to manage mental models. In a locally controlled organization, you have the fundamental challenge of learning how to help people make good decisions without coercing them into making _particular_ decisions. By managing mental models, we create "self-concluding" decisions—decisions that people come to themselves—which will result in deeper conviction, better implementation, and the ability to make better adjustments when the situation changes.

Senge: What concrete steps can top managers take to begin moving toward learning organizations?

O'Brien: Look at the signals you send through the organization. For example, one critical signal is how you spend your time. It's hard to build a learning organization if people are unable to take the time to think through important matters. I rarely set up an appointment for less than one hour. If the subject is not worth an hour, it shouldn't be on my calendar.

Senge: Why is this so hard for so many managers?

O'Brien: It comes back to what you believe about the nature of your work. The authoritarian manager has a "chain gang" mental model: "The speed of the boss is the speed of the gang. I've got to keep things moving fast, because I've got to keep people working." In a learning organization, the manager shoulders an almost sacred responsibility: to create conditions that enable people to have happy and productive lives. If you understand the effects the ideas we are discussing can have on the lives of people in your organization, you will take the time.

■

Sloan
Management
Review

21

Fall 1990

and reasoning that are leading to my concern over the project, and be open to Bill's views on both. The skills to carry on such conversations without invoking defensiveness take time to develop. But if both parties in a learning impasse start by doing their own left-hand column exercise and sharing them with each other, it is remarkable how quickly everyone recognizes their contribution to the impasse and progress starts to be made.

Learning Laboratories: Practice Fields for Management Teams

One of the most promising new tools is the learning laboratory or "microworld": constructed microcosms of real-life settings in which management teams can learn how to learn together.

The rationale behind learning laboratories can best be explained by analogy. Although most management teams have great difficulty learning (enhancing their collective intelligence and capacity to create), in other domains team learning is the norm rather than the exception — team sports and the performing arts, for example. Great basketball teams do not start off great. They learn. But the process by which these teams learn is, by and large, absent from modern organizations. The process is a continual movement between practice and performance.

The vision guiding current research in management learning laboratories is to design and construct effective practice fields for management teams. Much remains to be done, but the broad outlines are emerging.

First, since team learning in organizations is an individual-to-individual and individual-to-system phenomenon, learning laboratories must combine meaningful business issues with meaningful interpersonal dynamics. Either alone is incomplete.

Second, the factors that thwart learning about complex business issues must be eliminated in the learning lab. Chief among these is the inability to experience the long-term, systemic consequences of key strategic decisions. We all learn best from experience, but we are unable to experience the consequences of many important organizational decisions. Learning laboratories remove this constraint through system dynamics simulation games that compress time and space.

Third, new learning skills must be developed. One constraint on learning is the inability of managers to reflect insightfully on their assumptions, and to inquire effectively into each other's assumptions. Both skills can be enhanced in a learning laboratory, where people can practice surfacing assumptions in a low-risk setting. A note of caution: It is far easier to design an entertaining learning laboratory than it is to have an impact on real management practices and firm traditions outside the learning lab. Research on management simulations has shown that they often have greater entertainment value than educational value. One of the reasons appears to be that many simulations do not offer deep insights into systemic structures causing business problems. Another reason is that they do not foster new learning skills. Also, there is no connection between experiments in the learning lab and real life experiments. These are significant problems that research on learning laboratory design is now addressing.

Developing Leaders and Learning Organizations

In a recently published retrospective on organization development in the 1980s, Marshall Sashkin and N. Warner Burke observe the return of an emphasis on developing leaders who can develop or-

Learning
Organizations

22

Senge

ganizations.[29] They also note Schein's critique that most top executives are not qualified for the task of developing culture.[30] Learning organizations represent a potentially significant evolution of organizational culture. So it should come as no surprise that such organizations will remain a distant vision until the leadership capabilities they demand are developed. "The 1990s may be the period," suggest Sashkin and Burke, "during which organization development and (a new sort of) management development are reconnected."

I believe that this new sort of management development will focus on the roles, skills, and tools for leadership in learning organizations. Undoubtedly, the ideas offered above are only a rough approximation of this new territory. The sooner we begin seriously exploring the territory, the sooner the initial map can be improved—and the sooner we will realize an age-old vision of leadership:

> The wicked leader is he who the people despise.
> The good leader is he who the people revere.
> The great leader is he who the people say, "We did it ourselves."

— Lao Tsu ■

References

1
P. Senge, *The Fifth Discipline: The Art and Practice of the Learning Organization* (New York: Doubleday/Currency, 1990).

2
A.P. de Geus, "Planning as Learning," *Harvard Business Review*, March-April 1988, pp. 70–74.

3
B. Domain, *Fortune*, 3 July 1989, pp. 48–62.

4
The distinction between adaptive and generative learning has its roots in the distinction between what Argyris and Schon have called their "single-loop" learning, in which individuals or groups adjust their behavior relative to fixed goals, norms, and assumptions, and "double-loop" learning, in which goals, norms, and assumptions, as well as behavior, are open to change (e.g., see C. Argyris and D. Schon, *Organizational Learning: A Theory-in-Action Perspective* (Reading, Massachusetts: Addison-Wesley, 1978)).

5
All unattributed quotes are from personal communications with the author.

6
G. Stalk, Jr., "Time: The Next Source of Competitive Advantage," *Harvard Business Review*, July-August 1988, pp. 41–51.

7
Senge (1990).

8
The principle of creative tension comes from Robert Fritz' work on creativity. See R. Fritz, *The Path of Least Resistance* (New York: Ballantine, 1989) and *Creating* (New York: Ballantine, 1990).

9
M.L. King, Jr., "Letter from Birmingham Jail," *American Visions*, January-February 1986, pp. 52–59.

10
E. Schein, *Organizational Culture and Leadership* (San Francisco: Jossey-Bass, 1985).
Similar views have been expressed by many leadership theorists. For example, see:
P. Selznick, *Leadership in Administration* (New York: Harper & Row, 1957);
W. Bennis and B. Nanus, *Leaders* (New York: Harper & Row, 1985); and
N.M. Tichy and M.A. Devanna, *The Transformational Leader* (New York: John Wiley & Sons, 1986).

11
Selznick (1957)

12
J.W. Forrester, "A New Corporate Design," *Sloan Management Review* (formerly *Industrial Management Review*), Fall 1965, pp. 5–17.

13
See, for example, H. Mintzberg, "Crafting Strategy," *Harvard Business Review*, July-August 1987, pp. 66–75

14
R. Mason and I. Mitroff, *Challenging Strategic Planning Assumptions* (New York: John Wiley & Sons, 1981), p. 16.

15
P. Wack, "Scenarios: Uncharted Waters Ahead," *Harvard Business Review*, September-October 1985, pp. 73–89

16
de Geus (1988).

17
M. de Pree, *Leadership Is an Art* (New York: Doubleday, 1989) p. 9.

18
For example, see T. Peters and N. Austin, *A Passion for Excellence* (New York: Random House, 1985) and
J.M. Kouzes and B.Z. Posner, *The Leadership Challenge* (San Francisco: Jossey-Bass, 1987).

19
I. Mitroff, *Break-Away Thinking* (New York: John Wiley & Sons, 1988), pp. 66–67.

20
R.K. Greenleaf, *Servant Leadership: A Journey into the Nature of Legitimate Power and Greatness* (New York: Paulist Press, 1977).

21
L. Miller, *American Spirit: Visions of a New Corporate Culture* (New York: William Morrow, 1984), p. 15.

22

These points are condensed from the practices of the five disciplines examined in Senge (1990).

23

The ideas below are based to a considerable extent on the work of Chris Argyris, Donald Schon, and their Action Science colleagues:

C. Argyris and D. Schon, *Organizational Learning: A Theory-in-Action Perspective* (Reading, Massachusetts: Addison-Wesley, 1978);

C. Argyris, R. Putnam, and D. Smith, *Action Science* (San Francisco: Jossey-Bass, 1985);

C. Argyris, *Strategy, Change, and Defensive Routines* (Boston: Pitman, 1985); and

C. Argyris, *Overcoming Organizational Defenses* (Englewood Cliffs, New Jersey: Prentice-Hall, 1990)

24

I am indebted to Diana Smith for the summary points below.

25

The system archetypes are one of several systems diagraming and communication tools. See D.H. Kim, "Toward Learning Organizations: Integrating Total Quality Control and Systems Thinking" (Cambridge, Massachusetts: MIT Sloan School of Management, Working Paper No. 3037-89-BPS, June 1989).

26

This archetype is closely associated with the work of ecologist Garrett Hardin, who coined its label: G. Hardin, "The Tragedy of the Commons," *Science*, 13 December 1968

27

These templates were originally developed by Jennifer Kemeny, Charles Kiefer, and Michael Goodman of Innovation Associates, Inc., Framingham, Massachusetts.

28

C. Hampden-Turner, *Charting the Corporate Mind* (New York: The Free Press, 1990)

29

M. Sashkin and W.W. Burke, "Organization Development in the 1980s" and "An End-of-the-Eighties Retrospective," in *Advances in Organization Development*, ed. F. Masank (Norwood, New Jersey: Ablex, 1990)

30

E. Schein (1985)

Part II
Relationships

Introduction to Part II

Relationships

Dr John Potter

There seems to be a consensus of opinion in much of the current business literature that the role of the leader is changing and that much of this perceived change has occurred since 1990. The days when leaders at all levels could hide behind their position of power and operate solely with a command-and-control style seem to be over. The history of investigation into the nature of leadership would suggest that, until the mid-twentieth century, the subject was looked at from the perspective of the Great Man Theory initially and, more recently, as a mix between the individual leader and the situation. Not only is this politically incorrect as there have been notable female leaders throughout history, but it presupposes a selection-based model of leadership rather than a developmental one.

The concept of leadership as somewhat 'male, military and Western' appeared to be widely supported until serious research work on the leader–follower relationship began to be undertaken in the middle of the twentieth century. In 1953 the *Harvard Business Review* published a seminal essay by Robert Tannenbaum and Warren Schmidt, which related leadership style to communication patterns and decision-making. This set the scene for leadership to be viewed as involving a range of styles, rather than as a consequence of the personal power of the individual leader in terms of personality and social position, and for these reasons we have chosen it as the opening essay for Part II of this volume. Subsequently, during the 1960s, the work of Stogdill, Mouton and Blake, Hersey and Blanchard, and Fiedler then shifted attention in the USA towards how the leader operated in terms of behavioural style. In the UK, research into leadership was much less scientific and much more anecdotal. In particular, the work of John Adair in identifying the needs of the followers that the effective leader must satisfy became a fundamental tool in leadership development. These models were all somewhat mechanistic and attracted the criticism that they were artificial and ignored the fundamental emotional nature of leadership. This led to leadership becoming one of the most researched, yet least understood, aspects of human performance. The result of this lack of progress in understanding the true nature of leadership and the associated processes has been commented upon by a number of writers, and many have suggested that leadership entered a 'black hole' in terms of research in the 1980s when most effort seemed to go into either validating or disproving these mechanistic approaches rather than exploring new avenues of inquiry.

It was in 1990 that the situation started to change. Peter Senge wrote his ground-breaking essay 'The Leader's New Work' in the *Sloan Management Review* (see Chapter 5, this volume), focusing on redefining the leader's role from driving through change towards a clear vision to creating organizational capacity through developing the learning organization. This led to the formation of the Society for Organizational Learning and the development of complexity theory in terms of redefining leadership away from the heroic personality towards individuals who subsumed their own egos and focused instead on creating the organization which could adapt to future challenges. As a result, leadership began to be viewed as an emotionally-based process rather than as a purely mechanistic one which could be taught as a set of behaviours. Part II addresses this shift and focuses on the relationship aspects of leadership, particularly in terms of emotional factors. A great deal of work is currently being published on leader–member exchange, which looks at the relationship between leaders and their followers. Some of this work suggests that leaders have to become much more aware of the context in which their followers are working than is often the case at present.

Once the leader and the leadership role had been redefined, attention moved towards the emotional relationship between leaders and their followers. Much has been written on emotional intelligence by Daniel Goleman and his associates. Although some critics would say that Goleman merely restates and repackages what we have known for years in a more easily digested form, he has succeeded in shifting the emphasis from leaders and their personalities to their emotional impact on their followers. Goleman has written a number of essays on leadership and emotional intelligence and has effectively linked the elements of emotional intelligence with specific leadership styles. His essay 'Leadership that Gets Results', reprinted here as Chapter 7 and originally published in the *Harvard Business Review* in 2000, broke new ground in that, for the first time, it quantified the impact of various leadership styles on the organizational climate. His notable finding is that the traditionally-held view of leadership, relating to coercion and pacesetting, tends to produce a negative impact on the climate. Other approaches to the leader–follower relationship involving vision-based, democratic, affiliative and coaching styles all produced positive impacts on the organizational climate, providing further evidence that the relationship between the leader and the follower is changing. However, Goleman's published work, whilst pragmatic and useful, sometimes lacks the depth of fundamental research. Thus we have chosen to include a significant piece of research on emotional intelligence which seeks to understand the phenomenon in more depth. This essay, by Chi-Sum Wong and Kenneth Law, originally published in the *Leadership Quarterly*, notes that, although many scholars have reported that emotional intelligence is a core variable that affects leadership performance, relatively little in-depth research has been carried out on the subject – although, as already indicated, there is much in the way of pragmatic advice, offered by the work of Goleman and others. Wong and Law identify a number of key areas which need to be addressed if the concept of emotional intelligence is to be taken seriously as a tool for understanding leader–follower relationships.

One specific aspect of the leader–follower relationship is the concept of leader-distance. Practising leaders often refer to this in terms of the undesirability of getting 'too close' to your people. However, in today's virtual organizational world distance is not just a psychological issue but may also be related to physical distance – maybe even to the other side of the world. In psychological terms the notion of leader-distance has significance in terms of perceived change in the leader–follower relationship. There does seem to be a tendency for leaders to try to get psychologically closer and to appear on the same level, at least socially, as their people – a dilemma that is probably best addressed using the range of styles suggested by Tannenbaum and Schmidt in Chapter 6. At times, leaders need to be relatively distant in order to act in command-and-control mode. At other times, they almost need to bury themselves in the group following the style of the *laissez-faire* or 'covert' leader. In Chapter 9 John Antonakis and Leanne Atwater investigate the concept in its widest sense and discuss three aspects of distance: physical distance, perceived social distance and task interaction frequency. With the ever-increasing tendency for technology to accommodate physical distance and sometimes create social distance this is a subject which will attract considerable attention in the future.

So if the role of the leader is expanding from simply command-and-control based on a strong personality to a wider range of styles, what does this mean in practical terms? It means that leaders now and in the future will have to be persuasive, rather than coercive, individuals. One of the most explicit writers on this changing aspect of leadership is Jay Conger whose essay 'The Necessary Art of Persuasion' we have chosen for this aspect of the leader–follower relationship (see Chapter 10). Conger has based his work on three sources of data over some 12 years of research, looking at the performance of some 23 business leaders, 18 cross-functional leaders and 14 individuals known for their ability to persuade others in a constructive way. The relationship process is considered from the perspective of those things which cause persuasion not to be effective, and these include some basic errors frequently perpetrated by leaders at all levels. What is of more interest, however, is the set of characteristics portrayed by effective persuaders. The qualities of credibility, empathy, use of language and understanding of the emotional frame all provide the aspiring leader with a diagnostic tool that may be used in times of challenge as well as ideas for personal development in this very important area.

As well as the shift in the leader's role to a wider range of styles than simply command-and-control and the concept of leader-distance, there does seem to be a definite shift from boss to coach on the part of many organizational leaders. Although many may perceive this as Theory Y applied to excess, a considerable number of writers, scholars and practising managers will agree that coaching is a highly effective way of unlocking human potential in the organization. So here we can see another emerging theme in our concept of what the leader and leadership is all about – leader as coach. 'The Executive as Coach' (Chapter 11) is written by two business psychologists, James Waldroop and Timothy Butler, operating in both the academic and consulting sectors and, as such, reflects a very pragmatic view of the coaching process. Coaching can be a major part of the leader–follower process, and this essay outlines practical strategies for ensuring that the process is effective.

In an ideal world, relationships would always be positive. However, in practice this is seldom the case. Even the most admired leaders will sometimes find themselves in difficult social situations, having to give bad news, challenge people's behaviour and performance, and cope with verbal attacks. The final essay in Part II, 'Taking the Stress out of Stressful Conversations' (Chapter 12) by Holly Weeks, lays the foundation for understanding the nature of conversational conflict and provides a framework for preparing for difficult conversations. It then outlines techniques for handling the situation as it unfolds. Such awareness is a key part of emotional intelligence, and thus this set of five essays has a common theme – how to manage relationships more effectively and create win–win outcomes.

References

Adair, J.E. (1983), *Effective Leadership*, London: Pan.

Blake, R.R. and Mouton, J.S., (1964), *The Managerial Grid*, Houston: Gulf Publishing.

Fiedler, F.E., Chemers, M. and Mahar, L. (1976) *Improving Leadership Effectiveness: The Leader Match Concept*, New York: Wiley.

Hersey, P. and Blanchard, K.H. (1969), *Management of Organizational Behaviour*, Englewood Cliffs, NJ: Prentice-Hall.

Stogdill, R.M. (1974), *Handbook of Leadership: A Survey of Theory and Research*, London: Macmillan.

[6]

How to Choose a Leadership Pattern

Robert Tannenbaum and Warren H. Schmidt

Since its publication in HBR's March–April 1958 issue, this article has had such impact and popularity as to warrant its choice as an "HBR Classic." Mr. Tannenbaum and Mr. Schmidt succeeded in capturing in a few succinct pages the main ideas involved in the question of how managers should lead their organizations. For this publication, the authors have written a commentary, in which they look at their article from a 15-year perspective (see page 10.)

☐ "I put most problems into my group's hands and leave it to them to carry the ball from there. I serve merely as a catalyst, mirroring back the people's thoughts and feelings so that they can better understand them."

☐ "It's foolish to make decisions oneself on matters that affect people. I always talk things over with my subordinates, but I make it clear to them that I'm the one who has to have the final say."

☐ "Once I have decided on a course of action, I do my best to sell my ideas to my employees."

Mr. Tannenbaum is Professor of the Development of Human Systems at the Graduate School of Management, University of California, Los Angeles. He is also a Consulting Editor of the Journal of Applied Behavioral Science and coauthor (with Irving Weschler and Fred Massarik) of Leadership and Organization: A Behavioral Science Approach (New York, McGraw-Hill, 1961). Mr. Schmidt is also affiliated with the UCLA Graduate School of Management, where he is Senior Lecturer in Behavioral Science. Besides writing extensively in the fields of human relations and leadership and conference planning, Mr. Schmidt wrote the screenplay for a film, "Is It Always Right to be Right!" which won an Academy Award in 1970.

☐ "I'm being paid to lead. If I let a lot of other people make the decisions I should be making, then I'm not worth my salt."

☐ "I believe in getting things done. I can't waste time calling meetings. Someone has to call the shots around here, and I think it should be me."

Each of these statements represents a point of view about "good leadership." Considerable experience, factual data, and theoretical principles could be cited to support each statement, even though they seem to be inconsistent when placed together. Such contradictions point up the dilemma in which modern managers frequently find themselves.

New Problem

The problem of how modern managers can be "democratic" in their relations with subordinates and at the same time maintain the necessary authority and control in the organizations for which they are responsible has come into focus increasingly in recent years.

Earlier in the century this problem was not so acutely felt. The successful executive was generally pictured as possessing intelligence, imagination, initiative, the capacity to make rapid (and generally wise) decisions, and the ability to inspire subordinates. People tended to think of the world as being divided into "leaders" and "followers."

New focus: Gradually, however, from the social sciences emerged the concept of "group dynamics" with its focus on *members* of the group rather than solely on the leader. Research efforts of social scientists underscored the importance of employee involvement and participation in decision making. Evidence began to challenge the efficiency of highly directive leadership, and increasing attention was paid to problems of motivation and human relations.

Through training laboratories in group development that sprang up across the country, many of the newer notions of leadership began to exert an impact. These training laboratories were carefully designed to give people a firsthand experience in full participation and decision making. The designated "leaders" deliberately attempted to reduce their own power and to make group members as responsible as possible for setting their own goals and methods within the laboratory experience.

It was perhaps inevitable that some of the people who attended the training laboratories regarded this kind of leadership as being truly "democratic" and went home with the determination to build fully participative decison making into their own organizations. Whenever their bosses made a decision without convening a staff meeting, they tended to perceive this as authoritarian behavior. The true symbol of democratic leadership to some was the meeting—and the less directed from the top, the more democratic it was.

Some of the more enthusiastic alumni of these training laboratories began to get the habit of categorizing leader behavior as "democratic" or "authoritarian." Bosses who made too many decisions themselves were thought of as authoritarian, and their directive behavior was often attributed solely to their personalities.

New need: The net result of the research findings and of the human relations training based upon them has been to call into question the stereotype of an effective leader. Consequently, modern managers often find themselves in an uncomfortable state of mind.

Often they are not quite sure how to behave; there are times when they are torn between exerting "strong" leadership and "permissive" leadership. Sometimes new knowledge pushes them in one direction ("I should really get the group to help make this decision"), but at the same time their experience pushes them in another direction ("I really understand the problem better than the group and therefore I should make the decision"). They are not sure when a group decision is really appropriate or when holding a staff meeting serves merely as a device for avoiding their own decision-making responsibility.

The purpose of our article is to suggest a framework which managers may find useful in grappling with this dilemma. First, we shall look at the different patterns of leadership behavior that managers can choose from in relating to their subordinates. Then, we shall turn to some of the questions suggested by this range of patterns. For instance, how important is it for managers' subordinates to know what type of leadership they are using in a situation? What factors should they consider in deciding on a leadership pattern? What difference do their long-run objectives make as compared to their immediate objectives?

Range of Behavior

Exhibit I presents the continuum or range of possible leadership behavior available to managers.

Exhibit I   Continuum of Leadership Behavior

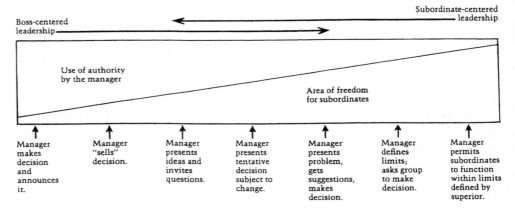

Each type of action is related to the degree of authority used by the boss and to the amount of freedom available to subordinates in reaching decisions. The actions seen on the extreme left characterize managers who maintain a high degree of control while those seen on the extreme right characterize managers who release a high degree of control. Neither extreme is absolute; authority and freedom are never without their limitations.

Now let us look more closely at each of the behavior points occurring along this continuum.

The manager makes the decision and announces it. In this case the boss identifies a problem, considers alternative solutions, chooses one of them, and then reports this decision to the subordinates for implementation. The boss may or may not give consideration to what he or she believes the subordinates will think or feel about the decision; in any case, no opportunity is provided for them to participate directly in the decision-making process. Coercion may or may not be used or implied.

The manager "sells" the decision. Here the manager, as before, takes responsibility for identifying the problem and arriving at a decision. However, rather than simply announcing it, he or she takes the additional step of persuading the subordinates to accept it. In doing so, the boss recognizes the possibility of some resistance among those who will be faced with the decision, and seeks to reduce this resistance by indicating, for example, what the employees have to gain from the decision.

The manager presents ideas, invites questions. Here the boss who has arrived at a decision and who seeks acceptance of his or her ideas provides an opportunity for subordinates to get a fuller explanation of his or her thinking and intentions. After presenting the ideas, the manager invites questions so that the associates can better understand what he or she is trying to accomplish. This "give and take" also enables the manager and the subordinates to explore more fully the implications of the decision.

The manager presents a tentative decision subject to change. This kind of behavior permits the subordinates to exert some influence on the decision. The initiative for identifying and diagnosing the problem remains with the boss. Before meeting with the staff, the manager has thought the problem through and arrived at a decision—but only a tentative one. Before finalizing it, he or she presents the proposed solution for the reaction of those who will be affected by it. He or she says in effect, "I'd like to hear what you have to say about this plan that I have developed. I'll appreciate your frank reactions but will reserve for myself the final decision."

The manager presents the problem, gets suggestions, and then makes the decision. Up to this point the boss has come before the group with a solution of his or her own. Not so in this case. The subordinates now get the first chance to suggest solutions. The manager's initial role involves identifying the problem. He or she might, for example, say something of this sort: "We are faced with a number of complaints from newspapers and the general public on our service policy. What is wrong here? What ideas do you have for coming to grips with this problem?"

The function of the group becomes one of increasing the manager's repertory of possible solutions to the problem. The purpose is to capitalize on the knowledge and experience of those who are on the "firing line." From the expanded list of alternatives developed by the manager and the subordinates, the manager then selects the solution that he or she regards as most promising.[1]

The manager defines the limits and requests the group to make a decision. At this point the manager passes to the group (possibly taking part as a member) the right to make decisions. Before doing so, however, he or she defines the problem to be solved and the boundaries within which the decision must be made.

An example might be the handling of a parking problem at a plant. The boss decides that this is something that should be worked on by the people involved, so they are called together. Pointing up the existence of the problem, the boss tells them:

"There is the open field just north of the main plant which has been designated for additional employee parking. We can build underground or surface multilevel facilities as long as the cost does not exceed $100,000. Within these limits we are free to work out whatever solution makes sense to us. After we decide on a specific plan, the company will spend the available money in whatever way we indicate."

The manager permits the group to make decisions within prescribed limits. This represents an extreme degree of group freedom only occasionally encountered in formal organizations, as, for instance, in many research groups. Here the team of managers or engineers undertakes the identification and diagnosis of the problem, develops alternative procedures for solving it, and decides on one or more of these alternative solutions. The only limits directly imposed on the group by the organization are those specified by the superior of the team's boss. If the boss participates in the decision-making process, deciding in advance to assist in implementing whatever decision the group makes, he or she attempts to do so with no more authority than any other member of the group.

---

1. For a fuller explanation of this approach, see Leo Moore, "Too Much Management, Too Little Change," HBR January–February 1956, p. 41.

Key Questions

As the continuum in Exhibit I demonstrates, there are a number of alternative ways in which managers can relate themselves to the group or individuals they are supervising. At the extreme left of the range, the emphasis is on the manager—on what *he* or *she* is interested in, how *he* or *she* sees things, how *he* or *she* feels about them. As we move toward the subordinate-centered end of the continuum, however, the focus is increasingly on the subordinates—on what *they* are interested in, how *they* look at things, how *they* feel about them.

When business leadership is regarded in this way, a number of questions arise. Let us take four of especial importance:

Can bosses ever relinquish their responsibility by delegating it to others? Our view is that managers must expect to be held responsible by their superiors for the quality of the decisions made, even though operationally these decisions may have been made on a group basis. They should, therefore, be ready to accept whatever risk is involved whenever they delegate decision-making power to subordinates. Delegation is not a way of "passing the buck." Also, it should be emphasized that the amount of freedom bosses give to subordinates cannot be greater than the freedom which they themselves have been given by their own superiors.

Should the manager participate with subordinates once he or she has delegated responsibility to them? Managers should carefully think over this question and decide on their role prior to involving the subordinate group. They should ask if their presence will inhibit or facilitate the problem-solving process. There may be some instances when they should leave the group to let it solve the problem for itself. Typically, however, the boss has useful ideas to contribute and should function as an additional member of the group. In the latter instance, it is important that he or she indicate clearly to the group that he or she is in a member role rather than an authority role.

How important is it for the group to recognize what kind of leadership behavior the boss is using? It makes a great deal of difference. Many relationship problems between bosses and subordinates occur because the bosses fail to make clear how they plan to use their authority. If, for example, the boss actually intends to make a certain decision, but the subordinate group gets the impression that he or she has delegated this authority, considerable confusion and resentment are likely to follow. Problems may also occur when the boss uses a "democratic" facade to conceal the fact that he or she has already made a decision which he or she hopes the group will accept as its own. The attempt

to "make them think it was their idea in the first place" is a risky one. We believe that it is highly important for managers to be honest and clear in describing what authority they are keeping and what role they are asking their subordinates to assume in solving a particular problem.

Can you tell how "democratic" a manager is by the number of decisions the subordinates make? The sheer *number* of decisions is not an accurate index of the amount of freedom that a subordinate group enjoys. More important is the *significance* of the decisions which the boss entrusts to subordinates. Obviously a decision on how to arrange desks is of an entirely different order from a decision involving the introduction of new electronic data-processing equipment. Even though the widest possible limits are given in dealing with the first issue, the group will sense no particular degree of responsibility. For a boss to permit the group to decide equipment policy, even within rather narrow limits, would reflect a greater degree of confidence in them on his or her part.

Deciding How to Lead

Now let us turn from the types of leadership which are possible in a company situation to the question of what types are *practical* and *desirable*. What factors or forces should a manager consider in deciding how to manage? Three are of particular importance:

☐ Forces in the manager.
☐ Forces in the subordinates.
☐ Forces in the situation.

We should like briefly to describe these elements and indicate how they might influence a manager's action in a decision-making situation.[2] The strength of each of them will, of course, vary from instance to instance, but managers who are sensitive to them can better assess the problems which face them and determine which mode of leadership behavior is most appropriate for them.

Forces in the manager: The manager's behavior in any given instance will be influenced greatly by the many forces operating within his or her own personality. Managers will, of course, perceive their leadership problems in a unique way on the basis of their background, knowledge, and experience. Among the important internal forces affecting them will be the following:

1. *Their value system.* How strongly do they feel that individuals should have a share in making the

---

2. See also Robert Tannenbaum and Fred Massarik, "Participation by Subordinates in the Managerial Decision-Making Process," *Canadian Journal of Economics and Political Science,* August 1950, p. 413.

decisions which affect them? Or, how convinced are they that the official who is paid to assume responsibility should personally carry the burden of decision making? The strength of their convictions on questions like these will tend to move managers to one end or the other of the continuum shown in Exhibit I. Their behavior will also be influenced by the relative importance that they attach to organizational efficiency, personal growth of subordinates, and company profits.[3]

2. *Their confidence in subordinates.* Managers differ greatly in the amount of trust they have in other people generally, and this carries over to the particular employees they supervise at a given time. In viewing his or her particular group of subordinates, the manager is likely to consider their knowledge and competence with respect to the problem. A central question managers might ask themselves is: "Who is best qualified to deal with this problem?" Often they may, justifiably or not, have more confidence in their own capabilities than in those of subordinates.

3. *Their own leadership inclinations.* There are some managers who seem to function more comfortably and naturally as highly directive leaders. Resolving problems and issuing orders come easily to them. Other managers seem to operate more comfortably in a team role, where they are continually sharing many of their functions with their subordinates.

4. *Their feelings of security in an uncertain situation.* Managers who release control over the decision-making process thereby reduce the predictability of the outcome. Some managers have a greater need than others for predictability and stability in their environment. This "tolerance for ambiguity" is being viewed increasingly by psychologists as a key variable in a person's manner of dealing with problems.

Managers bring these and other highly personal variables to each situation they face. If they can see them as forces which, consciously or unconsciously, influence their behavior, they can better understand what makes them prefer to act in a given way. And understanding this, they can often make themselves more effective.

Forces in the subordinate: Before deciding how to lead a certain group, managers will also want to consider a number of forces affecting their subordinates' behavior. They will want to remember that each employee, like themselves, is influenced by many personality variables. In addition, each subordinate has a set of expectations about how the boss should act in relation to him or her (the phrase "expected behavior" is one we hear more and more often these days at discussions of leadership and teaching). The better man-

agers understand these factors, the more accurately they can determine what kind of behavior on their part will enable subordinates to act most effectively.

Generally speaking, managers can permit subordinates greater freedom if the following essential conditions exist:

☐ If the subordinates have relatively high needs for independence. (As we all know, people differ greatly in the amount of direction that they desire.)

☆ If the subordinates have a readiness to assume responsibility for decision making. (Some see additional responsibility as a tribute to their ability; others see it as "passing the buck.")

☐ If they have a relatively high tolerance for ambiguity. (Some employees prefer to have clear-cut directives given to them; others prefer a wider area of freedom.)

☐ If they are interested in the problem and feel that it is important.

☐ If they understand and identify with the goals of the organization.

☐ If they have the necessary knowledge and experience to deal with the problem.

☐ If they have learned to expect to share in decision making. (Persons who have come to expect strong leadership and are then suddenly confronted with the request to share more fully in decision making are often upset by this new experience. On the other hand, persons who have enjoyed a considerable amount of freedom resent bosses who begin to make all the decisions themselves.)

Managers will probably tend to make fuller use of their own authority if the above conditions do *not* exist; at times there may be no realistic alternative to running a "one-man show."

The restrictive effect of many of the forces will, of course, be greatly modified by the general feeling of confidence which subordinates have in the boss. Where they have learned to respect and trust the boss, he or she is free to vary his or her own behavior. The boss will feel certain that he or she will not be perceived as an authoritarian boss on those occasions when he or she makes decisions alone. Similarly, the boss will not be seen as using staff meetings to avoid decision-making responsibility. In a climate of mutual confidence and respect, people tend to feel less threatened by deviations from normal practice, which in turn makes possible a higher degree of flexibility in the whole relationship.

Forces in the situation: In addition to the forces which exist in managers themselves and in the subordinates, certain characteristics of the general situation will also affect managers' behavior. Among the more critical environmental pressures that surround

---

3. See Chris Argyris, "Top Management Dilemma: Company Needs vs. Individual Development," *Personnel*, September 1955, pp. 123–134.

them are those which stem from the organization, the work group, the nature of the problem, and the pressures of time. Let us look briefly at each of these:

Type of organization—Like individuals, organizations have values and traditions which inevitably influence the behavior of the people who work in them. Managers who are newcomers to a company quickly discover that certain kinds of behavior are approved while others are not. They also discover that to deviate radically from what is' generally accepted is likely to create problems for them.

These values and traditions are communicated in numerous ways—through job descriptions, policy pronouncements, and public statements by top executives. Some organizations, for example, hold to the notion that the desirable executive is one who is dynamic, imaginative, decisive, and persuasive. Other organizations put more emphasis upon the importance of the executive's ability to work effectively with people—human relations skills. The fact that the person's superiors have a defined concept of what the good executive should be will very likely push the manager toward one end or the other of the behavioral range.

In addition to the above, the amount of employee participation is influenced by such variables as the size of the working units, their geographical distribution, and the degree of inter- and intra-organizational security required to attain company goals. For example, the wide geographical dispersion of an organization may preclude a practical system of participative decision making, even though this would otherwise be desirable. Similarly, the size of the working units or the need for keeping plans confidential may make it necessary for the boss to exercise more control than would otherwise be the case. Factors like these may limit considerably the manager's ability to function flexibly on the continuum.

Group effectiveness—Before turning decision-making responsibility over to a subordinate group, the boss should consider how effectively its members work together as a unit.

One of the relevant factors here is the experience the group has had in working together. It can generally be expected that a group which has functioned for some time will have developed habits of cooperation and thus be able to tackle a problem more effectively than a new group. It can also be expected that a group of people with similar backgrounds and interests will work more quickly and easily than people with dissimilar backgrounds, because the communication problems are likely to be less complex.

The degree of confidence that the members have in their ability to solve problems as a group is also a key consideration. Finally, such group variables as cohesiveness, permissiveness, mutual acceptance, and commonality of purpose will exert subtle but powerful influence on the group's functioning.

The problem itself—The nature of the problem may determine what degree of authority should be delegated by managers to their subordinates. Obviously, managers will ask themselves whether subordinates have the kind of knowledge which is needed. It is possible to do them a real disservice by assigning a problem that their experience does not equip them to handle.

Since the problems faced in large or growing industries increasingly require knowledge of specialists from many different fields, it might be inferred that the more complex a problem, the more anxious a manager will be to get some assistance in solving it. However, this is not always the case. There will be times when the very complexity of the problem calls for one person to work it out. For example, if the manager has most of the background and factual data relevant to a given issue, it may be easier for him or her to think it through than to take the time to fill in the staff on all the pertinent background information.

The key question to ask, of course, is: "Have I heard the ideas of everyone who has the necessary knowledge to make a significant contribution to the solution of this problem?"

The pressure of time—This is perhaps the most clearly felt pressure on managers (in spite of the fact that it may sometimes be imagined). The more that they feel the need for an immediate decision, the more difficult it is to involve other people. In organizations which are in a constant state of "crisis" and "crash programming" one is likely to find managers personally using a high degree of authority with relatively little delegation to subordinates. When the time pressure is less intense, however, it becomes much more possible to bring subordinates in on the decision-making process.

These, then, are the principal forces that impinge on managers in any given instance and that tend to determine their tactical behavior in relation to subordinates. In each case their behavior ideally will be that which makes possible the most effective attainment of their immediate goals within the limits facing them.

Long-Run Strategy

As managers work with their organizations on the problems that come up day to day, their choice of a leadership pattern is usually limited. They must take account of the forces just described and, within the restrictions those factors impose on them, do the best that they can. But as they look ahead months or even years, they can shift their thinking from tactics to large-scale strategy. No longer need they be fettered by all of the forces mentioned, for they can view many of them as variables over which they have some control. They can, for example, gain new insights or skills for themselves, supply training for individual subordinates, and provide participative experiences for their employee group.

In trying to bring about a change in these variables, however, they are faced with a challenging question: At which point along the continuum *should* they act?

Attaining objectives: The answer depends largely on what they want to accomplish. Let us suppose that they are interested in the same objectives that most modern managers seek to attain when they can shift their attention from the pressure of immediate assignments:

1. To raise the level of employee motivation.
2. To increase the readiness of subordinates to accept change.
3. To improve the quality of all managerial decisions.
4. To develop teamwork and morale.
5. To further the individual development of employees.

In recent years managers have been deluged with a flow of advice on how best to achieve these longer-run objectives. It is little wonder that they are often both bewildered and annoyed. However, there are some guidelines which they can usefully follow in making a decision.

Most research and much of the experience of recent years give a strong factual basis to the theory that a fairly high degree of subordinate-center behavior is associated with the accomplishment of the five purposes mentioned.[4] This does not mean that managers should always leave all decisions to their assis-

tants. To provide the individual or the group with greater freedom than they are ready for at any given time may very well tend to generate anxieties and therefore inhibit rather than facilitate the attainment of desired objectives. But this should not keep managers from making a continuing effort to confront subordinates with the challenge of freedom.

In summary, there are two implications in the basic thesis that we have been developing. The first is that successful leaders are those who are keenly aware of the forces which are most relevant to their behavior at any given time. They accurately understand themselves, the individuals and groups they are dealing with, and the company and broader social environment in which they operate. And certainly they are able to assess the present readiness for growth of their subordinates.

But this sensitivity or understanding is not enough, which brings us to the second implication. Successful leaders are those who are able to behave appropriately in the light of these perceptions. If direction is in order, they are able to direct; if considerable participative freedom is called for, they are able to provide such freedom.

Thus, successful managers of people can be primarily characterized neither as strong leaders nor as permissive ones. Rather, they are people who maintain a high batting average in accurately assessing the forces that determine what their most appropriate behavior at any given time should be and in actually being able to behave accordingly. Being both insightful and flexible, they are less likely to see the problems of leadership as a dilemma.

---

4. For example, see Warren H. Schmidt and Paul C. Buchanan, *Techniques that Produce Teamwork* (New London, Arthur C. Croft Publications, 1954); and Morris S. Viteles, *Motivation and Morale in Industry* (New York, W.W. Norton & Company, Inc., 1953).

Retrospective Commentary

Since this HBR Classic was first published in 1958, there have been many changes in organizations and in the world that have affected leadership patterns. While the article's continued popularity attests to its essential validity, we believe it can be reconsidered and updated to reflect subsequent societal changes and new management concepts.

The reasons for the article's continued relevance can be summarized briefly:

☐ The article contains insights and perspectives which mesh well with, and help clarify, the experiences of managers, other leaders, and students of leadership. Thus it is useful to individuals in a wide variety of organizations—industrial, governmental, educational, religious, and community.

☐ The concept of leadership the article defines is reflected in a continuum of leadership behavior (see Exhibit I in original article). Rather than offering a choice between two styles of leadership, democratic or authoritarian, it sanctions a range of behavior.

☐ The concept does not dictate to managers but helps them to analyze their own behavior. The continuum permits them to review their behavior within a context of other alternatives, without any style being labeled right or wrong.

(We have sometimes wondered if we have, perhaps, made it too easy for anyone to justify his or her style of leadership. It may be a small step between being nonjudgmental and giving the impression that all behavior is equally valid and useful. The latter was not our intention. Indeed, the thrust of our endorsement was for managers who are insightful in assessing relevant forces within themselves, others, and situations, and who can be flexible in responding to these forces.)

In recognizing that our article can be updated, we are acknowledging that organizations do not exist in a vacuum but are affected by changes that occur in society. Consider, for example, the implications for organizations of these recent social developments:

> The youth revolution that expresses distrust and even contempt for organizations identified with the establishment.

> The civil rights movement that demands all minority groups be given a greater opportunity for participation and influence in the organizational processes.

> The ecology and consumer movements that challenge the right of managers to make decisions without considering the interest of people outside the organization.

> The increasing national concern with the quality of working life and its relationship to worker productivity, participation, and satisfaction.

These and other societal changes make effective leadership in this decade a more challenging task, requiring even greater sensitivity and flexibility than was needed in the 1950's. Today's manager is more likely to deal with employees who resent being treated as subordinates, who may be highly critical of any organizational system, who expect to be consulted and to exert influence, and who often stand on the edge of alienation from the institution that needs their loyalty and commitment. In addition, the manager is frequently confronted by a highly turbulent, unpredictable environment.

In response to these social pressures, new concepts of management have emerged in organizations. Open-system theory, with its emphasis on subsystems' interdependency *and* on the interaction of an organization with its environment, has made a powerful impact on managers' approach to problems. Organization development has emerged as a new behavioral science approach to the improvement of individual, group, organizational, and interorganizational performance. New research has added to our understanding of motivation in the work situation. More and more executives have become concerned with social responsibility and have explored the feasibility of social audits. And a growing number of organizations, in Europe and in the United States, have conducted experiments in industrial democracy.

In light of these developments, we submit the following thoughts on how we would rewrite certain points in our original article.

The article described forces in the manager, subordinates, and the situation as givens, with the leadership pattern a result of these forces. We would now give more attention to the *interdependency* of these forces. For example, such interdependency occurs in: (a) the interplay between the manager's confidence in subordinates, their readiness to assume responsibility, and the level of group effectiveness; and (b) the impact of the behavior of the manager on that of subordinates, and vice versa.

In discussing the forces in the situation, we primarily identified organizational phenomena. We would now include forces lying outside the organization and would explore the relevant interdependencies between the organization and its environment.

In the original article, we presented the size of the rectangle in Exhibit I as a given, with its boundaries already determined by external forces—in effect, a closed system. We would now recognize the possibility of the manager and/or the subordinates taking the initiative to change those boundaries through interaction with relevant external forces—both within their own organization and in the larger society.

The article portrayed the manager as the principal and almost unilateral actor. He or she initiated and

(continued)

EXHIBIT II   Continuum of Manager-Nonmanager Behavior

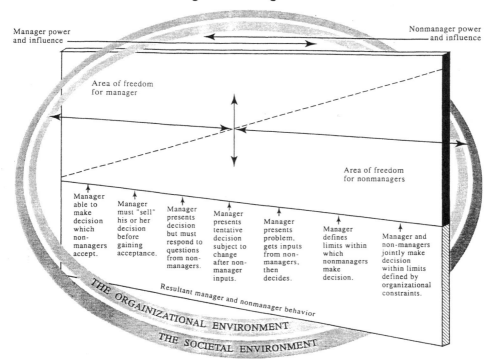

Manager power and influence ← → Nonmanager power and influence

Area of freedom for manager

Area of freedom for nonmanagers

| Manager able to make decision which non-managers accept. | Manager must "sell" his or her decision before gaining acceptance. | Manager presents decision but must respond to questions from non-managers. | Manager presents tentative decision subject to change after non-manager inputs. | Manager presents problem, gets inputs from non-managers, then decides. | Manager defines limits within which nonmanagers make decision. | Manager and non-managers jointly make decision within limits defined by organizational constraints. |

Resultant manager and nonmanager behavior

THE ORGANIZATIONAL ENVIRONMENT

THE SOCIETAL ENVIRONMENT

determined group functions, assumed responsibility, and exercised control. Subordinates made inputs and assumed power only at the will of the manager. Although the manager might have taken outside forces into account, it was *he* or *she* who decided where to operate on the continuum—that is, whether to announce a decision instead of trying to sell the idea to subordinates, whether to invite questions, to let subordinates decide an issue, and so on. While the manager has retained this clear prerogative in many organizations, it has been challenged in others. Even in situations where managers have retained it, however, the balance in the relationship between managers and subordinates at any given time is arrived at by interaction—direct or indirect—between the two parties.

Although power and its use by managers played a role in our article, we now realize that our concern with cooperation and collaboration, common goals, commitment, trust, and mutual caring limited our

vision with respect to the realities of power. We did not attempt to deal with unions, other forms of joint worker action, or with individual workers' expressions of resistance. Today, we would recognize much more clearly the power available to *all* parties and the factors that underlie the interrelated decisions on whether to use it.

In the original article, we used the terms "manager" and "subordinate." We are now uncomfortable with "subordinate" because of its demeaning, dependency-laden connotations and prefer "nonmanager." The titles "manager" and "nonmanager" make the terminological difference functional rather than hierarchical.

We assumed fairly traditional organizational structures in our original article. Now we would alter our formulation to reflect newer organizational modes which are slowly emerging, such as industrial democracy, intentional communities, and "phenomenarchy."* These new modes are based on observations such as the following:

(continued)

> Both manager and nonmanagers may be governing forces in their group's environment, contributing to the definition of the total area of freedom.

> A group can function without a manager, with managerial functions being shared by group members.

> A group, as a unit, can be delegated authority and can assume responsibility within a larger organizational context.

Our thoughts on the question of leadership have prompted us to design a new behavior continuum (see *Exhibit II*) in which the total area of freedom shared by manager and nonmanagers is constantly redefined by interactions between them and the forces in the environment.

The arrows in the exhibit indicate the continual flow of interdependent influence among systems and people. The points on the continuum designate the types of manager and nonmanager behavior that become possible with any given amount of freedom available to each. The new continuum is both more complex and more dynamic than the 1958 version, reflecting the organizational and societal realities of 1973.

---

*For a description of phenomenarchy, see Will McWhinney, "Phenomenarchy: A Suggestion for Social Redesign," *Journal of Applied Behavioral Science*, May 1973.

[7]

LEADERSHIP THAT GETS RESULTS

by Daniel Goleman

ASK ANY GROUP of businesspeople the question "What do effective leaders do?" and you'll hear a sweep of answers. Leaders set strategy; they motivate; they create a mission; they build a culture. Then ask "What *should* leaders do?" If the group is seasoned, you'll likely hear one response: the leader's singular job is to get results.

But how? The mystery of what leaders can and ought to do in order to spark the best performance from their people is age-old. In recent years, that mystery has spawned an entire cottage industry: literally thousands of "leadership experts" have made careers of testing and coaching executives, all in pursuit of creating businesspeople who can turn bold objectives – be they strategic, financial, organizational, or all three – into reality.

Still, effective leadership eludes many people and organizations. One reason is that until recently, virtually no quantitative research has demonstrated which precise leadership behaviors yield positive results. Leadership experts proffer advice based on inference, experience, and instinct. Sometimes that advice is right on target; sometimes it's not.

But new research by the consulting firm Hay/McBer, which draws on a random sample of 3,871 executives selected from a database of more than 20,000 executives worldwide, takes much of the mystery out of effective leadership. The research found six distinct leadership styles, each springing from different components of emotional intelligence. The styles, taken individually, appear to have a direct and unique impact on the working atmosphere of a company, division, or team, and in turn, on its financial performance. And perhaps most important, the research indicates that leaders with the best results do not rely on only one leadership style; they use most of them in a given week – seamlessly and in different measure – depending on the

Leadership That Gets Results

Emotional Intelligence: A Primer

Emotional intelligence – the ability to manage ourselves and our relationships effectively – consists of four fundamental capabilities: self-awareness, self-management, social awareness, and social skill. Each capability, in turn, is composed of specific sets of competencies. Below is a list of the capabilities and their corresponding traits.

Self-Awareness	Self-Management	Social Awareness	Social Skill
• *Emotional self-awareness:* the ability to read and understand your emotions as well as recognize their impact on work performance, relationships, and the like.	• *Self-control:* the ability to keep disruptive emotions and impulses under control.	• *Empathy:* skill at sensing other people's emotions, understanding their perspective, and taking an active interest in their concerns.	• *Visionary leadership:* the ability to take charge and inspire with a compelling vision.
• *Accurate self-assessment:* a realistic evaluation of your strengths and limitations.	• *Trustworthiness:* a consistent display of honesty and integrity.	• *Organizational awareness:* the ability to read the currents of organizational life, build decision networks, and navigate politics.	• *Influence:* the ability to wield a range of persuasive tactics.
• *Self-confidence:* a strong and positive sense of self-worth.	• *Conscientiousness:* the ability to manage yourself and your responsibilities.	• *Service orientation:* the ability to recognize and meet customers' needs.	• *Developing others:* the propensity to bolster the abilities of others through feedback and guidance.
	• *Adaptability:* skill at adjusting to changing situations and overcoming obstacles.		• *Communication:* skill at listening and at sending clear, convincing, and well-tuned messages.
	• *Achievement orientation:* the drive to meet an internal standard of excellence.		• *Change catalyst:* proficiency in initiating new ideas and leading people in a new direction.
	• *Initiative:* a readiness to seize opportunities.		• *Conflict management:* the ability to de-escalate disagreements and orchestrate resolutions.
			• *Building bonds:* proficiency at cultivating and maintaining a web of relationships.
			• *Teamwork and collaboration:* competence at promoting cooperation and building teams.

business situation. Imagine the styles, then, as the array of clubs in a golf pro's bag. Over the course of a game, the pro picks and chooses clubs based on the demands of the shot. Sometimes he has to ponder his selection, but usually it is automatic. The pro senses the challenge ahead, swiftly pulls out the right tool, and elegantly puts it to work. That's how high-impact leaders operate, too.

What are the six styles of leadership? None will shock workplace veterans. Indeed, each style, by name and brief description alone, will likely resonate with anyone who leads, is led, or as is the case with most of us, does both. *Coercive leaders* demand immediate compliance. *Authoritative leaders* mobilize people toward a vision. *Affiliative leaders* create emotional bonds and harmony. *Democratic leaders* build consensus through participation. *Pacesetting leaders* expect excellence and self-direction. And *coaching leaders* develop people for the future.

Close your eyes and you can surely imagine a colleague who uses any one of these styles. You most likely use at least one yourself. What is new in this research, then, is its implications for action. First, it offers a fine-grained understanding of how different leadership styles affect performance and results. Second, it offers clear guidance on when a manager

should switch between them. It also strongly suggests that switching flexibly is well advised. New, too, is the research's finding that each leadership style springs from different components of emotional intelligence.

Measuring Leadership's Impact

It has been more than a decade since research first linked aspects of emotional intelligence to business results. The late David McClelland, a noted Harvard University psychologist, found that leaders with strengths in a critical mass of six or more emotional intelligence competencies were far more effective than peers who lacked such strengths. For

---

Daniel Goleman is the author of Emotional Intelligence *(Bantam, 1995) and* Working with Emotional Intelligence *(Bantam, 1998). He is cochairman of the Consortium for Research on Emotional Intelligence in Organizations, which is based at Rutgers University's Graduate School of Applied Psychology in Piscataway, New Jersey. His article "What Makes a Leader?" appeared in the November–December 1998 issue of HBR. He can be reached at goleman@javanet.com.*

instance, when he analyzed the performance of division heads at a global food and beverage company, he found that among leaders with this critical mass of competence, 87% placed in the top third for annual salary bonuses based on their business performance. More telling, their divisions on average outperformed yearly revenue targets by 15% to 20%. Those executives who lacked emotional intelligence were rarely rated as outstanding in their annual performance reviews, and their divisions underperformed by an average of almost 20%.

Our research set out to gain a more molecular view of the links among leadership and emotional intelligence, and climate and performance. A team of McClelland's colleagues headed by Mary Fontaine and Ruth Jacobs from Hay/McBer studied data about or observed thousands of executives, noting specific behaviors and their impact on climate.[1] How did each individual motivate direct reports? Manage change initiatives? Handle crises? It was in a later phase of the research that we identified which emotional intelligence capabilities drive the six leadership styles. How does he rate in terms of self-control and social skill? Does a leader show high or low levels of empathy?

The team tested each executive's immediate sphere of influence for its climate. "Climate" is not an amorphous term. First defined by psychologists George Litwin and Richard Stringer and later refined by McClelland and his colleagues, it refers to six key factors that influence an organization's working environment: its *flexibility*—that is, how free employees feel to innovate unencumbered by red tape; their sense of *responsibility* to the organization; the level of *standards* that people set; the sense of accuracy about performance feedback and aptness of *rewards*; the *clarity* people have about mission and values; and finally, the level of *commitment* to a common purpose.

We found that all six leadership styles have a measurable effect on each aspect of climate. (For details, see the exhibit "Getting Molecular: The Impact of Leadership Styles on Drivers of Climate.") Further, when we looked at the impact of climate on financial results—such as return on sales, revenue growth, efficiency, and profitability—we found a direct correlation between the two. Leaders who used styles that positively affected the climate had decidedly better financial results than those who did not. That is not to say that organizational climate is the only driver of performance. Economic conditions

Getting Molecular: The Impact of Leadership Styles on Drivers of Climate

Our research investigated how each leadership style affected the six drivers of climate, or working atmosphere. The figures below show the correlation between each leadership style and each aspect of climate. So, for instance, if we look at the climate driver of flexibility, we see that the coercive style has a -.28 correlation while the democratic style has a .28 correlation, equally strong in the opposite direction. Focusing on the authoritative leadership style, we find that it has a .54 correlation with rewards—

strongly positive—and a .21 correlation with responsibility—positive, but not as strong. In other words, the style's correlation with rewards was more than twice that with responsibility.

According to the data, the authoritative leadership style has the most positive effect on climate, but three others—affiliative, democratic, and coaching—follow close behind. That said, the research indicates that no style should be relied on exclusively, and all have at least short-term uses.

	Coercive	Authoritative	Affiliative	Democratic	Pacesetting	Coaching
Flexibility	-.28	.32	.27	.28	-.07	.17
Responsibility	-.37	.21	.16	.23	.04	.08
Standards	.02	.38	.31	.22	-.27	.39
Rewards	-.18	.54	.48	.42	-.29	.43
Clarity	-.11	.44	.37	.35	-.28	.38
Commitment	-.13	.35	.34	.26	-.20	.27
Overall impact on climate	-.26	.54	.46	.43	-.25	.42

The Six Leadership Styles at a Glance

		Coercive	Authoritative
Our research found that leaders use six styles, each springing from different components of emotional intelligence. Here is a summary of the styles, their origin, when they work best, and their impact on an organization's climate and thus its performance.	The leader's modus operandi	Demands immediate compliance	Mobilizes people toward a vision
	The style in a phrase	"Do what I tell you."	"Come with me."
	Underlying emotional intelligence competences	Drive to achieve, initiative, self-control	Self-confidence, empathy, change catalyst
	When the style works best	In a crisis, to kick start a turnaround, or with problem employees	When changes require a new vision, or when a clear direction is needed
	Overall impact on climate	Negative	Most strongly positive

and competitive dynamics matter enormously. But our analysis strongly suggests that climate accounts for nearly a third of results. And that's simply too much of an impact to ignore.

The Styles in Detail

Executives use six leadership styles, but only four of the six consistently have a positive effect on climate and results. Let's look then at each style of leadership in detail. (For a summary of the material that follows, see the chart "The Six Leadership Styles at a Glance.")

The Coercive Style. The computer company was in crisis mode – its sales and profits were falling, its stock was losing value precipitously, and its shareholders were in an uproar. The board brought in a new CEO with a reputation as a turnaround artist. He set to work chopping jobs, selling off divisions, and making the tough decisions that should have been executed years before. The company was saved, at least in the short-term.

From the start, though, the CEO created a reign of terror, bullying and demeaning his executives, roaring his displeasure at the slightest misstep. The company's top echelons were decimated not just by his erratic firings but also by defections. The CEO's direct reports, frightened by his tendency to blame the bearer of bad news, stopped bringing him any news at all. Morale was at an all-time low – a fact reflected in another downturn in the business after the short-term recovery. The CEO was eventually fired by the board of directors.

It's easy to understand why of all the leadership styles, the coercive one is the least effective in most situations. Consider what the style does to an organization's climate. Flexibility is the hardest hit. The leader's extreme top-down decision making kills new ideas on the vine. People feel so disrespected that they think, "I won't even bring my ideas up – they'll only be shot down." Likewise, people's sense of responsibility evaporates: unable to act on their own initiative, they lose their sense of ownership and feel little accountability for their performance. Some become so resentful they adopt the attitude, "I'm not going to help this bastard."

Coercive leadership also has a damaging effect on the rewards system. Most high-performing workers are motivated by more than money – they seek the satisfaction of work well done. The coercive style erodes such pride. And finally, the style undermines one of the leader's prime tools – motivating people by showing them how their job fits into a grand, shared mission. Such a loss, measured in terms of diminished clarity and commitment, leaves people alienated from their own jobs, wondering, "How does any of this matter?"

Given the impact of the coercive style, you might assume it should never be applied. Our research, however, uncovered a few occasions when it worked masterfully. Take the case of a division president who was brought in to change the direction of a food company that was losing money. His first act was to have the executive conference room demolished. To him, the room – with its long marble table that looked like "the deck of the Starship Enterprise" – symbolized the tradition-bound formality that was paralyzing the company. The destruction of the room, and the subsequent move to a smaller, more informal setting, sent a message no one could

Affiliative	Democratic	Pacesetting	Coaching
Creates harmony and builds emotional bonds	Forges consensus through participation	Sets high standards for performance	Develops people for the future
"People come first."	"What do you think?"	"Do as I do, now."	"Try this."
Empathy, building relationships, communication	Collaboration, team leadership, communication	Conscientiousness, drive to achieve, initiative	Developing others, empathy, self-awareness
To heal rifts in a team or to motivate people during stressful circumstances	To build buy-in or consensus, or to get input from valuable employees	To get quick results from a highly motivated and competent team	To help an employee improve performance or develop long-term strengths
Positive	Positive	Negative	Positive

miss, and the division's culture changed quickly in its wake.

That said, the coercive style should be used only with extreme caution and in the few situations when it is absolutely imperative, such as during a turnaround or when a hostile takeover is looming. In those cases, the coercive style can break failed business habits and shock people into new ways of working. It is always appropriate during a genuine emergency, like in the aftermath of an earthquake or a fire. And it can work with problem employees with whom all else has failed. But if a leader relies solely on this style or continues to use it once the emergency passes, the long-term impact of his insensitivity to the morale and feelings of those he leads will be ruinous.

The Authoritative Style. Tom was the vice president of marketing at a floundering national restaurant chain that specialized in pizza. Needless to say, the company's poor performance troubled the senior managers, but they were at a loss for what to do. Every Monday, they met to review recent sales, struggling to come up with fixes. To Tom, the approach didn't make sense. "We were always trying to figure out why our sales were down last week. We had the whole company looking backward instead of figuring out what we had to do tomorrow."

Tom saw an opportunity to change people's way of thinking at an off-site strategy meeting. There, the conversation began with stale truisms: the company had to drive up shareholder wealth and increase return on assets. Tom believed those concepts didn't have the power to inspire a restaurant manager to be innovative or to do better than a good-enough job.

So Tom made a bold move. In the middle of a meeting, he made an impassioned plea for his colleagues to think from the customer's perspective. Customers want convenience, he said. The company was not in the restaurant business, it was in the business of distributing high-quality, convenient-to-get pizza. That notion – and nothing else – should drive everything the company did.

With his vibrant enthusiasm and clear vision – the hallmarks of the authoritative style – Tom filled a leadership vacuum at the company. Indeed, his concept became the core of the new mission statement. But this conceptual breakthrough was just the beginning. Tom made sure that the mission statement was built into the company's strategic planning process as the designated driver of growth. And he ensured that the vision was articulated so that local restaurant managers understood they were the key to the company's success and were free to find new ways to distribute pizza.

Changes came quickly. Within weeks, many local managers started guaranteeing fast, new delivery times. Even better, they started to act like entrepreneurs, finding ingenious locations to open new branches: kiosks on busy street corners and in bus and train stations, even from carts in airports and hotel lobbies.

Tom's success was no fluke. Our research indicates that of the six leadership styles, the authoritative one is most effective, driving up every aspect of climate. Take clarity. The authoritative leader is a visionary; he motivates people by making clear to them how their work fits into a larger vision for the organization. People who work for such leaders understand that what they do matters and why.

Leadership That Gets Results

Authoritative leadership also maximizes commitment to the organization's goals and strategy. By framing the individual tasks within a grand vision, the authoritative leader defines standards that revolve around that vision. When he gives performance feedback – whether positive or negative – the singular criterion is whether or not that performance furthers the vision. The standards for success are clear to all, as are the rewards. Finally, consider the style's impact on flexibility. An authoritative leader states the end but generally gives people plenty of leeway to devise their own means. Authoritative leaders give people the freedom to innovate, experiment, and take calculated risks.

Because of its positive impact, the authoritative style works well in almost any business situation. But it is particularly effective when a business is adrift. An authoritative leader charts a new course and sells his people on a fresh long-term vision.

The authoritative style, powerful though it may be, will not work in every situation. The approach fails, for instance, when a leader is working with a team of experts or peers who are more experienced than he is; they may see the leader as pompous or out-of-touch. Another limitation: if a manager trying to be authoritative becomes overbearing, he can undermine the egalitarian spirit of an effective team. Yet even with such caveats, leaders would be wise to grab for the authoritative "club" more often than not. It may not guarantee a hole in one, but it certainly helps with the long drive.

The Affiliative Style. If the coercive leader demands, "Do what I say," and the authoritative urges, "Come with me," the affiliative leader says, "People come first." This leadership style revolves around people – its proponents value individuals and their

> An authoritative leader states the end but gives people plenty of leeway to devise their own means.

emotions more than tasks and goals. The affiliative leader strives to keep employees happy and to create harmony among them. He manages by building strong emotional bonds and then reaping the benefits of such an approach, namely fierce loyalty. The style also has a markedly positive effect on communication. People who like one another a lot talk a lot. They share ideas; they share inspiration. And the

style drives up flexibility; friends trust one another, allowing habitual innovation and risk taking. Flexibility also rises because the affiliative leader, like a parent who adjusts household rules for a maturing adolescent, doesn't impose unnecessary strictures on how employees get their work done. They give people the freedom to do their job in the way they think is most effective.

As for a sense of recognition and reward for work well done, the affiliative leader offers ample positive feedback. Such feedback has special potency in the workplace because it is all too rare: outside of an annual review, most people usually get no feedback on their day-to-day efforts – or only negative feedback. That makes the affiliative leader's positive words all the more motivating. Finally, affiliative leaders are masters at building a sense of belonging. They are, for instance, likely to take their direct reports out for a meal or a drink, one-on-one, to see how they're doing. They will bring in a cake to celebrate a group accomplishment. They are natural relationship builders.

Joe Torre, the heart and soul of the New York Yankees, is a classic affiliative leader. During the 1999 World Series, Torre tended ably to the psyches of his players as they endured the emotional pressure cooker of a pennant race. All season long, he made a special point to praise Scott Brosius, whose father had died during the season, for staying committed even as he mourned. At the celebration party after the team's final game, Torre specifically sought out right fielder Paul O'Neill. Although he had received the news of his father's death that morning, O'Neill chose to play in the decisive game – and he burst into tears the moment it ended. Torre made a point of acknowledging O'Neill's personal struggle, calling him a "warrior." Torre also used the spotlight of the victory celebration to praise two players whose return the following year was threatened by contract disputes. In doing so, he sent a clear message to the team and to the club's owner that he valued the players immensely – too much to lose them.

Along with ministering to the emotions of his people, an affiliative leader may also tend to his own emotions openly. The year Torre's brother was near death awaiting a heart transplant, he shared his worries with his players. He also spoke candidly with the team about his treatment for prostate cancer.

The affiliative style's generally positive impact makes it a good all-weather approach, but leaders should employ it particularly when trying to build team harmony, increase morale, improve communication, or repair broken trust. For instance, one executive in our study was hired to replace a ruth-

84 ·

less team leader. The former leader had taken credit for his employees' work and had attempted to pit them against one another. His efforts ultimately failed, but the team he left behind was suspicious and weary. The new executive managed to mend the situation by unstintingly showing emotional honesty and rebuilding ties. Several months in, her leadership had created a renewed sense of commitment and energy.

Despite its benefits, the affiliative style should not be used alone. Its exclusive focus on praise can allow poor performance to go uncorrected; employees may perceive that mediocrity is tolerated. And because affiliative leaders rarely offer constructive advice on how to improve, employees must figure out how to do so on their own. When people need clear directives to navigate through complex challenges, the affiliative style leaves them rudderless. Indeed, if overly relied on, this style can actually steer a group to failure. Perhaps that is why many affiliative leaders, including Torre, use this style in close conjunction with the authoritative style. Authoritative leaders state a vision, set standards, and let people know how their work is furthering the group's goals. Alternate that with the caring, nurturing approach of the affiliative leader, and you have a potent combination.

The Democratic Style. Sister Mary ran a Catholic school system in a large metropolitan area. One of the schools – the only private school in an impoverished neighborhood – had been losing money for years, and the archdiocese could no longer afford to keep it open. When Sister Mary eventually got the order to shut it down, she didn't just lock the doors. She called a meeting of all the teachers and staff at the school and explained to them the details of the financial crisis – the first time anyone working at the school had been included in the business side of the institution. She asked for their ideas on ways to keep the school open and on how to handle the closing, should it come to that. Sister Mary spent much of her time at the meeting just listening.

She did the same at later meetings for school parents and for the community and during a successive series of meetings for the school's teachers and staff. After two months of meetings, the consensus was clear: the school would have to close. A plan was made to transfer students to other schools in the Catholic system.

The final outcome was no different than if Sister Mary had gone ahead and closed the school the day she was told to. But by allowing the school's constituents to reach that decision collectively, Sister Mary received none of the backlash that would have accompanied such a move. People mourned the loss of the school, but they understood its inevitability. Virtually no one objected.

Compare that with the experiences of a priest in our research who headed another Catholic school. He, too, was told to shut it down. And he did – by fiat. The result was disastrous: parents filed lawsuits, teachers and parents picketed, and local newspapers ran editorials attacking his decision. It took a year to resolve the disputes before he could finally go ahead and close the school.

Sister Mary exemplifies the democratic style in action – and its benefits. By spending time getting people's ideas and buy-in, a leader builds trust, respect, and commitment. By letting workers themselves have a say in decisions that affect their goals and how they do their work, the democratic leader drives up flexibility and responsibility. And by listening to employees' concerns, the democratic leader learns what to do to keep morale high. Finally, because they have a say in setting their goals and the standards for evaluating success, people operating in a democratic system tend to be very realistic about what can and cannot be accomplished.

However, the democratic style has its drawbacks, which is why its impact on climate is not as high as some of the other styles. One of its more exasperating consequences can be endless meetings where ideas are mulled over, consensus remains elusive, and the only visible result is scheduling more meetings. Some democratic leaders use the style to put off making crucial decisions, hoping that enough thrashing things out will eventually yield a blinding insight. In reality, their people end up feeling confused and leaderless. Such an approach can even escalate conflicts.

When does the style work best? This approach is ideal when a leader is himself uncertain about the best direction to take and needs ideas and guidance from able employees. And even if a leader has a strong vision, the democratic style works well to generate fresh ideas for executing that vision.

The democratic style, of course, makes much less sense when employees are not competent or informed enough to offer sound advice. And it almost goes without saying that building consensus is wrongheaded in times of crisis. Take the case of a CEO whose computer company was severely threatened by changes in the market. He always sought consensus about what to do. As competitors stole customers and customers' needs changed, he kept appointing committees to consider the situation. When the market made a sudden shift because of a new technology, the CEO froze in his tracks. The board replaced him before he could appoint yet another task force to consider the situation. The new CEO, while occasionally democratic and affiliative, relied heavily on the authoritative style, especially in his first months.

The Pacesetting Style. Like the coercive style, the pacesetting style has its place in the leader's repertory, but it should be used sparingly. That's not what we expected to find. After all, the hallmarks of the pacesetting style sound admirable. The leader sets extremely high performance standards and exemplifies them himself. He is obsessive about doing things better and faster, and he asks the same of everyone around him. He quickly pinpoints poor performers and demands more from them. If they don't rise to the occasion, he replaces them with people who can. You would think such an approach would improve results, but it doesn't.

In fact, the pacesetting style destroys climate. Many employees feel overwhelmed by the pacesetter's demands for excellence, and their morale drops. Guidelines for working may be clear in the leader's head, but she does not state them clearly; she expects people to know what to do and even thinks, "If I have to tell you, you're the wrong person for the job." Work becomes not a matter of doing one's best along a clear course so much as second-guessing what the leader wants. At the same time, people often feel that the pacesetter doesn't trust them to work in their own way or to take initiative. Flexibility and responsibility evaporate; work becomes so task focused and routinized it's boring.

As for rewards, the pacesetter either gives no feedback on how people are doing or jumps in to take over when he thinks they're lagging. And if the leader should leave, people feel directionless—they're so used to "the expert" setting the rules. Finally, commitment dwindles under the regime of a pacesetting leader because people have no sense of how their personal efforts fit into the big picture.

For an example of the pacesetting style, take the case of Sam, a biochemist in R&D at a large pharmaceutical company. Sam's superb technical expertise made him an early star: he was the one everyone turned to when they needed help. Soon he was promoted to head of a team developing a new product. The other scientists on the team were as competent and self-motivated as Sam; his métier as team leader became offering himself as a model of how to do first-class scientific work under tremendous deadline pressure, pitching in when needed. His team completed its task in record time.

But then came a new assignment: Sam was put in charge of R&D for his entire division. As his tasks expanded and he had to articulate a vision, coordinate projects, delegate responsibility, and help develop others, Sam began to slip. Not trusting that his subordinates were as capable as he was, he became a micromanager, obsessed with details and taking over for others when their performance slackened. Instead of trusting them to improve with guidance and development, Sam found himself working nights and weekends after stepping in to take over for the head of a floundering research team. Finally, his own boss suggested, to his relief, that he return to his old job as head of a product development team.

Although Sam faltered, the pacesetting style isn't always a disaster. The approach works well when all employees are self-motivated, highly competent, and need little direction or coordination—for example, it can work for leaders of highly skilled and self-motivated professionals, like R&D groups or legal teams. And, given a talented team to lead, pacesetting does exactly that: gets work done on time or even ahead of schedule. Yet like any leadership style, pacesetting should never be used by itself.

The Coaching Style. A product unit at a global computer company had seen sales plummet from twice as much as its competitors to only half as much. So Lawrence, the president of the manufacturing division, decided to close the unit and reassign its people and products. Upon hearing the news, James, the head of the doomed unit, decided to go over his boss's head and plead his case to the CEO.

What did Lawrence do? Instead of blowing up at James, he sat down with his rebellious direct report and talked over not just the decision to close the division but also James's future. He explained to James how moving to another division would help him develop new skills. It would make him a better leader and teach him more about the company's business.

Lawrence acted more like a counselor than a traditional boss. He listened to James's concerns and hopes, and he shared his own. He said he believed James had grown stale in his current job; it was, after all, the only place he'd worked in the company. He predicted that James would blossom in a new role.

The conversation then took a practical turn. James had not yet had his meeting with the CEO—the one he had impetuously demanded when he heard of his division's closing. Knowing this—and also knowing that the CEO unwaveringly supported the closing—Lawrence took the time to coach James on how to present his case in that meeting. "You don't get an audience with the CEO very often," he noted, "let's make sure you impress him with your thoughtfulness." He advised James not to plead his personal case but to focus on the business unit: "If he thinks you're in there for your own glory, he'll throw you out faster than you walked through the door." And he urged him to put his ideas in writing; the CEO always appreciated that.

Lawrence's reason for coaching instead of scolding? "James is a good guy, very talented and promising," the executive explained to us, "and I don't want this to derail his career. I want him to stay with the company, I want him to work out, I want him to learn, I want him to benefit and grow. Just because he screwed up doesn't mean he's terrible."

Lawrence's actions illustrate the coaching style par excellence. Coaching leaders help employees identify their unique strengths and weaknesses and tie them to their personal and career aspirations. They encourage employees to establish long-term development goals and help them conceptualize a plan for attaining them. They make agreements with their employees about their role and responsibilities in enacting development plans, and they give plentiful instruction and feedback. Coaching leaders excel at delegating; they give employees challenging assignments, even if that means the tasks won't be accomplished quickly. In other words, these leaders are willing to put up with short-term failure if it furthers long-term learning.

Of the six styles, our research found that the coaching style is used least often. Many leaders told us they don't have the time in this high-pressure economy for the slow and tedious work of teaching people and helping them grow. But after a first session, it takes little or no extra time. Leaders who ignore this style are passing up a powerful tool: its impact on climate and performance are markedly positive.

Admittedly, there is a paradox in coaching's positive effect on business performance because coaching focuses primarily on personal development, not on immediate work-related tasks. Even so, coaching improves results. The reason: it requires constant dialogue, and that dialogue has a way of pushing up every driver of climate. Take flexibility. When an employee knows his boss watches him and cares about what he does, he feels free to experiment. After all, he's sure to get quick and constructive feedback. Similarly, the ongoing dialogue of coaching guarantees that people know what is expected of them and how their work fits into a larger vision or strategy. That affects responsibility and clarity. As for commitment, coaching helps there, too, because the style's implicit message is, "I believe in you, I'm investing in you, and I expect your best efforts." Employees very often rise to that challenge with their heart, mind, and soul.

The coaching style works well in many business situations, but it is perhaps most effective when people on the receiving end are "up for it." For instance, the coaching style works particularly well when employees are already aware of their weaknesses and would like to improve their performance. Similarly, the style works well when employees realize how cultivating new abilities can help them advance. In short, it works best with employees who want to be coached.

> **L**eaders who have mastered four or more – especially the authoritative, democratic, affiliative, and coaching styles – have the best climate and business performance.

By contrast, the coaching style makes little sense when employees, for whatever reason, are resistant to learning or changing their ways. And it flops if the leader lacks the expertise to help the employee along. The fact is, many managers are unfamiliar with or simply inept at coaching, particularly when it comes to giving ongoing performance feedback that motivates rather than creates fear or apathy. Some companies have realized the positive impact of the style and are trying to make it a core competence. At some companies, a significant portion of annual bonuses are tied to an executive's development of his or her direct reports. But many organizations have yet to take full advantage of this leadership style. Although the coaching style may not scream "bottom-line results," it delivers them.

Leaders Need Many Styles

Many studies, including this one, have shown that the more styles a leader exhibits, the better. Leaders who have mastered four or more – especially the authoritative, democratic, affiliative, and coaching styles – have the very best climate and business performance. And the most effective leaders switch flexibly among the leadership styles as needed. Although that may sound daunting, we witnessed it more often than you might guess, at both large corporations and tiny start-ups, by seasoned veterans who could explain exactly how and why they lead and by entrepreneurs who claim to lead by gut alone.

Such leaders don't mechanically match their style to fit a checklist of situations – they are far more fluid. They are exquisitely sensitive to the impact they are having on others and seamlessly adjust their style to get the best results. These are leaders, for example, who can read in the first minutes of conversation that a talented but underperforming employee has been demoralized by an un-sympathetic, do-it-the-way-I-tell-you manager and needs to be inspired through a reminder of why her work matters. Or that leader might choose to reen-ergize the employee by asking her about her dreams and aspirations and finding ways to make her job more challenging. Or that initial conversation might signal that the employee needs an ultimatum: improve or leave.

For an example of fluid leadership in action, consider Joan, the general manager of a major division at a global food and beverage company. Joan was appointed to her job while the division was in a deep crisis. It had not made its profit targets for six years; in the most recent year, it had missed by $50 million. Morale among the top management team was miserable; mistrust and resentments were rampant. Joan's directive from above was clear: turn the division around.

Joan did so with a nimbleness in switching among leadership styles that is rare. From the start, she realized she had a short window to demonstrate effective leadership and to establish rapport and trust. She also knew that she urgently needed to be informed about what was not working, so her first task was to listen to key people.

Her first week on the job she had lunch and dinner meetings with each member of the management team. Joan sought to get each person's understanding of the current situation. But her focus was not so much on learning how each person diagnosed the problem as on getting to know each manager as a person. Here Joan employed the affiliative style: she explored their lives, dreams, and aspirations.

She also stepped into the coaching role, looking for ways she could help the team members achieve what they wanted in their careers. For instance, one manager who had been getting feedback that he was a poor team player confided his worries to her. He thought he was a good team member, but he was plagued by persistent complaints. Recognizing that he was a talented executive and a valuable asset to the company, Joan made an agreement with him to point out (in private) when his actions undermined his goal of being seen as a team player.

She followed the one-on-one conversations with a three-day off-site meeting. Her goal here was team building, so that everyone would own whatever solution for the business problems emerged. Her initial stance at the off-site meeting was that of a democratic leader. She encouraged everyone to express freely their frustrations and complaints.

Growing Your Emotional Intelligence

Unlike IQ, which is largely genetic – it changes little from childhood – the skills of emotional intelligence can be learned at any age. It's not easy, however. Growing your emotional intelligence takes practice and commitment. But the payoffs are well worth the investment.

Consider the case of a marketing director for a division of a global food company. Jack, as I'll call him, was a classic pacesetter: high-energy, always striving to find better ways to get things done, and too eager to step in and take over when, say, someone seemed about to miss a deadline. Worse, Jack was prone to pounce on anyone who didn't seem to meet his standards, flying off the handle if a person merely deviated from completing a job in the order Jack thought best.

Jack's leadership style had a predictably disastrous impact on

climate and business results. After two years of stagnant performance, Jack's boss suggested he seek out a coach. Jack wasn't pleased but, realizing his own job was on the line, he complied.

The coach, an expert in teaching people how to increase their emotional intelligence, began with a 360-degree evaluation of Jack. A diagnosis from multiple viewpoints is essential in improving emotional intelligence because those who need the most help usually have blind spots. In fact, our research found that top-performing leaders overestimate their strengths on, at most, one emotional intelligence ability, whereas poor performers overrate themselves on four or more. Jack was not that far off, but he did rate himself more glowingly than his direct reports, who gave him especially low grades

on emotional self-control and empathy.

Initially, Jack had some trouble accepting the feedback data. But when his coach showed him how those weaknesses were tied to his inability to display leadership styles dependent on those competencies – especially the authoritative, affiliative, and coaching styles – Jack realized he had to improve if he wanted to advance in the company. Making such a connection is essential. The reason: improving emotional intelligence isn't done in a weekend or during a seminar – it takes diligent practice on the job, over several months. If people do not see the value of the change, they will not make that effort.

Once Jack zeroed in on areas for improvement and committed himself to making the effort, he and his coach worked up a plan to turn his

The next day, Joan had the group focus on solutions: each person made three specific proposals about what needed to be done. As Joan clustered the suggestions, a natural consensus emerged about priorities for the business, such as cutting costs. As the group came up with specific action plans, Joan got the commitment and buy-in she sought.

With that vision in place, Joan shifted into the authoritative style, assigning accountability for each follow-up step to specific executives and holding them responsible for their accomplishment. For example, the division had been dropping prices on products without increasing its volume. One obvious solution was to raise prices, but the previous VP of sales had dithered and had let the problem fester. The new VP of sales now had responsibility to adjust the price points to fix the problem.

Over the following months, Joan's main stance was authoritative. She continually articulated the group's new vision in a way that reminded each member of how his or her role was crucial to achieving these goals. And, especially during the first few weeks of the plan's implementation, Joan felt that the urgency of the business crisis justified an occasional shift into the coercive style should someone fail to meet his or her responsibility. As she put it,

"I had to be brutal about this follow-up and make sure this stuff happened. It was going to take discipline and focus."

The results? Every aspect of climate improved. People were innovating. They were talking about the division's vision and crowing about their commitment to new, clear goals. The ultimate proof of Joan's fluid leadership style is written in black ink: after only seven months, her division exceeded its yearly profit target by $5 million.

Expanding Your Repertoire

Few leaders, of course, have all six styles in their repertoire, and even fewer know when and how to use them. In fact, as we have brought the findings of our research into many organizations, the most common responses have been, "But I have only two of those!" and, "I can't use all those styles. It wouldn't be natural."

Such feelings are understandable, and in some cases, the antidote is relatively simple. The leader can build a team with members who employ styles she lacks. Take the case of a VP for manufacturing. She successfully ran a global factory system largely by using the affiliative style. She

---

day-to-day job into a learning laboratory. For instance, Jack discovered he was empathetic when things were calm, but in a crisis, he tuned out others. This tendency hampered his ability to listen to what people were telling him in the very moments he most needed to do so. Jack's plan required him to focus on his behavior during tough situations. As soon as he felt himself tensing up, his job was to immediately step back, let the other person speak, and then ask clarifying questions. The point was to not act judgmental or hostile under pressure.

The change didn't come easily, but with practice Jack learned to defuse his flare-ups by entering into a dialogue instead of launching a harangue. Although he didn't always agree with them, at least he gave people a chance to make their case. At the same time, Jack also practiced giving his direct reports more positive feedback and reminding them of how their work

contributed to the group's mission. And he restrained himself from micromanaging them.

Jack met with his coach every week or two to review his progress and get advice on specific problems. For instance, occasionally Jack would find himself falling back on his old pacesetting tactics—cutting people off, jumping in to take over, and blowing up in a rage. Almost immediately, he would regret it. So he and his coach dissected those relapses to figure out what triggered the old ways and what to do the next time a similar moment arose. Such "relapse prevention" measures inoculate people against future lapses or just giving up. Over a six-month period, Jack made real improvement. His own records showed he had reduced the number of flare-ups from one or more a day at the beginning to just one or two a month. The climate had improved sharply, and the division's numbers were starting to creep upward.

Why does improving an emotional intelligence competence take months rather than days? Because the emotional centers of the brain, not just the neocortex, are involved. The neocortex, the thinking brain that learns technical skills and purely cognitive abilities, gains knowledge very quickly, but the emotional brain does not. To master a new behavior, the emotional centers need repetition and practice. Improving your emotional intelligence, then, is akin to changing your habits. Brain circuits that carry leadership habits have to unlearn the old ones and replace them with the new. The more often a behavioral sequence is repeated, the stronger the underlying brain circuits become. At some point, the new neural pathways become the brain's default option. When that happened, Jack was able to go through the paces of leadership effortlessly, using styles that worked for him – and the whole company.

was on the road constantly, meeting with plant managers, attending to their pressing concerns, and letting them know how much she cared about them personally. She left the division's strategy – extreme efficiency – to a trusted lieutenant with a keen understanding of technology, and she delegated its performance standards to a colleague who was adept at the authoritative approach. She also had a pacesetter on her team who always visited the plants with her.

An alternative approach, and one I would recommend more, is for leaders to expand their own style repertories. To do so, leaders must first understand which emotional intelligence competencies underlie the leadership styles they are lacking. They can then work assiduously to increase their quotient of them.

For instance, an affiliative leader has strengths in three emotional intelligence competencies: in empathy, in building relationships, and in communication. Empathy – sensing how people are feeling in the moment – allows the affiliative leader to respond to employees in a way that is highly congruent with that person's emotions, thus building rapport. The affiliative leader also displays a natural ease in forming new relationships, getting to know someone as a person, and cultivating a bond. Finally, the outstanding affiliative leader has mastered the art of interpersonal communication, particularly in saying just the right thing or making the apt symbolic gesture at just the right moment.

So if you are primarily a pacesetting leader who wants to be able to use the affiliative style more often, you would need to improve your level of empathy and, perhaps, your skills at building relationships or communicating effectively. As another example, an authoritative leader who wants to add the democratic style to his repertory might need to work on the capabilities of collaboration and communication. Such advice about adding capabilities may seem simplistic – "Go change yourself" – but enhancing emotional intelligence is entirely possible with practice. (For more on how to improve emotional intelligence, see the sidebar "Growing Your Emotional Intelligence.")

More Science, Less Art

Like parenthood, leadership will never be an exact science. But neither should it be a complete mystery to those who practice it. In recent years, research has helped parents understand the genetic, psychological, and behavioral components that affect their "job performance." With our new research, leaders, too, can get a clearer picture of what it takes to lead effectively. And perhaps as important, they can see how they can make that happen.

The business environment is continually changing, and a leader must respond in kind. Hour to hour, day to day, week to week, executives must play their leadership styles like a pro – using the right one at just the right time and in the right measure. The payoff is in the results.

---

1. Daniel Goleman consults with Hay/McBer on leadership development.

[8]

The effects of leader and follower emotional intelligence on performance and attitude: An exploratory study

Chi-Sum Wong[a,*], Kenneth S. Law[b,1]

[a]Department of Management, The Chinese University of Hong Kong, Shatin, N.T., Hong Kong, China
[b]Department of Management of Organizations, Hong Kong University of Science and Technology, Clear Water Bay Road, Hong Kong, China

Abstract

Recently, increasing numbers of scholars have argued that emotional intelligence (EI) is a core variable that affects the performance of leaders. In this study, we develop a psychometrically sound and practically short EI measure that can be used in leadership and management studies. We also provide exploratory evidence for the effects of the EI of both leaders and followers on job outcomes. Applying Gross' emotion regulation model, we argue that the EI of leaders and followers should have positive effects on job performance and attitudes. We also propose that the emotional labor of the job moderates the EI–job outcome relationship. Our results show that the EI of followers affects job performance and job satisfaction, while the EI of leaders affects their satisfaction and extra-role behavior. For followers, the proposed interaction effects between EI and emotional labor on job performance, organizational commitment, and turnover intention are also supported.

1. Introduction

Emotional intelligence (EI) is an emerging topic for psychological, educational, and management researchers and consultants (see, e.g., Shapiro, 1997; Weisinger, 1998). Many organizations have sent their employees to various EI training courses offered by manage-

---

* Corresponding author. Tel.: +852-2609-7794; fax: +852-2603-6840.
E-mail addresses: cswong@baf.msmail.cuhk.edu.hk (C.-S. Wong), mnlaw@ust.hk (K.S. Law).
[1] Tel.: +852-2358-7740; fax: +852-2335-5325.

244   *C.-S. Wong, K.S. Law / The Leadership Quarterly 13 (2002) 243–274*

ment consultants. Proponents of the EI concept argue that EI affects one's physical and mental health as well as one's career achievements (e.g., Goleman, 1995). Some emerging leadership theories also imply that emotional and social intelligence are even more important for leaders and managers because cognitive and behavioral complexity and flexibility are important characteristics of competent leaders (Boal & Whitehead, 1992). However, there is little empirical evidence in the literature about the relationship between the EI of both leaders and followers and their job outcomes. One of the reasons for this gap may be the lack of a psychologically sound yet practically short measure of EI that can be used in leadership and management studies. The project reported in this paper was designed to develop such a measure and provide exploratory evidence concerning the effect of the EI of both leaders and followers on job outcomes.

The purpose of this multisample, multistudy project is threefold. Firstly, the core concepts of EI and emotional labor are discussed and hypotheses are developed concerning their role in leadership and management research. EI is referred to as a set of interrelated abilities possessed by individuals to deal with emotions, while emotional labor is referred to as emotion-related job requirements imposed by organizations. Thus, EI is a particular set of an individual's abilities, while emotional labor represents a particular type of job demand.

Secondly, we develop a short but psychologically sound measure of EI for research on leadership and management in our first empirical study. Finally, in the second and third studies, we test the relationships between the EI of followers and leaders and their job outcomes, and the proposed moderating effects of emotional labor on the EI–job outcome relationship of followers.

This article is organized as follows. We first discuss the importance of EI for leaders as suggested in the leadership literature, and review the constructs of EI and emotional labor. Then, the potential moderating effect of emotional labor on the EI–job outcome relationship is discussed within the framework of the emotion regulation model. After proposing our hypotheses, we report Study 1 in which a 16-item EI scale is developed. In Study 2, this EI scale is applied to 149 supervisor–subordinate dyads and the follower EI–job outcome relationship and the moderating effects of emotional labor are tested. In Study 3, the EI scale is applied to another supervisor–subordinate dyad to examine the effect of leader EI on follower job outcomes. The article concludes with a discussion of the general contribution of this study to the management and leadership literature on EI.

1.1. EI as a leadership quality

Leadership concerns the interaction of leaders with other individuals. Once social interactions are involved, emotional awareness and emotional regulation become important factors affecting the quality of the interactions. As House and Aditya (1997) summarized, "contemporary research on intelligence offers renewed potential for leadership trait research. The notion of multiple intelligence and Sternberg's theory of triarchic intelligence have implications for managerial roles. Leadership is embedded in a social context, and the idea of social intelligence as a required leadership trait is a powerful one" (p. 418). Sternberg (1997) echoed House and Aditya's viewpoint by providing vivid examples to illustrate why social intelligence may be even more important in affecting the job success of managers and leaders than traditional general mental intelligence. Many leadership researchers have also argued that effective leadership behavior fundamentally depends upon the leader's ability to solve complex social problems that arise in organizations (e.g., Mumford, Zaccaro, Harding, Jacobs, & Fleishman, 2000; Zaccaro, Mumford, Connelly, Marks, & Gilbert, 2000).

By integrating EI into modern theories of leadership, Hooijberg, Hunt, and Dodge (1997) presented a framework of the cognitive, social, and behavioral complexities of leadership. They argued that the social aspect of a leader's capacity consisted of two components — social differentiation and social integration. Social differentiation was defined as "the ability of a managerial leader to discriminate and recognize the various facets, aspects, and significances of a given social situation over time. Social differentiation is a function of the leader's ability to discern existing and potential patterns of social relationships; the leader's ability to regulate emotions within self and recognize emotions in others; the number and degree of independence of a leaders' value preferences; and the leader's level of self-complexity" (p. 382). In other words, good leaders need to have a good understanding of their own emotions as well as those of others, and are able to regulate their own emotions when interacting with others.

This idea is reinforced by Boal and Hooijberg (2000) who highlighted the argument that behavioral complexity is a core element of leader effectiveness. Leaders needed to play different roles at different times, and more importantly, good leaders had the ability to select the right roles for the situation. Boal and Hooijberg argued that social intelligence was the underlying ability that governed the behavioral complexity of leaders.

Day (2000) also reinforced the importance of EI in leader effectiveness. While discussing the training and development of leaders in organizations, Day emphasized that "specific examples of the type of intrapersonal competence associated with leader development initiatives include self-awareness (e.g., emotional awareness, self confidence), self regulation (e.g., self-control, trustworthiness, adaptability), and self-motivation (e.g., commitment, initiative, optimism)." As we explain in the next section, emotional awareness, emotional control, and self-motivation are the basic dimensions of the EI construct. Based on the above discussion, it may be seen that EI is viewed in the leadership literature as a core variable that affects leader effectiveness. Before we actually test the effect of leader EI on the performance of followers and their attitudes, it is necessary to introduce the definition of EI used in this article.

1.2. The definition and domain of EI

EI has its roots in the concept of "social intelligence" that was first identified by Thorndike in 1920. Thorndike defined social intelligence as "the ability to understand and manage men and women, boys and girls — to act wisely in human relations." Following Thorndike, Gardner (1993) included social intelligence as one of the seven intelligence domains in his theory of multiple intelligences. According to Gardner, social intelligence is comprised of a person's interpersonal and intrapersonal intelligences. Intrapersonal intelligence relates to one's intelligence in dealing with oneself, and is the ability to "symbolize complex and highly differentiated sets of feelings." In contrast, interpersonal intelligence relates to one's intelligence in dealing with others and is the ability to "notice and make distinctions among other individuals and, in particular, among their moods, temperaments, motivations and intentions" (p. 239).

Salovey and Mayer (1990) were among the earliest to propose the name "emotional intelligence" to represent the ability of people to deal with their emotions. They defined emotional intelligence as "the subset of social intelligence that involves the ability to monitor one's own and others' feelings and emotions, to discriminate among them and to use this information to guide one's thinking and actions" (p. 189). Recently, Goleman (1995) adopted Salovey and Mayer's definition, and proposed that EI involves abilities that can be categorized as self-awareness, managing emotions, motivating oneself, empathy, and handling relationships.

In this study, we have used the Mayer and Salovey (1997) definition of EI as a set of interrelated skills concerning "the ability to perceive accurately, appraise, and express emotion; the ability to access and/or generate feelings when they facilitate thought; the ability to understand emotion and emotional knowledge; and the ability to regulate emotions to promote emotional and intellectual growth" (p. 10). Salovey and Mayer (1990) and Mayer and Salovey conceptualized EI as composed of four distinct dimensions:

1. *Appraisal and expression of emotion in the self (self emotional appraisal [SEA]).* This relates to the individual's ability to understand their deep emotions and be able to express these emotions naturally. People who have great ability in this area will sense and acknowledge their emotions well before most people.

2. *Appraisal and recognition of emotion in others (others' emotional appraisal [OEA]).* This relates to peoples' ability to perceive and understand the emotions of those people around them. People who are high in this ability will be much more sensitive to the feelings and emotions of others as well as reading their minds.

3. *Regulation of emotion in the self (regulation of emotion [ROE]).* This relates to the ability of people to regulate their emotions, which will enable a more rapid recovery from psychological distress.

4. *Use of emotion to facilitate performance (use of emotion [UOE]).* This relates to the ability of individuals to make use of their emotions by directing them towards constructive activities and personal performance.

1.3. The conceptual and theoretical basis of EI

While there has been much theoretical discussion about, and empirical evidence of, the interaction of the cognitive and noncognitive neural systems in the human brain, as well as how that affects emotions (see, e.g., Fischer, Shaver, & Carnochan, 1990; Izard, 1992, 1993), there is no theory that specifically discusses the role of EI and how it affects work outcomes. To understand the effect of EI on organizational outcomes, we borrow from Gross' model of emotion regulation (Gross, 1998a, 1998b) and develop possible hypotheses to be tested in our study.

C.-S. Wong, K.S. Law / The Leadership Quarterly 13 (2002) 243–274   247

Gross defines emotions as "adaptive behavioral and physiological response tendencies that are called forth directly by evolutionarily significant situations" (Gross, 1998b, p. 272). As emotions are response tendencies and may be modulated, they can be regulated and managed. Emotion regulation refers to "the processes by which individuals influence which emotions they have, when they have them, and how they experience and express these emotions" (Gross, 1998b, p. 275).

Gross' definition of emotion regulation matches our definition of EI. Before people can regulate their emotions, they should have a good understanding of these emotions (SEA). As many of our emotional responses are stimulated by the emotions of other individuals, our understanding of our own emotions is related to our ability to understand the emotions of others (OEA). Gross' emotion regulation model prescribes that one can modulate how one experiences these emotions (ROE) as well as how one expresses them (UOE). Therefore, according to the definitions of EI and emotional regulation, persons with high EI should be more able to modulate their response tendencies and have more effective emotion regulation processes. As a result, Gross' model of emotional regulation appears to be a reasonable theoretical basis for our investigation of the effects of EI in the workplace.

According to Gross (1988a, p. 225), emotional response tendencies can be regulated either by manipulating "the input to the system" (*antecedent-focused emotion regulation*) or by "its output" (*response-focused emotion regulation*). Antecedent-focused emotion regulation is accomplished by four steps: *situation selection*, in which one approaches or avoids certain people or situations on the basis of their likely emotional impact; *situation modification*, in which one modifies an environment so as to alter its emotional impact; *attention deployment*, in which one turns attention toward or away from something in order to influence one's emotions; and *cognitive change*, in which one reevaluates either the situation one is in or one's capacity to manage the situation so as to alter one's emotions. Similarly, response-focused emotion regulation also includes multiple steps. One may *intensify, diminish, prolong*, or *curtail* ongoing emotional experiences for specific purposes.

When this model is applied to EI in the organizational setting, employees will be able to modulate their perception of the work environment. Such perception affects their emotions, through antecedent-focused emotion regulation by being selective about the people they interact with, modifying the work environment, focusing on specific aspects of their work environment, or changing their evaluation of the work environment. These employees can also modulate the impact of emotional stimuli from the work environment after the fact through response-focused emotion regulation by intensifying, diminishing, prolonging, or curtailing certain emotions. People with high levels of EI can make use of this emotion regulation mechanism effectively to create positive emotions as well as to promote emotional and intellectual growth. In contrast, people with low levels of EI are not able to use antecedent- and response-focused emotion regulation effectively, and they have slower emotional growth.

1.4. The effects of EI on work outcomes in the workplace

Organizations are settings that require interpersonal interaction. Most of these interactions are related to the performance of job duties, for example, serving customers, receiving instructions and reporting to supervisors, or cooperating and coordinating with colleagues. Employees with high levels of EI are those who can make use of the antecedent- and response-focused emotional regulation effectively, and master their interactions with others in a more effective manner. Ashkanasy and Hooper (1999) utilized the proposition that affective commitment towards other people is a necessary component of social interaction and argued that the showing of positive emotions is associated with a high likelihood of success at work. Abraham (1999), based on her own earlier observation that optimistic insurance salesmen would perform better than pessimistic salesmen, proposed that EI is directly related to performance. These studies, together with the Goleman (1998) observation that EI is related to job performance, lead to our first hypothesis:

Hypothesis 1: Emotional intelligence is positively related to job performance.

EI should also be related to other affective job outcomes such as job satisfaction, organizational commitment, and turnover intention. The ability to apply antecedent- and response-focused emotion regulation should enable employees to have better relationships with coworkers and supervisors, as well as greater satisfaction in their jobs. The continual presence of positive emotional states of the employees will also lead to positive affection towards the work environment and the organization. As a result, the positive experience on the job and positive affective emotions also should make employees more committed to the organization and less likely to leave their jobs. Therefore, following the arguments of Abraham (1999), Ashkanasy and Hooper (1999), and Goleman (1998) we hypothesize that:

Hypothesis 2: Emotional intelligence is positively related to job satisfaction.

Hypothesis 3: Emotional intelligence is positively related to organizational commitment.

Hypothesis 4: Emotional intelligence is negatively related to turnover intention.

1.5. The EI–job outcome relationships of followers as moderated by emotional labor

While the above arguments about the effects of EI on job outcomes may be reasonable, it is difficult to argue that the effects of EI on job outcomes will be the same across job categories. There are many jobs that require extensive interaction with customers (e.g., in service industries) or coworkers (e.g., team-oriented jobs). In contrast, job incumbents in other occupations may undertake minimal interaction with others (e.g., production-line workers). We borrow the idea of "emotional labor" to represent the extent to which the job requires the management of emotions to achieve positive job outcomes and study the moderating effects of emotional labor on the EI–job outcome relationships.

Many scholars view emotions in the workplace as a commodity provided by the employees in exchange for individual rewards (e.g., Hochschild, 1983; Morris & Feldman, 1996, 1997; Sutton, 1991; Sutton & Rafaeli, 1988; Turner, 1986; Van Mannen & Kunda, 1989; Wharton & Erickson, 1995). According to these scholars, there are at least three types of "labor" to be offered to the organization in exchange for rewards. "Mental labor" refers to the cognitive skills and knowledge as well as the expertise of employees. "Physical labor" refers to the physical efforts of employees to achieve organizational goals. "Emotional labor" refers to the extent to which an employee is required to present an appropriate emotion in order to perform the job in an efficient and effective manner. Examples of jobs requiring a high level of emotional labor are flight attendants, who are required to be friendly to the customers even when the attendants are in a bad mood, or bill collectors, who have to be tough with debtors despite their inclination to sympathize with them.

Scholars have argued that the extent of emotional labor required may vary across occupations. Hochschild (1983, Appendix C) identified a set of 44 census occupations that involve important amounts of emotional labor. However, this view of emotional labor is not universally accepted. For example, Grandey (2000) defines emotional labor as "the process of regulating both feelings and expressions for the organizational goals" (p. 97). We do not use this definition of emotional labor for two reasons. Firstly, it is distinct from the original definition as proposed by Hochschild (1983). Secondly, this process definition of emotional labor intertwines it with EI. Therefore, we follow Hochschild and use of the concept of emotional labor to distinguish those jobs that require employees to manage their emotions for job performance. The above discussion leads to our fifth hypothesis:

Hypothesis 5: The emotional intelligence–job performance relationship is moderated by the extent of emotional labor required by the job. Specifically, the relationship is stronger for jobs that require high emotional labor.

Hypothesis 5 concerns the EI–job performance relationship. Based on our earlier discussion, the job satisfaction of incumbents, their organizational commitment, and their turnover intention are all directly affected by their ability to effectively regulate antecedent- and response-focused emotion. If that is the case, the EI of job incumbents in jobs that require them to manage their emotions frequently and extensively will have greater effect on their job satisfaction, commitment, and turnover intention than incumbents performing low emotional labor jobs. For example, social workers (whose jobs require great emotional labor) would hardly be satisfied with their jobs should they have low levels of EI, because they would have less chance of doing their jobs well. As a result, organizational commitment and turnover intention would be affected. In contrast, auto mechanics (whose jobs involve little emotional labor) could still be reasonably satisfied with their job despite a low level of EI. We, therefore, propose the following hypotheses:

Hypothesis 6: The emotional intelligence–job satisfaction relationship is moderated by the extent of emotional labor required by the job. This relationship will be stronger for jobs that require a high level of emotional labor.

Hypothesis 7: The emotional intelligence–organizational commitment relationship is moderated by the extent of emotional labor required by the job. This relationship will be stronger for jobs that require a high level of emotional labor.

250   *C.-S. Wong, K.S. Law / The Leadership Quarterly 13 (2002) 243–274*

Hypothesis 8: The emotional intelligence–turnover intention relationship is moderated by the extent of emotional labor required by the job. This relationship will be stronger for jobs that require a high level of emotional labor.

These eight hypotheses are summarized diagrammatically in Fig. 1.

1.6. Relationship between the EI of leaders and the job outcomes of followers

As already discussed, the literature indicates that the EI of leaders will influence their effectiveness. In addition, there is evidence (Fisher & Edwards, 1988) that the supportive behavior of leaders has a positive effect on the job satisfaction, and probably performance, of followers. Applying the social exchange theory to the area of leadership, some scholars have argued that followers will have stronger commitment and satisfaction should leaders treat them with psychological benefits such as approval, respect, esteem and affection (e.g., Hollander, 1979; Jacobs, 1970). Dansereau et al. (1995) have shown that leaders are able to affect the performance of their subordinates by supporting their feelings of self-worth. Furthermore, some leadership studies have shown that the emotional maturity of leaders is associated with their managerial effectiveness (Bass, 1990). From our definition of EI, supervisors with high EI and emotional maturity are more likely to use supportive behavior and treat their followers with psychological benefits, as they are more sensitive to feelings and emotions of themselves and their followers. This, high EI and emotional maturity should have a positive effect on the job outcomes of supervisors' followers. Hence, we hypothesize:

Hypothesis 9: The emotional intelligence of supervisors is positively related to the in-role behaviors (i.e., job performance) of their subordinates.

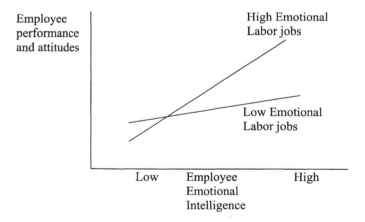

Fig. 1. The proposed moderating effect of emotional labor on the relationship between EI and job outcomes.

Hypothesis 10: The emotional intelligence of supervisors is positively related to the job satisfaction of their subordinates.

Hypothesis 11: The emotional intelligence of supervisors is positively related to the extra-role behavior (i.e., organizational citizenship behavior) of their subordinates.

2. Study 1: development of measurement items for EI

2.1. Development of an EI measure for research purposes

There are some existing measures of EI, but they are not suitable for research on the workplace. For example, Carson, Carson, and Philips (1997) developed a 14-item measure of EI, and Carson and Carson (1998) used this measure to examine the relationship between EI and career commitment in a sample of 75 nurses. However, the authors only reported the coefficient alpha of all 14 items as .79, without mentioning any other psychometric properties of the measure. Salovey, Mayer, Goldman, Turvey, and Palfai (1995) developed a 30-item Trait Meta-Mood Scale to measure EI. Martinez-Pons (1997) used this measure on 108 parents, teachers, and administrators in two public elementary schools. Unfortunately, the measure was designed to capture three components: attention to one's moods and emotions, emotional clarity (one's tendency to discriminate among one's emotions and moods), and emotional repair (or one's tendency to regulate one's feelings). These three components do not capture all of the EI dimensions as defined in this article.

BarOn (1997) introduced the BarOn EQ-i instrument, which contains 133 items. However, there is only validation evidence provided by the developer. BarOn's definition of EI also is slightly different from our own, which seems to be the current view of the EI construct, and the scale includes a number of dimensions that may not relate to EI directly (e.g., problem solving, social responsibility, etc.). Goleman (1995) developed a 10-item measure of EI without any validation evidence. Similarly, Weisinger (1998) developed a short EI instrument without any validation evidence. Mayer, Salovey, and Caruso (1997) developed the Multifacet Emotional Intelligence Scale (MEIS), which requires responses to more than 400 items and takes 1 to 2 hours to complete. Moreover, the psychometric properties of this measure have not been reported. The MEIS is also scored by a norm-referenced method. Respondents are considered high in EI when a majority of the subjects in the norm samples choose the same answer. The developer highlighted that the expert-referenced scoring method did not work as well as the norm-referenced method for this scale. Sosik and Megerian (1999) did not develop an EI measure, but considered various measures that appeared to capture some dimensions of EI. However, it is not clear whether these dimensions (e.g., self-monitoring and personal efficacy) can actually capture the dimensions summarized in our discussion. Although there are some measures of EI in the literature, it appears necessary for us to develop a simple, practical, and psychometrically sound measure of EI for organizational research purposes.

To develop a reasonable EI measure, we used three groups of independent samples to develop the items and test their psychometric properties. In the first group, one sample ($n=120$)

252   *C.-S. Wong, K.S. Law / The Leadership Quarterly 13 (2002) 243–274*

generated items, while quantitative evidence was gathered in the other sample ($n=189$) to select the appropriate items. In the second group, two cross-validated samples ($n=72$ and $n=146$) provided quantitative evidence to confirm the factorial structure of the four EI dimensions and their relationships with the external criterion variables. In the third group, another two samples ($n=110$ and $n=116$) were used to test the convergent, discriminant, and incremental validity of the measure by examining its relationships with some existing EI personality measures and the criterion variable.

2.2. Samples for item generation and selection

2.2.1. Samples and sampling procedures

We started the process of developing our own EI instrument by asking managers and students to generate items to capture the construct. Three groups of part-time MBA and undergraduate students ($n=120$) in a large Hong Kong university were first introduced to the four dimensions of EI defined in this study. They were then asked to generate self-reported items on each dimension that would describe a person with a high level of EI. Three types of items were deleted from the item pool based on the judgment of the two authors. They were: (1) overlapping or similar items suggested by different respondents; (2) items with unclear meaning; and (3) items that did not match the definition of EI due to misunderstandings of the students. We finally extracted nine items for each of the four EI dimensions, which resulted in a 36-item preliminary measure of EI.

These 36 items were then tested on a sample of 189 undergraduate students in Hong Kong by using a 7-point Likert-type scale ranging from strongly agree to strongly disagree. These students were second- and third-year business majors who were required to participate in an experiment to fulfill the basic requirement of a course on organizational behavior. On top of the 36 EI items, we also collected data on two groups of variables as external evidence of the validity of our EI measure. As indicated before, proponents of the EI construct have argued that one's EI level should have little relationship with one's general mental intelligence. Empirically, Ciarrochi, Chan, and Caputi (2000) and Pellitteri (1999) found a very low correlation between EI and IQ in their college student samples. We used a test developed by Eysenck (1990) to measure IQ.

We also examined the correlation between our EI measure and two constructs that are, conceptually, highly related to EI. These constructs are life satisfaction and feeling of powerlessness. Proponents of EI have argued that life satisfaction should be positively related to EI. Several empirical studies have provided evidence of this positive relationship (e.g., Ciarrochi et al., 2000; Martinez-Pons, 1997). We also argue that EI should be negatively related to a feeling of powerlessness. As described by Pearlin and Schooler (1978), powerlessness is the extent to which one regards one's life chances as being fatalistically ruled in contrast to being under one's own control. Theoretically, people with high EI will enjoy better relationships with others, have better control over their own lives, and be able to control negative emotions. Although no empirical study has investigated this relationship, it has been shown that a feeling of powerlessness is related to negative emotions such as sadness and fear (e.g., Roseman, Dhawan, Rettek, & Naidu, 1995). Thus, any EI measure developed should

C.-S. Wong, K.S. Law / The Leadership Quarterly 13 (2002) 243–274   253

have a negligible relationship with IQ, a positive relationship with life satisfaction, and a negative relationship with powerlessness.

2.2.2. Measures

Life satisfaction was measured with the nine items constructed by Campbell, Converse, and Rodgers (1976). The first eight items of this scale are pairs of opposite adjectives (e.g., interesting vs. boring, enjoyable vs. miserable) with a 7-point Likert-type scale of numbers between them. Respondents were requested to circle the number that best described their feelings towards their lives. The last item was a direct question asking about the level of satisfaction in life, namely: "how satisfied or dissatisfied are you with your life as a whole?" Internal consistency reliability (i.e., the coefficient alpha) was .91 for this sample. Power-lessness in life mastery was measured with the seven items constructed by Pearlin and Schooler (1978). The response format was a 7-point Likert type scale ranging from strongly disagree to strongly agree. Examples of these items include: "I have little control over the things that happen to me" and "there is really no way I can solve some of the problems I have." The internal consistency reliability was .67 for this sample.

IQ was measured by the fourth test devised by Eysenck (1990). This test consisted of 40 items. Respondents were required to finish the test within 30 minutes. A correct response to an item scored one point, and so the maximum possible score for the test was 40. The minimum score in our sample of 189 students was 6, and the maximum was 26. The average score was 15.3 and the standard deviation was 4.12.

2.2.3. Results of item selection and factorial structure

The major purpose of this first study was to develop a psychometrically sound self-report EI scale. As a result, our first job was to test the factorial structure of the instrument. We conducted an exploratory factor analysis of the 36 items using the maximum likelihood method with varimax rotation. A total of eight factors was identified with an eigenvalue greater than unity. From a detailed look at the factor loadings of these eight factors, it was found that the first four factors with the largest eigenvalues basically represented the four hypothesized EI dimensions. For example, seven out of the nine items measuring the first EI dimension of SEA loaded on the same factor with loadings larger than .50. Similarly, for the other three EI dimensions, at least six of the nine items loaded on their respective factor with loadings greater than .50. The remaining four factors captured only some random or error variances of individual items. All of the remaining four factors only consisted of a maximum of one item with a loading greater than .50.

To improve the psychometric properties of our EI scale, we selected only the four items with the largest factor loadings from each of the first four factors to represent the four EI dimensions. When a second factor analysis was conducted with only these 16 items, a clear four-factor structure emerged. The first part of Table 1 shows the results of this factor analysis. The average loadings of the 16 items on their respective EI dimensions was .80. Cross loadings were negligible. Internal consistency reliability for the four factors (each with four items) ranged from .83 to .90. The distribution of each item appeared to be

Table 1
Factor analysis and correlations for the item selection sample

(a) Factor analysis

Items	Factor 1	Factor 2	Factor 3	Factor 4
SEA1	.05	.89	.13	.06
SEA2	.04	.86	.01	.16
SEA3	.10	.74	.11	.07
SEA4	−.01	.87	.05	.17
ROE1	.07	−.01	.82	.20
ROE2	.10	.15	.76	.04
ROE3	.11	.08	.76	.13
ROE4	.04	.08	.80	.26
UOE1	.17	.22	.09	.76
UOE2	.12	.37	.09	.76
UOE3	.06	.08	.19	.83
UOE4	.03	−.06	.33	.66
OEA1	.85	.09	.15	.10
OEA2	.91	.03	.07	.07
OEA3	.88	.01	.05	−.04
OEA4	.83	.07	.08	.26
Eigenvalue	5.01	2.70	2.27	1.46
% of variance explained	31.3	16.9	14.2	9.1

(b) Correlation coefficients

	1	2	3	4	5	6	7	8
1. SEA	(.87)							
2. ROE	.20**	(.83)						
3. UOE	.34**	.42**	(.84)					
4. OEA	.13$^+$	.21**	.25**	(.90)				
5. LS	.38**	.46**	.33**	.16*	(.91)			
6. PWL	−.31**	−.29**	−.39**	−.13$^+$	−.38**	(.67)		
7. IQ	.06	−.16*	−.05	−.19*	−.06	.03	–	

SEA, OEA, ROE, UOE, LS, PWL, IQ stand for self-emotion appraisal, others' emotion appraisal, regulation of emotion, uses of emotion, life satisfaction, powerlessness, and intelligence as measured by Eysneck's test, respectively.
Numbers in the diagonal are coefficient alphas.
$n = 189$.
   * $P < .05$ (two-tailed tests).
   ** $P < .01$ (two-tailed tests).
   $^+$ $< .10$.

similar. The means ranged from 4.25 to 4.94, with standard deviations ranging from 1.20 to 1.43.

2.2.4. Results of scale correlation

The correlations among the four EI factors and the criterion variables were all within reasonable limits. The second part of Table 1 shows the correlation coefficients. The EI dimensions were all mildly correlated (ranging from $r = .13$ to .42), which indicated that they were related but not identical dimensions. All EI dimensions correlated significantly with life satisfaction. The correlation ranged from .16 to .46. All EI dimensions correlated moderately and negatively with the powerlessness measures. The correlation ranged from $-.13$ to $-.39$. Individuals with a high level of EI should have a low chance of experiencing powerlessness. Finally, as expected, the EI dimensions had minimal correlations with the IQ estimate. It is notable that OEA and ROE actually correlated negatively and significantly with Eysenck's IQ measure. In other words, individuals with a higher level of cognitive intelligence will be less able to recognize others' emotions.

2.3. Cross-validation samples on factor structure and relationship with criteria

2.3.1. Samples, sampling procedures, and measures

To assure that the factorial structure of the 16 EI items and the correlations of the EI dimensions with the criterion variables could be generalized to other samples, we collected data from two independent undergraduate samples in Hong Kong. The first sample consisted of 72 students. They were asked to respond to a questionnaire containing the 16 EI items as well as the powerlessness and life satisfaction items. The second sample consisted of another 146 undergraduate students who were asked to respond to the same measurement items.

2.3.2. Results of the first cross-validation sample

We conducted a confirmatory factor analysis of the EI items using the computer program LISREL (Jöreskog & Sörbom, 1993). With the specified four items loading on their respective EI dimensions, the model χ^2 of the confirmatory factor analysis was 132.41 ($df = 98$). The standardized RMR of the model was .08, the comparative fit index (CFI, Bentler, 1990) was .95, and the Tucker–Lewis Index (TLI, Tucker & Lewis, 1973) was .93. All model fit indices showed that the four-factor model fitted the data reasonably well. Correlations among the four EI dimensions, as well as their correlations with powerlessness and life satisfaction, are shown below the diagonal in Table 2.

All of the observed correlations matched well with our hypotheses. All EI dimensions were negatively correlated with powerlessness, and positively correlated with life satisfaction. In addition, the size of the correlations were similar to those found in the item-selection sample.

2.3.3. Results of the second cross-validation sample

The confirmatory factor analysis results for this cross-validation sample were similar to the first cross-validation sample. Model χ^2 for the four-factor model for the 16 EI items was 179.33 ($df = 98$). The standardized RMR was .07, the CFI was .91, and the TLI was .89. Again, all model fit indices showed that the four-factor model fitted the data reasonably well. Correlations of the four EI dimensions with powerlessness and life satisfaction are shown in the upper half of Table 2. The magnitudes of these correlations were extremely similar to those found in the first cross-validation sample, and quite similar to those in the first developmental sample. We concluded that the 16-item EI scale effectively captured the EI dimensions. The resulting 16 EI items are shown in Appendix A.

Table 2
Correlations among the EI dimensions and criterion variables for the cross-validation samples

	SEA	ROE	USE	OEA	PWL	LS
SEA	(.89/.87)	.45**	.28**	.34**	−.14	.23*
ROE	.35**	(.74/.71)	.33**	.29**	−.26**	.29**
UOE	.34**	.24*	(.87/.87)	.31**	−.29**	.40**
OEA	.34**	.34**	.37**	(.89/.88)	−.08	.12
PWL	−.27	−.14	−.28*	.03	(.91/.90)	−.37**
LS	.29*	.18	.31**	.26*	−.36**	(.71/.73)

$n = 72$ for the first validation sample (lower triangle); $n = 146$ for the second validation sample (upper triangle). Numbers in the diagonal are coefficient alphas and the first and second numbers are from the first and second validation sample, respectively.

SEA, OEA, ROE, UOE, LS, and PWL stand for self-emotion appraisal, others' emotion appraisal, regulation of emotion, uses of emotion, life satisfaction, powerlessness, respectively.

  * $P < .05$ (two-tailed test).
  ** $P < .01$ (two-tailed test).

2.4. Samples testing convergent, discriminant, and incremental validity

2.4.1. Samples, sampling procedures, and measures

Davies, Stankov, and Roberts (1998) argued that the construct of EI was illusive because self-reported EI measures had salient loadings on well-established Big Five personality factors. To test the convergent and discriminant validities of the 16-item EI scale developed, we collected additional data from two independent samples. The first sample consisted of 110 undergraduate business students. These students completed a questionnaire containing the 16 EI items, another existing measure of EI (the 30-item Trait Meta-Mood Scale by Salovey et al., 1995), the 80-item Big Five personality measure (McCrae & Costa, 1987), and the same life satisfaction scale as in our earlier samples. As with the previous samples, the response format for all measures was a 7-point scale.

The second sample consisted of 116 nonteaching employees from a Hong Kong university. To include a variety of employees from various jobs, questionnaires were distributed to different units to include administrative, clerical, and technical staff. These employees were selected from the telephone directory. They were contacted by telephone, and those who agreed to participate received, in person, a copy of the questionnaire from a research assistant. Respondents were instructed to complete the questionnaire within 1 week, and the research assistant collected the questionnaire in person. Two personality and EI measures were included in the questionnaire. The first personality scale consisted of the 60-item short form of the NEO Personality Inventory (Costa & McCrae, 1985) and the second was the adjective scale used in the previous sample.

To avoid a long questionnaire, we randomly selected six items for each Big Five personality dimension from the 80-item adjective scale used in the previous sample. The first EI scale was the 16-item developed in previous samples. The second scale consisted of 20 items from BarOn's EQ-i. Specifically, we randomly selected five items for each of the four dimensions of BarOn's EQ-i (i.e., emotional self-awareness, empathy, impulse control, and optimism), which appeared to be most relevant to our EI definition. Reliability estimates (coefficient alphas) for the four dimensions of self-emotion appraisal, uses of emotion, regulation of emotion, and others' emotion appraisal were .92, .91, .84, and .93, respectively.

2.4.2. Results of the first convergent, discriminant, and incremental validity sample

To test the convergent and discriminant validities of our measure, we conducted exploratory factor analysis on the EI and personality measures. Because of the large number of Big Five personality items compared to the sample size, we randomly averaged the items and formed two indicators for each personality dimension. Table 3 shows the results of the

Table 3
Exploratory factor analysis of Big-Five and EI indicators of the convergent, discriminant, and incremental validity sample

	Factor 1	Factor 2	Factor 3	Factor 4	Factor 5	Factor 6	Factor 7
NEURO1	−.18	−.57	−.18	−.26	−.21	−.05	.31
NEURO2	−.19	−.50	−.14	−.38	.01	−.03	.53
EXTRA1	.07	−.25	−.21	.29	.53	−.16	.31
EXTRA2	.11	.07	.09	.43	.46	.06	.03
OPEN1	.13	.02	−.06	−.07	.89	.13	.00
OPEN2	.09	.15	.16	.02	.85	.01	−.14
AGREE1	.14	.06	.04	.76	−.03	.15	−.17
AGREE2	.00	.07	.09	.87	.03	.04	.00
CONSC1	.21	.13	.64	.16	−.12	.07	−.59
CONSC2	.23	.25	.65	.26	.21	.07	−.44
ATTEND	.36	.40	.30	.36	.12	.04	.15
ATTEND	.28	.25	.24	.49	.17	.16	.17
CLARITY	.26	.00	.05	.02	−.02	.18	.42
CLARITY	.33	−.03	.02	.09	−.06	.30	.34
REPAIR	.71	.02	.09	−.04	.25	.15	−.07
REPAIR	.69	.14	.16	.06	.06	.17	−.01
SEA1	.71	.15	.15	.19	.01	.08	.14
SEA2	.77	.12	.05	.13	.08	.16	.01
UOE1	.09	.89	.23	.10	.02	−.03	−.07
UOE2	.11	.93	.05	−.01	−.01	.06	.02
ROE1	.12	.19	.82	.12	−.11	.02	.10
ROE2	.12	.10	.86	.03	.14	.04	−.02
OEA1	.32	.03	.07	.13	.02	.76	.05
OEA2	.22	.04	.03	.12	.12	.96	.08
Eigenvalue	2.79	5.33	1.96	1.79	1.68	1.72	.95
% of variance explained	11.6	22.2	8.2	7.5	7.0	7.2	4.0

ATTEND, CLARITY, and REPAIR are the three EI dimensions of the Trait–Meta Mood Scale. NEURO, EXTRA, OPEN, AGREE, CONSC stand for neuroticism, extraversion, openness, agreeableness, and conscientiousness of the Big five personality dimensions. SEA, OEA, ROE, VOE stands for self emotion appraisal, other's emotion appraisal, regulation of emotion. The number after each dimension represents the indicator used for the latent construct. For example, NEURO1 represents the first indicator of the Conscientiousness dimension of Big Five personality. *n*=110.

exploratory factor analysis. The Big Five personality indicators loaded heavily on their respective dimensions except for neuroticism and conscientiousness. The UOE dimension of EI and neuroticism both loaded on Factor 2. The ROE dimension of EI and conscientiousness loaded on the same Factor 3. The other two EI dimensions of SEA and OEA did not cross-load with the Big Five factors.

To show the incremental validity of our EI measure as compared with the Trait Meta-Mood Scale, we conducted hierarchical regression using life satisfaction and powerlessness as criterion variables. We first entered the Big Five personality dimensions as control variables. These were followed by the three Trait Meta-Mood dimensions. Finally, our four EI dimensions were entered into the regression equation as predictors. For life satisfaction as the dependent measure, the change in model R^2 when the three sets of predictors were entered hierarchically were .466 ($P < .01$), .029 ($P > .10$), and .077 ($P < .01$), respectively. The Big Five dimensions shared a statistically significant portion of the variances of life satisfaction. The Trait Meta-Mood dimensions did not explain incremental variances of life satisfaction on top of the Big Five dimensions. In contrast, our EI dimensions provided significant incremental contributions in predicting life satisfaction on top of the Big Five dimensions.

When powerlessness was used as the dependent measure, the change in the model R^2s when the three sets of predictors were entered hierarchically were .247 ($P < .01$), .077 ($P < .05$), and .059 ($P < .10$), respectively. Our EI measure still provided incremental variance explanation marginally on top of the Big Five dimensions and the Trait Meta-Mood scale. The first two columns in Table 4 show the beta coefficients for the final step of regression when life satisfaction and powerlessness were analyzed as dependent variables.

Table 4
Regression results for the discriminant, convergence, and incremental validity samples of study 1

	Sample 1 ($n=110$)		Sample 2 ($n=116$)
	Life satisfaction	Powerlessness	Life satisfaction
NEURO	−.13	.12	−.01
EXTRA	.19*	.00	−.03
OPEN	.06	−.10	−.00
AGREE	.20*	.09	−.01
CONSC	.20*	−.15	−.08
ATTEND	.05	−.28*	–
CLARITY	.03	.06	–
REPAIR	−.17*	.08	–
EQ-i	–	–	.22[+]
EI	.35**	−.22[+]	.23[+]
R^2	.57**	.38**	.20**

NEURO, EXTRA, OPEN, AGREE, CONSC stand for neuroticism, extraversion, openness, agreeableness, and conscientiousness of the Big Five personality dimensions. ATTEND, CLARITY, and REPAIR are the three EI dimensions of the Trait–Meta Mood Scale. EQ-i stands for the estimate of emotional intelligence by the Bar-On EQ-i items. EI stands for the estimate of emotional intelligence by the 16 items developed in this study.

 * $P < .05$ (two-tailed tests).
 ** $P < .01$ (two-tailed tests).
 [+] $< .10$.

2.4.3. Results of the second convergent, discriminant, and incremental validity sample

We conducted a confirmatory factor analysis with our 16 EI items and the Big Five personality dimensions. To avoid too many indicators for the Big Five measures, we formed three indicators for each dimension by randomly averaging two items from the respective dimension. Results show reasonably good fit for the nine-factor model (i.e., four EI and five personality factors). The model χ^2 was 591.59 ($df = 398$), the standardized RMR was .08, the CFI was .90, and the TLI was .89. These results indicate good convergent and discriminant validity between our EI and the Big Five personality dimensions.

To cross-validate the incremental predictive validity of our EI measure on the Big Five personality dimensions and the EQ-i, hierarchical regression was conducted on life satisfaction by entering the Big Five personality dimensions and EQ-i in the first step, and our EI measure in the second step. The change in model R^2s when the two sets of predictors were entered hierarchically were .099 ($P < .01$), and .023 ($P < .10$), respectively. Thus, the incremental validity was cross-validated in this non-student sample. The third column in Table 4 shows the beta coefficients for the final step of this regression analysis.

Finally, descriptive statistics and correlation among the measures for this sample are shown in Table 5. Table 5 may be regarded as a Multitrait Multimethod (MTMM) cor-

Table 5

Correlation matrix for the second convergent, discriminant and incremental validity sample (non-student sample with $n = 116$)

	Mean (S.D.)	1	2	3	4	5	6	7	8	9	10	11	12
1. NEURO1	3.06 (.57)	(.83)											
2. NEURO2	3.52 (.76)	.64	(.79)										
3. EXTRA1	3.17 (.42)	−.40	−.21	(.68)									
4. EXTRA2	3.91 (.68)	−.21	−.03	.69	(.77)								
5. OPEN1	3.17 (.40)	.14	.21	.08	.25	(.62)							
6. OPEN2	3.79 (.64)	−.01	.04	.18	.44	.36	(.72)						
7. AGREE1	3.26 (.42)	−.06	−.02	.14	.08	.16	−.02	(.67)					
8. AGREE2	4.31 (.63)	.09	.20	.18	.30	.06	.15	.58	(.78)				
9. CONSC1	3.33 (.46)	−.28	−.20	.15	.13	−.17	−.02	.32	.23	(.74)			
10. CONSC2	3.93 (.60)	−.27	−.17	.23	.34	−.01	.17	.27	.30	.59	(.70)		
11. EQ-i	4.86 (.54)	−.27	−.15	.22	.25	.04	.13	−.04	.04	.25	.30	(.78)	
12. LS	3.74 (.95)	−.17	−.08	.09	.10	.00	.05	.04	−.01	.25	.24	.39	(.92)
13. EI	4.95 (.79)	−.40	−.24	.24	.27	.07	.13	.17	.19	.50	.51	.63	.41

NEURO, EXTRA, OPEN, AGREE, CONSC stand for neuroticism, extraversion, openness, agreeableness, and conscientiousness of the Big Five personality dimensions. ATTEND, CLARITY, and REPAIR are the three EI dimensions of the Trait–Meta Mood Scale. The number after each dimension represents the indicator used for the latent construct. For example, NEURO1 represents the first indicator of the Conscientiousness dimension of Big Five personality. EQ-i stands for the estimate of EI by the BarOn EQ-i items. LS stands for life satisfaction. EI stands for the estimate intelligence by the 16 items developed in this study. Numbers in the diagonal are coefficient alphas; the first and second personality measures are the NEO Personality Inventory and the adjective scales, respectively. NEO Personality Inventory is measured by 5-point scale, and EQ-i and EI are measured by 7-point scales, while all others are measured by 6-point scales.
$n = 116$.

relation matrix, as we have two measures on both the Big Five personality dimensions and EI. The results clearly indicate the convergence between our EI measure and the EQ-i ($r = .63$) and its discriminant validity with the Big Five personality dimensions. The patterns of correlations between our EI measure and the EQ-i with the big-five personality dimensions were very similar, and they were all smaller than the correlation between the EI and EQ-i measures.

2.5. Estimation of the EI construct from its dimensions

Based on the above analyses of the three groups of samples showing evidence of factor structure, internal consistency, convergence, and discriminant and incremental validity, we concluded that our EI measure should be of reasonable reliability and validity to be adopted for further studies. However, as EI is a multidimensional construct, one final issue is the estimation of the overall EI construct from its dimensions. Law, Wong, and Mobley (1998) pointed out that there are three types of multidimensional constructs, namely: profile, aggregate, and latent. For the profile and aggregate types, individual dimensions of the multidimensional construct may be unrelated to each other. As the EI construct represent interrelated sets (dimensions) of abilities, it fits mostly the latent type. That is, the EI construct exists at a deeper level than its dimensions, and the dimensions should be interrelated because they are manifestations of the EI construct. This definition is also comparable to the traditional intelligence construct, which is defined as the common factor behind various sets (dimensions) of abilities in verbal comprehension, word fluency, space, number, memory, and reasoning (Eysenck, 1964).

To test whether the EI items that were developed fit this description, we followed the recommendation of Law et al. (1998) to perform a second-order confirmatory factor analysis on the EI items. Specifically, we compared the results of two confirmatory factor analyses. The first specified a single factor behind all the 16 items, while the second specified the four dimensions from their respective items and then a second-order factor behind the four EI dimensions. For all of the samples in Study 1, the results of the single-factor model were unacceptable, while the second-order model fitted the data reasonably well. For example, the non-student sample (i.e., the second convergent, discriminant, and incremental validity sample with $n = 116$) had an extremely poor fit for the single-factor model ($\chi^2 = 942.95$ with $df = 104$; CFI $= .44$; TLI $= .35$; standardized RMR $= .20$), while it fitted well the second-factor model ($\chi^2 = 211.85$ with $df = 100$; CFI $= .93$; TLI $= .91$; standardized RMR $= .08$). From these results, we conclude that the EI items developed in Study 1 can serve as a reasonable estimate of their dimensions, and that the dimensions in turn can represent an underlying multidimensional EI construct.

3. Study 2: testing the interaction between the EI of followers and their emotional labor

There are two limitations of the design in the series of analyses conducted in Study 1. Firstly, all of the dependent and independent variables are self-reported by the same

C.-S. Wong, K.S. Law / The Leadership Quarterly 13 (2002) 243–274   261

respondents. It is difficult to tell how much of the covariance between EI and the criterion variables (life satisfaction and powerlessness) are caused by the problem of common method variance. Secondly, all the samples except the last one used to test the EI scale developed are from undergraduate students. The results may not be generalizable to experienced workers in an organization. To deal with these two concerns, we conducted our second study with practicing managers to test the hypothesis that the EI of followers affects their job performance, and that the relationship is moderated by emotional labor.

3.1. Sample and procedures

The sample for this study consisted of 149 supervisor–subordinate dyads. The supervisors were 60 middle and upper-level managers enrolled in a part-time management diploma course at a large Hong Kong university. These managers were asked to evaluate the emotional labor and job performance of four of their subordinates. Respondents with less than four subordinates were asked to evaluate as many subordinates as they had. After completing the evaluations, the managers were asked to give a sealed envelope to each of their subordinates. The envelope contained: (1) a cover letter explaining the objectives of the study and a statement ensuring that responses would be confidential; (2) a stamped reply envelope addressed to the authors of this study; and (3) a short questionnaire containing our 16-item EI scale, and scales designed to measure emotional labor, job satisfaction, organizational commitment, and turnover intention. Each subordinate questionnaire was marked with an identification code so that the evaluation of the supervisors could be matched with the responses of their subordinates. The mean age of these subordinates was 29.02 (with a standard deviation of 6.97), and 52.8% were female.

3.2. Measures

3.2.1. Emotional intelligence

The 16 items developed from Study 1 were used to measure the EI of the incumbents. The response format was a 7-point Likert-type scale. Reliability estimates (coefficient alphas) for the four dimensions of self-emotion appraisal, uses of emotion, regulation of emotion, and others' emotion appraisal were .89, .88, .76, and .85, respectively.

3.2.2. Emotional labor: supervisor judgments

Because emotional labor is a requirement of the organization, and supervisors are responsible to ensure that their subordinates fulfill this requirement, we believe that supervisors should be the most reasonable people to judge the emotional labor of subordinates. Therefore, we trained the supervisors for about an hour in the concept of emotional labor.

After introducing the concept, we showed the supervisors the Adelmann (1989, pp. 22–24) tables, which contrast high and low emotional labor jobs in different occupations. The classification system was explained. Then samples of job descriptions were presented and the supervisors were asked to judge whether these jobs should be classified as high or low in emotional labor. The training session ended when the supervisors reached a consensus on the classification of these jobs. The supervisors were asked to judge whether the jobs of their subordinates should be classified as requiring a *high* (coded as 1) or *low* degree of emotional labor (coded as 0) before they evaluated the performance and organizational citizenship behavior of their subordinates. They were instructed to select subordinates with both high and low emotional labor jobs whenever possible.

3.2.3. Emotional labor: incumbent ratings

Past studies were either case studies (e.g., Rafaeli & Sutton, 1987; Sutton, 1991; Van Maanen & Kunda, 1989) or used an ad hoc measure that was suitable only for a particular occupation or sample (e.g., Morris & Feldman, 1997; Wharton, 1993; Wharton & Erickson, 1995). To provide cross-validation evidence for the supervisor judgments, we also included five emotional labor items in the incumbent questionnaire. We designed these items according to the Hochschild (1983) characteristics of jobs with a high degree of emotional labor, and the items used by Adelmann (1989). These five items are shown in Appendix A. The response format was a 7-point Likert-type scale, and the coefficient alpha of these five items was .69.

3.2.4. Job satisfaction

The four items from the Job Diagnostic Survey (Hackman & Oldham, 1976), which measure satisfaction with the work itself, were adopted. These items asked respondents to evaluate the extent of satisfaction in four dimensions of performing their jobs (including, for example, the amount of personal growth and development, and the feeling of worthwhile accomplishment). The response format was a 5-point Likert-type scale. The coefficient alpha of these four items was .77.

3.2.5. Organizational commitment

The six items measuring the affective commitment to the organization as developed by Meyer, Allen, and Smith (1993) were adopted. An example of such items is: "I really feel as if this organization's problems are my own." The response format was a 5-point Likert-type scale. The coefficient alpha of the six items was .74.

3.2.6. Turnover intention

The three items from Cammann, Fichman, Jenkins, and Klesh (1979) were modified so that a Likert-type response scale could be used. An example of such items is: "I will probably look for a new job in the next year." The response format was a 5-point Likert-type scale, and the coefficient alpha of the three items was .81.

3.2.7. Job performance

The five items developed by Williams (1988) and used by Hui, Law, and Chen (1999) were adopted. An example of such items is: "This subordinate always completes the duties specified in his/her job description." The response format was a 7-point Likert-type scale, and the coefficient alpha of the three items was .81.

3.3. Results

Two preliminary analyses were conducted to check the appropriateness of the EI and emotional labor measures. Using the LISREL program, confirmatory factor analysis was conducted on the 16 EI items to determine whether they conformed to the four-factor model as designed. To maximize our sample size, we invited the 60 supervisors to evaluate their own EI level, and we included these 60 data points in the confirmatory factor analysis. In other words, the total sample size of the confirmatory factor analysis was 209.

The results of the analysis showed that the four-factor model fitted the data very well. The model χ^2 was 233.53 ($df = 98$), the CFI was .94, the TLI was .92, and the standardized RMR was .05. The reliability estimates for each dimension (ranging from .76 to .89) were also acceptable. As with the samples in Study 1, the second-level model also resulted in a reasonably good fit ($\chi^2 = 243.59$, with $df = 100$; CFI = .93; TLI = .92; and standardized RMR = .07), while the single-factor model was unacceptable ($\chi^2 = 488.20$, with $df = 104$; CFI = .82; TLI = .80; and standardized RMR = .20). Thus, these dimensions may be combined to form an estimate of the underlying EI construct.

Moreover, the convergence of the supervisor judgments and incumbent ratings of emotional labor were examined. Since a supervisor's judgment is a dichotomous variable, the point–biserial correlation coefficient was calculated. It was .77 ($P < .01$) between the two ratings, which indicated strong agreement between the supervisors and incumbents concerning the emotional labor of incumbent jobs.

We conducted another preliminary analysis for the performance data because in our data, 41 supervisors rated the performance of more than one subordinate. Independence of the performance data may have created a problem in data analysis. Thus, we calculated the within-group interrater reliability for these 41 supervisors according to the formula provided by James and Demaree (1984). To be conservative, we did not consider any response bias and assumed a triangular null distribution. The mean interrater reliability for the 41 groups of performance ratings was .65 and its standard deviation was .31. Over half of these reliability coefficients (53.7%) were less than .70. George and Bettenhausen (1990) argued that an interrater reliability greater than .70 could be considered as an indicator of good within group agreement. From this result, we believe that the performance ratings may be regarded as independent and the results will not be affected significantly.

To test the proposed interaction effect between emotional labor and the EI of followers on their job performance and attitudes, moderated regression analyses were conducted for each job outcome using both the measures of emotional labor (supervisor and subordinate assessment). Specifically, the main and interaction effects were entered into the regression equation step by step, and the change in R^2s was examined when the interaction term was entered into the equation.

Descriptive statistics and correlations among variables are shown in Table 6. It should be noted that the judgments by supervisors of a low degree of emotional labor were coded as zero, and those of a high degree of emotional labor were coded as one. EI (as represented by the mean score across the four EI dimensions) had a significant correlation with job performance ($r = .21$, $P < .01$) and job satisfaction ($r = .40$, $P < .01$), but a nonsignificant

Table 6
Descriptive statistics and correlation among variables for Study 2

	$\bar{X}$	S.D.	1	2	3	4	5	6	7	8	9	10	11
1. SEA	4.70	.97	(.89)										
2. ROE	4.71	.91	.68**	(.76)									
3. UOE	4.50	.96	.73**	.60**	(.88)								
4. OEA	4.59	.96	.74**	.76**	.65**	(.85)							
5. EI	4.63	.83	.90**	.86**	.85**	.90**	(.94)						
6. EL (Sup)	.51	.50	.32**	.37**	.16	.39**	.35**	–					
7. EL (Incum)	4.42	.79	.44**	.47**	.33**	.49**	.49**	.77*	(.88)				
8. Job perf	5.00	.91	.15	.26**	.08	.27**	.21**	.31**	.25**	(.81)			
9. Job sat	3.27	.67	.34**	.45**	.27**	.36**	.40**	.29**	.44**	.27**	(.77)		
10. Orgl com	3.95	.78	.15	.17*	.14	.02	.14	.29**	.40**	.13	.45**	(.74)	
11. TI	3.78	1.31	-.00	-.01	.01	.11	.03	-.10	-.08	-.10	-.34**	-.53**	(.81)

SEA, OEA, ROE, UOE, LS, PWL, IQ stand for self-emotion appraisal, other's emotion appraisal, regulation of emotion, uses of emotion. EI = mean score of the four EI dimensions. EL (Sup) = emotional labor estimated by supervisor. EL (Incum) = emotional labor estimated by incumbents. Job perf = job performance. Orgl com = organizational commitment. TI = turnover intention. $n = 149$.

* $P < .05$ (two-tailed tests).
** $P < .01$ (two-tailed tests).

correlation with organizational commitment ($r = .14$, *ns*) and turnover intention ($r = .03$, *ns*). As a result, we conclude that Hypotheses 1 and 2 are supported, while Hypotheses 3 and 4 are not. EI is related to job performance and job satisfaction, but not to organizational commitment and turnover intention.

The results of the moderated regression analyses are shown in Table 7. As an exploratory effort, we conducted these analyses both for the overall measure of EI and its individual dimensions. As the results are quite similar, we focus on the mean EI score as a representation of the EI construct to simplify our discussion. As shown in the two parts of Table 7, the interaction terms are significant when organizational commitment and turnover intention are used as the dependent variables. It does not matter whether supervisor or job incumbent assessments of emotional labor are used. Therefore, Hypotheses 7 and 8 are strongly supported. Emotional labor is a significant moderator of the EI–job performance relationship when incumbent assessments of emotional labor are used. When supervisor assessments of emotional labor are used, the moderating term is marginally significant.

As a whole, we conclude that Hypothesis 5 is generally supported. In contrast, the product term is marginally significant when job satisfaction is used as the dependent variable and emotional labor is assessed by the supervisor. When emotional labor is assessed by incumbents, the product term is not significant. Therefore, Hypothesis 6 is not supported.

To examine the direction of the interaction effect, we calculated the intercepts (b_0), slope (b_1), and the correlation coefficients for the high and low emotional labor subgroups according to supervisor judgments of emotional labor. The results are shown in Table 8. These results provide strong support for our hypotheses.

The correlation between EI and job performance was virtually zero in the low emotional labor group, while it was highly significant ($r = .26$) in the high emotional labor group. The

Table 7
Change in the model R^2 of the moderated regression analysis ($n=149$)

	Dependent variables			
	Job performance	Job satisfaction	Organizational commitment	Turnover intention
(a) Using supervisor assessments of emotional labor				
SEA×EL	.02[+]	.02[+]	.06**	.06**
OEA×EL	.01	.01	.06**	.08**
ROE×EL	.02[+]	.01	.05**	.04*
UOE×EL	.01	.01	.07**	.06**
EI×EL	.02[+]	.02[+]	.09**	.08**
(b) Using job incumbent assessments of emotional labor				
SEA×EL	.03*	.00	.03*	.04*
OEA×EL	.03*	.00	.02[+]	.06**
ROE×EL	.02	.00	.04*	.06**
UOE×EL	.00	.01	.04**	.04*
EI×EL	.03*	.01	.04[+]	.06**

SEA, OEA, ROE, UOE, LS, PWL, IQ stand for self-emotion appraisal, others' emotion appraisal, regulation of emotion, uses of emotion. EL stands for emotional labor; EI is the total score of the four EI dimensions. $n=149$.
* $<.05$ (two-tailed tests).
** $P<.01$ (two-tailed tests).
[+] $<.10$.

results for organizational commitment and turnover intention are stronger yet. EI showed the expected positive correlation with organizational commitment ($r=.34$) and a negative correlation with turnover intention ($r=-.22$) only in the high emotional labor group. In the low emotional labor group, the observed correlations are opposite to the expected relationships. These differences in correlation coefficients are all statistically significant ($P<.05$).

Table 8
Beta coefficients for the regression of job outcomes on EI for the groups with high and low levels of emotional labor as judged by supervisors

	Low-EL group ($n=73$)			High-EL group ($n=76$)		
	b_o	b_1	R_{xy}	b_o	b_1	R_{xy}
Job performance	4.71	.00	.00	3.70	.32	.26
Organizational commitment	4.61	−.21	−.26	2.17	.41	.34
Turnover intention	1.76	.50	.36	5.85	−.45	−.22

The low- and high-EL groups stand for the incumbent jobs that were judged to be of low and high emotional labor, respectively, by their supervisors. b_o is the intercept of the regression line, and b_1 is the slope of the regression line; R_{xy} is the Pearson correlation between EI and the outcome variable.

266   *C.-S. Wong, K.S. Law / The Leadership Quarterly 13 (2002) 243–274*

4. Study 3: testing the influence of leader EI on followers' job outcomes

Study 2 demonstrated the influence of follower EI on job outcomes. In Study 3, we test the relationship between the EI of leaders and their effectiveness by examining the relationship between leader EI and follower job outcomes.

4.1. Sample and procedures

To control for organizational differences, the sample for this study consisted of 146 middle-level administrators in the Hong Kong Government. These administrators were asked to evaluate their own EI with the 16-item EI measure developed in Study 1, and the in-role and extra-role behaviors for one of their subordinates who reported to them directly. After completing the evaluations, these administrators were asked to give a short questionnaire containing the 16-item EI, job satisfaction, job characteristics, education level, and tenure with their organizations items to the subordinate that they evaluated. These subordinates were given the short questionnaire in a sealed envelop that contained a cover letter explaining the objectives of the study, a statement ensuring that responses would be confidential, and a stamped reply envelop addressed to the authors of this study. Respondents mailed the completed questionnaire directly to the authors. Each questionnaire was marked with an identification code so that supervisor evaluations could be matched with subordinate responses. The mean age of these subordinates was 28.90 (with a standard deviation of 6.30), and 61.9% were female.

4.2. Measures

4.2.1. Emotional intelligence
Reliability estimates (coefficient alphas) for the four dimensions of SEA, UOE, ROE, and OEA were .86, .85, .79, and .82, respectively, for the supervisor responses. These reliability estimates were .86, .85, .79, and .82, respectively, for the subordinate responses.

4.2.2. Job satisfaction
The 14 items from the Job Diagnostic Survey (Hackman & Oldham, 1976) that measures job satisfaction were adopted. The response format was a 5-point Likert-type scale, and coefficient alpha of these 14 items was .87.

4.2.3. Job perception
Although we chose a relatively homogenous sample in terms of organizational culture and reward systems, job characteristics were controlled because respondents came from different units of the government service. Thus, we measured their job characteristics by the 15 items of the Job Diagnostic Survey (Hackman & Oldham, 1976). The response format was a 7-point Likert-type scale, and the reliability for each dimension was: skills variety,0.73; job identity, .85; job significance, .80; autonomy, .80; and feedback, .61.

Table 9
Descriptive statistics and correlation among variables for Study 3

	Mean	S.D.	1	2	3	4	5	6	7
1. Incumbent's EI	4.84	.76	–						
2. Supervisor's EI	5.32	.72	.05	–					
3. Job perception	4.42	.93	.23**	.25**	–				
4. Job performance	5.07	.89	.05	.13	.14$^+$	–			
5. Job satisfaction	3.25	.52	.22**	.26**	.55**	.16$^+$	–		
6. Organizational citizenship behavior	4.39	.72	.15$^+$	.21*	.29**	.63**	.21*	–	
7. Education level	2.35	.55	.19*	−.13	−.09	−.01	−.14	.03	–
8. Tenure	45.54	46.34	−.11	.10	.05	.10	.12	−.07	−.28**

EI stands for emotional intelligence measured by the 16 items developed in this study.
$n=146$.
   * $P<.05$ (two-tailed tests).
  ** $P<.01$ (two-tailed tests).
  $^+$ $<.10$.

4.2.4. In-role and extra-role behavior

The five items used in Study 2 measuring in-role behavior (i.e., job performance) were adopted. The response format was a 7-point Likert-type scale, and the coefficient alpha in this sample was .81. Extra-role behavior (i.e., organizational citizenship behavior) was measured by items from Podsakoff, MacKenzie, Moorman, and Fetter (1990). These 36 items measured seven dimensions of organizational citizenship behaviors. The response format was a 7-point Likert-type scale, and the coefficient alphas were: altruism, .88; peace, .78; cheer leader, .92; cons, .84; civic virtue, .83; court, .83; and sportsmanship, .80.

Table 10
Results of regression analyses of leader EI on follower job outcomes

	Dependent variables					
	Job performance		Job satisfaction		Organizational citizenship behavior	
Independent variables	Model 1	Model 2	Model 1	Model 2	Model 1	Model 2
Job perception	.13	.10	.51**	.48**	.23**	.21*
Subordinate's EI	.02	.01	.14$^+$	.14$^+$	.08	.08
Education level	.04	.05	−.09	−.07	.03	.04
Tenure	.10	.09	.09	.08	−.08	−.09
Job satisfaction	–	–	–	–	.07	.04
Supervisor's EI	–	.122	–	.13$^+$	–	.18*
R^2	.026	.040	.333**	.348**	.100*	.128*
ΔR^2	–	.014	–	.015$^+$	–	.028*

EI stands for emotional intelligence measured by the 16 items developed in this study.
$n=146$.
   * $P<.05$ (two-tailed tests).
  ** $P<.01$ (two-tailed tests).
  $^+$ $<.10$.

268 *C.-S. Wong, K.S. Law / The Leadership Quarterly 13 (2002) 243–274*

4.2.5. Education and tenure with organization

Education level and job tenure were also controlled in this study. Education level was measured by a multiple-choice item. Primary, secondary, and tertiary education levels were coded as 1, 2, and 3. Tenure with organization was measured by an open question asking respondents to indicate their tenure with their organizations in terms of the number of months.

4.3. Results

Descriptive statistics and the correlations among measures are shown in Table 9. To test for the effects of leader EI on follower job outcomes, hierarchical regression was conducted. The results are shown in Table 10. After controlling for the subordinate job perceptions, EI, education level, and tenure with the organization, the EI of supervisors still has a marginal significant effect on the job satisfaction of subordinates and a significant effect on their extra-role behaviors. However, no effect was found with job performance. Thus, Hypothesis 9 was not supported, while Hypotheses 10 and 11 were supported.

5. Discussion and conclusion

Recently, increasing numbers of scholars have argued that EI is a core variable that affects the performance of leaders (see, e.g., Day, 2000; Sternberg, 1997). Unfortunately, there has been a lack of a psychometrically sound yet practically short EI measure for leadership and management research. There is also little evidence concerning the effects of leader and follower EI on job outcomes. The purpose of this study was to develop such a measure and provide evidence concerning the effects of EI on job outcomes to aid future leadership and management research.

Our study yielded some interesting results. Firstly, apart from acceptable reliability and validity, the EI measure developed shows good convergence with some of the past EI measures such as the Trait Meta-Mood and the EQ-i. However, our measure appears to perform better in predicting external criterion variables such as life satisfaction. As the EI measure developed is relatively simple, it may be beneficial for future leadership and management research.

For the EI of followers, our study has provided preliminary evidence that the EI–job outcome relationship is more complicated than recent proposals (e.g., Abraham, 1999; Ashkanasy & Hooper, 1999; Goleman, 1998). Specifically, job performance is significantly correlated with EI, and this relationship appears to be moderated by emotional labor, as proposed in Fig. 1. Job satisfaction is significantly correlated with EI, but emotional labor does not moderate the EI–job satisfaction relationship. In contrast, organizational commitment and turnover intention have a low and nonsignificant correlation with EI, but emotional labor strongly moderates the EI–commitment and EI–turnover intention relationship. In other words, EI has a strong positive effect on job satisfaction regardless of the nature of the job. In contrast, EI might only have a desirable effect on organizational commitment and turnover intention in jobs that require high emotional, labor while the effect is undesirable in jobs that require low emotional labor. Perhaps this is because employees with high EI find it difficult to commit to a work place that is not conducive to the emotional impact they consider good. Alternatively, they may feel that their abilities are not appreciated or are utilized in low emotional labor jobs. These results are sensible on a post hoc basis, although they were unexpected then the study was designed.

Our study provides some preliminary support for researchers who have proposed the importance of leader EI (e.g., Boal & Hooijberg, 2000; Hooijberg et al., 1997; Sternberg, 1997). Our results show that the EI of leaders is positively related to the job satisfaction and extra-role behavior of followers, as expected. However, no relationship between the EI of leaders and the job performance of their followers has been found. This may be due to our sample, which consists of government administrators who have a culture of distorting the performance ratings of their subordinates. Future research should use different samples to cross-validate this finding.

Despite these unexpected findings and limitations, we believe there are both theoretical and practical implications of this study. Theoretically, we have applied the emotion regulation model to explain the importance of EI in the social interactions in the workplace. As some or most of the social interactions in the workplace may be related to job duties, we hypothesize a positive relationship between EI and job outcomes. As an exploratory effort, we focus on demonstrating these relationships. As the results of this study provide support for these relationships, it is worthwhile to investigate further the role of emotion regulation in the workplace. For example, the emotion regulation model has specified two types of actions to regulate emotions, namely antecedent- and response-focused emotion regulation. It is worthwhile to investigate the specific actions taken by both the leaders and the incumbents in the workplace. What are the factors affecting the choices of actions made by leaders and in-cumbents? Will some actions be more effective under certain circumstances? Will some actions be more effective for some jobs? These are interesting questions that future leadership and management research should address.

Furthermore, new studies should be conducted to investigate the role of EI in the workplace. Proponents have argued for the benefit of hiring employees with high levels of EI. However, few empirical studies have been conducted to test this argument. The results of this exploratory study provide evidence that EI tends to be related to important job outcomes that management desires.

Results of this study also have certain practical implications. Firstly, it is generally believed that individuals with a high level of EI are better employees. For example, Goleman (1995) contends that IE should become increasingly valued in the workplace in the future. The results of this study suggest that although it may be nice to have leaders and employees with a high level of EI because these employees tend to have higher job satisfaction, it is still important to ensure the match employee levels of EI to job requirements. It may be a waste of resources and time to stress the importance of the level of employee EI when it is not required in the job.

Secondly, in contrast to our expectations, strong interaction effects were observed for organizational commitment and turnover intention. That is, the effects of follower EI on organizational commitment and turnover intention is detrimental for low emotional labor jobs. If this finding is further verified by future research, then it will mean that employees with high levels of EI who do not have the opportunity to use these skills in their jobs may be less committed to their organizations and have a higher chance of quitting. This finding is worthy of further research. It is also interesting that this strong interaction effect does not hold for other job outcomes such as job performance. Perhaps employees with a high level of EI are still able to concentrate on performing their jobs although they realize that their skills are underutilized. Thus, having employees with a high level of EI may be advantageous to the organization.

To conclude, this study has provided some preliminary evidence for the role of leader and follower EI, and for the interaction effect of employee EI and emotional labor on their job performance and attitudes towards their jobs. As an exploratory effort, we believe that we have provided sufficient evidence for future leadership and management research to investigate the role of emotions in the workplace. Thus, more research on the role of both leader and follower EI in the workplace is called for.

Acknowledgments

The work described in this paper was partially supported by a grant from the Research Grants Council of the Hong Kong Special Administrative Region (Project No. CUHK4038/00H).

Appendix A. Emotional intelligence and emotional labor items

A.1. Emotional intelligence items

Self-emotion appraisal (SEA)
1. I have a good sense of why I have certain feelings most of the time.
2. I have good understanding of my own emotions.
3. I really understand what I feel.
4. I always know whether or not I am happy.

Others' emotion appraisal (OEA)
5. I always know my friends' emotions from their behavior.
6. I am a good observer of others' emotions.
7. I am sensitive to the feelings and emotions of others.
8. I have good understanding of the emotions of people around me.

Use of emotion (UOE)
9. I always set goals for myself and then try my best to achieve them.
10. I always tell myself I am a competent person.

11. I am a self-motivated person.
12. I would always encourage myself to try my best.

Regulation of emotion (ROE)
13. I am able to control my temper and handle difficulties rationally.
14. I am quite capable of controlling my own emotions.
15. I can always calm down quickly when I am very angry.
16. I have good control of my own emotions.

A.2. Emotional labor items

To perform my job well, it is necessary for me to:
1. spend most of my work time interacting with people (e.g., customers, colleagues, and other workers in this organization).
2. spend a lot of time with every person whom I work with.
3. hide my actual feelings when acting and speaking with people.
4. be considerate and think from the point of view of others.
5. hide my negative feelings (e.g., anger and depression).

References

Abraham, R. (1999). Emotional intelligence in organizations: a conceptualization. *Genetic, Social, and General Psychology Monographs, 125* (2), 209–224.

Adelmann, P. K. (1989). *Emotional labor and employee well-being.* Unpublished doctoral dissertation, the University of Michigan.

Ashkanasy, N. M., Hooper, G. (1999). *Perceiving and managing emotion in the workplace: a research agenda based on neurophysiology.* Paper presented at the Third Australian Industrial and Organizational Psychology Conference, Brisbane, June, 1999.

BarOn, R. (1997). *BarOn EQ-i technical manual.* Toronto, Canada: Psychological Assessment Resources.

Bass, B. M. (1990). *Handbook of leadership: a survey of theory and research.* New York: Free Press.

Bentler, P. M. (1990). Comparative fit indexes in structural models. *Psychological Bulletin, 107*, 238–246.

Boal, K. B., & Hooijberg, R. (2000). Strategic leadership research: moving on. *The Leadership Quarterly Yearly Review of Leadership, 11* (4), 515–550.

Boal, K. B., & Whitehead, C. J. (1992). A critique and extension of the stratified systems theory perspective. In R. L. Phillips, & J. G. Hunt (Eds.), *Strategic leadership: a multiorganizational-level perspective* (pp. 237–255). Westport, CT: Quorum.

Cammann, C., Fichman, M., Jenkins, D., Klesh, J. (1979). *The Michigan Organizational Assessment Questionnaire.* Unpublished manuscript, University of Michigan, Ann Arbor, Michigan.

Campbell, A., Converse, P. E., & Rodgers, W. L. (1976). *The quality of American life: perceptions, evaluation and satisfaction.* New York: Russell Sage.

Carson, K. D., & Carson, P. P. (1998). Career commitment, competencies, and citizenship. *Journal of Career Assessment, 6* (2), 195–208.

Carson, K. D., Carson, P., & Philips, J. S. (1997). *The ABCs of collaborative change.* Chicago: American Library Association.

Ciarrochi, J. V., Chan, A. Y. C., & Caputi, P. (2000). A critical evaluation of the emotional intelligence construct. *Personality and Individual Differences, 28* (3), 539–561.

Costa, P. T., & McCrae, R. R. (1985). *The NEO personality inventory manual.* Odessa, FL: Psychological Assessment Resources.

Dansereau, F., Alutto, J. A., Nachman, S. A., Al-Kelabi, S. A., Yammarino, F. J., Newman, J., Naughton, T. J., Lee, S., Markham, S. E., Dumas, M., Kim, K., & Keller, T. (1995). Individualized leadership: a new multiple-level approach. *The Leadership Quarterly, 6* (3), 413–450.

Davies, M., Stankov, L., & Roberts, R. D. (1998). Emotional intelligence: in search of an elusive construct. *Journal of Personality and Social Psychology, 75* (4), 989–1015.

Day, D. V. (2000). Leadership development: a review in context. *The Leadership Quarterly Yearly Review of Leadership, 11* (4), 581–614.

Eysenck, H. J. (1964). *Know your own IQ.* Harmondsworth, England: Penguin.

Eysenck, H. J. (1990). *Check your own IQ.* (2nd ed.). Harmondsworth, England: Penguin.

Fischer, K. W., Shaver, P. R., & Carnochan, P. (1990). How emotions develop and how they organize development. *Cognition and Emotion, 4,* 81–127.

Fisher, B. M., & Edwards, J. E. (1988). Consideration and initiating structure and their relationships with leader effectiveness: a meta-analysis. *Proceedings of the Academy of Management, August, 1988,* 201–205.

Gardner, H. (1993). *Multiple intelligences: the theory in practice.* NY: Basic Books.

George, J. M., & Bettenhausen, K. (1990). Understanding prosaic behavior, sales performance, and turnover: a group-level analysis in a service context. *Journal of Applied Psychology, 75,* 698–709.

Goleman, D. (1995). *Emotional intelligence.* New York: Bantam Books.

Goleman, D. (1998). *Working with emotional intelligence.* New York: Bantam Books.

Grandey, A. A. (2000). Emotion regulation in the workplace: a new way to conceptualize emotional labor. *Journal of Occupational Health Psychology, 5* (1), 95–110.

Gross, J. J. (1998a). The emerging field of emotion regulation: an integrated review. *Review of General Psychology, 2* (3), 271–299.

Gross, J. J. (1998b). Antecedent- and response-focused emotion regulation: divergent consequences for experience, expression, and physiology. *Journal of Personality and Social Psychology, 74* (1), 224–237.

Hackman, J. R., & Oldham, G. R. (1976). Development of the job diagnostic survey. *Journal of Applied Psychology, 60* (2), 159–170.

Hochschild, A. R. (1983). *The managed heart: commercialization of human feeling.* Berkeley: University of California Press.

Hollander, E. P. (1979). Leadership and social exchange processes. In K. Gergen, M. S. Greenberg, & R. H. Wills (Eds.), *Social exchange: advances in theory and research.* New York: Winston-Wiley.

Hooijberg, R., Hunt, J. G., & Dodge, G. E. (1997). Leadership complexity and development of the leaderplex model. *Journal of Management, 23* (3), 375–408.

House, R. J., & Aditya, R. N. (1997). The social scientific study of leadership: quo vadis? *Journal of Management, 23* (3), 409–473.

Hui, C., Law, K. S., & Chen, Z. X. (1999). The structural equation model of the effect of negative affectivity, leader member exchange and perceived job mobility on in-role and extra-role performance: A Chinese case. *Organizational Behavior and Human Decision Process, 77,* 3–21.

Izard, C. E. (1992). Basic emotions, relations among emotions, and emotion–cognition relations. *Psychological Review, 99,* 561–565.

Izard, C. E. (1993). Four systems for emotion activation: cognitive and noncognitive processes. *Psychological Review, 100,* 68–90.

Jacobs, T. O. (1970). *Leadership and exchange in formal organizations.* Alexandria, VA: Human Resources Research Organization.

James, L. R., & Demaree, R. G. (1984). Estimating within-group interrater reliability with and without response bias. *Journal of Applied Psychology, 69* (1), 85–98.

Jöreskog, K. G., & Sörbom, D. (1993). *LISREL 8: structural equation modeling with the SIMPLIS command language.* Chicago: Scientific Software International.

Law, K. S., Wong, C. S., & Mobley, W. H. (1998). Toward a taxonomy of multidimensional constructs. *Academy of Management Review, 23* (4), 741–755.

Martinez-Pons, M. (1997). The relation of emotional intelligence with selected areas of personal functioning. *Imagination, Cognition and Personality, 17* (1), 3–13.

Mayer, J. D., & Salovey, P. (1997). What is emotional intelligence? In P. Salovey, & D. Sluyter (Eds.), *Emotional development and emotional intelligence: educational implications* (pp. 3–34). New York: Basic Books.

Mayer, J. D., Salovey, P., & Caruso, D. (1997). *Emotional IQ test. CD-ROM version.* Richard Viard (producer). Needham, MA: Virtual Entertainment.

McCrae, R. R., & Costa Jr., P. T. (1987). Validation of the five-factor model of personality across instruments and observers. *Journal of Personality and Social Psychology, 52* (1), 81–90.

Meyer, J. P., Allen, N. J., & Smith, C. A. (1993). Commitment to organizations and occupations: Extensions and test of a three-component conceptualization. *Journal of Applied Psychology, 78* (4), 538–555.

Morris, J. A., & Feldman, D. C. (1996). The dimensions, antecedents, and consequences of emotional labor. *Academy of Management Review, 21* (4), 986–1010.

Morris, J. A., & Feldman, D. C. (1997). Managing emotions in the workplace. *Journal of Managerial Issues, 9* (3), 257–274.

Mumford, M. D., Zaccaro, S. J., Harding, F. D., Jacobs, T. O., & Fleishman, E. A. (2000). Leadership skills for a changing world: solving complex social problems. *The Leadership Quarterly, 11* (1), 11–35.

Pearlin, L., & Schooler, C. (1978). The structure of coping. *Journal of Health and Social Behavior, 19,* 2–21.

Pellitteri, J. (1999). *The relationships between emotional intelligence, cognitive reasoning, and defense mechanisms.* Unpublished dissertation, New York University.

Podsakoff, P. M., Mackenzie, S. B., Moorman, R. H., & Fetter, R. (1990). Transformational leader behaviors and their effects on followers' trust in leader, satisfaction, and organizational citizenship behaviors. *The Leadership Quarterly, 1* (2), 107–142.

Rafaeli, A., & Sutton, R. I. (1987). Expression of emotion as part of the work role. *Academy of Management Review, 12,* 23–37.

Roseman, I. J., Dhawan, N., Rettek, S. I., & Naidu, R. K. (1995). Cultural differences and cross-cultural similarities in appraisals and emotional responses. *Journal of Cross-Cultural Psychology, 26* (1), 23–48.

Salovey, P., & Mayer, J. D. (1990). Emotional intelligence. *Imagination, Cognition and Personality, 9* (3), 185–211.

Salovey, P., Mayer, J. D., Goldman, S. L., Turvey, C., & Palfai, T. (1995). Emotional attention, clarity and repair: exploring emotional intelligence using the Trait Meta-Mood Scale. In J. W. Pennebaker (Ed.), *Emotion, disclosure, and health.* Washington, DC: American Psychological Association.

Shapiro, L. E. (1997). *How to raise a child with a high EQ: a parent's guide to emotional intelligence.* New York: HarperCollins.

Sosik, J. J., & Megerian, L. E. (1999). Understanding leader emotional intelligence and performance: the role of self-other agreement on transformational leadership perceptions. *Group and Organization Management, 24* (3), 367–390.

Sternberg, R. J. (1997). Managerial Intelligence: why IQ isn't enough. *Journal of Management, 23* (3), 475–493.

Sutton, R. I. (1991). Maintaining norms about expressed emotions: the case of bill collectors. *Administrative Science Quarterly, 36,* 245–268.

Sutton, R. I., & Rafaeli, A. (1988). Untangling the relationship between displayed emotions and organizational sales: the case of convenience stores. *Academy of Management Journal, 31,* 461–487.

Thorndike, E. L. (1920). Intelligence and its uses. *Harper's Magazine, 140,* 227–235.

Tucker, L. R., & Lewis, C. (1973). The reliability coefficient for maximum likelihood factor analysis. *Psychometrika, 28,* 1–10.

Turner, B. A. (1986). Sociological aspects of organizational symbolism. *Organizational Studies, 7,* 101–115.

Van Maanen, J., & Kunda, G. (1989). "Real feelings": emotional expression and organizational culture. *Research in Organizational Behavior, 11,* 43–103.

Weisinger, H. (1998). *Emotional intelligence at work: the untapped edge for success.* San Francisco: Jossey-Bass.

Wharton, A. S. (1993). The affective consequences of service work. *Work and Occupations, 20* (2), 205–232.

Wharton, A. S., & Erickson, R. J. (1995). The consequences of caring: exploring the links between women's job and family emotion work. *The Sociological Quarterly, 36* (2), 273–296.

Williams, L. J. (1988). *Affective and nonaffective components of job satisfaction and organizational commitment as determinants of organizational citizenship and in-role behaviors.* Unpublished doctoral dissertation, Indiana University, Bloomington.

Zaccaro, S. J., Mumford, M. D., Connelly, M. S., Marks, M. A., & Gilbert, J. A. (2000). Assessment of leader problem-solving capabilities. *The Leadership Quarterly, 11* (1), 37–64.

[9]

Leader distance: a review and a proposed theory

John Antonakis[a,*], Leanne Atwater[b]

[a]Department of Psychology, Yale University, New Haven, CT, USA
[b]School of Management, Arizona State University West, Phoenix, AZ, USA

Accepted 9 September 2002

Abstract

The concept of leader distance has been subsumed in a number of leadership theories; however, with few exceptions, leadership scholars have not expressly defined nor discussed leader distance, how distance is implicated in the legitimization of a leader, and how distance affects leader outcomes. We review available literature and demonstrate that integral to untangling the dynamics of the leadership influencing process is an understanding of leader–follower distance. We present distance in terms of three independent dimensions: leader–follower physical distance, perceived social distance, and perceived task interaction frequency. We discuss possible antecedents of leader–follower distance, including organizational and task characteristics, national culture, and leader/follower implicit motives. Finally, we use configural theory to present eight typologies (i.e., coexistence of a cluster or constellation of independent factors serving as a unit of analysis) of leader distance and propose an integrated cross-level model of leader distance, linking the distance typologies to leader outcomes at the individual and group levels of analysis.

1. Introduction

The embers of "leadership at a distance"—as initially proposed by Bogardus (1927)—smoldered for half a century. They were briefly fanned by Katz and Kahn (1978), who cursorily referred to the leadership-at-a-distance phenomenon. Others (e.g., Napier & Ferris,

* Corresponding author. Present address: Faculty of Economics and Business Administration (Ecoles des Hautes Etudes Commerciales—HEC), University of Lausanne, BFSH-1 Lausanne CH-1015, Switzerland. Tel.: +41-21-692-3300.
E-mail address: john.antonakis@hec.unil.ch (J. Antonakis).

1993; Shamir, 1995; Waldman & Yammarino, 1999; Yammarino, 1994) have rekindled the idea of leadership at a distance. In its various forms, leader distance has been considered as (a) a sine qua non of the emergence of charismatic leadership (Katz & Kahn, 1978); (b) a moderator of the type of charismatic leadership that might emerge (Shamir, 1995; Yagil, 1998); and (c) a neutralizer of leadership that reduces the effect that leader behaviors have on others (Howell, Bowen, Dorfman, Kerr, & Podsakoff, 1997; Kerr & Jermier, 1978).

Napier and Ferris (1993, p. 321) began their integrative review on distance and supervisory-level leadership in organizations as follows: "Understanding the role of inter-personal distance in organizations is fundamental to our comprehension of work place dynamics, yet no theory currently exists that integrates the various types of distance in organizations." A similar comment was echoed by Yammarino (1994) who examined indirect leadership. Almost a decade has passed since these two studies were conducted; however, the literature on leadership at a distance in the organizational domain has yet to generate much empirical work, let alone define and bound the phenomenon of "leader distance."

Why do we need to study leadership at a distance? Although our current understanding of leadership is quite broad, we still do not understand the fundamental processes undergirding the influencing effect of leadership. For example, Yukl (1999) noted that our understanding of certain leadership theories, for example, the full-range leadership theory (FRLT, i.e., transformational, transactional, and laissez-faire leadership) are limited in that the focus is generally on the dyadic level of analysis (i.e., direct leadership), instead of also group and organizational levels of analysis (i.e., indirect leadership). Hunt (1991), Shamir (1995), and Yammarino (1994) proposed that most theories of organizational leadership focus on supervisory-level leaders and their effects on immediate followers.

Political scientists have, of course, long viewed the impact of leaders on far-removed followers (e.g., Burns, 1978; Gardner, 1990; Willner, 1984). Paradoxically, political scientists typically examined what could be termed "distal leaders"; however, leadership theorists, with few exceptions (e.g., Sashkin, 1988; Waldman & Yammarino, 1999) have typically applied political science theories to explain the effects of what could be termed "proximal leaders" on followers.

The dynamics of the influencing process differ depending on how "close" or "distant" followers are from their leader. In other words, the types of leader behaviors that can affect followers and how those behaviors are evaluated by followers depend on how "close" or "distant" followers are from leaders. Briefly, we define leader distance as the configual effect (i.e., the coexistance of a cluster of independent factors–discussed later) of leader–follower physical distance, perceived social distance, and perceived interaction frequency. Thus, leaders can appear to be very distant to followers if leaders (a) are physically distant from followers, (b) maximize their status and power differentials by virtue of their elevated social position, and (c) maintain infrequent contact with followers. These three dimensions could, however, make leaders appear very close. We thus set out to answer the following questions in our article: Can both "distant" and "close" leaders influence followers? Can followers identify with and trust both types of leaders? What causes distance between leaders and followers? Is distance beneficial or detrimental to leader outcomes? Can we explain the linkages of "close" and "distant" leadership to individual and group level outcomes?

J. Antonakis, L. Atwater / The Leadership Quarterly 13 (2002) 673–704   675

As we argue here, leader effectiveness is contingent on matching the degree of closeness that followers expect of the leader in various contexts (e.g., Roberts & Bradley, 1988). Thus, a crucial component of the leadership phenomenon (i.e., how leaders are perceived, whether followers accept leaders, and the level of analysis at which leader outcomes are evident) can be partly explained by the distance that exists between leaders and their followers.

Furthermore, we argue that the construct of leader distance has abounded but has been implicitly subsumed in other leader constructs. Theoretical frameworks to guide research, however, are sparse. Conducting a review under such conditions was therefore especially challenging. As well as we can determine, after Napier and Ferris's (1993) review, our review is the second one dealing explicitly with distance and organizational leadership. Therefore, apart from reviewing the available literature we felt compelled to also define precisely what "leadership at a distance" is and the factors that comprise it. We also felt it necessary to integrate the disjointed findings and attempted to present a leader distance model (see Fig. 1) and testable propositions that we hope will guide future research. Indeed, as noted by Napier and Ferris (p. 325), "distance between supervisor and subordinate has been studied implicitly

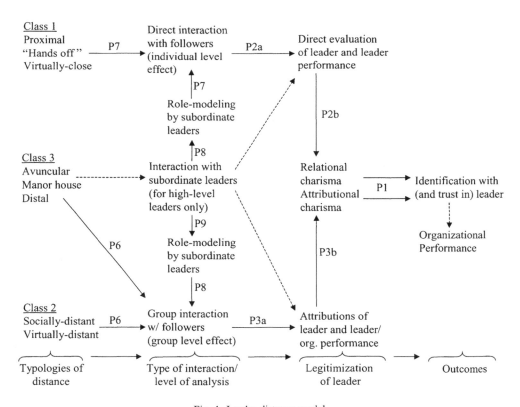

Fig. 1. Leader distance model.

by a variety of researchers, leading to a myriad of findings with limited theoretical support, confusing and diverse operationalizations of constructs, and few if any comprehensive conclusions."

2. Leadership as an influencing process

Leadership is an influencing process that results from follower perceptions of leader behavior and follower attributions of leader dispositional characteristics, behaviors, and performance (see Bass, 1990; Conger & Kanugo, 1998; House, 1977; Shamir, 1995; Waldman & Yammarino, 1999). One of the most popular theories of leadership is Bass and Avolio's (Bass, 1985; Bass & Avolio, 1994, 1997) transformational, transactional, and laissez-faire leadership theory or Full-Range Leadership Theory (FRLT), which has played a salient role in shifting the current paradigms of leadership towards neocharismatic and transformational leadership (Conger, 1999; Hunt, 1999; Yukl, 1999). As such, we will use the FRLT as an example concerning what behaviors leaders enact and how leader distance moderates the types of full-range leader behaviors that are visible and salient to followers.

Bass and Avolio argued that previous paradigms of leadership typically focused on the fulfillment of transactional obligations, and the types of leader behaviors associated with goal establishment, and the rewarding or sanctioning of follower behavior contingent on goal achievement. This type of leadership was referred to as transactional leadership, which was limited to inducing basic changes in followers. Following the work of Burn (1978), Bass and Avolio theorized that a more potent form of leadership was needed to elevate the influencing process to a higher level. By virtue of their visionary, inspirational, and charismatic behaviors, Bass and Avolio argued that transformational leaders focus on elevating followers' higher-order needs to achieve extraordinary and worthy feats, and to make followers aware of and believe in superordinate values and goals.

In its current form, Bass and Avolio (1997) argued that transactional leadership comprises (a) management-by-exception passive (i.e., a passive-corrective transaction), (b) management-by-exception active (i.e., an active-corrective transaction), and (c) contingent reward (i.e., a constructive transaction). Transformational leadership, which is seen as the most active and effective leader style, comprises (a) attributed idealized influence (i.e., attributed charisma), (b) behavioral idealized influence (i.e., behavioral charisma), (c) inspirational motivation (i.e., raising follower self-efficacy beliefs), (d) intellectual stimulation (i.e., encouragement of creative thinking and challenging the status quo), and (e) individualized consideration (i.e., individualized follower development). The FRLT is completed by laissez-faire leadership, which entails the absence of leadership and transactions. The FRLT is measured by the Multifactor Leadership Questionnaire Form 5X (Bass & Avolio, 1995).

Although the FRLT may be the flag bearer of the neocharismatic leadership movement, it omits important leader behaviors, which Antonakis and House (in press) referred to as instrumental leadership. Instrumental leadership theoretically accounts for leader behaviors that are independent of value-based or transactional behavior that are (a) strategic in nature (i.e., strategy formulation and implementation), impacting the organizational level of analysis;

and (b) focused on follower work facilitation (i.e., path-goal facilitation and outcome monitoring). Thus, our examples will be based on the extended Antonakis and House FRLT.

An important factor associated with how leadership as process impacts followers is leader hierarchical level, which, as we establish later, is associated with leader distance. High-level leaders display qualitatively different behaviors from low-level leaders (e.g., Antonakis & House, 2002; Hunt, 1991; Sashkin, 1988; Waldman & Yammarino, 1999; Westley & Mintzberg, 1988; Zaccaro, 2002). Thus, hierarchical level, as a contextual factor, should be considered as a boundary condition of leadership models. For example, Antonakis (2001) found support for the validity of the nine-factors of the FRLT; however, he demonstrated that the validity of the model depended on using data from contextually similar conditions, one of which included leader hierarchical level. In a meta-analysis, Lowe, Kroeck, and Sivasubra-maniam, (1996) established that the mean of the leadership factors were moderated by leader level. The implication of these findings is that leaders will enact different behaviors depending on the context in which those behaviors occur. Therefore, because the FRLT may not operate in the same manner across various hierarchical levels and within different degrees of leader–follower distance, it is important that we make explicit how distance may moderate the types of leader behaviors that may emerge or are visible.

2.1. Follower identification and trust

Before reviewing the dimensions of leader distance, we briefly discuss why followers identify with and trust charismatic/transformational leaders, and how the identification process may occur differently depending on leader distance. As we will argue, the legitimacy of a leader is moderated by leader distance. Furthermore, how followers come to identify with their leader or the collective is a function of leader distance. Because identification with the leader is a result of the leader's charisma (Bass, 1985; House, 1977), as a prelude to our detailed discussion on the dimensions of leader distance first, we briefly explore how leader charisma emerges and how charisma may be related to leader distance. For simplicity, when we refer to charisma we are referring to a leader's idealized influence as well as the leader's inspirational motivation, individualized consideration and intellectual stimulation. As argued by Antonakis and House (in press), current explications of transformational leadership are similar to the descriptions of charismatic and visionary leadership, and—apart from instrumental leadership—most of the dimensions of charismatic/visionary leadership are theoretically captured by the FRLT.

According to House (1977), a charismatic leader becomes a symbol of identification for followers, and commands loyalty, trust, and devotion from followers resulting from the leader's transcendent vision and the confidence the leader instills in followers that the vision is achievable. Others have argued that the charismatic leader's vision of a highly attractive future that challenges and breaks with the past creates follower identification with the leader (Bass, 1985; Conger & Kanugo, 1998).

In their self-concept based theory of charismatic leadership, Shamir, House, and Arthur (1993) argued that individuals are motivated to self-express, to enhance their self-worth, self-esteem and self-efficacy, and to establish an identity of who they are. If these self-concepts can be expressed in a charismatic leader or in a collective, individuals can come to identify with the charismatic leader and with the collective. That is, followers' self-concepts are affected and implicated by the charismatic leader—especially when the leader represents what followers and the group consider to be salient values—values that implicate the followers' social identity. According to Ashforth and Mael (1989, p. 21), identification with the collective is referred to as social identification or "the perception of oneness with or belongingness to some human aggregate." They noted further that individuals will "choose activities congruent with salient aspects of their identities and they support the institutions embodying those identities" (p. 25). Thus, Shamir et al. noted that followers become self-motivated to perform in conditions where the leader implicates their self-concepts and social identity.

Conger and Kanugo (1998, p. 38) noted that charisma "is both a relational and attributional phenomenon." The leader's charisma is thus legitimized by virtue of his or her actual behaviors and whether the behaviors are observable to followers (implying that leaders are "close" to followers; see Shamir, 1995), or attributions that followers make of the leader (implying that leaders are "distant" from followers") resulting from (a) the leader's impression management techniques (see Gardner & Avolio, 1998; Shamir, 1995; Waldman & Yammarino, 1999); (b) a social contagion effect, whereby followers' perceptions and attributions of the leader spread to others (see Meindl, 1990); (c) from the leader's social network, that is, "the social systems in which [followers] are embedded... and the thinking and behavior of other social actors to whom they are exposed" (see Pastor, Meindl, & Mayo, 2002, p. 410); (d) implicit leadership theories that followers have of leaders (see Eden and Leviatan, 1975); or (e) attributions of charisma followers make of high-level (and generally "distant" leaders) based on the organization's performance (see Shamir, 1995; Waldman & Yammarino, 1999).

However, it appears that these attributional effects depend on how much information followers have of leaders. For instance, attributional effects would be more prevalent for "distant" than for "close" charismatic leaders, because followers of distant leaders are more prone to leader image-building efforts and have less information on the leader (see Shamir, 1995; Howell & Shamir, 1998). Because individuals may not have enough information on a leader to make an accurate assessment of the leader's behavior and performance, they may make assumptions and attributions to rationalize and comprehend organizational outcomes (see Meindl & Ehrlich, 1987; Yukl, 1998). It follows, therefore, that the knowledge followers have of the leader's performance and how the leader's performance affects the organization is critical to whether they (a) directly evaluate the leader's performance or (b) whether they attribute organizational success to the leader's performance and image-building efforts. Further discussion on attributional and relational charisma is presented later in our coverage of social distance.

Proposition 1: *Followers will identify with leaders as a result of the leaders' relational or attributional charisma.*

Proposition 2a: *Followers who interact directly with their leaders are more able to directly evaluate the leader's performance than followers who interact indirectly with their leaders.*

Proposition 2b: *Followers who can directly evaluate their leader's performance will be more prone to the effects of relational leader charisma than to attributional charisma.*

Proposition 3a: *Followers who interact indirectly with their leaders will rely more on attributions of the leaders' performance than will followers who interact directly with their leaders.*

Proposition 3b: *Followers who cannot directly evaluate their leader's performance will be more prone to the effects of attributional leader charisma than to relational leader charisma.*

Note: "followers" in the above propositions can refer to immediate (e.g., subordinates or subordinate leaders) or nonimmediate followers (i.e., indirect followers) of a leader.

Apart from identification with the leader, follower trust in the leader has also been viewed as an outcome of charisma (Bass, 1985; House, 1977). As we argue later, trust may take on two forms (i.e., "close" and "distant" trust) as a function of leader distance. Thus, it is important here that we describe how trust develops, and its multidimensional nature, so that we can later link trust to leader distance.

Mayer, Davis, and Schoorman (1995) suggested that the propensity to trust an individual is a function of the trustee's (a) *ability* (i.e., expertise), (b) *benevolence* (i.e., altruism), and (c) *integrity* (i.e., consistency). *Ability* is related to instrumental leader behavior, because the latter is predicated on the leader's domain-relevant expertise and impacts follower and organizational performance (see Antonakis & House, 2002). *Benevolence* is related to a leader's socialized charisma (see Antonakis & House, in press), that is, the degree of overlap between leader and follower values such that that leader is acting congruent to the values of the collective, challenging the status quo for the better (i.e., using intellectual stimulation) demonstrating conviction that collective goals are achievable (i.e., using inspirational motivation), and finally empowering followers (i.e., using individualized consideration). *Integrity* is related to the leaders' honesty and reliability and whether they fulfill their transactional obligations (see Shamir, 1995).

Similar to our discussions above about the implications of distance to leader charisma, it becomes apparent that the dimensions of trust may not arise in the same manner because of leader distance, as we also discuss later. Briefly, a leader's ability and integrity is evident to followers if they have direct information on the leader's performance and behavior and are "close" to the leader; however, a leader's ability and integrity are not easily determined if followers do not have direct information on the leader and are "distant" from the leader. Therefore, the ways in which a leader is legitimized and trusted appears to be a function of leader distance.

3. "Close" and "distant" leadership

Distance, as it refers to leadership, has been generally discussed in terms of social or psychosocial distance (e.g., Bass, 1990; Bogardus, 1927; Shamir, 1995; Waldman & Yammarino, 1999), physical distance (Kerr & Jermier, 1978), in terms of the maintenance

680 *J. Antonakis, L. Atwater / The Leadership Quarterly 13 (2002) 673–704*

of frequent and direct contact of leader with followers (Hunt, 1991; Yagil, 1998; Yammarino, 1994), and in terms of hierarchical or cross-functional leadership (Bass & Avolio, 1993; Hunt, 1991; Yammarino, 1994). In this section, we discuss literature that has explicitly considered the effects of distance on leadership. We also include theories of leadership in which distance was implicitly assumed but not expressly discussed. In reviewing the literature, we concluded that distance can be manifested in three independent dimensions, that is, leader–follower physical distance, perceived social distance, and perceived leader–follower interaction frequency. The degree to which these three dimensions are manifested in the leader's behavior will affect the degree to which followers perceive the leader as "close" or "distant."

3.1. Distance in leadership theories

Many leadership scholars have based their theories of leadership on an assumption that some sort of distance, or lack thereof, is prevalent in leader–follower relationships. We review a few examples below.

In the Ohio State University studies, Halpin and Winer's (1957) definition of leader consideration implied that a leader was intimate and close to followers. Other conceptualizations inferring closeness include Blake and Mouton's (1964, p. 57) "country club" managerial style (i.e., high concern-for-people leaders), describing leaders as being friendly, informal, sociable, promoting togetherness, and reducing status differentials with followers. Also, the scale of "individualized consideration" in the FRLT refers to leader behaviors that provide individualized and personalized attention to followers implying leader–follower closeness and intimacy (Bass, 1985, 1998).

Some conceptualizations imply distance. Fiedler's (1967) least preferred coworker, based on the Assumed Similarity between Opposites Scale, referred in part, to the preferred psychological distance a leader wished to maintain from followers. White and Lippitt (1968) described authoritarian leaders as being aloof (i.e., socially distant) from their group of followers, whereas democratic leaders were more egalitarian and unconcerned by status differentials. House (1977) argued that charismatic leaders can either be, or can create the impressions to be, confident, dominant, and successful, thus implying that leaders create these impressions because followers cannot directly assess the leaders' behaviors and attitudes (i.e., the leader is "distant" from the followers).

Still other conceptualizations suggest that leaders may be either close or distant. LMX theory describes the quality of dyadic relations (i.e., leader–follower) that characterize whether the relationship is based primarily on the mutual fulfillment of contractual obligations (i.e., the "out group") or whether the relation will be based on trust, respect, and positive social exchange (i.e., the "in group") (Uhl-Bien, Graen, & Scandura, 2000). Kerr and Jermier (1978) noted that leadership may be unnecessary and that the degree of closeness of leader supervision will depend on various leader "substitutes," which include among others follower abilities and various organizational systems and processes.

Although some scholars have specifically examined the implication of distance on leadership, they generally have not explicitly defined what they meant by "distance." The only explicit definition of leader distance has been offered by Napier and Ferris (1993, p. 326), who referred to the distance between a leader and a follower as dyadic distance, "a multidimensional construct that describes the psychological, structural, and functional separation, disparity, or discord between a supervisor and a subordinate." They speculated that functional distance mediates the relations of psychological and structural distance in determining subordinate performance and satisfaction. The three dimensions of distance that Napier and Ferris identified included:

1. Psychological distance—this refers to the "psychological effects of actual and perceived... differences between the supervisor and subordinate" (pp. 328–329). These differences or similarities include (a) demographic distance, which refers to age, race, and gender differences (similar to how social distance has been defined, as discussed below); (b) power distance, which refers to follower acceptance of power differentials between the follower and the leader (also similar to social distance); (c) perceived similarity, which refers to "the degree to which an individual believes that s(he) is similar to a target individual" (p. 331), (also appears similar to social distance); and (d) values similarity, which refers to similarity of "beliefs, values, or attitudes" (p. 332) between followers and their leader (appears similar to our description of follower identification with the leader).
2. Structural distance—this refers to "aspects of distance brought about by physical structure (e.g., physical distance), as well as organizational structure (e.g., span of management control and management centralization) and supervision structure (e.g., frequency of leader–follower interaction)" (Napier & Ferris, 1993, p. 333). It is discussed in terms of propinquity (i.e., proximity). They stated further, "The conceptual link which binds (the above three) variables is that they all are associated with the amount of interaction in the dyad, which is allowed or encouraged" (p. 333).
3. Functional distance—refers to the "degree of closeness and quality of the functional working relationship between the supervisor and the subordinate; in essence, whether the subordinate is a member of the in-group or the out-group" (Napier & Ferris, 1993, p. 337), suggesting leader–follower intimacy. They argued that functional distance is comprised of affect, perceptual congruence (i.e., mutual understanding), and latitude (i.e., the degree of follower empowerment). Here, Napier and Ferris draw heavily upon LMX theory.

There are a number of ways we expand Napier and Ferris's (1993) model, which seems to be more normative than descriptive. First, Napier and Ferris suggest that functional distance is a negative predictor of subordinate outcomes, for example, "Subordinates who feel they have access to their supervisors, and who actually interact on a more frequent basis, are hypothesized to develop a better, closer working relationship" (p. 344). They stated further "less functional distance is proposed to lead to higher performance evaluations, higher subordinate satisfaction, and lower subordinate withdrawal" (p. 344). We believe this proposition is premature for the below reasons.

Their explication of distance relates in toto to leader–follower intimacy, which is not a necessary condition for the emergence of successful leadership. The type of charisma ascribed to a leader will vary depending on the degree of social distance (i.e., intimacy) prevalent in the leader–follower relationship (Shamir, 1995; Yagil, 1998). Intimacy is not a necessary condition for the emergence of successful charismatic leadership (Shamir, 1995). The closeness of leader–follower interaction depends on a variety of factors, for example, follower skills (House, 1971) and leader substitutes (Kerr & Jermier, 1978). Additionally, as discussed previously, affect for, identification with, and trust in the leader is predicated on numerous factors, and does not necessitate that a leader is intimate with his or her followers.

Second, Napier and Ferris (1993) argued that functional distance mediates the effect of psychological and structural distance in determining subordinate performance and satisfaction. Again, in focusing on supervisor-level leadership and only on a single unit of analysis, the dyadic follower–leader relation, they have not considered the effects of high-level leaders on groups and collectives.

Third, in contrast to Napier and Ferris (1993), we suggest that identification and social distance need to be considered as independent of each other. Identification with the leader is possible when leader–follower social distance is large or small.

Finally, Napier and Ferris (1993, p. 349) stated that factors that moderate the emergence of distance should be investigated, including "the nature of the task, the use of impression management behaviors, instrumental or expressive orientations, and other personality characteristics, size, or industry type and other organizational constraints, and location or culture of the organization." Although their commentary is very insightful, those recommendations were not included in the formulation of their normative model. Based in part on their work, we hope to present a more general model and distinct definitions of the multidimensional nature of distance.

In Sections 3.1.1–3.1.3, we present the three distance dimensions and relevant literature to support their conceptualization.

3.1.1. Perceived social or psychological distance

Social distance, which we generally equate to psychological distance (Napier & Ferris, 1993) or psychosocial distance (Bass, 1990), was first described by Park (1924, p. 339) to refer to degree of "understanding and intimacy which characterize personal and social relations." Social distance can include differentials in status depending upon the context in which they are observed (Bogardus, 1928; Park, 1924), and the degree to which individuals are personally acquainted with one another (Frank, 1974). We thus define social distance in the leadership domain as perceived differences in status, rank, authority, social standing, and power, which affect the degree of intimacy and social contact that develop between followers and their leader.

Bogardus (1927) first proposed that leadership entails a degree of social distance between a leader and followers, which he referred to as vertical social distance. He speculated that social distance is created because the leader is accorded recognition by followers for outstanding feats in a particular domain. By definition, therefore, leadership is accompanied by social distance. Bogardus (p. 177) was the first to note, "To the extent that leadership rests on sheer prestige, it is easily punctured by intimacy." In other words, leaders' influence and the respect they command diminish when the social distance between them and their followers is reduced, because followers can more easily see a leader's weaknesses.

As discussed below, however, in the presentation of Shamir's (1995) work, leader charisma can be evident both in socially distant and close situations. Shamir (p. 19) noted, "For many years, it was assumed that the concept of charisma was inapplicable to lower-level leaders or close leadership situations" (see Etzioni, 1961; Katz & Kahn, 1978). For example, Katz and Kahn (p. 546) noted explicitly "subordinates cannot build an aura of magic about [immediate leaders]. Day-to-day intimacy destroys illusion. But the [top-level] leader... is sufficiently distant from the membership to make a simplified and magical image possible."

Bogardus (1927) noted that, even in socially close situations, it is possible for leaders to maintain their influence if they are recognized for their unique expertise in a particular domain, or if their followers have a high degree of affection for them. We interpret affection in this context to refer to the identification of the followers with their leader, following our discussions about the charismatic effect. Indeed, Bogardus (p. 177) noted, "Great affection for a [leader] will cause [an individual] to remain a faithful follower despite gross weaknesses in the life and character of the leader." As noted by Bass (1990, p. 199), "Social distance between leaders and followers is not essential for the maintenance of the charismatic relationship." Rather, charisma is a function of ideal-based behavior and appeals to transcendent goals that arouse follower motives to pursue these goals as symbolized by the leader (see Bass, 1985; House, 1977).

Yagil (1998, p. 172) stated that followers view leader social (and physical) proximity as being beneficial, because proximity allows the leader to "deliver sensitive and individually tailored confidence-building communications [i.e., individualized consideration and inspirational motivation], which are probably more effective than messages addressed to the group as a whole." Yagil argued further that, apart from being more approachable, a leader that is physically close to followers has the opportunity to role model effective behaviors. Furthermore, following Aronson, Willerman, and Floyd (1966), Yagil argued that proximity may make the leader appear more human and fallible, thus, undergirding the identification effect. In fact, as demonstrated by Aronson et al., individuals to whom status was ascribed were viewed more favorably when committing a clumsy blunder of sorts as compared to individuals who are ascribed less status. However, Yagil also demonstrated that socially (and physically) distant leaders are still attributed charisma and have group-level effects as opposed to individual-level effects.

In his germinal article that related social distance to leadership, Shamir (1995) outlined important distinctions between socially close and socially distant charismatic leaders, but stressed that charisma may emerge in both case. Similarly, Yammarino (1994) argued that transformational leadership has a direct as well as an indirect effect on followers depending on leader hierarchy. In other words, transformational leadership or indeed other styles of leadership can work effectively even though the leader is not in direct contact with followers.

According to Shamir (1995), socially distant leaders will more readily invoke attributions of exceptional qualities because of organizational performance cues, image-building techniques, visionary behaviors, use of rhetoric, and articulation of ideology, which can create the charismatic effect and an idealized leader (we referred to this type of charisma as attributional charisma). Socially close leaders will mainly be ascribed charisma based on followers' observations of the leader's performance, and the personal examples the leaders set (we referred to this type of charisma as relational charisma).

Shamir (1995) also noted that the way trust develops in leaders is moderated by distance; socially close leaders can engage in transactional behavior, which, if mutually beneficial, serves to build trust and can undergird the charismatic effect (see Waldman & Yammarino, 1999). This effect is prevalent because through direct interactions "the leader's honesty, reliability, and trustworthiness can be directly manifested by the leader and assessed by close followers" (Shamir, p. 26). Furthermore, socially close leaders can empathize with followers and demonstrate individualized consideration—as opposed to socially distant leaders who do not have opportunities to practice such leader behaviors—which may further build trust in the leader. We refer to this type of trust as "close" trust. Distant leaders may develop trust as a function of attributions regarding the leader's ethical, moral, and altruistic orientations. Because distant leaders are more idealized, Shamir noted they are trusted unconditionally (i.e., blindly). We refer to this type of trust as "distant" trust.

As discussed, socially close or distant leadership does not preclude the identification of followers with leaders. The two types of leadership operate differently, but both types of leaders can be ascribed charisma. The distinction that Shamir (1995) made between socially close and distant leaders is also important in terms of determining the level at which leader outcomes are evident. Briefly, it appears that the outcomes of socially distant leaders would be theoretically evident is at the group level of analysis, because the leaders would tend to behave homogenously with followers; however, the outcomes of socially close leaders would theoretically be evident at the individual level of analysis, because the leaders would treat followers individually. We examine this issue in detail later in our discussion regarding levels of analysis.

Although Shamir (1995) did not precisely define what he meant by social distance, implicit in his explications is that socially distant leadership is prevalent in high-level leaders that are physically distant, who have infrequent and indirect contact with their followers, and whose followers cannot readily observe the day-to-day functioning of their leader (i.e., the leaders are inaccessible to followers). As will be evident later, this assumption may not be tenable because social distance can emerge regardless of leader level, leader proximity, and leader–follower contact. It thus becomes evident that Shamir's propositions do not include a provision for physically close leaders who maintain a high degree of social distance, but also frequent and direct contact with followers. Thus, perceived frequency of leader–follower interaction and physical distance must be included in a complete definition of distance.

3.1.2. Physical distance

We simply define physical distance as how far or how close followers are located from their leader. It is important that we differentiate physical distance from social distance, because some authors have suggested that the effects of these two constructs may operate in a similar manner (e.g., Howell & Hall-Merenda, 1999; Howell, Neufeld, & Avolio, 1998, 2002), and that social distance may imply that followers are physically distant from their leader (e.g., Shamir, 1995). Social distance and physical distance are distinct. For example, it is highly feasible for a leader to be proximally located, but to be socially distant. Furthermore, it is equally possible for a leader to be distally located, but to be socially close. Indeed, as acknowledged by Howell et al. (2002), theoretically, leadership could function differently in terms of the joint effects of social and physical distance.

Kerr and Jermier (1978, p. 396) noted that physical distance creates "circumstances in which effective leadership may be impossible." They noted further that physical distance neutralizes leadership behaviors, that is, "make it effectively *impossible* for relationship and/ or task-oriented leadership to make a difference" (p. 395). Howell et al. (1997, p. 389) noted that distance renders "many recommended leadership practices...nearly impossible to perform." Although in principle we agree that physical distance creates challenges for leaders and in certain situations may be negatively associated with leader outcomes, as we argue later, physical distance may indeed be a necessary requisite for effective leadership. We also believe that because of advances in technology, physical distance may not have the "neutralizing effect" that it did several decades ago when Kerr and Jermier proposed their theory.

Napier and Ferris (1993) argued that less functional distance should be associated with higher performance and follower satisfaction, and less subordinate withdrawal, which suggests that physical distance between followers and their leader should be minimized. Again, although in principle we agree with their position as it applies to certain situations, their proposition is limited given that Napier and Ferris dealt mostly with supervisory-level leadership. This criticism may also be directed to the majority of the findings below.

Regarding the effects of distance, Bass (1990) noted that distance has a negative effect on the quality of the exchange, and reduces the leader's influence. This effect may be prevalent because of the reduced richness of information transmission (see Daft & Lengel, 1984). Similarly, Bass (1998) proposed that physical distance may neutralize the effects of leaders as a result of reduced social interaction. It also becomes difficult for leaders to monitor outcomes, because leaders cannot directly observe follower behavior (Yagil, 1998). Consequently, administering timely rewards and punishments becomes challenging in these types of conditions. Podsakoff, Todor, Grover, and Huber (1984) demonstrated that use of noncontingent punishment increased along with an increase in physical distance. Podsakoff et al. further demonstrated that the use of contingent rewards was negatively related to physical distance. As argued by Howell and Hall-Merenda (1999), noncontingent management-by-exception may have more deleterious effects than does contingent management-by-exception. Furthermore, it may also be possible that lack of leader interaction may be perceived as the type of inactivity displayed by laissez-faire leaders, which as noted by Bass (1998) are the least effective leaders portrayed in the FRLT.

Physical distance may also make it difficult for a leader to monitor and rate follower performance. For example, Judge and Ferris (1993) demonstrated that the more opportunities leaders had to observe follower performance the higher they rated follower performance. Physical distance in the leader–follower relationship has been found to be positively related to perceptions of group role conflict and negatively related to group altruism (Podsakoff, MacKenzie, & Bommer, 1996a, 1996b). In their meta-analysis, Podsakoff et al. (1996b) also demonstrated that physical distance negatively impacted follower performance, conscientiousness, and civic virtue. Similarly, Burrows, Munday, Tunnell, and Seay (1996) found that physically distant leaders negatively impacted follower satisfaction. However, in contrast to the above findings, Howell et al. (1998, p. 29) found that distance strengthened the relation between charismatic leadership (i.e., idealized influence) and organizational performance, and stated, "physical proximity between charismatic leaders and followers appears to reduce the potency of the leader's visionary message." Because Howell et al. used an older version of the Multifactor Leadership Questionnaire, which did not draw a fine line between behavioral and attributional charisma, it is difficult to determine the role of the idealized influence components in these results.

Howell and Hall-Merenda (1999) argued that a key contextual moderator of the quality of leader follower relationships is physical distance. Howell and Hall-Merenda gathered measures of LMX, transformational leadership, contingent-reward leadership, management-by-exception active and management-by-exception passive, and rated performance of followers, and found that physical distance moderated the effectiveness of leadership behaviors. Specifically, transformational leadership was significantly more related to performance in close than in distant conditions (this finding was replicated by Howell et al., 2002), whereas contingent reward leadership was significantly more related to follower performance in distant than in close conditions. They also found that active management-by-exception was significantly related to performance in close but not distant leader conditions, and that passive management-by-exception was more negatively related to performance in close rather than in distant conditions. Interestingly, the relation between LMX and follower performance was not moderated by physical distance, which contradicts previous findings and theorizing that physical distance is detrimental to leader–follower relations and leader outcomes.

The impact of transformational leadership in the above study cannot be well understood because the transformational leadership items were aggregated across scales to form one overall measure of transformational leadership. As discussed previously, it is theoretically possible that the type of charisma ascribed to leaders and the types of full-range behaviors leaders can use (e.g., individualized consideration) are moderated by leader distance. Furthermore, it may be possible that the distant leaders in their sample were not rated highly in charisma, and close leaders were not rated highly on individualized consideration. The scale aggregations thus limit the interpretations we can make from these results.

In all, it appears that physical distance acts as a negative moderator on leadership outcomes. However, empirical results demonstrate that LMX is related to leader outcomes regardless of physical distance suggesting that the neutralizing effect of distance can be overcome. Furthermore, charismatic leadership (i.e., idealized influence in general) appears to have more of an impact when leader–follower physical distance is large.

3.1.3. Perceived frequency of leader–follower interaction

Following Napier and Ferris (1993), the third dimension of distance we propose is perceived leader–follower interaction frequency. This dimension is defined as the perceived degree to which leaders interact with their followers. Although this dimension does not connote "distance" of sorts, it directly impacts how "close" a leader may seem to a follower. In other words, followers who have frequent interactions with their leader have a "closer" relationship with their leader than followers who have infrequent interactions with their leader. This dimension is independent of social and physical distance. Although physical distance may make it more likely that leader–follower contact is infrequent, distance does not cause infrequent leader–follower contact. For example, it is theoretically possible that a proximally located leader maintains infrequent contact with followers. Furthermore, with the aid of technology, it is also possible that a distally located leader maintains frequent contact with followers.

A distinction that must also be made here too is that frequency of interaction does not necessarily imply good leader–member exchanges, as suggested by LMX theory. Although we would intuitively expect a relation, as suggested by House (1971), House and Dessler (1994), House and Mitchell (1974), and Kerr and Jermier (1978), the optimal degree of leader–follower interaction and follower satisfaction in a leader is contingent on situational variables. In certain situations (e.g., task ambiguity), followers would require frequent task or socioemotional interaction with their leader, whereas in other situations they may require less frequent interaction with their leader. Frequency of interaction, therefore, is related to the degree of direction and feedback followers will receive and seek. For instance, Ashford and Cummings (1985) noted that followers initiate feedback-seeking behaviors, especially when ambiguities regarding roles and tasks are presented in the working environment, or if followers are newly tenured and inexperienced.

Thus, frequency of interaction can operate independently of physical and social distance and contributes directly to follower perceptions of total leader distance. Higher frequency of interaction will be associated with leader closeness, whereas lower frequency of interaction will be associated with leader distance. Quality of interaction may not necessarily be related to quantity of interaction. Furthermore, the need for frequency of interaction will depend on contextual factors, as we discuss later.

Proposition 4: *Leader–follower physical distance, perceived social distance, and perceived interaction frequency are independent, measurable dimensions each describing an element of leader distance.*

3.2. Typologies of distant leadership

Apart from Shamir and Ben-Ari (1999) who briefly discussed the implications of socially and physically distant leadership, we did not locate any studies that addressed the combined nature of leader distance as a function of social and physical distance. By combined nature, we mean "the multidimensional constellation of conceptually distinct characteristics [in our case the three distance dimensions] that commonly occur together" (Meyer, Tsui, & Hinnings, 1993, p. 1175). That is, the three distance dimensions (i.e., leader–follower physical distance, perceived social distance, and perceived interaction frequency) are conceptually independent and, theoretically, can be found to occur concurrently in varying degrees.

688   *J. Antonakis, L. Atwater / The Leadership Quarterly 13 (2002) 673–704*

According to Meyer et al. (1993), what can be termed as the "configurational approach" to studying organizational, group, and individual-level phenomena typically leads to clusters of configurations or typologies that can be conceptually (e.g., Smith & Foti, 1998) or empirically derived (e.g., Jermier, Slocum, Fry, & Gaines, 1991). The typology— in this case, the "distance style" adopted by the leader—is useful as a unit of analysis because the variables of which it is comprised cannot be studied alone or additively (Meyer et al., 1993; Smith & Foti, 1998). Smith and Foti argued that leaders should be classified based on patterns of variables and not simply by the variables in isolation of each other. Smith and Foti classified leaders on three dispositional variables (i.e., dominance, self-efficacy, and intelligence) and used a median split to derive eight "multivariable patterns." Similarly, based on the occurrence of either a high or low value of the three distance dimensions, we conceptually identified eight typologies of distant leadership. Thus, data on the distance dimensions could be gathered on leaders, who could then be categorized according to one of the eight typologies. The data of leaders in the respective typologies could then be linked to various intermediate or dependent outcomes.

Where possible, we provide examples below of leaders that that fit our eight labels of leader distance. We have also named the typologies for ease of reference. Our descriptions of the eight typologies of leader distance below are not normative; that is, a particular typology is not necessarily better than another. The success of the type of distant leadership employed by the leader will depend on situational moderators (discussed later). The total permissible (i.e., normative) distance in the leader–follower relation will depend on the context. For example, Uhl-Bien et al. (2000) noted that conditions that characterize high leader–follower interdependence theoretically require "close" LMX relations, whereas low leader–follower interdependence could theoretically be accompanied by "distant" LMX relations.

Furthermore, it is possible that two individuals fit a particular typology, but that one leader is successful and the other is not. Some of the leaders that we present below were either authentic (e.g., F.D. Roosevelt) or inauthentic (e.g., Hitler). Also, it is possible that any of the major classes of leadership comprising the FRLT (i.e., transformational, instrumental, transactional, and laissez-faire leadership) can be used to describe the leadership styles of leaders within any of the eight typologies.

The eight typologies of distance include the following (note: H = high, L = low, P = physical distance, S = perceived social distance, and F = perceived leader–follower interaction frequency):

1. *Proximal leadership ($P = L$, $S = L$, $F = H$).* Kegan's (1987) portrayal of Alexander the Great is a good example of the proximal leader who commanded great respect and loyalty from his followers. Although Alexander was a hierarchically high leader, he led by example, maintained close contact with his soldiers, treated them as equals, led them personally into battle, and fought shoulder-to-shoulder with his soldiers, many of whom he knew personally. He made a point of personally communicating with his troops at critical times, for example, by repeating his battle speech so that all his troops could personally hear his intent.
2. *Hands-off leadership ($P = L$, $S = L$, $F = L$).* These leaders are physically and socially close but maintain infrequent contact with their followers. An example is the type leader that is

accessible to followers and can speak intimately with followers, but does not interact frequently with followers as a result of "leader substitutes," that exist in the organization (e.g., Howell, Bowen, Dorfman, & Kerr, 1990).

3. *Virtually close leadership (P=H, S=L, F=H)*. This type of leader is what Avolio, Kahai, and Dodge (2001) referred to as an "e-leader." Although operating in a low technology epoch, Ulysses Grant fits our label of this type of leader. According to Kegan (1987), Grant maintained frequent contact with his subordinates and empathized with them. Grant, though, hated the site of blood and battle, was always distant from the front lines, and led from behind. As such, he made frequent use of technology—dispatch and telegraph—to keep in touch with his subordinates and to be informed of battle developments. Grant was modest and very courteous to subordinates and considered his subordinates as equals. According to Kegan, Grant "often ate more simply than his staff" (p. 204), and "his accustomed outfit was a private's coat, on which he pinned his general's stars" (p. 206).

4. *Socially distant leadership (P=L, S=H, F=H)*. The Duke of Wellington is a good example of a socially distant leader. Kegan (1987) described Wellington as maintaining frequent contact with his soldiers, and commanding from close at hand. However, he was "icy, distant, loftily contemptuous, the voice of someone speaking across an unbridgeable gap set between him and the groundlings.... Wellington really did not seem to love his soldiers, or perhaps even to know them" (p. 127). Wellington maintained a stiff upper lip, and was always well composed. He was "aloof and supervisory in bivouacs or on the line of march" (Kegan, 1987, p. 155).

5. *Virtually distant leadership (P=H, S=H, F=H)*. These types of leaders, physically and socially distant, but with heavy reliance on technology, are able to maintain frequent contact with followers. As a description of the "digitized" military of the future, Shamir and Ben-Ari (1999) referred to this type of leadership as teleleadership, that "de-emphasizes the social and human elements... and presents a very 'cold' prototype of a technical manager in place of a... leader" (p. 17).

6. *Avuncular leadership (P=H, S=L, F=L)*. Although a high-level, physically distant political figure, F.D. Roosevelt typified the avuncular leader; he championed the cause of the commoners, paid attention to them (e.g., through town meetings), emphasized social equality, used colloquial and folksy phrases, and appeared to be warm hearted (Willner, 1984). In other words, he created the impression of being socially close to common citizens even though he did not interact often with them.

7. *Manor house leadership (P=L, S=H, F=L)*. An example of this type of leader is Waldman and Yammarino's (1999) description of a typical CEO, who, although he or she may be proximally located with followers, is socially distant from them and generally interacts with followers indirectly (and with subordinate leaders directly).[1] These types of

---

[1] Waldman and Yammarino did not specifically address physical proximity; however, our explanation of manor house leaders rests on the assumption that the leader is physically co-located, as with many cases of high-level strategic leaders. In the event that a strategic-level leader is distally located, the befitting label becomes distal leadership, which, as discussed from a levels-of-analysis perspective, has the same outcome as manor house leadership.

leaders do not, and cannot, know their followers intimately, nor do they share personal information about themselves with their followers.
8. *Distal leadership (P=H, S=H, F=L).* Adolf Hitler is a good example of a distal leader. Kegan (1987) portrayed Hitler being physically and socially distant from his troops. Contact with his soldiers was infrequent and staged. He was disinvolved from them, was aloof, and primarily interacted with his subordinate leaders.

The type of distance perceived by a follower will thus be a function of how the leadership style of the leader is perceived. For example, Hede and Wear (1996) demonstrated that the transformational or transactional leadership styles of high-level political leaders varied, depending on the vantage point from which the leader was observed (i.e., how close or distant the follower is from the leader). This suggests that (a) by virtue of their contextualized (i.e., tacit) knowledge, (i.e., implicit knowledge derived experientially, see Antonakis, Hedlund, Pretz, & Sternberg, 2002), leaders can alternate from being distant to close, depending on situational requirements; (b) close and distant followers perceive the leader differently (as discussed previously); or (c) both (a) and (b). Thus, subordinate leaders of a CEO may see the CEO as a proximal leader, because the CEO may be physically and socially close to them, and maintain a high degree of leader–follower interaction. However, low-level, indirect followers may see the CEO as a manor house or distal leader, depending on the physical location of the CEO. Therefore, in describing the typologies of distant leadership above, we labeled Grant as a virtually close leader in terms of his interaction with his direct subordinate leaders. However, nonimmediate followers of Grant would have perceived him as an avuncular leader, as could be the case for other high-level leaders.

3.3. Levels of analysis and distance

Bass and Avolio (1993) argued that the behaviors described in the FRLT can impact three levels of analysis: (a) the microlevel, that is, the impact of leadership on immediate followers; (b) the macrolevel, that is, the impact of leadership on organizations; and (c) metalevel, that is, the impact of leadership on large social systems. However, not much research has uncovered the level of analysis at which the leadership phenomenon may operate. As mentioned by Waldman and Yammarino (1999, p. 266), the confusion surrounding leader outcomes has stemmed because "organizational behavior theorists generally have confined leadership and its effects to the individual, dyadic, or small group levels of analysis." Following Klein, Dansereau, and Hall (1994), Waldman and Yammarino argued that leader outcomes may be evident across various levels of analysis, measurement, and management, depending on leader hierarchical level. Waldman and Yammarino argued that levels of analysis refer to the level at which theoretical constructs are being measured. For example, leader behavior can be viewed at the individual level but may impact individual, group, or organizational levels of analysis. They referred to levels of measurement reflecting the precision of measurement required to ensure that the effects operate at the assumed level. Finally, levels of management refer to hierarchical levels ranging from supervisory level to strategic leadership.

J. Antonakis, L. Atwater / The Leadership Quarterly 13 (2002) 673–704 691

Klein and House (1998) argued that charismatic leadership has an individual and group level effect. They stated further that the more charismatic leaders treat the followers homogenously, the more the effects of charisma will be evident on a group level. Following Howell and Shamir (1998), it is apparent that they failed to make a distinction between hierarchical leadership levels, or to take social distance into consideration, which could explain why the outcomes of leadership could vary from the individual to the group level of analysis.

Leader hierarchical level is a defining element implicating the level of analysis at which leader outcomes will be evident. Although leader hierarchical level may not necessarily cause leader distance (i.e., a high-level leader could interact individually with followers and reduce social distance, as with Alexander the Great), we would expect a moderate correlation between leader distance and leader hierarchy. For instance, a collective-level impact would be more prevalent in leaders who primarily have interactions with followers at the group level (e.g., socially and virtually distant leaders), or where hierarchical level and physical distance (i.e., structural organizational characteristics) may prevent high-level leaders from interacting individually and frequently with low-level followers (e.g., avuncular, manor house, and distal leaders). However, an individual level impact would be more prevalent in leaders who primarily interact with followers at the individual level (e.g., proximal, "hands-off," and virtually close leadership).

Yagil (1998), for example, theorized and found that socially (and physically) distant leaders impacted group-level efficacy more than they did individual-level efficacy, because socially distant leaders have more information on the group than the individuals comprising the group. Yagil also demonstrated that socially (and physically) close leaders have an impact on individual-level efficacy because they custom-design their behaviors towards individual followers. Thus, our understanding of leader distance necessitates understanding the level of analysis at which leader outcomes should be measured.

Following the above discussions, and for the development of a parsimonious model, we grouped the eight typologies of distance into three broad classes, depending on the level of analysis at which the leader's behavior is theoretically evident. Class 1 comprises proximal, "hands off," and virtually close leadership. These types of leaders are socially close to followers and, because of their close physical proximity or high frequency of contact, have individualized and direct interactions with followers. Leader outcomes are visible at the individual level of analysis. Class 2 comprises socially and virtually distant leaders. Here, leadership operates at the group level because of leader social (and physical) distance. Class 3 comprises avuncular, manor house, and distal leadership. The primary commonality in this case is that leaders cannot maintain frequent and direct interaction with followers, and are either socially and/or physically distant. Depending on the leaders' hierarchical level, Class 3 leaders will either (a) have individual or group-level interaction with subordinate leaders who emulate the leader's behavior and, in turn, interact with followers on an individual or group level; or (b) they will interact homogenously at the group level with followers; or (c) both (a) and (b). The role-modeling of the active components of a leader's behavior (i.e., transformational and constructive transactional leadership) has been referred to as the "cascading effect" as demonstrated empirically by Bass, Waldman, Avolio, and Bebb (1987) (for further

692   *J. Antonakis, L. Atwater / The Leadership Quarterly 13 (2002) 673–704*

discussion on the cascading effect, see Klein & House, 1998; Rainey & Watson, 1996; Shamir et al., 1993; Shamir, Zakay, Brainin, & Popper, 2000; Yammarino, 1994).

Proposition 5: *The level of analysis at which the effect of leadership is evident will vary as a function of leader–follower distance.*

Proposition 6: *Outcomes of Class 2 leaders on immediate followers or of Class 3 leaders on indirect followers will be more evident at the group level of analysis than at the individual level of analysis.*

Proposition 7: *Outcomes of Class 1 leaders on immediate followers will be more evident at the individual level of analysis than at the group level of analysis.*

Proposition 8: *Subordinate leaders of active leaders will role-model their leaders' behaviors.*

3.4. Antecedents of the emergence of leader distance

In this section, we review contextual variables that theoretically cause the dimensions of leader distance to emerge. Whether the actual leader distance that is prevalent in a certain context is equal to follower's expectations of how much distance a leader should maintain depends on whether the leader–follower distance is complementary to the contextual condition in which leadership is viewed. In other words, the behavior of a leader is successful to followers if the behavior matches followers' expected leader prototypes (see Lord, Foti, & De Vader, 1984).

Apart from the structural characteristics of the organization (e.g., the physical design of the organization and physical layout of work areas) that may affect the degree of physical distance that emerges (Napier & Ferris, 1993), we describe four factors that could theoretically affect the degree to which the three distance dimensions could emerge. We present each of the factors separately; however, it is probable that the factors could interact in determining total leader distance.

3.4.1. Span of control

The leaders' span of control could theoretically affect the degree of interaction with followers (Napier & Ferris, 1993). For instance, Judge and Ferris (1993) argued that a large span of control is associated with less leader–follower contact, because it theoretically becomes increasingly difficult for the leader to spend more time with his/her followers. According to Bass (1998), when leaders supervise a greater number of followers, they may be obliged to use more management-by-exception behaviors, which is a less active form of leadership than is transformational or constructive transactional leadership. Furthermore, a large span of control could be associated with larger social distance, because the leader would treat followers more homogenously and with less individualized attention.

Proposition 9: *Span of leader control will be negatively associated with leader–follower interaction and positively associated with social distance.*

3.4.2. Task characteristics and follower abilities

Based on the propositions of House's (1971) path-goal theory, the degree of leader–follower interaction—whether directive or developmentally centered—is contingent on task characteristics and follower abilities. Howell et al. (1997) made a similar point. House and Mitchell (1974, p. 88) noted, "when goals and paths to desired goals are apparent because of the routine nature of the task, clear group norms or objective controls of the formal authority systems, attempts by the leader to clarify paths and goals will be both redundant and seen by subordinates as imposing unnecessary close control." House and Mitchell also noted "Where the subordinate's perceived ability is high, [leader directiveness and coaching behavior] is likely to have little positive effect on the motivation of the subordinate and to be perceived as excessively close control" (p. 87). For example, Cardinal and Hatfield (2000) demonstrated that research facilities of pharmaceutical companies were more innovative when distally located from corporate headquarters, because top management did not meddle in the work of highly qualified research scientists.

Proposition 10: *High follower ability and clear follower task demands will be negatively associated with perceived leader–follower interaction frequency.*

3.4.3. National and organizational culture

As discussed before, followers accept leaders as a function of followers' perceptions of the leaders' behaviors, and whether these behaviors match the followers' expected leader prototypes in certain contexts. Context must therefore be taken into consideration because it is likely that implicit leader prototypes will vary depending on cultural context (Gerstner & Day, 1994; Lord, Brown, Harvey, & Hall, 2001). As noted by House, Wright, and Aditya (1997, p. 600), implicit theories allow members of a common group to "constrain, moderate, or facilitate the exercise of leadership, the acceptance of leaders, and the perception of leaders as influential, acceptable, and effective." Therefore, individuals (and leaders) that are bound together by a common culture will have similar implicit notions of how leaders should behave.

Hofstede (1980, p. 25) defined culture to be "the collective programming of the mind which distinguishes the members of one human group from another." He offered a similar definition of organizational culture, which he defined as being "the collective programming of the mind which distinguishes the members of one organization from another," including the history of the organization, its rites and rituals (pp. 179–180). Because national and organizational culture operate in a similar manner in terms of how they influence individuals, and because organizational culture is in part a function of national culture (e.g., see Bochner & Hesketh, 1994; Hofstede, 1980; Offermann & Hellmann, 1997; Pavett & Morris, 1995; Smith, Dugan, & Trompenaars, 1996; van Muijen & Koopman, 1994), below we will describe only how national culture may affect the degree to which leader distance is prevalent in the organization.

Den Hartog, House, Hanges, Ruiz-Quintanilla, and Dorfman (1999) found that various elements of transformational/charismatic leadership were perceived as effective across 62 cultures. Following Bass (1997), Antonakis and House (in press) argued that transformational and transactional leadership may indeed be universal; however, the manner in which directive and participative leader behaviors are enacted will vary by culture, and will depend in part, on PD and collectivism (see Hofstede, 1980, 1991). Power Distance (PD) refers to how society deals with and views inequalities in power distribution among the members of society. Inequalities in societies can occur in terms of social status, prestige, power, and rights. Hofstede's definition of PD thus appears to largely parallel our definition of social distance. Hofstede found that organizations of high PD cultures tended to be more centralized and relied on more hierarchical levels than did organizations in low PD cultures. Also, high PD leaders were more autocratic and directive than were low PD leaders.

Individualism is the degree to which members of a group are individualistic in their goals and objectives in life. Collectivism refers to the extent that individual goals are more aligned with those of the collectivity (Hofstede, 1980, 1991). Because of the high correlation between PD and collectivism ($r=.76$; Hofstede, 1980, p. 221), from a practical perspective, Triandis (1993) argued that the two dimensions could be assumed to have a common effect. Triandis stated that collectivist societies value hierarchy, whereas individualists value autonomy. The former value collective goals and interdependency, whereas the latter value individual goals and independence. Thus, it follows that in high power-distance/collectivist societies, leaders are more autocratic, directive, and inaccessible, and organizations are more mechanistic and hierarchically tall. Low PD cultures should, however, support more democratic, participative, and accessible leaders, and more organic and flat organizational structures (e.g., see Bakhtari, 1995; Bochner & Hesketh, 1994; Javidan & House, 2001; Mead, 1967; Offermann & Hellmann, 1997; Pavett & Morris, 1995; Yammarino & Jung, 1998).

In terms of the level of analysis at which the effect of leadership will be evident, and following the above reasoning, Yammarino and Jung (1998, p. 54) proposed that high PD cultures "adopt a person–group (leader–followers) model—an independent higher status person of power (leader) essentially directs through equal treatment a group of loyal followers who accept this status difference." In other words, the effect of leadership is evident at the group level of analysis resulting from the homogenous behavior of leaders towards followers. Yammarino and Jung (p. 54) argued that low PD cultures would value leader–follower relationships that are "dyadic and balanced... because they are not predicated on unequal or differing power status." In other words, given the individualized contact between leaders and their followers, the effect of leadership is evident at the individual level of analysis.

Following the above discussion, leaders in high PD and collectivist societies would therefore maintain a higher degree of social distance with their followers and treat them more homogenously. Moreover, the level of analysis at which leader outcomes will be visible is at the group level of analysis. Leaders in low PD and individualistic societies would maintain a lower degree of social distance with their followers and treat followers individually. Thus, the level of analysis at which leader outcomes will be visible is at the individual level of analysis.

Proposition 11: *High PD (and collectivism) will be positively associated with high social distance.*

Proposition 12: *In high PD (and collectivist) cultures, the level of analysis at which leadership outcomes will be evident is at the group level of analysis.*

Proposition 13: *In low PD (and individualist) cultures, the level of analysis at which leadership outcomes will be evident is at the individual level of analysis.*

3.4.4. Leader and follower implicit motives

Implicit (nonconscious) motives refer to conditions that individuals wish to bring about or avoid (Winter, John, Stewart, Klohnen, & Duncan, 1998). Three types of implicit motives guide behavior (McClelland, 1975): (a) need for power, which refers to the degree to which individuals wish to influence or have an impact on other individuals or social systems; (b) need for achievement, which refers the degree to which individuals wish to surpass standards of performance and to achieve excellence; and (c) need for affiliation, which refers to the degree to which individuals wish be friendly with others and their desire to be affiliated with a social group. Leader and follower motives could theoretically affect the distance that is prevalent in leader–follower relations. Following Howell et al. (2002), it is possible that the amount of distance tolerated or desired by leaders may be linked to their motive patterns.

Leaders with a high need for affiliation would theoretically strive to minimize social distance with followers. Because "someone who is eager for power is *less* likely to be friendly with others," McClelland (1975, p. 322) argued that need for power is negatively correlated with need for affiliation. Thus, leaders with a high need for power would probably be socially distant from their followers. Achievement-oriented leaders have been found to be effective in small task-oriented groups and at low levels of management (Litwin & Stringer, 1968; McClelland, 1962; McClelland & Boyatzis, 1982) and would tend to micromanage (Winter, 2002). Thus, we would expect achievement-oriented leaders to maintain high frequency of contact with followers.

As regards follower motives, leader behavior is viewed as satisfactory to followers if the behavior is instrumental to follower satisfaction or success (House & Dessler, 1994). Thus, an element of follower satisfaction related to leadership may be the fulfillment of implicit follower motives, because followers "with high needs for affiliation and social approval would see friendly, considerate leader behavior as an immediate source of satisfaction" (House & Dessler, 1994, p. 31). Thus, these types of followers would expect low social distance from their leader. It would follow that leaders, would in turn, attempt to satisfy follower expectations by behaving more or less socially close or distant with followers.

Proposition 14: *High need for power leaders will maintain greater social distance from followers than will low need for power leaders.*

Proposition 15: *High need for affiliation leaders will maintain less social distance from followers than will low need for affiliation leaders.*

Proposition 16: *High need for achievement leaders will maintain higher interaction frequency with followers than will low need for achievement leaders.*

696   *J. Antonakis, L. Atwater / The Leadership Quarterly 13 (2002) 673–704*

Proposition 17: *High need for affiliation followers would expect their leaders to act less socially distant than would low need for affiliation followers.*

4. A model of leader distance

Based on Waldman and Yammarino's (1999) model describing the socially close and distant leadership of high-level (CEO) leaders, and following our propositions, we have developed an integrated cross-level model of leader distance (see Fig. 1). Causal relations in solid-line arrows follow our propositions and are labeled according to the relevant proposition. As suggested in the model, the typology of leader distance that emerges is associated with leader behavior affecting the individual and/or group level of analysis. The level at which leader outcomes are evident determines how the leader is legitimized and the type of charisma that will emerge. The latter, in turn, leads to follower identification with (and trust in) the leader. The model is based on the assumptions that the leadership presented in all cases is effective and authentic (see Avolio, 1999; Bass, 1998), and that the role-modeling behaviors of subordinate leaders support and emulate the behaviors of the leader.

As discussed before, what constitutes a follower is important in terms of which typology is used to describe a leader. For example, indirect followers may see the leader as a distal leader; however, direct followers may see the leader as a proximal leader. Thus, in the case of Class 3 leaders, leader outcomes may be evident at the individual level of analysis (i.e., on subordinate leaders, following Proposition 7) or at the group level of analysis (i.e., on subordinate leaders or on indirect followers, following Proposition 6). Thus, the direct effect of leaders on subordinate leaders could also be considered in the model, linking subordinate leader interaction with direct evaluation of the leader (as per Proposition 2a) or with attributions of the leader (as per Proposition 3a), as depicted with the two dotted-lined arrows in the center of the figure. However, for simplicity, we will exclude leader outcomes on subordinate leaders.

As suggested in the model, the leader's influence flows from the three following sources: (a) from individual-level relations that the leader has with immediate followers as with Class 1 leaders; (b) from individual or group-level relations that the subordinate leaders have with followers, resulting from the cascading effect leader behaviors have on distant followers through the leader's subordinate leaders, as with Class 3 hierarchically high level leaders; (c) from group-level relations that the leader has with followers as with Classes 2 and 3 leaders.

Followers who can directly evaluate a leader's behaviors and performance will accept the leader based on their direct observations and intimate knowledge of the leader. Because the leader has an effect at the individual level of analysis, as a result of the leader's relational charisma, self-concepts will be implicated at the individual level, leading to identification with, and "close" trust in, the leader.

Attributional charisma will emerge from attributions of the leader or subordinate leaders that followers make based on the leaders' homogenous behaviors towards followers, the impression management techniques they use, and how followers perceive the leader's socialized charisma. Because the leader has an effect at the group level of analysis, self-concepts will be implicated at the collective level leading to social identification and identification with, and "distant" trust in, the leader.

Finally, as has been established empirically, followers of charismatic leaders will exert more effort in ensuring that organizational goals are realized than will followers of noncharismatic leaders (see Avolio, 1999; Bass, 1990, 1998 for reviews). However, this effort needs to be coordinated. According to Katz and Kahn (1978), the roles of leaders are to ensure the systemic functioning of their organizations by synthesizing and integrating its human resources, and by compensating for deficiencies in the system and changes in the environment.

Similarly, Waldman and Yammarino (1999) argued that due to the inherent conflicting nature of certain organizational processes, the role of top-level leaders is to use their vision and values to ensure that organizational resources are used to achieve the organization's intended objectives. The strategic coordination function of top-level leaders is integral to coordinated organizational effectiveness; however, efforts that lead to organizational effectiveness are not restricted to top-level leaders and can be evident throughout the hierarchy of the organization. At lower hierarchical levels, values and vision also play a role, but different instrumental leader behaviors (e.g., path-goal facilitation and outcome monitoring) will contribute to organizational performance (Antonakis & House, in press).

5. Discussion

The central thesis of this article was that total leader distance plays an important role in explaining the leadership influencing process and how trust and identification in the leader develop. Our intention was to build on previous frameworks that used distance as a central theoretical concept. Our study was mainly explanatory; we discussed how intermediate outcomes of leadership were a function of total leader distance, and how leaders' behaviors may affect various levels of analysis. Our intention was to demonstrate that functional distance, as defined by Napier and Ferris (1993), is not a necessary condition for effective leadership. Rather, leader success is contingent on actively managing the degree of distance leaders maintain from followers, depending on contextual factors. That is, leader–follower distance can contribute to or detract from leader effectiveness.

Beyond the theoretical considerations in our article there are practical implications of physical distance that we discuss briefly below. As noted by Howell et al. (1997), physical distance in organizations will become increasingly prevalent as firms internationalize, and because of the increase in amount of service–sector employees working from home. Our closing remarks will thus focus on the implications of physical distance on leaders. As discussed previously, physical distance creates conditions that may not be conducive for leadership because it makes it difficult for leaders and followers to interact with each other. However, advances in communications technology can facilitate communication that occurs between leaders and followers that previously was hindered by physical distance. Situations in which the leader is physically distant from followers who require frequent interaction with the leader necessitates that either the leader can deliver the interaction that followers require using communications technology or that there are adequate substitutes for leadership that can allow followers to be effective without the leader. For example, Howell et al. (1997) noted that feedback generated by information technology systems and closely knit teams can provide appropriate substitutes for leadership.

Virtual communication may bring several advantages and disadvantages. Avolio, Kahai, Dumdum, and Sivasubramaniam (2001, p. 337) noted that modern technologies "have enabled organizations to rapidly form teams that are not restricted by geography, time, or organizational boundaries." Avolio et al. (2001) also argued that virtual leaders, whose communication is mediated by electronic means, can create conditions which induce followers to transcend their self-interest for the good of the group. We have some evidence that leadership, and in particular certain styles of leadership (e.g., transformational leadership), can have an impact on followers when leader–follower interaction is mediated by technology, and that individuals can perceive differences in leadership styles in computer-mediated communication environments (e.g., Kahai, Sosik, & Avolio, 1997; Sosik, 1997; Sosik, Avolio, & Kahai, 1997; Sosik, Avolio, Kahai, & Jung, 1998).

Another advantage of technology-mediated environments using asynchronous communication systems (e.g., electronic brainstorming) is that it "frees participants from the social rules typically associated with face-to-face communication (e.g., waiting for someone to finish speaking before you speak), as well as cognitive constraints (e.g., thinking along narrow lines)" (Kahai et al., 1997, p. 125). Furthermore, Weisband and Atwater (1999) stated that virtual communication may eliminate affect bias of others because individuals lack cues and information associated with face-to-face interactions.

However, virtual leader–follower contexts will create conditions that are increasingly challenging for leaders to manage. Shamir (1999) noted that it is unclear whether individuals can identify with and trust virtual leaders due to the cold, deemphasized social and human context of interaction in such situations. As noted by Daft and Lengel (1984), the medium of information (e.g., face-to-face, telephone, etc.) affects the richness of information such that highly complex problems are best understood by transmitting information using very rich information media (e.g., face-to-face). Information richness also affects how a message is delivered. For example, Awamleh and Gardner (1999) suggested that, although vision content plays a role in promoting a better image of the leader and charismatic attributions that followers make of the leader, the way in which a leader delivers his or her vision has a greater impact on follower perceptions than does the actual content of the message and other organizational performance cues. They noted further "a weak delivery acts like 'noise' which undermines the impact of the leader's speech, no matter how inspirational its content may be" (p. 360). Thus, communicating at a distance may make it especially difficult for leaders to be inspirational, unless followers can see and hear the leader. Indeed, Hitler disliked using the telephone because he felt that it "minimized his magnetism" (Kegan, 1987, p. 327).

Shamir and Ben-Ari (1999) further noted that it would be very difficult for virtually distant leaders to inspire confidence in followers especially through the display of exemplary acts,

J. Antonakis, L. Atwater / The Leadership Quarterly 13 (2002) 673–704 699

role modeling, or other symbolic gestures. Sosik, Avolio, and Kahai (1997) made a similar point and stated that nonverbal cues, which characterize an important element of charismatic leadership would be restricted if leaders–follower interaction was mediated solely by written electronic means. Also, as indicated by Weisband and Atwater (1999) social interactions in virtual teams typically lack nonverbal cues, and thus the degree to which interpersonal relations may develop between individuals is reduced.

Interactions that occur in virtual team contexts also complicate how trust may be developed. As we discussed previously, whether trust emerges, and what type of trust that emerges depends on various factors. Jarvenpaa and Leidner (1999) argued that trust between organizational players in virtual teams (i.e., geographically displaced teams that have been assembled for short-term projects) does not operate in the same manner virtually as it does in face-to-face encounters. In virtual settings, trust has more of a temporary nature and needs to be formed swiftly, that is, "members act as if trust is present from the start" (Jarvenpaa, Knoll, & Leider, 1998, p. 56).

Thus, identifying responsibilities of team members, maintaining frequent contact, and promoting team-related aims may lead to increased trust (Jarvenpaa & Leider, 1999), suggesting that the role of a leader in a virtual team context plays an important role. Furthermore, Jarvenpaa et al. (1998, p. 32) argued that because virtual team members may not know each other, and because of communication channels that are impersonal (e.g., e-mail), "Trust in a virtual-team context might therefore be more strongly related to ability and integrity, and less to benevolence." They suggest the use of team exercises to increase perception of ability and integrity (but also of benevolence), by the exchange of information early in the collaboration.

In conclusion, we hope that leader distance will be considered in future theoretical frameworks and that empirical work will result, in part, from our review. The distance that a leader maintains from followers appears to be a defining element of the leadership influencing process. It is our hope that we have brought the concept of leader distance a little closer.

Acknowledgements

We would like to thank Jerry Hunt, LQ Senior Editor, for his helpful comments and encouragement. We are also grateful for the feedback of the LQ 2002 Symposium Distinguished Scholar Panel, participating LQ Editors, and attendees.

References

Antonakis, J. (2001). The validity of the transformational, transactional, and laissez-faire leadership model as measured by the Multifactor Leadership Questionnaire (MLQ5X). *Dissertation Abstracts International*. University Microfilms No. 3000380.

Antonakis, J., Hedlund, J., Pretz, J. E., & Sternberg, R. J. (2002). *Exploring the nature and acquisition of tacit knowledge for military leadership*. Army Research Institute for the Behavioral and Social Sciences. Research Note 2002-04, Alexandria, VA.

700   *J. Antonakis, L. Atwater / The Leadership Quarterly 13 (2002) 673–704*

Antonakis, J., & House, R. J. (2002). A reformulated full-range leadership theory. Manuscript in preparation.

Antonakis, J., & House, R. J. (in press). An analysis of the full-range leadership theory: the way forward. In B. J. Avolio & F. J. Yammarino (Eds.), *Transformational and charismatic leadership: the road ahead.* Oxford, UK: Elsevier Science.

Aronson, E., Willerman, B., & Floyd, J. (1966). The effect of pratfall on increasing interpersonal attractiveness. *Psychonomic Science, 4*(6), 227–228.

Ashford, S. J., & Cummings, L. L. (1985). Proactive feedback seeking: the instrumental use of the information environment. *Journal of Occupational Psychology, 58,* 67–79.

Ashforth, B. E., & Mael, F. (1989). Social identity theory and the organization. *Academy of Management Review, 14*(1), 20–39.

Avolio, B. J. (1999). *Full leadership development: building the vital forces in organizations.* Thousand Oaks, CA: Sage Publications.

Avolio, B. J., Kahai, S., & Dodge, G. E. (2001). E-leadership: implications for theory, research, and practice. *Leadership Quarterly, 11*(4), 615–668.

Avolio, B. J., Kahai, S., Dumdum, R., & Sivasubramaniam, N. (2001). Virtual teams: implications for e-leadership and team development. In M. London (Ed.), *How people evaluate others in organizations* (pp. 337–358). Mahwah, NJ: Lawrence Erlbaum Associates.

Awamleh, R., & Gardner, W. L. (1999). Perceptions of leader charisma and effectiveness: the effects of vision content, delivery, and organizational performance. *Leadership Quarterly, 10*(3), 345–373.

Bakhtari, H. (1995). Cultural effects on management style. *International Studies of Management and Organiza-tion, 25*(3), 97–118.

Bass, B. M. (1985). *Leadership and performance beyond expectations.* New York: Free Press.

Bass, B. M. (1990). *Bass and Stogdill's handbook of leadership* (3rd ed.). New York: Free Press.

Bass, B. M. (1997). Does the transactional–transformational leadership paradigm transcend organizational boun-daries? *American Psychologist, 52*(2), 130–139.

Bass, B. M. (1998). *Transformational leadership: industrial, military, and educational impact.* Mahwah, NJ: Lawrence Erlbaum Associates.

Bass, B. M., & Avolio, B. J. (1993). Transformational leadership: a response to critiques. In M. M. Chemers, & R. Ayman (Eds.), *Leadership theory and research: perspectives and directions* (pp. 49–80). San Diego: Academic Press.

Bass, B. M., & Avolio, B. J. (Eds.) (1994). *Improving organizational effectiveness through transformational leadership.* Thousand Oaks, CA: Sage Publications.

Bass, B. M., & Avolio, B. J. (1995). *MLQ Multifactor leadership questionnaire for research.* Redwood City, CA: Mindgarden.

Bass, B. M., & Avolio, B. J. (1997). *Full range leadership development: manual for the multifactor leadership questionnaire.* Palo Alto, CA: Mindgarden.

Bass, B. M., Waldman, D. A., Avolio, B. J., & Bebb, M. (1987). Transformational leadership and the falling dominoes effect. *Group and Organization Studies, 12*(1), 73–87.

Blake, R. R., & Mouton, J. S. (1964). *The managerial grid.* Houston: Gulf Publishing Group.

Bochner, S., & Hesketh, B. (1994). Power distance, individualism/collectivism, and job-related attitudes in a culturally diverse work group. *Journal of Cross-Cultural Psychology, 25*(2), 233–257.

Bogardus, E. S. (1927). Leadership and social distance. *Sociology and Social Research, 12,* 173–178.

Bogardus, E. S. (1928). Occupational distance. *Sociology and Social Research, 13,* 73–81.

Burns, J. M. (1978). *Leadership.* New York: Harper and Row.

Burrows, L., Munday, R., Tunnell, J., & Seay, R. (1996). Leadership substitutes: their effects on teacher organiza-tional commitment and job satisfaction. *Journal of Instructional Psychology, 23,* 3–8.

Cardinal, L. B., & Hatfield, D. E. (2000). Internal knowledge generation: the research laboratory and innovative productivity in the pharmaceutical industry. *Journal of Engineering and Technology Management, 17,* 247–271.

Conger, J. A. (1999). Charismatic and transformational leadership in organizations: an insider's perspective on these developing streams of research. *Leadership Quarterly, 10*(2), 145–179.

J. Antonakis, L. Atwater / The Leadership Quarterly 13 (2002) 673–704 701

Conger, J. A., & Kanugo, R. N. (1998). *Charismatic leadership in organizations*. Thousand Oaks, CA: Sage Publications.

Daft, R. L., & Lengel, R. H. (1984). Information richness: a new approach to managerial behavior and organizational design. In B. M. Staw, & L. L. Cummings (Eds.), *Research in organizational behavior, vol. 6* (pp. 191–233). Greenwich, CT: JAI Press.

Den Hartog, D. N., House, R. J., Hanges, P. J., Ruiz-Quintanilla, S. A., Dorfman, P. W. (1999). Culture specific and cross-cultural generalizable implicit leadership theories: are attributes of charismatic/transformational leadership universally endorsed? *Leadership Quarterly, 10*(2), 219–256.

Eden, D., & Leviatan, U. (1975). Implicit leadership theory as a determinant of the factor structure underlying supervisory behavior scales. *Journal of Applied Psychology, 60*(6), 736–741.

Etzioni, A. (1961). *A comparative analysis of complex organizations*. New York: Free Press.

Fiedler, F. E. (1967). *A theory of leadership effectiveness*. New York: McGraw-Hill.

Frank, A. W. (1974). Social distance. *Encyclopedia of sociology* (pp. 269–270). Guilford, CT: Dushkin Publishing Group.

Gardner, J. W. (1990). *On leadership*. New York: Free Press.

Gardner, W. L., & Avolio, B. J. (1998). The charismatic relationship: a dramaturgical perspective. *Academy of Management Review, 23*(1), 32–58.

Gerstner, C. R., & Day, D. V. (1994). Cross-cultural comparisons of leadership prototypes. *Leadership Quarterly, 5*(2), 121–134.

Halpin, A. W., & Winer, B. J. (1957). A factorial study of the leader behavior descriptions. In R. M. Stogdill, & A. E. Coons (Eds.), *Leader behavior: its description and measurement* (pp. 39–51). Columbus, OH: Ohio State University Bureau of Business Research. Research Monograph Number 88.

Hede, A., & Wear, R. (1996). Dimensions of political and organisational leadership. In K. W. Parry (Ed.), *Leadership research and practice: emerging themes and new challenges* (pp. 65–75). Warriewood, Australia: Business and Professional Publishing.

Hofstede, G. (1980). *Culture's consequences: international differences in work-related values*. Beverly Hills, CA: Sage Publications.

Hofstede, G. (1991). *Cultures and organizations: software of the mind*. Berkshire, England: McGraw-Hill.

House, R. J. (1971). A path-goal theory of leadership effectiveness. *Administrative Science Quarterly, 16*, 321–328.

House, R. J. (1977). A 1976 theory of charismatic leadership. In J. G. Hunt, & L. L. Larson (Eds.), *Leadership: the cutting edge* (pp. 189–207). Carbondale: Southern Illinois Univ. Press.

House, R. J., & Dessler, G. (1994). The path-goal theory of leadership: some post hoc and a priori tests. In R. J. Hunt, & L. L. Larson (Eds.), *Contingency approaches to leadership* (pp. 29–55). Carbondale: Southern Illinois Univ. Press.

House, R. J., & Mitchell, T. R. (1974). Path-goal theory of leadership. *Journal of Contemporary Business, 3*(4), 81–97.

House, R. J., Wright, N. S., & Aditya, R. N. (1997). Cross-cultural research on organizational leadership: a critical analysis and a proposed theory. In P. C. Earley, & M. Erez (Eds.), *New perspectives on international industrial/ organizational psychology*. San Francisco: New Lexington Press.

Howell, J. M., & Hall-Merenda, K. (1999). The ties that bind: the impact of leader–member exchange, transformational and transactional leadership, and distance on predicting follower performance. *Journal of Applied Psychology, 84*, 680–694.

Howell, J. M., Neufeld, D. J., & Avolio, B. J. (1998). Leadership at a distance: the effects of physical distance, charismatic leadership, and communication style on predicting business unit performance. Unpublished manuscript, University of Western Ontario, Canada.

Howell, J. M., Neufeld, D. J., & Avolio, B. J. (2002). A longitudinal study of the effects of transformational and contingent reward leadership, communication style, and physical distance on business unit performance. Manuscript submitted for publication.

Howell, J. M., & Shamir, B. (1998). Pockets of fire: the potential and the risk. In F. Dansereau, & F. J. Yammarino

(Eds.), *Leadership: the multiple-level approach (contemporary and alternative)* (pp. 37–44). Stamford, CT: Jai Press.

Howell, J. P., Bowen, D. E., Dorman, P. W., & Kerr, S. (1990). Substitutes for leadership: effective alternatives to ineffective leadership. *Organizational Dynamics, 19*(1), 21–38.

Howell, J. P., Bowen, D. E., Dorfman, P. W., Kerr, S., & Podsakoff, P. M. (1997). Substitutes for leadership: effective alternatives to ineffective leadership. In R. P. Vecchio (Ed.), *Leadership: understanding the dynamics of power and influence in organizations* (pp. 381–395). Notre Dame, IN: University of Notre Dame Press.

Hunt, J. G. (1991). *Leadership: a new synthesis*. Newbury Park, CA: Sage Publications.

Hunt, J. G. (1999). Transformational/charismatic leadership's transformation of the field: an historical essay. *Leadership Quarterly, 10*(2), 129–144.

Jarvenpaa, S., Knoll, K., & Leidner, D. (1998). Is anybody out there? Antecedents of trust in global virtual teams. *Journal of Management Information Systems, 14*, 29–64.

Jarvenpaa, S. L., & Leidner, D. E. (1998). Communication and trust in global virtual teams. *Organization Science, 10*(6), 791–815.

Javidan, M., & House, R. J. (2001). Cultural acumen for the global manager: lessons from Project GLOBE. *Organizational Dynamics, 29*(4), 289–305.

Jermier, J. M., Slocum, J. W., Fry, L. W., & Gaines, J. (1991). Organizational subcultures in a soft bureaucracy: resistance behind the myth and façade of an official culture. *Organizational Science, 2*(2), 170–194.

Judge, T. A., & Ferris, G. R. (1993). Social context of performance evaluation decisions. *Academy of Management Journal, 36*(1), 80–105.

Kahai, S. S., Sosik, J. J., & Avolio, B. J. (1997). Effects of leadership style and problem structure on work group process and outcomes in an electronic meeting system environment. *Personnel Psychology, 50*(1), 121–146.

Katz, D., & Kahn, R. L. (1978). *The social psychology of organizations*. New York: Wiley.

Kegan, J. (1987). *The mask of command*. New York: Penguin Books.

Kerr, S., & Jermier, J. M. (1978). Substitutes for leadership: their meaning and measurement. *Organizational Behavior and Human Performance, 22*, 375–403.

Klein, K. J., Dansereau, F., & Hall, R. J. (1994). Levels issues in theory development, data collection and analysis. *Academy of Management Review, 19*(2), 195–229.

Klein, K. J., & House, R. J. (1998). On fire: charismatic leadership and levels of analysis. In F. Dansereau, & F. J. Yammarino (Eds.), *Leadership: the multiple-level approaches* (pp. 3–21). Stamford, CT: Jai Press.

Litwin, G. H., & Stringer Jr., R. A. (1968). *Motivation and organizational climate*. Boston: Harvard Business School Press.

Lord, R. G., Brown, D. J., Harvey, J. L., & Hall, R. J. (2001). Contextual constraints on prototype generation and their multilevel consequences for leadership perceptions. *Leadership Quarterly, 12*, 311–338.

Lord, R. G., Foti, R. J., & De Vader, C. L. (1984). A test of leadership categorization theory: internal structure, information processing, and leadership perceptions. *Organizational Behavior and Human Performance, 34*, 343–378.

Lowe, K. B., Kroeck, K. G., & Sivasubramaniam, N. (1996). Effectiveness correlates of transformational and transactional leadership: a meta-analytic review of the literature. *Leadership Quarterly, 7*(3), 385–425.

Mayer, R. C., Davis, J. H., & Schoorman, F. D. (1995). An integrative model of organizational trust. *Academy of Management Review, 20*(3), 709–734.

McClelland, D. C. (1962). Business drive and national achievement. *Harvard Business Review, 40*(4), 99–112.

McClelland, D. C. (1975). *Power: the inner experience*. New York: Halsted Press.

McClelland, D. C., & Boyatzis, R. E. (1982). Leadership motive pattern and long-term success in management. *Journal of Applied Psychology, 67*(6), 737–743.

Mead, R. D. (1967). An experimental study of leadership in India. *Journal of Social Psychology, 72*(1), 35–43.

Meindl, J. R. (1990). On leadership: an alternative to the conventional wisdom. In B. M. Staw, & L. L. Cummings (Eds.), *Research in organizational behavior, vol. 12* (pp. 159–203). Greenwich, CT: JAI Press.

Meindl, J. R., & Ehrlich, S. B. (1987). The romance of leadership and the evaluation of organizational performance. *Academy of Management Journal, 30*(1), 91–109.

Meyer, A. D., Tsui, A. S., & Hinings, C. R. (1993). Configural approaches to organizational analysis. *Academy of Management Journal, 36*(6), 1175–1195.

Napier, B. J., & Ferris, G. R. (1993). Distance in organizations. *Human Resource Management Review, 3*(4), 321–357.

Offermann, L. R., & Hellmann, P. S. (1997). Culture's consequences for leadership behavior: national values in action. *Journal of Cross-Cultural Psychology, 28*(3), 342–351.

Park, R. E. (1924). The concept of social distance. *Journal of Applied Sociology, 8*(5), 339–344.

Pastor, J. C., Meindl, J. R., & Mayo, M. C. (2002). A networks effects model of charisma attributions. *Academy of Management Journal, 45*(2), 410–420.

Pavett, C., & Morris, T. (1995). Management styles within a multinational corporation: a five country comparative study. *Human Relations, 48*(10), 1171–1191.

Podsakoff, P. M., MacKenzie, S. B., & Bommer, W. H. (1996a). Transformational leader behaviors and substitutes for leadership as determinants of employee satisfaction, commitment, trust, and organizational citizenship behaviors. *Journal of Management, 22*(2), 259–298.

Podsakoff, P. M., MacKenzie, S. B., & Bommer, W. H. (1996b). Meta-analysis of the relationships between Kerr and Jermier's substitutes for leadership and employee job attitudes, role perceptions, and performance. *Journal of Applied Psychology, 81*(4), 380–399.

Podsakoff, P. M., Todor, W. D., Grover, R. A., & Huber, V. L. (1984). Situational moderators of leader reward and punishment behaviors: fact or fiction? *Organizational Behavior and Human Performance, 34*, 21–63.

Rainey, H. G., & Watson, S. A. (1996). Transformational leadership and middle management: towards a role for mere mortals. *International Journal of Public Administration, 19*(6), 763–800.

Roberts, N. C., & Bradley, R. T. (1988). Limits of charisma. In J. A. Conger, & R. N. Kanugo (Eds.), *Charismatic leadership: the elusive factor in organizational effectiveness* (pp. 253–275). San Francisco: Jossey-Bass Publishers.

Sashkin, M. (1988). The visionary leader. In J. A. Conger, & R. N. Kanugo (Eds.), *Charismatic leadership: the elusive factor in organizational effectiveness* (pp. 122–160). San Francisco: Jossey-Bass Publishers.

Shamir, B. (1995). Social distance and charisma: theoretical notes and an exploratory study. *Leadership Quarterly, 6*(1), 19–47.

Shamir, B. (1999). Leadership in boundaryless organizations: disposable or indispensable. *European Journal of Work and Organizational Psychology, 8*(1), 49–71.

Shamir, B., & Ben-Ari, E. (1999). Leadership in an open army? Civilian connections, interorganizational frameworks and changes in military leadership. In J. G. Hunt, G. E. Dodge, & L. Wong (Eds.), *Out-of-the-box leadership: transforming the twenty-first-century army and other top-performing organizations* (pp. 15–40). Stamford, CT: JAI Press.

Shamir, B., House, R. J., & Arthur, M. B. (1993). The motivational effects of charismatic leadership: a self-concept based theory. *Organization Science, 4*(4), 577–594.

Shamir, B., Zakay, E., Brainin, E., & Popper, M. (2000). Leadership and social identification in military units: direct and indirect relationships. *Journal of Applied Social Psychology, 30*(3), 612–640.

Smith, P. B., Dugan, S., & Trompenaars, F. (1996). National culture and the values of organizational employees: a dimensional analysis across 43 nations. *Journal of Cross-Cultural Psychology, 27*(2), 231–264.

Smith, J. A., & Foti, R. J. (1998). A pattern approach to the study of leader emergence. *Leadership Quarterly, 9*(2), 147–160.

Sosik, J. J. (1997). Effects of transformational leadership and anonymity on idea generation in computer-mediated groups. *Group and Organization Management, 22*(4), 460–487.

Sosik, J. J., Avolio, B. J., & Kahai, S. S. (1997). Effects of leader style and anonymity on group potency and effectiveness in a group decision support system environment. *Journal of Applied Psychology, 82*, 89–103.

Sosik, J. J., Avolio, B. J., Kahai, S. S., & Jung, D. I. (1998). Computer-supported work group potency and effectiveness: the role of transformational leadership, anonymity, and task interdependence. *Computers in Human Behavior, 14*(3), 491–511.

Triandis, H. C. (1993). The contingency model in cross-cultural perspective. In M. M. Chemers, & R. Ayman (Eds.), *Leadership theory and research: perspectives and directions* (pp. 167–188). San Diego: Academic Press.

Uhl-Bien, M., Graen, G. B., & Scandura, T. (2000). Implications of Leader–Member Exchange (LMX) for strategic human resource management systems: relationships as social capital for competitive advantage. In G. Ferris (Ed.), *Research in personnel and human resource management, vol. 18* (pp. 137–185). Greenwich, CT: JAI Press.

van Muijen, J. J., & Koopman, P. L. (1994). The influence of national culture on organizational culture: a comparative study between 10 countries. *European Work and Organizational Psychologist, 4*(4), 367–380.

Waldman, D. A., & Yammarino, F. J. (1999). CEO charismatic leadership: levels-of-management and levels-of-analysis effects. *Academy of Management Review, 24*(2), 266–285.

Weisband, S., & Atwater, L. (1999). Evaluating self and others in electronic and face-to-face groups. *Journal of Applied Psychology, 84,* 632–639.

Westley, F. R., & Mintzberg, H. (1988). Profiles of strategic vision: levesque and Iacocca. In J. A. Conger, & R. N. Kanugo (Eds.), *Charismatic leadership: the elusive factor in organizational effectiveness* (pp. 161–212). San Francisco: Jossey-Bass Publishers.

White, R., & Lippitt, R. (1968). Leader behavior and member reaction in three "social climates". In D. Cartwright, & A. Zander (Eds.), *Group dynamics* (pp. 318–335). New York: Harper and Row.

Willner, A. R. (1984). *The spellbinders: charismatic political leadership.* New Haven: Yale Univ. Press.

Winter, D. G. (2002). The motivational dimensions of leadership: power, achievement and affiliation. In R. E. Riggio, S. E. Murphy, & F. J. Pirozzolo (Eds.), *Multiple intelligences and leadership* (pp. 119–138). Mahwah, NJ: Lawrence Erlbaum Associates.

Winter, D. G., John, O. P., Stewart, A. J., Klohnen, E. C., & Duncan, L. E. (1998). Traits and motives: toward an integration of two traditions in personality research. *Psychological Review, 105*(2), 230–250.

Yagil, D. (1998). Charismatic leadership and organizational hierarchy: attribution of charisma to close and distant leaders. *Leadership Quarterly, 9*(2), 161–176.

Yammarino, F. J. (1994). Indirect Leadership: transformational leadership at a distance. In B. M. Bass, & B. J. Avolio (Eds.), *Improving organizational effectiveness through transformational leadership* (pp. 26–47). Thousand Oaks, CA: Sage Publications.

Yammarino, F. J., & Jung, D. I. (1998). Asian Americans and leadership: a levels of analysis perspective. *Journal of Applied Behavioral Science, 34*(1), 47–57.

Yukl, G. (1998). *Leadership in organizations* (4th ed.). Englewood Cliffs, NJ: Prentice Hall.

Yukl, G. (1999). An evaluation of conceptual weaknesses in transformational and charismatic leadership theories. *Leadership Quarterly, 10*(2), 285–305.

Zaccaro, S. J. (2002). *The nature of executive leadership.* Washington, DC: American Psychological Association.

[10]
THE NECESSARY ART OF
PERSUASION

BY JAY A. CONGER

I F THERE EVER WAS A TIME for businesspeople to learn the fine art
of persuasion, it is now. Gone are the command-and-control days of
executives managing by decree. Today businesses are run largely by
cross-functional teams of peers and populated by baby boomers and
their Generation X offspring, who show little tolerance for unquestioned authority. Electronic communication and globalization have
further eroded the traditional hierarchy, as ideas and people flow more
freely than ever around organizations and as decisions get made closer
to the markets. These fundamental changes, more than a decade in
the making but now firmly part of the economic landscape, essentially
come down to this: work today gets done in an environment where

THE NECESSARY ART OF PERSUASION

TWELVE YEARS OF WATCHING AND LISTENING

The ideas behind this article spring from three streams of research.

For the last 12 years as both an academic and as a consultant, I have been studying 23 senior business leaders who have shown themselves to be effective change agents. Specifically, I have investigated how these individuals use language to motivate their employees, articulate vision and strategy, and mobilize their organizations to adapt to challenging business environments.

Four years ago, I started a second stream of research exploring the capabilities and characteristics of successful cross-functional team leaders. The core of my database comprised interviews with and observations of 18 individuals working in a range of U.S. and Canadian companies. These were not senior leaders as in my earlier studies but low- and middle-level managers. Along with interviewing the colleagues of these people, I also compared their skills with those of other team leaders – in particular, with the leaders of less successful cross-functional teams engaged in similar initiatives within the same companies. Again, my focus was on language, but I also studied the influence of interpersonal skills.

The similarities in the persuasion skills possessed by both the change-agent leaders and effective team leaders prompted me to explore the academic literature on persuasion and rhetoric, as well as on the art of gospel preaching. Meanwhile, to learn how most managers approach the persuasion process, I observed several dozen managers in company meetings, and I employed simulations in company executive-education programs where groups of managers had to persuade one another on hypothetical business objectives. Finally, I selected a group of 14 managers known for their outstanding abilities in constructive persuasion. For several months, I interviewed them and their colleagues and observed them in actual work situations.

people don't just ask What should I do? but Why should I do it?

To answer this why question effectively is to persuade. Yet many businesspeople misunderstand persuasion, and more still underutilize it. The reason? Persuasion is widely perceived as a skill reserved for selling products and closing deals. It is also commonly seen as just another form of manipulation – devious and to be avoided. Certainly, persuasion can be used in selling and deal-clinching situations, and it can be misused to manipulate people. But exercised constructively and to its full potential, persuasion supersedes sales and is quite the opposite of deception. Effective persuasion becomes a negotiating and learning process through which a persuader leads colleagues to a problem's shared solution. Persuasion does indeed involve moving people to a position they don't currently hold, but not by begging or cajoling. Instead, it involves careful preparation, the proper framing of arguments, the presentation of vivid supporting evidence, and the effort to find the correct emotional match with your audience.

Jay A. Conger is a professor of organizational behavior at the University of Southern California's Marshall School of Business in Los Angeles, where he directs the Leadership Institute. He is the author of Winning 'Em Over: A New Model for Managing in the Age of Persuasion *(Simon & Schuster, 1998).*

Effective persuasion is a difficult and time-consuming proposition, but it may also be more powerful than the command-and-control managerial model it succeeds. As AlliedSignal's CEO Lawrence Bossidy said recently, "The day when you could yell and scream and beat people into good performance is over. Today you have to appeal to them by helping them see how they can get from here to there, by establishing some credibility, and by giving them some reason and help to get there. Do all those things, and they'll knock down doors." In essence, he is describing persuasion – now more than ever, the language of business leadership.

Think for a moment of your definition of persuasion. If you are like most businesspeople I have encountered (see the insert "Twelve Years of Watching and Listening"), you see persuasion as a relatively straightforward process. First, you strongly state your position. Second, you outline the supporting arguments, followed by a highly assertive, data-based exposition. Finally, you enter the deal-making stage and work toward a "close." In other words, you use logic, persistence, and personal enthusiasm to get others to buy a good idea. The reality is that following this process is one surefire way to fail at persuasion. (See the insert "Four Ways Not to Persuade.")

What, then, constitutes effective persuasion? If persuasion is a learning and negotiating process, then in the most general terms it involves phases of

ARTWORK BY DAVID JOHNSON

discovery, preparation, and dialogue. Getting ready to persuade colleagues can take weeks or months of planning as you learn about your audience and the position you intend to argue. Before they even start to talk, effective persuaders have considered their positions from every angle. What investments in time and money will my position require from others? Is my supporting evidence weak in any way? Are there alternative positions I need to examine?

Dialogue happens before and during the persuasion process. Before the process begins, effective persuaders use dialogue to learn more about their audience's opinions, concerns, and perspectives. During the process, dialogue continues to be a form of learning, but it is also the beginning of the negotiation stage. You invite people to discuss, even debate, the merits of your position, and then to offer honest feedback and suggest alternative solutions. That may sound like a slow way to achieve your goal, but effective persuasion is about testing and revising ideas in concert with your colleagues' concerns and needs. In fact, the best persuaders not only listen to others but also incorporate their perspectives into a shared solution.

Persuasion, in other words, often involves – indeed, demands – compromise. Perhaps that is why the most effective persuaders seem to share a common trait: they are open-minded, never dogmatic. They enter the persuasion process prepared to adjust their viewpoints and incorporate others' ideas. That approach to persuasion is, interestingly, highly persuasive in itself. When colleagues see that a persuader is eager to hear their views and willing to make changes in response to their needs and concerns, they respond very positively. They trust the persuader more and listen more attentively. They don't fear being bowled over or manipulated. They see the persuader as flexible and are thus more willing to make sacrifices themselves. Because that is such a powerful dynamic, good persuaders often enter the persuasion process with judicious compromises already prepared.

Four Essential Steps

Effective persuasion involves four distinct and essential steps. First, effective persuaders establish credibility. Second, they frame their goals in a way

FOUR WAYS NOT TO PERSUADE

In my work with managers as a researcher and as a consultant, I have had the unfortunate opportunity to see executives fail miserably at persuasion. Here are the four most common mistakes people make:

1. They attempt to make their case with an up-front, hard sell. I call this the John Wayne approach. Managers strongly state their position at the outset, and then through a process of persistence, logic, and exuberance, they try to push the idea to a close. In reality, setting out a strong position at the start of a persuasion effort gives potential opponents something to grab onto – and fight against. It's far better to present your position with the finesse and reserve of a lion tamer, who engages his "partner" by showing him the legs of a chair. In other words, effective persuaders don't begin the process by giving their colleagues a clear target in which to set their jaws.

2. They resist compromise. Too many managers see compromise as surrender, but it is essential to constructive persuasion. Before people buy into a proposal, they want to see that the persuader is flexible enough to respond to their concerns. Compromises can often lead to better, more sustainable shared solutions.

By not compromising, ineffective persuaders unconsciously send the message that they think persuasion is a one-way street. But persuasion is a process of give-and-take. Kathleen Reardon, a professor of organizational behavior at the University of Southern California, points out that a persuader rarely changes another person's behavior or viewpoint without altering his or her own in the process. To persuade meaningfully, we must not only listen to others but also incorporate their perspectives into our own.

3. They think the secret of persuasion lies in presenting great arguments. In persuading people to change their minds, great arguments matter. No doubt about it. But arguments, per se, are only one part of the equation. Other factors matter just as much, such as the persuader's credibility and his or her ability to create a proper, mutually beneficial frame for a position, connect on the right emotional level with an audience, and communicate through vivid language that makes arguments come alive.

4. They assume persuasion is a one-shot effort. Persuasion is a process, not an event. Rarely, if ever, is it possible to arrive at a shared solution on the first try. More often than not, persuasion involves listening to people, testing a position, developing a new position that reflects input from the group, more testing, incorporating compromises, and then trying again. If this sounds like a slow and difficult process, that's because it is. But the results are worth the effort.

THE NECESSARY ART OF PERSUASION

that identifies common ground with those they intend to persuade. Third, they reinforce their positions using vivid language and compelling evidence. And fourth, they connect emotionally with their audience. As one of the most effective executives in our research commented, "The most valuable lesson I've learned about persuasion over the years is that there's just as much strategy in how you present your position as in the position itself. In fact, I'd say the strategy of presentation is the more critical."

Establish credibility. The first hurdle persuaders must overcome is their own credibility. A persuader can't advocate a new or contrarian position without having people wonder, Can we trust this individual's perspectives and opinions? Such a reaction is understandable. After all, allowing oneself to be persuaded is risky, because any new initiative demands a commitment of time and resources. Yet even though persuaders must have high credibility, our research strongly suggests that most managers overestimate their own credibility – considerably.

In the workplace, credibility grows out of two sources: expertise and relationships. People are considered to have high levels of expertise if they have a history of sound judgment or have proven themselves knowledgeable and well informed about their proposals. For example, in proposing a new product idea, an effective persuader would need to be perceived as possessing a thorough understanding of the product – its specifications, target markets, customers, and competing products. A history of prior successes would further strengthen the per-

time – that they can be trusted to listen and to work in the best interests of others. They have also consistently shown strong emotional character and integrity; that is, they are not known for mood extremes or inconsistent performance. Indeed, people who are known to be honest, steady, and reliable have an edge when going into any persuasion situation. Because their relationships are robust, they are more apt to be given the benefit of the doubt. One effective persuader in our research was considered by colleagues to be remarkably trustworthy and fair; many people confided in her. In addition, she generously shared credit for good ideas and provided staff with exposure to the company's senior executives. This woman had built strong relationships, which meant her staff and peers were always willing to consider seriously what she proposed.

If expertise and relationships determine credibility, it is crucial that you undertake an honest assessment of where you stand on both criteria before beginning to persuade. To do so, first step back and ask yourself the following questions related to expertise: How will others perceive my knowledge about the strategy, product, or change I am proposing? Do I have a track record in this area that others know about and respect? Then, to assess the strength of your relationship credibility, ask yourself, Do those I am hoping to persuade see me as helpful, trustworthy, and supportive? Will they see me as someone in sync with them – emotionally, intellectually, and politically – on issues like this one? Finally, it is important to note that it is not enough to get your own read on these matters. You must also test your answers with colleagues you trust to give you a reality check. Only then will you have a complete picture of your credibility.

In most cases, that exercise helps people discover that they have some measure of weakness, either on the expertise or on the relationship side of credibility. The challenge then becomes to fill in such gaps.

In general, if your area of weakness is on the expertise side, you have several options:
- First, you can learn more about the complexities of your position through either formal or informal education and through conversations with knowledgeable individuals. You might also get more relevant experience on the job by asking, for instance, to be assigned to a team that would increase your insight into particular markets or products.
- Another alternative is to hire someone to bolster your expertise – for example, an industry consultant or a recognized outside expert, such as a profes-

Research strongly suggests that most managers are in the habit of overestimating their own credibility – often considerably.

suader's perceived expertise. One extremely successful executive in our research had a track record of 14 years of devising highly effective advertising campaigns. Not surprisingly, he had an easy time winning colleagues over to his position. Another manager had a track record of seven successful new-product launches in a period of five years. He, too, had an advantage when it came to persuading his colleagues to support his next new idea.

On the relationship side, people with high credibility have demonstrated – again, usually over sor. Either one may have the knowledge and experience required to support your position effectively. Similarly, you may tap experts within your organization to advocate your position. Their credibility becomes a substitute for your own.

■ You can also utilize other outside sources of information to support your position, such as respected business or trade periodicals, books, independently produced reports, and lectures by experts. In our research, one executive from the clothing industry successfully persuaded his company to reposition an entire product line to a more youthful market after bolstering his credibility with articles by a noted demographer in two highly regarded journals and with two independent market-research studies.

■ Finally, you may launch pilot projects to demonstrate on a small scale your expertise and the value of your ideas.

As for filling in the relationship gap:

■ You should make a concerted effort to meet one-on-one with all the key people you plan to persuade. This is not the time to outline your position but rather to get a range of perspectives on the issue at hand. If you have the time and resources, you should even offer to help these people with issues that concern them.

■ Another option is to involve like-minded coworkers who already have strong relationships with your audience. Again, that is a matter of seeking out substitutes on your own behalf.

For an example of how these strategies can be put to work, consider the case of a chief operating officer of a large retail bank, whom we will call Tom Smith. Although he was new to his job, Smith ardently wanted to persuade the senior management team that the company was in serious trouble. He believed that the bank's overhead was excessive and would jeopardize its position as the industry entered a more competitive era. Most of his colleagues, however, did not see the potential seriousness of the situation. Because the bank had been enormously successful in recent years, they believed changes in the industry posed little danger. In addition to being newly appointed, Smith had another problem: his career had been in financial services, and he was considered an outsider in the world of retail banking. Thus he had few personal connections to draw on as he made his case, nor was he perceived to be particularly knowledgeable about marketplace exigencies.

As a first step in establishing credibility, Smith hired an external consultant with respected credentials in the industry who showed that the bank was indeed poorly positioned to be a low-cost producer. In a series of interactive presentations to the bank's top-level management, the consultant revealed how the company's leading competitors were taking aggressive actions to contain operating costs. He made it clear from these presentations that not

A persuader should make a concerted effort to meet one-on-one with all the key people he or she plans to persuade.

cutting costs would soon cause the bank to fall drastically behind the competition. These findings were then distributed in written reports that circulated throughout the bank.

Next, Smith determined that the bank's branch managers were critical to his campaign. The buy-in of those respected and informed individuals would signal to others in the company that his concerns were valid. Moreover, Smith looked to the branch managers because he believed that they could increase his expertise about marketplace trends and also help him test his own assumptions. Thus, for the next three months, he visited every branch in his region of Ontario, Canada–135 in all. During each visit, he spent time with branch managers, listening to their perceptions of the bank's strengths and weaknesses. He learned firsthand about the competition's initiatives and customer trends, and he solicited ideas for improving the bank's services and minimizing costs. By the time he was through, Smith had a broad perspective on the bank's future that few people even in senior management possessed. And he had built dozens of relationships in the process.

Finally, Smith launched some small but highly visible initiatives to demonstrate his expertise and capabilities. For example, he was concerned about slow growth in the company's mortgage business and the loan officers' resulting slip in morale. So he devised a program in which new mortgage customers would make no payments for the first 90 days. The initiative proved remarkably successful, and in short order Smith appeared to be a far more savvy retail banker than anyone had assumed.

Another example of how to establish credibility comes from Microsoft. In 1990, two product-development managers, Karen Fries and Barry Linnett,

THE NECESSARY ART OF PERSUASION

came to believe that the market would greatly welcome software that featured a "social interface." They envisioned a package that would employ animated human and animal characters to show users how to go about their computing tasks.

Inside Microsoft, however, employees had immediate concerns about the concept. Software programmers ridiculed the cute characters. Animated characters had been used before only in software for children, making their use in adult environments

Massena. With Massena, they developed a set of prototypes to demonstrate that they did indeed understand the software's technology and could make it work. They then tested the prototypes in market research, and users responded enthusiastically. Finally, and most important, they enlisted two Stanford University professors, Clifford Nass and Bryon Reeves, both experts in human-computer interaction. In several meetings with Microsoft senior managers and Gates himself, they presented a rigorously compiled and thorough body of research that demonstrated how and why social-interface software was ideally suited to the average computer user. In addition, Fries and Linnett asserted that considerable jumps in computing power would make more realistic cartoon characters an increasingly malleable technology. Their product, they said, was the leading edge of an incipient software rev-

In some situations, no shared advantages are readily apparent. In these cases, effective persuaders adjust their positions.

hard to envision. But Fries and Linnett felt their proposed product had both dynamism and complexity, and they remained convinced that consumers would eagerly buy such programs. They also believed that the home-computer software market – largely untapped at the time and with fewer software standards – would be open to such innovation.

Within the company, Fries had gained quite a bit of relationship credibility. She had started out as a recruiter for the company in 1987 and had worked directly for many of Microsoft's senior executives. They trusted and liked her. In addition, she had been responsible for hiring the company's product and program managers. As a result, she knew all the senior people at Microsoft and had hired many of the people who would be deciding on her product.

Linnett's strength laid in his expertise. In particular, he knew the technology behind an innovative tutorial program called PC Works. In addition, both Fries and Linnett had managed Publisher, a product with a unique help feature called Wizards, which Microsoft's CEO, Bill Gates, had liked. But those factors were sufficient only to get an initial hearing from Microsoft's senior management. To persuade the organization to move forward, the pair would need to improve perceptions of their expertise. It hurt them that this type of social-interface software had no proven track record of success and that they were both novices with such software. Their challenge became one of finding substitutes for their own expertise.

Their first step was a wise one. From within Microsoft, they hired respected technical guru Darrin

olution. Convinced, Gates approved a full product-development team, and in January 1995, the product called BOB was launched. BOB went on to sell more than half a million copies, and its concept and technology are being used within Microsoft as a platform for developing several Internet products.

Credibility is the cornerstone of effective persuading; without it, a persuader won't be given the time of day. In the best-case scenario, people enter into a persuasion situation with some measure of expertise and relationship credibility. But it is important to note that credibility along either lines can be built or bought. Indeed, it must be, or the next steps are an exercise in futility.

Frame for common ground. Even if your credibility is high, your position must still appeal strongly to the people you are trying to persuade. After all, few people will jump on board a train that will bring them to ruin or even mild discomfort. Effective persuaders must be adept at describing their positions in terms that illuminate their advantages. As any parent can tell you, the fastest way to get a child to come along willingly on a trip to the grocery store is to point out that there are lollipops by the cash register. That is not deception. It is just a persuasive way of framing the benefits of taking such a journey. In work situations, persuasive framing is obviously more complex, but the underlying principle is the same. It is a process of identifying shared benefits.

Monica Ruffo, an account executive for an advertising agency, offers a good example of persuasive framing. Her client, a fast-food chain, was instituting a promotional campaign in Canada; menu

90

items such as a hamburger, fries, and cola were to be bundled together and sold at a low price. The strategy made sense to corporate headquarters. Its research showed that consumers thought the company's products were higher priced than the competition's, and the company was anxious to overcome this perception. The franchisees, on the other hand, were still experiencing strong sales and were far more concerned about the short-term impact that the new, low prices would have on their profit margins.

A less experienced persuader would have attempted to rationalize headquarters' perspective to the franchisees – to convince them of its validity. But Ruffo framed the change in pricing to demonstrate its benefits to the franchisees themselves. The new value campaign, she explained, would actually improve franchisees' profits. To back up this point, she drew on several sources. A pilot project in Tennessee, for instance, had demonstrated that under the new pricing scheme, the sales of french fries and drinks – the two most profitable items on the menu – had markedly increased. In addition, the company had rolled out medium-sized meal packages in 80% of its U.S. outlets, and franchisees' sales of fries and drinks had jumped 26%. Citing research from a respected business periodical, Ruffo also showed that when customers raised their estimate of the value they receive from a retail establishment by 10%, the establishment's sales rose by 1%. She had estimated that the new meal plan would increase value perceptions by 100%, with the result that franchisee sales could be expected to grow 10%.

Ruffo closed her presentation with a letter written many years before by the company's founder to the organization. It was an emotional letter extolling the values of the company and stressing the importance of the franchisees to the company's success. It also highlighted the importance of the company's position as the low-price leader in the industry. The beliefs and values contained in the letter had long been etched in the minds of Ruffo's audience. Hearing them again only confirmed the company's concern for the franchisees and the importance of their winning formula. They also won Ruffo a standing ovation. That day, the franchisees voted unanimously to support the new meal-pricing plan.

The Ruffo case illustrates why – in choosing appropriate positioning – it is critical first to identify your objective's tangible benefits to the people you are trying to persuade. Sometimes that is easy. Mutual benefits exist. In other situations, however, no shared advantages are readily apparent – or meaningful. In these cases, effective persuaders adjust their positions. They know it is impossible to en-

When a fast-food chain needed to persuade its franchisees to buy into a meal-pricing plan that had the potential to eat into profits, headquarters framed the initiative to accent the positive.

gage people and gain commitment to ideas or plans without highlighting the advantages to all the parties involved.

At the heart of framing is a solid understanding of your audience. Even before starting to persuade, the best persuaders we have encountered closely study the issues that matter to their colleagues. They use conversations, meetings, and other forms of dialogue to collect essential information. They are good at listening. They test their ideas with trusted confidants, and they ask questions of the people they will later be persuading. Those steps help them think through the arguments, the evidence, and the perspectives they will present. Oftentimes, this process causes them to alter or compromise their own plans before they even start persuading. It is through this thoughtful, inquisitive approach they develop frames that appeal to their audience.

Consider the case of a manager who was in charge of process engineering for a jet engine manufacturer. He had redesigned the work flow for routine turbine maintenance for airline clients in a manner

Numbers do not make an emotional impact, but stories and vivid language do.

that would dramatically shorten the turnaround time for servicing. Before presenting his ideas to the company's president, he consulted a good friend in the company, the vice president of engineering, who knew the president well. This conversation revealed that the president's prime concern would not be speed or efficiency but profitability. To get the president's buy-in, the vice president explained, the new system would have to improve the company's profitability in the short run by lowering operating expenses.

At first this information had the manager stumped. He had planned to focus on efficiency and had even intended to request additional funding to make the process work. But his conversation with the vice president sparked him to change his position. Indeed, he went so far as to change the work-flow design itself so that it no longer required new investment but rather drove down costs. He then carefully documented the cost savings and profitability gains that his new plan would produce and presented this revised plan to the president. With his initiative positioned anew, the manager persuaded the president and got the project approved.

Provide evidence. With credibility established and a common frame identified, persuasion becomes a matter of presenting evidence. Ordinary evidence, however, won't do. We have found that the most effective persuaders use language in a particular way. They supplement numerical data with examples, stories, metaphors, and analogies to make their positions come alive. That use of language paints a vivid word picture and, in doing so, lends a compelling and tangible quality to the persuader's point of view.

Think about a typical persuasion situation. The persuader is often advocating a goal, strategy, or initiative with an uncertain outcome. Karen Fries and Barry Linnett, for instance, wanted Microsoft to invest millions of dollars in a software package with chancy technology and unknown market demand. The team could have supported its case solely with market research, financial projections, and the like. But that would have been a mistake, because research shows that most people perceive such reports as not entirely informative. They are too abstract to be completely meaningful or memorable. In essence, the numbers don't make an emotional impact.

By contrast, stories and vivid language do, particularly when they present comparable situations to the one under discussion. A marketing manager trying to persuade senior executives to invest in a new product, for example, might cite examples of similar investments that paid off handsomely. Indeed, we found that people readily draw lessons from such cases. More important, the research shows that listeners absorb information in proportion to its vividness. Thus it is no wonder that Fries and Linnett hit a home run when they presented their case for BOB with the following analogy:

Imagine you want to cook dinner and you must first go to the supermarket. You have all the flexibility you want – you can cook anything in the world as long as you know how and have the time and desire to do it. When you arrive at the supermarket, you find all these overstuffed aisles with cryptic single-word headings like "sundries" and "ethnic food" and "condiments." These are the menus on typical computer interfaces. The question is whether salt is under condiments or ethnic food or near the potato chip section. There are surrounding racks and wall spaces, much as our software interfaces now have support buttons, tool bars, and lines around the perimeters. Now after you have collected everything, you still need to put it all together in the correct order to make a meal. If you're a good cook, your meal will probably be good. If you're a novice, it probably won't be.

We [at Microsoft] have been selling under the supermarket category for years, and we think there is a big opportunity for restaurants. That's what we are trying to do now with BOB: pushing the next step with software that is more like going to a restaurant, so the user doesn't spend all of his time searching for the ingredients. We find and put the ingredients together. You sit down, you get comfortable. We bring you a menu. We do the work, you relax. It's an enjoyable experience. No walking around lost trying to find things, no cooking.

Had Fries and Linnett used a literal description of BOB's advantages, few of their highly computer-

92   HARVARD BUSINESS REVIEW   May–June 1998

literate colleagues at Microsoft would have personally related to the menu-searching frustration that BOB was designed to eliminate. The analogy they selected, however, made BOB's purpose both concrete and memorable.

A master persuader, Mary Kay Ash, the founder of Mary Kay Cosmetics, regularly draws on analogies to illustrate and "sell" the business conduct she values. Consider this speech at the company's annual sales convention:

> Back in the days of the Roman Empire, the legions of the emperor conquered the known world. There was, however, one band of people that the Romans never conquered. Those people were the followers of the great teacher from Bethlehem. Historians have long since discovered that one of the reasons for the sturdiness of this folk was their habit of meeting together weekly. They shared their difficulties, and they stood side by side. Does this remind you of something? The way we stand side by side and share our knowledge and difficulties with each other in our weekly unit meetings? I have so often observed when a director or unit member is confronted with a personal problem that the unit stands together in helping that sister in distress. What a wonderful circle of friendships we have. Perhaps it's one of the greatest fringe benefits of our company.

Through her vivid analogy, Ash links collective support in the company to a courageous period in Christian history. In doing so, she accomplishes several objectives. First, she drives home her belief that collective support is crucial to the success of the organization. Most Mary Kay salespeople are independent operators who face the daily challenges of direct selling. An emotional support system of fellow salespeople is essential to ensure that self-esteem and confidence remain intact in the face of rejection. Next she suggests by her analogy that solidarity against the odds is the best way to stymie powerful oppressors – to wit, the competition. Finally, Ash's choice of analogy imbues a sense of a heroic mission to the work of her sales force.

You probably don't need to invoke the analogy of the Christian struggle to support your position, but effective persuaders are not afraid of unleashing the immense power of language. In fact, they use it to their utmost advantage.

Connect emotionally. In the business world, we like to think that our colleagues use reason to make their decisions, yet if we scratch below the surface we will always find emotions at play. Good persuaders are aware of the primacy of emotions and are responsive to them in two important ways.

First, they show their own emotional commitment to the position they are advocating. Such expression is a delicate matter. If you act too emotional, people may doubt your clearheadedness. But you must also show that your commitment to a goal is not just in your mind but in your heart and gut as well. Without this demonstration of feeling, people may wonder if you actually believe in the position you're championing.

Perhaps more important, however, is that effective persuaders have a strong and accurate sense of their audience's emotional state, and they adjust the tone of their arguments accordingly. Sometimes that means coming on strong, with forceful points. Other times, a whisper may be all that is required. The idea is that whatever your position, you match your emotional fervor to your audience's ability to receive the message.

Effective persuaders seem to have a second sense about how their colleagues have interpreted past events in the organization and how they will probably interpret a proposal. The best persuaders in our study would usually canvass key individuals who had a good pulse on the mood and emotional expectations of those about to be persuaded. They would ask those individuals how various proposals might affect colleagues on an emotional level – in essence, testing possible reactions. They were also quite effective at gathering information through informal conversations in the hallways or at lunch. In the end, their aim was to ensure that the emotional appeal behind their persuasion matched what their audience was already feeling or expecting.

To illustrate the importance of emotional matchmaking in persuasion, consider this example. The president of an aeronautics manufacturing company strongly believed that the maintenance costs

A persuader must match his or her emotional fervor to the audience's ability to receive the message.

and turnaround time of the company's U.S. and foreign competitors were so much better than his own company's that it stood to lose customers and profits. He wanted to communicate his fear and his urgent desire for change to his senior managers. So one afternoon, he called them into the boardroom. On an overhead screen was the projected image of a smiling man flying an old-fashioned biplane with his scarf blowing in the wind. The right half of the

THE NECESSARY ART OF PERSUASION

transparency was covered. When everyone was seated, the president explained that he felt as this pilot did, given the company's recent good fortune. The organization, after all, had just finished its most successful year in history. But then with a deep sigh, he announced that his happiness was quickly vanishing. As the president lifted the remaining portion of the sheet, he revealed an image of the pilot flying directly into a wall. The president then faced his audience and in a heavy voice said, "This is what I see happening to us." He asserted that the company was headed for a crash if people didn't take action fast. He then went on to lecture the group about the steps needed to counter this threat.

The reaction from the group was immediate and negative. Directly after the meeting, managers gathered in small clusters in the hallways to talk about the president's "scare tactics." They resented what they perceived to be the president's overstatement of the case. As the managers saw it, they had exerted enormous effort that year to break the company's records in sales and profitability. They were proud of their achievements. In fact, they had entered the meeting expecting it would be the moment of recognition. But to their absolute surprise, they were scolded.

The president's mistake? First, he should have canvassed a few members of his senior team to ascertain the emotional state of the group. From that, he would have learned that they were in need of thanks and recognition. He should then have held a separate session devoted simply to praising the team's accomplishments. Later, in a second meeting, he could have expressed his own anxieties about the coming year. And rather than blame the team for ignoring the future, he could have calmly described what he saw as emerging threats to the company and then asked his management team to help him develop new initiatives.

Now let us look at someone who found the right emotional match with his audience: Robert Marcell, head of Chrysler's small-car design team. In the early 1990s, Chrysler was eager to produce a new subcompact – indeed, the company had not introduced a new model of this type since 1978. But senior managers at Chrysler did not want to go it alone. They thought an alliance with a foreign manufacturer would improve the car's design and protect Chrysler's cash stores.

Marcell was convinced otherwise. He believed that the company should bring the design and production of a new subcompact in-house. He knew

that persuading senior managers would be difficult, but he also had his own team to contend with. Team members had lost their confidence that they would ever again have the opportunity to create a good car. They were also angry that the United States had once again given up its position to foreign competitors when it came to small cars.

Marcell decided that his persuasion tactics had to be built around emotional themes that would

It's important for people to understand persuasion for what it is – not convincing and selling but learning and negotiating.

touch his audience. From innumerable conversations around the company, he learned that many people felt as he did – that to surrender the subcompact's design to a foreign manufacturer was to surrender the company's soul and, ultimately, its ability to provide jobs. In addition, he felt deeply that his organization was a talented group hungry for a challenge and an opportunity to restore its self-esteem and pride. He would need to demonstrate his faith in the team's abilities.

Marcell prepared a 15-minute talk built around slides of his hometown, Iron River, a now defunct mining town in Upper Michigan, devastated, in large part, by foreign mining companies. On the screen flashed recent photographs he had taken of his boarded-up high school, the shuttered homes of his childhood friends, the crumbling ruins of the town's ironworks, closed churches, and an abandoned railroad yard. After a description of each of these places, he said the phrase, "We couldn't compete" – like the refrain of a hymn. Marcell's point was that the same outcome awaited Detroit if the production of small cars was not brought back to the United States. Surrender was the enemy, he said, and devastation would follow if the group did not take immediate action.

Marcell ended his slide show on a hopeful note. He spoke of his pride in his design group and then challenged the team to build a "made-in-America" subcompact that would prove that the United States could still compete. The speech, which echoed the exact sentiments of the audience, rekindled the group's fighting spirit. Shortly after the speech, group members began drafting their ideas for a new car.

Marcell then took his slide show to the company's senior management and ultimately to Chrysler chairman Lee Iacocca. As Marcell showed his slides, he could see that Iacocca was touched. Iacocca, after all, was a fighter and a strongly patriotic man himself. In fact, Marcell's approach was not too different from Iacocca's earlier appeal to the United States Congress to save Chrysler. At the end of the show, Marcell stopped and said, "If we dare to be different, we could be the reason the U.S. auto industry survives. We could be the reason our kids and grandkids don't end up working at fast-food chains." Iacocca stayed on for two hours as Marcell explained in greater detail what his team was planning. Afterward, Iacocca changed his mind and gave Marcell's group approval to develop a car, the Neon.

With both groups, Marcell skillfully matched his emotional tenor to that of the group he was addressing. The ideas he conveyed resonated deeply with his largely Midwestern audience. And rather than leave them in a depressed state, he offered them hope, which was more persuasive than promising doom. Again, this played to the strong patriotic sentiments of his American-heartland audience.

No effort to persuade can succeed without emotion, but showing too much emotion can be as unproductive as showing too little. The important point to remember is that you must match your emotions to your audience's.

The Force of Persuasion

The concept of persuasion, like that of power, often confuses and even mystifies businesspeople. It is so complex – and so dangerous when mishandled – that many would rather just avoid it altogether. But like power, persuasion can be a force for enormous good in an organization. It can pull people together, move ideas forward, galvanize change, and forge constructive solutions. To do all that, however, people must understand persuasion for what it is – not convincing and selling but learning and negotiating. Furthermore, it must be seen as an art form that requires commitment and practice, especially as today's business contingencies make persuasion more necessary than ever.   ⊖

[11]

The Executive as Coach

by James Waldroop and Timothy Butler

ow do you deal with the talented manager whose perfectionism paralyzes his or her direct reports? Or the high-performing expert who disdains teamwork under any circumstances? What about the sensitive manager who avoids confrontation of any kind? Do you ignore the problems? Get rid of the managers? Or do you coach them? Coaching requires understanding someone's problem behavior in context, deciding whether the problem can be remedied, and encouraging the person to adapt. Coaching – helping to change the behaviors that threaten to derail a valued manager – is often the best way to help that manager succeed.

So why are some executives reluctant to coach? Coaching can take a lot of time; the process is a bit of a mystery; and the results are not guaranteed. On a deeper level, executives may fear overstepping personal boundaries, assuming too much responsibility, or playing the role of psychiatrist. Let us be clear: Good coaching is simply good management. It requires many of the same skills that are critical to effective management, such as keen powers of observation, sensible judgment, and an ability to take appropriate action. Similarly, the goal of coaching is the goal of good management: to make the most of an organization's valuable resources. It sounds simple, yet many executives don't know where to begin.

In helping executives become better coaches, we have learned a few lessons that we would like to pass along. An effective coach knows what questions to ask when evaluating a situation, assessing problem behaviors, and calibrating his or her own coaching abilities. An effective coach also draws on a wide variety of techniques to help a manager change problem behaviors.

o identify what's really going on, it is critical to observe the dynamics between the manager in question and those around him. The focus, of course, is on the manager's behavior, but behavior never takes place in a vacuum. An important part of what you assess is the impact that problem behaviors have on the other members of the organization. A systematic way to understand a problem behavior in its context is to ask the same questions a journalist would ask when gathering information for a story: Who, what, when, where, how, and (if possible) why?

Consider, for example, the analytically brilliant but overbearing manager. Look for opportunities to see her in action, and pay attention to how she behaves under various circumstances. Whom does she attempt to dominate? Whom does she seem to respect? Is her behavior apparently influenced by the gender, status, or ethnic background of those around her? Does she have difficulties with one specific person? What exactly does she do that is overbearing? When does she act out that behavior?

James Waldroop and Timothy Butler are business psychologists who direct M.B.A. career-development programs at the Harvard Business School in Boston, Massachusetts. They are principals in Waldroop Butler Associates, a consulting firm in Brookline, Massachusetts, that specializes in executive coaching and career development counseling for business professionals. The authors recently completed their book, Discovering Your Career in Business, *to be published by Addison-Wesley in January 1997.*

COACHING

Always? During times of stress? When asked to perform outside her area of expertise? Does her behavior depend on where she is? Is she more or less overbearing outside her familiar territory? How does the behavior affect those around her and her ability to get her work done? Can you begin to understand why she behaves in an overbearing manner?

It is often very difficult to uncover the underlying reasons for a problem behavior. If the behavior is new, it may help to consider what else in the manager's life could be affecting her. Is she getting divorced? Suffering an illness? Struggling with a financial setback? Adjusting to married life? Finding out what's going on in the individual's personal life may provide you with key insights into the problem behavior. Of course, establishing rapport is not always easy to do and is generally possible only after you have entered into a coaching relationship with the manager.

Keeping track of effective behaviors as well as ineffective ones will help you develop a full picture of the person in question. Sometimes executives tend to focus only on the bad and overlook the good. The goal of coaching, however, is to help someone be more effective, not to build a case for the prosecution. Depending on the frequency of the problem behavior, the period of observation may go on for three months or longer, although it is sometimes possible to reach a conclusion sooner. Our rule of thumb is that one event makes one event, two events make two events, and three events make a pattern. How long the period of observation lasts must depend on your own judgment that enough information has been gathered.

To evaluate the effect of the problem behavior on the rest of the organization, it helps to answer some simple questions: How many of the problems that you have dealt with in the past three months centered on this person's behavior? When the organization tolerates negative behavior, what does it signal to other employees? What would life be like without the individual in the organization? What is life like when the manager is out on vacation?

It may be helpful to draw on the observations of other people you trust to round out your own understanding. Obviously, this information gathering must be conducted with great sensitivity. For example, you should not ask leading questions of the manager's peers or subordinates. Suppose, for example, that you are concerned that one of your managers controls information too tightly and finds delegation next to impossible. What kind of conversation could you have with his direct reports that would leave them confident in his leadership? Highlighting his problem behavior in any way risks undermining his effectiveness. If he finds out that you are talking about his problem behaviors with his peers and subordinates, he will almost certainly feel betrayed. Then your chances of establishing a healthy coaching relationship with him will be slim. Of course, employees who come to you with comments or complaints should be given an ear regardless of their status in the organization, or they will justifiably feel ignored.

As a general rule, confine your discussions about the manager to your own peers. They may have useful observations and advice. In one company we worked with, for instance, the general counsel had a very good sense of what was going on in the organization and often served as the senior executive's sounding board and confidant.

Once you have evaluated the situation, you must determine how bad the behavior is. "We are what we repeatedly do," wrote Aristotle more than 2,300 years ago. "Excellence, then, is not an act but a habit." Most commonly observed behaviors are habits in some form. The question you have to answer is, How entrenched is the habit? Stubbornly ingrained or something that can easily be changed? Truly expressive of the manager's character or a reflex without profound significance? Part of her substance or part of her style?

The answers to those questions have important implications. Consider the newly promoted vice president who is perceived as arrogant. Through his bluster, he may unwittingly be expressing a fear of failing in his new position. A good coach can help him identify his fears as normal and encourage him to behave more modestly. Alternatively, the manager may be deliberately acting arrogantly in the mistaken belief that arrogance is respected. A coach can help him dispose of that myth. The third possibility is that the manager is, in fact, incorrigible. A wise executive will recognize that the manager's behavior is not likely to change, because he is simply expressing his true character.

Three tests reveal whether or not a problem behavior is based in character. First, the behavior is part of a pattern seen in different contexts. For example, a person with low self-esteem may mask it by buying an expensive car, getting herself invited to the "right" parties, or sending her children to the "right" schools. She likely evaluates other people professionally and socially on the basis of status and generally avoids taking risks that might jeopardize her own standing.

Second, the problem behavior is generally observable over a long period. Has one manager always cheated on her income taxes or did she cheat just once when she was desperately short of cash? Has another always dodged responsibility or is he simply overwhelmed right now and temporarily unable to cope?

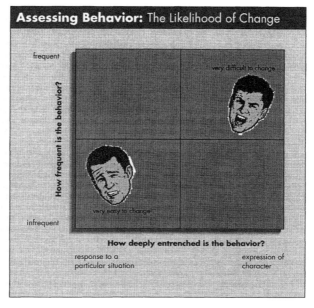

Assessing Behavior: The Likelihood of Change

How frequent is the behavior? — frequent / infrequent

very difficult to change

very easy to change

How deeply entrenched is the behavior?

response to a particular situation — expression of character

Third, character flaws tend to express themselves in a complex array of behaviors rather than in a single one. Changing one or two of these behaviors will not make much of a difference because too many other negative behaviors will likely remain. Imagine trying to coach the socially awkward technological wizard to prepare her for a senior sales-management position. You may succeed in some superficial ways – for instance, by training her to stand farther away from others at cocktail parties or to dress a bit better – but you cannot hope to change the myriad other behaviors that express her core being and mark her as a techno-nerd. The manager will never be able to engage in small talk when she really wants to talk bits and bytes. And she will never suffer fools gladly simply to make a sale. Even if you could identify and work on the many behaviors that express the very core of her character, such efforts would demand constant attention. She would revert to old habits unless she relentlessly monitored them, just as a car straightens out of a turn without a steady hand on the wheel. A manager can sometimes change character-driven behaviors, but only with constant effort and limits to success. Such be-

haviors are a lot like crabgrass: deeply rooted and difficult to weed out.

A simple conceptual framework can help you classify the type of the behavioral problem you are facing. (See the chart "Assessing Behavior: The Likelihood of Change.") The framework allows you to map the manager's behavior along two key dimensions: how frequently it occurs and how deeply

Character-driven behaviors are like crabgrass: deeply rooted and difficult to weed out.

rooted it is. The key questions that the framework then helps answer are as follows:

Can the problem behavior be changed? In cases at the extreme right of the continuum, consider the behavior to be unchangeable. The question then becomes, Can we live with that behavior? The decision whether or not to keep a manager depends on how profound the negative effect is. Does the behavior occur too frequently to be ignored? Does the behavior occur infrequently but with such impact

COACHING

that the person cannot succeed in the organization? A character trait such as dishonesty need express itself only rarely to derail a manager permanently. Do the negatives of a set of behaviors clearly outweigh the positives of the individual's contributions to the organization? If the negative aspects are too great, the answer may be to suggest that the person move to a place where the character trait is not a liability but a potential asset. For example, the verbally aggressive manager on the genteel corporate staff might be encouraged to join a new venture that would welcome his energy and shrug off his edge.

If the behavior can be changed, is the person willing to try to change it? Behavioral change is possible only when it is voluntary, and willingness to change even a superficial behavior at the far left of our chart depends on the individual. Some people will go to great lengths to change any behavior that inhibits their effectiveness. Other people consider any suggestion to change an assault on their entire being. The best predictor of future flexibility is flexibility in the past. Has the person previously been open to feedback and willing to change and grow? If so, you can expect him to do the same in the current situation.

Even if the individual's history suggests an unwillingness to change behaviors that are in fact changeable, you should assume that change is possible. One of management's most important jobs is to motivate, and inspiring a flawed but valuable player to accomplish something as difficult as significant behavioral change constitutes one mark of a fine executive. You are, in effect, resurrecting a valuable human resource that your organization might otherwise lose. It's worth a try.

 ecoming an effective coach requires introspection. Ironically, coaching someone else may require behavioral changes on your own part as great as the change you expect of the person you are coaching. Successful coaching behaviors run counter to many traditionally successful executive behaviors—behaviors that you will still need to use in other business contexts but may need to suspend for coaching. In effect, you need to figure out which of your own reflexes may get in the way as you begin to coach.

What are the typical behaviors of a successful senior executive? Not every executive has emerged from the same mold, of course, but top-level executives as a class tend to be very competitive and quick to think, judge, act, and speak. Concerned with the complex needs of the business, they are pressed for time and can afford to tolerate few excuses from their subordinates. Given the pressures on them from their boards and from Wall Street, most executives focus their attention on the business in the near term and don't have a great deal of time to spend on building warm and fuzzy relationships with their subordinates. Because of the meeting and travel schedules most executives keep today, it is hard for them to develop and maintain relationships.

Compare that profile with the characteristics of an effective coach. The coach must adopt the approach of teacher, not competitor; of helpful colleague, not judge. The coach observes first to understand, and only after understanding is he able to criticize. The intent of any criticism is to help the person improve. The coach reflects before acting and encourages the individual he is coaching to do the same. Although the ultimate goal of coaching is to improve business performance, the focus is less on the immediate task and more on the long term. In addition to pointing out problems, a wise coach knows when to give positive strokes to provide support and structures a collaborative relationship through regular meetings.

If you had to, could you do all that tomorrow? Could you stand some of your most prized behaviors on their head? Think of what that would mean. The coaching relationship would receive as high a priority as any other important business challenge. Would you be willing to set aside other business obligations temporarily? Coach and manager need to meet regularly and frequently. Could you meet for at least an hour every other week? Are you willing to put these meetings on your calendar and guard that time?

Coaching requires confronting some unpleasant truths about a key member of your team. Are you able to deal with an imperfection in one of your managers? Can you suspend judgment long enough to figure out how to help? Perhaps the problem behavior annoys you as much as it bothers everyone else. Will you be able to put that feeling of irritation aside to be a helpful coach? For example, we know of one hard-driving, analytical, supremely organized executive faced with coaching a brilliant, creative, very disorganized manager who did excellent work but could not meet a deadline. The executive's struggle with himself was as great as his struggle with the subordinate. He had to face and overcome his fundamental distaste for the other's style even before he could consider coaching. The executive ultimately succeeded as a coach because he was very clear about the standards that he wanted met and did not compromise them. The behavioral objective he set for the manager was clear and unambiguous: be brilliant and creative, but change the perfectionist behaviors that get in the way of meeting deadlines.

Coaches who define their purpose as saving a valuable resource for the long-term benefit of the organization are more successful than coaches who get caught up in the immediacy of the coaching relationship. This long-term view keeps them out of personality conflicts and reminds them that coaching is a legitimate business responsibility. To maintain this kind of positive attitude, it helps to remember two other things. First, sometimes even the strongest performers need assistance to grow into a new position. Coaching is as much about ensuring success as it is about staving off failure. Second, most people want to be effective, especially the goal-oriented individuals who are key to your organization. The message to send is not, Nobody likes you. It is instead, You're less effective than you could be.

 etting up the first meeting in which you introduce the idea of coaching requires great care. You should schedule it as you would any other business meeting, broaching the subject of the meeting gently: "Let's get together and talk about the Chan deal. There were some problems with it that we've seen before, and I'd like to talk to you about them." Remember that confronting the manager in immediate reaction to a specific incident is a mistake because the atmosphere will still be too fraught with tension.

You may want to create a rough script for the meeting. What do you want to say? In what order? When would it make sense to pause to let a point sink in? When should you wait to allow for a reaction? It may be helpful to practice out loud, as if you were preparing for any other important business presentation. Speaking in the first person makes it clear that both of you are dealing with perceptions, not objective reality: "Here's how I observe you..." "Here is what I'm seeing..." "If I were in that person's shoes, I might think..." Be truthful, calm, and supportive.

The manager must emerge from the first conversation with her ego intact. She needs to feel that she is appreciated but has room to grow. Sandwiching negative feedback between two genuinely positive messages softens the blow. At the close of the conversation, you need to be able to say, "I don't want you to leave this meeting without going back to my opening comments. You are very important to us, and we would not be having this conversation if I did not value you and your contribution very highly. There is a real problem here, and I want to work on it with you so that you have a rewarding future in our organization."

Despite your best efforts, many managers confronted with their behaviors for the first time will resist the feedback and deny the behaviors. If that happens, remain calm and say, "You need to understand how other people experience working with you." The message to send at the outset is that you are accurately relating what you and others experience in their relationship with the individual. If the manager continues to resist, let go. In the words of the fly fisherman, sometimes you have to let the fish run. A day or two of reflection can greatly increase a manager's receptivity to coaching advice. Once you broach the subject, however, you must follow through with it. Nothing will be gained by avoiding the issue.

You will need to find a useful balance between carrot and stick. The deciding factor is the sensitivity of the individual. If he is fragile, use more carrot: "You are so valuable that we really want you to succeed. I understand that it's not easy to shift into a new job. I certainly needed help when I was promoted to this level. Let's get together every once in a while and talk about how things are going. I know that you'll do a great job." Of course, if you are too positive, the manager may not grasp the serious need to change; however, if you overemphasize the negative, you can scare a valuable player into jumping ship. The situation may seem too desperate.

If the person in question is very bullheaded (or simply dense), you may be forced to use more stick.

When coaching, you need to find a balance between carrot and stick.

COACHING

Sometimes a manager confronted with his problem behavior simply shrugs and lets you know that he frankly doesn't care. You might try this answer: "I don't care if you think you have a problem or not. *I'm* your boss, and *I* think you have a problem, so you have a problem. Work on this behavior and make it go away, or you are out of here." In general, it makes sense to err on the side of the carrot because you cannot erase wounds once they have been inflicted. But it is just as big a mistake to avoid confronting someone who does not realize his effect on other people.

Finally, separate the coaching experience from the formal performance-review process. Of course, they are related – the behavioral issue may be the root cause of a performance issue – but you should present the coaching experience as a developmental opportunity for the benefit of both manager and organization.

Practicing a number of coaching techniques can help you be more effective in your new role. Both coach and manager need to agree on the ultimate goal, be it reducing the number of sarcastic outbursts, repairing relationships across organizational boundaries, allowing subordinates to speak freely – the potential list is endless. It is likely that you will be working on more than one line of development in a single individual. Unfortunately, few people in need of coaching exhibit only one troublesome behavior at a time.

Any plan of action for remedying problems must be behaviorally specific, but lasting change also requires the manager to reflect on her own actions and to learn from them. When developing a plan of action with a manager, do not devise a to-do list with boxes to check off. Instead, create together a thoughtful program that encourages learning. We have found some relatively simple techniques to be helpful in the coaching meetings themselves.

Practice active listening. Play back to the person what you heard her say, paraphrasing in your own words so that the person knows you truly understood her – or so that you can clarify any misunderstandings if you didn't. This discipline also helps you better articulate to yourself what you are hearing and exemplifies a good behavior for the manager to use in her own work.

Support learning through action and reflection. The coach needs to support the manager's learning process by taking time after a specific event or during the scheduled coaching meeting to ask, "What happened? What did you do? How successful do you think the action was? How did you feel before, dur-

ing, and after? How did other people react? Did you get any feedback? Do you need to follow up?" One goal of the coach in the action-and-reflection cycle is to make the manager realize how his behaviors affect his ability to succeed. The best way to accomplish that is to ask him to imagine how others might be reacting to his behavior.

Move from easy to hard. One of the best pieces of advice that we can give to an executive is to move from easy to hard, much as learning to ski on the beginner slopes gives a skier the skills and confidence to advance to intermediate runs. Do not expect the behavioral goal to be reached without some trial and error along the way. If you need to work on several behaviors, pick the one that is likeliest to change quickly and with the least amount of trauma. Then move on to successively more entrenched behaviors.

Set microgoals. A very effective technique that allows for practicing a new behavior with minimal risk is to set what we call *microgoals*. These goals approximate the ultimate goal and form the basis for reflection and discussion between coach and manager. For example, if the ultimate goal is to be a more trusted and approachable manager, successive microgoals for the manager might be to ask a staff assistant how his weekend went, to solicit other people's opinions about a decision and to follow up with them afterward, to ask more people out to lunch, and to take notes about how a particularly nettlesome relationship is progressing. If the ultimate goal is to stop overly controlling behavior, a series of microgoals might encourage the manager to hold back her opinion in a meeting until everyone else has spoken, to delegate an important piece of work, and to practice active listening.

Use tape delay. Another helpful technique for a coach to use is what we call *tape delay*. The coach encourages the manager who gets into trouble by speaking before thinking to wait for five seconds before reacting in meetings, just as live television

delays broadcast by a few seconds to allow network censors to delete any profanity.

Practice script writing and role-playing. The coach can help the manager who has problems communicating by encouraging him to write scripts and then to play out possible scenarios.

Set up relationship-repair meetings. The coach must ask many questions of the manager to find out what is happening in a bad relationship. When the manager is ready to work on the relationship, the coach may help him script and play out a first meeting. It also may be of benefit if the coach acts as meeting facilitator.

Encourage more positive feedback. Executives and managers have an understandable tendency to focus on problems more than on successes. When coaching, don't just dwell on the negative, and encourage the manager you are coaching to avoid this error as well. Napoleon stressed how everyone responds to rewards when he said, "Men don't risk their lives for their country. Men risk their lives for medals." Human nature has not changed.

The essence of coaching is to be imaginative and to look for a variety of solutions. Coaching must reflect the complexity and difficulty of genuine efforts to change behavior. Behavioral change requires understanding one's effect on other people – a process that can be painful. Change requires endurance: it may take place over months, not weeks or days. Change requires faith: progress in the beginning may come in small increments as the manager moves from minor modifications to more noticeable differences. Change takes vigilance and self-discipline: sliding backward is almost always easier than moving forward. Change means deferring gratification: expect no applause; even after a behavior changes for the better, few people will notice until new behavioral patterns are well established. Change is not linear: allow for the occasional slip backward as well as the leap forward.

Successful executives often tell us that when they were in business school, they considered the quantitative "hard" subjects, such as finance and operations management, to be the most important topics they studied; they had little respect for the "soft" subjects, such as organizational behavior and human resources management. Fifteen or 20 years later, however, those same executives recognize that it is their people management skills – working with and developing people–that have been the key both to their personal success and to that of their business. Being an effective coach is one essential part of that key to success.   ☋

[12]

TAKING THE STRESS OUT OF STRESSFUL CONVERSATIONS

We all get caught in conversations
fraught with emotion. Usually, these
interactions end badly – but they
don't have to, thanks to a handful of
techniques you can apply unilaterally.

by Holly Weeks

W E LIVE BY TALKING. That's just the kind of animal we are. We chatter and tattle and gossip
and jest. But sometimes – more often than
we'd like – we have stressful conversations, those sensitive exchanges that can hurt or haunt us in ways no
other kind of talking does. Stressful conversations are
unavoidable in life, and in business they can run the
gamut from firing a subordinate to, curiously enough,
receiving praise. But whatever the context, stressful
conversations differ from other conversations because
of the emotional loads they carry. These conversations
call up embarrassment, confusion, anxiety, anger, pain,

or fear – if not in us, then in our counterparts. Indeed, stressful conversations cause such anxiety that most people simply avoid them. This strategy is not necessarily wrong. One of the first rules of engagement, after all, is to pick your battles. Yet sometimes it can be extremely costly to dodge issues, appease difficult people, and smooth over antagonisms because the fact is that avoidance usually makes a problem or relationship worse.

Since stressful conversations are so common – and so painful – why don't we work harder to improve them? The reason is precisely because our feelings are so enmeshed. When we are not emotionally entangled in an issue, we know that conflict is normal, that it can be resolved – or at least managed. But when feelings get stirred up, most of us are thrown off balance. Like a quarterback who chokes in a tight play, we lose all hope of ever making it to the goal line.

For the past 20 years, I have been teaching classes and conducting workshops at some of the top corporations and universities in the United States on how to communicate during stressful conversations. With classrooms as my laboratory, I have learned that most people feel incapable of talking through sensitive issues. It's as though all our skills go out the window and we can't think usefully about what's happening or what we could do to get good results.

Stressful conversations, though, need not be this way. I have seen that managers can improve difficult conversations unilaterally if they approach them with greater self-awareness, rehearse them in advance, and apply just three proven communication techniques. Don't misunderstand me: There will never be a cookie-cutter approach to stressful conversations. There are too many variables and too much tension, and the interactions between people in difficult situations are always unique. Yet nearly every stressful conversation can be seen as an amalgam of a limited number of basic conversations, each with its own distinct set of problems. In the following pages, we'll explore how you can anticipate and handle those problems. But first, let's look at the three basic stressful conversations that we bump up against most often in the workplace.

"I Have Bad News for You"

Delivering unpleasant news is usually difficult for both parties. The speaker is often tense, and the listener is apprehensive about where the conversation is headed. Consider David, the director of a nonprofit institution. He was in the uncomfortable position of needing to talk with an ambitious researcher, Jeremy, who had a much higher opinion of his job performance than others in the organization did. The complication for David was that, in the past, Jeremy had received artificially high evaluations. There were several reasons for this. One had to do with the organization's culture: The nonprofit was not a

confrontational kind of place. Additionally, Jeremy had tremendous confidence in both his own abilities and the quality of his academic background. Together with his defensive response to even the mildest criticism, this confidence led others – including David – to let slide discussions of weaknesses that were interfering with Jeremy's ability to deliver high-quality work. Jeremy had a cutting sense of humor, for instance, which had offended people inside and outside his unit. No one had ever said anything to him directly, but as time passed, more and more people were reluctant to work with him. Given that Jeremy had received almost no concrete criticism over the years, his biting style was now entrenched and the staff was restive.

In conversations like this, the main challenge is to get off to the right start. If the exchange starts off reasonably well, the rest of it has a good chance of going well. But if the opening goes badly, it threatens to bleed forward into the rest of the conversation. In an effort to be gentle, many people start these conversations on a light note. And that was just what David did, opening with, "How about those Red Sox?"

Naturally Jeremy got the wrong idea about where David was heading; he remained his usual cocky, superior self. Sensing this, David felt he had to take off the velvet gloves. The conversation quickly became brutally honest, and David did almost all the talking. When the monologue was over, Jeremy stared icily at the floor. He got up in stiff silence and left. David was relieved. From his point of view, the interaction had been painful but swift. There was not too much blood on the floor, he observed wryly. But two days later, Jeremy handed in his resignation, taking a lot of institutional memory – and talent – with him.

"What's Going On Here?"

Often we have stressful conversations thrust upon us. Indeed, some of the worst conversations – especially for people who are conflict averse – are the altogether unexpected ones that break out like crackling summer storms. Suddenly the conversation becomes intensely charged emotionally, and electricity flies in all directions. What's worse, nothing makes sense. We seem to have been drawn into a black cloud of twisted logic and altered sensibilities.

Consider the case of Elizabeth and Rafael. They were team leaders working together on a project for a major consulting firm. It seemed that everything that could have gone wrong on the project had, and the work was badly bogged down. The two consultants were meeting to revise their schedule, given the delays, and to divide up the discouraging tasks for the week ahead. As they talked, Eliza-

Holly Weeks is an independent consultant and the president of WritingWorks and SpeakingWorks in Cambridge, Massachusetts. She also teaches at the Radcliffe Institute of Harvard University in Cambridge.

beth wrote and erased on the white board. When she had finished, she looked at Rafael and said matter-of-factly, "Is that it, then?"

Rafael clenched his teeth in frustration. "If you say so," he sniped.

Elizabeth recoiled. She instantly replayed the exchange in her mind but couldn't figure out what had provoked Rafael. His reaction seemed completely disconnected from her comment. The most common reaction of someone in Elizabeth's place is to guiltily defend herself by denying Rafael's unspoken accusation. But Elizabeth was uneasy with confrontation so she tried appeasement. "Rafael," she stammered, "I'm sorry. Is something wrong?"

"Who put you in charge?" he retorted. "Who told you to assign work to me?"

Clearly, Rafael and Elizabeth have just happened into a difficult conversation. Some transgression has occurred, but Elizabeth doesn't know exactly what it is. She feels blindsided – her attempt to expedite the task at hand has clearly been misconstrued. Rafael feels he's been put in a position of inferiority by what he sees as Elizabeth's controlling behavior. Inexplicably, there seem to be more than two people taking part in this conversation, and the invisible parties are creating lots of static. What childhood experience, we may wonder, is causing Elizabeth to assume that Rafael's tension is automatically her fault? And who is influencing Rafael's perception that Elizabeth is taking over? Could it be his father? His wife? It's impossible to tell. At the same time, it's hard for us to escape the feeling that Rafael is overreacting when he challenges Elizabeth about her alleged need to take control.

Elizabeth felt Rafael's resentment like a wave and she apologized again. "Sorry. How do you want the work divided?" Deferring to Rafael in this way smoothed the strained atmosphere for the time being. But it set a precedent for unequal status that neither Elizabeth nor the company believed was correct. Worse, though Rafael and Elizabeth remained on the same team after their painful exchange, Elizabeth chafed under the status change and three months later transferred out of the project.

"You Are Attacking Me!"

Now let's turn our attention to aggressively stressful conversations, those in which people use all kinds of psychological and rhetorical mechanisms to throw their counterparts off balance, to undermine their positions, even to expose and belittle them. These "thwarting tactics" take many forms – profanity, manipulation, shouting – and not everyone is triggered or stumped by the same ones. The red zone is not the thwarting tactic alone but the pairing of the thwarting tactic with individual vulnerability.

Consider Nick and Karen, two senior managers working at the same level in an IT firm. Karen was leading a

presentation to a client, and the information was weak and disorganized. She and the team had not been able to answer even basic questions. The client had been patient, then quiet, then clearly exasperated. When the presentation really started to fall apart, the client put the team on the spot with questions that made them look increasingly inadequate.

On this particular day, Nick was not part of the presenting team; he was simply observing. He was as surprised as the client at Karen's poor performance. After the client left, he asked Karen what happened. She lashed out at him defensively: "You're not my boss, so don't start patronizing me. You always undercut me no matter what I do." Karen continued to shout at Nick, her antagonism palpable. Each time he spoke, she interrupted him with accusations and threats: "I can't wait to see how you like it when people leave you flailing in the wind." Nick tried to remain reasonable, but Karen didn't wind down. "Karen," he said, "pull yourself together. You are twisting every word I say."

Here, Nick's problem is not that Karen is using a panoply of thwarting tactics, but that all her tactics – accusation, distortion, and digression – are aggressive. This raises the stakes considerably. Most of us are vulnerable to aggressive tactics because we don't know whether, or how far, the aggression will escalate. Nick wanted to avoid Karen's aggression, but his insistence on rationality in the face of emotionalism was not working. His cool approach was trumped by Karen's aggressive one. As a result, Nick found himself trapped in the snare of Karen's choosing. In particular, her threats that she would pay him back with the client rattled him. He couldn't tell whether she was just huffing or meant it. He finally turned to the managing director, who grew frustrated, and later angry, at Nick and Karen for their inability to resolve their problems. In the end, their lack of skill in handling their difficult conversations cost them dearly. Both were passed over for promotion after the company pinned the loss of the client directly on their persistent failure to communicate.

Preparing for a Stressful Conversation

So how can we prepare for these three basic stressful conversations before they occur? A good start is to become aware of your own weaknesses to people and situations. David, Elizabeth, and Nick were unable to control their counterparts, but their stressful conversations would have gone much better if they had been more usefully aware of their vulnerabilities. It is important for those who are vulnerable to hostility, for example, to know how they react to it. Do they withdraw or escalate – do they clam up or retaliate? While one reaction is not better than the other, knowing how you react in a stressful situation will teach you a lot about your vulnerabilities, and it can help you master stressful situations.

Recall Nick's problem. If he had been more self-aware, he would have known that he acts stubbornly rational in the face of aggressive outbursts such as Karen's. Nick's choice of a disengaged demeanor gave Karen control over the conversation, but he didn't have to allow Karen – or anyone else – to exploit his vulnerability. In moments of calm self-scrutiny, when he's not entangled in a live stressful conversation, Nick can take time to reflect on his inability to tolerate irrational aggressive outbursts. This self-awareness would free him to prepare himself – not for Karen's unexpected accusations but for his own predictable vulnerability to any sudden assault like hers.

Though it might sound like it, building awareness is not about endless self-analysis. Much of it simply involves making our tacit knowledge about ourselves more explicit. We all know from past experience, for instance, what kinds of conversations and people we handle badly. When you find yourself in a difficult conversation, ask yourself whether this is one of those situations and whether it involves one of those people. For instance, do you bare your teeth when faced with an overbearing competitor? Do you shut down when you feel excluded? Once you know what your danger zones are, you can anticipate your vulnerability and improve your response.

Explicit self-awareness will often help save you from engaging in a conversation in a way that panders to your feelings rather than one that serves your needs. Think back to David, the boss of the nonprofit institution, and Jeremy, his cocky subordinate. Given Jeremy's history, David's conversational game plan – easing in, then when that didn't work, the painful-but-quick bombshell – was doomed. A better approach would have been for David to split the conversation into two parts. In a first meeting, he could have raised the central issues of Jeremy's biting humor and disappointing performance. A second meeting could have been set up for the discussion itself. Handling the situation incrementally would have allowed time for both David and Jeremy to prepare for a two-way conversation instead of one of them delivering a monologue. After all, this wasn't an emergency; David didn't have to exhaust this topic immediately. Indeed, if David had been more self-aware, he might have recognized that the approach he chose was dictated less by Jeremy's character than by his own distaste for conflict.

An excellent way to anticipate specific problems that you may encounter in a stressful conversation is to rehearse with a neutral friend. Pick someone who doesn't have the same communication problems as you. Ideally, the friend should be a good listener, honest but nonjudgmental. Start with content. Just tell your friend what you want to say to your counterpart without worrying about tone or phrasing. Be vicious, be timid, be sarcastically witty, jump around in your argument, but get it out. Now

go over it again and think about what you would say if the situation weren't emotionally loaded. Your friend can help you because he or she is not in a flush of emotion over the situation. Write down what you come up with together because if you don't, you'll forget it later.

Now fine-tune the phrasing. When you imagine talking to the counterpart, your phrasing tends to be highly charged – and you can think of only one way to say anything. But when your friend says, "Tell me how you want to say this," an interesting thing happens: your phrasing is often much better, much more temperate, usable. Remember, you can say what you want to say, you just can't say it *like that.* Also, work on your body language with your friend. You'll both soon be laughing because of the expressions that sneak out unawares – eyebrows skittering up and down, legs wrapped around each other like licorice twists, nervous snickers that will certainly be misinterpreted. (For more on preparing for stressful conversations, see the sidebar "The DNA of Conversation Management.")

Managing the Conversation

While it is important to build awareness and to practice before a stressful conversation, these steps are not enough. Let's look at what you can do as the conversation unfolds. Consider Elizabeth, the team leader whose colleague claimed she was usurping control. She couldn't think well on her feet in confrontational situations, and she knew it, so she needed a few hip-pocket phrases – phrases she could recall on the spot so that she wouldn't have to be silent or invent something on the spur of the moment. Though such a solution sounds simple, most of us don't have a tool kit of conversational tactics ready at hand. Rectifying this gap is an essential part of learning how to handle stressful conversations better. We need to learn communications skills, in the same way that we learn CPR: well in advance, knowing that when we need to use them, the situation will be critical and tense. Here are three proven conversational gambits. The particular wording may not suit your style, and that's fine. The important thing is to understand how the techniques work, and then choose phrasing that is comfortable for you.

Honor thy partner. When David gave negative feedback to Jeremy, it would have been refreshing if he had begun with an admission of regret and some responsibility for his contribution to their shared problem. "Jeremy," he might have said, "the quality of your work has been undercut – in part by the reluctance of your colleagues to risk the edge of your humor by talking problems through with you. I share responsibility for this because I have been reluctant to speak openly about these difficulties with you, whom I like and respect and with whom I have worked a long time." Acknowledging responsibility as a technique – particularly as an opening – can be effective because it immediately focuses attention, but without

The DNA of Conversation Management

The techniques I have identified for handling stressful conversations all have tucked within them three deceptively simple ingredients that are needed to make stressful conversations succeed. These are clarity, neutrality, and temperance, and they are the building blocks of all good communication. Mastering them will multiply your chances of responding well to even the most strained conversation. Let's take a look at each of the components in turn.

Clarity means letting words do the work for us. Avoid euphemisms or talking in circles – tell people clearly what you mean: "Emily, from your family's point of view, the Somerset Valley Nursing Home would be the best placement for your father. His benefits don't cover it." Unfortunately, delivering clear content when the news is bad is particularly hard to do. Under strained circumstances, we all tend to shy away from clarity because we equate it with brutality. Instead, we often say things like: "Well, Dan, we're still not sure yet what's going to happen with this job, but in the future we'll keep our eyes open." This is a roundabout – and terribly misleading – way to inform someone that he didn't get the promotion he was seeking. Yet there's nothing inherently brutal about honesty. It is not the content but the delivery of the news that makes it brutal or humane. Ask a surgeon; ask a priest; ask a cop. If a message is given skillfully – even though the news is bad – the content may still be tolerable. When a senior executive, for example, directly tells a subordinate that "the promotion has gone to someone else," the news is likely to be highly unpleasant, and the appropriate reaction is sadness, anger, and anxiety. But if the content is clear, the listener can better begin to process the information. Indeed, bringing clarity to the content eases the burden for the counterpart rather than increases it.

Tone is the nonverbal part of delivery in stressful conversations. It is intonation, facial expressions, conscious and unconscious body language. Although it's hard to have a neutral tone when overcome by strong feelings, neutrality is the desired norm in crisis communications, including stressful conversations. Consider the classic neutrality of NASA. Regardless of how dire the message, NASA communicates its content in uninflected tones: "Houston, we have a problem." It takes practice to acquire such neutrality. But a neutral tone is the best place to start when a conversation turns stressful.

Temperate phrasing is the final element in this triumvirate of skills. English is a huge language, and there are lots of different ways to say what you need to say. Some of these phrases are temperate, while others baldly provoke your counterpart to dismiss your words – and your content. In the United States, for example, some of the most intemperate phrasing revolves around threats of litigation: "If you don't get a check to me by April 23, I'll be forced to call my lawyer." Phrases like this turn up the heat in all conversations, particularly in strained ones. But remember, we're not in stressful conversations to score points or to create enemies. The goal is to advance the conversation, to hear and be heard accurately, and to have a functional exchange between two people. So next time you want to snap at someone – "Stop interrupting me!" – try this: "Can you hold on a minute? I want to finish before I lose my train of thought." Temperate phrasing will help you take the strain out of a stressful conversation.

One of the most common occurrences in stressful conversations is that we all start relying far too much on our intentions. As the mercury in the emotional thermometer rises, we presume that other people automatically understand what we mean. We assume, for instance, that people know we mean well. Indeed, research shows that in stressful conversations, most speakers assume cerely by the speaker; nevertheless, most people automatically react by stiffening inwardly, anticipating something at least mildly offensive or antagonistic. And that is exactly the reaction that phrase is always going to get. Because the simplest rule about stressful conversations is that people don't register intention despite words; we register intention through words. In stressful conversations in particular, the emphasis is on what Of course, in difficult conversations we may all wish that we didn't have to be so explicit. We may want the other person to realize what we mean even if we don't spell it out. But that leads to the wrong division of labor–with the listener interpreting rather than the speaker communicating. In all conversations, but especially in stressful ones, we are all responsible for getting across to one an-

The Gap Between Communication and Intent

that the listener believes that they have good intentions, regardless of what they say. Intentions can never be that powerful in communications – and certainly not in stressful conversations.

To see what I mean, just think of the last time someone told you not to take something the wrong way. This may well have been uttered quite sin-

ticular, the emphasis is on what is actually said, not on what we intend or feel. This doesn't mean that participants in stressful conversations don't have feelings or intentions that are valid and valuable. They do. But when we talk about people in stressful communication, we're talking about communication between people–and not about intentions.

other precisely what we want to say. In the end, it's far more dignified for an executive to come right out and tell an employee: "Corey, I've arranged a desk for you–and six weeks of outplacement service–because you won't be with us after the end of July." Forcing someone to guess your intentions only prolongs the agony of the inevitable.

provocation, on the difficult things the speaker needs to say and the listener needs to hear.

Is this always a good technique in a difficult conversation? No, because there is never any one good technique. But in this case, it effectively sets the tone for David's discussion with Jeremy. It honors the problems, it honors Jeremy, it honors their relationship, and it honors David's responsibility. Any technique that communicates honor in a stressful conversation–particularly a conversation that will take the counterpart by surprise–is to be highly valued. Indeed, the ability to act with dignity can make or break a stressful conversation. More important, while Jeremy has left the company, he can still do harm by spreading gossip and using his insider's knowledge against the organization. The more intolerable the conversation with David has been, the more Jeremy is likely to make the organization pay.

Disarm by restating your intentions. Part of the difficulty in Rafael and Elizabeth's "What's Going On Here?" conversation is that Rafael's misinterpretation of Eliza-

beth's words and actions seems to be influenced by instant replays of other stressful conversations that he has had in the past. Elizabeth doesn't want to psychoanalyze Rafael; indeed, exploring Rafael's internal landscape would exacerbate this painful situation. So what can Elizabeth do to defuse the situation unilaterally?

Elizabeth needs a technique that doesn't require her to understand the underlying reasons for Rafael's strong reaction but helps her handle the situation effectively. "I can see how you took what I said the way you did, Rafael. That wasn't what I meant. Let's go over this list again." I call this the clarification technique, and it's a highly disarming one. Using it, Elizabeth can unilaterally change the confrontation into a point of agreement. Instead of arguing with Rafael about his perceptions, she grants him his perceptions–after all, they're his. Instead of arguing about her intentions, she keeps the responsibility for aligning her words with her intentions on her side. And she goes back into the conversation right where they left off. (For a fuller discussion of the disconnect between what we mean and what we say, see the sidebar "The Gap Between Communication and Intent.")

This technique will work for Elizabeth regardless of Rafael's motive. If Rafael innocently misunderstood what she was saying, she isn't fighting him. She accepts his take on what she said and did and corrects it. If his motive is hostile, Elizabeth doesn't concur just to appease him. She accepts and retries. No one loses face. No one scores points off the other. No one gets drawn off on a tangent.

Fight tactics, not people. Rafael may have baffled Elizabeth, but Karen was acting with outright malice toward Nick when she flew off the handle after a disastrous meeting with the client. Nick certainly can't prevent her from using the thwarting tactics with which she has been so successful in the past. But he can separate Karen's character from her behavior. For instance, it's much more useful for him to think of Karen's reactions as thwarting tactics rather than as personal characteristics. If he thinks of Karen as a distorting, hostile, threatening person, where does that lead? What can anyone ever do about another person's character? But if Nick sees Karen's behavior as a series of tactics that she is using with him because they have worked for her in the past, he can think about using countering techniques to neutralize them.

The best way to neutralize a tactic is to name it. It's much harder to use a tactic once it is openly identified. If Nick, for instance, had said, "Karen, we've worked together pretty well for a long time. I don't know how to talk about what went wrong in the meeting when your take on what happened, and what's going on now, is so different from mine," he would have changed the game completely. He neither would have attacked Karen nor remained the pawn of her tactics. But he would have made Karen's tactics in the conversation the dominant problem.

Openly identifying a tactic, particularly an aggressive one, is disarming for another reason. Often we think of an aggressive counterpart as persistently, even endlessly, contentious, but that isn't true. People have definite levels of aggression that they're comfortable with – and they are reluctant to raise the bar. When Nick doesn't acknowledge Karen's tactics, she can use them unwittingly, or allegedly

so. But if Nick speaks of them, it would require more aggression on Karen's part to continue using the same tactics. If she is at or near her aggression threshold, she won't continue because that would make her uncomfortable. Nick may not be able to stop Karen, but she may stop herself.

People think stressful conversations are inevitable. And they are. But that doesn't mean they have to have bad resolutions. Consider a client of mine, Jacqueline, the only woman on the board of an engineering company. She was sensitive to slighting remarks about women in business, and she found one board member deliberately insensitive. He repeatedly ribbed her about being a feminist and, on this occasion, he was telling a sexist joke.

This wasn't the first time that something like this had happened, and Jacqueline felt the usual internal cacophony of reactions. But because she was aware that this was a stressful situation for her, Jacqueline was prepared. First, she let the joke hang in the air for a minute and then went back to the issue they had been discussing. When Richard didn't let it go but escalated with a new poke – "Come on, Jackie, it was a *joke*" – Jacqueline stood her ground. "Richard," she said, "this kind of humor is frivolous to you, but it makes me feel pushed aside." Jacqueline didn't need to say more. If Richard had continued to escalate, he would have lost face. In fact, he backed down: "Well, I wouldn't want my wife to hear about my bad behavior a second time," he snickered. Jacqueline was silent. She had made her point; there was no need to embarrass him.

Stressful conversations are never easy, but we can all fare better if, like Jacqueline, we prepare for them by developing greater awareness of our vulnerabilities and better techniques for handling ourselves. The advice and tools described in this article can be helpful in unilaterally reducing the strain in stressful conversations. All you have to do is try them. If one technique doesn't work, try another. Find phrasing that feels natural. But keep practicing – you'll find what works best for you.   ♉

Part III
Power and Leadership

Introduction to Part III

Power and Leadership

David Pearce and Alan Hooper

Power is an inevitable constituent of leadership. However, modern Western leaders are surprisingly coy about acknowledging the word 'power', and until recently it has been quite difficult to find straightforward accounts of leadership and power in modern management literature. Perhaps power smacks too much of ideology, self-aggrandizement and repression – all the things that are considered bad, both in a democracy and in modern people-centred organizations.

Nevertheless, the most cursory reflection on leadership and followership is likely to lead to the conclusion that an understanding of power is essential to achieve any form of successful outcome in a situation that requires the exercise of leadership by an individual or by a group. It is also increasingly becoming recognized that the balanced use of power by followers is an essential part of the exercise of power by mature leaders.

In the Preface to his book *Power in Organizations* (1981) Jeffrey Pfeffer asserts that 'Power, influence, and political activity all exist' in organizations (1981, p. x). He finds that '[t]he literature on power is not particularly large, and the empirical study of power and politics is unfortunately a rare event' (ibid.) and adds that '[a]s part of any study of influence, the topic of power and the political activities through which power is acquired and exercised is important'(ibid., p. ix).

In 1981 the dominant words that were used to describe the exercise of power in organizations referred to an underlying assumption of rationality of decision-making in the managerial and administrative processes of control. However, we shall show later that Rosabeth Moss Kanter was ahead of her time in 1979 when she connected power to leaders and leadership rather than to managers and management. Recently there has been a growing reference in the literature on organizations to leaders and also to the implications of power in the exercise of leadership.

In the purely political arena, referring to the leaders of states, countries and empires, power has always been associated with the exercise of leadership, whether for selfish or more altruistic ends. In *The Republic*, Plato rendered the exercise of power a respectable, laudable and inevitable aspect of running a state. However, it can be argued, in contrast, that Machiavelli rendered power an unacceptable topic, because of his advocacy of an extreme use of power in the selfish and brutal (by our standards) service of *The Prince*.

Powerful leadership can lead to bad, as well as good, outcomes. Quite clearly, a number of great leaders have produced a great deal of harmful effects. Throughout history leaders have regularly used their power to put themselves in a win–lose position. One of the challenges for modern political and organizational leaders is to use their power in such a way as to achieve a win–win outcome for all sides. A fine example of its exposition can be found in the book *Getting to Yes: Negotiating Agreement Without Giving In* (Fisher, Ury and Patton, 1991).

Baritz also demonstrates that power was covertly on the agenda in 1960:

> American management came to believe in the importance of understanding human behaviour because it became convinced that this was one sure way of improving its main weapon in the struggle for power, the profit margin. (Baritz, 1960, pp. 191–92).

Turning now to the essays selected for this chapter, we have focused on the central importance of power in the exercise of leadership, as demonstrated by seven well-known thinkers and writers. Although no specific essay by Pfeffer has been included, his influence is considerable and is worthy of further study.

In his essay 'Power and Organization' (Chapter 14), J.K. Galbraith quotes Max Weber's definition of power: 'the possibility of imposing one's will upon the behaviour of other persons' (p. 204), but then points out that, although it is assumed that most people understand the meaning of the word 'power', there is little mention in most references 'as to how will is imposed, how the acquiescence of others is achieved' (p. 204).

He then proceeds to argue that power is related to three traits: condign, compensatory and conditional. In turn, behind these traits lie the three sources of power: personality, property (or wealth) and organization (p. 206).

In his succinct essay on 'The Forms of Power', Bertrand Russell (Chapter 13) examines these forms through various classifications, supported by appropriate examples. He is particularly effective in linking together the various classifications. For instance, when referring to 'naked power' he states that '[c]onquest by the force of arms has had more to do with the spread of civilization than any other single agency' and then illustrates this by pointing out that Christianity could not have been preached throughout the Roman Empire without the preceding conquests of Julius Caesar (p. 195).

In 'Power and the Control of Behavior' (Chapter 15) Robert Dahl traces the origins of theories of power going back to Aristotle and strides through history right up to the ideas of the Chicago School in the mid-1940s and 1950s. He also considers a number of characteristics (such as resources, skill, motivation and cost) as viewed by both those who are in control and those who are dependent.

Gareth Morgan complements Dahl's work in his book, *Images of Organization* (1986), and in a chapter from this book, 'Exploring Power', reproduced as Chapter 16, he explores 14 sources of power. This is a comprehensive listing, which he further elucidates with a series of explanations and examples. He begins with formal authority and notes concrete examples such as the control of scarce resources, of decision processes and of technology with further abstract items such as the ability to cope with uncertainty, symbolism and the management of meaning through to the 'power one already has'.

Morgan also refers to the leadership positions in organizations, thereby making the connection between power and leadership:

> By monitoring and controlling boundary transactions people are able to build up considerable power ... Most people in leadership positions at all levels of an organization can engage in this kind of boundary management in a way that contributes to their power. (p. 169)

In his section on 'Gender and the management of gender relations' he demonstrates that sources of power can change over time. At the time when he was writing, the traditional male and female stereotypes were changing '[u]nder the influence of the "gender revolution"' (p. 179).

Morgan notes that it is not only the biographies of eminent politicians in public life where the exercise of power is a route to control. It also applies to politicians in organizations. In relation to the effects of power on followers, he states that '[p]ower, like honey, is a perpetual source of sustenance and attraction among the worker bees' (p.264).

In their seminal essay 'Power is the Great Motivator' (Chapter 17), David McClelland and David Burnham assert that the 'need for power' is an essential part of the motivation of an effective manager. However, they are aware that power is not sufficient by itself for effective management; it has to be associated with a 'need for achievement' and a 'need for affiliation'. They also discover that '"power motivation" refers not to dictatorial behavior but to a desire to have an impact, to be strong and influential' (p. 274) and further propose that '[t]he better managers, as judged by the morale of those working for them, tended to score even higher in power motivation' (ibid.).

The final essay in Part III is by Rosabeth Moss Kanter, 'Power Failure in Management Circuits'. In this she proposes a similar thesis: '[w]here the power is "on," the system can be productive; where the power is "off", the system bogs down' (p. 281). She has also discovered that '[i]f organizational power can "ennoble," then, recent research shows, organizational powerlessness can (with apologies to Lord Acton) "corrupt"' (ibid.).

All these writers lead us to the conclusion that, in the twenty-first century, power and leadership are essential components of the agenda of organizations, nations and the world order. Furthermore, the way in which power is used will largely determine the types and styles of leadership that will evolve.

References

Baritz, L. (1960), *The Servants of Power: A History of the Use of Social Science in American Industry*, Middletown, CT: Wesleyan University Press.

Fisher, R.L., Ury, W.L. and Patton, B.M. (1991), *Getting to Yes: Negotiating Agreement Without Giving In* (2nd edn), Boston, MA: Houghton Mifflin.

Morgan, Gareth (1986), *Images of Organization*, London: Sage Publications.

Pfeffer, Jeffrey (1981), *Power in Organizations*, Marshfield, MA: Pitman Publishing.

[13]

The Forms of Power

BERTRAND RUSSELL

Power may be defined as the production of intended effects. It is thus a quantitative concept: given two men with similar desires, if one achieves all the desires that the other achieves, and also others, he has more power than the other. But there is no exact means of comparing the power of two men of whom one can achieve one group of desires, and another another; e.g. given two artists of whom each wishes to paint good pictures and become rich, and of whom one succeeds in painting good pictures and the other in becoming rich, there is no way of estimating which has the more power. Nevertheless, it is easy to say, roughly, that A has more power than B, if A achieves many intended effects and B only a few.

There are various ways of classifying the forms of power, each of which has its utility. In the first place, there is power over human beings and power over dead matter or non-human forms of life. I shall be concerned mainly with power over human beings, but it will be necessary to remember that the chief cause of change in the modern world is the increased power over matter that we owe to science.

Power over human beings may be classified by the manner of influencing individuals, or by the type of organization involved.

An individual may be influenced: (a) by direct physical power over his body, e.g. when he is imprisoned or killed; (b) by rewards and punishments as inducements, e.g. in giving or withholding employment; (c) by influence on opinion, i.e. propaganda in its broadest sense. Under this last head I should include the opportunity for creating desired habits in others, e.g. by military drill, the only difference being that in such cases action follows without any such mental intermediary as could be called opinion.

20   *Bertrand Russell*

These forms of power are most nakedly and simply displayed in our dealings with animals, where disguises and pretences are not thought necessary. When a pig with a rope round its middle is hoisted squealing into a ship, it is subject to direct physical power over its body. On the other hand, when the proverbial donkey follows the proverbial carrot, we induce him to act as we wish by persuading him that it is to his interest to do so. Intermediate between these two cases is that of performing animals, in whom habits have been formed by rewards and punishments; also, in a different way, that of sheep induced to embark on a ship, when the leader has to be dragged across the gangway by force, and the rest then follow willingly.

All these forms of power are exemplified among human beings.

The case of the pig illustrates military and police power.

The donkey with the carrot typifies the power of propaganda.

Performing animals show the power of 'education'.

The sheep following their unwilling leader are illustrative of party politics, whenever, as is usual, a revered leader is in bondage to a clique or to party bosses.

Let us apply these Aesopian analogies to the rise of Hitler. The carrot was the Nazi programme (involving, e.g. the abolition of interest); the donkey was the lower middle class. The sheep and their leader were the Social Democrats and Hindenburg. The pigs (only so far as their misfortunes are concerned) were the victims in concentration camps, and the performing animals are the millions who make the Nazi salute.

The most important organizations are approximately distinguishable by the kind of power that they exert. The army and the police exercise coercive power over the body; economic organizations, in the main, use rewards and punishments as incentives and deterrents; schools, churches, and political parties aim at influencing opinion. But these distinctions are not very clear-cut, since every organization uses other forms of power in addition to the one which is most characteristic.

The power of the Law will illustrate these complexities. The ultimate power of the Law is the coercive power of the State. It is the characteristic of civilized communities that direct physical coercion is (with some limitations) the prerogative of the State, and the Law is a set of rules according to which the State exercises this prerogative in dealing with its own citizens. But the Law uses punishment, not only for the purpose of making undesired actions physically impossible, but also as an inducement; a fine, for example, does not make an action impossible, but only unattractive.

The Forms of Power   21

Moreover – and this is a much more important matter – the Law is almost powerless when it is not supported by public sentiment, as might be seen in the United States during Prohibition, or in Ireland in the eighties, when moonlighters had the sympathy of a majority of the population. Law, therefore, as an effective force, depends upon opinion and sentiment even more than upon the powers of the police. The degree of feeling in favour of Law is one of the most important characteristics of a community.

This brings us to a very necessary distinction, between traditional power and newly acquired power. Traditional power has on its side the force of habit; it does not have to justify itself at every moment, nor to prove continually that no opposition is strong enough to overthrow it. Moreover it is almost invariably associated with religious or quasi-religious beliefs purporting to show that resistance is wicked. It can, accordingly, rely upon public opinion to a much greater degree than is possible for revolutionary or usurped power. This has two more or less opposite consequences: on the one hand, traditional power, since it feels secure, is not on the lookout for traitors, and is likely to avoid much active political tyranny; on the other hand, where ancient institutions persist, the injustices to which holders of power are always prone have the sanction of immemorial custom, and can therefore be more glaring than would be possible under a new form of government which hoped to win popular support. The reign of terror in France illustrates the revolutionary kind of tyranny, the *corvée* the traditional kind.

Power not based on tradition or assent I call 'naked' power. Its characteristics differ greatly from those of traditional power. And where traditional power persists, the character of the regime depends, to an almost unlimited extent, upon its feeling of security or insecurity.

Naked power is usually military, and may take the form either of internal tyranny or of foreign conquest. Its importance, especially in the latter form, is very great indeed – greater, I think, than many modern 'scientific' historians are willing to admit. Alexander the Great and Julius Caesar altered the whole course of history by their battles. But for the former, the Gospels would not have been written in Greek, and Christianity could not have been preached throughout the Roman Empire. But for the latter, the French would not speak a language derived from Latin, and the Catholic Church could scarcely have existed. The military superiority of the white man to the American Indian is an even more undeniable example of the power of the sword. Conquest by force of arms has had more to do with the spread of civilization than any other single agency.

22 *Bertrand Russell*

Nevertheless, military power is, in most cases, based upon some other form of power, such as wealth, or technical knowledge, or fanaticism. I do not suggest that this is always the case; for example, in the War of the Spanish Succession Marlborough's genius was essential to the result. But this is to be regarded as an exception to the general rule.

When a traditional form of power comes to an end, it may be succeeded, not by naked power, but by a revolutionary authority commanding the willing assent of the majority or a large minority of the population. So it was, for example, in America in the War of Independence. Washington's authority had none of the characteristics of naked power. Similarly, in the Reformation, new Churches were established to take the place of the Catholic Church, and their success was due much more to assent than to force. A revolutionary authority, if it is to succeed in establishing itself without much use of naked power, requires much more vigorous and active popular support than is needed by a traditional authority. When the Chinese Republic was proclaimed in 1911, the men of foreign education decreed a parliamentary Constitution, but the public was apathetic, and the regime quickly became one of naked power under warring Tuchuns (military governors). Such unity as was afterwards achieved by the Kuo-Min-Tang depended on nationalism, not parliamentarianism. The same sort of thing has happened frequently in Latin America. In all these cases, the authority of Parliament, if it had had sufficient popular support to succeed, would have been revolutionary; but the purely military power which was in fact victorious was naked.

The distinction between traditional, revolutionary, and naked power is psychological. I do not call power traditional merely because it has ancient forms: it must also command respect which is partly due to custom. As this respect decays, traditional power gradually passes over into naked power. The process was to be seen in Russia in the gradual growth of the revolutionary movement up to the moment of its victory in 1917.

I call power revolutionary when it depends upon a large group united by a new creed, programme, or sentiment, such as Protestantism, Communism, or desire for national independence. I call power naked when it results merely from the power-loving impulses of individuals or groups, and wins from its subjects only submission through fear, not active cooperation. It will be seen that the nakedness of power is a matter of degree. In a democratic country, the power of the government is not naked in relation to opposing political parties, but is naked in relation to a convinced

The Forms of Power 23

anarchist. Similarly, where persecution exists, the power of the Church is naked in relation to heretics, but not in relation to orthodox sinners.

Another division of our subject is between the power of organizations and the power of individuals. The way in which an organization acquires power is one thing, and the way in which an individual acquires power within an organization is quite another. The two are, of course, interrelated: if you wish to be Prime Minister, you must acquire power in your Party, and your Party must acquire power in the nation. But if you had lived before the decay of the hereditary principle, you would have had to be the heir of a king in order to acquire political control of a nation; this would, however, not have enabled you to conquer other nations, for which you would have needed qualities that kings' sons often lack. In the present age, a similar situation still exists in the economic sphere, where the plutocracy is largely hereditary. Consider the two hundred plutocratic families in France against whom French Socialists agitate. But dynasties among the plutocracy have not the same degree of permanence as they formerly had on thrones, because they have failed to cause the widespread acceptance of the doctrine of Divine Right. No one thinks it impious for a rising financial magnate to impoverish one who is the son of his father, provided it is done according to the rules and without introducing subversive innovations.

Different types of organization bring different types of individuals to the top, and so do different states of society. An age appears in history through its prominent individuals, and derives its apparent character from the character of these men. As the qualities required for achieving prominence change, so the prominent men change. It is to be presumed that there were men like Lenin in the twelfth century, and that there are men like Richard Coeur de Lion at the present time; but history does not know of them. Let us consider for a moment the kinds of individuals produced by different types of power.

Hereditary power has given rise to our notion of a 'gentleman'. This is a somewhat degenerate form of a conception which has a long history, from magic properties of chiefs, through the divinity of kings, to knightly chivalry and the blue-blooded aristocrat. The qualities which are admired, where power is hereditary, are such as result from leisure and unquestioned superiority. Where power is aristocratic rather than monarchical, the best manners include courteous behaviour towards equals as an addition to bland self-assertion in dealing with inferiors. But whatever the prevalent

24   *Bertrand Russell*

conception of manners may be, it is only where power is (or lately was) hereditary that men will be judged by their manners. The *bourgeois gentilhomme* is only laughable when he intrudes into a society of men and women who have never had anything better to do than study social niceties. What survives in the way of admiration of the 'gentleman' depends upon inherited wealth, and must rapidly disappear if economic as well as political power ceases to pass from father to son.

A very different type of character comes to the fore where power is achieved through learning or wisdom, real or supposed. The two most important examples of this form of power are traditional China and the Catholic Church. There is less of it in the modern world than there has been at most times in the past; apart from the Church, in England, very little of this type of power remains. Oddly enough, the power of what passes for learning is greatest in the most savage communities, and steadily decreases as civilization advances. When I say 'learning' I include, of course, reputed learning, such as that of magicians and medicine men. Twenty years of study are required in order to obtain a Doctor's Degree at the University of Lhasa, which is necessary for all the higher posts except that of Dalai Lama. This position is much what it was in Europe in the year 1000, when Pope Silvester II was reputed a magician because he read books, and was consequently able to increase the power of the Church by inspiring metaphysical terrors.

The intellectual, as we know him, is a spiritual descendant of the priest; but the spread of education has robbed him of power. The power of the intellectual depends upon superstition: reverence for a traditional incantation or a sacred book. Of these, something survives in English-speaking countries, as is seen in the English attitude to the Coronation Service and the American reverence for the Constitution: accordingly, the Archbishop of Canterbury and the Supreme Court Judges still have some of the traditional power of learned men. But this is only a pale ghost of the power of Egyptian priests or Chinese Confucian scholars.

While the typical virtue of the gentleman is honour, that of the man who achieves power through learning is wisdom. To gain a reputation for wisdom a man must seem to have a store of recondite knowledge, a mastery over his passions, and a long experience of the ways of men. Age alone is thought to give something of these qualities; hence 'presbyter', 'seigneur', 'alderman', and 'elder' are terms of respect. A Chinese beggar addresses passers-by as 'great old sire'. But where the power of wise men is organized, there is a corporation of priests or literati, among whom all wisdom is held to

The Forms of Power 25

be concentrated. The sage is a very different type of character from the knightly warrior, and produces, where he rules, a very different society. China and Japan illustrate the contrast.

We have already noted the curious fact that, although knowledge plays a larger part in civilization now than at any former time, there has not been any corresponding growth of power among those who possess the new knowledge. Although the electrician and the telephone man do strange things that minister to our comfort (or discomfort), we do not regard them as medicine-men, or imagine that they can cause thunderstorms if we annoy them. The reason for this is that scientific knowledge, though difficult, is not mysterious, but open to all who care to take the necessary trouble. The modern intellectual, therefore, inspires no awe, but remains a mere employee; except in a few cases, such as the Archbishop of Canterbury, he has failed to inherit the glamour which gave power to his predecessors.

The truth is that the respect accorded to men of learning was never bestowed for genuine knowledge, but for the supposed possession of magical powers. Science, in giving some real acquaintance with natural processes, has destroyed the belief in magic, and therefore the respect for the intellectual. Thus it has come about that, while men of science are the fundamental cause of the features which distinguish our time from former ages, and have, through their discoveries and inventions, an immeasurable influence upon the course of events, they have not, as individuals, as great a reputation for wisdom as may be enjoyed in India by a naked fakir or in Melanesia by a medicine-man. The intellectuals, finding their prestige slipping from them as a result of their own activities, become dissatisfied with the modern world. Those in whom the dissatisfaction is least take to Communism; those in whom it goes deeper shut themselves up in their ivory tower.

The growth of large economic organizations has produced a new type of powerful individual: the 'executive', as he is called in America. The typical 'executive' impresses others as a man of rapid decisions, quick insight into character, and iron will; he must have a firm jaw, tightly closed lips, and a habit of brief and incisive speech. He must be able to inspire respect in equals, and confidence in subordinates who are by no means nonentities. He must combine the qualities of a great general and a great diplomatist: ruthlessness in battle, but a capacity for skilful concession in negotiation. It is by such qualities that men acquire control of important economic organizations.

Political power, in a democracy, tends to belong to men of a type

26   *Bertrand Russell*

which differs considerably from the three that we have considered
hitherto. A politician, if he is to succeed, must be able to win the
confidence of his machine, and then to arouse some degree of
enthusiasm in a majority of the electorate. The qualities required
for these two stages on the road to power are by no means identical,
and many men possess the one without the other. Candidates for
the Presidency in the United States are not infrequently men who
cannot stir the imagination of the general public, though they
possess the art of ingratiating themselves with party managers.
Such men are, as a rule, defeated, but the party managers do not
foresee their defeat. Sometimes, however, the machine is able to
secure the victory of a man without 'magnetism'; in such cases, it
dominates him after his election, and he never achieves real power.
Sometimes, on the contrary, a man is able to create his own
machine; Napoleon III, Mussolini, and Hitler are examples of this.
More commonly, a really successful politician, though he uses an
already existing machine, is able ultimately to dominate it and
make it subservient to his will.

The qualities which make a successful politician in a democracy
vary according to the character of the times; they are not the same
in quiet times as they are during war or revolution. In quiet times, a
man may succeed by giving an impression of solidity and sound
judgement, but in times of excitement something more is needed. At
such times, it is necessary to be an impressive speaker – not
necessarily eloquent in the conventional sense, for Robespierre and
Lenin were not eloquent, but determined, passionate, and bold. The
passion may be cold and controlled, but must exist and be felt. In
excited times, a politican needs no power of reasoning, no apprehension of impersonal facts, and no shred of wisdom. What he
must have is the capacity of persuading the multitude that what
they passionately desire is attainable, and that he, through his
ruthless determination, is the man to attain it.

The most successful democratic politicians are those who succeed
in abolishing democracy and becoming dictators. This, of course, is
only possible in certain circumstances; no one could have achieved
it in nineteenth-century England. But when it is possible, it requires
only a high degree of the same qualities as are required by democratic politicians in general, at any rate in excited times. Lenin,
Mussolini, and Hitler owed their rise to democracy.

When once a dictatorship has been established, the qualities by
which a man succeeds a dead dictator are totally different from
those by which the dictatorship was originally created. Wire-pull-
ing, intrigue, and Court favour are the most important methods

The Forms of Power   27

when heredity is discarded. For this reason, a dictatorship is sure to change its character very considerably after the death of its founder. And since the qualities by which a man succeeds to a dictatorship are less generally impressive than those by which the regime was created, there is a likelihood of instability, palace revolutions, and ultimate reversion to some different system. It is hoped, however, that modern methods of propaganda may successfully counteract this tendency, by creating popularity for the Head of the State without the need for any display of popular qualities on his part. How far such methods can succeed it is as yet impossible to say.

There is one form of the power of individuals which we have not yet considered, namely, power behind the scenes: the power of courtiers, intriguers, spies, and wire-pullers. In every large organization, where the men in control have considerable power, there are other less prominent men (or women) who acquire influence over the leaders by personal methods. Wire-pullers and party bosses belong to the same type, though their technique is different. They put their friends, quietly, into key positions, and so, in time, control the organization. In a dictatorship which is not hereditary, such men may hope to succeed to the dictator when he dies; but in general they prefer not to take the front of the stage. They are men who love power more than glory; often they are socially timid. Sometimes, like eunuchs in Oriental monarchies, or kings' mistresses elsewhere, they are, for one reason or another, debarred from titular leadership. Their influence is greatest where nominal power is hereditary, and least where it is the reward of personal skill and energy. Such men, however, even in the most modern forms of government, inevitably have considerable power in those departments which average men consider mysterious. Of these the most important, in our time, are currency and foreign policy. In the time of the Kaiser William II, Baron Holstein (permanent Head of the German Foreign Office) had immense power, although he made no public appearances. How great is the power of the permanent officials in the British Foreign Office at the present day, it is impossible for us to know; the necessary documents may become known to our children. The qualities required for power behind the scenes are very different from those required for all other kinds, and as a rule, though not always, they are undesirable qualities. A system which accords much power to the courtier or the wire-puller is, therefore, in general not a system likely to promote the general welfare.

[14]

Power and Organization

JOHN KENNETH GALBRAITH

THE ANATOMY OF POWER: AN OVERVIEW

The subject [is] not . . . remote, philosophical, or esoteric.

Adolf A. Berle, Jr, *Power*

1

Few words are used so frequently with so little seeming need to reflect on their meaning as power, and so it has been for all the ages of man. In association with kingship and glory it was included in the ultimate scriptural accolade to the Supreme Being; millions still offer it every day. Bertrand Russell was led to the thought that power, along with glory, remains the highest aspiration and the greatest reward of humankind.[1]

Not many get through a conversation without a reference to power. Presidents or prime ministers are said to have it or to lack it in the requisite amount. Other politicians are thought to be gaining in power or losing it. Corporations and trade unions are said to be powerful, and multinational corporations dangerously so. Newspaper publishers, the heads of the broadcasting networks, and the more articulate, uninhibited, intelligent, or notorious of their editors, columnists, and commentators are the powers that be. The Reverend Billy Sunday is remembered as a powerful voice; the Reverend Billy Graham is now so described. So is the Reverend Jerry Falwell; indeed, such has been his seeming power as a moral leader that he has been thought by some to be giving morality a bad name.

J.K. Galbraith, *The Anatomy of Power*, London: Hamish Hamilton, 1984, chapter 1 'The Anatomy of Power: An Overview', pp. 1–13, and chapter 14 'The Age of Organization', pp. 131–43.

212   *John Kenneth Galbraith*

The references continue. The United States is a large and otherwise important country; so is the Soviet Union. But it is their power that evokes the common notice; they are the great powers, or the superpowers. Britain, once also a great power, is no longer powerful. All know that in recent times the United States has been losing some of its industrial power to Germany and Japan. None of these and the myriad other references to power is ever thought to require explanation. However diversely the word is used, the reader or listener is assumed to know what is meant.

And doubtless most do – to a point. Max Weber, the German sociologist and political scientist (1864–1920), while deeply fascinated by the complexity of the subject, contented himself with a definition close to everyday understanding: power is 'the possibility of imposing one's will upon the behavior of other persons'.[2] This, almost certainly, is the common perception; someone or some group is imposing its will and purpose or purposes on others, including on those who are reluctant or adverse. The greater the capacity so to impose such will and achieve the related purpose, the greater the power. It is because power has such a commonsense meaning that it is used so often with so little seeming need for definition.

But little more about power is so simple. Unmentioned in nearly all references to it is the highly interesting question as to how the will is imposed, how the acquiescence of others is achieved. Is it the threat of physical punishment, the promise of pecuniary reward, the exercise of persuasion, or some other, deeper force that causes the person or persons subject to the exercise of power to abandon their own preferences and to accept those of others? In any meaningful reference to power, this should be known. And one should also know the sources of power – what it is that differentiates those who exercise it from those who are subject to the authority of others. By what license do some have the right, whether in large matters or small, to rule? And what causes others to be ruled? It is these questions – how power is enforced, what accords access to the methods of enforcement – that this book [*The Anatomy of Power*] addresses.

2

The instruments by which power is exercised and the sources of the right to such exercise are interrelated in complex fashion. Some use of power depends on its being concealed – on their submission not being evident to those who render it. And in modern industrial

Power and Organization 213

society both the instruments for subordinating some people to the will of others and the sources of this ability are subject to rapid change. Much of what is believed about the exercise of power, deriving as it does from what was true in the past, is obsolete or obsolescent in the present.

Nonetheless, as Adolf Berle observed, the subject is not a remote or esoteric thing. No one should venture into it with the feeling that it is a mystery that only the privileged can penetrate. There is a form of scholarship that seeks not to extend knowledge but to exclude the unknowing. One should not surrender to it and certainly not on a subject of such great practical importance as this. All conclusions on power can be tested against generally acceptable historical evidence and most of them against everyday observation and uncomplicated common sense. It will help, however, to have the basic facts of power in mind at the outset and thus to proceed with a clear view of its essential character – its anatomy.

3

Power yields strongly, in a secular way, to the rule of three. There are three instruments for wielding or enforcing it. And there are three institutions or traits that accord the right to its use.

It is a measure of how slightly the subject of power has been analyzed that the three reasonably obvious instruments of its exercise do not have generally accepted names. These must be provided: I shall speak of condign, compensatory, and conditioned power.

Condign power wins submission by the ability to impose an alternative to the preferences of the individual or group that is sufficiently unpleasant or painful so that these preferences are abandoned. There is an overtone of punishment in the term, and this conveys the appropriate impression.[3] It was the undoubted preference of the galley slave to avoid his toil, but his prospective discomfort from the lash for any malingering at the oars was sufficiently unpleasant to ensure the requisite, if also painful, effort. At a less formidable level, the individual refrains from speaking his or her mind and accepts the view of another because the expected rebuke is otherwise too harsh.

Condign power wins submission by inflicting or threatening appropriately adverse consequences. Compensatory power, in contrast, wins submission by the offer of affirmative reward – by the giving of something of value to the individual so submitting. In an earlier stage of economic development, as still in elementary rural economies, the compensation took varied forms – including pay-

214   *John Kenneth Galbraith*

ments in kind and the right to work a plot of land or to share in the product of the landlord's fields. And as personal or public rebuke is a form of condign power, so praise is a form of compensatory power. However, in the modern economy, the most important expression of compensatory power is, of course, pecuniary reward – the payment of money for services rendered, which is to say for submission to the economic or personal purposes of others. On occasion, where reference to pecuniary payment conveys a more exact meaning, this term will be used.

It is a common feature of both condign and compensatory power that the individual submitting is aware of his or her submission – in the one case compelled and in the other for reward. Conditioned power, in contrast, is exercised by changing belief. Persuasion, education, or the social commitment to what seems natural, proper, or right causes the individual to submit to the will of another or of others. The submission reflects the preferred course; the fact of submission is not recognized. Conditioned power, more than condign or compensatory power, is central, as we shall see, to the functioning of the modern economy and polity, and in capitalist and socialist countries alike.

4

Behind these three instruments for the exercise of power lie the three sources of power – the attributes or institutions that differentiate those who wield power from those who submit to it. These three sources are personality, property (which, of course, includes disposable income), and organization.

Personality – leadership in the common reference – is the quality of physique, mind, speech, moral certainty, or other personal trait that gives access to one or more of the instruments of power. In primitive societies this access was through physical strength to condign power; it is a source of power still retained in some households or youthful communities by the larger, more muscular male. However, personality in modern times has its primary association with conditioned power – with the ability to persuade or create belief.

Property or wealth accords an aspect of authority, a certainty of purpose, and this can invite conditioned submission. But its principal association, quite obviously, is with compensatory power. Property – income – provides the wherewithal to purchase submission.

Organization, the most important source of power in modern societies, has its foremost relationship with conditioned power. It is taken for granted that when an exercise of power is sought or needed, organization is required. From the organization, then, come the requisite persuasion and the resulting submission to the purposes of the organization. But organization, as in the case of the state, also has access to condign power – to diverse forms of punishment. And organized groups have greater or lesser access to compensatory power through the property of which they are possessed.

This brings up a final point. As there is a primary but not exclusive association between each of the three instruments by which power is exercised and one of the sources, so there are also numerous combinations of the sources of power and the related instruments. Personality, property, and organization are combined in various strengths. From this comes a varying combination of instruments for the enforcement of power. The isolation or disentangling of the sources and instruments in any particular exercise of power, the assessment of their relative importance, and the consideration of the changes in relative importance over time are the task of this book.

In earliest Christian days, power originated with the compelling personality of the Savior. Almost immediately an organization, the Apostles, came into being, and in time the Church as an organization became the most influential and durable in all the world. Not the least of its sources of power was its property and the income thus disposed. From the combination of personality (those of the Heavenly Presence and a long line of religious leaders), the property, and, above all, the unique organization came the conditioned belief, the benefices or compensation, and the threat of condign punishment either in this world or the next that, in the aggregate, constituted the religious power. Such is the complex of factors incorporated in and, in great measure, concealed by that term. Political power, economic power, corporate power, military power, and other such references similarly and deeply conceal an equally diverse interrelationship. When they are mentioned, their inner nature is not pursued.[4] My present concern is with what is so often kept hidden.

5

As with much concerning power, the purposes for which it is sought are widely sensed but more rarely articulated. Individuals

John Kenneth Galbraith

and groups seek power to advance their own interests, including, notably, their own pecuniary interest. And to extend to others their personal, religious, or social values. And to win support for their economic or other social perception of the public good. The business-man buys the submission of his workers to serve his economic purposes – to make money. The religious leader persuades his congregation or his radio or television audience because he thinks his beliefs should be theirs. The politician seeks the support, which is to say the submission, of voters so that he may remain in office. Preferring clean to dirty air, the conservationist seeks to enforce respect for his preference on those who make automobiles or own factories. The latter seek submission to their own desire for lower costs and less regulation. Conservatives seek submission to their view of the economic and social order and the associated action; liberals or socialists seek similar submission to theirs. In all cases organization – the coming together of those with similar interests, values, or perceptions – is integral to the winning of such submission, to the pursuit of power.

Everyday language comments regularly on the reasons for which power is being pursued. If it is narrowly confined to the interest of an individual or group, one says it is being sought for selfish ends; if it reflects the interest or perception of a much larger number of people, those involved are thought inspired leaders or statemen.

It is also recognized that the purposes for which power is being sought will often be extensively and thoughtfully hidden by artful misstatement. The politician who seeks office on behalf of the pecuniary interests of affluent supporters will be especially eloquent in describing himself as a public benefactor, even a diligent and devoted friend of the poor. The adequately educated businessman no longer employs workers to enhance his profit; his deeper pur-pose is to provide employment, advance community well-being, and ensure the success of the free enterprise system. The more fervent evangelist is overtly concerned with the salvation of sinners, bringing the unrighteous to grace; anciently he has been known to have his eye on the collection plate. A deeply ingrained and exceed-ingly valuable cynicism is the appropriate and frequent response to all avowals of the purposes of power; it is expressed in the omnipre-sent question, 'What is he really after?'

Much less appreciated is the extent to which the purpose of power is the exercise of power itself.[5] In all societies, from the most primitive to the ostensibly most civilized, the exercise of power is profoundly enjoyed. Elaborate rituals of obeisance – admiring multitudes, applauded speeches, precedence at dinners and banquets, a place in the motorcade, access to the corporate jet, the military salute – celebrate the possession of power. These rituals are greatly rewarding; so are the pleas and intercessions of those who seek to influence others in the exercise of power; and so, of course, are the acts of exercise – the instructions to subordinates, the military commands, the conveying of court decisions, the statement at the end of the meeting, when the person in charge says, 'Well, this is what we'll do.' A sense of self-actuated worth derives from both the context and the exercise of power. On no other aspect of human existence is vanity so much at risk; in William Hazlitt's words, 'The love of power is the love of ourselves.' It follows that power is pursued not only for the service it renders to personal interests, values, or social perceptions but also for its own sake, for the emotional and material rewards inherent in its possession and exercise.

However, that power is thus wanted for its own sake cannot, as a matter of basic decency, be too flagrantly conceded. It is accepted that an individual can seek power to impose his moral values on others, or to further a vision of social virtue, or to make money. And, as noted, it is permissible to disguise one purpose with another – self-enrichment can be hidden behind great community service, sordid political intent behind a passionate avowal of devotion to the public good. But it is not permissible to seek power merely for the very great enjoyment that it accords.[6]

Yet while the pursuit of power for the sake of power cannot be admitted, the reality is, as ever, part of the public consciousness. Politicians are frequently described as 'power-hungry'; the obvious implication is that they seek power to satisfy an appetite. Corporations take over other corporations not in pursuit of profits but in pursuit of the power that goes with the direction of a yet larger enterprise. This, too, is recognized. American politicians – senators, congressmen, cabinet officers, and Presidents – regularly sacrifice wealth, leisure, and much else to the rigors of public office. That the nonspecific exercise of power and the access to its rituals are part of the reason is fairly evident. Perhaps only from those so rewarded are the pleasures of power for its own sake extensively concealed.

6

A reference to power is rarely neutral; there are few words that produce such admiring or, in the frequent case, indignant response. A politician can be seen by some as a powerful and thus effective leader; seen by others, he is dangerously ruthless. Bureaucratic power is bad, but public servants with power to render effective public service are very good. Corporate power is dangerous; so, however, is a weakly administered enterprise. Unions in their exercise of power indispensably defend the rights of the workers; otherwise perceived, they are deeply in conflict with the liberty of their members and the well-being of employers and the public at large.

Much obviously depends on the point of view – on the differential responses arising from whose submission is being sought, whose ox is being gored. The politician who wins a tax reform of which one approves has engaged in a wise exercise of power; to those who must pay, it is or can be arbitrary, even unconscionable. The admiration for the exercise of power that wins a new airport is not shared by the people whose property abuts the landing strip.

The response to power is also, in substantial measure, a legacy of its past. Until nearly within living memory, black workers in the United States and white serfs in Imperial Russia were impelled to the will of the overseer, owner, or landlord by application of the whip. Power meant condign power of a particularly painful and sanguinary sort. The world has also had thousands of years of harsh experience with condign enforcement by military organization, an experience that is not yet at an end. It is this history and more that has given power its chilling name.

Further, much exercise of power depends on a social conditioning that seeks to conceal it. The young are taught that in a democracy all power resides in the people. And that in a free enterprise system all authority rests with the sovereign consumer operating through the impersonal mechanism of the market. Thus is hidden the public power of organization – of the Pentagon, the weapons firms, and other corporations and lobbyists. Similarly concealed by the mystique of the market and consumer sovereignty is the power of corporations to set or influence prices and costs, to suborn or subdue politicians, and to manipulate consumer response. But eventually it becomes apparent that organizations *do* influence government, bend it and therewith the people to their need and will. And that corporations are not subordinate to the market; instead the market that is supposed to regulate them is, in some measure, an instrument in their hands for setting their prices and incomes. All this being in conflict with social conditioning, it evokes indignation. Power thus concealed by social conditioning and then revealed seems deeply illegitimate.

Yet power, *per se*, is not a proper subject for indignation. The exercise of power, the submission of some to the will of others, is inevitable in modern society; nothing whatever is accomplished without it. It is a subject to be approached with a skeptical mind but not with one that has a fixation of evil. Power can be socially malign; it is also socially essential.[7] Judgement thereon must be rendered, but no general judgement applying to all power can possibly serve.

THE AGE OF ORGANIZATION

1

The social conditioning of high capitalism was broad and deep. So was the countering response it engendered. And both continue influential to this day. The market remains to many the solvent of industrial power; the modern corporation is still thought to be led as by an invisible hand to what is socially the best. The Marxist ideas are still a specter of evil – or hope. And herein lies one of the problems of social conditioning as an instrument of power: it is accepted as the reality by those who employ it, but then, as underlying circumstances change, the conditioning does not. Since it is considered *the* reality, it conceals the new reality. So it is in the most recent great movement in the dynamics of power – the rise of organization as a source of power and the concurrent lessening in the comparative roles of personality and property. The older vision of the economic order is still avowed, and for it policy is still prescribed. Meanwhile a new order has arrived and has the modern relevance. Over this the older social conditioning spreads a deep disguise.

The rise of organization in modern times is, for those who are willing to see it, clearly visible. Its influence is felt in the economy, in the polity, and in the special and somber case of the military power; it manifests itself in a hundred forms of citizen and (as it is called) special-interest effort to win the submission of others, either directly or by way of the state. The management-controlled corporation, the trade union, the modern bureaucratic state, groups of farmers and oil producers working in close alliance with governments, trade associations, and lobbies – all are manifestations of the age of organization. All attest to a relative decline in the importance of both personality and, though in lesser measure, property as sources of power. And all signify a hugely increased reliance on social conditioning as an instrument for the enforcement of power. Property, as earlier observed, has much of its remaining importance as a source of power not in the submission it

John Kenneth Galbraith

purchases directly but in the special conditioning by way of the media — television commercials, radio commercials, newspaper advertising, and the artistry of advertising agencies and public relations firms — for which it can pay.

2

The shift in the sources of power in the modern business enterprise is of the most striking clarity. The dominant personalities of high capitalism have disappeared. During the last century and into the present one, the names of the great entrepreneurs were synonymous with the American industrial scene. And the case was the same, if less dramatically so, in the other industrial countries. Now, outside the particular industry and not always therein, no one knows the name of the head of General Motors, Ford, Exxon, Du Pont, or the other large corporations. The powerful personality has been replaced by the management team; the entrepreneur has yielded to the faceless organization man. Thus the decline of personality as a source of power.

The role of property has similarly declined. In the age of high capitalism none could doubt the power originating in the ownership of capital. It was this property that accorded the right to run the business, and it was this that gave access to influence in legislatures, over Presidents and prime ministers, and with the public at large. Property as a source of industrial power is not negligible now — as ever in these matters there are no perfect cases — but it has, nonetheless, suffered a major relative decline. The thousand largest industrial enterprises in the United States, all vast organizations, currently contribute about two thirds of all private production of goods and services, and the concentration of economic activity has followed a similar course in the other industrial countries. In few of these corporations and in none of the biggest does ownership by the individual stockholder give access to authority within the firm. This has long been so; it is fifty years since the pioneering scholars Adolf A. Berle, Jr, and Gardiner C. Means concluded that in the majority of the largest two hundred corporations in the United States control had passed to the management, which is to say the managers elected the board of directors, which then, in an incestuous way, selected the management that had selected them.[8] The continuing transfer of power from owners to managers — from property to organization — has been a pervasively characteristic feature of industrial development ever since.

Two factors contributed to the decline of property in relation to management. With the passage of time, ownership holdings in the enterprise were dispersed by inheritance, including, inevitably, to some heirs eminently disqualified by disposition or intelligence to exercise the power that property conferred. And, at the same time, the industrial tasks became increasingly complex. Corporate size, sophisticated technology, and the need for specialized management and marketing skills united to exclude from decision-making those whose principal qualification was the ownership of the property. Power passed beyond the intellectual reach of the nonparticipant and thus beyond his or her capacity to intervene effectively. And increasingly within the enterprise, decisions emerged not from the single competence of any one individual but from the several contributions of specialists meeting in committee or close daily association.[9]

The decline of property in relation to organization as a source of power has not been accepted easily. A certain legitimacy is still thought to be attached to property. Its importance is affirmed by quasi-religious observances; the young are still told that *ultimate* power in the modern corporation rests with the stockholder. 'When, for example, John purchased a new issue of stock from the Keim Corporation last year . . . [it gave] him a voice in the decision of "his" firm's management when he meets with other stockholders at annual meetings'.[10] University faculties and students labor under the belief that, by the exercise of its vote in stockholders' meetings, their institution can substantially affect corporate decisions. At such yearly meetings a repetitively devout obeisance is accorded to property ownership; the obligatory reference, as indicated by the Department of Commerce pamphlet quoted above, is to 'your company'. No important management decisions are ever altered by any of these observances.[11]

3

With the shift in the sources of power from personality and property to organization went a marked diminution in the relative effectiveness of compensatory power and, as might be expected, a very great increase in the exercise of conditioned power. This was evident, among other places, in the relationship of the industrial firm to the union, of which earlier mention has been made. The trade union, as a countervailing exercise of power in the purchase of labor, had emerged before the age of organization. We have seen that it met with a far more adamant opposition from the early entrepreneurs — in the United States from Henry Clay Frick, Henry

Ford, and Sewell Avery[12] – than from the organization men. The property-owning industrialist was frequently interested in power for its own sake, in subduing the workers as an act of personal will and purpose; a vice president in charge of labor relations, on the other hand, is measured in part by his ability to keep the peace. And – a not insignificant point – he is not defending his own personal property from the aggressions of the workers. The age of organization[13] has thus brought a major easing of the compensatory power once exercised over the labor force.

When it came to the exercise of the same kind of power over consumers or customers, the change with the rise of organization was rather more subtle and, in some respects, contradictory in practical effect. Here, as with the employment of workers, power consists at its greatest in getting the most submission for the least cost. Much can be had for little if the buyer's need is great and if alternatives are not available; the consumer is exploited, as is the worker in the parallel case of submission. The classic example of such exercise of power is the monopoly of some essential or much-desired product for which there is no clear substitute; there being no alternative seller, the need and power are large. Competition enters as the remedy; hence its reputation as the basic solvent of power.

Organization and associated industrial development have had a marked, even profound, effect on both competition and monopoly. A major purpose of the great industrial enterprise, the labor union, the farm organization, the organization of petroleum-exporting states, or the professional or trade association, is to restrain or eliminate price competition – to ensure, so far as may be possible, that there is no alternative at a lower price. In the case of modern industrial enterprises, this does not require formal communication; it is sufficient that there be a common understanding that price competition, if allowed to get out of hand, will be at cost to the power of all. Even the classical tradition in economics has come generally to concede the commitment to such implicit restraint – to what is called oligopoly pricing. Thus a primary purpose of organization has been to escape the power-limiting tendencies, otherwise called the discipline, of the market, and this has been widely successful.

But opposing influences have also been at work. The affluence associated with modern industrial development has greatly diminished the pressure of any given consumer need; the expansion in the number and variety of products and services has directly increased the alternatives available to the consumer. The choice among consumer products is infinitely greater than in the last century and therewith the sources of enjoyment and ostentation. Consequently, monopoly has ceased to be the ogre that it was in the earlier days of compensatory power. Those who might be subject to its force have the possibility now of buying something else or not buying at all. A little-noticed but highly significant result is that monopoly as a social ill has ceased, in recent times, to be an important subject of agitation in the industrial lands.

The consequence of this development has been a major shift from compensatory to conditioned power. One answer to the excessive availability of alternatives is to persuade people that they are not *real* alternatives — to cultivate the belief that the product or service in question has qualities that are unique. From this comes the massive modern commitment to commercial advertising. Advertising is not, as some would suggest, a new and vital form of market competition. Rather, it seeks through conditioned power to retain some of the authority over the buyer that was earlier associated with compensatory power.

The change here is evident in the symmetrical response of consumers to the power of sellers of goods and services. When they were subject to compensatory power — to the power that required of them much for little — they established cooperatives or buying associations to exercise a compensatory power of their own in return. These groups sought to buy more for less, developed alternative sources of supply, or appealed to the government to regulate prices or otherwise dissolve the market power of the seller. The price of the product, the index of relative compensatory power, was the central concern. This is so no longer. The preoccupation of the modern consumer is now all but exclusively with the advertising of the product, with countering the exercise of conditioned power in order to learn what is true or what is deemed to be true. This is also manifest in the actions of government agencies on behalf of the consumer. Prices are best an afterthought; central to all concern is the validity of advertising claims, what passes for truth in advertising. This is the modern purpose of the consumer movement; it is the predictable response to the passage from the exercise of compensatory power to the exercise of conditioned power.

4

When the modern industrial enterprise seeks support for its purposes from the state, conditioned power is again the instrument that it invokes or that is ultimately involved. The forthright purchase of legislators and other public officials is not unknown; however, it is now regarded as offending the finer ethical sense, and, to a considerable extent, it has also been suppressed by law. The major exercise of power by the corporation over the legislator or public official is by cultivating belief in its needs or purposes either directly or in the constituency to which he is beholden. What is called a powerful lobby is one skilled in such direct conditioning or one that can appeal effectively to sizable responsive groups and associations and through them to their political representatives.[14] No one can suppose that pecuniary resources – property – are unimportant in this connection. However, they have their importance not in direct compensatory action but, as earlier noted, in the larger social conditioning they can buy, including that which may be used on behalf of a pliable or supportive legislator or against one who is adversely inclined.

The exercise of conditioned power in the modern state – the persuasion of legislators, public officials, or their constituencies – is no slight thing. It assails the eyes and ears and is a subject of major political comment and concern. However, it is probably not as efficient as the direct purchase, or compensatory power, that was commonplace in the era of high capitalism. Also, as we have already seen, compensatory power had its inescapable nexus with property, and property, in turn, was possessed in largest amount by the industrial capitalists. Conditioned power also requires pecuniary resources to pay for the diverse forms of persuasion – television, radio, and newspaper advertising, speeches, personal blandishment – on which it relies. But even granting this need, it is more generally available than the compensatory power it replaces. Resources can be found; money can be raised. In some measure, if often very slight, conditioned power is available to all who can form an organization.

5

Not only is conditioned power more widely available in the age of organization, but that available to the modern large corporation is, in some respects at least, weaker than the conditioned power associated with the pre-eminence of capital or property in the last century.

As massive organization manifested in the great industrial enterprise has become the basic fact of modern industrial life, the social conditioning on which its power extensively depends has not, as already noted, kept pace. Instead, it has remained basically

Power and Organization 225

unchanged from the age of classical capitalism. Power is still held to be dissolved by the market and by competition. And it is assumed that power, whatever its intention, is always guided to socially desirable ends by the miracle of the market and the competitive struggle therein. In consequence, the social conditioning of the last century is perpetuated in circumstances of increasing implausibility in the world of great organizations.

The continuing use of the earlier conditioning is vividly evident in economic instruction. The real world is one of great interacting organizations – corporations, unions, and the state. The interaction between union wage claims and corporate prices has become the principal modern cause of inflation. But a textbook that took as its point of departure the reality of such interaction would not be acceptable for college or university use, and, significantly, it would not lend itself to the geometrical and other mathematical refinements that are compatible with the assumption of market competition and without which the teaching of economics is not considered wholly reputable.

The social conditioning that is sustained by this instruction does have a certain effect. Hundreds of thousands of otherwise intelligent young people have their thoughts guided innocuously away from the exercise of industrial power. We have seen that power is served in many ways and that no service is more useful than the cultivation of the belief that it does not exist. 'To recognize that micro-economics must now deal with a world of pervasive oligopoly . . . would threaten some basic ideological defences of the *laissez-faire* system.'[15]

But social conditioning, however deep and pervasive, cannot collide too obviously with reality. The presence and power of the modern great corporations – Exxon, General Motors, Shell, Philips – are hidden only with increasing difficulty behind the market façade. In consequence, a reference to neoclassical economics, the conditioning medium of instruction, has come to have a vaguely pejorative sound; something no longer quite real is implied. Once economic instruction is perceived not as the reality but as the guidance away from the reality, its conditioning value is, not surprisingly, impaired.

The conflict with reality becomes greater when the classical social conditioning passes out of the field of education into everyday executive expression and the public relations and advertising effort of the large industrial firm. Then qualifications disappear; the power-dissolving role of the market becomes an absolute; Exxon is held to be indistinguishable from the corner grocery or the village pharmacy in its exercise of power. As a consequence, the persuasive effect is confined to the unduly susceptible, those capable of believing anything today, who, accordingly, will believe something else tomorrow. For yet others an important effect of the social conditioning of corporate propaganda, as significantly it is often called, is to cultivate disbelief. There must be some misuse of power when those who so obviously possess it are so at pains to deny having it. In the industrial countries it is now a minor mark of sophistication that one does not believe what one reads or hears in the public-interest advertising of the great corporation. The conditioned and compensatory power of the modern business enterprise remains considerable, but it cannot be supposed that it rivals the forthright compensatory power of the great capitalist firm in the age of high capitalism.

There is a further indication of this decline in the relation of the modern corporation to the state. In the last century, when the state was an ally, an adversary relationship between government and business would have been unthinkable. Now government and business are widely regarded as mutual enemies. The social conditioning of the modern corporate enterprise is extensively concerned with the intrusive, limiting, and otherwise malign tendencies of the state. (Only in the area of military power is there full harmony between government and its dependent corporate enterprises.) In important measure, the reason lies in the shift from compensatory to conditioned power. Compensatory power was the clear monopoly of the business firm. The legislators and public officials it purchased were not likely to show hostility to their paymasters. Conditioned power allows many more interests access to the state; some of these are hostile to the business power and thus contribute to the adversary relationship, seeming or real, between corporate enterprise and modern government.

But the state also has changed; in contrast with its role in the last century, it is much less the instrument of those who seek its power, much more a power in its own right. Organization and conditioned power are again the operative forces. The modern state encompasses a large organization – bureaucracy – which, in turn, has made the state extensively the instrument of its own purposes.

NOTES

1 'Of the infinite desires of man, the chief are the desires for power and glory', *Power: A New Social Analysis* (W. W. Norton, New York, 1938), p. 11.

2 Max Weber on *Law in Economy and Society* (Harvard University Press, Cambridge, Mass., 1954), p. 323. See Reinhard Bendix. *Max Weber: An Intellectual Portrait* (Doubleday, Garden City, New York, 1960), pp. 294–300. Elsewhere Weber said of power that it is the ability of one or more persons to 'realize their own will in a communal act against the will of others who are participating in the same act'.

3 I have taken some liberties in the selection and use of this term. According to strict dictionary usage, *condign* has an adjectival relationship to *punishment*. A condign punishment is, broadly speaking, an appropriate or fitting one. Were one scrupulously pedantic, the reference here and throughout would be to *condign punishment*. I omit the latter word with the thought, first articulated by Lewis Carroll, that one can have a word mean what one chooses it to mean – 'neither more nor less'. A tempting alternative would have been 'coercive' power as used by Dennis H. Wrong in *Power: Its Forms, Bases and Uses* (Harper Colophon Books, New York, 1980). His discussion of coercive authority (pp. 41–4) parallels in a general way my use of *condign power*. However, it less specifically implies the instrument to which the individual (or group) surrenders, that which brings the submission.

4 As others have held, 'Perhaps no subject in the entire range of the social sciences is more important, and at the same time so seriously neglected, as the role of power in economic life', Melville J. Ulmer, 'Economic power and vested interests', in *Power in Economics*, edited by K. W. Rothschild (Penguin Books, Harmondsworth, 1971), p. 245.

5 'The healthy individual who gains power loves it', Dr Harvey Rich (a Washington, DC, psychoanalyst, quoted in the *New York Times*, 9 November 1982). Bertrand de Jouvenel puts the matter more vividly: 'The leader of any group of men . . . feels thereby an almost physical enlargement of himself. . . . Command is a mountain top. The air breathed there is different, and the perspectives seen there are different, from those of the valley of obedience.' (*On Power: Its Nature and the History of Its Growth* (Viking Press, New York, 1949), p. 116.)

6 John F. Kennedy, a man of some candor in public expression, nearly did so. 'I run for President', he said, 'because that is where the action is.' By *action* he was close to meaning power.

7 'Power has two aspects . . . It is a social necessity . . . It is also a social menace', De Jouvenel, *On Power*, p. 283.

8 *The Modern Corporation and Private Property* (Macmillan, New York, 1933). The shift in power was further affirmed by the studies of R. A. Gordon, among them *Business Leadership in the Large Corporation* (Bookings Institution, Washington, DC, 1945), and in the more general writings of James Burnham. See *The Managerial Revolution* (John Day, New York, 1941). The bureaucratization of modern economic enterprise was strongly emphasized by Joseph A. Schumpeter – 'it is an inevitable complement to modern economic development' – in *Capitalism, Socialism, and Democracy*, 2nd edn (Harper and Brothers, New York, 1947), p. 206. It is obvious that the shift from property to

228   *John Kenneth Galbraith*

organization as the prime source of power in the industrial enterprise is not a discovery of recent date. For a comprehensive contemporary treatment of this subject see Edward S. Herman, *Corporate Control, Corporate Power*, A Twentieth Century Fund Study (Cambridge University Press, Cambridge, 1981).

9 These are matters with which I have dealt in *The New Industrial State*, 3rd edn (Houghton Mifflin, Boston, 1978). C. Wright Mills made the point some 25 years ago: 'Decision-making . . . at the top [of the corporation] is slowly being replaced by the worried-over efforts of committees, who judge ideas tossed before them, usually from below the top levels' (*The Power Elite* (Oxford University Press, New York, 1956), p. 134.)

10 From 'Do You Know Your Economic ABC's? Profits in the American Economy', an instructional pamphlet on economics (Washington, DC: United States Department of Commerce, 1965), pp. 17–18.

11 '[S]tockholders, though still politely called "owners", are passive. They have the right to receive only. The condition of their being is that they do not interfere in management. Neither in law nor, as a rule, in fact do they have that capacity.' Adolf A. Berle, Jr., *Power Without Property: A New Development in American Political Economy* (Harcourt, Brace, New York, 1959), p. 74.

12 Of Carnegie become United States Steel, the Ford Motor Company, and Montgomery Ward, respectively.

13 Along, of course, with the effect of higher wages, unemployment compensation, and Social Security, all of which have widened the gap between condign and compensatory power and lowered the level of compulsion associated with the latter.

14 Thus in the United States the power for their own purposes of war veterans, people living on Social Security, and members of the National Rifle Association.

15 Thomas Balogh, *The Irrelevance of Conventional Economics* (Weidenfeld and Nicolson, London, 1982), p. 60.

[15]

Power as the Control of Behavior

ROBERT DAHL

In approaching the study of politics through the analysis of power, one assumes, at a minimum, that relations of power are among the significant aspects of a political system. This assumption, and therefore the analysis of power, can be applied to any kind of political system, international, national, or local, to associations and groups of various kinds, such as the family, the hospital, and the business firm, and to historical developments.

At one extreme, an analysis of power may simply postulate that power relations are one feature of politics among a number of others – but nonetheless a sufficiently important feature to need emphasis and description. At the other extreme, an analyst may hold that power distinguishes 'politics' from other human activity; to analysts of this view 'political science, as an empirical discipline, is the study of the shaping and sharing of power'.[1]

In either case, the analyst takes it for granted that differences between political systems, or profound changes in the same society, can often be interpreted as differences in the way power is distributed among individuals, groups, or other units. Power may be relatively concentrated or diffused, and the share of power held by different individuals, strata, classes, professional groups, ethnic, racial, or religious groups, etc., may be relatively great or small. The analysis of power is often concerned, therefore, with the identification of elites and leadership, the discovery of the ways in which power is allocated to different strata, relations among leaders and between leaders and non-leaders, and so forth.

Although the approach to politics through the study of power relations is sometimes thought to postulate that everyone seeks power as the highest value, analysts of power generally reject this

38   *Robert Dahl*

assumption as psychologically untenable; the analysis of power does not logically imply any particular psychological assumptions. Sometimes critics also regard the analysis of power as implying that the pursuit of power is morally good or at any rate that it should not be condemned. But an analysis of power may be neutral as to values; or the analyst may be concerned with power, not to glorify it, but in order to modify the place it holds in human relations and to increase the opportunities for dignity, respect, freedom, or other values.[2]

Indeed, it would be difficult to explain the extent to which political theorists for the past 25 centuries have been concerned with relations of power and authority were it not for the moral and practical significance of power to any person interested in political life, whether as observer or activist. Some understanding of power is usually thought to be indispensable for moral or ethical appraisals of political systems. From a very early time – certainly since Socrates, and probably before – men have been inclined to judge the relative desirability of different types of political systems by, among other characteristics, the relations of power and authority in these systems. In addition, intelligent *action* to bring about a result of some kind in a political system, such as a change in a law or a policy, a revolution, or a settlement of an international dispute requires knowledge of how to produce or 'cause' these results. In political action, as in other spheres of life, we try to produce the results we want by acting appropriately on the relevant causes. As we shall see, power relations can be viewed as causal relations of a particular kind.

It therefore seems most unlikely that the analysis of power will disappear as an approach to the study of politics. However, the fact that this approach is important and relevant does not shield it from some serious difficulties. These have become particularly manifest as the approach has been more earnestly and systematically employed.

ORIGINS

The attempt to study and explain politics by analyzing relations of power is, in a loose sense, ancient. To Aristotle, differences in the location of power, authority, or rule among the citizens of a political society served as one criterion for differentiating among actual constitutions, and it entered into his distinction between good constitutions and bad ones. With few exceptions (most nota-

Power as the Control of Behavior 39

bly Thomas Hobbes) political theorists did not press their investigations very far into certain aspects of power that have seemed important to social scientists in the twentieth century. For example, most political theorists took it for granted, as did Aristotle, that key terms like *power, influence, authority,* and *rule* (let us call them 'power terms') needed no great elaboration, presumably because the meaning of these words was clear to men of common sense. Even Machiavelli, who marks a decisive turning point from classical–normative to modern–empirical theory, did not consider political terms in general as particularly technical. Moreover, he strongly preferred the concrete to the abstract. In his treatment of power relations Machiavelli frequently described a specific event as an example of a general principle; but often the general principle was only implied or barely alluded to, and he used a variety of undefined terms such as *imperio, forza, potente,* and *autorità.*

From Aristotle to Hobbes political theorists were mainly concerned with power relations within a given community. But external relations even more than internal ones force attention to questions of relative power. The rise of the modern nation-state therefore compelled political theorists to recognize the saliency of power in politics, and particularly, of course, in international politics.[3]

Thus political 'realists' found it useful to define, distinguish, and interpret the state in terms of its power. Max Weber both reflected this tradition of 'realism' and opened the way for new developments in the analysis of power. '"Power" (*Macht*) is the probability that one actor within a social relationship will be in a position to carry out his own will despite resistance, regardless of the basis on which this probability rests.'[4] This definition permitted Weber to conclude that 'the concept of power is highly comprehensive from the point of view of sociology. All conceivable . . . combinations of circumstances may put him [the actor] in a position to impose his will in a given situation.' It follows that the state is not distinguishable from other associations merely because it employs a special and peculiarly important kind of power–force. In a famous and highly influential definition, Weber characterized the state as follows: 'A compulsory political association with continuous organization (*politischer Anstaltsbetrieb*) will be called a "state" if and in so far as its administrative staff successfully upholds a claim to the *monopoly* of the *legitimate* use of physical force in the enforcement of its order.'

In his well-known typologies and his analyses of political systems, however, Weber was less concerned with power in general

40   *Robert Dahl*

than with a special kind that he held to be unusually important —
legitimate power, or authority.

Later theorists, practically all of whom were directly or indirectly
influenced by Weber, expanded their objectives to include a fuller
range of power relations. In the United States attempts to suggest or
develop systematic and comprehensive theories of politics centring
about power relations appeared in books by Catlin,[5] an important
essay by Goldhamer and Shils,[6] and numerous works of the Chicago school – principally Merriam,[7] Lasswell,[8] and, in international
politics, Morgenthau.[9] In the decade after World War II the ideas of
the Chicago school were rapidly diffused throughout American
political science.

ELEMENTS IN THE ANALYSIS OF POWER

Power terms evidently cover a very broad category of human
relations. Considerable effort and ingenuity have gone into schemes
for classifying these relations into various types, labelled power,
influence, authority, persuasion, dissuasion, inducement, coercion,
compulsion, force, and so on, all of which we shall subsume under
the collective label power terms. The great variety and heteroge-
neity of these relations may, in fact, make it impossible – or at any
rate not very fruitful – to develop general theories of power
intended to cover them all.

At the most general level, power terms in modern social science
refer to *subsets of relations among social units such that the behaviors of one or more units* (the responsive units, R) *depend in some
circumstances on the behavior of other units* (the controlling units,
C). (In the following discussion, R will always symbolize the
responsive or dependent unit, C the controlling unit. These symbols
will be used throughout and will be substituted even in direct
quotations where the authors themselves have used different letters.) By this broad definition, then, power terms in the social
sciences exclude relations with inanimate or even non-human
objects; the control of a dog by his master or the power of a
scientist over 'nature' provided by a nuclear reactor would fall, by
definition, in a different realm of discourse. On the other hand, the
definition could include the power of one nation to affect the
actions of another by threatening to use a nuclear reactor as a bomb
or by offering to transfer it by gift or sale.

If power-terms include *all* relations of the kind just defined, then
they spread very widely over the whole domain of human relations.
In practice, analysts of power usually confine their attention to

smaller subsets. One such subset consists, for example, of relations in which 'severe sanctions . . . are expected to be used or are in fact applied to sustain a policy against opposition' — a subset that Lasswell and Kaplan call power.[10] However, there is no agreement on the common characteristics of the various subsets covered by power terms, nor are different labels applied with the same meaning by different analysts.

Despite disagreement on how the general concept is to be defined and limited, the variety of smaller subsets that different writers find interesting or important, and the total lack of a standardized classification scheme and nomenclature, there is nonetheless some underlying unity in the various approaches to the analysis of power. In describing and explaining patterns of power, different writers employ rather similar elements.[11] What follows is an attempt to clarify these common elements by ignoring many differences in terminology, treatment, and emphasis.

Some Descriptive Characteristics

For purposes of exposition it is convenient to think of the analysis of power in terms of the familiar distinction between dependent and independent variables. The attempt to understand a political system may then be conceived of as an effort to *describe* certain characteristics of the system: the dependent variables; and to *explain* why the system takes on these particular characteristics, by showing the effects on these characteristics of certain other factors: the independent variables. Some of the characteristics of a political system that analysts seek to explain are the *magnitude* of the power of the C's with respect to the R's, how this power is *distributed* in the system, and the *scope*, and *domain*, of control that different individuals or actors have, exercise, or are subject to.

Magnitude

Political systems are often characterized explicitly or implicitly by the differences in the 'amounts' of power (over the actions of the government or state) exercised by different individuals, groups, or strata. The magnitude of C's power with respect to R is thought of as measurable, in some sense, by at least an ordinal scale; frequently, indeed, a literal reading would imply that power is subject to measurement by an interval scale. How to compare and measure different magnitudes of power poses a major unsolved problem; we shall return to it briefly later on. Meanwhile, we shall accept the assumption of practically every political theorist for several thousand years, that it is possible to speak meaningfully of different amounts of power. Thus a typical question in the analysis of a political system would be: Is control over government highly concentrated or relatively diffused?

Distribution

An ancient and conventional way of distinguishing among political systems is according to the way control over the government or the state is distributed to individuals or groups in the systems. Aristotle, for example, stated: 'The proper application of the term "democracy" is to a constitution in which the free-born and poor control the government – being at the same time a majority; and similarly the term "oligarchy" is properly applied to a constitution in which the rich and better-born control the government – being at the same time a minority'.[12]

Control over government may be conceived as analogous to income, wealth, or property; and in the same way that income or wealth may be distributed in different patterns, so too the distribution of power over government may vary from one society or historical period to another. One task of analysis, then, is to classify and describe the most common distributions and to account for the different patterns. Typical questions would be: What are the characteristics of the C's and of the R's? How do the C's and R's compare in numbers? Do C's and R's typically come from different classes, strata, regions, or other groups? What historical changes have occurred in the characteristics of C and R?

Scope

What if C's are sometimes not C's, or C's sometimes R's, or R's sometimes C's? The possibility cannot be ruled out that individuals or groups who are relatively powerful with respect to one kind of activity may be relatively weak with respect to other activities. Power need not be general; it may be specialized. In fact, in the absence of a single world ruler, some specialization is inevitable; in any case, it is so commonplace that analysts of power have frequently insisted that a statement about the power of an individual, group, state, or other actor is practically meaningless unless it specifies the power of actor C with respect to some class of R's activities. Such a class of activities is sometimes called the range[12]

Power as the Control of Behavior 43

or the scope of C's power.[13] There is no generally accepted way of defining and classifying different scopes. However, a typical question about a political system would be: Is power generalized over many scopes, or is it specialized? If it is specialized, what are the characteristics of the C's, the elites, in the different scopes? Is power specialized by individuals in the sense that C_a and C_b exercise power over different scopes, or is it also specialized by classes, social strata, skills, professions, or other categories?

Domain

C's power will be limited to certain individuals: the R's over whom C has or exercises control constitute what is sometimes called the 'domain', or 'extension', of C's power.[14] Typical questions thus might be: Who are the R's over whom C has control? What are their characteristics? How numerous are they? How do they differ in numbers or characteristics from the R's not under C's control?

Given the absence of any standard unit of measure for amounts, distributions, scopes, domains, and other aspects of power, and the variety of ways of describing these characteristics, it is not at all surprising that there is an abundance of schemes for classifying political systems according to some characteristic of power. Most such schemes use, implicitly or explicitly, the idea of a *distribution of power over the behavior of government*. The oldest, most famous, and most enduring of these is the distinction made by the Greeks between rule by one, the few, and the many.[15] Some variant of this scheme frequently reappears in modern analyses of power.[16] Often, as with Aristotle himself, the distribution of power is combined with one or more other dimensions.[17] Rough dichotomous schemes are common. One based on 'the degree of autonomy and interdependence of the several power holders' distinguishes two polar types, called autocracy and constitutionalism.[18] American community studies have in recent years called attention to differences between 'pluralistic' systems and unified or highly stratified 'power structures'. In one study that compares four communities the authors developed a more complex typology of power structures by combining a dimension of 'distribution of political power among citizens' with the degree of convergence or divergence in the ideology of leaders; the four types of power structures produced by dichotomizing these two dimensions are in turn distinguished from regimes.[19]

44   *Robert Dahl*

Some Explanatory Characteristics

Given the different types of political systems, how are the differences among them to be explained? If, for example, control over government is sometimes distributed to the many, often to the few, and occasionally to one dominant leader, how can we account for the differences? Obviously these are ancient, enduring, and highly complex problems; and there is slight agreement on the answers. However, some factors that are often emphasized in modern analysis can be distinguished.

Resources

Differences in patterns or structures of power may be attributed primarily, mainly, or partly to the way in which 'resources', or 'base values', are distributed among the individuals, strata, classes and groups in different communities, countries, societies and historical periods. This is an ancient, distinguished, widespread and persuasive mode of explanation, used by Aristotle in Greece in the fourth century BC, by James Harrington in seventeenth-century England, by the fathers of the American constitution in the late eighteenth century, by Marx and Engels in the nineteenth century, and by a great many social scientists in the twentieth century. A central hypothesis in most of these theories is that the greater one's resources, the greater one's power. Although explanations of this kind do not always go beyond tautology (by defining power in terms of resources), logical circularity is certainly not inherent in this mode of explanation. However, there is no accepted way of classifying resources or bases. Harold Lasswell has constructed a comprehensive scheme of eight base values which, although not necessarily exhaustive, are certainly inclusive; these are power (which can serve as a base for more power), respect, rectitude or moral standing, affection, well-being, wealth, skill, and enlightenment.[20] Other writers choose more familiar categories to classify resources: for example, in trying to account for the patterns of influence in one community, the author described the patterns of social standing; the distribution of cash, credit and wealth; access to legality, popularity and control over jobs; and control over sources of information.[21]

Skill

Two individuals with access to approximately the same resources

Power as the Control of Behavior   45

may not exercise the same degree of power (over, let us say, government decisions). Indeed, it is a common observation that individuals of approximately equal wealth or social status may differ greatly in power. To be sure, this might be accounted for by differences in access to other resources, such as the greater legality, bureaucratic knowledge, and public affection that fall to any individual who is chosen, say, to be prime minister of Britain or president of the United States. Another factor, however, one given particular prominence by Machiavelli, is political skill. Formally, skill could be treated as another resource. Nonetheless, it is generally thought to be of critical importance in explaining differences in the power of different leaders – different presidents, for example, as in Neustadt's comparison of presidents Roosevelt, Truman, and Eisenhower.[22] However, despite many attempts at analysis, from Machiavelli to the present day, political skill has remained among the more elusive aspects in the analysis of power.

Motivations

Two individuals with access to the same resources may exercise different degrees of power (with respect to some scope) because of different motivations: the one may use his resources to increase his power; the other may not. Moreover, since power is a relationship between C's and R's, the motivations not only of the C's but also of the R's are important. One person may worship authority, while another may defy it. A number of writers have explored various aspects of motivations involved in power relations.[23]

Costs

Motivations can be related to resources by way of the economists' language of cost – a factor introduced into the analysis of power by a mathematical economist.[24] In order to control R, C may have to use some of his resources. Thus C's supply of resources is likely to have a bearing on how far he is willing to go in trying to control R. And variations in C's resources are likely to produce variations in C's power. C's *opportunity costs* in controlling R – that is, what C must forgo or give up in other opportunities as a result of using some of his resources to control R – are less (other things being equal) if he is rich in resources than if he is poor in resources. In concrete terms, to a rich man the sacrifice involved in a campaign contribution of \$100 is negligible; to a poor man the sacrifice entailed in a contribution of \$100 is heavy. C's willingness to use

46   *Robert Dahl*

his resources to control R will also depend on the value to C of R's response; the value of R's response is, in turn, dependent in part on C's motivations. The relationship may also be examined from R's point of view. R's opportunity costs consist of what he is then unable to do if he complies with C. In R's case, as in C's, his supply of resources and his motivations help determine his opportunity costs. Thus a power relation can be interpreted as a sort of transaction between C and R.

PROBLEMS OF RESEARCH

Like all other approaches to an understanding of complex social phenomena, the analysis of power is beset with problems. At a very general level, attempts to analyze power share with many – perhaps most – other strategies of inquiry in the social sciences the familiar dilemma of rigor versus relevance, and the dilemma has led to familiar results. Attempts to meet high standards of logical rigor or empirical verification have produced some intriguing experiments and a good deal of effort to clarify concepts and logical relationships but not rounded and well-verified explanations of complex political systems in the real world. Conversely, attempts to arrive at a better understanding of the more concrete phenomena of political life and institutions often sacrifice a good deal in rigor of logic and verification in order to provide more useful and reliable guides to the real world.

There are, however, a number of more specific problems in the analysis of power, many of which have only been identified in the last few decades. Relevant work is quite recent and seeks (1) to clarify the central concepts, partly by expanding on the analogy between power relations and causal relations, (2) to specify particular subsets that are most interesting for social analysis, (3) to develop methods of measurement, and (4) to undertake empirical investigations of concrete political phenomena.

Power and Cause

The closest equivalent to the power relation is the causal relation. For the assertion 'C has power over R', one can substitute the assertion, 'C's behavior causes R's behavior'. If one can define the causal relation, one can define influence, power, or authority, and vice-versa.[25]

Since the language of cause is no longer common in the formal theoretical language of the natural sciences, it might be argued that

Power as the Control of Behavior 47

social scientists should also dispense with that language and that insofar as power is merely a term for a causal relation involving human beings, power-terms should simultaneously be dispensed with. But it seems rather unlikely that social scientists will, in fact, reject causal language. For the language of cause, like the language of power, is used to interpret situations in which there is the possibility that some event will intervene to change the order of other events. In medical research it is natural and meaningful to ask, Does cigarette smoking cause lung cancer and heart disease? In social situations the notion of cause is equally or even more appropriate. What makes causal analysis important to us is our desire to act on causes in the real world in order to bring about effects — reducing death rates from lung cancer, passing a civil-rights bill through Congress, or preventing the outbreak of war.

To interpret the terms *power, influence, authority*, etc., as instances of causal relations means, however, that the attempt to detect true rather than spurious power relations must run into the same difficulties that have beset efforts to distinguish true from spurious causal relations. Some analysts have confronted the problem; others have noted it only to put it aside; most have ignored it entirely, perhaps on the assumption that if social scientists tried to solve the unsolved problems of philosophy they would never get around to the problems of the social sciences. Yet if power is analogous to cause — or if power relations are logically a subset of causal relations — then recent analyses of causality must have relevance to the analysis of power.

In the first place, properties used to distinguish causation also serve to define power relations: covariation, temporal sequence, and asymmetry, for example. The appropriateness of these criteria has in fact been debated, not always conclusively, by various students of power.[26]

Thus, the problem whether *A* can be said to cause *B* if *A* is a necessary condition for *B*, or a sufficient condition, or *both* necessary *and* sufficient, has also plagued the definition of power-terms. Some writers have explicitly stated or at least implied that relations of power mean that some action by *C* is a necessary condition for *R*'s response.[27] Oppenheim has argued, however, that such definitions permit statements that run flatly counter to common sense; he holds that it would be more appropriate to require only that *C*'s action be sufficient to produce *R*'s response.[28] Riker has suggested in turn that 'the customary definition of power be revised . . . to reflect the necessary-and-sufficient condition theory of causality'.[29] However, Blalock in his *Causal Inferences in Non-experimental*

48   *Robert Dahl*

Research[30] has shown that defining cause in terms of necessary and sufficient conditions leads to great practical difficulties in research. 'In real-life situations we seldom encounter instances where *B* is present if and only if *A* is also present'; moreover, specifying necessary and sufficient conditions requires the researcher 'to think always in terms of attributes and dichotomies', whereas 'there are most certainly a number of variables which are best conceived as continuously distributed, even though we may find it difficult to measure them operationally in terms of a specified unit of some kind.' 'The use of "necessary and sufficient" terminology . . . may work well for the logician but not [for] the social scientist.' Blalock's criticism, and indeed his whole effort to explore problems of causal inference in non-experimental research, are highly relevant to the analysis of power.

Aside from these somewhat rarefied philosophical and definitional questions, which many social scientists are prepared to abandon to metaphysicians or philosophers of science, the analogy between power and cause argues that the problem of distinguishing cause from correlation, or true from spurious causation, is bound to carry over into the analysis of power. And indeed it does. The difficulty of distinguishing true from spurious power relations has proved to be quite formidable.

The most rigorous method of distinguishing true from spurious causation is, of course, experimentation, and this would be the most rigorous method for distinguishing true from spurious power relations, provided the proper experimental conditions were present. Unfortunately, however, as in many areas of the social sciences, so too in the analysis of power, experimental methods have so far been of limited value, and for similar reasons. In non-experimental situations the optimal requirements for identifying causal relations seem to be the existence of satisfactory interval measures, a large supply of good data employing these measures, and an exhaustive analysis of alternative ways of accounting for the observations.[31] Unfortunately, in the analysis of power, existing methods of measurement are rather inadequate, the data are often inescapably crude and limited, a variety of simple alternative explanations seem to fit the data about equally well, and in any case the complexity of the relations requires extraordinarily complex models.

The shortage of relevant models of power may disappear in time. In fact, the causal analogue suggests that the development of a great array of carefully described alternative models to compare with observations is probably a prerequisite for further development in

Power as the Control of Behavior   49

the analysis of power. Again, the analogy between power and cause readily reveals why this would seem to be the case. In trying to determine the cause of a phenomenon it is of course impossible to know whether all the relevant factors in the real world are actually controlled during an investigation. Consequently, it is never possible to demonstrate causality.

> It is possible to make causal *inferences* concerning the adequacy of causal models, at least in the sense that we can proceed by eliminating inadequate models that make predictions that are not consistent with the data. . . . [Such] causal models involve (1) a finite set of explicitly defined variables, (2) certain asumptions about how these variables are interrelated causally, and (3) assumptions to the effect that outside variables, while operating, do not have confounding influences that disturb the causal patterning among the variables explicitly being considered.[32]

If power relations are a subset of causal relations, these requirements would also be applicable in the analysis of power.

In analyzing power, why have analysts so rarely attempted to describe, in rigorous language at any rate, the alternative causal models relevant to their inquiry? There seem to be several reasons. First, students of power have not always been wholly aware that distinguishing true from spurious power relations requires intellectual strategies at a rather high level of sophistication. Second, the crude quality of the observations usually available in studying power may discourage efforts to construct elegant theoretical models. Third, until recent times the whole approach to power analysis was somewhat speculative: there were a good many impressionistic works but few systematic empirical studies of power relations. Of the empirical studies now available most are investigations of power relations in American communities undertaken since 1950. These community studies have provoked a good deal of dispute over what are, in effect, alternative models of causation. So far, however, investigators have usually not described clearly the array of alternative models that might be proposed to explain their data, nor have they clearly specified the criteria they use for rejecting all the alternatives except the one they accept as their preferred explanation.

Theories about power relations in various political systems are of course scattered through the writings of a number of analysts.[33] But a straightforward presentation of an empirical theory of power

50   *Robert Dahl*

relations in political systems is a rarity. A notable exception is
offered by March's formulation of six models of social choice that
involve, in some sense, relationships of power.

The analogy between cause and power calls attention to one
further point: any attempt to develop an empirical theory of power
will run headlong into the fact that a causal chain has many links;
that the links one specifies depend on what one wishes to explain;
and that what one wishes to explain depends, in part, on the theory
with which one begins. In causal analysis, it is usually

> possible to insert a very large number of additional variables
> between any two supposedly directly related factors. We must
> stop somewhere and consider the theoretical system closed.
> Practically, we may choose to stop at the point 'where the
> additional variables are either difficult or expensive to
> measure, or where they have not been associated with any
> operations at all. . . . A relationship that is direct in one
> theoretical system may be indirect in another, or it may even
> be taken as spurious.[34]

Some of the links that a power analyst may take as 'effects' to be
explained by searching for causes are the outcomes of specific
decisions; the current values, attitudes, and expectations of decision
makers; their earlier or more fundamental attitudes and values; the
attitudes and values of other participants – or non-participants –
whose participation is in some way significant; the processes of
selection, self-selection, recruitment, or entry by which decision
makers arrive at their locations in the political system; the rules of
decision making, the structures, the constitutions. No doubt a
'complete' explanation of power relations in a political system
would try to account for all of these effects, and others. Yet this is
an enormously ambitious task. Meanwhile, it is important to specify which effects are at the focus of an explanatory theory and
which are not. A good deal of confusion, and no little controversy,
are produced when different analysts focus on different links in the
chain of power and causation without specifying clearly what
effects they wish to explain; and a good deal of criticism of dubious
relevance is produced by critics who hold that an investigator has
focused on the 'wrong' links or did not provide a 'complete'
explanation.

Classifying Types of Power

Even though the analysis of power has not produced many rigorous causal models, it has spawned a profusion of schemes for classifying types of power relations.[35]

Among the characteristics most often singled out for attention are (1) legitimacy: the extent to which R feels normatively obliged to comply with C; (2) the nature of the sanctions: whether C uses rewards or deprivations, positive or negative sanctions; (3) the magnitude of the sanctions: extending from severe coercion to no sanctions at all; (4) the means or channels employed: whether C controls R only by means of information that changes R's intentions or by actually changing R's situation or his environment of rewards and deprivations. These and other characteristics can be combined to yield many different types of power relations.

As we have already indicated, no single classification system prevails, and the names for the various categories are so completely unstandardized that what is labeled power in one scheme may be called coercion or influence in another. Detached from empirical theories, these schemes are of doubtful value. In the abstract it is impossible to say why one classification system should be preferred over another.

Nonetheless, there are some subsets of power relations — types of power, as they are often called — that call attention to interesting problems of analysis and research. One of these is the distinction between *having* and *exercising* power or influence.[36] This distinction is also involved in the way anticipated reactions function as a basis for influence and power.[37]

To illustrate the problem by example, let us suppose that even in the absence of any previous communication from the president to Senator R, or indeed any previous action of any kind by the president, Senator R regularly votes *now* in a way he thinks will insure the president's favor *later*. The senator calculates that if he loses the next election, he may, as a result of the president's favorable attitude, be in line to receive a presidential appointment to a federal court. Thus, while Senator R's voting behavior is oriented toward future rewards, expected or hoped for, his votes are not the result of any specific action by the president.

If one holds that C cannot be a cause of R if C follows R in time, then no act of the incumbent president *need* be a cause of Senator R's favorable vote. Obviously this does not mean that Senator R's actions are 'uncaused'. The immediate determinant of his vote is his expectations. If we ask what 'caused' his expectations, there are many possible answers. For example, he might have concluded that in American society if favors are extended to C, this makes it more likely that C will be indulgent later on. Or he may have acquired

52   *Robert Dahl*

from political lore the understanding that the general rule applies specifically to relations of senators and presidents. Thus, the causal chain recedes into the senator's previous learning – but not necessarily to any specific *past* act of the incumbent president or any other president.

This kind of phenomenon is commonplace, important, and obviously relevant to the analysis of power. Yet some studies, critics have said, concentrate on the exercise of power and fail to account for individuals or groups in the community who, though they do not exercise power, nonetheless have power, in the sense that many people try assiduously to anticipate their reactions.[38] This failure may be a result of certain paradoxical aspects of having power that can make it an exceedingly difficult phenomenon to study.

For in the limiting case of anticipated reactions, it appears, paradoxically, that it is not the president who controls the senator, but the senator who controls the president – i.e., it is the senator who, by his loyal behavior, induces the president to appoint him to a federal court. Thus, it is not C who controls or even attempts to control R, but R who attempts to control C – and to the extent that R anticipates C's reactions correctly, R does in fact control C. It is, then, not the king who controls the courtier but the courtier who controls the king.

Now if we examine this paradox closely we quickly discover that it arises simply because we have tried to describe the relationship between king and courtier, president and senator, C and R by distinguishing only one aspect, namely, the exercise of power. The courtier does indeed exercise power over the king by successfully anticipating the reactions of the monarch and thereby gaining a duchy. But it was not this that we set out to explain. For it is the king who has, holds, or possesses the capacity to confer that dukedom, and even though he does not *exercise* his power, he gains the willing compliance of the courtier.

What is it, then, that distinguishes having power from exercising power? The distinction could hinge upon the presence or absence of a manifest intention. We could define the *exercise* of power in such a way as to require C to manifest an intention to act in some way in the future, his action to be contingent on R's behavior. By contrast, C might be said to *have* power when, though he does not manifest an intention, R imputes an intention to him and shapes his behaviour to meet the imputed intention. If one were to accept this distinction, then in studying the *exercise* of power, one would have to examine not only R's perceptions and responses but also C's intentions and actions. In studying relationships in which C is thought to *have* power, even though he does not exercise it, one would in principle need only to study R's perceptions, the intentions R imputes to C, and the bearing of these on R's behavior. Carried to the extreme, then, this kind of analysis could lead to the discovery of as many different power structures in a political system as there are individuals who impute different intentions to other individuals, groups, or strata in the system.

The distinction between having and exercising power could also turn on the directness involved in the relation between C and R and on the specificity of the actions. In the most direct relationship R's response would be tripped off by a signal directly from C. In this case, C is exercising power. But some relationships are highly indirect; for example, C may modify R's environment in a more or less lasting way, so that R continues to respond as C had intended, even though C makes no effort to control R. In these cases, one might say that although C does not exercise control over R, he does *have* control over R. There are a variety of these indirect, or 'roundabout', controls.[39]

Measuring Power

Even more than with power terms themselves, notions of 'more' or 'less' power were in classical theory left to the realm of common sense and intuition. Efforts to develop systematic measures of power date almost wholly from the 1950s. Of those, some are stated partly in mathematical formulas, some entirely in non-mathematical language. Since the essential features can be suggested without mathematics, we shall describe these measures in ordinary language.[40]

In a rough way, the various criteria for measuring power can be classified into three types: game-theoretical, Newtonian, and economic.

Game-theoretical Criteria

Shapley, a mathematician, and Shubik, an econometrician, have jointly formulated a 'method for evaluating the distribution of power in a committee system'.[41] This is intended to measure the power accruing to a voter where the outcome or decision is determined exclusively by voting. In these cases the rules prescribe what proportion of votes constitutes a winning proportion (e.g., a simple majority of all committee members). Thus each member has a

Robert Dahl

certain abstract probability of casting the last vote that would be
needed to complete a winning coalition, in other words to occupy a
pivotal position with respect to the outcome. By adding his vote at
this crucial juncture, a voter may be conceived of as having made a
particularly decisive contribution to the outcome; thus, gaining his
vote might have considerable value to the other members of a
coalition that would lose without his vote. Shapley and Shubik
proposed measuring the power of a voter by the probability that he
would be the pivotal voter in a winning coalition. Because their
measure is entirely limited to voting situations and excludes all
outcomes other than the act of voting itself, the utility of the
measure is limited to cases where most of the other familiar elements of political life – various forms of persuasion, inducement,
and coercion – are lacking.

Newtonian Criteria

On the analogy of the measurement of force in classical mechanics,
a number of analysts propose to measure power by the amount of
change in R attributable to C. The greater the change in R, the
greater the power of C; thus C_a is said to exert more power than C_b
if C_a induces more change in R_a than C_b induces in R_a (or in some
other R). Measures of this kind have been more frequently proposed than any other.[42]

'Change in R' is not, however, a single dimension, since many
different changes in R may be relevant. Some of the important
dimensions of the 'change in R' brought about by C that have been
suggested for measuring the amount of C's power are (1) the
probability that R will comply; (2) the number of persons in R; (3)
the number of distinct items, subjects, or values in R; (4) the
amount of change in R's position, attitudes, or psychological state;
(5) the speed with which R changes; (6) the reduction in the size of
the set of outcomes or behaviors available to R; and (7) the degree
of R's threatened or expected deprivation.

Economic Criteria

Where the game-theoretical measure focuses on the pivotal position
of C, and Newtonian measures on changes in R, a third proposal
would include 'costs' to both C and R in measuring C's power.
Harsanyi has argued that a complete measure of power should
include (1) the opportunity costs to C of attempting to influence R,
which Harsanyi calls the *costs* of C's power, and (2) the opportu-

Power as the Control of Behavior 55

nity costs to R of refusing to comply with C, which Harsanyi calls the *strength* of C's power over R.[43] The measure Harsanyi proposes is not inherently limited to the kinds of cost most familiar to economists but could be extended – at least in principle – to include psychological costs of all kinds.

Designing Operational Definitions

Empirical studies discussed by Cartwright,[44] March,[45] and others, and particularly community studies, have called attention to the neglected problem of designing acceptable operational definitions.

The concepts and measures discussed in this article have not been clothed in operational language. It is not yet clear how many of them can be. Yet the researcher who seeks to observe, report, compare, and analyze power in the real world, in order to test a particular hypothesis or a broader theory, quickly discovers urgent need for operationally defined terms. Research so far has called attention to three kinds of problems. First, the gap between concept and operational definition is generally very great, so great, indeed, that it is not always possible to see what relation there is between the operations and the abstract definition. Thus a critic is likely to conclude that the studies are, no doubt, reporting something in the real world, but he might question whether they are reporting the phenomena we mean when we speak of power. Second, different operational measures do not seem to correlate with one another,[46] which suggests that they may tap different aspects of power relations. Third, almost every measure proposed has engendered controversy over its validity.

None of these results should be altogether surprising or even discouraging. For despite the fact that the attempt to understand political systems by analyzing power relations is ancient, the systematic empirical study of power relations is remarkably new.

NOTES

1 Harold D. Lasswell and Abraham Kaplan, *Power and Society: A Framework for Political Enquiry*, Yale Law School Studies, vol. 2 (Yale University Press, New Haven, 1950; paperback edn 1963), p. xiv.

2 Lasswell and Kaplan, *Power and Society*; Bertrand de Jouvenel, *Power: The Natural History of its Growth* (Batchworth, London, 1952; first published in French). See also Felix E. Oppenheim, *Dimensions of Freedom: An Analysis* (St. Martins, New York; Macmillan, London, 1961), chapters 8 and 9.

56 *Robert Dahl*

3 Friedrich Meinecke, *Machiavellism: The Doctrine of Raison d'État and its Place in Modern History* (Yale University Press, New Haven, 1957, first published as *Die Idee der Staatsräson in der neueren Geschichte*, 1924).

4 Max Weber, *The Theory of Social and Economic Organization*, ed. Talcott Parsons (The Free Press, Glencoe, Ill., 1957; first published as part 1 of *Wirtschaft und Gesellschaft*, 1922), p. 152. Further quotations from pp. 153, 154.

5 George E. G. Catlin, *The Science and Method of Politics* (Knopf, New York; Routledge, London, 1927) and *A Study of the Principles of Politics, Being an Essay Towards Political Rationalization* (Macmillan, New York, 1930).

6 Herbert Goldhamer and Edward Shils, 'Types of power and status', *American Journal of Sociology*, 45 (1939), pp. 171–82.

7 Charles E. Merriam, *Political Power: Its Composition and Incidence* (McGraw-Hill, New York, 1934; paperback edn 1964 by Collier).

8 Harold D. Lasswell, *Politics: Who Gets What When, How?* (McGraw-Hill, New York, 1936).

9 Hans J. Morgenthau, *Politics Among Nations: The Struggle for Power and Peace*, 4th edn (Knopf, New York, 1967).

10 Lasswell and Kaplan, *Power and Society*, pp. 74–5.

11 Compare Dorwin Cartwright, 'Influence, leadership, control' in James G. March (ed.), *Handbook of Organizations* (Rand McNally, Chicago, 1965), pp. 1–47.

12 Aristotle, *The Politics of Aristotle*, translated and edited by Ernest Barker (Oxford University Press, New York, 1962), p. 164.

13 Lasswell and Kaplan, *Power and Society*, p. 73.

14 Lasswell and Kaplan, *Power and Society*, p. 73; John C. Harsanyi, 'Measurement of social power, opportunity costs, and the theory of two-person bargaining games', *Behavioral Science*, 7 (1962), pp. 67–80, esp. p. 67.

15 Aristotle, *The Politics of Aristotle*, pp. 110 ff.

16 Lasswell and Kaplan, *Power and Society*, p. 218.

17 Robert A. Dahl, *Modern Political Analysis* (Prentice-Hall, Englewood Cliffs, N.J., 1963), p. 38.

18 Karl Loewenstein, *Political Power and the Governmental Process* (University of Chicago Press, Chicago, 1957), p. 29.

19 Robert E. Agger, Daniel Goldrich and Bert Swanson, *The Rulers and the Ruled: Political Power and Impotence in American Communities* (Wiley, New York, 1964), pp. 73 ff.

20 Lasswell and Kaplan, *Power and Society*, p. 87.

21 Robert A. Dahl, *Who Governs? Democracy and Power in an American City* (Yale University Press, New Haven, 1961, 1963), pp. 229 ff.

22 Richard E. Neustadt, *Presidential Power: The Politics of Leadership* (Wiley, New York, 1960, paperback edn 1962), pp. 152 ff.

23 E.g. Harold D. Lasswell, *Psychopathology and Politics*, new edn, with afterthoughts by the author (Viking, New York, 1960); Arnold A.

Power as the Control of Behavior 57

Rogow and Harold D. Lasswell, *Power, Corruption and Rectitude* (Prentice-Hall, Englewood Cliffs, N.J., 1963); Dorwin Cartwright (ed.), *Studies in Social Power*, Research Center for Group Dynamics, publication no. 6 (University of Michigan, Institute for Social Research, Ann Arbor, 1959).

24 Harsanyi, 'Measurement of social power, opportunity costs, etc.'; John C. Harsanyi, 'Measurement of social power in *n*-person reciprocal power situations', *Behavioral Science*, 7 (1962), pp. 81–91.

25 Herbert A. Simon, *Models of Man: Social and Rational; Mathematical Essays on Rational Human Behavior in a Social Setting* (Wiley, New York, 1947–56, 1957), p. 5.

26 Simon, *Models of Man*, pp. 5, 11, 12, 66; Robert A. Dahl, 'The concept of power', *Behavioral Science*, 2 (1957), pp. 201–15, esp. p. 204; Cartwright, *Studies in Social Power*, p. 197; Oppenheim, *Dimensions of Freedom*, p. 104.

27 Herbert A. Simon, 'Notes on the observation and measurement of political power', *Journal of Politics*, 15 (1953), pp. 500–16, esp. p. 504; James G. March, 'An introduction to the theory and measurement of influence', *American Political Science Review*, 49 (1955), pp. 431–51, esp. p. 435; Dahl, 'The concept of power', p. 203.

28 Oppenheim, *Dimensions of Freedom*, p. 41.

29 William H. Riker, 'Some ambiguities in the notion of power', *American Political Science Review*, 58 (1964), pp. 341–9, esp. p. 348.

30 Hubert M. Blalock Jr, *Causal Inferences in Nonexperimental Research* (University of North Carolina Press, Chapel Hill, 1964), quotations from pp. 30, 32, 34.

31 Blalock, *Causal Inferences*.

32 Ibid., p. 62.

33 E.g. Vilfredo Pareto, *The Mind and Society: A Treatise on General Sociology*, 4 vols (Dover, New York, 1963; first published as *Trattato di sociologia generale*. Volume 1: *Non-logical Conduct*. Volume 2: *Theory of Residues*. Volume 3: *Theory of Derivations*. Volume 4: *The General Form of Society*), vol. 4; C. Wright Mills, *The Power Elite* (Oxford University Press, New York, 1956) *passim*; Lasswell and Kaplan, *Power and Society*, chapters 9 and 10. See also Dahl, *Who Governs?*; Gaetano Mosca, *The Ruling Class* (McGraw-Hill, New York 1939, first published as *Elementi di scienza politica*, 1896); Peter H. Rossi, 'Power and community structure', *Midwest Journal of Political Science*, 4 (1960), pp. 390–401; Nelson W. Polsby, *Community Power and Political Theory*, Yale Studies in Political Science, vol. 7 (Yale University Press, New Haven, 1963); Talcott Parsons, 'On the concept of influence', *Public Opinion Quarterly*, 27 (1963), pp. 37–62 (a comment by J. S. Coleman appears on pp. 63–83; a communication by R. A. Bauer on pp. 83–6; and a rejoinder by Talcott Parsons on pp. 87–92); Talcott Parsons, 'On the concept of political power', *American Philosophical Society, Proceedings*, 107 (1963), pp. 232–62.

34 Blalock, *Causal Inferences*, p. 18.

58 *Robert Dahl*

35 Oppenheim, *Dimensions of Freedom*; Cartwright, 'Influence, leadership, control'; Parsons, 'On the concept of influence'; Parsons, 'On the concept of political power'; John R. P. French and Bertram Raven, 'The bases of social power', in Dorwin Cartwright (ed.) *Studies in Social Power*, Research Center for Group Dynamics, publication no. 6 (University of Michigan, Institute for Social Research, Ann Arbor, 1959), pp. 150–67.

36 Lasswell and Kaplan, *Power and Society*, p. 71; Oppenheim, *Dimensions of Freedom*, chapters 2 and 3.

37 Carl J. Friedrich, *Man and His Government: An Empirical Theory of Politics* (McGraw-Hill, New York, 1963), chapter 11.

38 Peter Bachrach and Morton Baratz, 'Two faces of power', *American Political Science Review*, 56 (1962), pp. 947–52.

39 Robert A. Dahl and Charles E. Lindblom, *Politics, Economics, and Welfare: Planning and Politico-economic Systems Resolved into Basic Social Processes* (Harper, New York, 1953; paperback edn 1963), pp. 110 ff.

40 The reader should consult the sources cited for the precise formulations. Most of the best-known measures are presented and discussed in Riker, 'Some ambiguities'.

41 L. S. Shapley and Martin Shubik, 'A method for evaluating the distribution of power in a committee system', *American Political Science Review*, 48 (1954), pp. 787–92.

42 See Oppenheim, *Dimensions of Freedom*, chapter 8; Dahl, *Modern Political Analysis*, chapter 5; Cartwright, *Studies in Social Power*; Simon, *Models of Man*; Dahl, 'The concept of power'; James G. March, 'Measurement concepts in the theory of influence', *Journal of Politics*, 19 (1957), pp. 202–26.

43 Harsanyi, 'Measurement of social power, opportunity costs, etc.', pp. 68 ff.

44 Cartwright, 'Influence, leadership, control'.

45 James G. March (ed.) *Handbook of Organizations* (Rand McNally, Chicago, 1965).

46 James G. March, 'Influence measurement in experimental and semi-experimental groups', *Sociometry*, 19 (1956), pp. 260–71.

[16]

EXPLORING POWER

Gareth Morgan

Power is the medium through which conflicts of interest are ultimately resolved. Power influences who gets what, when, and how.

In recent years organization and management theorists have become increasingly aware of the need to recognize the importance of power in explaining organizational affairs. However, no really clear and consistent definition of power has emerged. While some view power as a resource, i.e., as something one possesses, others view it as a social relation characterized by some kind of dependency, i.e., as an influence *over* something or someone. Most organization theorists tend to take their point of departure from the definition of power offered by American political scientist Robert Dahl, who suggests that power involves an ability to get another person to do something that he or she would not otherwise have done. For some theorists this definition leads to a study of the "here and now" conditions under which one person, group, or organization becomes dependent on another, while for others it leads to an examination of the historical forces that shape the stage of action on which contemporary power relations are set. As listed in Exhibit 6.3, the sources of power are rich and varied, providing those who wish to wheel and deal in the pursuit of their interests with many ways of doing so. In the following discussion we will examine how these sources of power are used to shape the dynamics of organizational life. In so doing we will be creating an analytical frame-

---

The following are among the most important sources of power:

1. FORMAL AUTHORITY
2. CONTROL OF SCARCE RESOURCES
3. USE OF ORGANIZATIONAL STRUCTURE, RULES, AND REGULATIONS
4. CONTROL OF DECISION PROCESSES
5. CONTROL OF KNOWLEDGE AND INFORMATION
6. CONTROL OF BOUNDARIES
7. ABILITY TO COPE WITH UNCERTAINTY
8. CONTROL OF TECHNOLOGY
9. INTERPERSONAL ALLIANCES, NETWORKS, AND CONTROL OF "INFORMAL ORGANIZATION"
10. CONTROL OF COUNTERORGANIZATIONS
11. SYMBOLISM AND THE MANAGEMENT OF MEANING
12. GENDER AND THE MANAGEMENT OF GENDER RELATIONS
13. STRUCTURAL FACTORS THAT DEFINE THE STAGE OF ACTION
14. THE POWER ONE ALREADY HAS

These sources of power provide organizational members with a variety of means for enhancing their interests and resolving or perpetuating organizational conflict.

Exhibit 6.3. Sources of power in organizations

work that can help us to understand the power dynamics within an organization, and to identify the ways in which organizational members can attempt to exert their influence.

Formal authority. The first and most obvious source of power in an organization is formal authority, a form of legitimized power that is respected and acknowledged by those with whom one interacts. As sociologist Max Weber has noted, legitimacy is a form of social approval that is essential for stabilizing power relations, and arises when people recognize that a person has a right to rule some area of human life, and when the ruled consider it their duty to obey. Historically, legitimate authority has been underpinned by one or more of three characteristics: charisma, tradition, or the rule of law (see Exhibit 9.1 for further details). Charismatic authority arises when people respect the special qualities of an individual (charisma means "gift of grace") and see those qualities as defining the right of the individual to act on their behalf. Traditional authority arises when people respect the custom and practices of the past and vest authority in those who symbolize and embody these traditional values. Monarchs and others who rule because of some kind of inherited status acquire their right to rule through this kind of principle. Bureaucratic or rational-legal authority arises when people insist that the exercise of power depends on the correct application of formal rules and procedures. Those that exercise bureaucratic authority must win their rights to power through procedural means, for example by demonstrating ownership or property rights in a corporation, through election in a democratic system, or by demonstrating appropriate professional or technical qualifications in a meritocracy.

Each of these three kinds of formal authority may be found in modern organizations. A hero figure may acquire immense charismatic power that allows him or her to control and direct others as he or she wishes. The owner of a family firm may exercise authority as a result of his or her membership in the founding family. A bureaucrat may exercise power as a result of the formal office that he or she holds. So long as those who are subject to the kind of authority in use respect and accept the nature of that authority, the authority serves as a form of power. If it is not respected, the authority becomes vacuous, and power depends on the other sources named in Exhibit 6.3.

The most obvious type of *formal* authority in most organizations is bureaucratic and is typically associated with the position one holds, whether as sales manager, accountant, project coordinator, secretary, factory supervisor, or machine operator. These different organizational positions are usually defined in terms of rights and obligations, which create a field of influence within which one can legitimately operate with the formal support of those with whom one works. A factory supervisor is given a "right" to instruct those under his or her control. A sales manager is given the "right" to influence policy on sales campaigns—but not on financial accounting. The latter falls within the field of discretion and influence delegated to the accounting manager. The formal positions on an organization chart thus define spheres of delegated authority. To the extent that authority is translated into power through the assent of those falling under the pattern of command, the authority structure is also a power structure. Though the authority is often seen as flowing down from the top of the organization chart, being delegated by one's superior, our discussion of the nature of legitimacy suggests that this is only partly true. For the authority becomes effective only to the extent that it is legitimized from below. The pyramid of power represented in an organization chart thus builds on a base where considerable power belongs to those at the bottom of the pyramid as well as to those at the top. Trade unionization has of course recognized this, channeling the power existing at the lower levels of the pyramid to challenge the power at the top. To the extent that trade-union power is legitimized by the rule of law and the right to unionize, it too represents a type of formal authority. We will have more to say on this later in our discussion of "counterorganizations."

Control of scarce resources. All organizations depend for their continued existence on an adequate flow of resources, such as money, materials, technology, personnel, and support from customers, suppliers, and the community at large. An ability to exercise control over any of these resources can thus provide an important source of power within and between organizations. Access to funds, possession of a crucial skill or raw material, control of access to some valued computer program or new technology, or even access to a special customer or supplier can lend individuals considerable organizational power. If the resource is in scarce supply and someone is dependent on its availability, then it can almost certainly be translated into power. Scarcity and dependence are the keys to resource power!

When we begin to talk about the power associated with resources, attention usually focuses on the role of money. For money is among the most liquid of all resources, and can usually be converted into the others. A person with a valued skill, a supplier with a precious raw material, or a person holding information on a new project opportunity can often be persuaded to exchange their valued resource for an attractive price. Money can also be converted into promotions, patronage, threats, promises, or favors to buy loyalty, service, support, or raw compliance.

No wonder therefore that so much organizational politics surrounds the process of budgeting and the control and allocation of financial resources. As Jeffrey Pfeffer of Stanford University has suggested, the use of such power is critically linked with one's ability to control the *discretionary* use of funds. It is not necessary to have full control over financial decisions. One needs to have just enough control to pull the crucial strings that can create changes at the margin. The reason for this is that most of the financial resources available to an organization are committed to sustain current operations. Changes to these operations are usually incremental, decisions being made to increase or reduce current expenditure. It is the ability to increase or decrease this flow of funds that gives power. Hence if a manager can acquire access to uncommitted resources that he or she can use in a discretionary way, e.g., as a slush fund, he or she can exert a major influence over future organizational development and at the same time buy commitment from those who benefit from this use of funds. Similarly, someone outside an organization who is responsible for deciding whether his or her financial support to that organization should be continued is in a position to exercise considerable influence on the policies and practices of the organization. Often this influence is out of all proportion with the amount actually given, since organizations are often critically dependent on marginal funds to create room to maneuver. Organizations often have a tendency to use their slack in one year in ways that create commitments or expectations for the next year—e.g., by giving a raise in salary that will be expected to be repeated next year, by appointing staff whose appointments will need to be renewed, or by launching a new program that staff will wish to continue—thus lending considerable power to the marginal funder.

The principles that we have discussed in relation to the use of financial power apply to other kinds of resource power as well. The important point is that power rests in controlling resources on which the organization is dependent for current operations or for creating new initiatives. There must be a dependence before one is able to control; and such control always derives its power from there being a scarcity of, or limited access to, the resource in question. Whether we are talking about the control of finance, skills, materials, or personnel, or even the provision of emotional support to a key decision maker who has come to value one's support and friendship, the principles remain the same. The more Machiavellian among us will quickly see how these principles point the way to a strategy for increasing power by *creating* dependence through the planned control of critical resources.

One's power can also be increased by reducing one's dependence on others. This is why many managers and organizational units like to have their own pockets of resources. The seemingly needless duplication of resources in an organization, where each department has the same underemployed machine or set of experts or a stockpile of staff that can be used in rush periods, is often a result of attempts to reduce one's dependence on the resources of others.

Use of organizational structure, rules, and regulations. Most often, organizational structure, rules, regulations, and procedures are viewed as rational instruments intended to aid task performance. A political view of these arrangements, however, suggests that in many situations they are often best understood as products and reflections of a struggle for political control.

Consider the following example drawn from research that I conducted on British "new town" development corporations. The corporation in question was established in the early 1960s to develop a new town in an old industrial area. A functional organization was established with separate departments (finance, law, administration, commercial development, housing, architecture and planning, and engineering services) reporting to a general manager, who reported to the board. In the late 1960s an energetic businessman became chairman of the board. He made the corporation's chief legal officer the new general manager and split the now vacant legal officer's post into two parts, creating the post of corporation secretary and leaving the new legal officer with a narrower range of functions. The secretary's post was filled by a nominee of the chairman who had worked with him in a similar capacity at another organization. The chairman and secretary began to work closely together, and the board eventually agreed that the secretary should have direct access to the board without having to go through the general manager. The chairman involved himself in the day-to-day running of the organization, often bypassing the general manager, whose role became very difficult to perform.

This situation came to a rather abrupt end after just one year, with the surprise resignation of the chairman in response to a controversy over policy issues. With the appointment of a new chairman who was interested in delegating the task of running the organization to the general manager, power relations within the corporation changed dramatically. The general manager gradually established his control over his department heads, many of whom had become quite powerful through the interventions of the former chairman. His approach was to bring many of the functions that had been allocated to the secretary under his own control, and to reorganize other departmental responsibilities. For example, he split the functions of the architecture and planning department, establishing a new planning department and a new department dealing with surveys. This move left the chief architect, who had become a strong executive during the reign of the previous chairman, with but a fraction of the department he once ran. These structural redesigns were later accompanied by further changes that in effect demoted the heads of the functional departments, and it was not long before a number left the organization, including the secretary and the chief architect.

While these structural changes were justified in technical terms, they were also motivated by political considerations relating to issues of control. The initial changes created by the corporation's energetic chairman were designed to enhance his own control of the organization by weakening that of the general manager. The changes introduced after the chairman's resignation were primarily designed to help the general manager regain control over powerful department heads. Structural change was part of a power play to limit the role and influence of other key individuals.

The circumstances of this case may be unique, but the pattern is quite general, since organizational structure is frequently used as a political instrument. Plans for organizational differentiation and integration, designs for centralization and decentralization, and the tensions that can arise in matrix organizations often entail hidden agendas related to the power, autonomy, or interdependence of departments and individuals. The size and status of a group or department within an organization often provides an indication of its power within the overall structure, since one obvious tactic of control is to downgrade the importance of a function or group of individuals, or to adopt a divide-and-rule strategy that fragments potential power bases. This tactic is illustrated in the case study discussed above and was also present in a number of other "new town" corporations included in my research. For example, in one corporation the community-development function, which often achieved departmental status in other corporations, was relegated to a small subdivision under the control of the chief legal officer—someone who had little knowledge of or interest in this kind of work. The community development staff, who usually took radical stands on planning matters, were correct in their perception that their unusual location within the organizational structure reflected the general manager's desire to reduce their influence and exclude them from meetings among department heads. The same general manager attempted to stifle the development of project teams across middle levels of the hierarchy, which would have led the organization toward a matrix rather than bureaucratic structure. The general manager wished to exercise strong authoritarian control through his department heads by discouraging project teams and making his department heads responsible for cross-departmental integration. Many of the middle-rank planning professionals became extremely discouraged by their lack of autonomy and influence and soon left the organization in large numbers.

The tensions surrounding the process of organizational design and redesign thus provide many insights on organizational power structures. And the rigidity and inertia of organizational structures can do the same, since people often preserve existing structures in order to protect the power that they derive from them. For example, people and departments often cling to outdated job descriptions or organizational designs, e.g., by resisting adoption of computer technology, because their power and status within the organization is so closely tied with the old order. One of the ironies of bureaucratic organization is that job and departmental designs that were originally introduced to control the work of employees can also be used by employees to control their superiors.

The same is true in relation to rules, regulations, and other kinds of formal procedures. Just as a job description can be used by an employee to define what he or she is *not* prepared to do ("that's not part of my job," or "I'm not paid to do that"), rules and regulations often prove to be two-edged swords. One outstanding example is found in the case of British Rail, where employees have discovered the power of "working to rule." Rather than going on strike to further a claim or address a grievance, a process that proves costly to employees since they forfeit their pay, the union often declares a "work to rule" whereby employees do exactly what is required by the regulations developed by the railway authorities. The result is that hardly any train leaves on time, schedules go haywire, and the whole railway system quickly slows to a snail's pace if not to a halt. The rules of course were created to control employees, to protect the safety of passengers, and, equally important, to protect the railway authorities, since in the event of a major accident a clear structure of rules and responsibilities can help allocate blame. The only trouble is that there are so many rules that they render the railway system almost inoperable. Normal functioning thus requires that employees find shortcuts or at least streamline procedures. British Rail is of course not unique in this regard. Many organizations have similar rules that, as many employees know, are not routinely applied.

The importance of these rules for their creators is clearly illustrated in the public investigations that follow major accidents, where investigators compare the evidence of events with the norms prescribed in formal regulations to find who is in error. Sometimes gaps in the rules are found. Sometimes gross negligence is discovered. But often the accident is no more than what Charles Perrow of Yale University calls a "normal accident," in the sense that its probability is built into the nature of the system. The broken rules that accompany the accident have often been broken thousands of times before as part of normal work practice, since normal work is impossible without breaking the rules. The railwaymen in Britain, like others who have adopted the "work to rule" practice, have discovered how they can use a weapon designed to control and possibly punish them to control and punish others.

Rules and regulations are thus often created, invoked, and used in either a proactive or retrospective fashion as part of a power play. All bureaucratic regulations, decision-making criteria, plans and schedules, promotion and job-evaluation requirements, and other rules that guide organizational functioning give potential power to both the controllers and those controlled. Rules designed to guide and streamline activities can almost always be used to block activities. Just as lawyers make a profession out of finding a new angle on what appears to be a clear-cut rule, many organizational members are able to invoke rules in ways that no one ever imagined possible. An ability to use the rules to one's advantage is thus an important source of organizational power and, as in the case of organizational structures, defines a contested terrain that is forever being negotiated, preserved, or changed.

Control of decision processes. An ability to influence the outcomes of decision-making processes is a well-recognized source of power, and one that has attracted considerable attention in the organization-theory literature. Since organizations are in large measure decision-making systems, an individual or group that can exert a major influence on decision processes can exert a great influence on the affairs of his or her organization. No wonder, therefore, the time, energy, and meticulous attention that so many power-hungry men and women devote to endless strings of meetings. These "politicos," as they are often known, are wheeling and dealing in terms of agendas that are often hidden to create the decision outcomes that they desire. It is these hidden agendas that allow many of them to emerge triumphant after hours of circular discussion that ends in stalemate. For the politics of organizational decision making often involves preventing crucial decisions from being made, as well as fostering those that one actually desires.

In discussing the kinds of power utilized in decision making it is useful to distinguish between control of three interrelated elements: decision *premises*, decision *processes*, and decision *issues and objectives*. One of the most effective ways of getting a decision is to allow it to be made by default. Hence much of the political activity within an organization hinges on the control of agendas and other decision premises that influence how a particular decision will be approached, perhaps in ways that prevent certain core issues from surfacing at all. By avoiding explicit discussion of an issue, one may be able to get precisely what one wants. For example, in an organization where members wish to form a trade union, or where there is a growing coalition in favor of opening up a new program area, these key decisions can often be avoided or delayed by making marginal though significant changes elsewhere in order to redirect attention. This tactic of preventing certain subjects from becoming hot issues that *must* command attention often proves popular with those who wish to preserve the status quo.

In addition to the conscious manipulation of decision premises there is also often a large unconscious or socialized element of control. As Charles Perrow has noted, much unobtrusive control is built into vocabularies, structures of communication, attitudes, beliefs, rules, and procedures that, though unquestioned, exert a decisive influence on decision outcomes. These factors shape decision premises by shaping the way we think and act. Visions of what the problems and issues are and how they can be tackled often act as mental straitjackets that prevent us from seeing other ways of formulating our basic concerns and the alternative courses of action that are available. Many of these constraints are built into organizational assumptions, beliefs, and practices about "who we are" and "the way we do things around here."

Control of decision-making *processes* is usually more visible than the control of decision premises. How should a decision be made? Who should be involved? When will the decision be made? By determining whether a decision can be taken and then reported to appropriate quarters, whether it must go before a committee, and which committee, whether it must be supported by a full report, whether it will appear on an agenda where it is likely to receive a rough ride (or an easy passage), the order of an agenda, and even whether the decision should be discussed at the beginning or end of a meeting, a manager can have a considerable impact on decision outcomes. The ground rules that are to guide decision making are thus important variables that organization members can manipulate and use to stack the deck in favor of or against a given action.

A final way of controlling decision making is to influence the *issues and objectives* to be addressed and the evaluative criteria to be employed. An individual can shape issues and objectives most directly through preparing the reports and contributing to the discussion on which the decision will be based. By emphasizing the importance of particular constraints, selecting and evaluating the alternatives on which a decision will be made, and highlighting the importance of certain values or outcomes, decision makers can exert considerable influence on the decision that emerges from discussion. Eloquence, command of the facts, passionate commitment, or sheer tenacity or endurance can in the end win the day, adding to a person's power to influence the decisions with which he or she is involved.

Control of knowledge and information.
Evident in much of the above discussion, particularly with regard to the control of decision premises, is the idea that power accrues to the person who is able to structure attention to issues in a way that in effect defines the reality of the decision-making process. This draws attention to the key importance of knowledge and information as sources of power. By controlling these key resources a person can systematically influence the definition of organizational situations and can create patterns of dependency. Both these activities deserve attention on their own account.

The American social psychologist W. I. Thomas once observed that if people define situations as real, they are real in their consequences. Many skillful organizational politicians put this dictum into practice on a daily basis by controlling information flows and the knowledge that is made available to different people, thereby influencing their perception of situations and hence the ways they act in relation to those situations. These politicians are often known as "gatekeepers," opening and closing channels of communication and filtering, summarizing, analyzing, and thus shaping knowledge in accordance with a view of the world that favors their interests. Many aspects of organizational structure, especially hierarchy and departmental divisions, influence how information flows and are readily used by unofficial gatekeepers to advance their own ends. Even by the simple process of slowing down or accelerating particular information flows, thus making knowledge available in a timely manner or too late for it to be of use to its recipients, the gatekeeper can wield considerable power.

Often the quest for control of information in an organization is linked to questions of organizational structure. For example, many battles have been fought over the control and use of centralized computer systems, because control of the computer often carried with it control over information flows and the design of information systems. The power of many finance and other information-processing departments is tied up with this fact. Finance staff are important not only because they control resources, but because they also define and control information about the use of resources. By influencing the design of budgeting and cost-control information systems they are able to influence what is perceived as being important within the organization, both on the part of those who use the information as a basis for control and among those who are subject to these controls. Just as decision-making premises influence the kind of decisions that are made, the hidden and sometimes unquestioned assumptions that are built into the design of information systems can be of crucial importance in structuring day-to-day activity.

Many of the hot issues regarding the merits and problems of micro-processing hinge on the question of power. The new information-processing technology creates the possibility of multiple points of access to common data bases and the possibility of local rather than centralized information systems. In principle the technology can be used to increase the power of those at the periphery or local levels of the organization by providing them with more comprehensive, immediate, and relevant data relating to their work, facilitating self-control rather than centralized control. In practice the technology is often used to increase power at the center. The designers and users of such systems have been acutely aware of the power in information, decentralizing certain activities while centralizing ongoing surveillance over their performance. Thus executives in remote parts of the world, airline reservation staff in unsupervised offices, and workers on the factory floor perform under the watchful eye of the computer, which reports almost every move to someone at the heart of the information system.

In addition to shaping definitions of organizational realities or exercising control, knowledge and information can be used to weave patterns of dependency. By possessing the right information at the right time, by having exclusive access to key data, or by simply demonstrating the ability to marshal and synthesize facts in an effective manner, organizational members can increase the power they wield within an organization. Many people develop these skills in a systematic way, and jealously guard or block access to crucial knowledge to enhance their indispensability and "expert" status. Obviously, other organizational members have an interest in breaking such exclusivity and widening access. There is thus usually a tendency in organizations to routinize valued skills and abilities whenever possible. There is also a tendency to break down dependencies on specific individuals and departments by acquiring one's own experts. Thus departments often prefer to have their own specialist skills on hand, even if this involves duplication and some redundancy of specialisms within the organization as a whole.

A final aspect of expert power relates to the use of knowledge and expertise as a means of legitimizing what one wishes to do. "The expert" often carries an aura of authority and power that can add considerable weight to a decision that rests in the balance but that has already been made in the minds of key actors.

Control of boundaries. Any discussion of power in organizations must give attention to what is sometimes known as "boundary management." The notion of boundary is used to refer to the interface between different elements of an organization. Thus we can talk about the boundary between different work groups or departments, or between an organization and its environment. By monitoring and controlling boundary transactions people are able to build up considerable power. For example, it becomes possible to monitor changes occurring outside one's group, department, or organization and initiate timely responses. One acquires knowledge of critical interdependencies over which one may be able to secure a degree of control. Or one gains access to critical information that places one in a particularly powerful position to interpret what is happening in the outside world, and thus to help define the organizational reality that will guide action. One can also control transactions across boundaries by performing a buffering function that allows or even encourages certain transactions while blocking others.

Most people in leadership positions at all levels of an organization can engage in this kind of boundary management in a way that contributes to their power. The process is also an important element of many organizational roles, such as those of a secretary, special assistant, or project coordinator, and of liaison people of all kinds. People in such roles are often able to acquire power that goes well beyond their formal status. For example, many secretaries and special assistants are able to exert a major impact on the way their boss views the reality of a given situation by determining who is given access to the manager and when, and by managing information in a way that highlights or downplays the importance of events and activities occurring elsewhere in the organization. One outstanding example of boundary management is found in the management of the White House under the Nixon administration, where Nixon's top aides Richard Erlichman and Bob Haldeman exercised tight control over access to the president. In doing so it seems that they were able to manage the president's view of what was happening in the White House and elsewhere. One of the main issues in the notorious Watergate affair and the collapse of the presidency was whether Nixon's aides had allowed him to receive the critical information regarding the Watergate burglary. Erlichman and Haldeman were experts at boundary management, and their basic strategy for acquiring power is found in many different kinds of organizations all over the world.

Boundary management can help integrate a unit with the outside world, or it can be used to isolate that unit so that it can function in an autonomous way. The quest for autonomy—by individuals, groups, and even departments—is a powerful feature of organizational life, because many people like to be in full control over their life space. Boundary management aids this quest, since it often shows ways in which a unit can acquire the resources necessary to create autonomy and points to strategies that can be used to fend off threats to autonomy. Groups and departments often attempt to incorporate key skills and resources within their boundaries and to control admissions through selective recruitment. They also often engage in what sociologist Erving Goffman has described as "avoidance rituals," steering clear of issues and potential problems that will threaten their independence.

The quest for autonomy is, however, often countered by opposing strategies initiated by managers elsewhere in the system. They may attempt to break down the cohesiveness of the group by nominating their own representatives or allies to key positions, find ways of minimizing the slack resources available to the group, or encourage organizational redesigns that increase interdependence and minimize the consequences of autonomous actions. Boundary transactions are thus often characterized by competing strategies for control and countercontrol. Many groups and departments are successful in acquiring considerable degrees of autonomy, and in defending their position in a way that makes the organization a system of loosely coupled groups and departments rather than a highly integrated unit.

Ability to cope with uncertainty. One source of power implicit in much that has been discussed above is the ability to cope with the uncertainties that influence the day-to-day operation of an organization. Organization implies a certain degree of interdependence, so that discontinuous or unpredictable situations in one part of an organization have considerable implications for operations elsewhere. An ability to deal with these uncertainties gives an individual, group, or subunit considerable power in the organization as a whole.

The ability to cope with uncertainty is often intimately connected with one's place in the overall division of labor in an organization. Generally speaking, uncertainty is of two kinds. Environmental uncertainties (e.g., with regard to markets, sources of raw materials, or finance) can provide great opportunities for those with the contacts or skills to tackle the problems and thus minimize their effects on the organization as a whole. Operational uncertainties within the organization (such as from the breakdown of critical machinery used in factory production or data processing) can help troubleshooters, maintenance staff, or others with the requisite skills and abilities acquire power and status as a result of their ability to restore normal operations. The degree of power that accrues to people who can tackle both these kinds of uncertainty depends primarily on two factors. First, the degree to which their skills are substitutable, and hence the ease with which they can be replaced. Second, the centrality of their functions to the operations of the organization as a whole.

Organizations generally try to reduce uncertainties whenever possible, usually by "buffering" or through processes of routinization. For example, stocks of critical resources may be built up from different sources, maintenance programs may be developed to minimize technological failures, and people may be trained to deal with environmental contingencies. However, some uncertainty almost always remains, since by nature, uncertain situations cannot always be accurately predicted and forestalled. In addition, those who see the power deriving from their capacity to deal with uncertainty often preserve their power base by ensuring that the uncertainties continue, and sometimes by manipulating situations so that they appear more uncertain than they actually are.

In understanding the impact of uncertainty on the way an organization operates, we thus have an important means of understanding the power relations between different groups and departments. We also get a better understanding of the conditions under which the power of the expert or troubleshooter comes into play, and of the importance of the various kinds of power deriving from the control of resources that we discussed earlier. The existence of uncertainty and an ability to cope with uncertainty are often reasons explaining why and when these other kinds of power become so critical in shaping organizational affairs.

Control of technology. From the beginning of history technology has served as an instrument of power, enhancing the ability of humans to manipulate, control, and impose themselves on their environment. The technology employed in modern organizations performs a similar function. It provides its users with an ability to achieve amazing results in productive activity, and it also provides them with an ability to manipulate this productive power and make it work effectively for their own ends.

Organizations usually become vitally dependent on some form of core technology as a means of converting organizational inputs into outputs. This may be a factory assembly line; a telephone switchboard; a centralized computer or record-keeping system; or perhaps a capital-intensive plant like those used in oil refining, the production of chemicals, or power stations. The kind of technology employed influences the patterns of interdependence within an organization and hence the power relations between different individuals and departments. For example, in organizations where the technology creates patterns of sequential interdependence, as in a mass-production assembly line where task A must be completed before B, which must be completed before C, the people controlling any one part of the technology possess considerable power to disrupt the whole. In organizations where the technology involves more autonomous systems of production, the ability of one individual or group to influence the operation of the whole is much more limited.

The fact that technology has a major impact on power relations is an important reason why attempts to change technology often create major conflicts between managers and employees and between different groups within an organization. For the introduction of a new technology can alter the balance of power. The introduction of assembly-line production into industry, designed to increase managerial control over the work process, also had the unintended effect of increasing the power of factory workers and their unions: in standardizing jobs the technology standardized employee interests in a way that encouraged collective action, and also gave employees the power over the production process to make that action extremely effective. A strike on any part of an assembly line can bring the work of hundreds or even thousands of people to a complete halt. The technology is designed in a way that makes collective action by a small group of people extremely effective. The system of production based on the use of autonomous work groups and other forms of "cellular technology," on the other hand, fragments the interests of workers. Work and rewards accrue to the work team as a primary organizational unit. The interests of an employee thus often become more closely associated with those of his team than with those of a general type of employee or occupational group, making unionization and collective action much more difficult, especially since competitive relations may develop between different work teams. Since under the group system a withdrawal of work does not affect overall operations unless other work groups do the same, the power of workers and their unions over the organization as a whole tends to be reduced quite substantially.

The introduction of new production methods, machines, computing facilities, or any kind of technological change that will increase the power of one group or department at the expense of another thus tends to develop into a hot political issue. Groups of employees usually have a clear understanding of the power relations inherent in current work arrangements and are usually ready to marshal all their resources and ingenuity to fight changes that threaten their position.

The power associated with the control of technology becomes most visible in confrontations and negotiations surrounding organizational change, or when groups are attempting to improve their lot within the organization. However, it also operates in more subtle ways. In working with a particular machine or work system an employee learns the ins and outs of its operation in a way that often lends him or her considerable power. Earlier in this chapter we discussed how machine operators were able to use their knowledge of their machines to outwit the work-study experts attempting to set work standards. They were able to control the use of their technology to improve their wages and control their pace of work. This kind of process is used for many purposes in different kinds of work settings every day. People manipulate and control their technology, just as they twist and turn rules, regulations, and job descriptions. Technology designed to direct and control the work of employees frequently becomes a tool of workers' control!

Interpersonal alliances, networks, and control of "informal organization." Friends in high places; sponsors; mentors; coalitions of people prepared to trade support and favors to further their individual ends; and informal networks for touching base, sounding out, or merely shooting the breeze—all provide a source of power to those involved. Through various kinds of interlocking networks an individual can acquire advance notice of developments that are relevant to his or her interests, exert various forms of interpersonal influence to shape these developments in a manner that he or she desires, and prepare the way for proposals he or she is interested in advancing. The skilled organizational politician systematically builds and cultivates such informal alliances and networks, incorporating whenever possible the help and influence of all those with an important stake in the domain in which he or she is operating. Alliances and coalitions are not necessarily built around an identity of interests; rather, the requirement for these forms of informal organization is that there be a basis for some form of mutually beneficial exchange. Successful networking or coalition building involves an awareness that in addition to winning friends it is necessary to incorporate and pacify potential enemies, and an ability to see beyond immediate issues and find ways of trading help in the present for promises in the future. The successful coalition builder recognizes that the currency of coalition building is one of mutual dependency and exchange.

The coalitions, alliances, and networks built through these processes may remain highly informal and to a degree invisible. The coalition building may occur over the telephone, through old-boy networks and other friendship groups, through the golf club, or through chance contacts. For example, people sharing a meeting on one project may find that they share an interest in relation to another area of their work, and use informal exchanges at the meeting to lay the ground for cooperative action elsewhere. Much of the coalition building found in organizational life occurs through this kind of chance encounter, or through planned informal meetings such as lunches and receptions. Sometimes, however, alliances and networks are forged through various kinds of institutionalized exchange, such as meetings of professional groups and associations, and may themselves eventually become institutionalized in enduring forms such as project teams, advisory boards, joint ventures, or cartellike organizations. As will be clear from the above examples, networks may be internal to an organization or extend to include key people outside. Sometimes they are explicitly interorganizational, such as interlocking directorships where the same people serve on the boards of different organizations. In all networks, some players may take an active central role while others may operate at the fringes. Some will contribute to and derive power from the network more than others, according to the pattern of mutual dependence on which the alliance builds.

In addition to drawing power from networking and coalition building, many members of an organization may draw power from their role in the social networks known as the "informal organization." All organizations have informal networks where people interact in ways that meet various kinds of social needs. Groups of coworkers may make a habit of going to lunch together or drinking on Fridays after work, or may evolve means of enhancing the quality of their life at work. Informal group leaders may become as powerful an influence on their group as any rule, regulation, or manager, and become forces to be recognized and respected for the way their area of the organization operates. The attention currently given to the importance of corporate culture in determining an organization's success highlights the power possessed by leaders and other members of social groups who are in a position to shape the values and attitudes of the particular subculture to which they belong.

One other variant of informal organization arises in situations where one member of an organization develops a psychological or emotional dependency on another. This becomes particularly significant when the dependent party draws considerable power from other sources. The history of corporate and public life is full of examples where a key decision maker has become critically dependent on his or her spouse, lover, secretary, or trusted aide, or even on a self-proclaimed prophet or mystic. In the power-behind-the-throne syndrome that results, the informal collaborator exerts a critical influence on how the decision maker's power is used. While such relations often develop by chance, it is by no means uncommon for people to rise to power by cultivating such dependencies in a Machiavellian way.

Control of counterorganizations. Another route to power in organizations rests in the establishment and control of what can be called "counterorganizations." Trade unions are the most obvious of these. Whenever a group of people manages to build a concentration of power in relatively few hands it is not uncommon for opposing forces to coordinate their actions to create a rival power bloc. Economist John Kenneth Galbraith has described the process as one involving the development of "countervailing power." Thus unions develop as a check on management in industries where there is a high degree of industrial concentration; government and other regulatory agencies develop as a check on the abuse of monopoly power; and the concentration of production is often balanced by the development of large organizations in the field of distributions, e.g., chain stores often develop in ways that balance the power exercised by the large producers and suppliers.

The strategy of exercising countervailing power thus provides a way of influencing organizations where one is not part of the established power structure. By joining and working for a trade union, consumers' association, social movement, cooperative, or lobby group—or by exercising citizen's rights and pressuring the media, one's political representative, or a government agency—one has a way of balancing power relations. Many people make a career out of doing this. Thus a shop-floor worker may spend a major part of his leisure time working for his union, perhaps rising through the ranks of the union bureaucracy to a level at which he deals with senior management face to face. For many people at the lowest levels of an organization the only effective way that they can influence their work life is through this form of countervailing power. Consumer advocate Ralph Nader has been able to have a much greater influence on American industry by acting as critic and champion of consumer rights than he would have had as an employee of any of the organizations he has criticized. Many socially conscious lawyers, journalists, academics, and members of other professional groups have also found an effective route to influence by criticizing rather than joining the organizations that are the object of their concern. The principle of countervailing power is also often employed by the leaders of large conglomerates, who in effect play a form of chess with their environment, buying and selling organizations as corporate pawns. More than one multinational has attempted to counter the power of its competitors or bargain with its host government with the principle of countervailing power in mind.

Symbolism and the management of meaning. Another important source of power in organizations rests in one's ability to persuade others to enact realities that further the interests one wishes to pursue. Leadership ultimately involves an ability to define the reality of others. While the authoritarian leader attempts to "sell," "tell," or force a reality on his or her subordinates, more democratic leaders allow definitions of a situation to evolve from the views of others. The democratic leader's influence is far more subtle and symbolic. He or she spends time listening, summarizing, integrating, and guiding what is being said, making key interventions and summoning images, ideas, and values that help those involved to make sense of the situation with which they are dealing. In managing the meanings assigned to a situation, the leader in effect wields a form of symbolic power that exerts a decisive influence on how people perceive their realities and hence the way they act. Charismatic leaders seem to have a natural ability to shape meaning in this way.

We will focus upon three related aspects of symbolic management: the use of imagery, the use of theater, and the use of gamesmanship.

Images, language, symbols, stories, ceremonies, rituals, and all the other attributes of corporate culture discussed in Chapter 5 are tools that can be used in the management of meaning and hence in shaping power relations in organizational life. Many successful managers and leaders are aware of the power of evocative imagery and instinctively give a great deal of attention to the impact their words and actions have on those around them. For example, they often encourage the idea that the organization is a team and the environment a competitive jungle, talk about problems in terms of opportunities and challenges, symbolize the importance of a key activity or function by giving it high priority and visibility on their own personal agenda, or find other ways of creating and massaging the systems of belief deemed necessary to achieve their aims. In managing the meaning of organizational situations in these ways, they can do much to shape patterns of corporate culture and subculture that will help them achieve desired aims and objectives.

Many organizational members are also keenly aware of the way in which theater—including physical settings, appearances, and styles of behavior—can add to their power; and many deserve organizational Oscars for their performances. We have all walked into senior executives' offices that exude power in terms of decor and layout, shouting out that someone of considerable influence works there. An executive's office is the stage on which he or she performs and is often carefully organized in ways that will help that performance. In one area we may find a formal desk with a thronelike chair where the executive plays authoritarian roles. In another we may find casual chairs around a coffee table, setting a more convivial scene. When one is summoned to such an office, one often senses the likely tone of the meeting according to where one is seated. If you are guided to a low-level chair facing a desk where the manager can physically look down and thus dominate you, you can almost be sure that you are in for a hard time. Situations often speak louder than words, and do much to express and reproduce the power relations existing within an organization.

Appearances can also count for a great deal. For example, most people in an organization soon learn the rules of dress and other unwritten requirements for successful progress to higher ranks. In some organizations it is possible to distinguish marketing people, accountants, or even those who work on a certain floor according to their choice of fashion and general demeanor. Many aspiring young executives quickly learn the value of carrying the *Wall Street Journal* to work and ensuring that it is always visible, even if they never actually manage to read it. Some people symbolize their activity with paper-strewn desks, and others demonstrate their control and mastery of their work with a desk where no trace of paper is ever seen. In organizational contexts, there is usually more to appearance than meets the eye.

Style also counts. It's amazing how you can symbolize power by being a couple of minutes late for that all-important meeting where everyone depends on your presence, or how visibility in certain situations can enhance your status. For example, in many organizations senior executives dramatize their presence at high-profile events but fade into the woodwork at low-status functions. It is reported that in the White House people often dramatize their access to the president by making sure that they arrive at least half an hour early so that others can see that they are seeing the president. Access to the president is itself both a reflection and a source of power, but if others know that you have such access, it can usually be used to acquire even more power. Those who are aware of how symbolism can enhance power often spend a great deal of time dramatizing their work, utilizing "impression management" to influence the systems of meaning surrounding them and their activities.

Finally, we must note the skills of "gamesmanship." The organizational game player comes in many forms. Sometimes he is reckless and ruthless, shooting from the hip at targets that he dislikes, engaging in boardroom brawls when he's certain that he's the best around. In doing so, he increases his visibility and asserts his power and superiority over his competitors. Other kinds of gamesmen may be as crafty and low in profile as a fox, making their way through the organization in a more subtle manner, shaping key impressions at every turn. In seeing organization—with its rewards of success, status, power, and influence—as a game to be played according to their own sets of unwritten rules, organizational game players often have a significant influence on the structure of power relations.

Gender and the management of gender relations. It often makes a great deal of difference if you're a man or a woman! Many organizations are dominated by gender-related values that bias organizational life in favor of one sex over another. Thus, as many feminist writers have emphasized, organizations often segment opportunity structures and job markets in ways that enable men to achieve positions of prestige and power more easily than women, and often operate in ways that produce gender-related biases in the way organizational reality is created and sustained on a day-to-day basis. This is most obvious in situations of open discrimination and various forms of sexual harassment, but often pervades the culture of an organization in a way that is much less visible.

Consider, for example, some of the links between gender stereotypes and traditional principles of organization. Exhibit 6.4 counterposes a series of characteristics that are often used to differentiate between male and female. The links between the male stereotype and the values that dominate many ideas about the nature of organization are striking. Organizations are often encouraged to be rational, analytical, strategic, decision-oriented, tough, and aggressive, and so are men. This has important implications for women who wish to operate in this kind of world, for insofar as they attempt to foster these values, they are often seen as breaking the traditional female stereotype in a way that opens them to criticism, e.g., for being "overly assertive" and "trying to play a male role." Of course, in organizations that cultivate values that are closer to those of the female stereotype, women can have an advantage, reversing the traditional imbalance.

These and other gender biases are also found in the language, rituals, myths, stories, and other modes of symbolism that shape an organization's culture. General conversation and day-to-day ritual can serve to include or to exclude and is sometimes constructed to achieve this end. A lone man or woman can quickly feel outnumbered or "out on a limb" when others talk about matters that he or

Relations between men and women are frequently shaped by prede-fined stereotypes and images as to how they are expected to behave. Here are some of the more common traits traditionally associated with being male and female in Western society:

The Male Stereotype	The Female Stereotype
Logical	Intuitive
Rational	Emotional
Aggressive	Submissive
Exploitative	Empathic
Strategic	Spontaneous
Independent	Nurturing
Competitive	Cooperative
"A leader and decision-maker"	"A loyal supporter and follower"

Under the influence of the "gender revolution" these stereotypes are now in flux and transition.

Exhibit 6.4. Traditional male and female stereotypes

she cannot share, or when language and jokes assume a derogatory form. He or she can miss important conversation by not being in the same locker room, and can be subjected to all kinds of subtle degrada-tion through the stories and myths that circulate on the organiza-tional grapevine. All the factors shaping corporate culture discussed in Chapter 5 are relevant for understanding the gender realities con-structed in an organization. They also identify the means through which a person can begin to counter and reshape the power relations thus produced.

The subtleties associated with gender often create different experi-ences of the same organizational situation and present many practical problems for the way men and women interact on a daily basis. Some-times the difficulties created are so significant that they give rise to con-scious and unconscious strategies for "gender management."

Consider the following situation, drawn from research conducted by my colleague Deborah Sheppard:

Susan Jones is a marketing research manager in a male-dominated industry. She frequently has to give presentations to her male col-leagues, and feels a need to ensure that she "blends in" by managing her appearance and behavior so that conventional expectations and norms relating to sex-roles are maintained. She strives to be "credible," while not overly challenging the status quo, and monitors herself on a continuing basis. She is particularly careful not to act in a malelike way, and much of her "impression management" rests in avoiding giving offense because she is a woman. Thus, in her oral presentations she tries to demonstrate competence while avoiding being assertive. She stands in the same place rather than engaging in the more aggressive act of walking around, even if the presentation lasts three hours. She attempts to get her ideas across gently. She does not raise her voice, finding other ways of emphasizing critical points, e.g., by using over-heads, but being sure never to use a pointer. She avoids wearing pants or three piece suits with a vest, and is always careful to balance her more formal attire with a feminine blouse.

Susan Jones works in a male-dominated reality, and spends a lot of her time living on other people's terms. Ms. Jones knows exactly what she is doing: She feels that to succeed in her organization she must try and fit in as best she can.

Many people would challenge her style of gender management, and suggest that she should be more assertive and confront and change the status quo. And many women in organizations do this very effectively. But the point about the case for present purposes rests in the fact that it shows how life in organizations is often guided by subtle and not so subtle power relations that guide attention and behavior in one direction rather than another. To do a good job Susan Jones has to put a much greater effort into accomplishing everyday reality than her male colleagues.

Exhibit 6.5 presents an evocative illustration of some of the implicit role models that men and women sometimes adopt in dealing with these gender-related issues. Whether or not gender is perceived as a factor shaping power relations, the choice or inclination toward one gender management strategy rather than another can have a major ef-fect on one's success and general influence within an organization. We shall have more to say about the source and nature of gender biases in Chapter 7, when we discuss the role of repressed sexuality, the influ-ence of the patriarchal family, and the general role of ideology in corpo-rate life.

Structural factors that define the stage of action. One of the surprising things one discovers in talking with members of an organization is that hardly anyone will admit to having any real power. Even chief executives often say that they feel highly constrained, that they have few significant options in decision making, and that the power they wield is more apparent than real. Everyone usually feels in some degree hemmed in, either by forces within the organization or in terms of requirements posed by the environment. Given the numerous and varied sources of power already discussed, these attitudes present us with a paradox. How is it that there can be so many sources of power, yet so many feelings of powerlessness?

One possible answer is that access to power is so open, wide, and varied that to a large extent power relations become more or less balanced. While some people may be able to amass considerable personal power, this is offset by the power of others, and even the powerful thus feel constrained. We will give more attention to this "pluralist" view later in the chapter.

Another possible explanation rests in the idea that it is important to distinguish between the surface manifestations and the deep structure of power. This view is linked with perspectives on organization to be explored in Chapters 8 and 9. It suggests that while organizations and society may at any one time comprise a variety of political actors drawing on a variety of power bases, the stage on which they engage in their various kinds of power play is defined by the logic of change shaping the social epoch in which they live. This view summons the idea that organization and society must be understood from a historical perspective. To illustrate let us examine an analogy from the natural world. Suppose that we are considering the ecology of a river valley. We can understand that ecology in terms of the "power relations" between the various species of tree, shrub, fern, and undergrowth and the soil from which they draw sustenance. But these power relations are underpinned by the basic structure of the river valley, as determined by the impact of glaciation millennia before. One species of tree may be more powerful and thus dominate another, but the conditions of this domination are structurally determined.

Applying this analogy to organizational life, we see how underlying structures or logics of change underpin power relations. A manager may control an important budget, have access to key information, and be excellent at impression management, and be a powerful person for all these reasons. But his ability to draw on and use these sources of power is underpinned by various structural factors, such as the invested capital that sustains the organization. Similarly a factory worker may possess considerable power to disrupt production as a result of his or her role on an assembly line. His or her knowledge of the way in which production can be disrupted is the immediate source of power, but the ultimate source is the structure of productive activity that makes such power significant. These considerations encourage us to see people as agents or carriers of power relations embedded in the wider structure of society. As such people may be no more than semi-autonomous pawns moving themselves around in a game where they

As one looks around the organizational world it is possible to identify different ways in which people manage gender relations. Here are a variety of popular strategies. Each can be successful or unsuccessful, according to the persons and situations involved.

Some Female Strategies

Queen Elizabeth I	— Rule with a firm hand, surrounding one-self as far as possible by submissive men. Margaret Thatcher provides a modern example.
The First Lady	— Be content to exercise power behind the throne: a tactic adopted by many "corporate wives" such as executive secretaries and special assistants.
The Invisible Woman	— Adopt a low profile and try and blend with one's surroundings, exercising influence in whatever ways one can.
The Great Mother	— Consolidate power through caring and nurturing.
The Liberationist	— Play rough and give as good as you get; be outspoken and always make a stand in favor of the role of women.
The Amazon	— Be a leader of women. This style is especially successful when one can build a powerful coalition by placing like-minded women in influential positions.
Delilah	— Use the powers of seduction to win over key figures in male-dominated organizations.
Joan of Arc	— Use the power of a shared cause and mission to transcend the fact that you are a woman, and gain widespread male support.
The Daughter	— Find a "father figure" prepared to act as sponsor and mentor.

can learn to understand the rules but have no power to change them. This phenomenon may explain why even the powerful often feel that they have little real choice as to how they should behave. For example, a chief executive may face some of these wider rules of the game in terms of the economic conditions that influence the survival of her organization. Insofar as she wishes the organization to survive, she may perceive herself as having no real options about what must be done to ensure its survival.

Some Male Strategies

The Warrior	— Frequently adopted by busy executives caught up in fighting corporate battles. Often used to bind women into roles as committed supporters.
The Father	— Often used to win the support of younger women searching for a mentor.
King Henry VIII	— Use of absolute power to get what one wants, attracting and discarding female supporters according to their usefulness.
The Playboy	— Use of sex appeal (both real and imagined) to win support and favor from female colleagues. A role often adopted by executives lacking a more stable power base.
The Jock	— Based on various kinds of "display behavior" concerned to attract and convince women of one's corporate prowess. Often used to develop admiration and support from women in subordinate or lateral positions.
The Little Boy	— Often used to try and "get one's way" in difficult situations, especially in relation to female co-workers and subordinates. The role may take many forms, e.g., the "angry little boy" who throws a temper to create a stir and force action; the "frustrated or whining little boy" who tries to cultivate sympathy; and the "cute little boy" who tries to curry favor, especially when he's in a jam.
The Good Friend	— Often used to develop partnerships with female colleagues, either as confidants or as key sources of information and advice.
The Chauvinist Pig	— Often used by men who feel threatened by the presence of women. Characterized by use of various "degradation" rituals, which seek to undermine the status of women and their contributions.

Exhibit 6.5. Some strategies for the management of gender relations

This view of the deep structure of power leads us to recognize the importance of factors such as class relations in determining the role we occupy within organizations and hence the kind of opportunity structure and power to which we have access. It draws attention to the way educational systems and other processes of socialization shape basic elements of culture. It draws attention to the logic of capital accumulation, which shapes the structure of industry, levels of employment, patterns of economic growth, and the ownership and distribution of wealth. We will be considering these underlying factors in some detail in the following chapters. They define the stage on which organizational members act, and moderate the significance and influence of the other sources of power to which one has access.

The power one already has. Power is a route to power, and one can often use power to acquire more. The biographies of many consummate politicians illustrate this fact. For example, politicians within organizations and in public life frequently tie the use of power to informal IOU agreements where help or favor begs its return in kind at a later date. Thus a manager may use his or her power to support X in a struggle with Y, knowing that when X is successful it will be possible to call upon similar (if not more) support from X: "Remember last July. Your future was on the line, and I risked everything to help out. Surely you'll now do a small favor for me?" Often the exchanges are more subtle than this, but the message is essentially the same. Power used in a judicious way takes the form of an investment and, like money, often becomes useful on a rainy day.

It is also possible to take advantage of the honey-pot characteristic of power. The presence of power attracts and sustains people who wish to feed off that power, and actually serves to increase the power holder's power. In the hope of gaining favor, people may begin to lend the power holder uninvited support or buy into his or her way of thinking so that he or she can see that they're on the same side. When the time comes for the power holder to recognize this interest with active support, people then actually become indebted to the power holder, with all kinds of IOUs coming into play. Power, like honey, is a perpetual source of sustenance and attraction among the worker bees.

Finally, there is the empowering aspect of power. When people experience progress or success, they are often energized to achieve further progress and success. In this way a sense of power can actually lead to more power. This kind of potential or transformative power is overlooked in most contemporary discussions of power relations but is vital in understanding the kind of dynamism and energy that can develop from very small and insignificant beginnings. The process is perhaps most evident in those situations in which people who believe that they have absolutely no power fight and win a small victory. Very soon they realize that one victory can lead to another and feel as if they are being carried on the crest of a wave. Action itself can be an empowering force, and many organizations and communities have been transformed by its effects in quite unexpected ways.

The ambiguity of power. While we have identified numerous sources of power, which are probably far from being exhaustive, it is difficult to tie down exactly what the phenomenon is. We know that it has a great deal to do with asymmetrical patterns of dependence whereby one person or unit becomes dependent on another in an unbalanced way, and that it also has a great deal to do with an ability to define the reality of others in ways that lead them to perceive and enact relations that one desires. However, it is far from clear whether power should be understood as an interpersonal behavioral phenomenon or as the manifestation of deep-seated structural factors. It is not clear whether people have and exercise power as autonomous human beings or are simply carriers of power relations that are the product of more fundamental forces. These and other issues—such as whether power is a resource or a relationship, whether there is a distinction between power and processes of societal domination and control, whether power is ultimately linked to the control of capital and the structuring of the world economy, or whether it is important to distinguish between actual manifest power and potential power—continue to be the subject of considerable interest and debate among those interested in the sociology of organization.

These problems aside, however, it is clear that our discussion of possible sources and uses of power provides us with an inventory of ideas through which we can begin to decode power plays and political dynamics in organizational contexts. Like our analysis of interests and our discussion of conflict, it provides us with a working tool through which we can analyze organizational politics and, if we so wish, orient our action in a politicized way.

[17]

Power Is the
Great Motivator

by David C. McClelland and David H. Burnham

Most HBR articles on motivation speak to managers about the people whose work they oversee. Curiously, the writers assume that the motivation of managers themselves – that is to say, of our readers – is so well aligned with organizational goals that it needs no examination. David McClelland and his colleague David Burnham knew better.

They found that managers fall into three motivational groups. Those in the first, affiliative managers, need to be liked more than they need to get things done. Their decisions are aimed at increasing their own popularity rather than promoting the goals of the organization. Managers motivated by the need to achieve – the second group – aren't worried about what people think of them. They focus on setting goals and reaching them, but they put their own achievement and recognition first. Those in the third group – institutional managers – are interested above all in power. Recognizing that you get things done inside organizations only if you can influence the people around you, they focus on building power through influence rather than through their own individual achievement. People in this third group are the most effective, and their direct reports have a greater sense of responsibility, see organizational goals more clearly, and exhibit more team spirit.

Contrary to popular opinion, the best managers are the ones who like power – and use it.

WHAT MAKES OR MOTIVATES a good manager? The question is enormous in scope. Some people might say that a good manager is one who is successful – and by now most business researchers and businesspeople know what motivates people who successfully run their own small businesses. The key to their success has turned out to be what psychologists call the need for achievement, the desire to do something better or more efficiently than it has been done before. Any number of books and articles summarize research studies explaining how the achievement motive is necessary for a person to attain success.

But what has achievement motivation got to do with good management? There is no reason on theoretical grounds why a person who has a strong need to be more efficient should make a good manager. While it sounds as if everyone ought to have the need to achieve, in fact, as psychologists define and measure achievement motivation, the need to achieve leads people to behave in ways that do not necessarily engender good management.

For one thing, because they focus on personal improvement, achievement-motivated people want to do things themselves. For another, they want concrete short-term feedback on their performance so that they can tell how well they are doing. Yet managers, particularly in large, complex organizations, cannot perform by themselves all the tasks necessary for success. They must manage others to perform for the organization. And they must be willing to do without immediate and personal feedback since tasks are spread among many people.

The manager's job seems to call more for someone who can influence people than for someone who does things better alone. In motivational terms, then, we might expect the successful manager to have a greater need for power than a need to achieve. But there must be other qualities besides the need for power that go into the makeup of a good manager. We will discuss here just what these qualities are and how they interrelate.

To measure the motivations of managers, we studied a number of individuals in different large U.S. corporations who were participating in management workshops designed to improve their managerial effectiveness. (See the sidebar "Workshop Techniques.") We concluded that the top manager of a company must possess a high need for power—that is, a concern for influencing people. However, this need must be disciplined and controlled so that it is directed toward the benefit of the institution as a whole and not toward the

The late *David C. McClelland was a professor of psychology at Harvard University in Cambridge, Massachusetts, in 1976 when this article first appeared. David H. Burnham was at that time the president and chief executive officer of McBer & Company, a behavioral science consulting firm. He is currently a principal of the Burnham Rosen Group, a strategic consulting and leadership-training firm in Boston.*

manager's personal aggrandizement. Moreover, the top manager's need for power ought to be greater than his or her need to be liked.

Measuring Managerial Effectiveness

What does it mean when we say that a good manager has a greater need for power than for achievement? Consider the case of Ken Briggs, a sales manager in a large U.S. corporation who joined one of our managerial workshops. (The names and details of all the cases that follow have been disguised.) About six years ago, Ken Briggs was promoted to a managerial position at headquarters, where he was responsible for salespeople who serviced his company's largest accounts.

In filling out his questionnaire at the workshop, Ken showed that he correctly perceived what his job required of him – namely, that he should influence others' success more than achieve new goals himself or socialize with his subordinates. However, when asked, with other members of the workshop, to write a story depicting a managerial situation, Ken unwittingly revealed through his fiction that he did not share those concerns. Indeed, he discovered that his need for achievement was very high – in fact, higher than the 90th percentile – and his need for power was very low, in about the 15th percentile. Ken's high need to achieve was no surprise – after all, he had been a very successful salesman – but obviously his desire to influence others was much less than his job required. Ken was a little disturbed but thought that perhaps the measuring instruments were not accurate and that the gap between the ideal and his score was not as great as it seemed.

Then came the real shocker. Ken's subordinates confirmed what his stories revealed: He *was* a poor manager, having little positive impact on those who worked for him. They felt that little responsibility had been delegated to them. He never rewarded them but only criticized them. And the office was

poorly organized, confused, and chaotic. On all those scales, his office rated in the tenth to 15th percentile relative to national norms.

As Ken talked the results of the survey over privately with a workshop leader, he became more and more upset. He finally agreed, however, that the results confirmed feelings he had been afraid to admit to himself or others. For years, he had been miserable in his managerial role. He now knew the reason: He simply did not want, and he had not

> Do our findings suggest
> that the good manager
> is one who cares for power
> and is not at all concerned
> about the needs of other
> people? Not quite.

been able, to influence or manage others. As he thought back, he realized he had failed every time he had tried to influence his staff, and he felt worse than ever.

Ken had responded to failure by setting very high standards – his office scored in the 98th percentile on this scale – and by trying to do most things himself, which was close to impossible. His own activity and lack of delegation consequently left his staff demoralized. Ken's experience is typical of those who have a strong need to achieve but little desire for power. They may become very successful salespeople and, as a consequence, may be promoted into managerial jobs for which they, ironically, are unsuited.

If the need to achieve does not make a good manager, what motive does? It is not enough to suspect that power motivation may be important; one needs hard evidence that people who are better managers than Ken Briggs is are in fact more highly motivated by power and perhaps score higher in

Workshop Techniques

We derived the case studies and data used in this article from a number of workshops we conducted, during which executives learned about their managerial styles and abilities, as well as how to change them. The workshops also provided an opportunity for us to study which motivation patterns in people make for the best managers.

At the workshops and in this article, we use the technical terms "need for achievement," "need for affiliation," and "need for power." The terms refer to measurable factors indicating motivation in groups and individuals. Briefly, those characteristics are measured by coding managers' spontaneous responses relating to how often they think about doing something better or more efficiently than before (need for achievement), about establishing or maintaining friendly relations with others (need for affiliation), or about having an impact on others (need for power). When we talk about power, we are not talking about dictatorial power but about the need to be strong and influential.

When the managers first arrived at the workshops, they were asked to fill out a questionnaire about their jobs. Each participant analyzed his or her job, explaining what he or she thought it required. The managers were asked to write a number of stories about pictures of various work situations we showed them. The stories were coded according to how concerned an individual was with achievement, affiliation, or power, as well as for the amount of inhibition or self-control they revealed. We then compared the results against national norms. The differences between a person's job requirements and his or her motivational patterns can often help assess whether the person is in the right job, is a candidate for promotion to another job, or is likely to be able to adjust to fit the present position.

To find out what kind of managerial style the participants had, we then gave them another questionnaire in which they had to choose how they would handle various realistic work situations in office settings. We divided their answers into six management styles, or ways of dealing with work situations. The styles were "democratic," "affiliative," "pacesetting," "coaching," "coercive," and "authoritarian." The managers were asked to comment on the effectiveness of each style and to name the style they preferred.

One way to determine how effective managers are is to ask the people who work for them. Thus, to isolate the characteristics that good managers have, we asked at least three subordinates of each manager at the workshop questions about their work situations that revealed characteristics of their supervisors according to six criteria: 1) the amount of conformity to rules the supervisor requires, 2) the amount of responsibility they feel they are given, 3) the emphasis the department places on standards of performance, 4) the degree to which rewards are given for good work compared with punishment when something goes wrong, 5) the degree of organizational clarity in the office, and 6) its team spirit.[1] The managers who received the highest morale scores (organizational clarity plus team spirit) from their subordinates were considered to be the best managers, possessing the most desirable motive patterns.

We also surveyed the subordinates six months later to see if morale scores rose after managers completed the workshop.

We measured participants on one other characteristic deemed important for good management: maturity. By coding the stories that the managers wrote, which revealed their attitudes toward authority and the kinds of emotions displayed over specific issues, we were able to pinpoint managers at one of four stages in their progress toward maturity. People in stage 1 are dependent on others for guidance and strength. Those in stage 2 are interested primarily in autonomy. In stage 3, people want to manipulate others. In stage 4, they lose their egotistic desires and wish to serve others selflessly.[2]

The conclusions we present in this article are based on workshops attended by more than 500 managers from some 25 U.S. corporations. We drew the examples in the charts from one of those companies.

---

1. Based on George H. Litwin and Robert A. Stringer's *Motivation and Organizational Climate* (Harvard University Press, 1968).

2. Based on work by Abigail Stewart, as reported in David C. McClelland's *Power: The Inner Experience* (Irvington Publishers, 1979).

other characteristics as well. But how does one decide who is the better manager?

Real-world performance measures are hard to come by if one is trying to rate managerial effectiveness in production, marketing, finance, or research and development. In trying to determine who the better managers were in Ken Briggs's company, we did not want to rely only on their superiors. For a variety of reasons, superiors' judgments of their subordinates' real-world performance may be inaccurate. In the absence of some standard measure of performance, we decided that the next best index of a manager's effectiveness would be the climate he or she creates in the office, reflected in the morale of subordinates.

Almost by definition, a good manager is one who, among other things, helps subordinates feel strong and responsible, rewards them properly for good performance, and sees that things are organized so that subordinates feel they know what they should be doing. Above all, managers should foster among subordinates a strong sense of team spirit, of pride in working as part of a team. If a manager creates and encourages this spirit, his or her subordinates certainly should perform better.

In the company Ken Briggs works for, we have direct evidence of a connection between morale and performance in the one area where performance measures are easy to find – namely, sales. In April 1973, at least three employees from each of this company's 16 sales districts filled out questionnaires that rated their office for organizational clarity and team spirit. Their scores were averaged and totaled to give an overall morale score for each office. Then, the percentage gains or losses in sales in 1973 were compared with those for 1972 for each district. The difference in sales figures by district ranged from a gain of nearly 30% to a loss of 8%, with a median gain of about 14%. The graph "The Link Between Morale and Sales" shows how, in Ken Briggs's company at least,

high morale at the beginning of the year became a good index of how well the sales division would actually perform throughout the year. Moreover, it seems likely that the manager who can create high morale among salespeople can also do the same for employees in other areas (production, design, and so on), which leads to better overall performance. What characteristics, then, does a manager need to create that kind of morale?

The Power Factor

To find out, we surveyed more than 50 managers in both high- and low-morale units in all sections of a single large company. We found that the power motivation scores for most of the managers – more than 70% – were higher than those of the average person. This finding confirms that power motivation is important to management. (Remember that as we use the term, "power motivation" refers not to dictatorial behavior but to a desire to have an impact, to be strong and influential.) The better managers, as judged by the morale of those working for them, tended to score even higher in power motivation. But the most important determining factor of high morale turned out to be not how their need for power compared with their need to achieve but whether it was higher than their need to be liked. This relationship existed for 80% of the better sales managers but for only 10% of the poorer managers. And the same held true for other managers in nearly every part of the organization.

In the research, product development, and operations divisions, 73% of the better managers had a stronger need for power than need to be liked, as compared with only 22% of the poorer managers, who tended to be what we term "affiliative managers" – whose strongest drive is to be liked. Why should this be so?

Sociologists have long argued that for a bureaucracy to function effectively, those who manage it must apply rules

universally: that is, if they make exceptions for the particular needs of individuals, the whole system will break down. The manager with a high need to be liked is precisely the one who wants to stay on good terms with everybody and, therefore, is the one most likely to make exceptions for particular needs. If an employee asks for time off to stay home and look after a sick spouse and the kids, the affiliative manager agrees almost without thinking, out of compassion for the employee's situation. When former President Gerald Ford remarked in pardoning Richard Nixon that Nixon had "suffered enough," he was responding as an affiliative manager would because he was empathizing primarily with Nixon's needs and feelings.

Sociological theory and our findings both argue, however, that the person

The affiliative manager wants to stay on good terms with everybody and, therefore, is the one most likely to make exceptions for particular needs.

whose need for affiliation is high does not make a good manager. This kind of person creates low morale because he or she does not understand that other people in the office will tend to regard exceptions to the rules as unfair to themselves, just as many U.S. citizens felt that it was unfair to let Nixon off and punish others who were less involved than he was in the Watergate scandal.

So far, our findings are a little alarming. Do they suggest that the good manager is one who cares for power and is not at all concerned about the needs of other people? Not quite, for the good manager has other characteristics that must still be taken into account. Above all, the good manager's power motivation is not oriented toward personal aggrandizement but toward the institution that he or she serves.

In another major research study, we found that the signs of controlled action, or inhibition, that appear when a person exercises imagination in writing stories tell a great deal about the kind of power that person needs.[1] We discovered that if a high power motivation score is balanced by high inhibition, stories about power tend to be altruistic. That is, the heroes in the story exercise power on behalf of someone else. This is the socialized face of power, as distinguished from the concern for personal power, which is characteristic of individuals whose stories are loaded with power imagery but show no sign of inhibition or self-control. In our earlier study, we found ample evidence that the latter individuals exercise their power impulsively. They are more often rude to other people, they drink too much, they try to exploit others sexually, and they collect symbols of personal prestige such as fancy cars or big offices.

Individuals high in power and in control, on the other hand, are more institution minded; they tend to get elected to more offices, to control their drinking, and to have a desire to serve others. Not surprisingly, we found in the workshops that the better managers in the corporation also tend to score high on both power and inhibition.

Three Kinds of Managers

Let us recapitulate what we have discussed so far and have illustrated with data from one company. The better managers we studied – what we call *institutional managers* – are high in power motivation, low in affiliation motivation, and high in inhibition. They care about institutional power and use it to stimulate their employees to be more productive. Now let us compare them with *affiliative managers* (those people for whom the need for affiliation is higher than the need for power) and with the *personal-power managers* (those

in whom the need for power is higher than the need for affiliation but whose inhibition score is low).

In the sales division of the company we chose to use as an illustration, there are managers who match the three types fairly closely. The chart "Which Manager Is Most Effective?" shows how their subordinates rated the offices they worked in on responsibility, organizational clarity, and team spirit. Managers who are concerned about being liked tend to have subordinates who feel that they have little personal responsibility, believe that organizational procedures are not clear, and have little pride in their work group. In short, as we expected, affiliative managers make so many ad hominem and ad hoc decisions that they almost totally abandon orderly procedures. Their disregard for procedure leaves employees feeling weak, irresponsible, and without a sense of what might happen next, of where they stand in relation to their manager, or even of what they ought to be doing. In this company, the group of affiliative managers portrayed in the chart falls

below the 40th percentile in all three measures of morale.

The managers who are motivated by a need for personal power are somewhat more effective. They are able to engender a greater sense of responsibility in their divisions and, above all, create a greater team spirit. They can be thought of as managerial equivalents of successful tank commanders such as General George Patton, whose own daring inspired admiration in his troops. But notice how in the chart these people are still only around the 40th percentile in the amount of organizational clarity they create, whereas the institutional managers – the high-power, low-affiliation, high-inhibition managers – score much higher.

Managers motivated by personal power are not disciplined enough to be good institution builders, and often their subordinates are loyal to them as individuals rather than to the institution they serve. When a personal-power manager leaves, disorganization often follows. The strong group spirit that the manager has personally inspired

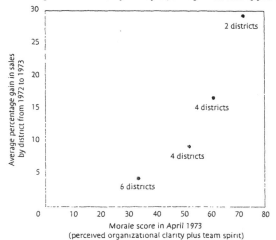

The Link Between Morale and Sales

The higher the morale early in the year, the higher the sales by year end.

(y-axis) Average percentage gain in sales by district from 1972 to 1973

- 2 districts
- 4 districts
- 4 districts
- 6 districts

(x-axis) Morale score in April 1973
(perceived organizational clarity plus team spirit)

deflates. The subordinates do not know what to do by themselves.

Of all the managerial types, the institutional manager is the most successful in creating an effective work climate. Subordinates feel that they have more responsibility. Also, those kinds of managers create high morale because they produce the greatest sense of organizational clarity and team spirit. If such a manager leaves, he or she can be more readily replaced by another because the employees have been encouraged to be loyal to the institution rather than to a particular person.

Since it seems undeniable that a manager with a power orientation creates better morale in subordinates than one with a people orientation, we must consider that a concern for power is essential to good management.

Our findings seem to fly in the face of a long and influential tradition of organizational psychology, which insists that authoritarian management is what is wrong with most businesses in the United States. Let us say frankly that we think the bogeyman of authoritarianism has been wrongly used to downplay the importance of power in management. After all, management is an influence game. Some proponents of democratic management seem to have forgotten this fact, urging managers to be more concerned with people's personal needs than with helping them to get things done.

But much of the apparent conflict between our findings and those of other behavioral scientists in this area stems from the fact that we are talking about *motives,* and behaviorists are often talking about *actions.* What we are saying is that managers must be interested in playing the influence game in a controlled way. That does not necessarily mean that they are or should be authoritarian in action. On the contrary, it appears that power-motivated managers make their subordinates feel strong rather than weak. The true authoritarian in action would have the reverse effect, making people feel weak and powerless.

Thus another important ingredient in the profile of a manager is managerial style. In our example, 63% of the better managers (those whose subordinates had higher morale) scored higher on the democratic or coaching styles of management as compared with only 22% of the poorer managers. By contrast, the latter scored higher on authoritarian or

> Power without discipline
> is often directed toward
> the manager's personal
> aggrandizement, not toward
> the benefit of the institution.

coercive management styles. Since the better managers were also higher in power motivation, it seems that in action they express their power motivation in a democratic way, which is more likely to be effective.

To see how motivation and style interact, consider the case of George Prentice, a manager in the sales division of another company. George had exactly the right combination of motives to be an institutional manager. He was high in the need for power, low in the need for affiliation, and high in inhibition. He exercised his power in a controlled, organized way. The stories he wrote reflected this fact. In one story, for instance, he wrote, "The men sitting around the table were feeling pretty good; they had just finished plans for reorganizing the company; the company has been beset with a number of organizational problems. This group, headed by a hard-driving, brilliant young executive, has completely reorganized the company structurally with new jobs and responsibilities...."

This described how George himself was perceived by the company, and shortly after the workshop, he was promoted to vice president in charge of all sales. But George was also known to his colleagues as a monster, a tough guy who

would "walk over his grandmother" if she stood in the way of his advancement. He had the right motive combination and, in fact, was more interested in institutional growth than he was in personal power, but his managerial style was all wrong. Taking his cue from some of the top executives in the corporation, he told people what they had to do, and he threatened them with dire consequences if they did not do it.

When George was confronted with his authoritarianism in a workshop, he recognized that this style was counterproductive – in fact, in another part of the study we found that it was associated with low morale – and he subsequently began to act more like a coach, which was the style for which he scored the lowest, initially. George saw more clearly that his job was not to force other people to do things but rather to help them figure out ways of getting their jobs done better for the company.

Profile of the Institutional Manager

One reason it was easy for George Prentice to change his managerial style was that, as we saw in his imaginative stories, he was already thinking about helping others – a characteristic of people with the institution-building motivational pattern. In further examining institution builders' thoughts and actions, we found they have four major characteristics:

· Institutional managers are more organization minded; that is, they tend to join more organizations and to feel responsible for building up those organizations. Furthermore, they believe strongly in the importance of centralized authority.

· They report that they like to work. This finding is particularly interesting because our research on achievement motivation has led many commentators to argue that achievement motivation promotes the Protestant work ethic. Almost the precise opposite is true. People who have a high need to achieve like to reduce their work by becoming more efficient. They would like to see the same result obtained in less time or with less effort. But managers who have a need for institutional power actually seem to like the discipline of work. It satisfies their need for getting things done in an orderly way.

· They seem quite willing to sacrifice some of their own self-interest for the welfare of the organization they serve.

· They have a keen sense of justice. It is almost as if they feel that people who work hard and sacrifice for the good of the organization should and will get a just reward for their effort.

It is easy to see how each of these four characteristics helps a person become a good manager, concerned about what the institution can achieve.

We discovered one more fact in studying the better managers at George Prentice's company. They were more mature. Mature people can be most simply described as less egotistic. Somehow their

positive self-image is not at stake in their jobs. They are less defensive, more willing to seek advice from experts, and have a longer-range view. They accumulate fewer personal possessions and seem older and wiser. It is as if they have awakened to the fact that they are not going to live forever and have lost some of the feeling that their own personal future is all that important.

Many U.S. businesspeople fear this kind of maturity. They suspect that it will make them less hard driving, less expansion minded, and less committed to organizational effectiveness. Our data do not support their fears.

Those fears are exactly the ones George Prentice had before he went to the workshop. Afterward, he was a more effective manager, not despite his loss of some of the sense of his own importance but because of it. The reason is simple: His subordinates believed afterward that he was genuinely more con-

cerned about the company than he was about himself. Whereas once they respected his confidence but feared him, they now trust him. Once, he supported their image of him as a "big man" by talking about the new Porsche and Honda he had bought; when we saw him recently, he said, almost as an aside, "I don't buy things anymore."

Altering Managerial Style

George Prentice was able to change his managerial style after learning more about himself. But does self-knowledge generally improve managerial behavior?

Consider the results shown in the chart "Managers *Can* Change Their Styles," where employee morale scores are compared before and after their managers attended workshop training. To judge by their subordinates' responses, the managers were clearly more effective after coming to terms with their styles. The subordinates felt that they received more rewards, that the organizational procedures were clearer, and that morale was higher.

But what do those differences mean in human terms? How did the managers change? Sometimes they decided they should get into another line of work. This happened to Ken Briggs, for example, who found that the reason he was doing so poorly as a manager was because he had almost no interest in influencing others. He understood how he would have to change in order to do well in his present job but in the end decided, with the help of management, that he would prefer to work back into his first love, sales.

Ken Briggs moved into remaindering, helping retail outlets for his company's products get rid of last year's stock so that they could take on each year's new styles. He is very successful in this new role; he has cut costs, increased dollar volume, and in time worked himself into an independent role selling some of the old stock on his own in a way that is quite satisfactory to the business. And he does not have to manage anybody anymore.

Which Manager Is Most Effective?

Subordinates of managers with different motive profiles report different levels of responsibility, organizational clarity, and team spirit.

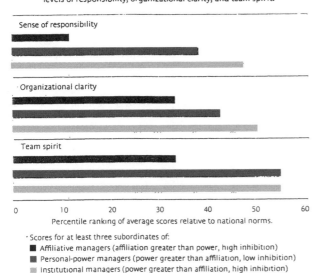

Sense of responsibility

· Organizational clarity

Team spirit

0   10   20   30   40   50   60

Percentile ranking of average scores relative to national norms.

· Scores for at least three subordinates of:

■ Affiliative managers (affiliation greater than power, high inhibition)

■ Personal-power managers (power greater than affiliation, low inhibition)

▒ Institutional managers (power greater than affiliation, high inhibition)

In George Prentice's case, less change was needed. He obviously was a very competent manager with the right motive profile for a top company position. When he was promoted, he performed even more successfully than he had previously because he realized that he needed to become more positive in his approach and less coercive in his managerial style.

But what about a person who does not want to change jobs and discovers that he or she does not have the right motive profile to be a manager? The case of Charlie Blake is instructive. Charlie was as low in power motivation as Ken Briggs, his need to achieve was about average, and his affiliation motivation was above average. Thus he had the affiliative manager profile, and, as expected, the morale among his subordinates was very low. When Charlie learned that his subordinates' sense of responsibility and perception of a reward system were in the tenth percentile and that team spirit was in the 30th, he was shocked. When shown a

film depicting three managerial climates, Charlie said he preferred what turned out to be the authoritarian climate. He became angry when the workshop trainer and other members in the group pointed out the limitations of this managerial style. He became obstructive to the group process, and he objected strenuously to what was being taught.

In an interview conducted much later, Charlie said, "I blew my cool. When I started yelling at you for being all wrong, I got even madder when you pointed out that, according to my style questionnaire, you bet that that was just what I did to my salespeople. Down underneath, I knew something must be wrong. The sales performance for my division wasn't so good. Most of it was due to me anyway and not to my salespeople. Obviously, their reports that they felt I delegated very little responsibility to them and didn't reward them at all had to mean something. So I finally decided to sit down and try to figure what I could do about it. I knew I had to

start being a manager instead of trying to do everything myself and blowing my cool at others because they didn't do what I thought they should. In the end, after I calmed down, on the way back from the workshop, I realized that it is not so bad to make a mistake; it's bad not to learn from it."

After the course, Charlie put his plans into effect. Six months later, his subordinates were asked to rate him again. He attended a second workshop to study the results and reported, "On the way home, I was nervous. I knew I had been working with those guys and not selling so much myself, but I was afraid of what they would say about how things were going in the office. When I found out that the team spirit and some of those other low scores had jumped from around the 30th to the 55th percentile, I was so delighted and relieved that I couldn't say anything all day long."

When he was asked how his behavior had changed, Charlie said, "In previous years when corporate headquarters said we had to make 110% of our original goal, I had called the salespeople in and said, in effect, 'This is ridiculous; we are not going to make it, but you know perfectly well what will happen if we don't. So get out there and work your tails off.' The result was that I worked 20 hours a day, and they did nothing.

"This time I approached the salespeople differently. I told them three things. First, they were going to have to do some sacrificing for the company. Second, working harder is not going to do much good because we are already working about as hard as we can. What will be required are special deals and promotions. You are going to have to figure out some new angles if we are to make it. Third, I'm going to back you up. I'm going to set a realistic goal with each of you. If you make that goal but don't make the company goal, I'll see to it that you are not punished. But if you do make the company goal, I'll see to it that you will get some kind of special rewards."

Managers *Can* Change Their Styles

Training managers clearly improves their employees' morale.

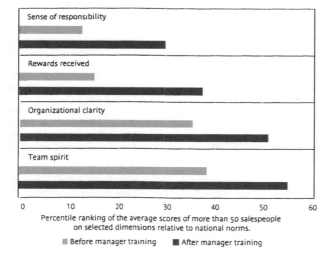

Percentile ranking of the average scores of more than 50 salespeople on selected dimensions relative to national norms.

▓ Before manager training   ▇ After manager training

The salespeople challenged Charlie, saying he did not have enough influence to give them rewards. Rather than becoming angry, Charlie promised rewards that were in his power to give – such as longer vacations.

Note that Charlie has now begun to behave in a number of ways that we

training. When morale was checked some six months later, it had not improved. Overall sales gains subsequently reflected this fact – only 2% above the previous year's figures.

Oddly enough, Henry's problem was that he was so well liked by everybody he felt little pressure to change. Always

where in his or her organization. The top managers shown here have a need for power greater than their interest in being liked. The manager's concern for power should be socialized – controlled so that the institution as a whole, not only the individual, benefits. People and nations with this motive profile are empire builders; they tend to create high morale and to expand the organizations they head. But there is also danger in this motive profile; as in countries, empire building can lead to imperialism and authoritarianism in companies. The same motive pattern that produces good power management can also lead a company to try to dominate others, ostensibly in the interests of organizational expansion. Thus it is not surprising that big business has had to be regulated periodically by federal agencies.

Institutional managers create high morale because they produce the greatest sense of organizational clarity and team spirit.

found to be characteristic of the good institutional manager. He is, above all, higher in power motivation – the desire to influence his salespeople – and lower in his tendency to try to do everything himself. He asks people to sacrifice for the company. He does not defensively chew them out when they challenge him but tries to figure out what their needs are so that he can influence them. He realizes that his job is more one of strengthening and supporting his subordinates than of criticizing them. And he is keenly interested in giving them just rewards for their efforts.

The changes in his approach to his job have certainly paid off. The sales for his office in 1973 were more than 16% higher than those of the previous year, and they rose still further in 1974. In 1973, his office's gain over the previous year ranked seventh in the nation; in 1974, it ranked third. And he wasn't the only one in his company to change managerial styles. Overall sales at his company were up substantially in 1973, an increase that played a large part in turning the overall company performance around from a $15 million loss in 1972 to a $3 million profit in 1973. The company continued to improve its performance in 1974 with a further 11% gain in sales and a 38% increase in profits.

Of course, everybody can't always be reached by a workshop. Henry Carter managed a sales office for a company that had very low morale (around the 20th percentile) before he went for

the life of the party, he was particularly popular because he supplied other managers with special hard-to-get brands of cigars and wines at a discount. He used his close ties with everyone to bolster his position in the company, even though it was known that his office did not perform as well as others.

His great interpersonal skills became evident at the workshop when he did very poorly at one of the business games. When the discussion turned to why he had done so badly and whether he acted that way on the job, two prestigious participants immediately sprang to his defense, explaining away Henry's failure by arguing that the way he did things was often a real help to others and the company. As a result, Henry did not have to cope with such questions at all. He had so successfully developed his role as a likable, helpful friend to everyone in management that, even though his salespeople performed badly, he did not feel under any pressure to change the way he managed.people.

What have we learned from Ken Briggs, George Prentice, Charlie Blake, and Henry Carter? We have discovered what motives make an effective manager – and that change is possible if a person has the right combination of qualities.

Oddly enough, the good manager in a large company does not have a high need for achievement, as we define and measure that motive, although there must be plenty of that motive some- ·

Similarly, the best managers possess two characteristics that act as regulators – a greater emotional maturity, where there is little egotism, and a democratic, coaching managerial style. If a manager's institutional power motivation is checked by maturity, it does not lead to an aggressive, egotistic expansiveness. That means managers can control their subordinates and influence others around them without having to resort to coercion or to an authoritarian management style.

Summarized in this way, what we have found out through empirical and statistical investigations may sound like good common sense. But it is more than common sense; now we can say objectively what the characteristics of the good manager are. Managers of corporations can select those who are likely to be good managers and train those already in managerial positions to be more effective with more confidence.   ▽

1. David C. McClelland, William N. Davis, Rudolf Kalin, and Eric Wanner, *The Drinking Man: Alcohol and Human Motivation* (Free Press, 1972).

[18]

Power Failure
in Management Circuits

by Rosabeth Moss Kanter

Power is America's last dirty word. It is easier to talk about money – and much easier to talk about sex – than it is to talk about power. People who have it deny it; people who want it do not want to appear to hunger for it; and people who engage in its machinations do so secretly.

Yet, because it turns out to be a critical element in effective managerial behavior, power should come out from undercover. Having searched for years for those styles or skills that would identify capable organization leaders, many analysts, like myself, are rejecting individual traits or situational appropriateness as key and finding the sources of a leader's real power.

Access to resources and information and the ability to act quickly make it possible to accomplish more and to pass on more resources and information to subordinates. For this reason, people tend to prefer bosses with "clout." When employees perceive their manager as influential upward and outward, their status is enhanced by association and they generally have high morale and feel less critical or resistant to their boss.[1] More powerful leaders are also more likely to delegate (they are too busy to do it all themselves), to reward talent, and to build a team that places subordinates in significant positions.

Powerlessness, in contrast, tends to breed bossiness rather than true leadership. In large organiza-

Ms. Kanter is professor of sociology and organization and management at Yale University, where she conducts research on organization design and change processes. She is the author of Men and Women of the Corporation (New York: Basic Books, 1977) and numerous other articles and books on life in today's organizations.

tions, at least, it is powerlessness that often creates ineffective, desultory management and petty, dictatorial, rules-minded managerial styles. Accountability without power – responsibility for results without the resources to get them – creates frustration and failure. People who see themselves as weak and powerless and find their subordinates resisting or discounting them tend to use more punishing forms of influence. If organizational power can "ennoble," then, recent research shows, organizational powerlessness can (with apologies to Lord Acton) "corrupt."[2]

So perhaps power, in the organization at least, does not deserve such a bad reputation. Rather than connoting only dominance, control, and oppression, *power* can mean efficacy and capacity – something managers and executives need to move the organization toward its goals. Power in organizations is analogous in simple terms to physical power: it is the ability to mobilize resources (human and material) to get things done. The true sign of power, then, is accomplishment – not fear, terror, or tyranny. Where the power is "on," the system can be productive; where the power is "off," the system bogs down.

But saying that people need power to be effective in organizations does not tell us where it comes from or why some people, in some jobs, systematically seem to have more of it than others. In this article I want to show that to discover the sources of productive power, we have to look not at the

1. Donald C. Pelz, "Influence: A Key to Effective Leadership in the First-Line Supervisor," Personnel, November 1952, p. 209.

2. See my book, Men and Women of the Corporation (New York: Basic Books, 1977), pp. 164-205; and David Kipnis, The Powerholders (Chicago: University of Chicago Press, 1976).

POWER FAILURE

person – as conventional classifications of effective managers and employees do – but at the *position* the person occupies in the organization.

Where Does Power Come From?

The effectiveness that power brings evolves from two kinds of capacities: first, access to the resources, information, and support necessary to carry out a task; and, second, ability to get cooperation in doing what is necessary. (*Exhibit I* identifies some symbols of an individual manager's power.)

Both capacities derive not so much from a leader's style and skill as from his or her location in the formal and informal systems of the organization – in both job definition and connection to other important people in the company. Even the ability to get cooperation from subordinates is strongly defined by the manager's clout outward. People are more responsive to bosses who look as if they can get more for them from the organization.

We can regard the uniquely organizational sources of power as consisting of three "lines":

1. *Lines of supply.* Influence outward, over the environment, means that managers have the capacity to bring in the things that their own organizational domain needs – materials, money, resources to distribute as rewards, and perhaps even prestige.

2. *Lines of information.* To be effective, managers need to be "in the know" in both the formal and the informal sense.

3. *Lines of support.* In a formal framework, a manager's job parameters need to allow for nonordinary action, for a show of discretion or exercise of judgment. Thus managers need to know that they can assume innovative, risk-taking activities without having to go through the stifling multilayered approval process. And, informally, managers need the backing of other important figures in the organization whose tacit approval becomes another resource they bring to their own work unit as well as a sign of the manager's being "in."

Note that productive power has to do with *connections* with other parts of a system. Such systemic aspects of power derive from two sources – job activities and political alliances:

1. Power is most easily accumulated when one has a job that is designed and located to allow *discretion* (nonroutinized action permitting flexible, adaptive, and creative contributions), *recognition* (visibility and notice), and *relevance* (being central to pressing organizational problems).

2. Power also comes when one has relatively close contact with *sponsors* (higher-level people who confer approval, prestige, or backing), *peer networks* (circles of acquaintanceship that provide reputation and information, the grapevine often being faster than formal communication channels), and *subordinates* (who can be developed to relieve managers of some of their burdens and to represent the manager's point of view).

When managers are in powerful situations, it is easier for them to accomplish more. Because the tools are there, they are likely to be highly motivated and, in turn, to be able to motivate subordinates. Their activities are more likely to be on target and to net them successes. They can flexibly interpret or shape policy to meet the needs of particular areas, emergent situations, or sudden environmental shifts. They gain the respect and cooperation that attributed power brings. Subordinates' talents are resources rather than threats. And, because powerful managers have so many lines of connection and thus are oriented outward, they tend to let go of control downward, developing more independently functioning lieutenants.

The powerless live in a different world. Lacking the supplies, information, or support to make things happen easily, they may turn instead to the ultimate weapon of those who lack productive power – oppressive power: holding others back and punishing with whatever threats they can muster.

Exhibit II summarizes some of the major ways in which variables in the organization and in job design contribute to either power or powerlessness.

Positions of Powerlessness

Understanding what it takes to have power and recognizing the classic behavior of the powerless can immediately help managers make sense out of a number of familiar organizational problems that are usually attributed to inadequate people:

☐ The ineffectiveness of first-line supervisors.

☐ The petty interest protection and conservatism of staff professionals.

☐ The crises of leadership at the top.

Instead of blaming the individuals involved in organizational problems, let us look at the positions people occupy. Of course, power or powerlessness in a position may not be all of the problem. Sometimes incapable people *are* at fault and need to be retrained or replaced. (See the ruled insert, "Women Managers Experience Special Power Failures," for a

3. Pehr G. Gyllenhammar, *People at Work* (Reading, Mass.: Addison-Wesley, 1977), p. 133.

4. William E. Fulmer, "Supervisory Selection: The Acid Test of Affirmative Action," *Personnel*, November-December 1976, p. 40.

5. See my chapter (coauthor, Barry A. Stein), "Life in the Middle: Getting In, Getting Up, and Getting Along," in *Life in Organizations*, eds. Rosabeth M. Kanter and Barry A. Stein (New York: Basic Books, 1979).

discussion of another special case, women.) But where patterns emerge, where the troubles associated with some units persist, organizational power failures could be the reason. Then, as Volvo President Pehr Gyllenhammar concludes, we should treat the powerless not as "villains" causing headaches for everyone else but as "victims."[3]

First-line supervisors. Because an employee's most important work relationship is with his or her supervisor, when many of them talk about "the company," they mean their immediate boss. Thus a supervisor's behavior is an important determinant of the average employee's relationship to work and is in itself a critical link in the production chain.

Yet I know of no U.S. corporate management entirely satisfied with the performance of its supervisors. Most see them as supervising too closely and not training their people. In one manufacturing company where direct laborers were asked on a survey how they learned their job, on a list of seven possibilities "from my supervisor" ranked next to last. (Only company training programs ranked worse.) Also, it is said that supervisors do not translate company policies into practice – for instance, that they do not carry out the right of every employee to frequent performance reviews or to career counseling.

In court cases charging race or sex discrimination, first-line supervisors are frequently cited as the "discriminating official."[4] And, in studies of innovative work redesign and quality of work life projects, they often appear as the implied villains; they are the ones who are said to undermine the program or interfere with its effectiveness. In short, they are often seen as "not sufficiently managerial."

The problem affects white-collar as well as blue-collar supervisors. In one large government agency, supervisors in field offices were seen as the source of problems concerning morale and the flow of information to and from headquarters. "Their attitudes are negative," said a senior official. "They turn people against the agency; they put down senior management. They build themselves up by always complaining about headquarters, but prevent their staff from getting any information directly. We can't afford to have such attitudes communicated to field staff."

Is the problem that supervisors need more management training programs or that incompetent people are invariably attracted to the job? Neither explanation suffices. A large part of the problem lies in the position itself – one that almost universally creates powerlessness.

First-line supervisors are "people in the middle," and that has been seen as the source of many of their problems.[5] But by recognizing that first-line

Exhibit I
Some common symbols of a manager's organizational power (influence upward and outward)

To what extent a manager can—

Intercede favorably on behalf of someone in trouble with the organization

Get a desirable placement for a talented subordinate

Get approval for expenditures beyond the budget

Get above-average salary increases for subordinates

Get items on the agenda at policy meetings

Get fast access to top decision makers

Get regular, frequent access to top decision makers

Get early information about decisions and policy shifts

Exhibit II
Ways organizational factors contribute to power or powerlessness

	Generates power when factor is	Generates powerlessness when factor is
Rules inherent in the job	few	many
Predecessors in the job	few	many
Established routines	few	many
Task variety	high	low
Rewards for reliability/predictability	few	many
Rewards for unusual performance/innovation	many	few
Flexibility around use of people	high	low
Approvals needed for nonroutine decisions	few	many
Physical location	central	distant
Publicity about job activities	high	low
Relationship of tasks to current problem areas	central	peripheral
Focus of tasks	outside work unit	inside work unit
Interpersonal contact in the job	high	low
Contact with senior officials	high	low
Participation in programs, conferences, meetings	high	low
Participation in problem-solving task forces	high	low
Advancement prospects of subordinates	high	low

supervisors are caught between higher management and workers, we only begin to skim the surface of the problem. There is practically no other organizational category as subject to powerlessness.

First, these supervisors may be at a virtual dead end in their careers. Even in companies where the job used to be a stepping stone to higher-level

Women Managers Experience Special Power Failures

The traditional problems of women in management are illustrative of how formal and informal practices can combine to engender powerlessness. Historically, women in management have found their opportunities in more routine, low-profile jobs. In staff positions, where they serve in support capacities to line managers but have no line responsibilities of their own, or in supervisory jobs managing "stuck" subordinates, they are not in a position either to take the kinds of risks that build credibility or to develop their own team by pushing bright subordinates.

Such jobs, which have few favors to trade, tend to keep women out of the mainstream of the organization. This lack of clout, coupled with the greater difficulty anyone who is "different" has in getting into the information and support networks, has meant that merely by organizational situation women in management have been more likely than men to be rendered structurally powerless. This is one reason those women who have achieved power have often had family connections that put them in the mainstream of the organization's social circles.

A disproportionate number of women managers are found among first-line supervisors or staff professionals; and they, like men in those circumstances, are likely to be organizationally powerless. But the behavior of other managers can contribute to the powerlessness of women in management in a number of less obvious ways.

One way other managers can make a woman powerless is by patronizingly overprotecting her: putting her in "a safe job," not giving her enough to do to prove herself, and not suggesting her for high-risk, visible assignments. This protectiveness is sometimes born of "good" intentions to give her every chance to succeed (why stack the deck against her?). Out of managerial concerns, out of awareness that a woman may be up against situations that men simply do not have to face, some very well-meaning managers protect their female managers ("It's a jungle, so why send her into it?").

Overprotectiveness can also mask a manager's fear of association with a woman should she fail. One senior bank official at a level below vice president told me about his concerns with respect to a high-performing, financially experienced woman reporting to him.

Despite *his* overwhelmingly positive work experiences with her, he was still afraid to recommend her for other assignments because he felt it was a personal risk. "What if other managers are not as accepting of women as I am?" he asked. "I know I'd be sticking my neck out; they would take her more because of my endorsement than her qualifications. And what if she doesn't make it? My judgment will be on the line."

Overprotection is relatively benign compared with rendering a person powerless by providing obvious signs of lack of managerial support. For example, allowing someone supposedly in authority to be bypassed easily means that no one else has to take him or her seriously. If a woman's immediate supervisor or other managers listen willingly to criticism of her and show they are concerned every time a negative comment comes up and that they assume she must be at fault, then they are helping to undercut her. If managers let other people know that they have concerns about this person or that they are testing her to see how she does, then they are inviting other people to look for signs of inadequacy or failure.

Furthermore, people assume they can afford to bypass women because they "must be uninformed" or "don't know the ropes." Even though women may be respected for their competence or expertise, they are not necessarily seen as being informed beyond the technical requirements of the job. There may be a grain of historical truth in this. Many women come to senior management positions as "outsiders" rather than up through the usual channels.

Also, because until very recently men have not felt comfortable seeing women as businesspeople (business clubs have traditionally excluded women), they have tended to seek each other out for informal socializing. Anyone, male or female, seen as organizationally naive and lacking sources of "inside dope" will find his or her own lines of information limited.

Finally, even when women are able to achieve some power on their own, they have not necessarily been able to translate such personal credibility into an organizational power base. To create a network of supporters out of individual clout requires that a person pass on and share power, that subordinates and peers be empowered by virtue of their connection with that

management jobs, it is now common practice to bring in MBAs from the outside for those positions. Thus moving from the ranks of direct labor into supervision may mean, essentially, getting "stuck" rather than moving upward. Because employees do not perceive supervisors as eventually joining the

leadership circles of the organization, they may see them as lacking the high-level contacts needed to have clout. Indeed, sometimes turnover among supervisors is so high that workers feel they can outwait – and outwit – any boss.

Second, although they lack clout, with little in

person. Traditionally, neither men nor women have seen women as capable of sponsoring others, even though they may be capable of achieving and succeeding on their own. Women have been viewed as the *recipients* of sponsorship rather than as the sponsors themselves.

(As more women prove themselves in organizations and think more self-consciously about bringing along young people, this situation may change. However, I still hear many more questions from women managers about how they can benefit from mentors, sponsors, or peer networks than about how they themselves can start to pass on favors and make use of their own resources to benefit others.)

Viewing managers in terms of power and powerlessness helps explain two familiar stereotypes about women and leadership in organizations: that no one wants a woman boss (although studies show that anyone who has ever had a woman boss is likely to have had a positive experience), and that the reason no one wants a woman boss is that women are "too controlling, rules-minded, and petty."

The first stereotype simply makes clear that power is important to leadership. Underneath the preference for men is the assumption that, given the current distribution of people in organizational leadership positions, men are more likely than women to be in positions to achieve power and, therefore, to share their power with others. Similarly, the "bossy woman boss" stereotype is a perfect picture of powerlessness. All of these traits are just as characteristic of men who are powerless, but women are slightly more likely, because of circumstances I have mentioned, to find themselves powerless than are men. Women with power in the organization are just as effective – and preferred – as men.

Recent interviews conducted with about 600 bank managers show that, when a woman exhibits the petty traits of powerlessness, people assume that she does so "because she is a woman." A striking difference is that, when a man engages in the same behavior, people assume the behavior is a matter of his own individual style and characteristics and do not conclude that it reflects on the suitability of men for management.

the way of support from above, supervisors are forced to administer programs or explain policies that they have no hand in shaping. In one company, as part of a new personnel program supervisors were required to conduct counseling interviews with employees. But supervisors were not trained to do this and were given no incentives to get involved. Counseling was just another obligation. Then managers suddenly encouraged the workers to bypass their supervisors or to put pressure on them. The personnel staff brought them together and told them to demand such interviews as a basic right. If supervisors had not felt powerless before, they did after that squeeze from below, engineered from above.

The people they supervise can also make life hard for them in numerous ways. This often happens when a supervisor has himself or herself risen up from the ranks. Peers that have not made it are resentful or derisive of their former colleague, whom they now see as trying to lord it over them. Often it is easy for workers to break rules and let a lot of things slip.

Yet first-line supervisors are frequently judged according to rules and regulations while being limited by other regulations in what disciplinary actions they can take. They often lack the resources to influence or reward people; after all, workers are guaranteed their pay and benefits by someone other than their supervisors. Supervisors cannot easily control events; rather, they must react to them.

In one factory, for instance, supervisors complained that performance of their job was out of their control: they could fill production quotas only if they had the supplies, but they had no way to influence the people controlling supplies.

The lack of support for many first-line managers, particularly in large organizations, was made dramatically clear in another company. When asked if contact with executives higher in the organization who had the potential for offering support, information, and alliances diminished their own feelings of career vulnerability and the number of headaches they experienced on the job, supervisors in five out of seven work units responded positively. For them *contact* was indeed related to a greater feeling of acceptance at work and membership in the organization.

But in the two other work units where there was greater contact, people perceived more, not less, career vulnerability. Further investigation showed that supervisors in these business units got attention only when they were in trouble. Otherwise, no one bothered to talk to them. To these particular supervisors, hearing from a higher-level manager was a sign not of recognition or potential support but of danger.

It is not surprising, then, that supervisors frequently manifest symptoms of powerlessness: overly close supervision, rules-mindedness, and a tendency to do the job themselves rather than to train their people (since job skills may be one of the few remaining things they feel good about). Perhaps

POWER FAILURE

this is why they sometimes stand as roadblocks between their subordinates and the higher reaches of the company.

Staff professionals. Also working under conditions that can lead to organizational powerlessness are the staff specialists. As advisers behind the scenes, staff people must sell their programs and bargain for resources, but unless they get themselves entrenched in organizational power networks, they have little in the way of favors to exchange. They are seen as useful adjuncts to the primary tasks of the organization but inessential in a day-to-day operating sense. This disenfranchisement occurs particularly when staff jobs consist of easily routinized administrative functions which are out of the mainstream of the currently relevant areas and involve little innovative decision making.

Furthermore, in some organizations, unless they have had previous line experience, staff people tend to be limited in the number of jobs into which they can move. Specialists' ladders are often very short, and professionals are just as likely to get "stuck" in such jobs as people are in less prestigious clerical or factory positions.

Staff people, unlike those who are being groomed for important line positions, may be hired because of a special expertise or particular background. But management rarely pays any attention to developing them into more general organizational resources. Lacking growth prospects themselves and working alone or in very small teams, they are not in a position to develop others or pass on power to them. They miss out on an important way that power can be accumulated.

Sometimes staff specialists, such as house counsel or organization development people, find their work being farmed out to consultants. Management considers them fine for the routine work, but the minute the activities involve risk or something problematic, they bring in outside experts. This treatment says something not only about their expertise but also about the status of their function. Since the company can always hire talent on a temporary basis, it is unclear that the management really needs to have or considers important its own staff for these functions.

And, because staff professionals are often seen as adjuncts to primary tasks, their effectiveness and therefore their contribution to the organization are often hard to measure. Thus visibility and recognition, as well as risk taking and relevance, may be denied to people in staff jobs.

Staff people tend to act out their powerlessness by becoming turf-minded. They create islands within the organization. They set themselves up as the only ones who can control professional standards and judge their own work. They create sometimes false distinctions between themselves as experts (no one else could possibly do what they do) and lay people, and this continues to keep them out of the mainstream.

One form such distinctions take is a combination of disdain when line managers attempt to act in areas the professionals think are their preserve and of subtle refusal to support the managers'·efforts. Or staff groups battle with each other for control of new "problem areas," with the result that no one really handles the issue at all. To cope with their essential powerlessness, staff groups may try to elevate their own status and draw boundaries between themselves and others.

When staff jobs are treated as final resting places for people who have reached their level of competence in the organization – a good shelf on which to dump managers who are too old to go anywhere but too young to retire – then staff groups can also become pockets of conservatism, resistant to change. Their own exclusion from the risk-taking action may make them resist *anyone's* innovative proposals. In the past, personnel departments, for example, have sometimes been the last in their organization to know about innovations in human resource development or to be interested in applying them.

Top executives. Despite the great resources and responsibilities concentrated at the top of an organization, leaders can be powerless for reasons that are not very different from those that affect staff and supervisors: lack of supplies, information, and support.

We have faith in leaders because of their ability to make things happen in the larger world, to create possibilities for everyone else, and to attract resources to the organization. These are their supplies. But influence outward – the source of much credibility downward – can diminish as environments change, setting terms and conditions out of the control of the leaders. Regardless of top management's grand plans for the organization, the environment presses. At the very least, things going on outside the organization can deflect a leader's attention and drain energy. And, more detrimental, decisions made elsewhere can have severe consequences for the organization and affect top management's sense of power and thus its operating style inside.

In the go-go years of the mid-1960s, for example, nearly every corporation officer or university president could look – and therefore feel – successful. Visible success gave leaders a great deal of credibility inside the organization, which in turn gave them the power to put new things in motion.

In the past few years, the environment has been strikingly different and the capacity of many organization leaders to do anything about it has been severely limited. New "players" have flexed their power muscles: the Arab oil bloc, government regulators, and congressional investigating committees. And managing economic decline is quite different from managing growth. It is no accident that when top leaders personally feel out of control, the control function in corporations grows.

As powerlessness in lower levels of organizations can manifest itself in overly routinized jobs where performance measures are oriented to rules and absence of change, so it can at upper levels as well. Routine work often drives out nonroutine work. Accomplishment becomes a question of nailing down details. Short-term results provide immediate gratifications and satisfy stockholders or other constituencies with limited interests.

It takes a powerful leader to be willing to risk short-term deprivations in order to bring about desired long-term outcomes. Much as first-line supervisors are tempted to focus on daily adherence to rules, leaders are tempted to focus on short-term fluctuations and lose sight of long-term objectives. The dynamics of such a situation are self-reinforcing. The more the long-term goals go unattended, the more a leader feels powerless and the greater the scramble to prove that he or she is in control of daily events at least. The more he is involved in the organization as a short-term Mr. Fix-it, the more out of control of long-term objectives he is, and the more ultimately powerless he is likely to be.

Credibility for top executives often comes from doing the extraordinary: exercising discretion, creating, inventing, planning, and acting in nonroutine ways. But since routine problems look easier and more manageable, require less change and consent on the part of anyone else, and lend themselves to instant solutions that can make any leader look good temporarily, leaders may avoid the risky by taking over what their subordinates should be doing. Ultimately, a leader may succeed in getting all the trivial problems dumped on his or her desk. This can establish expectations even for leaders attempting more challenging tasks. When Warren Bennis was president of the University of Cincinnati, a professor called him when the heat was down in a classroom. In writing about this incident, Bennis commented, "I suppose he expected me to grab a wrench and fix it."[6]

People at the top need to insulate themselves from the routine operations of the organization in order to develop and exercise power. But this very insulation can lead to another source of powerlessness – lack of information. In one multinational corporation, top executives who are sealed off in a large, distant office, flattered and virtually babied by aides, are frustrated by their distance from the real action.[7]

At the top, the concern for secrecy and privacy is mixed with real loneliness. In one bank, organization members were so accustomed to never seeing the top leaders that when a new senior vice president went to the branch offices to look around, they had suspicion, even fear, about his intentions.

Thus leaders who are cut out of an organization's information networks understand neither what is really going on at lower levels nor that their own isolation may be having negative effects. All too often top executives design "beneficial" new employee programs or declare a new humanitarian policy (e.g., "Participatory management is now our style") only to find the policy ignored or mistrusted because it is perceived as coming from uncaring bosses.

The information gap has more serious consequences when executives are so insulated from the rest of the organization or from other decision makers that, as Nixon so dramatically did, they fail to see their own impending downfall. Such insulation is partly a matter of organizational position and, in some cases, of executive style.

For example, leaders may create closed inner circles consisting of "doppelgängers," people just like themselves, who are their principal sources of organizational information and tell them only what they want to know. The reasons for the distortions are varied: key aides want to relieve the leader of burdens, they think just like the leader, they want to protect their own positions of power, or the familiar "kill the messenger" syndrome makes people close to top executives reluctant to be the bearers of bad news.

Finally, just as supervisors and lower-level managers need their supporters in order to be and feel powerful, so do top executives. But for them sponsorship may not be so much a matter of individual endorsement as an issue of support by larger sources of legitimacy in the society. For top executives the problem is not to fit in among peers; rather, the question is whether the public at large and other organization members perceive a common interest which they see the executives as promoting.

If, however, public sources of support are withdrawn and leaders are open to public attack or if inside constituencies fragment and employees see their interests better aligned with pressure groups

---

6. Warren Bennis, *The Unconscious Conspiracy: Why Leaders Can't Lead* (New York: AMACOM, 1976).

7. See my chapter, "How the Top is Different," in *Life in Organizations*.

than with organizational leadership, then power-lessness begins to set in.

When common purpose is lost, the system's own politics may reduce the capacity of those at the top to act. Just as managing decline seems to create a much more passive and reactive stance than managing growth, so does mediating among conflicting interests. When what is happening outside and inside their organizations is out of their control, many people at the top turn into decline managers and dispute mediators. Neither is a particularly empowering role.

Thus when top executives lose their own lines of supply, lines of information, and lines of support, they too suffer from a kind of powerlessness. The temptation for them then is to pull in every shred of power they can and to decrease the power available to other people to act. Innovation loses out in favor of control. Limits rather than targets are set. Financial goals are met by reducing "overhead" (people) rather than by giving people the tools and discretion to increase their own productive capacity. Dictatorial statements come down from the top, spreading the mentality of powerlessness farther until the whole organization becomes sluggish and people concentrate on protecting what they have rather than on producing what they can.

When everyone is playing "king of the mountain," guarding his or her turf jealously, then king of the mountain becomes the only game in town.

To Expand Power, Share It

In no case am I saying that people in the three hierarchical levels described are always powerless, but they are susceptible to common conditions that can contribute to powerlessness. *Exhibit III* summarizes the most common symptoms of powerlessness for each level and some typical sources of that behavior.

I am also distinguishing the tremendous concentration of economic and political power in large corporations themselves from the powerlessness that can beset individuals even in the highest positions in such organizations. What grows with organizational position in hierarchical levels is not necessarily the power to accomplish – productive power – but the power to punish, to prevent, to sell off, to reduce, to fire, all without appropriate concern for consequences. It is that kind of power – oppressive power – that we often say corrupts.

The absence of ways to prevent individual and social harm causes the polity to feel it must surround people in power with constraints, regulations, and laws that limit the arbitrary use of their authority. But if oppressive power corrupts, then so does the absence of productive power. In large organizations, powerlessness can be a bigger problem than power.

David C. McClelland makes a similar distinction between oppressive and productive power:

"The negative...face of power is characterized by the dominance-submission mode: if I win, you lose.... It leads to simple and direct means of feeling powerful [such as being aggressive]. It does not often lead to effective social leadership for the reason that such a person tends to treat other people as pawns. People who feel they are pawns tend to be passive and useless to the leader who gets his satisfaction from dominating them. Slaves are the most inefficient form of labor ever devised by man. If a leader wants to have far-reaching influence, he must make his followers feel powerful and able to accomplish things on their own.... Even the most dictatorial leader does not succeed if he has not instilled in at least some of his followers a sense of power and the strength to pursue the goals he has set."[8]

Organizational power can grow, in part, by being shared. We do not yet know enough about new organizational forms to say whether productive power is infinitely expandable or where we reach the point of diminishing returns. But we do know that sharing power is different from giving or throwing it away. Delegation does not mean abdication.

Some basic lessons could be translated from the field of economics to the realm of organizations and management. Capital investment in plants and equipment is not the only key to productivity. The productive capacity of nations, like organizations, grows if the skill base is upgraded. People with the tools, information, and support to make more informed decisions and act more quickly can often accomplish more. By empowering others, a leader does not decrease his power; instead he may increase it – especially if the whole organization performs better.

This analysis leads to some counterintuitive conclusions. In a certain tautological sense, the principal problem of the powerless is that they lack power. Powerless people are usually the last ones to whom anyone wants to entrust more power, for fear of its dissipation or abuse. But those people are precisely the ones who might benefit most from an injection of power and whose behavior is likely to change as new options open up to them.

Also, if the powerless bosses could be encouraged to share some of the power they do have, their power would grow. Yet, of course, only those leaders

8. David C. McClelland, *Power: The Inner Experience* (New York: Irvington Publishers, 1975), p. 263. Quoted by permission.

Exhibit III

Common symptoms and sources of powerlessness for three key organizational positions

Position	Symptoms	Sources
First-line supervisors	Close, rules-minded supervision	Routine, rules-minded jobs with little control over lines of supply
	Tendency to do things oneself, blocking of subordinates' development and information	Limited lines of information
		Limited advancement or involvement prospects for oneself/subordinates
	Resistant, underproducing subordinates	
Staff professionals	Turf protection, information control	Routine tasks seen as peripheral to "real tasks" of line organization
	Retreat into professionalism	Blocked careers
	Conservative resistance to change	Easy replacement by outside experts
Top executives	Focus on internal cutting, short-term results, "punishing"	Uncontrollable lines of supply because of environmental changes
	Dictatorial top-down communications	Limited or blocked lines of information about lower levels of organization
	Retreat to comfort of like-minded lieutenants	Diminished lines of support because of challenges to legitimacy (e.g., from the public or special interest groups)

who feel secure about their own power outward – their lines of supply, information, and support – can see empowering subordinates as a gain rather than a loss. The two sides of power (getting it and giving it) are closely connected.

There are important lessons here for both subordinates and those who want to change organizations, whether executives or change agents. Instead of resisting or criticizing a powerless boss, which only increases the boss's feeling of powerlessness and need to control, subordinates instead might concentrate on helping the boss become more powerful. Managers might make pockets of ineffectiveness in the organization more productive not by training or replacing individuals but by structural solutions such as opening supply and support lines.

Similarly, organizational change agents who want a new program or policy to succeed should make sure that the change itself does not render any other level of the organization powerless. In making changes, it is wise to make sure that the key people in the level or two directly above and in neighboring functions are sufficiently involved, informed, and taken into account, so that the program can be used to build their own sense of power also. If such involvement is impossible, then it is better to move these people out of the territory altogether than to leave behind a group from whom some power has been removed and who might resist and undercut the program.

In part, of course, spreading power means educating people to this new definition of it. But words alone will not make the difference; managers will need the real experience of a new way of managing.

Here is how the associate director of a large corporate professional department phrased the lessons that he learned in the transition to a team-oriented, participatory, power-sharing management process:

"Get in the habit of involving your own managers in decision making and approvals. But don't abdicate! Tell them what you want and where you're coming from. Don't go for a one-boss grass roots 'democracy.' Make the management hierarchy work for you in participation...

"Hang in there, baby, and don't give up. Try not to 'revert' just because everything seems to go sour on a particular day. Open up – talk to people and tell them how you feel. They'll want to get you back on track and will do things to make that happen – because they don't really want to go back to the way it was.... Subordinates will push you to 'act more like a boss,' but their interest is usually more in seeing someone else brought to heel than getting bossed themselves."

Naturally, people need to have power before they can learn to share it. Exhorting managers to change their leadership styles is rarely useful by itself. In one large plant of a major electronics company, first-line production supervisors were the source of numerous complaints from managers who saw them as major roadblocks to overall plant productivity and as insufficiently skilled supervisors. So the plant personnel staff undertook two pilot programs to increase the supervisors' effectiveness. The first program was based on a traditional competency and training model aimed at teaching the specific skills of successful supervisors. The second program, in contrast, was designed to empower the supervisors by directly affecting their flexibility, access to resources, connections with higher-level officials, and control over working conditions.

After an initial gathering of data from supervisors and their subordinates, the personnel staff held meetings where all the supervisors were given tools for developing action plans for sharing the data with their people and collaborating on solutions to perceived problems. But then, in a departure from common practice in this organization, task forces of supervisors were formed to develop new systems for handling job and career issues common to them and their people. These task forces were given budgets, consultants, representation on a plantwide project steering committee alongside managers at much higher levels, and wide latitude in defining the nature and scope of the changes they wished to make. In short, lines of supply, information, and support were opened to them.

As the task forces progressed in their activities, it became clear to the plant management that the hoped-for changes in supervisory effectiveness were taking place much more rapidly through these structural changes in power than through conventional management training; so the conventional training was dropped. Not only did the pilot groups design useful new procedures for the plant, astonishing senior management in several cases with their knowledge and capabilities, but also, significantly, they learned to manage their own people better.

Several groups decided to involve shop-floor workers in their task forces; they could now see from their own experience the benefits of involving subordinates in solving job-related problems. Other supervisors began to experiment with ways to implement "participatory management" by giving subordinates more control and influence without relinquishing their own authority.

Soon the "problem supervisors" in the "most troubled plant in the company" were getting the highest possible performance ratings and were considered models for direct production management. The sharing of organizational power from the top made possible the productive use of power below.

One might wonder why more organizations do not adopt such empowering strategies. There are standard answers: that giving up control is threatening to people who have fought for every shred of it; that people do not want to share power with those they look down on; that managers fear losing their own place and special privileges in the system; that "predictability" often rates higher than "flexibility" as an organizational value; and so forth.

But I would also put skepticism about employee abilities high on the list. Many modern bureaucratic systems are designed to minimize dependence on individual intelligence by making routine as many decisions as possible. So it often comes as a genuine surprise to top executives that people doing the more routine jobs could, indeed, make sophisticated decisions or use resources entrusted to them in intelligent ways.

In the same electronics company just mentioned, at the end of a quarter the pilot supervisory task forces were asked to report results and plans to senior management in order to have their new budget requests approved. The task forces made sure they were well prepared, and the high-level executives were duly impressed. In fact, they were *so* impressed that they kept interrupting the presentations with compliments, remarking that the supervisors could easily be doing sophisticated personnel work.

At first the supervisors were flattered. Such praise from upper management could only be taken well. But when the first glow wore off, several of them became very angry. They saw the excessive praise as patronizing and insulting. "Didn't they think we could think? Didn't they imagine we were capable of doing this kind of work?" one asked. "They must have seen us as just a bunch of animals. No wonder they gave us such limited jobs."

As far as these supervisors were concerned, their abilities had always been there, in latent form perhaps, but still there. They as individuals had not changed – just their organizational power. ⊟

Part IV
Leadership, Identity and Difference

Introduction to Part IV

Leadership, Identity and Difference

Martin Wood and Pat Lyons

> ... a person is a fluid process, not a fixed and static entity; a flowing river of change, not a block of solid material; a continually changing constellation of potentialities, not a fixed quantity of traits. (Rogers, this volume, p. 312)

By the term 'leadership' we usually mean any of the personal qualities and capabilities of a few key people occupying top positions in a hierarchy. We may be thinking of business gurus, policy-makers, political leaders, spiritual teachers, fashion icons, pop idols and sporting heroes, but in all these senses the 'leader' (as post-holder) is promoted as the source of leadership. The leader is seen to act as an energizer, catalyst and visionary, equipped with a set of abilities that can be applied across a diverse range of situations and contexts.

Such individuals are often promoted as 'leaderful' to the extent that their conduct and attitudes resemble some already-held exemplar or archetype. Alternatively, leadership is referred to as the activities of individuals and their relationships with particular situations and contexts, which, when aligned, can help achieve business objectives and deliver improved organizational performance. Whilst contingency and situational factors may be seen as barriers to an individual's ability to lead, the problem is one of 'fit', and may be solved by finding another leader with the right package of skills and, simultaneously, finding another position for the individual.

As Jeffrey Pfeffer shows in Chapter 22, a number of interconnected issues and key questions can be introduced to debate the prevalence and dominance of an approach to leadership, which attributes causation to individual social actors. Leadership studies typically rest on 'a belief in natural individuals not arriving through social production, but posited by nature' (Marx, 1973, p. 83). But, how, precisely, are these individual social actors identified? And what if their apparently objective appearance turns out to be a phenomenological construct? Do leaders serve as important symbols representing the choice of a social collectivity? Might this lead to the selection of only those individuals who match the socially constructed image of the leader? Does this suggest the primacy of social relations above individual causation? Is what is at stake, in all of these issues and questions, the nature and definition of the concept of leadership itself?

Part IV is organized around a key reading taken from Carl Rogers' (1967) classic discussion of the process of becoming a person. Subsequent essays each take a particular perspective on the way in which the nature and definition of leadership is identified. Employing theoretical tools from cultural symbolism, dialectical materialism, phenomenological experience, post-structuralism, psychotherapy and transformative systems, they each elucidate a particular aspect of the becoming of leadership, rather than seeking simply to endorse some already fixed quantity of traits or essential characteristics.

Rogers (Chapter 19) offers us an accessible overview of the experience of the development of personal identity. He does so in a way that sees the individual as constantly in a *process of becoming* – a living, breathing, fluctuating process. There are a number of interrelated implications of this focus. The first has to do with the experience of feeling. The reality of the individual social actor is determined in the way s/he experiences/feels that which, at an organic level, s/he *is*; the individual in such a moment is coming to *be* what s/he *is*. This reflective attitude leads to a second process of self-discovery in experience. To become themselves individual social actors must find the goal they most wish to achieve – the pattern, the underlying order, which exists in the ceaselessly changing flow of their experience. The process of becoming a person, therefore, involves dropping the false fronts, or the masks, or the roles, with which the individual has faced their life. Rogers reminds us that this is deeply disturbing if it involves removing false faces that the individual did not know were false and opening their self to their experience, able to take in evidence of their situation *as it is* at *this moment*, rather than distorting it to fit some fixed state or fixed goals. According to Rogers, the real self is discovered in one's experiences. The individual becomes open to their experience and so becomes more content to be a process rather than some fixed state or product. In opening to all the elements of one's experience one is more likely to develop trust in one's own organism, recognize that one is the locus of evaluation, learn to live as a participant in a fluid, ongoing process, and be continually discovering new aspects of oneself in the flow of this experience.

In Chapter 20 Peter Drucker sounds a clarion call for the development of the reflective mindset, recognized as essential by Rogers. Drucker points to some key issues, which are central to recent questions of leadership identity – issues such as personal evaluation and continuous learning. His essay importantly draws attention to our need to develop reflective relationships in order to manage others and ourselves. Set within a brief review of leadership thought, the next essay by Robert Goffee and Gareth Jones (Chapter 21) asks an important question at the core of the current leadership identity debate: what makes an inspirational leader? Again, the emphasis is on self-reflection and its role in establishing role authenticity, together with 'selective' recognition of the 'weaknesses' that characterize practising leaders. Their essay underscores the key point, however, that leadership practice may usefully articulate some of the things that a person does, is, or aspires to, but simply doing these things may still do little to get effective leadership done.

At best, we can arrive at a list of features that are common to this group, which may be necessary, but are hardly sufficient to constitute the rarefied plant envisaged within earlier debates. I may endeavour to know myself – my strengths, my values, how I best perform and what I should contribute. I may even be visionary, communicative and honest, balance respect for the individual with the task at hand, and yet still find leadership to be elusive. So these qualities turn out to be descriptive (not necessarily of leadership, but of some qualities associated with people in the top jobs). A potential weakness of Drucker's and Goffee's and Jones's approach is they present these qualities as prescriptive. For example: 'Leaders *need* vision, energy, authority, and strategic direction' (Goffee and Jones, p. 325, emphasis added). Where leadership is lacking the boss may well need to envision, but simply envisioning does not conjure up 'leadership'. In fact, the list of things a leader *ought* to be (for example, visionary, energetic) might be experienced as yet another imposition.

Both Drucker and Goffee and Jones point out that being a leader is about 'being yourself' more than being 'different'. As Drucker (p. 319) warns, 'do not try to change yourself – you are unlikely to succeed'. Each introduces the concept of difference as a negative – the active negation of something else, as being different from something else. Great achievers, for example, are distinguished from most people by their talents and their accomplishments. It is their exceptional qualities and abilities that set them apart or grade them as different. Yet, a consideration of great achievers and inspirational leaders may simply mark an avowed return to neo-traitism, elevating those activities that 'engage people and rouse their commitment to company goals' (Goffee and Jones, p. 325) and so represent a blatant retreat to the 'discredited heroics' (Gronn, 2002, p. 426) of standalone leaders.

An important question is whether Drucker and Goffee and Jones each overstate a causal link between individual leadership behaviour and goal achievement, and ultimately organizational success. In Chapter 22 – a classic rebuke, first published in 1977 in the *Academy of Management Review* – Jeffrey Pfeffer argues that the meaning and behavioural attributes of leadership remain ambiguous and that the literature assessing the magnitude of the effects of leadership is equivocal. He points out 'there are few meaningful distinctions between leadership and other concepts of social influence' (p. 334). The belief in leadership effects, he continues, only 'provides a simple causal framework and a justification for the structure of the social collectivity' (p. 339). The implication is that Drucker's and Goffee's and Jones's focus on the exceptional actions of one person (guru, teacher, icon or hero) may cause a failure to recognize the importance of a given social context. Their enthusiasm for attributing *causation* to individual social actors may be a little injudicious. It might be that the importance of leadership is in fact an *outcome* of various social processes, leading to the selection of only those who match the constructed image of the leader.

One exciting facet of Pfeffer's argument 'is that leadership is of interest primarily as a phenomenological construct' (p. 333). His assertion that the construction of the importance of leadership in a given social context is the outcome of various social processes and that these processes 'can be empirically examined' (p. 339) presents an open field for research.

In the final essay of Part IV, Richard Barker attempts to provide important metaphysical support for this endeavour. With a definite nod to Pfeffer, Barker, too, believes that the problem of studying the properties of exceptional or self-reflective individuals lies in the inevitable error of separating leaders from 'the complex, reciprocal relationships of people and institutions' that surround and suffuse them (p. 357). He also argues that the error is made with the assumption that isolating a single leader can explain the complex and continuous 'nature of leadership'. Leadership, as we experience it, he continues, is in fact a continuous social process. In this he is also in agreement with Rogers, for whom, as we recall, an existing individual is constantly in the process of becoming. Barker's approach, however, extends beyond the individual striving to become himself to the claim that it is precisely the complex and continuous relationships of people and institutions which 'must be the foci of the explanation of leadership' (ibid.). He proposes a 'new framework for leadership studies', one 'built upon a direct, phenomenological experience of leadership' (ibid.) as a 'dissipative system ... continuously renew[ing] itself within a dynamic context (p. 361). Barker defines a dissipative (transforming or chaotic) system as a 'spontaneous formation of structures in open systems which exchange energy and matter with their environment' (Jantsch, 1980 cited in Barker, p. 360). The 'structure' of a dissipative system is not a solid, tangible structure, but a process structure: what Jantsch refers to as a dynamic regime. Whatever we experience as leadership transforms as a part of the system; the macro-system changes as a part of the transformation. Therefore, Barker concludes, it makes little sense to discuss any constant quality of the leader as the source of leadership. Instead, he identifies leadership as a process of transformative change.

Our discussion of leadership identity is not directed towards a location of essence or the distinguishing of a state but, rather, towards the identification of an essential movement, an incompletion in the process of production. What endures is leadership's continual difference and not the sameness of a leader's individual identity.

References

Gronn, P. (2002), 'Distributed Leadership as a Unit of Analysis', *Leadership Quarterly*, **13**, pp. 423–51.

Jantsch, Erich (1980), *The Self-Organizing Universe: The Scientific and Human Implication of the Emerging Paradigm of Evolution*, New York: Pergamon.

Marx, Karl (1973), *Grundrisse*, trans. Martin Nicolaus, London: Penguin.

[19]

What It Means
to Become a Person

Carl R. Rogers

*This chapter was first given as a talk to a meeting at Oberlin
College in 1954. I was trying to pull together in more completely organized form, some of the conceptions of therapy which
had been growing in me. I have revised it slightly.*

*As is customary with me, I was trying to keep my thinking close
to the grass roots of actual experience in therapeutic interviews, so
I drew heavily upon recorded interviews as the source of the generalizations which I make.*

IN MY WORK at the Counseling Center of the University of Chicago, I have the opportunity of working with people who present
a wide variety of personal problems. There is the student concerned
about failing in college; the housewife disturbed about her marriage;
the individual who feels he is teetering on the edge of a complete
breakdown or psychosis; the responsible professional man who
spends much of his time in sexual fantasies and functions inefficiently

in his work; the brilliant student, at the top of his class, who is paralyzed by the conviction that he is hopelessly and helplessly inadequate; the parent who is distressed by his child's behavior; the popular girl who finds herself unaccountably overtaken by sharp spells of black depression; the woman who fears that life and love are passing her by, and that her good graduate record is a poor recompense; the man who has become convinced that powerful or sinister forces are plotting against him; — I could go on and on with the many different and unique problems which people bring to us. They run the gamut of life's experiences. Yet there is no satisfaction in giving this type of catalog, for, as counselor, I know that the problem as stated in the first interview will not be the problem as seen in the second or third hour, and by the tenth interview it will be a still different problem or series of problems.

I have however come to believe that in spite of this bewildering horizontal multiplicity, and the layer upon layer of vertical complexity, there is perhaps only one problem. As I follow the experience of many clients in the therapeutic relationship which we endeavor to create for them, it seems to me that each one is raising the same question. Below the level of the problem situation about which the individual is complaining — behind the trouble with studies, or wife, or employer, or with his own uncontrollable or bizarre behavior, or with his frightening feelings, lies one central search. It seems to me that at bottom each person is asking, "Who am I, *really?* How can I get in touch with this real self, underlying all my surface behavior? How can I become myself?"

THE PROCESS OF BECOMING

GETTING BEHIND THE MASK

Let me try to explain what I mean when I say that it appears that the goal the individual most wishes to achieve, the end which he knowingly and unknowingly pursues, is to become himself.

When a person comes to me, troubled by his unique combination of difficulties, I have found it most worth while to try to create a relationship with him in which he is safe and free. It is my purpose to understand the way he feels in his own inner world, to accept him as he is, to create an atmosphere of freedom in which he can move in his thinking and feeling and being, in any direction he desires. How does he use this freedom?

It is my experience that he uses it to become more and more himself. He begins to drop the false fronts, or the masks, or the roles, with which he has faced life. He appears to be trying to discover something more basic, something more truly himself. At first he lays aside masks which he is to some degree aware of using. One young woman student describes in a counseling interview one of the masks she has been using, and how uncertain she is whether underneath this appeasing, ingratiating front there is any real self with convictions.

I was thinking about this business of standards. I somehow developed a sort of knack, I guess, of — well — habit — of trying to make people feel at ease around me, or to make things go along smoothly. There always had to be some appeaser around, being sorta the oil that soothed the waters. At a small meeting, or a little party, or something — I could help things go along nicely and appear to be having a good time. And sometimes I'd surprise myself by arguing against what I really thought when I saw that the person in charge would be quite unhappy about it if I didn't. In other words I just wasn't ever — I mean, I didn't find myself ever being set and definite about things. Now the reason why I did it probably was I'd been doing it around home so much. I just didn't stand up for my own convictions, until I don't know whether I have any convictions to stand up for. I haven't been really honestly being myself, or actually knowing what my real self is, and I've been just playing a sort of false role.

You can, in this excerpt, see her examining the mask she has been using, recognizing her dissatisfaction with it, and wondering how to get to the real self underneath, if such a self exists.

In this attempt to discover his own self, the client typically uses the relationship to explore, to examine the various aspects of his own experience, to recognize and face up to the deep contradictions which he often discovers. He learns how much of his behavior, even how much of the feeling he experiences, is not real, is not something which flows from the genuine reactions of his organism, but is a façade, a front, behind which he has been hiding. He discovers how much of his life is guided by what he thinks he *should* be, not by what he is. Often he discovers that he exists only in response to the demands of others, that he seems to have no self of his own, that he is only trying to think, and feel, and behave in the way that others believe he *ought* to think, and feel and behave.

In this connection I have been astonished to find how accurately the Danish philosopher, Søren Kierkegaard, pictured the dilemma of the individual more than a century ago, with keen psychological insight. He points out that the most common despair is to be in despair at not choosing, or willing, to be oneself; but that the deepest form of despair is to choose "to be another than himself." On the other hand "to will to be that self which one truly is, is indeed the opposite of despair," and this choice is the deepest responsibility of man. As I read some of his writings I almost feel that he must have listened in on the statements made by our clients as they search and explore for the reality of self — often a painful and troubling search.

This exploration becomes even more disturbing when they find themselves involved in removing the false faces which they had not known were false faces. They begin to engage in the frightening task of exploring the turbulent and sometimes violent feelings within themselves. To remove a mask which you had thought was part of your real self can be a deeply disturbing experience, yet when there is freedom to think and feel and be, the individual moves toward such a goal. A few statements from a person who had completed a series of psychotherapeutic interviews, will illustrate this. She uses many metaphors as she tells how she struggled to get to the core of herself.

As I look at it now, I was peeling off layer after layer of defenses. I'd build them up, try them, and then discard them when you remained the same. I didn't know what was at the bottom and I was very much afraid to find out, but I *had* to keep on trying. At first I felt there was nothing within me — just a great emptiness where I needed and wanted a solid core. Then I began to feel that

I was facing a solid brick wall, too high to get over and too thick to go through. One day the wall became translucent, rather than solid. After this, the wall seemed to disappear but beyond it I discovered a dam holding back violent, churning waters. I felt as if I were holding back the force of these waters and if I opened even a tiny hole I and all about me would be destroyed in the ensuing torrent of feelings represented by the water. Finally I could stand the strain no longer and I let go. All I did, actually, was to succumb to complete and utter self pity, then hate, then love. After this experience, I felt as if I had leaped a brink and was safely on the other side, though still tottering a bit on the edge. I don't know what I was searching for or where I was going, but I felt then as I have always felt whenever I really lived, that I was moving forward.

I believe this represents rather well the feelings of many an individual that if the false front, the wall, the dam, is not maintained, then everything will be swept away in the violence of the feelings that he discovers pent-up in his private world. Yet it also illustrates the compelling necessity which the individual feels to search for and become himself. It also begins to indicate the way in which the individual determines the reality in himself — that when he fully experiences the feelings which at an organic level he *is*, as this client experienced her self-pity, hatred, and love, then he feels an assurance that he is being a part of his real self.

THE EXPERIENCING OF FEELING

I would like to say something more about this experiencing of feeling. It is really the discovery of unknown elements of self. The phenomenon I am trying to describe is something which I think is quite difficult to get across in any meaningful way. In our daily lives there are a thousand and one reasons for not letting ourselves experience our attitudes fully, reasons from our past and from the present, reasons that reside within the social situation. It seems too dangerous, too potentially damaging, to experience them freely and fully. But in the safety and freedom of the therapeutic relationship, they can be experienced fully, clear to the limit of what they are. They can be and are experienced in a fashion that I like to think of as a "pure culture," so that for the moment the person *is* his fear, or he *is* his anger, or he *is* his tenderness, or whatever.

Perhaps again I can clarify this by giving an example from a client which will indicate and convey something of what I mean. A young man, a graduate student who is deep in therapy, has been puzzling over a vague feeling which he senses in himself. He gradually identifies it as a frightened feeling of some kind, a fear of failing, a fear of not getting his Ph.D. Then comes a long pause. From this point on we will let the recorded interview speak for itself.

> *Client:* I was kinda letting it seep through. But I also tied it in with you and with my relationship with you. And that's one thing I feel about it is kind of a fear of it going away; or that's another thing — it's so hard to get hold of — there's kind of two pulling feelings about it. Or two "me's" somehow. One is the scared one that wants to hold on to things, and that one I guess I can feel pretty clearly right now. You know, I kinda need things to hold on to — and I feel kinda scared.
>
> *Therapist:* M-hm. That's something you can feel right this minute, and have been feeling and perhaps *are* feeling in regard to our relationship, too.
>
> *C:* Won't you let me *have* this, because, you know, I kinda *need* it. I can be so lonely and scared without it.
>
> *T:* M-hm, m-hm. Let me hang on to this because I'd be terribly scared if I didn't. Let me *hold* on to it. (*Pause*)
>
> *C:* It's kinda the same thing — *W on't* you let me have my thesis or my Ph.D. so then . . . 'Cause I kinda *need* that little world. I mean. . . .
>
> *T:* In both instances it's kind of a pleading thing too, isn't it? Let me *have* this because I need it *badly*. I'd be awfully frightened without it. (*Long pause.*)
>
> *C:* I get a sense of . . . I can't somehow get much further . . . It's this kind of *pleading* little boy, somehow, even . . . What's this gesture of begging? (*Putting his hands together as if in prayer*) Isn't it funny? 'Cause that . . .

T: You put your hands in sort of a supplication.

C: Ya, that's right! Won't you *do* this for me, kinda . . . Oh, that's *terrible!* Who, me, *beg?*

Perhaps this excerpt will convey a bit of the thing I have been talking about, the experiencing of a feeling all the way to the limit. Here he is, for a moment, experiencing himself as nothing but a pleading little boy, supplicating, begging, dependent. At that moment he is nothing but his pleadingness, all the way through. To be sure he almost immediately backs away from this experiencing by saying "Who, me, *beg?*" but it has left its mark. As he says a moment later, "It's such a wondrous thing to have these new things come out of me. It amazes me so much each time, and then again there's that same feeling, kind of feeling scared that I've so much of this that I'm keeping back or something." He realizes that this has bubbled through, and that for the moment he *is* his dependency, in a way which astonishes him.

It is not only dependency that is experienced in this all-out kind of fashion. It may be hurt, or sorrow, or jealousy, or destructive anger, or deep desire, or confidence and pride, or sensitive tenderness, or outgoing love. It may be any of the emotions of which man is capable.

What I have gradually learned from experiences such as this, is that the individual in such a moment, is coming to *be* what he *is*. When a person has, throughout therapy, experienced in this fashion all the emotions which organismically arise in him, and has experienced them in this knowing and open manner, then he has experienced *himself*, in all the richness that exists within himself. He has become what he is.

THE DISCOVERY OF SELF IN EXPERIENCE

Let us pursue a bit further this question of what it means to become one's self. It is a most perplexing question and again I will try to take from a statement by a client, written between interviews, a suggestion of an answer. She tells how the various façades by which she has been living have somehow crumpled and collapsed, bringing a feeling of confusion, but also a feeling of relief. She continues:

> You know, it seems as if all the energy that went into holding the arbitrary pattern together was quite unnecessary — a waste. You think you have to make the pattern yourself; but there are so many pieces, and it's so hard to see where they fit. Sometimes you put them in the wrong place, and the more pieces mis-fitted, the more effort it takes to hold them in place, until at last you are so tired that even that awful confusion is better than holding on any longer. Then you discover that left to themselves the jumbled pieces fall quite naturally into their own places, and a living pattern emerges without any effort at all on your part. Your job is just to discover it, and in the course of that, you will find yourself and your own place. You must even let your own experience tell you its own meaning; the minute *you* tell it what it means, you are at war with yourself.

Let me see if I can take her poetic expression and translate it into the meaning it has for me. I believe she is saying that to be herself means to find the pattern, the underlying order, which exists in the ceaselessly changing flow of her experience. Rather than to try to hold her experience into the form of a mask, or to make it be a form or structure that it is not, being herself means to discover the unity and harmony which exists in her own actual feelings and reactions. It means that the real self is something which is comfortably discovered in one's experiences, not something imposed upon it.

Through giving excerpts from the statements of these clients, I have been trying to suggest what happens in the warmth and understanding of a facilitating relationship with a therapist. It seems that gradually, painfully, the individual explores what is behind the masks he presents to the world, and even behind the masks with which he has been deceiving himself. Deeply and often vividly he experiences the various elements of himself which have been hidden within. Thus to an increasing degree he becomes himself — not a façade of conformity to others, not a cynical denial of all feeling, nor a front of intellectual rationality, but a living, breathing, feeling, fluctuating process — in short, he becomes a person.

The Person Who Emerges

I imagine that some of you are asking, "But what *kind* of a person does he become? It isn't enough to say that he drops the façades. What kind of person lies underneath?" Since one of the most obvious facts is that each individual tends to become a separate and distinct and unique person, the answer is not easy. However I would like to point out some of the characteristic trends which I see. No one person would fully exemplify these characteristics, no one person fully achives the description I will give, but I do see certain generalizations which can be drawn, based upon living a therapeutic relationship with many clients.

Openness to Experience

First of all I would say that in this process the individual becomes more open to his experience. This is a phrase which has come to have a great deal of meaning to me. It is the opposite of defensiveness. Psychological research has shown that if the evidence of our senses runs contrary to our picture of self, then that evidence is distorted. In other words we cannot see all that our senses report, but only the things which fit the picture we have.

Now in a safe relationship of the sort I have described, this defensiveness or rigidity, tends to be replaced by an increasing openness to experience. The individual becomes more openly aware of his own feelings and attitudes as they exist in him at an organic level, in the way I tried to describe. He also becomes more aware of reality as it exists outside of himself, instead of perceiving it in preconceived categories. He sees that not all trees are green, not all men are stern fathers, not all women are rejecting, not all failure experiences prove that he is no good, and the like. He is able to take in the evidence in a new situation, *as it is*, rather than distorting it to fit a pattern which he already holds. As you might expect, this increasing ability to be open to experience makes him far more realistic in dealing with new people, new situations, new problems. It means that his beliefs are not rigid, that he can tolerate ambiguity. He can receive much conflicting evidence without forcing closure upon the situation. This openness of awareness to what exists at *this moment* in *oneself* and in *the situation* is, I believe, an important element in the description of the person who emerges from therapy.

Perhaps I can give this concept a more vivid meaning if I illustrate it from a recorded interview. A young professional man reports in the 48th interview the way in which he has become more open to some of his bodily sensations, as well as other feelings.

> *C:* It doesn't seem to me that it would be possible for anybody to relate all the changes that you feel. But I certainly have felt recently that I have more respect for, more objectivity toward my physical makeup. I mean I don't expect too much of myself. This is how it works out: It feels to me that in the past I used to fight a certain tiredness that I felt after supper. Well, now I feel pretty sure that I really *am tired* — that I am not making myself tired — that I am just physiologically lower. It seemed that I was just constantly criticizing my tiredness.
>
> *T:* So you can let yourself *be* tired, instead of feeling along with it a kind of criticism of it.
>
> *C:* Yes, that I shouldn't be tired or something. And it seems in a way to be pretty profound that I can just not fight this tiredness, and along with it goes a real feeling of *I've* got to slow down, too, so that being tired isn't such an awful thing. I think I can also kind of pick up a thread here of why I should be that way in the way my father is and the way he looks at some of these things. For instance, say that I was sick, and I would report this, and it would seem that overtly he would want to do something about it but he would also communicate, "Oh, my gosh, more trouble." You know, something like that.
>
> *T:* As though there were something quite annoying really about being physically ill.
>
> *C:* Yeah, I'm sure that my father has the same disrespect for his own physiology that I have had. Now last summer I twisted my back, I wrenched it, I heard it snap and everything. There was real pain there all the time at first, real sharp. And I had the doctor look at it and he said it wasn't serious, it should heal by itself as

long as I didn't bend too much. Well this was months ago — and I have been noticing recently that — hell, this is a real pain and it's still there — and it's not my fault.

T: It doesn't prove something bad about you —

C: No — and one of the reasons I seem to get more tired than I should maybe is because of this constant strain, and so — I have already made an appointment with one of the doctors at the hospital that he would look at it and take an X ray or something. In a way I guesss you could say that I am just more accurately sensitive — or objectively sensitive to this kind of thing. . . . And this is really a profound change as I say, and of course my relationship with my wife and the two children is — well, you just wouldn't recognize it if you could see me inside — as you have — I mean — there just doesn't seem to be anything more wonderful than really and genuinely — really *feeling* love for your own children and at the same time receiving it. I don't know how to put this. We have such an increased respect — both of us — for Judy and we've noticed just — as we participated in this — we have noticed such a tremendous change in her — it seems to be a pretty deep kind of thing.

T: It seems to me you are saying that you can listen more accurately to yourself. If your body says it's tired, you listen to it and believe it, instead of criticizing it; if it's in pain, you can listen to that; if the feeling is really loving your wife or children, you can *feel* that, and it seems to show up in the differences in them too.

Here, in a relatively minor but symbolically important excerpt, can be seen much of what I have been trying to say about openness to experience. Formerly he could not freely feel pain or illness, because being ill meant being unacceptable. Neither could he feel tenderness and love for his child, because such feelings meant being weak, and he had to maintain his façade of being strong. But now he can be genuinely open to the experiences of his organism — he can be tired when he is tired, he can feel pain when his organism is in pain, he can freely experience the love he feels for his daughter, and he can also feel and express annoyance toward her, as he goes on to say in the next portion of the interview. He can fully live the experiences of his total organism, rather than shutting them out of awareness.

Trust in One's Organism

A second characteristic of the persons who emerge from therapy is difficult to describe. It seems that the person increasingly discovers that his own organism is trustworthy, that it is a suitable instrument for discovering the most satisfying behavior in each immediate situation.

If this seems strange, let me try to state it more fully. Perhaps it will help to understand my description if you think of the individual as faced with some existential choice: "Shall I go home to my family during vacation, or strike out on my own?" "Shall I drink this third cocktail which is being offered?" "Is this the person whom I would like to have as my partner in love and in life?" Thinking of such situations, what seems to be true of the person who emerges from the therapeutic process? To the extent that this person is open to all of his experience, he has access to all of the available data in the situation, on which to base his behavior. He has knowledge of his own feelings and impulses, which are often complex and contradictory. He is freely able to sense the social demands, from the relatively rigid social "laws" to the desires of friends and family. He has access to his memories of similar situations, and the consequences of different behaviors in those situations. He has a relatively accurate perception of this external situation in all of its complexity. He is better able to permit his total organism, his conscious thought participating, to consider, weigh and balance each stimulus, need, and demand, and its relative weight and intensity. Out of this complex weighing and balancing he is able to discover that course of action which seems to come closest to satisfying all his needs in the situation, long-range as well as immediate needs.

In such a weighing and balancing of all of the components of a given life choice, his organism would not by any means be infallible. Mistaken choices might be made. But because he tends to be open to his experience, there is a greater and more immediate awareness of unsatisfying consequences, a quicker correction of choices which are in error.

It may help to realize that in most of us the defects which interfere with this weighing and balancing are that we include things that are not a part of our experience, and exclude elements which are. Thus an individual may persist in the concept that "I can handle liquor," when openness to his past experience would indicate that this is scarcely correct. Or a young woman may see only the good qualities of her prospective mate, where an openness to experience would indicate that he possesses faults as well.

In general then, it appears to be true that when a client is open to his experience, he comes to find his organism more trustworthy. He feels less fear of the emotional reactions which he has. There is a gradual growth of trust in, and even affection for the complex, rich, varied assortment of feelings and tendencies which exist in him at the organic level. Consciousness, instead of being the watchman over a dangerous and unpredictable lot of impulses, of which few can be permitted to see the light of day, becomes the comfortable inhabitant of a society of impulses and feelings and thoughts, which are discovered to be very satisfactorily self-governing when not fearfully guarded.

An Internal Locus of Evaluation

Another trend which is evident in this process of becoming a person relates to the source or locus of choices and decisions, or evaluative judgments. The individual increasingly comes to feel that this locus of evaluation lies within himself. Less and less does he look to others for approval or disapproval; for standards to live by; for decisions and choices. He recognizes that it rests within himself to choose; that the only question which matters is, "Am I living in a way which is deeply satisfying to me, and which truly expresses me?" This I think is perhaps *the* most important question for the creative individual.

Perhaps it will help if I give an illustration. I would like to give a brief portion of a recorded interview with a young woman, a graduate student, who had come for counseling help. She was initially very much disturbed about many problems, and had been contemplating suicide. During the interview one of the feelings she discovered was her great desire to be dependent, just to let someone else take over the direction of her life. She was very critical of those who had not given her enough guidance. She talked about one after another of her professors, feeling bitterly that none of them had taught her anything with deep meaning. Gradually she began to realize that part of the difficulty was the fact that she had taken no initiative in *participating* in these classes. Then comes the portion I wish to quote.

I think you will find that this excerpt gives you some indication of what it means in experience to accept the locus of evaluation as being within oneself. Here then is the quotation from one of the later interviews with this young woman as she has begun to realize that perhaps she is partly responsible for the deficiencies in her own education.

C: Well now, I wonder if I've been going around doing that, getting smatterings of things, and not getting hold, not really getting down to things.

T: Maybe you've been getting just spoonfuls here and there rather than really digging in somewhere rather deeply.

C: M-hm. That's why I say — (*slowly and very thoughtfully*) well, with that sort of a foundation, well, it's really up to *me*. I mean, it seems to be really apparent to me that I *can't depend on someone else* to give me an education. (*Very softly*) I'll really have to get it myself.

T: It really begins to come home — there's only one person that can educate you — a realization that perhaps nobody else *can give* you an education.

C: M-hm. (*Long pause — while she sits thinking*) I have all the symptoms of fright. (*Laughs softly*)

T: Fright? That this is a scary thing, is that what you mean?

C: M-hm. (*Very long pause — obviously struggling with feelings in herself*).

T: Do you want to say any more about what you mean by that? That it really does give you the symptoms of fright?

C: (*Laughs*) I, uh — I don't know whether I quite know. I mean — well it really seems like I'm cut loose (*pause*), and it seems that I'm very — I don't know — in a vulnerable position, but I, uh, I brought this up and it, uh, somehow it almost came out without my saying it. It seems to be — it's something I let out.

T: Hardly a part of you.

C: Well, I felt surprised.

T: As though, "Well for goodness sake, did I say that?" (*Both chuckle.*)

C: Really, I don't think I've had that feeling before. I've — uh, well, this really feels like I'm saying something that, uh, *is* a part of me really. (*Pause*) Or, uh, (*quite perplexed*) it feels like I sort of have, uh, I don't know. I have a feeling of *strength*, and yet, I have a feeling of — realizing it's so sort of fearful, of fright.

T: That is, do you mean that saying something of that sort gives you at the same time a feeling of, of strength in saying it, and yet at the same time a frightened feeling of *what* you have said, is that it?

C: M-hm. I am feeling that. For instance, I'm feeling it internally now — a sort of surging up, or force or outlet. As if that's something really big and strong. And yet, uh, well at first it was almost a physical feeling of just being out alone, and sort of cut off from a — a support I had been carrying around.

T: You feel that it's something deep and strong, and surging forth, and at the same time, you just feel as though you'd cut yourself loose from any support when you say it.

C: M-hm. Maybe that's — I don't know — it's a disturbance of a kind of pattern I've been carrying around, I think.

T: It sort of shakes a rather significant pattern, jars it loose.

C: M-hm. (*Pause, then cautiously, but with conviction*) I, I think — I don't know, but I have the feeling that then I am going to begin to *do* more things that I know I should do. . . . There are so many things that I need to do. It seems in so many avenues of my living I have to work out new ways of behavior, but — maybe — I can see myself doing a little better in some things

I hope that this illustration gives some sense of the strength which is experienced in being a unique person, responsible for oneself, and also the uneasiness that accompanies this assumption of responsibility. To recognize that "I am the one who chooses" and "I am the one who determines the value of an experience for me" is both an invigorating and a frightening realization.

WILLINGNESS TO BE A PROCESS

I should like to point out one final characteristic of these individuals as they strive to discover and become themselves. It is that the individual seems to become more content to be a *process* rather than a *product*. When he enters the therapeutic relationship, the client is likely to wish to achieve some fixed state: he wants to reach the point where his problems are solved, or where he is effective in his work, or where his marriage is satisfactory. He tends, in the freedom of the therapeutic relationship to drop such fixed goals, and to accept a more satisfying realization that he is not a fixed entity, but a process of becoming.

One client, at the conclusion of therapy, says in rather puzzled fashion, "I haven't finished the job of integrating and reorganizing myself, but that's only confusing, not discouraging, now that I realize this is a continuing process. . . . It's exciting, sometimes upsetting, but deeply encouraging to feel yourself in action, apparently knowing where you are going even though you don't always consciously know where that is." One can see here both the expression of trust in the organism, which I have mentioned, and also the realization of self as a process. Here is a personal description of what it seems like to accept oneself as a stream of becoming, not a finished product. It means that a person is a fluid process, not a fixed and static entity; a flowing river of change, not a block of solid material; a continually changing constellation of potentialities, not a fixed quantity of traits.

Here is another statement of this same element of fluidity or existential living, "This whole train of experiencing, and the meanings that I have thus far discovered in it, seem to have launched me on a process which is both fascinating and at times a little frightening. It seems to mean letting my experiences carry me on, in a direction which appears to be forward, towards goals that I can but dimly define, as I try to understand at least the current meaning of that experience. The sensation is that of floating with a complex stream of experience, with the fascinating possibility of trying to comprehend its ever-changing complexity."

CONCLUSION

I have tried to tell you what has seemed to occur in the lives of people with whom I have had the privilege of being in a relationship as they struggled toward becoming themselves. I have endeavored to describe, as accurately as I can, the meanings which seem to be involved in this process of becoming a person. I am sure that this process is *not* one that occurs only in therapy. I am sure that I do not see it clearly or completely, since I keep changing my comprehension and understanding of it. I hope you will accept it as a current and tentative picture, not as something final.

One reason for stressing the tentative nature of what I have said is that I wish to make it clear that I am *not* saying, "This is what you should become; here is the goal for you." Rather, I am saying that these are some of the meanings I see in the experiences that my clients and I have shared. Perhaps this picture of the experience of others may illuminate or give more meaning to some of your own experience.

I have pointed out that each individual appears to be asking a double question: "Who am I?" and "How may I become myself?" I have stated that in a favorable psychological climate a process of becoming takes place; that here the individual drops one after another of the defensive masks with which he has faced life; that he experiences fully the hidden aspects of himself; that he discovers in these experiences the stranger who has been living behind these masks, the stranger who is himself. I have tried to give my picture of the characteristic attributes of the person who emerges; a person who is more open to all of the elements of his organic experience; a person who is developing a trust in his own organism as an instrument of sensitive living; a person who accepts the locus of evaluation as residing within himself; a person who is learning to live in his life as a participant in a fluid, ongoing process, in which he is continually discovering new aspects of himself in the flow of his experience. These are some of the elements which seem to me to be involved in becoming a person.

[20]

MANAGING ONESELF

by Peter F. Drucker

H ISTORY'S GREAT ACHIEVERS — A Napoleon, a daVinci, a Mozart — have always managed themselves. That, in large measure, is what makes them great achievers. But they are rare exceptions, so unusual both in their talents and their accomplishments as to be considered outside the boundaries of ordinary human existence. Now, most of us, even those of us with modest endowments, will have to learn to manage

Peter F. Drucker is the Marie Rankin Clarke Professor of Social Science and Management at Claremont Graduate University in Claremont, California. This article is an excerpt from his forthcoming book Management Challenges for the 21st Century *(HarperCollins, May 1999).*

ourselves. We will have to learn to develop ourselves. We will have to place ourselves where we can make the greatest contribution. And we will have to stay mentally alert and engaged during a 50-year working life, which means knowing how and when to change the work we do.

What Are My Strengths?

Most people think they know what they are good at. They are usually wrong. More often, people know what they are not good at – and even then more people are wrong than right. And yet, a person can perform only from strength. One cannot build performance on weaknesses, let alone on something one cannot do at all.

Throughout history, people had little need to know their strengths. A person was born into a position and a line of work: the peasant's son would also be a peasant; the artisan's daughter, an artisan's wife, and so on. But now people have choices. We need to know our strengths in order to know where we belong.

The only way to discover your strengths is through feedback analysis. Whenever you make a key decision or take a key action, write down what you expect will happen. Nine or 12 months later, compare the actual results with your expectations. I have been practicing this method for 15 to 20 years now, and every time I do it, I am surprised. The feedback analysis showed me, for instance –

To stay mentally alert and engaged during a 50-year working life, one must know how and when to change the work one does.

and to my great surprise – that I have an intuitive understanding of technical people, whether they are engineers or accountants or market researchers. It also showed me that I don't really resonate with generalists.

Feedback analysis is by no means new. It was invented sometime in the fourteenth century by an otherwise totally obscure German theologian and picked up quite independently, some 150 years later, by John Calvin and Ignatius Loyola, each of whom incorporated it into the practice of his followers. In fact, the steadfast focus on performance and results that this habit produces explains why the institu-·

tions these two men founded, the Calvinist church and the Jesuit order, came to dominate Europe within 30 years.

Practiced consistently, this simple method will show you within a fairly short period of time, maybe two or three years, where your strengths lie – and this is the most important thing to know. The method will show you what you are doing or failing to do that deprives you of the full benefits of your strengths. It will show you where you are not particularly competent. And finally, it will show you where you have no strengths and cannot perform.

Several implications for action follow from feedback analysis. First and foremost, concentrate on your strengths. Put yourself where your strengths can produce results.

Second, work on improving your strengths. Analysis will rapidly show where you need to improve skills or acquire new ones. It will also show the gaps in your knowledge – and those can usually be filled. Mathematicians are born, but everyone can learn trigonometry.

Third, discover where your intellectual arrogance is causing disabling ignorance and overcome it. Far too many people – especially people with great expertise in one area – are contemptuous of knowledge in other areas or believe that being bright is a substitute for knowledge. First-rate engineers, for instance, tend to take pride in not knowing anything about people. Human beings, they believe, are much too disorderly for the good engineering mind. Human resource professionals, by contrast, often pride themselves on their ignorance of elementary accounting or of quantitative methods altogether. But taking pride in such ignorance is self-defeating. Go to work on acquiring the skills and knowledge you need to fully realize your strengths.

It is equally essential to remedy your bad habits – the things you do or fail to do that inhibit your effectiveness and performance. Such habits will quickly show up in the feedback. For example, a planner may find that his beautiful plans fail because he does not follow through on them. Like so many brilliant people, he believes that ideas move mountains. But bulldozers move mountains; ideas show where the bulldozers should go to work. This planner will have to learn that the work does not stop when the plan is completed. He must find people to carry out the plan and explain it to them. He must adapt and change it as he puts it into action. And finally, he must decide when to stop pushing the plan.

At the same time, feedback will also reveal when the problem is a lack of manners. Manners are the lubricating oil of an organization. It is a law of nature that two moving bodies in contact with each other create friction. This is as true for human beings as it is for inanimate objects. Manners – simple things like saying "please" and "thank you" and knowing a person's name or asking after her family – enable two people to work together whether they like each other or not. Bright people, especially bright young people, often do not understand this. If analysis shows that someone's brilliant work fails again and again as soon as cooperation from others is required, it probably indicates a lack of courtesy – that is, a lack of manners.

Comparing your expectations with your results also indicates what not to do. We all have a vast number of areas in which we have no talent or skill and little chance of becoming even mediocre. In those areas a person – and especially a knowledge worker – should not take on work, jobs, and assignments. One should waste as little effort as possible on improving areas of low competence. It takes far more energy and work to improve from incompetence to mediocrity than it takes to improve from first-rate performance to excellence. And yet most people – especially most teachers and most organizations – concentrate on making incompetent performers into mediocre ones. Energy, resources, and time should go instead to making a competent person into a star performer.

How Do I Perform?

Amazingly few people know *how* they get things done. Indeed, most of us do not even know that different people work and perform differently. Too many people work in ways that are not their ways, and that almost guarantees nonperformance. For knowledge workers, How do I perform? may be an even more important question than What are my strengths?

Like one's strengths, how one performs is unique. It is a matter of personality. Whether personality be a matter of nature or nurture, it surely is formed long before a person goes to work. And how a person performs is a given, just as *what* a person is good at or not good at is a given. A person's way of performing can be slightly modified, but it is unlikely to be completely changed – and certainly not easily. Just as people achieve results by doing what they are good at, they also achieve results by work-

ing in ways that they best perform. A few common personality traits usually determine how a person performs.

Am I a reader or a listener? The first thing to know is whether you are a reader or a listener. Far too few people even know that there are readers and listeners and that people are rarely both. Even fewer know which of the two they themselves are. But some examples will show how damaging such ignorance can be.

When Dwight Eisenhower was commander in chief of the Allied forces in Europe, he was the darling of the press. His press conferences were famous

It takes far more energy to improve from incompetence to mediocrity than to improve from first-rate performance to excellence.

for their style – General Eisenhower showed total command of whatever question he was asked, and he was able to describe a situation and explain a policy in two or three beautifully polished and elegant sentences. Ten years later, the same journalists who had been his admirers held President Eisenhower in open contempt. He never addressed the questions, they complained, but rambled on endlessly about something else. And they constantly ridiculed him for butchering the King's English in incoherent and ungrammatical answers.

Eisenhower apparently did not know that he was a reader, not a listener. When he was commander in chief in Europe, his aides made sure that every question from the press was presented in writing at least half an hour before a conference was to begin. And then Eisenhower was in total command. When he became president, he succeeded two listeners, Franklin D. Roosevelt and Harry Truman. Both men knew themselves to be listeners and both enjoyed free-for-all press conferences. Eisenhower may have felt that he had to do what his two predecessors had done. As a result, he never even heard the questions journalists asked. And Eisenhower is not even an extreme case of a nonlistener.

A few years later, Lyndon Johnson destroyed his presidency, in large measure, by not knowing that he was a listener. His predecessor, John Kennedy, was a reader who had assembled a brilliant group of writers as his assistants, making sure that they wrote to him before discussing their memos in person. Johnson kept these people on his staff – and they kept on writing. He never, apparently, understood one word of what they wrote. Yet as a senator, Johnson had been superb; for parliamentarians have to be, above all, listeners.

Few listeners can be made, or can make themselves, into competent readers – and vice versa. The listener who tries to be a reader will, therefore, suffer the fate of Lyndon Johnson, whereas the reader who tries to be a listener will suffer the fate of Dwight Eisenhower. They will not perform or achieve.

How do I learn? The second thing to know about how one performs is to know how one learns. Many first-class writers – Winston Churchill is but one example – do poorly in school. They tend to remember their schooling as pure torture. Yet few of their classmates remember it the same way. They may not have enjoyed the school very much, but the worst they suffered was boredom. The explanation is that writers do not, as a rule, learn by listening and reading. They learn by writing. Because schools do not allow them to learn this way, they get poor grades.

Schools everywhere are organized on the assumption that there is only one right way to learn and that it is the same way for everybody. But to be forced to learn the way a school teaches is sheer hell for students who learn differently. Indeed, there are probably half a dozen different ways to learn.

There are people, like Churchill, who learn by writing. Some people learn by taking copious notes.

Do not try to change yourself – you are unlikely to succeed. Work to improve the way you perform.

Beethoven, for example, left behind an enormous number of sketchbooks, yet he said he never actually looked at them when he composed. Asked why he kept them, he is reported to have replied, "If I don't write it down immediately, I forget it right away. If I put it into a sketchbook, I never forget it and I never have to look it up again." Some people learn by doing. Others learn by hearing themselves talk.

A chief executive I know who converted a small and mediocre family business into the leading company in its industry was one of those people who learn by talking. He was in the habit of calling his entire senior staff into his office once a week and then talking at them for two or three hours. He would raise policy issues and argue three different positions on each one. He rarely asked his associates for comments or questions; he simply needed an audience to hear himself talk. That's how he learned. And although he is a fairly extreme case, learning through talking is by no means an unusual method. Successful trial lawyers learn the same way, as do many medical diagnosticians (and so do I).

Of all the important pieces of self-knowledge, understanding how you learn is the easiest to acquire. When I ask people, "How do you learn?" most of them know the answer. But when I ask, "Do you act on this knowledge?" few answer yes. And yet, acting on this knowledge is the key to performance; or rather, *not* acting on this knowledge condemns one to nonperformance.

How do I perform? and How do I learn? are the first questions to ask. But they are by no means the only ones. To manage yourself effectively, you also have to ask, Do I work well with people or am I a loner? And if you do work well with people, you then must ask, In what relationship?

Some people work best as subordinates. General George Patton, the great American military hero of World War II, is a prime example. Patton was America's top troop commander. Yet when he was proposed for an independent command, General George Marshall, the U.S. chief of staff – and probably the most successful picker of men in U.S. history – said, "Patton is the best subordinate the American army has ever produced, but he would be the worst commander."

Some people work best as team members. Others work best alone. Some are exceptionally talented as coaches and mentors; others are simply incompetent as mentors.

Another crucial question is, Do I produce results as a decision maker or as an adviser? A great many people perform best as advisers but cannot take the burden and pressure of making the decision. A good many other people, by contrast, need an adviser to force themselves to think; then they can make decisions and act on them with speed, self-confidence, and courage.

This is a reason, by the way, that the number two person in an organization often fails when promoted to the number one position. The top spot requires a decision maker. Strong decision makers often put somebody they trust into the number two spot as their adviser – and in that position the person is outstanding. But in the number one spot, the same person fails. He or she knows what the decision should be but cannot accept the responsibility of actually making it.

Other important questions to ask include, Do I perform well under stress or do I need a highly structured and predictable environment? Do I work best in a big organization or a small one? Few people work well in all kinds of environments. Again and again, I have seen people who were very successful in large organizations flounder miserably when they moved into smaller ones. And the reverse is equally true.

The conclusion bears repeating: do not try to change yourself – you are unlikely to succeed. But work hard to improve the way you perform. And try not to take on work you cannot perform or will only perform poorly.

What Are My Values?

To be able to manage yourself, you finally have to ask, What are my values? This is not a question of ethics. With respect to ethics, the rules are the same for everybody, and the test is a simple one. I call it the "mirror test."

In the early years of this century, the most highly respected diplomat of all the great powers was the German ambassador in London. He was clearly destined for great things – to become his country's foreign minister, at least, if not its federal chancellor. Yet in 1906 he abruptly resigned rather than preside over a dinner given by the diplomatic corps for Edward VII. The king was a notorious womanizer and made it clear what kind of dinner he wanted. The ambassador is reported to have said, "I refuse to see a pimp in the mirror in the morning when I shave."

That is the mirror test. Ethics requires that you ask yourself, What kind of person do I want to see in the mirror in the morning? What is ethical behavior in one kind of organization or situation is ethical behavior in another. But ethics are only part of a value system – especially of an organization's value system.

To work in an organization whose value system is unacceptable or incompatible with one's own condemns a person both to frustration and to nonperformance.

Consider the experience of a highly successful human resources executive whose company was acquired by a bigger organization. After the acquisition, she was promoted to do the kind of work she did best, which included selecting people for important positions. The executive deeply believed that a company should hire people for such positions from the outside only after exhausting all the inside possibilities. But her new company believed in first looking outside "to bring in fresh blood." There is something to be said for both approaches – in my experience, the proper one is to do some of both. They are, however, fundamentally incompatible – not as policies but as values. They bespeak different views of the relationship between organizations and people; different views of the responsibility of an organization to its people and their development; and different views of a person's most important contribution to an enterprise. After several years of frustration, the executive quit – at considerable financial loss. Her values and the values of the organization simply were not compatible.

Similarly, whether a pharmaceutical company tries to obtain results by making constant, small improvements or by achieving occasional, highly expensive, and risky "breakthroughs" is not primarily an economic question. The results of either strategy may be pretty much the same. At bottom, there is a conflict between a value system that sees the company's contribution in terms of helping physicians do better what they already do and a value system that is oriented toward making scientific discoveries.

Whether a business should be run for short-term results or with a focus on the long term is likewise a question of values. Financial analysts believe that businesses can be run for both simultaneously. Successful businesspeople know better. To be sure, every company has to produce short-term results. But in any conflict between short-term results and long-term growth, each company will determine its own priority. This is not primarily a disagreement about economics. It is fundamentally a value conflict regarding the function of a business and the responsibility of management.

Value conflicts are not limited to business organizations. One of the fastest-growing pastoral churches in the United States measures success by the number of new parishioners. Its leadership believes that what matters is how many newcomers join the congregation. The Good Lord will then minister to their spiritual needs or at least to the needs of a sufficient percentage. Another pastoral, evangelical church believes that what matters is people's spiritual growth. The church eases out newcomers who join but do not enter into its spiritual life.

Again, this is not a matter of numbers. At first glance, it appears that the second church grows more slowly. But it retains a far larger proportion of newcomers than the first one does. Its growth, in other words, is more solid. This is also not a theological problem, or only secondarily so. It is a prob-

MANAGING ONESELF

lem about values. In a public debate, one pastor argued, "Unless you first come to church, you will never find the gate to the Kingdom of Heaven."

"No," answered the other. "Until you first look for the gate to the Kingdom of Heaven, you don't belong in church."

Organizations, like people, have values. To be effective in an organization, a person's values must be compatible with the organization's values. They do not need to be the same, but they must be close

What one does well – even very well and successfully – may not fit with one's value system.

enough to coexist. Otherwise, the person will not only be frustrated but also will not produce results.

A person's strengths and the way that person performs rarely conflict; the two are complementary. But there is sometimes a conflict between a person's values and his or her strengths. What one does well – even very well and successfully – may not fit with one's value system. In that case, the work may not appear to be worth devoting one's life to (or even a substantial portion thereof).

If I may, allow me to interject a personal note. Many years ago, I too had to decide between my values and what I was doing successfully. I was doing very well as a young investment banker in London in the mid-1930s, and the work clearly fit my strengths. Yet I did not see myself making a contribution as an asset manager. People, I realized, were what I valued, and I saw no point in being the richest man in the cemetery. I had no money and no other job prospects. Despite the continuing Depression, I quit – and it was the right thing to do. Values, in other words, are and should be the ultimate test.

Where Do I Belong?

A small number of people know very early where they belong. Mathematicians, musicians, and cooks, for instance, are usually mathematicians, musicians, and cooks by the time they are four or five years old. Physicians usually decide on their careers in their teens, if not earlier. But most people, especially highly gifted people, do not really know where they belong until they are well past their mid-twenties. By that time, however, they should know the answers to the three questions: What are my strengths? How do I perform? and, What are my

values? And then they can and should decide where they belong.

Or rather, they should be able to decide where they do *not* belong. The person who has learned that he or she does not perform well in a big organization should have learned to say no to a position in one. The person who has learned that he or she is not a decision maker should have learned to say no to a decision-making assignment. A General Patton (who probably never learned this himself) should have learned to say no to an independent command.

Equally important, knowing the answer to these questions enables a person to say to an opportunity, an offer, or an assignment, "Yes, I will do that. But this is the way I should be doing it. This is the way it should be structured. This is the way the relationships should be. These are the kind of results you should expect from me, and in this time frame, because this is who I am."

Successful careers are not planned. They develop when people are prepared for opportunities because they know their strengths, their method of work, and their values. Knowing where one belongs can transform an ordinary person – hard-working and competent but otherwise mediocre – into an outstanding performer.

What Should I Contribute?

Throughout history, the great majority of people never had to ask the question, What should I contribute? They were told what to contribute, and their tasks were dictated either by the work itself – as it was for the peasant or artisan – or by a master or a mistress, as it was for domestic servants. And until very recently, it was taken for granted that most people were subordinates who did as they were told. Even in the 1950s and 1960s, the new knowledge workers (the so-called organization men) looked to their company's personnel department to plan their careers.

Then in the late 1960s, no one wanted to be told what to do any longer. Young men and women began to ask, What do *I* want to do? And what they heard was that the way to contribute was to "do your own thing." But this solution was as wrong as the organization men's had been. Very few of the people who believed that doing one's own thing would lead to contribution, self-fulfillment, and success achieved any of the three.

But still, there is no return to the old answer of doing what you are told or assigned to do. Knowledge workers in particular have to learn to ask a question that has not been asked before: What *should* my contribution be? To answer it, they must address three distinct elements: What does the situation require? Given my strengths, my way of performing, and my values, how can I make the greatest contribution to what needs to be done? And finally, What results have to be achieved to make a difference?

Consider the experience of a newly appointed hospital administrator. The hospital was big and prestigious, but it had been coasting on its reputation for 30 years. The new administrator decided that his contribution should be to establish a standard of excellence in one important area within two years. He chose to focus on the emergency room, which was big, visible, and sloppy. He decided that every patient who came into the ER had to be seen by a qualified nurse within 60 seconds. Within 12 months, the hospital's emergency room had become a model for all hospitals in the United States, and within another two years, the whole hospital had been transformed.

As this example suggests, it is rarely possible – or even particularly fruitful – to look too far ahead. A plan can usually cover no more than 18 months and still be reasonably clear and specific. So the question in most cases should be, Where and how can I achieve results that will make a difference within the next year and a half? The answer must balance several things. First, the results should be hard to achieve – they should require "stretching," to use the current buzzword. But also, they should be within reach. To aim at results that cannot be achieved – or that can be only under the most unlikely circumstances – is not being ambitious; it is being foolish. Second, the results should be meaningful. They should make a difference. Finally, results should be visible and, if at all possible, measurable. From this will come a course of action: what to do, where and how to start, and what goals and deadlines to set.

Responsibility for Relationships

Very few people work by themselves and achieve results by themselves – a few great artists, a few great scientists, a few great athletes. Most people work with others and are effective with other peo-

ple. That is true whether they are members of an organization or independently employed. Managing yourself requires taking responsibility for relationships. This has two parts.

The first is to accept the fact that other people are as much individuals as you yourself are. They perversely insist on behaving like human beings. This means that they too have their strengths; they too have their ways of getting things done; they too have their values. To be effective, therefore, you

Knowing where one belongs can transform an ordinary person – hardworking but otherwise mediocre – into an outstanding performer.

have to know the strengths, the performance modes, and the values of your coworkers.

That sounds obvious, but few people pay attention to it. Typical is the person who was trained to write reports in his or her first assignment because that boss was a reader. Even if the next boss is a listener, the person goes on writing reports that, invariably, produce no results. Invariably the boss will think the employee is stupid, incompetent, and lazy, and he or she will fail. But that could have been avoided if the employee had only looked at the new boss and analyzed how *this* boss performs.

Bosses are neither a title on the organization chart nor a "function." They are individuals and are entitled to do their work in the way they do it best. It is incumbent on the people who work with them to observe them, to find out how they work, and to adapt themselves to what makes their bosses most effective. This, in fact, is the secret of "managing" the boss.

The same holds true for all your coworkers. Each works his or her way, not your way. And each is entitled to work in his or her way. What matters is whether they perform and what their values are. As for how they perform – each is likely to do it differently. The first secret of effectiveness is to understand the people you work with and depend on so that you can make use of their strengths, their ways of working, and their values. Working relationships are as much based on the people as they are on the work.

The second part of relationship responsibility is taking responsibility for communication. Whenever I, or any other consultant, start to work with an organization, the first thing I hear about are all the personality conflicts. Most of these arise from the fact that people do not know what other people are doing and how they do their work, or what contribution the other people are concentrating on and what results they expect. And the reason they do not know is that they have not asked and therefore have not been told.

This failure to ask reflects human stupidity less than it reflects human history. Until recently, it was unnecessary to tell any of these things to anybody. In the medieval city, everyone in a district plied the same trade. In the countryside, everyone in a valley planted the same crop as soon as the frost was out of the ground. Even those few people who did things that were not "common" worked alone, so they did not have to tell anyone what they were doing.

Today the great majority of people work with others who have different tasks and responsibilities. The marketing vice president may have come out of sales and know everything about sales, but she knows nothing about the things she has never done – pricing, advertising, packaging, and the like. So the people who do these things must make sure that the marketing vice president understands what they are trying to do, why they are trying to do it, how they are going to do it, and what results to expect.

If the marketing vice president does not understand what these high-grade knowledge specialists

are doing, it is primarily their fault, not hers. They have not educated her. Conversely, it is the marketing vice president's responsibility to make sure that all of her coworkers understand how she looks at marketing: what her goals are, how she works, and what she expects of herself and of each one of them.

Even people who understand the importance of taking responsibility for relationships often do not communicate sufficiently with their associates. They are afraid of being thought presumptuous or inquisitive or stupid. They are wrong. Whenever someone goes to his or her associates and says, "This is what I am good at. This is how I work. These are my values. This is the contribution I plan to concentrate on and the results I should be expected to deliver," the response is always, "This is most helpful. But why didn't you tell me earlier?"

And one gets the same reaction – without exception, in my experience – if one continues by asking, "And what do I need to know about your strengths, how you perform, your values, and your proposed contribution?" In fact, knowledge workers should request this of everyone with whom they work, whether as subordinate, superior, colleague, or team member. And again, whenever this is done, the reaction is always, "Thanks for asking me. But why didn't you ask me earlier?"

Organizations are no longer built on force but on trust. The existence of trust between people does not necessarily mean that they like one another. It means that they understand one another. Taking responsibility for relationships is therefore an absolute necessity. It is a duty. Whether one is a member of the organization, a consultant to it, a supplier, or a distributor, one owes that responsibility to all one's coworkers: those whose work one depends on as well as those who depend on one's own work.

The Second Half of Your Life

When work for most people meant manual labor, there was no need to worry about the second half of your life. You simply kept on doing what you had always done. And if you were lucky enough to survive 40 years of hard work in the mill or on the railroad, you were quite happy to spend the rest of your life doing nothing. Today, however, most work is knowledge work, and knowledge workers are not "finished" after 40 years on the job, they are merely bored.

We hear a great deal of talk about the midlife crisis of the executive. It is mostly boredom. At 45, most executives have reached the peak of their business careers, and they know it. After 20 years of doing very much the same kind of work, they are very good at their jobs. But they are not learning or contributing or deriving challenge and satisfaction from the job. And yet they are still likely to face another 20 if not 25 years of work. That is why managing oneself increasingly leads one to begin a second career.

There are three ways to develop a second career. The first is actually to start one. Often this takes nothing more than moving from one kind of organization to another: the divisional controller in a large corporation, for instance, becomes the controller of a medium-sized hospital. But there are also growing numbers of people who move into different lines of work altogether: the business executive or government official who enters the ministry at 45, for instance; or the midlevel manager who leaves corporate life after 20 years to attend law school and become a small-town attorney.

We will see many more second careers undertaken by people who have achieved modest success in their first jobs. Such people have substantial skills, and they know how to work. They need a community – the house is empty with the children gone – and they need income as well. But above all, they need challenge.

The second way to prepare for the second half of your life is to develop a parallel career. Many people who are very successful in their first careers stay in the work they have been doing, either on a full-time or a part-time or consulting basis. But in addition, they create a parallel job, usually in a nonprofit organization, that takes another ten hours of work a week. They might take over the administration of their church, for instance, or the presidency of the local Girl Scouts Council. They might run the battered women's shelter, work as a children's librarian for the local public library, sit on the school board, and so on.

Finally, there are the social entrepreneurs. These are usually people who have been very successful in their first careers. They love their work, but it no longer challenges them. In many cases they keep on doing what they have been doing all along but spend less and less of their time on it. They also start another activity, usually a nonprofit. My friend Bob Buford, for example, built a very successful television company that he still runs. But he has also founded and built a successful nonprofit organization that works with Protestant churches, and he is building another to teach social entrepreneurs how to manage their own nonprofit ventures while still running their original businesses.

People who manage the second half of their lives may always be a minority. The majority may "retire on the job" and count the years until their actual retirement. But it is this minority, the men and women who see a long working-life expectancy as an opportunity both for themselves and for society, who will become leaders and models.

There is one prerequisite for managing the second half of your life: you must begin long before you enter it. When it first became clear 30 years ago that working-life expectancies were lengthening very fast, many observers (including myself) believed that retired people would increasingly become volunteers for nonprofit institutions. That has not happened. If one does not begin to volunteer before one is 40 or so, one will not volunteer once past 60.

Similarly, all the social entrepreneurs I know began to work in their chosen second enterprise long before they reached their peak in their original business. Consider the example of a successful lawyer, the legal counsel to a large corporation, who has started a venture to establish model schools in his state. He began to do volunteer legal work for the schools when he was around 35. He was elected to the school board at age 40. At age 50, when he had amassed a fortune, he started his own enterprise to build and to run model schools. He is, however, still working nearly full-time as the lead counsel in the company he helped found as a young lawyer.

There is another reason to develop a second major interest, and to develop it early. No one can expect to live very long without experiencing a serious setback in his or her life or work. There is the competent engineer who is passed over for promo-

> There is one prerequisite for managing the second half of your life: you must begin doing so long before you enter it.

tion at age 45. There is the competent college professor who realizes at age 42 that she will never get a professorship at a big university, even though she may be fully qualified for it. There are tragedies in one's family life: the breakup of one's marriage or the loss of a child. At such times, a second major interest – not just a hobby – may make all the difference. The engineer, for example, now knows that he has not been very successful in his job. But in his outside activity – as church treasurer, for example –

MANAGING ONESELF

he is a success. One's family may break up, but in that outside activity there is still a community.

In a society in which success has become so terribly important, having options will become increasingly vital. Historically, there was no such thing as "success." The overwhelming majority of people did not expect anything but to stay in their "proper station," as an old English prayer has it. The only mobility was downward mobility.

In a knowledge society, however, we expect everyone to be a success. This is clearly an impossibility. For a great many people, there is at best an absence of failure. Wherever there is success, there has to be failure. And then it is vitally important for the individual, and equally for the individual's family, to have an area in which he or she can contribute, make a difference, and be *somebody*. That means finding a second area – whether in a second career, a parallel career, or a social venture – that offers an opportunity for being a leader, for being respected, for being a success.

The challenges of managing oneself may seem obvious, if not elementary. And the answers may seem self-evident to the point of appearing naïve. But managing oneself requires new and unprecedented things from the individual, and especially from the knowledge worker. In effect, managing oneself demands that each knowledge worker think and behave like a chief executive officer. Further, the shift from manual workers who do as they are told to knowledge workers who have to manage themselves profoundly challenges social structure. Every existing society, even the most individualistic one, takes two things for granted, if only subconsciously: that organizations outlive workers, and that most people stay put.

But today the opposite is true. Knowledge workers outlive organizations, and they are mobile. The need to manage oneself is therefore creating a revolution in human affairs.   ∇

[21]

Why Should Anyone Be Led by You?

by Robert Goffee and Gareth Jones

If you want to silence a room of executives, try this small trick. Ask them, "Why would anyone want to be led by you?" We've asked just that question for the past ten years while consulting for dozens of companies in Europe and the United States. Without fail, the response is a sudden, stunned hush. All you can hear are knees knocking.

Executives have good reason to be scared. You can't do anything in business without followers, and followers in these "empowered" times are hard to find. So executives had better know what it takes to lead effectively—they must find ways to engage people and rouse their commitment to company goals. But most don't know how, and who can blame them? There's simply too much advice out there. Last year alone, more than 2,000 books on leadership were published, some of them even repackaging Moses and Shakespeare as leadership gurus.

We've yet to hear advice that tells the whole truth about leadership. Yes, everyone agrees that leaders need vision, energy, author-ity, and strategic direction. That goes without saying. But we've discovered that inspirational leaders also share four unexpected qualities:

- **They selectively show their weaknesses.** By exposing some vulnerability, they reveal their approachability and humanity.

- **They rely heavily on intuition to gauge the appropriate timing and course of their actions.** Their ability to collect and interpret soft data helps them know just when and how to act.

- **They manage employees with something we call tough empathy.** Inspirational leaders empathize passionately—and realistically—with people, and they care intensely about the work employees do.

- **They reveal their differences.** They capitalize on what's unique about themselves.

You may find yourself in a top position without these qualities, but few people will want to be led by you.

Our theory about the four essential qualities of leadership, it should be noted, is not about results per se. While many of the leaders we have studied and use as examples do in fact post superior financial returns, the focus of our research has been on leaders who excel at inspiring people—in capturing hearts, minds, and souls. This ability is not everything in business, but any experienced leader will tell you it is worth quite a lot. Indeed, great results may be impossible without it.

Our research into leadership began some 25 years ago and has followed three streams since then. First, as academics, we ransacked the prominent leadership theories of the past century to develop our own working model of effective leadership. (For more on the history of leadership thinking, see the sidebar "Leadership: A Small History of a Big Topic.") Second, as consultants, we have tested our theory with thousands of executives in workshops worldwide and through observations with dozens of clients. And third, as executives ourselves, we have vetted our theories in our own organizations.

Reveal Your Weaknesses

When leaders reveal their weaknesses, they show us who they are—warts and all. This may mean admitting that they're irritable on Monday mornings, that they are somewhat disorganized, or even rather shy. Such admissions work because people need to see leaders own up to some flaw before they participate willingly in an endeavor. Exposing a weakness establishes trust and thus helps get folks on board. Indeed, if executives try to communicate that they're perfect at everything, there will be no need for anyone to help them with anything. They won't need followers. They'll signal that they can do it all themselves.

Beyond creating trust and a collaborative atmosphere, communicating a weakness also builds solidarity between followers and leaders. Consider a senior executive we know at a global management consultancy. He agreed to give a major presentation despite being badly afflicted by physical shaking caused by a medical condition. The otherwise highly critical audience greeted this courageous display of weakness with a standing ovation. By giving the talk, he had dared to say, "I am just like you—imperfect." Sharing an imperfection is so effective because it underscores a human being's authenticity. Richard Branson, the founder of Virgin, is a brilliant businessman and a hero in the United Kingdom. (Indeed,

the Virgin brand is so linked to him personally that succession is a significant issue.) Branson is particularly effective at communicating his vulnerability. He is ill at ease and fumbles incessantly when interviewed in public. It's a weakness, but it's Richard Branson. That's what revealing a weakness is all about: showing your followers that you are genuine and approachable—human and humane.

Another advantage to exposing a weakness is that it offers a leader valuable protection. Human nature being what it is, if you don't show some weakness, then observers may invent one for you. Celebrities and politicians have always known this. Often, they deliberately give the public something to talk about, knowing full well that if they don't, the newspapers will invent something even worse. Princess Diana may have aired her eating disorder in public, but she died with her reputation intact, indeed even enhanced.

That said, the most effective leaders know that exposing a weakness must be done carefully. They own up to *selective* weaknesses. Knowing which weakness to disclose is a highly honed art. The golden rule is never to expose a weakness that will be seen as a fatal flaw—by which we mean a flaw that jeopardizes central aspects of your professional role. Consider the new finance director of a major corporation. He can't suddenly confess that he's never understood discounted cash flow. A leader should reveal only a tangential flaw—and perhaps even several of them. Paradoxically, this admission will help divert attention away from major weaknesses.

Another well-known strategy is to pick a weakness that can in some ways be considered a strength, such as being a workaholic. When leaders expose these limited flaws, people won't see much of anything and little harm will come to them. There is an important caveat, however: if the leader's vulnerability is not perceived to be genuine, he won't gain anyone's support. Instead he will open himself up to derision and scorn. One scenario we saw repeatedly in our research was one in which a CEO feigns absentmindedness to conceal his inconsistency or even dishonesty. This is a sure way to alienate followers who will remember accurately what happened or what was said.

Become a Sensor

Inspirational leaders rely heavily on their in-

Robert Goffee is a professor of organizational behavior at London Business School. **Gareth Jones** is the director of human resources and internal communications at the British Broadcasting Corporation and a former professor of organizational development at Henley Management College in Oxfordshire, England. Goffee and Jones are the founding partners of Creative Management Associates, an organizational consulting firm in London.

Leadership: A Small History of a Big Topic

People have been talking about leadership since the time of Plato. But in organizations all over the world—in dinosaur conglomerates and new-economy startups alike—the same complaint emerges: we don't have enough leadership. We have to ask ourselves, Why are we so obsessed with leadership?

One answer is that there is a crisis of belief in the modern world that has its roots in the rationalist revolution of the eighteenth century. During the Enlightenment, philosophers such as Voltaire claimed that through the application of reason alone, people could control their destiny. This marked an incredibly optimistic turn in world history. In the nineteenth century, two beliefs stemmed from this rationalist notion: a belief in progress and a belief in the perfectibility of man. This produced an even rosier world view than before. It wasn't until the end of the nineteenth century, with the writings first of Sigmund Freud and later of Max Weber, that the chinks in the armor appeared. These two thinkers destroyed Western man's belief in rationality and progress. The current quest for leadership is a direct consequence of their work.

The founder of psychoanalysis, Freud theorized that beneath the surface of the rational mind was the unconscious. He supposed that the unconscious was responsible for a fair proportion of human behavior. Weber, the leading critic of Marx and a brilliant sociologist, also explored the limits of reason. Indeed, for him, the most destructive force operating in institutions was something he called technical rationality—that is, rationality without morality.

For Weber, technical rationality was embodied in one particular organizational form—the bureaucracy. Bureaucracies, he said, were frightening not for their inefficiencies but for their efficiencies and their capacity to dehumanize people. The tragic novels of Franz Kafka bear stark testimony to the debilitating effects of bureaucracy. Even more chilling was the testimony of Hitler's lieutenant Adolf Eichmann that "I was just a good bureaucrat." Weber believed that the only power that could resist bureaucratization was charismatic leadership. But even this has a very mixed record in the twentieth century. Although there have been inspirational and transformational wartime leaders, there have also been charismatic leaders like Hitler, Stalin, and Mao Tse-tung who committed horrendous atrocities.

By the twentieth century, there was much skepticism about the power of reason and man's ability to progress continuously. Thus, for both pragmatic and philosophic reasons, an intense interest in the concept of leadership began to develop. And indeed, in the 1920s, the first serious research started. The first leadership theory—trait theory—attempted to identify the common characteristics of effective leaders. To that end, leaders were weighed and measured and subjected to a battery of psychological tests. But no one could identify what effective leaders had in common. Trait theory fell into disfavor soon after expensive studies concluded that effective leaders were either above-average height or below.

Trait theory was replaced by style theory in the 1940s, primarily in the United States. One particular style of

leadership was singled out as having the most potential. It was a hail-fellow-well-met democratic style of leadership, and thousands of American executives were sent to training courses to learn how to behave this way. There was only one drawback. The theory was essentially capturing the spirit of FDR's America—open, democratic, and meritocratic. And so when McCarthyism and the Cold War surpassed the New Deal, a completely new style was required. Suddenly, everyone was encouraged to behave like a Cold War warrior! The poor executive was completely confused.

Recent leadership thinking is dominated by contingency theory, which says that leadership is dependent on a particular situation. That's fundamentally true, but given that there are endless contingencies in life, there are endless varieties of leadership. Once again, the beleaguered executive looking for a model to help him is hopelessly lost.

For this article, we ransacked all the leadership theories to come up with the four essential leadership qualities. Like Weber, we look at leadership that is primarily antibureaucratic and charismatic. From trait theory, we derived the qualities of weaknesses and differences. Unlike the original trait theorists, however, we do not believe that all leaders have the same weaknesses; our research only showed that all leaders expose some flaws. Tough empathy grew out of style theory, which looked at different kinds of relationships between leaders and their followers. Finally, context theory set the stage for needing to know what skills to use in various circumstances.

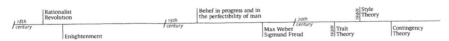

| 18th century | Rationalist Revolution | 19th century | Belief in progress and in the perfectibility of man | 20th century | | 1940s | Style Theory |
| | Enlightenment | | | | Max Weber / Sigmund Freud | 1920s Trait Theory | Contingency Theory |

stincts to know when to reveal a weakness or a difference. We call them good situation sensors, and by that we mean that they can collect and interpret soft data. They can sniff out the signals in the environment and sense what's going on without having anything spelled out for them.

Franz Humer, the CEO of Roche, is a classic sensor. He is highly accomplished in detecting shifts in climate and ambience; he can read subtle cues and sense underlying currents of opinion that elude less perceptive people. Humer says he developed this skill as a tour guide in his mid-twenties when he was responsible for groups of 100 or more. "There was no salary, only tips," he explains. "Pretty soon, I knew how to hone in on particular groups. Eventually, I could predict within 10% how much I could earn from any particular group." Indeed, great sensors can easily gauge unexpressed feelings; they can very accurately judge whether relationships are working or not. The process is complex, and as anyone who has ever encountered it knows, the results are impressive.

Consider a human resources executive we worked with in a multinational entertainment company. One day he got news of a distribution problem in Italy that had the potential to affect the company's worldwide operations. As he was thinking about how to hide the information temporarily from the Paris-based CEO while he worked on a solution, the phone rang. It was the CEO saying, "Tell me, Roberto, what the hell's going on in Milan?" The CEO was already aware that something was wrong. How? He had his networks, of course. But in large part, he was gifted at detecting information that wasn't aimed at him. He could read the silences and pick up on nonverbal cues in the organization.

Not surprisingly, the most impressive business leaders we have worked with are all very refined sensors. Ray van Schaik, the chairman of Heineken in the early 1990s, is a good example. Conservative and urbane, van Schaik's genius lay in his ability to read signals he received from colleagues and from Freddie Heineken, the third-generation family member who was "always there without being there." While some senior managers spent a lot of time second-guessing the major shareholder, van Schaik developed an ability to "just know" what Heineken wanted. This abil-

Sensing can create problems. In making fine judgments about how far they can go, leaders risk losing their followers.

ity was based on many years of working with him on the Heineken board, but it was more than that—van Schaik could read Heineken even though they had very different personalities and didn't work together directly.

Success stories like van Schaik's come with a word of warning. While leaders must be great sensors, sensing can create problems. That's because in making fine judgments about how far they can go, leaders risk losing their followers. The political situation in Northern Ireland is a powerful example. Over the past two years, several leaders—David Trimble, Gerry Adams, and Tony Blair, together with George Mitchell—have taken unprecedented initiatives toward peace. At every step of the way, these leaders had to sense how far they could go without losing their electorates. In business, think of mergers and acquisitions. Unless organizational leaders and negotiators can convince their followers in a timely way that the move is positive, value and goodwill quickly erode. This is the situation recently faced by Vodafone and France Telecom in the sale and purchase of Orange.

There is another danger associated with sensing skills. By definition, sensing a situation involves projection—that state of mind whereby you attribute your own ideas to other people and things. When a person "projects," his thoughts may interfere with the truth. Imagine a radio that picks up any number of signals, many of which are weak and distorted. Situation sensing is like that; you can't always be sure what you're hearing because of all the static. The employee who sees her boss distracted and leaps to the conclusion that she is going to be fired is a classic example. Most skills become heightened under threat, but particularly during situation sensing. Such oversensitivity in a leader can be a recipe for disaster. For this reason, sensing capability must always be framed by reality testing. Even the most gifted sensor may need to validate his perceptions with a trusted adviser or a member of his inner team.

Practice Tough Empathy

Unfortunately, there's altogether too much hype nowadays about the idea that leaders *must* show concern for their teams. There's nothing worse than seeing a manager return from the latest interpersonal-skills training program with "concern" for others. Real leaders don't need a training program to convince their employees that they care. Real leaders empathize fiercely with the people they lead. They also care intensely about the work their employees do.

Consider Alain Levy, the former CEO of Polygram. Although he often comes across as a rather aloof intellectual, Levy is well able to close the distance between himself and his followers. On one occasion, he helped some junior record executives in Australia choose singles off albums. Picking singles is a critical task in the music business: the selection of a song can make or break the album. Levy sat down with the young people and took on the work with passion. "You bloody idiots," he added his voice to the melee, "you don't know what the hell you're talking about; we always have a dance track first!" Within 24 hours, the story spread throughout the company; it was the best PR Levy ever got. "Levy really knows how to pick singles," people said. In fact, he knew how to identify with the work, and he knew how to enter his followers' world—one where strong, colorful language is the norm—to show them that he cared.

Clearly, as the above example illustrates, we do not believe that the empathy of inspira-

tional leaders is the soft kind described in so much of the management literature. On the contrary, we feel that real leaders manage through a unique approach we call tough empathy. Tough empathy means giving people what they need, not what they want. Organizations like the Marine Corps and consulting firms specialize in tough empathy. Recruits are pushed to be the best that they can be; "grow or go" is the motto. Chris Satterwaite, the CEO of Bell Pottinger Communications and a former chief executive of several ad agencies, understands what tough empathy is all about. He adeptly handles the challenges of managing creative people while making tough decisions. "If I have to, I can be ruthless," he says. "But while they're with me, I promise my people that they'll learn."

At its best, tough empathy balances respect for the individual and for the task at hand. Attending to both, however, isn't easy, especially when the business is in survival mode. At such times, caring leaders have to give selflessly to the people around them and know when to pull back. Consider a situation at Unilever at a time when it was developing Persil Power, a detergent that eventually had to be removed from the market because it destroyed clothes

---

Four Popular Myths About Leadership

In both our research and consulting work, we have seen executives who profoundly misunderstand what makes an inspirational leader. Here are four of the most common myths:

Everyone can be a leader.
Not true. Many executives don't have the self-knowledge or the authenticity necessary for leadership. And self-knowledge and authenticity are only part of the equation. Individuals must also want to be leaders, and many talented employees are not interested in shouldering that responsibility. Others prefer to devote more time to their private lives than to their work. After all, there is more to life than work, and more to work than being the boss.

Leaders deliver business results.
Not always. If results were always a matter of good leadership, picking leaders would be easy. In every case, the best strategy would be to go after people in companies with the best results. But clearly, things are not that

simple. Businesses in quasi-monopolistic industries can often do very well with competent management rather than great leadership. Equally, some well-led businesses do not necessarily produce results, particularly in the short term.

People who get to the top are leaders.
Not necessarily. One of the most persistent misperceptions is that people in leadership positions are leaders. But people who make it to the top may have done so because of political acumen, not necessarily because of true leadership quality. What's more, real leaders are found all over the organization, from the executive suite to the shop floor. By definition, leaders are simply people who have followers, and rank doesn't have much

to do with that. Effective military organizations like the U.S. Navy have long realized the importance of developing leaders throughout the organization.

Leaders are great coaches.
Rarely. A whole cottage industry has grown up around the teaching that good leaders ought to be good coaches. But that thinking assumes that a single person can both inspire the troops and impart technical skills. Of course, it's possible that great leaders may also be great coaches, but we see that only occasionally. More typical are leaders like Steve Jobs whose distinctive strengths lie in their ability to excite others through their vision rather than through their coaching talents.

that were laundered in it. Even though the product was showing early signs of trouble, CEO Niall FitzGerald stood by his troops. "That was the popular place to be, but I should not have been there," he says now. "I should have stood back, cool and detached, looked at the whole field, watched out for the customer." But caring with detachment is not easy, especially since, when done right, tough empathy is harder on you than on your employees. "Some theories of leadership make caring look effortless. It isn't," says Paulanne Mancuso, president and CEO of Calvin Klein Cosmetics. "You have to do things you don't want to do, and that's hard." It's tough to be tough.

Tough empathy also has the benefit of impelling leaders to take risks. When Greg Dyke took over at the BBC, his commercial competitors were able to spend substantially more on programs than the BBC could. Dyke quickly realized that in order to thrive in a digital world, the BBC needed to increase its expenditures. He explained this openly and directly to the staff. Once he had secured their buy-in, he

began thoroughly restructuring the organization. Although many employees were let go, he was able to maintain people's commitment. Dyke attributed his success to his tough empathy with employees: "Once you have the people with you, you can make the difficult decisions that need to be made."

One final point about tough empathy: those more apt to use it are people who really care about something. And when people care deeply about something—anything—they're more likely to show their true selves. They will not only communicate authenticity, which is the precondition for leadership, but they will show that they are doing more than just playing a role. People do not commit to executives who merely live up to the obligations of their jobs. They want more. They want someone who cares passionately about the people and the work—just as they do.

Dare to Be Different

Another quality of inspirational leaders is that they capitalize on what's unique about themselves. In fact, using these differences to great advantage is the most important quality of the four we've mentioned. The most effective leaders deliberately use differences to keep a social distance. Even as they are drawing their followers close to them, inspirational leaders signal their separateness.

Often, a leader will show his differences by having a distinctly different dress style or physical appearance, but typically he will move on to distinguish himself through qualities like imagination, loyalty, expertise, or even a handshake. Anything can be a difference, but it is important to communicate it. Most people, however, are hesitant to communicate what's unique about themselves, and it can take years for them to be fully aware of what sets them apart. This is a serious disadvantage in a world where networking is so critical and where teams need to be formed overnight.

Some leaders know exactly how to take advantage of their differences. Take Sir John Harvey-Jones, the former CEO of ICI—what was once the largest manufacturing company in the United Kingdom. When he wrote his autobiography a few years ago, a British newspaper advertised the book with a sketch of Harvey-Jones. The profile had a moustache, long hair, and a loud tie. The drawing was in black and white, but everyone knew who it was. Of

---

Can Female Leaders Be True to Themselves?

Gender differences can be used to either positive or negative effect. Women, in particular, are prone to being stereotyped according to differences—albeit usually not the ones that they would choose. Partly this is because there are fewer women than men in management positions. According to research in social psychology, if a group's representation falls below 20% in a given society, then it's going to be subjected to stereotyping whether it likes it or not. For women, this may mean being typecast as a "helper," "nurturer," or "seductress"—labels that may prevent them from defining their own differences.

In earlier research, we discovered that many women—particularly women in their fifties—try to avoid this dynamic by disappearing. They try to make themselves invisible. They wear clothes that disguise their bodies; they try to blend in with men by talking tough. That's certainly one way to avoid negative stereotyping, but the problem is that it re-

duces a woman's chances of being seen as a potential leader. She's not promoting her real self and differences.

Another response to negative stereotyping is to collectively resist it—for example, by mounting a campaign that promotes the rights, opportunities, and even the number of women in the workplace. But on a day-to-day basis, survival is often all women have time for, therefore making it impossible for them to organize themselves formally.

A third response that emerged in our research was that women play into stereotyping to personal advantage. Some women, for example, knowingly play the role of "nurturer" at work, but they do it with such wit and skill that they are able to benefit from it. The cost of such a strategy?

It furthers harmful stereotypes and continues to limit opportunities for other women to communicate their genuine personal differences.

course, John Harvey-Jones didn't get to the top of ICI because of eye-catching ties and long hair. But he was very clever in developing differences that he exploited to show that he was adventurous, entrepreneurial, and unique—he was John Harvey-Jones.

There are other people who aren't as aware of their differences but still use them to great effect. For instance, Richard Surface, former managing director of the UK-based Pearl Insurance, always walked the floor and overtook people, using his own pace as a means of communicating urgency. Still other leaders are fortunate enough to have colleagues point out their differences for them. As the BBC's Greg Dyke puts it, "My partner tells me, 'You do things instinctively that you don't understand. What I worry about is that in the process of understanding them you could lose them!'" Indeed, what emerged in our interviews is that most leaders start off not knowing what their differences are but eventually come to know— and use—them more effectively over time. Franz Humer at Roche, for instance, now realizes that he uses his emotions to evoke reactions in others.

Most of the differences we've described are those that tend to be apparent, either to the leader himself or to the colleagues around him. But there are differences that are more subtle but still have very powerful effects. For instance, David Prosser, the CEO of Legal and General, one of Europe's largest and most successful insurance companies, is an outsider. He is not a smooth city type; in fact, he comes from industrial South Wales. And though generally approachable, Prosser has a hard edge, which he uses in an understated but highly effective way. At a recent cocktail party, a rather excitable sales manager had been claiming how good the company was at cross-selling products. In a low voice, Prosser intervened: "We may be good, but we're not good enough." A chill swept through the room. What was Prosser's point? Don't feel so close you can relax! I'm the leader, and I make that call. Don't you forget it. He even uses this edge to good effect with the top team—it keeps everyone on their toes.

Inspirational leaders use separateness to motivate others to perform better. It is not that they are being Machiavellian but that they recognize instinctively that followers will push themselves if their leader is just a little

Executives can overdifferentiate themselves in their determination to express their separateness.

aloof. Leadership, after all, is not a popularity contest.

One danger, of course, is that executives can overdifferentiate themselves in their determination to express their separateness. Indeed, some leaders lose contact with their followers, and doing so is fatal. Once they create too much distance, they stop being good sensors, and they lose the ability to identify and care. That's what appeared to happen during Robert Horton's tenure as chairman and CEO of BP during the early 1990s. Horton's conspicuous display of his considerable—indeed, daunting—intelligence sometimes led others to see him as arrogant and self-aggrandizing. That resulted in overdifferentiation, and it eventually contributed to Horton's dismissal just three years after he was appointed to the position.

Leadership in Action

All four of the qualities described here are necessary for inspirational leadership, but they cannot be used mechanically. They must become or must already be part of an executive's personality. That's why the "recipe" business books—those that prescribe to the Lee Iacocca or Bill Gates way—often fail. No one can just ape another leader. So the challenge facing prospective leaders is for them to be themselves, but with more skill. That can be done by making yourself increasingly aware of the four leadership qualities we describe and by manipulating these qualities to come up with a personal style that works for you. Remember, there is no universal formula, and what's needed will vary from context to context. What's more, the results are often subtle, as the following story about Sir Richard Sykes, the highly successful chairman and CEO of Glaxo Wellcome, one of the world's leading pharmaceutical companies, illustrates.

When he was running the R&D division at Glaxo, Sykes gave a year-end review to the company's top scientists. At the end of the presentation, a researcher asked him about one of the company's new compounds, and the two men engaged in a short heated debate. The question-answer session continued for another 20 minutes, at the end of which the researcher broached the subject again. "Dr. Sykes," he began in a loud voice, "you have still failed to understand the structure of the new compound." You could feel Sykes's temper rise through the soles of his feet. He marched to the back of the room and displayed his anger before the intellectual brainpower of the entire company. "All right, lad," he yelled, "let us have a look at your notes!"

The Sykes story provides the ideal framework for discussing the four leadership qualities. To some people, Sykes's irritability could have seemed like inappropriate weakness. But in this context, his show of temper demonstrated Sykes's deep belief in the discussion about basic science—a company value. Therefore, his willingness to get angry actually cemented his credibility as a leader. He also showed that he was a very good sensor. If Sykes had exploded earlier in the meeting, he would have quashed the debate. Instead, his anger was perceived as defending the faith. The story also reveals Sykes's ability to identify with his colleagues and their work. By talking to the researcher as a fellow scientist, he was able to create an empathic bond with his audience. He really cared, though his caring was clearly tough empathy. Finally, the story indicates Sykes's own willingness to show his differences. Despite being one of the United Kingdom's most successful businessmen, he has not conformed to "standard" English. On the contrary, Sykes proudly retains his distinc-

tive northern accent. He also doesn't show the typical British reserve and decorum; he radiates passion. Like other real leaders, he acts and communicates naturally. Indeed, if we were to sum up the entire year-end review at Glaxo Wellcome, we'd say that Sykes was being himself—with great skill.

Unraveling the Mystery

As long as business is around, we will continue to pick apart the underlying ingredients of true leadership. And there will always be as many theories as there are questions. But of all the facets of leadership that one might investigate, there are few so difficult as understanding what it takes to develop leaders. The four leadership qualities are a necessary first step. Taken together, they tell executives to be authentic. As we counsel the executives we coach: "Be yourselves—more—with skill." There can be no advice more difficult to follow than that.   ▽

[22]

The Ambiguity of Leadership [1]

JEFFREY PFEFFER

University of California, Berkeley

Problems with the concept of leadership are addressed: (a) the ambiguity of its definition and measurement, (b) the issue of whether leadership affects organizational performance, and (c) the process of selecting leaders, which frequently emphasizes organizationally-irrelevant criteria. Leadership is a process of attributing causation to individual social actors. Study of leaders as symbols and of the process of attributing leadership might be productive.

Leadership has for some time been a major topic in social and organizational psychology. Underlying much of this research has been the assumption that leadership is causally related to organizational performance. Through an analysis of leadership styles, behaviors, or characteristics (depending on the theoretical perspective chosen), the argument has been made that more effective leaders can be selected or trained or, alternatively, the situation can be configured to provide for enhanced leader and organizational effectiveness.

Three problems with emphasis on leadership as a concept can be posed: (a) ambiguity in definition and measurement of the concept itself; (b) the question of whether leadership has discernible effects on organizational outcomes; and (c) the selection process in succession to leadership positions, which frequently uses organizationally irrelevant criteria and which has implications for normative theories of leadership. The argument here is that leadership is of interest primarily as a phenomenological construct. Leaders serve as symbols for representing personal causation of social events. How and why are such attributions of personal effects made? Instead of focusing on leadership and its effects, how do people make

Jeffrey Pfeffer (Ph.D. — Stanford University) is Associate Professor in the School of Business Administration and Associate Research Sociologist in the Institute of Industrial Relations at the University of California, Berkeley.

Received 12/17/75, Accepted 2/27/76; Revised 4/20/76.

1   An earlier version of this paper was presented at the conference, Leadership: Where Else Can We Go?, Center for Creative Leadership, Greensboro, North Carolina, June 30 - July 1, 1975.

Academy of Management Review-January 1977   105

inferences about and react to phenomena labelled as leadership (5)?

The Ambiguity of the Concept

While there have been many studies of leadership, the dimensions and definition of the concept remain unclear. To treat leadership as a separate concept, it must be distinguished from other social influence phenomena. Hollander and Julian (24) and Bavelas (2) did not draw distinctions between leadership and other processes of social influence. A major point of the Hollander and Julian review was that leadership research might develop more rapidly if more general theories of social influence were incorporated. Calder (5) also argued that there is no unique content to the construct of leadership that is not subsumed under other, more general models of behavior.

Kochan, Schmidt, and DeCotiis (33) attempted to distinguish leadership from related concepts of authority and social power. In leadership, influence rights are voluntarily conferred. Power does not require goal compatability — merely dependence — but leadership implies some congruence between the objectives of the leader and the led. These distinctions depend on the ability to distinguish voluntary from involuntary compliance and to assess goal compatibility. Goal statements may be retrospective inferences from action (46, 53) and problems of distinguishing voluntary from involuntary compliance also exist (32). Apparently there are few meaningful distinctions between leadership and other concepts of social influence. Thus, an understanding of the phenomena subsumed under the rubric of leadership may not require the construct of leadership (5).

While there is some agreement that leadership is related to social influence, more disagreement concerns the basic dimensions of leader behavior. Some have argued that there are two tasks to be accomplished in groups — maintenance of the group and performance of some task or activity — and thus leader behavior might

be described along these two dimensions (1, 6, 8, 25). The dimensions emerging from the Ohio State leadership studies — consideration and initiating structure — may be seen as similar to the two components of group maintenance and task accomplishment (18).

Other dimensions of leadership behavior have also been proposed (4). Day and Hamblin (10) analyzed leadership in terms of the closeness and punitiveness of the supervision. Several authors have conceptualized leadership behavior in terms of the authority and discretion subordinates are permitted (23, 36, 51). Fiedler (14) analyzed leadership in terms of the least-preferred-co-worker scale (LPC), but the meaning and behavioral attributes of this dimension of leadership behavior remain controversial.

The proliferation of dimensions is partly a function of research strategies frequently employed. Factor analysis on a large number of items describing behavior has frequently been used. This procedure tends to produce as many factors as the analyst decides to find, and permits the development of a large number of possible factor structures. The resultant factors must be named and further imprecision is introduced. Deciding on a summative concept to represent a factor is inevitably a partly subjective process.

Literature assessing the effects of leadership tends to be equivocal. Sales (45) summarized leadership literature employing the authoritarian-democratic typology and concluded that effects on performance were small and inconsistent. Reviewing the literature on consideration and initiating structure dimensions, Korman (34) reported relatively small and inconsistent results, and Kerr and Schriesheim (30) reported more consistent effects of the two dimensions. Better results apparently emerge when moderating factors are taken into account, including subordinate personalities (50), and situational characteristics (23, 51). Kerr, et al. (31) list many moderating effects grouped under the headings of subordinate considerations, supervisor considerations, and task considerations. Even if each set of considerations consisted of only one factor (which it does not), an attempt to account for the effects of leader behavior would necessitate considering four-way interactions. While social reality is complex and contingent, it seems desirable to attempt to find more parsimonious explanations for the phenomena under study.

The Effects of Leaders

Hall asked a basic question about leadership: is there any evidence on the magnitude of the effects of leadership (17, p. 248)? Surprisingly, he could find little evidence. Given the resources that have been spent studying, selecting, and training leaders, one might expect that the question of whether or not leaders matter would have been addressed earlier (12).

There are at least three reasons why it might be argued that the observed effects of leaders on organizational outcomes would be small. First, those obtaining leadership positions are selected, and perhaps only certain, limited styles of behavior may be chosen. Second, once in the leadership position, the discretion and behavior of the leader are constrained. And third, leaders can typically affect only a few of the variables that may impact organizational performance.

Homogeneity of Leaders

Persons are selected to leadership positions. As a consequence of this selection process, the range of behaviors or characteristics exhibited by leaders is reduced, making it more problematic to empirically discover an effect of leadership. There are many types of constraints on the selection process. The attraction literature suggests that there is a tendency for persons to like those they perceive as similar (3). In critical decisions such as the selections of persons for leadership positions, compatible styles of behavior probably will be chosen.

Selection of persons is also constrained by the internal system of influence in the organization. As Zald (56) noted, succession is a critical decision, affected by political influence and by environmental contingencies faced by the or-

ganization. As Thompson (49) noted, leaders may be selected for their capacity to deal with various organizational contingencies. In a study of characteristics of hospital administrators, Pfeffer and Salancik (42) found a relationship between the hospital's context and the characteristics and tenure of the administrators. To the extent that the contingencies and power distribution within the organization remain stable, the abilities and behaviors of those selected into leadership positions will also remain stable.

Finally, the selection of persons to leadership positions is affected by a self-selection process. Organizations and roles have images, providing information about their character. Persons are likely to select themselves into organizations and roles based upon their preferences for the dimensions of the organizational and role characteristics as perceived through these images. The self-selection of persons would tend to work along with organizational selection to limit the range of abilities and behaviors in a given organizational role.

Such selection processes would tend to increase homogeneity more within a single organization than across organizations. Yet many studies of leadership effect at the work group level have compared groups within a single organization. If there comes to be a widely shared, socially constructed definition of leadership behaviors or characteristics which guides the selection process, then leadership activity may come to be defined similarly in various organizations, leading to the selection of only those who match the constructed image of a leader.

Constraints on Leader Behavior

Analyses of leadership have frequently presumed that leadership style or leader behavior was an independent variable that could be selected or trained at will to conform to what research would find to be optimal. Even theorists who took a more contingent view of appropriate leadership behavior generally assumed that with proper training, appropriate behavior could be produced (51). Fiedler (13), noting how hard it

Academy of Management Review-January 1977   107

was to change behavior, suggested changing the situational characteristics rather than the person, but this was an unusual suggestion in the context of prevailing literature which suggested that leadership style was something to be strategically selected according to the variables of the particular leadership theory.

But the leader is embedded in a social system, which constrains behavior. The leader has a role set (27), in which members have expectations for appropriate behavior and persons make efforts to modify the leader's behavior. Pressures to conform to the expectations of peers, subordinates, and superiors are all relevant in determining actual behavior.

Leaders, even in high-level positions, have unilateral control over fewer resources and fewer policies than might be expected. Investment decisions may require approval of others, while hiring and promotion decisions may be accomplished by committees. Leader behavior is constrained by both the demands of others in the role set and by organizationally prescribed limitations on the sphere of activity and influence.

External Factors

Many factors that may affect organizational performance are outside a leader's control, even if he or she were to have complete discretion over major areas of organizational decisions. For example, consider the executive in a construction firm. Costs are largely determined by operation of commodities and labor markets; and demand is largely affected by interest rates, availability of mortgage money, and economic conditions which are affected by governmental policies over which the executive has little control. School superintendents have little control over birth rates and community economic development, both of which profoundly affect school system budgets. While the leader may react to contingencies as they arise, or may be a better or worse forecaster, in accounting for variation in organizational outcomes, he or she may account for relatively little compared to external factors.

Second, the leader's success or failure may be partly due to circumstances unique to the organization but still outside his or her control. Leader positions in organizations vary in terms of the strength and position of the organization. The choice of a new executive does not fundamentally alter a market and financial position that has developed over years and affects the leader's ability to make strategic changes and the likelihood that the organization will do well or poorly. Organizations have relatively enduring strengths and weaknesses. The choice of a particular leader for a particular position has limited impact on these capabilities.

Empirical Evidence

Two studies have assessed the effects of leadership changes in major positions in organizations. Lieberson and O'Connor (35) examined 167 business firms in 13 industries over a 20 year period, allocating variance in sales, profits, and profit margins to one of four sources: year (general economic conditions), industry, company effects, and effects of changes in the top executive position. They concluded that compared to other factors, administration had a limited effect on organizational outcomes.

Using a similar analytical procedure, Salancik and Pfeffer (44) examined the effects of mayors on city budgets for 30 U.S. cities. Data on expenditures by budget category were collected for 1951-1968. Variance in amount and proportion of expenditures was apportioned to the year, the city, or the mayor. The mayoral effect was relatively small, with the city accounting for most of the variance, although the mayor effect was larger for expenditure categories that were not as directly connected to important interest groups. Salancik and Pfeffer argued that the effects of the mayor were limited both by absence of power to control many of the expenditures and tax sources, and by construction of policies in response to demands from interests in the environment.

If leadership is defined as a strictly interpersonal phenomenon, the relevance of these two studies for the issue of leadership effects becomes problematic. But such a conceptualization seems unduly restrictive, and is certainly inconsistent with Selznick's (47) conceptualization of leadership as strategic management and decision making. If one cannot observe differences when leaders change, then what does it matter who occupies the positions or how they behave?

Pfeffer and Salancik (41) investigated the extent to which behaviors selected by first-line supervisors were constrained by expectations of others in their role set. Variance in task and social behaviors could be accounted for by role-set expectations, with adherence to various demands made by role-set participants a function of similarity and relative power. Lowin and Craig (37) experimentally demonstrated that leader behavior was determined by the subordinate's own behavior. Both studies illustrate that leader behaviors are responses to the demands of the social context.

The effect of leadership may vary depending upon level in the organizational hierarchy, while the appropriate activities and behaviors may also vary with organizational level (26, 40). For the most part, empirical studies of leadership have dealt with first line supervisors or leaders with relatively low organizational status (17). If leadership has any impact, it should be more evident at higher organizational levels or where there is more discretion in decisions and activities.

The Process of Selecting Leaders

Along with the suggestion that leadership may not account for much variance in organizational outcomes, it can be argued that merit or ability may not account for much variation in hiring and advancement of organizational personnel. These two ideas are related. If competence is hard to judge, or if leadership competence does not greatly affect organizational outcomes, then other, person-dependent criteria may be sufficient. Effective leadership styles may not predict career success when other variables such as social background are controlled.

Belief in the importance of leadership is frequently accompanied by belief that persons occupying leadership positions are selected and trained according to how well they can enhance the organization's performance. Belief in a leadership effect leads to development of a set of activities oriented toward enhancing leadership effectiveness. Simultaneously, persons managing their own careers are likely to place emphasis on activities and developing behaviors that will enhance their own leadership skills, assuming that such a strategy will facilitate advancement.

Research on the bases for hiring and promotion has been concentrated in examination of academic positions (e.g., 7, 19, 20). This is possibly the result of availability of relatively precise and unambiguous measures of performance, such as number of publications or citations. Evidence on criteria used in selecting and advancing personnel in industry is more indirect.

Studies have attempted to predict either the compensation or the attainment of general management positions of MBA students, using personality and other background information (21, 22, 54). There is some evidence that managerial success can be predicted by indicators of ability and motivation such as test scores and grades, but the amount of variance explained is typically quite small.

A second line of research has investigated characteristics and backgrounds of persons attaining leadership positions in major organizations in society. Domhoff (11), Mills (38), and Warner and Abbeglin (52) found a strong preponderance of persons with upper-class backgrounds occupying leadership positions. The implication of these findings is that studies of graduate success, including the success of MBA's, would explain more variance if the family background of the person were included.

A third line of inquiry uses a tracking model. The dynamic model developed is one in which access to elite universities is affected by social status (28) and, in turn, social status and attendance at elite universities affect later career outcomes (9, 43, 48, 55).

Unless one is willing to make the argument

Academy of Management Review-January 1977   109

that attendance at elite universities or coming from an upper class background is perfectly correlated with merit, the evidence suggests that succession to leadership positions is not strictly based on meritocratic criteria. Such a conclusion is consistent with the inability of studies attempting to predict the success of MBA graduates to account for much variance, even when a variety of personality and ability factors are used.

Beliefs about the bases for social mobility are important for social stability. As long as persons believe that positions are allocated on meritocratic grounds, they are more likely to be satisfied with the social order and with their position in it. This satisfaction derives from the belief that occupational position results from application of fair and reasonable criteria, and that the opportunity exists for mobility if the person improves skills and performance.

If succession to leadership positions is determined by person-based criteria such as social origins or social connections (16), then efforts to enhance managerial effectiveness with the expectation that this will lead to career success divert attention from the processes of stratification actually operating within organizations. Leadership literature has been implicitly aimed at two audiences. Organizations were told how to become more effective, and persons were told what behaviors to acquire in order to become effective, and hence, advance in their careers. The possibility that neither organizational outcomes nor career success are related to leadership behaviors leaves leadership research facing issues of relevance and importance.

The Attribution of Leadership

Kelley conceptualized the layman as:

an applied scientist, that is, as a person concerned about applying his knowledge of causal relationships in order to exercise control of his world (29, p. 2).

Reviewing a series of studies dealing with the attributional process, he concluded that persons were not only interested in understanding their world correctly, but also in controlling it.

The view here proposed is that attribution processes are to be understood not only as a means of providing the individual with a veridical view of his world, but as a means of encouraging and maintaining his effective exercise of control in that world (29, p. 22).

Controllable factors will have high salience as candidates for causal explanation, while a bias toward the more important causes may shift the attributional emphasis toward causes that are not controllable (29, p. 23). The study of attribution is a study of naive psychology — an examination of how persons make sense out of the events taking place around them.

If Kelley is correct that individuals will tend to develop attributions that give them a feeling of control, then emphasis on leadership may derive partially from a desire to believe in the effectiveness and importance of individual action, since individual action is more controllable than contextual variables. Lieberson and O'Connor (35) made essentially the same point in introducing their paper on the effects of top management changes on organizational performance. Given the desire for control and a feeling of personal effectiveness, organizational outcomes are more likely to be attributed to individual actions, regardless of their actual causes.

Leadership is attributed by observers. Social action has meaning only through a phenomenological process (46). The identification of certain organizational roles as leadership positions guides the construction of meaning in the direction of attributing effects to the actions of those positions. While Bavelas (2) argued that the functions of leadership, such as task accomplishment and group maintenance, are shared throughout the group, this fact provides no simple and potentially controllable focus for attributing causality. Rather, the identification of leadership positions provides a simpler and more readily changeable model of reality. When causality is lodged in one or a few persons rather than being a function of a complex set of interactions among all group members, changes can be made by replacing or influencing the occupant of the leadership position. Causes of organizational actions are readily identified in this simple causal structure.

Even if, empirically, leadership has little effect, and even if succession to leadership positions is not predicated on ability or performance, the belief in leadership effects and meritocratic succession provides a simple causal framework and a justification for the structure of the social collectivity. More importantly, the beliefs interpret social actions in terms that indicate potential for effective individual intervention or control. The personification of social causality serves too many uses to be easily overcome. Whether or not leader behavior actually influences performance or effectiveness, it is important because people believe it does.

One consequence of the attribution of causality to leaders and leadership is that leaders come to be symbols. Mintzberg (39), in his discussion of the roles of managers, wrote of the symbolic role, but more in terms of attendance at formal events and formally representing the organization. The symbolic role of leadership is more important than implied in such a description. The leader as a symbol provides a target for action when difficulties occur, serving as a scapegoat when things go wrong. Gamson and Scotch (15) noted that in baseball, the firing of the manager served a scapegoating purpose. One cannot fire the whole team, yet when performance is poor, something must be done. The firing of the manager conveys to the world and to the actors involved that success is the result of personal actions, and that steps can and will be taken to enhance organizational performance.

The attribution of causality to leadership may be reinforced by organizational actions, such as the inauguration process, the choice process, and providing the leader with symbols and ceremony. If leaders are chosen by using a random number table, persons are less likely to believe in their effects than if there is an elaborate search or selection process followed by an elaborate ceremony signifying the changing of control, and if the leader then has a variety of perquisites and symbols that distinguish him or

her from the rest of the organization. Construction of the importance of leadership in a given social context is the outcome of various social processes, which can be empirically examined.

Since belief in the leadership effect provides a feeling of personal control, one might argue that efforts to increase the attribution of causality to leaders would occur more when it is more necessary and more problematic to attribute causality to controllable factors. Such an argument would lead to the hypothesis that the more the *context* actually effects organizational outcomes, the more efforts will be made to ensure attribution to *leadership*. When leaders really do have effects, it is less necessary to engage in rituals indicating their effects. Such rituals are more likely when there is uncertainty and unpredictability associated with the organization's operations. This results both from the desire to feel control in uncertain situations and from the fact that in ambiguous contexts, it is easier to attribute consequences to leadership without facing possible disconfirmation.

The leader is, in part, an actor. Through statements and actions, the leader attempts to reinforce the operation of an attribution process which tends to vest causality in that position in the social structure. Successful leaders, as perceived by members of the social system, are those who can separate themselves from organizational failures and associate themselves with organizational successes. Since the meaning of action is socially constructed, this involves manipulation of symbols to reinforce the desired process of attribution. For instance, if a manager knows that business in his or her division is about to improve because of the economic cycle, the leader may, nevertheless, write recommendations and undertake actions and changes that are highly visible and that will tend to identify his or her behavior closely with the division. A manager who perceives impending failure will attempt to associate the division and its policies and decisions with others, particularly persons in higher organizational positions, and to disassociate himself or herself from the division's

Academy of Management Review–January 1977

performance, occasionally even transferring or moving to another organization.

Conclusion

The theme of this article has been that analysis of leadership and leadership processes must be contingent on the intent of the researcher. If the interest is in understanding the causality of social phenomena as reliably and accurately as possible, then the concept of leadership may be a poor place to begin. The issue of the effects of leadership is open to question. But examination of situational variables that accompany more or less leadership effect is a worthwhile task.

The more phenomenological analysis of leadership directs attention to the process by which social causality is attributed, and focuses on the distinction between causality as perceived by group members and causality as assessed by an outside observer. Leadership is associated with a set of myths reinforcing a social construction of meaning which legitimates leadership role occupants, provides belief in potential mobility for those not in leadership roles, and attributes social causality to leadership roles, thereby providing a belief in the effectiveness of individual control. In analyzing leadership, this mythology and the process by which such mythology is created and supported should be separated from analysis of leadership as a social influence process, operating within constraints.

REFERENCES

1. Bales, R.F. *Interaction Process Analysis: A Method for the Study of Small Groups* (Reading, Mass.: Addison-Wesley, 1950).
2. Bavelas, Alex. "Leadership: Man and Function," *Administrative Science Quarterly*, Vol. 4 (1960), 491-498.
3. Berscheid, Ellen, and Elaine Walster. *Interpersonal Attraction* (Reading, Mass.: Addison-Wesley, 1969).
4. Bowers, David G., and Stanley E. Seashore. "Predicting Organizational Effectiveness with a Four-Factor Theory of Leadership," *Administrative Science Quarterly*, Vol. 11 (1966), 238-263.
5. Calder, Bobby J. "An Attribution Theory of Leadership," in B. Staw and G. Salancik (Eds.), *New Directions in Organizational Behavior* (Chicago: St. Clair Press, 1976), in press.
6. Cartwright, Dorwin C., and Alvin Zander. *Group Dynamics: Research and Theory*, 3rd ed. (Evanston, Ill.: Row, Peterson, 1960).
7. Cole, Jonathan R., and Stephen Cole. *Social Stratification in Science* (Chicago: University of Chicago Press, 1973).
8. Collins, Barry E., and Harold Guetzkow. *A Social Psychology of Group Processes for Decision-Making* (New York: Wiley, 1964).
9. Collins, Randall. "Functional and Conflict Theories of Stratification," *American Sociological Review*, Vol. 36 (1971), 1002-1019.
10. Day, R. C., and R. L. Hamblin. "Some Effects of Close and Punitive Styles of Supervision," *American Journal of Sociology*, Vol. 69 (1964), 499-510.
11. Domhoff, G. William. *Who Rules America?* (Englewood Cliffs, N.J.: Prentice-Hall, 1967).

12. Dubin, Robert. "Supervision and Productivity: Empirical Findings and Theoretical Considerations," in R. Dubin, G. C. Homans, F. C. Mann, and D. C. Miller (Eds.), *Leadership and Productivity* (San Francisco: Chandler Publishing Co., 1965), pp. 1-50.
13. Fiedler, Fred E. "Engineering the Job to Fit the Manager," *Harvard Business Review*, Vol. 43 (1965), 115-122.
14. Fiedler, Fred E. *A Theory of Leadership Effectiveness* (New York: McGraw-Hill, 1967).
15. Gamson, William A., and Norman A. Scotch. "Scapegoating in Baseball," *American Journal of Sociology*, Vol. 70 (1964), 69-72.
16. Granovetter, Mark. *Getting a Job* (Cambridge, Mass.: Harvard University Press, 1974).
17. Hall, Richard H. *Organizations: Structure and Process* (Englewood Cliffs, N.J.: Prentice-Hall, 1972).
18. Halpin, A. W., and J. Winer. "A Factorial Study of the Leader Behavior Description Questionnaire," in R. M. Stogdill and A. E. Coons (Eds.), *Leader Behavior: Its Description and Measurement* (Columbus, Ohio: Bureau of Business Research, Ohio State University, 1957), pp. 39-51.
19. Hargens, L. L. "Patterns of Mobility of New Ph.D.'s Among American Academic Institutions," *Sociology of Education*, Vol. 42 (1969), 18-37.
20. Hargens, L. L., and W. O. Hagstrom. "Sponsored and Contest Mobility of American Academic Scientists," *Sociology of Education*, Vol. 40 (1967), 24-38.
21. Harrell, Thomas W. "High Earning MBA's," *Personnel Psychology*, Vol. 25 (1972), 523-530.

22. Harrell, Thomas W., and Margaret S. Harrell. "Predictors of Management Success." *Stanford University Graduate School of Business, Technical Report No. 3 to the Office of Naval Research.*

23. Heller, Frank, and Gary Yukl. "Participation, Managerial Decision-Making, and Situational Variables," *Organizational Behavior and Human Performance,* Vol. 4 (1969), 227-241.

24. Hollander, Edwin P., and James W. Julian. "Contemporary Trends in the Analysis of Leadership Processes," *Psychological Bulletin,* Vol. 71 (1969), 387-397.

25. House, Robert J. "A Path Goal Theory of Leader Effectiveness," *Administrative Science Quarterly,* Vol. 16 (1971), 321-338.

26. Hunt, J. G. "Leadership-Style Effects at Two Managerial Levels in a Simulated Organization," *Administrative Science Quarterly,* Vol. 16 (1971), 476-485.

27. Kahn, R. L., D. M. Wolfe, R. P. Quinn, and J. D. Snoek. *Organizational Stress: Studies in Role Conflict and Ambiguity* (New York: Wiley, 1964).

28. Karabel, J., and A. W. Astin. "Social Class, Academic Ability, and College 'Quality'," *Social Forces,* Vol. 53 (1975), 381-398.

29. Kelley, Harold H. *Attribution in Social Interaction* (Morristown, N.J.: General Learning Press, 1971).

30. Kerr, Steven, and Chester Schriesheim. "Consideration, Initiating Structure and Organizational Criteria—An Update of Korman's 1966 Review," *Personnel Psychology,* Vol. 27 (1974), 555-568.

31. Kerr, S., C. Schriesheim, C. J. Murphy, and R. M. Stogdill, "Toward A Contingency Theory of Leadership Based Upon the Consideration and Initiating Structure Literature," *Organizational Behavior and Human Performance,* Vol. 12 (1974), 62-82.

32. Kiesler, C., and S. Kiesler. *Conformity* (Reading, Mass.: Addison-Wesley, 1969).

33. Kochan, T. A., S. M. Schmidt, and T. A. DeCotiis. "Superior-Subordinate Relations: Leadership and Headship," *Human Relations,* Vol. 28 (1975), 279-294.

34. Korman, A. K. "Consideration, Initiating Structure, and Organizational Criteria—A Review," *Personnel Psychology,* Vol. 19 (1966), 349-362.

35. Lieberson, Stanley, and James F. O'Connor. "Leadership and Organizational Performance: A Study of Large Corporations," *American Sociological Review,* Vol. 37 (1972), 117-130.

36. Lippitt, Ronald. "An Experimental Study of the Effect of Democratic and Authoritarian Group Atmospheres," *University of Iowa Studies in Child Welfare,* Vol. 16 (1940), 43-195.

37. Lowin, A., and J. R. Craig. "The Influence of Level of Performance on Managerial Style: An Experimental Object-Lesson in the Ambiguity of Correlational Data," *Organizational Behavior and Human Performance,* Vol. 3 (1968), 440-458.

38. Mills, C. Wright. "The American Business Elite: A Collective Portrait," in C. W. Mills, *Power, Politics, and People* (New York: Oxford University Press, 1963), pp. 110-139.

39. Mintzberg, Henry. *The Nature of Managerial Work* (New York: Harper and Row, 1973).

40. Nealey, Stanley M., and Milton R. Blood. "Leadership Performance of Nursing Supervisors at Two Organizational Levels," *Journal of Applied Psychology,* Vol. 52 (1968), 414-442.

41. Pfeffer, Jeffrey, and Gerald R. Salancik. "Determinants of Supervisory Behavior: A Role Set Analysis," *Human Relations,* Vol. 28 (1975), 139-154.

42. Pfeffer, Jeffrey, and Gerald R. Salancik. "Organizational Context and the Characteristics and Tenure of Hospital Administrators," *Academy of Management Journal,* Vol. 20 (1977), in press.

43. Reed, R. H., and H. P. Miller. "Some Determinants of the Variation in Earnings for College Men," *Journal of Human Resources,* Vol. 5 (1970), 117-190.

44. Salancik, Gerald R., and Jeffrey Pfeffer. "Constraints on Administrator Discretion: The Limited Influence of Mayors on City Budgets," *Urban Affairs Quarterly,* in press.

45. Sales, Stephen M. "Supervisory Style and Productivity: Review and Theory," *Personnel Psychology,* Vol. 19 (1966), 275-286.

46. Schutz Alfred. *The Phenomenology of the Social World* (Evanston, Ill.: Northwestern University Press, 1967)

47. Selznick, P. *Leadership in Administration* (Evanston, Ill.: Row, Peterson, 1957).

48. Spaeth, J. L., and A. M. Greeley. *Recent Alumni and Higher Education* (New York: McGraw-Hill, 1970).

49. Thompson, James D. *Organizations in Action* (New York: McGraw-Hill, 1967).

50. Vroom, Victor H. "Some Personality Determinants of the Effects of Participation," *Journal of Abnormal and Social Psychology,* Vol. 59 (1959), 322-327.

51. Vroom, Victor H., and Phillip W. Yetton. *Leadership and Decision-Making* (Pittsburgh: University of Pittsburgh Press, 1973).

52. Warner, W. L., and J. C. Abbeglin. *Big Business Leaders in America* (New York: Harper and Brothers, 1955).

53. Weick, Karl E. *The Social Psychology of Organizing* (Reading, Mass.: Addison-Wesley, 1969).

54. Weinstein, Alan G., and V. Srinivasan. "Predicting Managerial Success of Master of Business Administration (MBA) Graduates," *Journal of Applied Psychology,* Vol. 59 (1974), 207-212.

55. Wolfle, Dael. *The Uses of Talent* (Princeton: Princeton University Press, 1971).

56. Zald, Mayer N. "Who Shall Rule? A Political Analysis of Succession in a Large Welfare Organization," *Pacific Sociological Review,* Vol. 8 (1965), 52-60.

[23]

The nature of leadership

Richard A. Barker

ABSTRACT   Trait/characteristic theories and empirical approaches to the study of leadership have been supported by mounds of data, graphic models, and regression statistics. While there has been criticism of these mainstream approaches, there has been little in the way of metaphysical support developed for either side of the argument. This paper attempts to address the 'science' of leadership study at its most fundamental level.

KEYWORDS   ethics ▪ leadership ▪ social evolution ▪ transformative systems

Leadership studies in the past few decades have come under increasing criticism for maintaining outmoded constructs and for bearing less than scholastic integrity (Barker, 1997; Burns, 1978; Foster, 1986; Gemmill & Oakley, 1992; Rost, 1991). At a recent leadership conference, faculty members of internationally known leadership education programs involved themselves in a discussion about what to call leadership: is it an art, a study, a discipline, a theoretical construct, what? The discussion was interrupted by the dinner speaker who inadvertently answered the question by declaring that leadership is an industry. This answer may indicate something about the mounting criticism, that is, that the selling of leadership training and education has created an a priori agenda for research and conclusions about leadership. Would that the problems of leadership study were as simple as that.

Just as most English-speaking people use the word 'classical' to refer to any music associated with symphonic or chamber ensembles, most people use the word 'leadership' to refer to any activities or relationships associated

470   **Human Relations 54(4)**

with persons occupying top positions in a hierarchy. Yet the words 'classical' and 'leadership' are indicative each of a specific phenomenon. Music scholars ignore popular terminology and carefully specify and define music according to its style, to its form, to its content, and to its function, conceptually separating the experience of what is 'Classical' from what is 'Baroque' and from what is 'Romantic'. Most leadership scholars have no such clearly defined taxonomy of activities or functions, and make no serious attempt to distinguish what they are studying from popular misconceptions (Rost, 1991).

There are those who would argue that distinguishing 'charismatic leadership' from, say, 'servant leadership' has accomplished the goal of classification. But, to use the music analogy, it is the same as distinguishing one of Mozart's symphonies from one of Haydn's symphonies. They are both examples of the same Classical form with differences which do not distinguish the form from other forms. Classical is one of many forms of music organization, which can be distinguished from other sound phenomena. Leadership is one of many forms of social organization, which can be distinguished from other human behavior phenomena. The need to distinguish leadership from other forms of social organization, such as management, is roughly the same as the need to distinguish Classical music from other forms of music organization. The distinction must be made using analysis that is consistent with its experiential nature, yet sufficient to make the distinction. In short, it must be phenomenological and metaphysical, and not merely quantitative.

At the end of his massive compilation of leadership research, Bass (1990) asserted that those who bemoan the inconclusiveness of the evidence and the subsequent dearth of understanding of leadership should be quieted by the sheer volume of pages of leadership findings. Yet, nowhere in his book did Bass make a serious attempt to articulate a metaphysical foundation for leadership study. While he acknowledged the existence of other views, Bass, like so many others, relied upon the dominant paradigm to be self-evident, and to be the view of choice for the future. This reliance is the result of a vested interest in the old thinking. Could it be that leadership scholars are not really scholars, but marketing representatives, developing programs for consumption by persons with business and political ambitions? Or, are leadership scholars simply less sophisticated than their counterparts in the physical sciences?

It is possible that the concept of leadership provides a 'social defense whose central aim is to repress uncomfortable needs, emotions, and wishes that emerge when people attempt to work together' (Gemmill & Oakley, 1992: 114). Gemmill and Oakley made an excellent case for the notion that leadership is an ideology designed to support the existing social order by providing both a rationale for dysfunction and a direction in which to shift blame. Given that this is the case, there is no need for scholars to define leadership specifically. Indeed, there is incentive to avoid any precision that would explode the myth that certain individuals in a social system are entitled to a greater share of the wealth and power by virtue of their 'leadership abilities'.

However, there is a plethora of new thinking in the physical sciences and in philosophy that is challenging the historic, philosophical foundations of scientific theories. Old theories of leadership, management, and administration are contained within the Newtonian language and logical positivism of the old physical sciences that are not consistent with new ideas about the nature of reality and of life. As a result, there is a loosely coupled set of ideas and findings that indicate some fundamental transitions in our thinking about a new administrative science (Overman, 1996). These new sciences demand an examination of old assumptions, and the application of new perspectives. This paper is an attempt to distinguish the phenomenon of 'leadership' from the activities, functions, and relationships often labeled as leadership by those who have not carefully considered that there should be a distinction.

The scientific approach to understanding leadership

Scientific study is accomplished by the creation of a metaphysical canon of consistency used primarily for structuring research and for developing educational curricula to perpetuate the study (Harré, 1970; Kuhn, 1970). The canon of industrial-era leadership theories is an adaptation of the hierarchical view of the universe adopted by the early Christian Church, and presumes that leadership is all about the person at the top of the hierarchy, this person's exceptional qualities and abilities to manage the structure of the hierarchy, and the activities of this person in relation to goal achievement. This canon has been incorporated into pragmatic application of theory.

The canon of any discipline is the conceptual basis for the professional language, and is founded in specific metaphysical assumptions that are defended and perpetuated as the 'truth' or *conventional knowledge* (Harré, 1970). As with any model of science, the language used to discuss leadership consists of specific descriptive terms that are designed to regulate the discipline by copying or representing a particular paradigm – terms such as transformational leadership, servant leadership, charismatic leadership, and strategic leadership. Each of these descriptive terms perpetuates the dominant paradigm by indicating some variation of the industrial model of leadership.

472   **Human Relations 54(4)**

Social sciences have developed with many of the fundamental assumptions about reality used in the physical sciences (Harré et al., 1985). The ultimate purpose of social science is to predict behavior. To facilitate prediction, Cartesian science assumes the existence of mechanistic, deterministic, cause–effect relationships that can be replicated in equivalent circumstances because they follow immutable laws. These relationships depend for their analysis upon distinctions between subjects and objects. It makes no sense to discuss one thing causing another unless the two 'things' can be distinguished. Two 'things' are distinguished by the nature of their substance; they have distinctive properties.

The problem of studying the properties of complex and continuous social processes lies in an inevitable error made by the human mind when it contemplates conceptual elements of a continuous phenomenon rather than the whole (Tolstoy, 1952: Book 11, Chapter 1). The error is made with the assumption that each conceptual increment of the phenomenon has a beginning and an end, which necessarily separates them by a boundary. Analysis of such discrete elements fails to account for their inherent connections, and does not abide their continuous nature.

Leadership, as we experience it, is a continuous social process. But industrial leadership studies are usually conducted by isolating a single event or a bounded series of events as though this event has a definable beginning and end, and by analysing as though this element is subject to cause–effect relationships. There are two errors inherent in the studies of leadership described by Bass (1990). The first error is the assumption that an analysis of a collection of these discrete events is equivalent to an analysis of continuous leadership. The second error of this leadership study is the assumption that the actions of one person (king, CEO, advocate, etc.) are the equivalent of many individual wills and the cause of outcomes. Both these errors result directly from the application of empirical methods to the study of leadership.

Empiricism begins with a direct observation, which is to say that it begins with a human perception of a phenomenon. If an instrument is used, the properties of the phenomenon are verified by a perception of data supplied by the instrument. Observations do not exist independent of the observer (Pirsig, 1991). A direct observation is necessarily founded in a particular *value* that is experienced before the observation itself or any abstract intellectualization or analysis can begin. Some value, for example, is behind the observer's attention to the phenomenon in the first place.

To illustrate the role of values in empirical science, Pirsig (1991) used the example of a scientist sitting on a hot stove. Regardless of the scientist's philosophical persuasion, the scientist will jump off the hot stove and exclaim some oaths, thus declaring that the phenomenon has negative value. The declaration of negative value is not a metaphysical abstraction, or a subjective judgement, or a description of a subjective experience; it is a predictable, verifiable, empirical observation. In other words, the *value* is present before the 'observation' takes place. According to Pirsig, the value lies between the stove and the exclamation. The scientist's behavior is more likely caused by the value than by the stove, but in any case the reality of causation is constructed after the phenomenon occurs. Empirical observations are perceptions of value.

Substance apart from its properties cannot be proven to exist; substance is what it is experienced to be (Locke, 1947). Substance is verified through human perception of patterns of data. Pirsig suggested that we strike the term *substance* and instead use the phrase *stable pattern of value*. Rather than using properties of substance to distinguish a 'thing' like leadership from other things, one can use a pattern of value to make the same distinction and to establish the reality of the 'thing'. The essential nature of leadership can be determined through patterns of value, both stable and dynamic. Patterns of value are contained within and defined by conventional knowledge.

The role of convention in the study and practice of leadership

Conventional knowledge is the common rationality as applied to human actions within a cultural milieu (Giddens, 1987). As with all other constructs, the understanding of leadership as applied to industrial society depends upon conventional 'theories' to support its internal integrity, and to establish its truth. Mainstream leadership study is designed to establish the conventional knowledge needed by actors in this specific social system. Leadership scholars discuss The Four Is, or Transformational Leadership, or Leader–Member Exchange theory, and practitioners adopt the roles specified within these models as the correct approach to the practice of leadership.

But, conventional understanding of leadership has been systematically constructed from other conventional knowledge about social hierarchies, and about their command and control structures. This knowledge is then used to validate leadership theories without further critical analysis. The development of leadership 'truth' has been a cyclical process of using convention that has been the source of development also as the source of validation.

Mainstream leadership scholars most consistently agree upon one thing: leaders are supposed to 'motivate' followers/subordinates to accomplish organizational goals. House and Aditya (1997) summarized the history of leadership study, discussing different approaches to assessing the leader's

ability to motivate subordinates, but without addressing specific sources of
motivation. Most theories of motivation attribute that which energizes and
sustains behavior to internally experienced needs. Many leadership theories
cited by House and Aditya hold that it is the leader's job to orient and/or to
satisfy those needs in such a way as to extract the desired goal-oriented
behavior from subordinates. The assumption that leaders can manipulate
subordinate motivation, and the recommendations for accomplishing that
manipulation, probably oversimplify the whole issue of motivational forces,
but they are exemplary of conventional ideas that place the leader in control
of outcomes. The simple assertion that the leader is responsible for achieving goals is used to verify the leader's involvement in motivation.

House and Aditya did not attempt to establish a definition of leadership, but concluded with the following statement: 'A problem with current
leadership study is that it continues to focus excessively on superior–
subordinate relationships to the exclusion of several functions that leaders
perform and to the exclusion of organizational and environmental variables
that are crucial to effective leadership performance' (p. 460). While these
authors are attempting to stimulate new approaches to leadership study, in
this rather typical statement they reinforce the key elements of conventional
leadership wisdom: (a) leadership is all about the leaders and their 'functions'
in the organization, (b) leadership is the sum total of the leader's performance, and (c) performance is the result of some characteristics of the leader
vis-a-vis conditions of the environment.

The aim of industrial leadership is to serve institutional needs. Pursuant
to this aim, knowledge of institutions has been one source for the development of leadership theory. Unlike critical philosophy, critical history, or critical science, leadership theories have not generally been examined for
anything other than the extent of their contribution toward their aim. In this
way, they constitute conventional knowledge, but not a science.

The pursuit of institutional needs proceeds under the presumption that
the satisfied institution ultimately will meet individual wants and needs. Conventional experience of leadership is thought to be consistent with the degree
to which a given individual experiences the satisfaction of needs. But the
study of leadership tends to overlook the effect of the potential dichotomy
between individual needs and institutional needs. In fact, the dichotomy itself
is seen as a 'leadership challenge'. One goal for industrial leaders is to persuade 'followers' to replace their desire to pursue individual needs with the
desire to pursue institutional needs. Further, institutional 'leaders' have
slowly but surely facilitated a deterioration of an individual's ability to meet
his or her own needs independent of institutions.

Given that many leadership scholars do not define leadership (Rost,

1991), they must necessarily be relying upon conventional knowledge to assess the validity of 'leadership' activities. Those who act out 'leadership' need not fully understand the minutia of convention to be in a position to contribute to this validation. Giddens (1987) used the example of writing a check to demonstrate the possibility of acting within the boundaries and with knowledge of convention without necessarily understanding it completely. One does not need to have an elaborate understanding of the banking system to have and to use a checking account. Further, asked about conventional ideas, actors are rarely able to articulate them; we all know what money is until someone asks us to define it specifically. We all know what leadership is until someone asks us to define it specifically.

When one writes a check, one does so within the context of a complex array of concepts about what credit is, what account balance is, and so on. Those who act out leadership do so armed with an array of concepts about what work is, what justice is, what success is, what cooperation is, what goals are, what responsibility is, and so forth. If someone were to act out leadership with different concepts, such as a different cultural definition of success or of responsibility, then a different construct of leadership could be expected to govern the assessment of action.

Leadership research in its traditional form is ultimately a ponderous confirmation of conventional knowledge and little else. Whether leadership study is intended to be a marketing tool or is simply the hapless result of unscrutinized conventional dogma, its future is changing.

Conventional knowledge about leadership

In his *Handbook of leadership*, Bass (1990) organized the work on leadership study into eight sections. The first section includes various concepts, definitions, and theories of leadership. Each concept is presented, some are related to each other, but none is developed to indicate a conceptual framework or theme for the remainder of the book. There is no discussion of metaphysical foundations for leadership study or any attempt to clarify a definition. The first section gives a brief look at famous people in history, behavior of animals (pecking order and such), and sets the tone for the remainder of the book by insisting that 'leaders do make a difference' (p. 8).

The second section is devoted to personal attributes of leaders. The third considers power and legitimacy, but the consideration emphasizes the leader's skill or ability to manage power and conflict rather than presenting power and conflict as a contextual issue. The fourth is about transactional exchange, where leadership is understood as the result of exchanges of valued

476   **Human Relations 54(4)**

things and leaders are defined by their ability to bargain. The fifth is about leadership and management style, and centers upon the personal values and activities of the person in charge. The sixth discusses situational moderators, but these moderators are viewed as things that enhance or inhibit elements of a leader's style and not as a general context for leadership or social processes to develop. The seventh is about diverse groups, but it is more about individual (cultural) differences in leadership style than about what leadership might mean in different cultures. The final section is about leadership study in the future and will be discussed later.

Bass legitimized and defended conventional knowledge about the industrial paradigm of leadership. The industrial paradigm of leadership, as described by Rost (1991), is based in an obsession with the persona of kings and conquerors that can be traced at least as far back as Biblical times. Until the Age of Enlightenment, people thought that 'the anointed one' in charge was actually ordained by God. For Thomas Aquinas (1952), unquestioning obedience to those in authority was a moral obligation because God had given them power.

In the early 16th century, the church condemned Machiavelli (1514/1981) because he removed leadership from the realm of God and placed it within the sphere of human activities, thereby setting the stage for industrial theories of leadership. He had carefully examined the behavior of princes and circumstances surrounding successful and unsuccessful principalities to create a theory of leadership. Machiavelli's audacity was to suggest that common people could become princes by virtue of their abilities and through the skillful application of specific principles: the successful leader:

> . . . must have no other object or thought, nor acquire skill in anything, except war, its organization, and its discipline. The art of war is all that is expected of a ruler; and it is so useful that besides enabling hereditary princes to maintain their rule it frequently enables ordinary citizens to become rulers.
>
> (p. 87)

The essential theme of waging war is still evident in conventional leadership theory. Its order is centered about an image of a powerful, male-like leader who sits atop a hierarchical structure and who controls all outcomes that emanate from that structure. The leader's power is thought to be based in knowledge, control, and the ability to win (war). The leader's will is imposed through the direct or indirect threat of violence. In the industrial world, violence is often economic in nature, relating to the acquisition of market share, and financial and material assets.

Since the time of Machiavelli, leadership theorists have incorporated dimensions of context and of 'followers,' but for the most part they have sought an explanation of leadership as the relationship between the persona (abilities, traits, characteristics, and actions) of the 'man in charge', and the outcomes of the social milieu within which 'he' appears to operate (his governance). This presumed cause–effect relationship is the source of conventional knowledge about leadership. On the one hand, trait theories are often criticized as inadequate means for understanding leadership (Bass, 1981; Bennis, 1959; Mintzberg, 1982; Rost, 1991; Stogdill, 1948), while on the other hand leadership scholars are flailing away at mounds of traits. In one survey of the literature, Fleishman et al. (1991) listed 499 traits or dimensions of leader behavior from 65 different systems.

Kotter (1988) defined leadership as 'the process of moving a group (or groups) of people in some direction through (mostly) noncoercive means' (p. 16). Kotter acknowledged that the word *leadership* sometimes refers to people who occupy the roles where leadership by the first definition is expected. Kotter then characterized 'good' or 'effective' leadership as a process that 'moves people in a direction that is genuinely in their real long-term best interests' (p. 17). As an example of effective leadership, Kotter chose Lee Iacocca. His rationale for this choice was Iacocca's apparent role in 'an extraordinarily dramatic and very impressive turnaround' (p. 17).

Despite Kotter's use of the word *process* in his definition, he was clearly relying upon a great man doing great things to verify his construct. In addition, if effective leadership moves people toward their own best interests, then we are left to assume that the 'processes' at Chrysler during the Iacocca era mobilized organizational activities and resources toward pursuit of the best interests of all of its employees. If leadership is fundamentally non-coercive, then we can be assured that these employees cheerfully carried out their organizational assignments with vivid images, perhaps even direct experience, of their common good.

The argument against questioning such applications of conventional knowledge is similar to that used in other institutionalized disciplines: any theoretical development that does not pay homage to the narrative or empirical traditions in the field is not valid. One hundred years of leadership theory development based upon the assumption that leadership is necessarily a function of the persona of the leader cannot be summarily dismissed, so the argument goes, because this development has been the result of sincere and thoughtful effort by brilliant and capable scholars.

But the most sincere and thoughtful scholarship can be dismissed if its foundation assumptions are contradictory, poorly supported, or simply wrong. For example, several hundred years' worth of sincere scholarship was

478   **Human Relations 54(4)**

founded on the assumption that the earth was the center of the universe. Just as geocentric theory was based in the understandable but incorrect perception of the sun and stars circling the earth, leadership theory has been based in the understandable but incorrect perception of a direct cause–effect relationship between the leader's abilities, traits, actions and leadership outcomes.

When leadership is defined, the definition usually addresses the nature of the *leader*, and not the nature of *leadership*. For example, Wills (1994), after a lengthy discussion of what *leadership* is about, why *leadership* is important, and what *leadership* concerns, boldly declared 'it is time for a definition: the leader is one who mobilizes others toward a goal shared by leaders and followers' (p. 17). This definition, incidentally, was not developed further, but taken to be self-evident.

The assumption that the leader is the source of leadership also implies that the leader is defined by position in a hierarchy: 'There he discovers that Leo, whom he had known first as *servant*, was in fact the titular head of the Order, its guiding spirit, a great and noble *leader*' (Greenleaf, 1995: 19, emphasis in original). This statement about the plot of Hermann Hesse's *Journey to the East* was used by Greenleaf to illustrate how he concluded that leaders are servants first. Greenleaf suggested that Leo was a great leader because of a particular trait; he was 'by nature a servant' (p. 19). But, even when he was the servant, 'Leo was actually the leader all of the time' (p. 19). While leaders may practice humility, they are still presumed to be in charge. Attempts to refute the assumption of hierarchy only serve to confuse the issue: 'Leadership is, as you know, not a position but a job' (DePree, 1992: 7).

While, some time ago, traits were thought to be insufficient to explain leadership (Stogdill, 1948), they have made a comeback as a primary explanation of leadership (Gemmill & Oakley, 1992; Kirkpatrick & Locke, 1991). Gemmill and Oakley likened the fascination with traits to a 'ghost dance' intended to restore and to prevent disintegration of a civilization that is slipping away. Alarm about a 'lack of leadership' is a sign of increasing social despair and massive learned helplessness.

Kirkpatrick and Locke identified six traits they believe differentiate leaders from other people: drive, motivation, honesty and integrity, self-confidence, cognitive ability, and knowledge of business. The assumption behind this form of research is that people will change their personalities and world views to adopt these traits and to become successful leaders (Rost, 1993). But, as Rost pointed out, the traits and abilities that presumably identify an effective leader cannot be substantially differentiated from those that define an effective manager, or an effective person. How can we be sure these are the right traits? Do people who do not have these traits become effective leaders? What about Franklin D. Roosevelt and Mahatma Ghandi? Both these individuals have been identified by Bennis and Nanus (1985), Burns (1978), and others as successful leaders. But, were FDR's honesty and integrity substantially higher than everyone else's? Of what business did Ghandi have intimate knowledge? Further, when did scholars who identified these traits know they were measuring the traits of leaders? Did the identification of leaders take place first by virtue of position or of success, or did a comprehensive measurement of traits indicate who might be correctly evaluated as a leader?

In the first four pages of their book, in or around a section proposing a 'new theory' of leadership, Bennis and Nanus (1985) identified 22 historic figures as great leaders. Like many others, Bennis and Nanus defined leadership by defining characteristics and activities of the leader. On page 5, they stated flatly that the great man theories of leadership failed to explain leadership, but, throughout their book, they used CEOs and famous people as examples of good leadership.

Bass (1990), in the eighth section of his tome, acknowledged new paradigms in leadership thinking:

> Recent developments in the mathematics of dealing with irregularities, reversals in trends, and seemingly chaotic conditions may be applied to modeling the natural discontinuities in leader–follower relationships. The physical sciences may suggest new ways of looking at short-lived phenomena, for example, the emergence of instant leadership in a crisis followed by its equally instant disappearance. The willingness to accept two distinctive ways of dealing with the same phenomenon, as is common in wave and particle physics, may lead leadership theorists to treat simultaneously the leader's and subordinates' different rationales for what is happening. Cause-and-effect analysis may be seen as the exception to mutual interactions between leader and group outcomes.
>
> (p. 882)

Following this rather close encounter with the metaphysics of science, Bass declared 'in the new paradigm, the transformational leader moved the followers to transcend their own interests for the good of the group, organization, or society ... transformational leaders, like charismatics, attract strong feelings of identification from their subordinates' (p. 902). Bass presented this statement as the view for the 21st century. His statement of 'the new paradigm' still clings to the idea that leadership is about leaders supervising subordinates, about subordinates working hard toward institutional objectives as the primary goal for leadership, and about the leader's ability to persuade/inspire/motivate subordinates to release their own needs to work toward the interests of the leader or the institution that the leader represents.

Another golden opportunity to examine conventional knowledge of the study of leadership and to explore the new paradigm was handed to Yukl and Van Fleet (1992). In the second edition of Marvin Dunnette's *Handbook of industrial and organizational psychology*, Yukl and Van Fleet wrote the section on theory and research in leadership. They began the section with an overview of the literature, with 'an emphasis on recent trends and developments likely to dominate the field through the turn of the century' (p. 148). They acknow-ledged that 'some theorists believe that leadership is inherent in the social influ-ence processes occurring among members of a group or organization, and leadership is a collective process shared among the members' (p. 148). But they chose to adopt the opposing view 'that all groups have role specialization, including a specialized leadership role wherein one person has more influence than other members and carries out some leadership functions that cannot be shared without jeopardizing the success of the group's mission' (p. 148).

The implication of the view adopted by Yukl and Van Fleet is that the group's mission is the same as organizational objectives. If the mission were truly their own, all group members could be trusted to pursue it without jeop-ardy. While it is possible for the group to develop its own mission, little dis-cussion was devoted to that possibility. This assumption regarding the source of mission determines whether research will center on the attributes, skills, abilities, and actions of a single leader carrying out assignments, or on reci-procal influence processes and integrative functions performed by a variety of people in the organization.

Yukl and Van Fleet's response to the general criticism of scholars who do not define leadership was the following:

> Definitions are somewhat arbitrary, and controversies about the best way to define leadership usually cause confusion and animosity rather than providing new insights into the nature of the process. At this point in the development of the field, it is not necessary to resolve the con-troversy over the appropriate definition of leadership.
>
> (p. 149)

So, rather than causing confusion and animosity, the authors chose to present the 'theories' developed over the past century and the best way to validate those theories through research methodology without defining the 'thing' that is being studied. If definitions are arbitrary, it is only because they have not been developed or supported.

Despite their reluctance to cause controversy, Yukl and Van Fleet offered this as an undeveloped definition: 'Leadership is viewed as a process that includes influencing the task objectives and strategies of a group or organization, influencing people in the organization to implement the strategies and achieve the objectives, influencing group maintenance and identification, and influencing the culture of the organization' (p. 149). The authors added that they would use the terms leadership and management interchangeably throughout their discussion without reference to the various arguments that they are different 'things' to define and to study (further discussion of differences can be found in Barker, 1997). Therefore, the 'new' theory of leadership, according to Yukl and Van Fleet, is founded on the assumption that leadership is all about influencing people to perform tasks and to implement strategies to, as Rost (1991) has nicely put it, do the leader's wishes, and that leadership is the same as management. This view of leadership is conventional.

The most recent books and articles on leadership claiming to offer new perspectives generally do not show much deviation from convention. Most books with the word *leadership* in the title are either self-help books, promoting self-efficacy labeled as leadership, or pop management books that agree with Yukl and Van Fleet that leadership and management are the same thing. For example, the book *Virtual leadership*, by Kostner (1994) is a novel about a modern 'project leader' who is charged with extracting performance out of a geographically distributed work team. He is mentored by 'the most legendary multi-site leader of all time – King Arthur of Camelot' (p. 1), and achieves business success upon the advice of a medieval king. While the book has many valuable management insights, it is a paragon of feudal wisdom, and provides nothing beyond conventional thinking.

Leadership and the new science by Wheatley (1994) fulfills its promise of an application of the new science, but the application is directed toward management. The word *leadership* is rarely mentioned outside the title, much less defined.

More typical is a book edited by Shelton (1997) entitled *A new paradigm of leadership* that contains 54 sections written by different authors – some well-known leadership scholars, some practitioners. Each section is a collection of tips on how to manage organizations, and how to get employees to do what the boss wants them to do to achieve higher levels of performance. No section offers a definition of leadership.

Scholastic journal articles tend to follow the same line of conventional thinking. Sparrowe and Liden (1997) insisted that 'leaders form different types of exchange relationships with their subordinates' (p. 522). Leader–Member Exchange Theory (LMX), as exemplified in this article, is

482   **Human Relations 54(4)**

focused on the ability of the leader to extract member performance by skillful exchange of valued things. The focus of this article is on exchange behavior relative to job assignments. While leadership is not defined, leaders are
characterized as those who socialize and orient members in the ways of institutional needs.

A discussion of 'international leadership' by Peterson and Hunt (1997)
focused on international and multicultural perceptions of leaders and heroes.
While the discussion raises some important issues regarding the generalization of what is largely ethnocentric social science conducted in the US, there
is no basis presented for a definition of leadership, and leadership is assumed
to be a function of how leaders conduct themselves in different cultural settings.

Pawar and Eastman (1997) claim in the title of their article to be providing a conceptual examination of transformational leadership, but they
limit their discussion to the top level of the organization and to the CEO's
ability to create and to manage change. Leadership is not defined, but is
characterized as a mechanism for accomplishing goals: 'The transformational
leader effects organizational change through the articulation of the leader's
vision, the acceptance of the vision by followers, and the creation of a congruence between followers' self-interests and the vision' (p. 82). The successful transformational leader finds a way to convince followers to align
their self-interests and subsequent actions with organizational structure and
goals.

One approach to leadership study that initially appeared promising
was the formulation of 'democratic leadership' by Kurt Lewin (1950). Lewin
was attempting to establish a substantive distinction among authoritarian
leadership, democratic leadership, and laissez-faire management. Unfortunately, Lewin and his colleagues ended their exploration with leader style, as
a characteristic of the leader, and seem to have done more to define management than to define leadership. Subsequent exploration of the same idea has
been confounded by the need for measurable variables, even though it has
popular support by those who value democracy.

A more comprehensive explanation of democratic leadership was conducted by Gastil (1994), who adopted Lewin's central idea that democratic
leadership is the outcome of the influence of the leader's behavior on people
in a manner consistent with democratic principles. Gastil's elaboration of this
idea included the relationship between authority and leadership, the functions of democratic leadership, the distribution of leadership, the roles of
democratic followers, and the appropriate settings for democratic leadership.
Aside from the old assumptions that leadership is a function of the leader
and that democratic leadership is one of many styles that can be applied or

not by choice, there is some ancient baggage that prevents this idea from being viable as a process explanation of leadership outcomes.

Ancient Greece was the birthplace of modern administrative thinking, and specifically associated with democracy. Plato implanted the idea that democracy is dangerous because the hegemony of demos would disrupt all classes of society (Takala, 1998). Plato was certain that a class structure in society with a ruling class of philosopher-kings would be the preferable alternative. Democracy invites change that Plato felt would interfere with the structure of society and would threaten the continuity of justice. As a counter to Athenian democracy as it existed, Plato promoted the transcendental abilities of the philosopher-king, who is possessed of magical skills and of superhuman wisdom. In short, modern leadership theory, even the theory of democratic leadership, is still attempting to make a case for Plato's philosopher-king.

A different approach

The relationship between action and structure must be mitigated by, what Giddens (1982) called, *the duality of structure*. Structural properties of social systems are both medium and outcomes of the practices and activities that comprise those systems. The complex, reciprocal relationships of people and institutions, then, must be the foci of the explanation of leadership. The duality of structure ultimately connects that which constitutes the leader and that which creates outcomes in a way that cannot be explained by defining the leader.

There is a difference between what we have defined as leadership and what we experience as leadership (Rost, 1991). Burns (1978) expressed the belief that the experience of leadership is centered on a striving to satisfy our mutual wants and needs. Are these wants and needs mutual among human beings, or is the mutuality we expect between human beings and social institutions?

A new framework for leadership studies can be built upon a direct, phenomenological experience of leadership that occurs prior to the creation or adaptation of conventional knowledge. Instead of cause–effect relationships, this experience can be assessed through value preferences. As opposed to the view, for example, that leader authenticity (A) causes morale (B), one can hold the view that followers value authentic leaders. Instead of A causing B, B prefers a precondition of A; B may go in some other direction (Pirsig, 1991).

Value is understood beyond preferential relationships as the source of

484   **Human Relations 54(4)**

those relationships. The question for leadership study is *what motivates people to modify their self-interest to work collectively toward common goals?* The conventional answer is to identify the leader as the source of motivation, or, if not the source, at least the stimulus. But, motivation is thought by most motivation theorists to be internally generated by needs. So, does that mean the source of leadership is internal?

The context of leadership

Hunt (1991) purported to offer a new synthesis – an extended model – of leadership. The discussion focused upon an analysis of the context of leadership, but developed no foundation for a definition. Given the context, leadership was divided into three domains: systems leadership (top level), organizational leadership (intermediate level), and direct leadership (bottom level). The extensive analysis of 'immensely complex environmental and societal–culture/values forces facing leaders at the highest levels' (p. 27) was impressive, but did not employ a metaphysical framework sufficient to organize an understanding of that complexity. In a large sense, the discussion of the context was bounded by assumptions that the leader is the source of leadership, and that the context is an obstacle with which the leader must cope. Indeed, Chapter 6 was devoted to the individual background factors and capabilities needed by leaders to cope with contextual issues.

Contemplation of the context of leadership is confounded by the same reductionism that has confounded physical science. Physical science is thought to be understandable only if all phenomena are reduced to the same level of inquiry (Jantsch, 1980). Reductionism depends upon a spatial structure where pieces can be disassembled and then reassembled. The structure is understood when key relationships among various combinations of components or subsystems are discovered. This view assumes that micro-systems are simply sub-systems of macro-systems, and that the latter is an unchanging 'environment' of the former. In order to make sense of micro-systems, the macro-system must be static or stable. If the macro-system changes, micro-systems are disrupted. Key relationships within a micro-system cannot be influenced by change in the macro-system, or they become different relationships.

Leader-centered theories of leadership are reductionistic; the leader represents a micro-system, and the task is to explain the nature of the leader – disassembling and reassembling the leader, if you will. The 'environment' of leadership, then, is some form of social milieu, such as a society, an organization, or a small group that has specific influences upon how the leader formulates leadership. These theories depend for their integrity on stable and consistent measurements of both the macro- and micro-systems; it is presumed that relationships among system components (traits, abilities, actions, etc.) are established within a stable environment. A change in the environment will require new definitions (or at least reverification) of these relationships.

Social systems are not static systems, and are not likely to remain stable for long periods of time. To begin with, people in a large social system can influence each other if they never meet, or if they have no knowledge of each other's existence. An accounting of this form of relationship is not possible by traditional measurements of group parameters. In addition, not all properties of macro-systems necessarily follow from the properties of their sub-systems or components – it cannot be stated that outcomes in society are properties of leadership. Rather, some properties of macro-systems are the result of dynamic interactions with sub-systems; they change at the same time, and sometimes in unpredictable ways. Reductionism does not account for these dynamic interactions. Therefore, studies of social process, like leadership, must be approached upon different levels of inquiry.

Jantsch (1980) distinguished three levels of inquiry that are irreducible to each other: (a) classical or Newtonian dynamics, (b) an equilibrium-seeking systems model based in laws of thermodynamics, and (c) dissipative structures. Newtonian science operates under an assumption of purity and exclusivity – behavior can be isolated and studied without reference to other entities. It is this view of systems that has predominated leadership studies in particular, and management theory and social science in general. The universe (macro-system) and all of its sub-systems are thought to be stable, orderly, and predictable. It is presumed that control of the system or organization can be attained through the measurement of phenomena and the prediction of change. Change can be made predictable even if it is not mechanistic because it can be minimized or incrementalized through measurement and control. Leadership, within this view of change, is characterized as mechanistic, linear, predictable, and subject to definition through numeric constants. The stability of the classical system (as applied to organizations) is accomplished through the imposition of structure and standard operating procedures that are assumed to provide the organization with stability and the leader with control. Taylor (1911), Weber (1947), and others have applied the classical system to management and to theories of administration because it provides some degree of certainty.

A thermodynamic system is always evolving toward a state of equilibrium, which in turn provides the sole reference point for defining the system. The origin and extinction of an equilibrium-seeking system are determined by some degree of disruption which causes the system to change energy levels. A key concept of the thermodynamic system is *entropy*. Entropy is a complex

486   **Human Relations 54(4)**

idea that is used to explain the conservation of energy. Thermodynamic systems increase their entropy when they lose energy, or when energy becomes unavailable for work. In organizations, entropy results from disruption, and managers seek out sources of entropy for correction.

The equilibrium-seeking, or structure-preserving, organization is one in which certainty and stability are important goals, but complete stability or control is not expected because some degree of change that will result in energy loss is either unpredictable or uncontrollable. Spurts of dynamic change are thought to be contained within predictable patterns of variation. Leadership is assumed to be centered, rather than in linear control, in some form of stable or predictable oscillation. For this type of system, unpredictable change (loss of energy) is assumed to be continuous, and is met by managers with adaptation and with reorientation. Managers tend to assume that change is incremental in nature, and that adaptation or minimizing energy loss can be facilitated through sequential shifting of structure.

A dissipative (transforming or chaotic) system is defined by a 'spontaneous formation of structures in open systems which exchange energy and matter with their environment' (Jantsch, 1980: 26). There are three characteristics: (1) they are open to the environment, (2) they are far from equilibrium, and (3) they necessarily include autocatalytic steps. The dissipative system can release entropy to its environment, and can dissipate or self-energize. The 'accounting' for entropy must include the environment. The environment changes with the micro-system in a mutually influencing way. The 'structure' of a dissipative system is not a solid, tangible structure, but a process structure: what Jantsch referred to as a dynamic regime.

Technically, chaotic systems can only be defined statistically by identifying discontinuous collections of data points on a graph, called strange attractors (Kiel, 1994). The presence of strange attractors signals that the system is chaotic and not random. As applied to leadership or to theories of management and administration, chaos theory should be understood as metaphorical and not statistical. Still, the term *chaos* can be misleading. One application of chaos theory to management is deterministic, in the sense of classical and thermodynamic models. This view provides managers with answers to problems and methods for finding those answers. Another view is what Overman (1996) called *quantum administration*. The quantum view holds that reality emerges from a perception of the changing order, and that what managers do to obtain an answer will influence the nature of the answer. 'Quantum administration is a world with different foci: on energy, not matter; on becoming, not being; on coincidence, not causes; on constructivism, not determinism; and on new states of awareness and consciousness' (p. 489).

Chaos theory is the study of complex, deterministic, nonlinear, dynamic systems (Kellert, 1993). Dissipative or transforming change is very complex, very dynamic, and necessarily discontinuous. A system is transforming when the existing structures of the system dissipate and transform into new forms or structures. Within this dynamic system, there is an internal capacity to reconfigure in response to gradual or to sudden change whether it is predicted or not. This internal capacity is not necessarily correlated with any given set of consistently identifiable or measurable variables. A dissipative system continuously renews itself within a dynamic context.

Rather than seeking to preserve its structure in some form, the transforming system evolves into new modes of operation, new orders of structure, and new relationships with its environment. Reorganizing a hierarchical (organizational) structure into a new hierarchy is not necessarily a transformation. If an anthill is leveled and a new one built, the result is not a transformation but merely an adaptation to change. Two key differences that distinguish the transforming system are that this system (a) is not organized by strategic, rational thought, and (b) responds to change not as a disruptive irregularity, but as an integral element of the environment. If the ants sprouted wings and moved to the trees instead of rebuilding in the ground, the result would be a transformation.

A quick illustration of the relationship of these three levels of inquiry to leader-centered views of leadership can be made by using the analogy of a person carrying a bowl of water. In the classical system, the leader's role is to minimize the disturbance or ripples in the bowl. In order to minimize ripples, the leader will change as little as possible to maximize control. There is an implicit assumption that the leader can isolate the elements of the system, avoid outside interference and disruptive change, and maintain stability through prediction and control. A bowl of ripples is thought, within this view, to indicate an incompetent leader.

If the system is equilibrium-seeking, the leader's role then is to be reactionary and adaptive in nature – goal oriented, but driven to some extent by changing environmental demands, like a changing market or a changing technology. The equilibrium system is a deterministic system that is acknowledged to be subject to unavoidable and commonly unanticipated disturbances from outside (and perhaps from inside) the system. The person in charge must change to meet demands for action, but is still focused on stabilizing the system as much as possible because equilibrium is still considered to be the desired state of existence for the system. Here, our water carrier is moving rapidly to keep up, while being jostled from all sides, trying to minimize the amount of water lost from the bowl. An unacceptable level of loss will signal the extinction of the system, and is thought to indicate an incompetent leader.

488   **Human Relations 54(4)**

In the transforming system, the leader's role cannot be defined in advance, but emerges from the dissipative or transforming processes. The bowl of water is expelled into the air, and whatever comes down is fundamentally and structurally different from what it was before; this is transformation. In the transforming system, there cannot be any form of control, any theory of prediction, or any form of measurable constant (such as traits, structures, and so forth) as determinants of leadership. In fact, in a transforming system, whatever we experience as leadership is itself transforming as a part of the system; the macro-system changes as a part of the transformation. Therefore, it makes little sense to discuss any constant quality of the leader as the source of leadership. While chaotic systems may be known and managed by way of experience (Overman, 1996), leadership in a transforming system may not be associated with any form of deliberate control or pre-selected specific goals for outcomes. Part of understanding chaos theory is perceiving organizational phenomena within new frameworks, and using a new language to order and to communicate those perceptions.

Imagine a carnival. There are various attractions set up in a structured way, but the crowd responds to the structure of the environment by creating, dissolving, and recreating its own structure. While the structure of the attractions has influence on the crowd, its patterns are influenced by the direct application of value. From a single vantage point, the crowd appears chaotic sometimes and orderly at other times. As different attractions change activity levels, lines form and then dissipate and reform somewhere else. Taken as a whole, the crowd appears to be a mass of people milling about randomly. But careful observation will reveal groupings of people waxing and waning in what may eventually become predictable patterns of structure. This predictability is not the result of a priori, cause–effect relationships, but emerges from collected observations of the results of applied values over time. The patterns formed at any one time eventually change in form, not mechanistically but organically; they do not shift, they bloom. The people in motion are reciprocally linked to the context within which they move, and their movement can adequately be explained only by referring to the values they apply to the choices of movement they make. The values governing movement of people in the crowd are energized to some extent by qualities of the environment: displays, pitches, activity, etc.

A ready example contrasting two levels of inquiry might be found in what is commonly called *military leadership*. Wills (1994), in his discussion of military leadership, used Napoleon as an example of a military leader, and George McClellan as an example of an antitype. Wills obviously assumed that any person holding the title of *General* must necessarily be assessed as a military leader. While Napoleon was clearly a good military combat general,

McClellan did not satisfy anyone's definition of a combat general. McClellan was good at organizing the military and preparing it for combat. In fact, some historians have suggested that the success of the Army of the Potomac was due at least in part to McClellan's skill at preparation (Foote, 1958).

If any social context can be described as a linear system, military training fits that description. Military drills are very highly structured, as is military life in general. If any context can be described as a transforming system, combat can be, as any combat soldier will verify. Wills seems to have unwittingly distinguished management from a classical system perspective from what leadership might be as experienced in a transforming system. While he recognized that one differed from the other, he did not adopt a framework or a language suitable for explaining the difference. Leadership has much more to do with action based upon perceptions of emerging structure in systems where order is periodically breaking down and reforming than it does with the imposition of structure and control relative to an a priori configuration. The 'leader' has no more influence on the emerging structure than the carnival barker has on the crowd.

At this point, it is possible to make a few tentative statements about the context of leadership: (1) leadership is more likely to be associated with a transforming or chaotic system than with a classical system – leadership is not about control; (2) the context of leadership as a dissipative system is irreducible – knowing the system does not mean that its elements are known (Jantsch, 1980); (3) the context of leadership is irreversible – progressive and not repetitive (Overman, 1996); (4) the higher level order in the leadership process may be perceived only by a few individuals, and perhaps by no one; (5) leadership, like perceived order, emerges from the system; (6) micro-systems, such as organizations or leaders themselves, exchange energy with their environment and cannot be understood apart from the macro-system. Process and not structure is the vessel of leadership; chaos and complexity are not problems to be solved, they are the engines of evolution, adaptation, and renewal.

The nature of leadership

'To study the laws of history, we must completely change the subject of our observation; must leave aside kings, ministers, and generals, and study the common and infinitesimally small elements by which the masses are moved' (Tolstoy, 1952: 470). The infinitesimally small elements by which the masses are moved are their individual wills – their personal values, their needs, or more specifically their ethics. An ethic (from the Greek word *ethos*) is a foundation of values that defines one's character and provides individuals with a sense of purpose and direction. Ethics are spiritual definitions of life that, for

490   **Human Relations 54(4)**

the individual, answer the question of *my needs* or 'what is life's greatest good?' Morals (from the Latin word *mos*) are customs and behavioral standards that patronize *society's needs*, or what one should do to fulfill one's purpose and to bring about life's greatest good. This distinction between ethics and morals – between *my needs* and *society's needs* – is crucial to understanding the difference between structure and energy in social systems.

Leadership scholars have been searching for structures to predict and to control, and not for dynamic value (energy). Dynamic value in social processes is created by spontaneously varying combinations of individual values. Structures in society emerge from dynamic value, and may in turn be swallowed up again. The values of individuals influence collective values, which then reciprocate; ethics create mores, which in turn create ethics – people meeting their own needs create institutions which are supposed to meet individual needs. Dynamic change in a classical system is thought to be a deviation from normal static patterns, and becomes something to be explained and controlled. But, in a self-organizing system, unpredicted and dynamic change is the essential composition of the system.

Although dissipative systems are unpredictable, they obey rules. Specifically, the rules are established through some principle of self-organization and they create the internal consistency that differentiates chaotic systems from random behavior. The basis for evolution within these systems is a balance between generation and degeneration, and between deviation and convention. The function of a dissipative system embraces its processes as they unfold when its function is self-renewal. Leadership scholars have always assumed that a 'vision' or goal must be present first before the processes are shaped toward the achievement of the goal. Perhaps it would be more instructive to take the position that the 'vision' emerges, at least in part, out of the dynamics of the unfolding processes.

While management can be understood as an activity of building, leadership must be understood as a process of unfolding. Building has as its goal the creation of hierarchical structure from bottom to top–top to bottom. 'Unfolding, in contrast, implies the interweaving of processes which lead simultaneously to phenomena of structuration at different hierarchical levels' (Jantsch, 1980: 75). What we experience as leadership is a process that organizes discontinuous cycles of energy exchanges that extend through the social milieu.

Leadership defined

Defining leadership as a social process is certainly not a new idea. Gemmill and Oakley (1992) defined leadership as 'a process of dynamic collaboration, where individuals and organization members authorize themselves and others to interact in ways that experiment with new forms of intellectual and emotional meaning' (p. 124). This definition was offered as a remedy to the view of leadership based in the traits of the leader, which functions as a means for followers to avoid responsibility and initiative. Gemmill and Oakley used a framework of alienation and learned helplessness as a context for their discussion of leadership. While this approach has considerable merit, it can be further clarified by incorporating an understanding of context through multiple levels of inquiry.

Without belaboring points made above, there are a few key ideas that may help to establish a broad definition of leadership as a process. First, leadership is a process that is not specifically a function of the person in charge. Leadership is a function of individual wills and of individual needs, and the result of the dynamics of collective will organized to meet those various needs. Second, leadership is a process of adaptation and of evolution; it is a process of dynamic exchange and the interchanges of value. Leadership is deviation from convention. Third, leadership is a process of energy, not structure. In this way, leadership is different from management – managers pursue stability, while leadership is all about change (Barker, 1997). Leadership, then, can be defined as *a process of transformative change where the ethics of individuals are integrated into the mores of a community as a means of evolutionary social development*.

Transformative change is structural change. While this form of change is possible and desirable in organizations, there are times and situations when it is disruptive and undesirable. If there is no need for change, there is no need for leadership. Management is used to maintain stability. When individuals understand that they can pursue their own needs by joining the collective movement, this motivates them to adapt their self-interest to shared goals. The 'leader' may only symbolize that adaptation, and not necessarily become the source of it. An individual's commitment to community goals and to structure can only emanate from the individual, not from the individual's boss. The individual may be inspired by the boss, but no one works hard to make someone else rich.

It should be clear that empirical verification of the proposed definition will not be easy, if it is in fact possible. Parry (1998) made a good case for using grounded theory as a method of researching the process of leadership. Does leadership evolve as a consequence of the environment responding to its demands, or as a creator of the environment, or both? What is the purpose of leadership, and how is it entwined with the purpose of life and the adult search for meaning? Social science research often assumes purpose or goals without actually attempting to define them

492   **Human Relations 54(4)**

because they are not observable. The assessment of progress is necessarily a matter of value.

A new view of science and of empirical study must be incorporated in conjunction with the new definition. Instead of cause–effect relationships, we must look for challenge–response relationships. A great deal more thought must be devoted to the metaphysical issues of measurement: 'I'm whatever your questions turn me into. Don't you see that? It's your questions that make me who I am' (Pirsig, 1991: 220).

References

Aquinas, T. Summa theologica (Fathers of the English Dominican Province). In R.M. Hutchins (Ed.), *Great books of the Western world.* Chicago: Encyclopedia Britannica, 1952.

Barker, R.A. How can we train leaders if we do not know what leadership is? *Human Relations*, 1997, *50*(4), 343–62.

Bass, B.M. *Stogdill's handbook of leadership* (rev. ed.). New York: The Free Press, 1981.

Bass, B.M. *Bass & Stogdill's handbook of leadership* (3rd ed.). New York: The Free Press, 1990.

Bennis, W.G. Leadership theory and administrative behavior: The problem with authority. *Administrative Science Quarterly*, 1959, *4*, 259–301.

Bennis, W.G. & Nanus, B. *Leaders: The strategies for taking charge.* New York: Harper & Row, 1985.

Burns, J.M. *Leadership.* New York: Harper & Row, 1978.

DePree, M. *Leadership jazz.* New York: Dell, 1992.

Fleishman, E.A., Mumford, M.D., Zaccaro, S.J., Levin, K.Y., Korotkin, A.L. & Hein, M.B. Taxonomic efforts in the description of leadership behavior: A synthesis and functional interpretation. *The Leadership Quarterly*, 1991, *2*, 245–87.

Foote, S. *The Civil War: A narrative.* New York: Random House, 1958.

Foster, W. *The reconstruction of leadership.* Victoria: Deakin University Press, 1986.

Gastil, J. A definition and illustration of democratic leadership. *Human Relations*, 1994, *47*, 953–75.

Gemmill, G. & Oakley, J. Leadership: An alienating social myth? *Human Relations*, 1992, *45*, 113–29.

Giddens, A. *Profiles and critiques in social theory.* Berkeley, CA: University of California Press, 1982.

Giddens, A. *Social theory and modern sociology.* Stanford, CA: Stanford University Press, 1987.

Greenleaf, R.K. Servant leadership. In J.T. Wren (Ed.), *The leader's companion: Insights on leadership through the ages.* New York: The Free Press, 1995, pp. 18–23.

Harré, R. *The principles of scientific thinking.* Chicago: University of Chicago Press, 1970.

Harré, R., Clarke, D. & DeCarlo, N. *Motives and mechanisms.* London: Methuen, 1985.

House, R.J. & Aditya, R.M. The social scientific study of leadership: Quo vadis? *Leadership Quarterly*, 1997, *23*(3), 409–64.

Hunt, J.G. *Leadership: A new synthesis.* Newbury Park, CA: Sage, 1991.

Jantsch, E. *The self-organizing universe: Scientific and human implications of the emerging paradigm of evolution.* Elmsford, NY: Pergamon, 1980.

Kellert, S.H. *In the wake of chaos.* Chicago, IL: University of Chicago Press, 1993.

Kiel, L.D. *Managing chaos and complexity in government.* San Francisco, CA: Jossey-Bass, 1994.

Kirkpatrick, S.A. & Locke, E.A. Leadership: Do traits matter? *Academy of Management Executive,* 1991, *5,* 48–60.

Kostner, J. *Virtual leadership.* New York: Warner Books, 1994.

Kotter, J.P. *The leadership factor.* New York: The Free Press, 1988.

Kuhn, T.S. *The structure of scientific revolutions* (2nd ed.). Chicago, IL: University of Chicago Press, 1970.

Lewin, K. The consequences of an authoritarian and democratic leadership. In A.W. Gouldner (Ed.), *Studies in leadership.* New York: Harper & Row, 1950, pp. 409–17.

Locke, J. *An essay concerning human understanding* (Edited by R. Wilburn). New York: Dutton, 1947.

Machiavelli, N. *The prince* (Translated by G. Bull). Harmondsworth: Penguin Books, 1514/1981.

Mintzberg, H. If you're not serving Bill and Barbara, then you're not serving leadership. In J.G. Hunt, U. Sekaran and C.A. Schriesheim (Eds), *Leadership: Beyond establishment views.* Carbondale, IL: Southern Illinois University Press, 1982, pp. 239–50.

Overman, E.S. The new sciences of administration: Chaos and quantum theory. *Public Administration Review,* 1996, *56,* 487–91.

Parry, K.W. Grounded theory and social process: A new direction for leadership research. *Leadership Quarterly,* 1998, *9*(1), 85–106.

Pawar, B.S. & Eastman, K.K. The nature and implications of contextual influences on transformational leadership: A conceptual examination. *Academy of Management Review,* 1997, *22*(1), 80–109.

Peterson, M.F. & Hunt, J.G. International perspectives on international leadership. *Leadership Quarterly,* 1997, *8*(3) 203–32.

Pirsig, R.M. (1991) *Lila: An inquiry into morals.* New York: Bantam, 1991.

Rost, J.C. *Leadership for the twenty-first century.* New York: Praeger, 1991.

Rost, J.C. Leadership development in the new millennium. *The Journal of Leadership Studies,* 1993, *1*(1), 92–110.

Shelton, K. (Ed.) *A new paradigm of leadership.* Provo, UT: Executive Excellence Publishing, 1997.

Sparrowe, R.T. & Liden, R.C. Process and structure in leader–member exchange. *Academy of Management Review,* 1997, *22*(2), 522–52.

Stogdill, R.M. (1948). Personal factors associated with leadership: A survey of the literature. *Journal of Psychology,* 1948, *25,* 35–71.

Takala, T. Plato on leadership. *Journal of Business Ethics,* 1998, *17*(7), 785–98.

Taylor, F.W. *Principles of scientific management.* New York: Harper & Brothers, 1911.

Tolstoy, L. War and peace (Translated by L. Maude and A. Maude). In R.M. Hutchins (Ed.), *Great books of the Western world.* Chicago, IL: Encyclopedia Britannica, 1952.

Weber, M. *The theory of social and economic organization* (Translated by A.M. Henderson and T. Parsons). New York: The Free Press, 1947.

Wheatley, M.J. *Leadership and the new science.* San Francisco, CA: Berrett-Koehler Publishers, 1994.

Wills, G. *Certain trumpets.* New York: Simon & Schuster, 1994.

Yukl, G. & Van Fleet, D.D. Theory and research on leadership in organizations. In M.D. Dunnette and L.M. Hough (Eds), *Handbook of industrial and organizational psychology, Vol. 3* (2nd ed.). Palo Alto, CA: Consulting Psychologists Press, Inc., 1992, pp. 147–97.

Richard Barker is Associate Professor of Management at Upper Iowa University, where he teaches leadership, OB, HRM, management theory, research design, and strategic planning at graduate and undergraduate levels. Before joining the faculty at UIU, he was a member of the faculty at Marist College. Previous to that, he worked for 15 years in the aerospace industry, in the areas of personnel, industrial engineering, production, and material, as an engineer, program manager, administrator, and organizational change agent. He has published articles in the areas of leadership, organizational culture, and business ethics.
[E-mail: rbarker@dubuque.net]

Part V
Imagination

Introduction to Part V

Imagination

Dan Archer and Peter Case

Many people look to leaders to guide them through both relatively stable and turbulent times, but what forms of leadership are inspirational and help organizations and communities achieve the ideals to which they aspire? Imaginative leaders are often believed to hold the key to the dreams of those they lead. Yet is this commonly-held belief accurate? According to some of the thinkers represented in Part V of this book, imagination – like leadership itself – is not simply in the gift of senior authority figures or something to be disseminated in a top-down fashion. Often it is *dispersed* within an organization or community and stems from the interaction between individuals, whether they are charismatic and larger than life or quiet, humble unsung heroes. Imagination, we are told, comes from every direction; pushing, pulling and adapting, chameleon-like, to the environment. It comes in many varieties and sometimes hails from the most unlikely of sources. On the other hand, some writers on leadership emphasize the heroic role of the individual leader in coming up with frame-breaking, imaginative innovations. The following essays were chosen to reflect this diversity of opinion. They offer new and old, classic and contemporary, scientific and philosophical perspectives on the relationship between leadership and imagination.

We begin by exploring the role of the brain, the source of our imagination, through the work of Henry Mintzberg. Our chosen piece (see Chapter 26) contrasts the intricacies of the two hemispheres of the brain and looks at how their differing functions influence the practice of leadership. The left-hand side processes information linearly, one piece of information after another, whereas the right-hand side of the brain simultaneously processes many bits of information. The more developed side of the brain controls how we behave, think and act. The 'Eastern' philosophies, such as Zen and Yoga are linked to the intuitive right hemisphere whilst Western philosophies look at the logical intellectual left side. Mintzberg describes how formal planning is logical and sequential, following a path of known steps that have been tried and tested and are devoid of intuition, requiring only dependable and solid logic. Management, however, focuses more on intuition and complexity and less on analytical techniques. As Mintzberg puts it:

> The great powers that appear to be associated with the right hemisphere are clearly useless without the faculties of the left ... . Truly outstanding managers are no doubt the ones who can couple effectiveness processes of the right (hunch, intuition, synthesis) with effective processes of the left (articulateness, logic, analysis). (p. 424)

Imaginative leadership, by its nature, is contradictory. Leaders needs to be imaginative in their own ideas, but must put them aside in order to develop and stimulate others' problem-solving.

More often than not, a leader must look to the unknown and let their team lead them to the goal, albeit with a little encouragement and moulding along the way.

Such an approach is exemplified by Keith Grint who, in his book *The Arts of Leadership* (2000), looks at the role of followers and how leaders create an environment in which followers thrive. Our chosen extract from this book (see Chapter 24) outlines how leaders create a community and how this affects people, their emotions, their thoughts and, to some extent, their logic in order for them to identify with their community. Grint stresses how people can become constrained by their pre-existing world, customs and their 'normality' and how the leader's imagination must focus on the possibility of 'perfection' and the transcendental ideal of a 'better future'. This dimension of leadership entails creating an imaginative vision and persuading others to enact it. Thus the persuasive leader must always be seen to be striving for more and offer strategic visions that followers can readily 'buy into'. Followers will often enact the personal goal of a leader not for the furtherance of that leader's needs, but because it will further what they perceive to be their own and the wider community's interests.

Having emphasized its dispersed nature, we should also recognize that imagination sometimes favours the individual. Certain writers on leadership argue that it is only through one individual wanting to break the mould of preconceived ideas and functional organizations that creative alternatives can start to develop. In other words, this individual must challenge the taken-for-granted assumptions and collective conditioning of the organizational environment. It is only when imagination and leadership are mixed within an individual that the potential for the system to be changed through their efforts can be realized.

The importance of being able to break out from our self-imposed boundaries and learn to see the same thing in different ways in order to generate new insights is demonstrated admirably by Gareth Morgan (1993) in an appendix to his book, *Imaginization* which is reproduced here as Chapter 27. He deals with how we can metaphorically encapsulate our boundaries within our lifestyle and our culture, outlining how people are trapped by their own self-imposed boundaries created from their perspectives and assumptions. Morgan draws on examples from the Industrial Revolution and later scientific advances to illustrate how individuals sometimes have to break free from existing paradigms. How could Einstein have developed his theory of relativity had he not left old assumptions behind and dared to think for himself? How could the pioneers of the Industrial Age have been so successful had they not broken established moulds and imagined new forms of 'progress'? Morgan stresses that to grow to our full potential we must develop our skills of framing and reframing, so that we can learn to see the same situation in different ways, so that we can remain open and flexible to multiple meanings, and so that we can generate new insights and become comfortable with the paradox that the same situation can mean different things at the same time:

> Imaginization ... builds around the paradox that any given situation may have multiple dimensions and multiple meanings, which acquire significance in the context of interpretation. None of these is necessarily absolute or 'true'. (p. 442)

Many imaginative leaders would probably appear two-faced to an outsider. On the one hand, they are playing the traditional organizational game so that they can stay in the system and continue to do something with it. On the other, they are moving ahead, gaining credits and being generally outrageous. It is this constant changing of ideas and standards that sets imaginative leaders apart. Some may see them as constantly moving their goalposts and hypocritical in their beliefs; however, such leaders are often just trying to develop what they have into something better.

In his book *Adventures of Ideas*, first published in 1933, Alfred North Whitehead adopts a philosophical approach to leadership, arguing that a dynamic equilibrium must be found between organizational stability, on the one hand, and imaginative change on the other. In the extract we have chosen from this book (see Chapter 28) he describes imaginative leaders as 'special creatures' whose natural foresight is the key, based on a natural understanding of a situation. This in turn suggests that foresight is a product of insight thereby demonstrating a detailed understanding of a whole system, not just a single part. In a similar vein to Grint and Morgan, he asserts that, 'routine is the god of every social system' and that, to function, a society must be based on routine so that every organism within that system knows its place, its function and its immediate role. This order, however, has to be counterbalanced by innovation. Over 70 years ago Whitehead saw that the communities of the day had become more fluid and transitory and warned that:

> ... routine is more fundamental than understanding, that is to say, routine modified by minor flashes of short range intelligence. Indeed the notion of complete understanding controlling action is an ideal in the clouds, grotesquely at variance with practical life. (pp. 458–59)

Imaginative leaders are often the catalyst for creativity and not a creative source in themselves. Within any organization, competition, conflict and the fight for survival are often the necessary catalyst to spark off the ingenuity that lies dormant within individuals. Familiarity is the enemy. Imaginative solutions involve the emotions of humans, not just their cognition. It is the discerning ability to seek this out that makes imaginative leaders so valuable.

Finally, an essay by Iain Mangham (Chapter 25), draws together imagination and society and links it with drama. Specifically, it contrasts a scene from *Waiting for Godot* with a team development meeting for a group of senior managers, and focuses on the nature of the experiences of the respective audiences and not on the instrumental value of the performances. Particular emphasis is placed upon the concept of art as 'unconcealment' and upon the notion of imaginative and present truth. Mangham suggests that what we do and show on the outside reflects our true nature, and who we are on the inside. He offers the view that there are two types of information we send out: the things we say and the things we do. The first is what we want to offer and the second is what we have no control over. People may check our motives by matching up what we say to what we do and how image becomes everything. *Performance*, in a dramaturgical sense, is everything, and central to Mangham's perspective is the idea that theatre and our lives are very much the same:

> Dramaturgy, as a perspective on social life, has existed for several hundred years. The notion that social life resembles theatre was a cliché as early as the sixteenth century. Jacques' use of it in Shakespeare's *As You Like It* is but a confirmation of what passed for an everyday analogy then:
>
> > All the world's a stage
> > And all the men and women merely players:
> > They have their exits and their entrances:
> > And one man in his time plays many parts. (p. 401)

As editors, we find the variety of ideas and perspectives represented in the extracts and essays selected for this section energizing and helpful in thinking about the relationship between leadership and imagination. We hope and trust that you, too, will find the collection stimulating and valuable.

References

Grint, Keith (2000), *The Arts of Leadership*, Oxford: Oxford University Press.
Morgan, Gareth (1993), *Imaginization: New Mindsets of Seeing, Organizing and Managing*, London: Sage.
Whitehead, Alfred North (1933/1985), *Adventures of Ideas*, New York: Macmillan.

[24]

The Who Question:
Constructing Identity and the
Construction of Truth

KEITH GRINT

Leadership is not simply about leaders. Leadership is an essentially social phenomenon: without followers there are no leaders. What leaders must do, therefore, is construct an imaginary community that followers can feel part of. In this case the imagination of the followers is critical, because few will ever know their fellow community members well enough really to know whether they have anything in common either with them or their putative leader (Anderson 1991: 6). We can probably take this further to suggest—ironically—that imaginary communities may well be considerably stronger than 'real' communities. By this I mean, for example, that we may feel we have more in common with a community that we do not know intimately than with one that we do. Take, for instance, the problem of moving house: if I think about moving locally—within my 'real' community—I know that I should avoid living in 'that' part of town or down 'this' particular street or next door to 'them' because I *know* what kind of people live there. But if I intend to move a hundred or a thousand miles away, I am quite happy to live near anyone because I *don't know* what they are like. Thus, in my imagination, I construct my unknown destination rather more generously than I do my known destination. Paradoxically, then, when I am called to defend my national community against 'foreigners' (who have allegedly invaded a country that I had not heard of until the invasion), I again have to imagine that I have more in common with my fellow nationals than with 'the enemy'—even if my lifestyle, chances, and culture are actually much closer to those in the 'enemy' camp than in my own. It was precisely this 'objective' reality across social classes that persuaded Marx to believe that the unity between the same social classes across national boundaries was stronger than the solidarity between different social classes in the same country. Marx was wrong, and he was wrong partly because solidarity is constructed in the imagination and does not mechanically reflect the material similarity of conditions. As Anderson (1991: 7) suggests, 'regardless of the actual inequality and exploitation that may prevail in each, the nation is always conceived as a deep, horizontal comradeship'.

Leaders, then, must spend at least some of their time constructing not just followers, but a *community* of followers. Whether that community is held together by love of the leader or of the community, by hate of the 'other', by greed, or by honour is less relevant than that identity is an issue that successful leaders address. Yet few people will ever really know their leader, least of all those at a national level. As Machiavelli (1981: 56) pointed out: 'Men in general judge by their eyes rather than their hands; because everyone is in a position to watch, few are in a position to come in close touch with you. Everyone sees what you appear to be, few experience what you really are. And those few dare not gainsay the many who are backed by the majesty of the state.'

The significance of this can be seen in the public reaction to the death of Diana, Princess of Wales, in 1997. Literally millions of people around the world were touched by the events of the death and the funeral, but there cannot have been more than a few hundred people who knew her personally and only a handful would have been able to experience what she 'really' was. Her mourners had to imagine themselves into a community that knew her. Here the double meaning of 'imagined' is especially pertinent. On the one hand, the British public did indeed seem to unite in grief and the national media duly recorded—that is, *revealed*—that collective grief; through a collective leap of imagination, Britain's social, cultural, and political divisions were stripped away to reveal the bedrock consensus that holds Britain together. On the other hand, the unity also appears imaginary in the sense that the media *constructed*, rather than *revealed*, the national consensus. For example, the British Film Institute's research suggests that half the population was *not* profoundly affected by the death. In fact, 40 per cent thought the media coverage excessive, while many who were affected saw Diana's life and death as a vehicle to analyse their own personal troubles rather than one solely concerned with that of the princess (Willis and Turnock 1998: 8–9).

It is but a short distance from the imaginative construction of a community of followers to the distorting invention of a community of fanatics, and much of that distance is routed directly through the emotional underpinnings of identity and the identity of the 'other'. For example, Adolf Hitler was reluctant to engage in war with the British, not because he was particularly concerned with British military prowess—he was not—but because he regarded the British as second only to the Germans in their 'Aryan' purity. Ironically he usually referred to the British as the English but, amongst all the nationalities making up the British, the English have probably the least claim to a definitive ethnic identity. Indeed, one consequence of the wars in the twentieth century has been that the very idea of a British identity has been cast into doubt as the empire collapsed, Europe arose, and the various elements of the United Kingdom showed clear signs of imminent separation, with Scottish and Welsh devolution and some degree of independence returning to Northern Ireland. But the identity of all these groups has long

8   INTRODUCTION:THE ARTS OF LEADERSHIP

been a contested arena. Historically, linguistically, and ethnically, the component parts of the 'Celtic fringe' have little in common, other than being 'not-English'. Indeed, S. James (1999) has argued that much of the ancient history of the Celts as a discrete ethnic people is a myth, constructed for political purposes in the early eighteenth century by the Welsh patriot Edward Lhuyd. And Daniel Defoe's albeit satirical *The True-Born Englishman*, with its eighteenth-century account of the ethnically diverse origins of the English—'a mongrel half-bred race', as he describes it—casts doubt upon all those who suggest there was a time when English identity was both clear and ethnically 'pure'. The force of Defoe's dissent draws its vitriol from a denial of clear boundaries between groups, for Sahlins is surely right to suggest that 'National identity, like ethnic or communal identity, is contingent and relational: it is defined by the social and territorial boundaries drawn to distinguish the collective self and its implicit negation, the other' (Sahlins 1989: 271, quoted in Colley 1994: 5–6).

Defoe's point also reminds us that collective identity is imagined, for if to be 'English' implies having a whole raft of things in common with every other English person, then the diversity of people living in Britain needs to be transcended through what Anderson refers to as a collective leap of the imagination. In effect, because the English—or any other population—hardly know each other, they have to imagine the similarities that apparently bind them together. But, to follow Jenkins (1996: 28), to say that something is imagined does not mean that it is imaginary. In effect, identity is constructed not discovered; it is imposed upon a population rather than emerging from one; it does not reflect what is a deep essence within a people but is essentially steeped upon a people. It is not an event but a process, for 'social identities exist and are acquired, claimed and allocated within power relations. Identity is something over which struggles take place and with which strategies are advanced: it is means and end in politics . . . Social identity is a practical accomplishment, a process' (Jenkins 1996: 25). Because of this, identities tend to become relatively stable in and through conflicts over boundaries (Douglas 1966)—that is to say, they are doubly 'forged'. First, in the sense that conflict generates heat and violence, identities are often 'forged' through war—as, for instance, British and French identities were forged through their interminable wars with each other, especially in the late eighteenth and early nineteenth centuries (Colley 1994; Pears 1997).

War is a particularly powerful crucible for identity construction because it often denudes the possibilities of difference; it makes us choose between them and us, between being for us or against us. As Jabri (1996: 5) reminds us: 'To be a dissenting voice is to be an outsider . . . what would previously have been blurred social boundaries become sharpened primarily through a discursive focus upon features, both symbolic and material, which divide communities.'

A further consequence of this 'forging' is a tendency for the complete stripping of all critical faculties, such that an identity based in a balanced construction of the admirable and distasteful elements of a group becomes rendered down to an infatuation, where the group or nation can do no wrong. In effect, there is a transition from a 'warts-and-all' patriotism to a xenophobic 'engulfment' (Scheff 1994). It is not far from such an engulfment to an assumption that 'the other' is the epitome of evil whose shaming and humiliation of one's own society can be revoked only by the annihilation of that same 'other' (Cooley 1922; Lewis 1971; Elias 1989; Scheff 1994).

Secondly, they are 'forged' in the sense of being 'not a true likeness', in that national identities are superimposed upon a myriad of competing local, regional, class, religious, ethnic, status, and any other identities that pre-exist the national construction. They are also 'forged' in the sense that identities do not exist as 'facts' or as 'things'—that is, independently of people; rather they have to be reproduced by people if they are to survive, though identities, like groups, may survive irrespective of who the particular individuals are that make them persist (Barth 1969). In the latter form we might note how the recent eruptions of violence over ethnic identity (in Rwanda, Turkey, Northern Ireland, and what used to be Yugoslavia, for example) appear in one form to be manifestations of resistance against 'false' identities imposed by 'the other' (Tutsis resisting Hutu identity, Kurds resisting Turkish identity, Nationalists resisting Loyalist identity, and Croats and Bosnians resisting first Yugoslav and then Serbian identity. In 1999 the very identities of the Kosovan Albanians were removed by the destruction of their official papers by the Serbian forces.) Here we have apparently 'true' identities— that is, they reflect *essentially* different ethnic groups with historically legitimate claims to their own culture and land: the 'real' and often 'innate' conditions generate 'real' identities, that then become manifest in national stereotypes. On the other hand, the history that they proclaim is itself littered with ambiguities and imagined times: for before Belgian intervention the Tutsis and Hutus lived relatively harmoniously together; at the same time, Turks and Kurds fought together under the same banner of the Ottoman Empire; while Irish history is a veritable jumble of eras when different groups at various times have either consorted with each other or attempted to eliminate each other (Sadowski 1998). In ex-Yugoslavia, Croat and Serb intermarriage was quite common before the break-up of the federal state, and the power of that state to 'suppress' the 'simmering' pot of ethnic violence appears to have been much exaggerated. Kosovo's territory is as disputed as its ethnic identity, for it has been ruled, in sequence, by Bulgarians, Byzantines, Serbs, Ottomans, Austrians, Serbs, Italians, Germans, Yugoslavians, and latterly, Serbs again (Malcolm 1999). Similarly, it is an open question whether the Soviet Union collapsed *because* it could not hold together the disparate ethnic groups whose identities it had coercively and vigorously repressed or *because*, as a consequence of the USSR falling apart, those left in the ruins were forced to construct new identities for themselves (albeit, often on the basis of previous ones) (Keitner 1997). In other words, the only essential element of identities are that they are essentially contested, and that contestation is the context within which leaders vie to impose their own version of identity upon populations.

This particular approach to identity owes much to constructivism. Constructivism in its most radical formats rejects the notion of essences entirely

10   INTRODUCTION: THE ARTS OF LEADERSHIP

(see Grint and Woolgar 1997). That is to say, it rejects the idea that we can ever have an objective account of an individual or a situation or a technology—or, in this case, an identity—because all such accounts are derived from linguistic reconstructions; they are not, in effect, transparent reproductions of the truth. Instead the approach suggests that what the identity (or situation or leader or whatever) actually is, is a consequence of various accounts and interpretations, all of which vie for domination. In effect, we know what an identity or leader or situation actually is only because some particular version of it or him or her has secured prominence. The relativism at the heart of the approach does not mean that all interpretations are equal—and that what the leader/context is, is wholly a matter of the whim of the observer—because some interpretations do appear, to misquote Orwell, to be more equal than others. For example, my version of an identity—individual or collective—must fight for dominance along with others. Similarly, my account of a popular individual may be that he or she is an incompetent charlatan, but, if the popularity of this person rests upon the support of more powerful 'voices' (including material resources), then my negative voice will carry little or no weight. The critical issue for this approach, then, is not what the identity or leader or the context 'really' is, but what are the processes by which these phenomena are constructed into successes or failures, crises or periods of calm. For example, when the CEO declares an impending crisis based on information that must remain confidential to prevent the crisis deepening, how are we mere ignorant subordinates to evaluate the claim? When governments declare military 'incidents' to be 'the mother of all victories', how are we to judge the situation? [1] Do we ever really know what happened? When the media represent all the leaders of a particular country or area as villains or heroes, do we really know enough about them to agree or disagree? The point of this approach, therefore, is to suggest that we may never know what the true essence of an identity, a leader, or a situation actually is, and must often base our actions and beliefs on the accounts of others from whom we can (re)constitute our version of events.

Furthermore, even the most powerful leaders are restricted by the social discourses within which they operate. In other words, leaders cannot invent a completely new world or identity but are constrained by the language, the customs, the social mores, the dress codes, and so on with which we all operate. For example, the discourse of marriage is primarily, but not only, a set of words and phrases that encourage those within it to perceive themselves and to act in certain ways: they are 'wives' or 'husbands' or 'spouses' rather than 'partners'; they are 'widows' or 'widowers', 'divorced' or 'separated' or whatever. The marriage discourse does not *force* people to think and act 'appropriately', but it operates as a kind of 'default'—we have to make conscious decisions to step outside it if we want to challenge the status quo. These categories are clearly not 'objectively real' in the sense that husbands or wives can be scientifically proven to look different or act differently from those not involved in marriage, but discourses do appear to take on a life of their own—they reify the world, they make something appear real when it is merely a cultural convention. A gardening example might clarify this better. Trying to define 'weeds' in a scientific way is impossible, because weeds are merely plants that are in the 'wrong' place. To some people poppies are weeds, but I consider them flowers; to encourage consumers, seed-sellers label them 'wild flowers'. The difficulty is that the form of discourse encourages us to consider plants as 'weeds' or 'not weeds', as if they were objectively different; indeed, children are frequently bemused when seeing adults 'weeding' the garden, because it is far from clear what criteria are being employed to differentiate between wanted and unwanted green things. Thus the identity of a green thing cannot be secured against an objective weed-measurer; it is culturally constructed. However, the gardening discourse encourages us to identify plants in this bipolar way—weed/not weed—in precisely the same way that we appear to perceive people as one identity or another.

This would not be the case if we could get to the world, in this case the plant or the person, without first going through language, but we can get to them only through the words that describe them or explain them or categorize them and so on. The implication of this mediated approach to the world is that our assessment of the validity of the account lies not in the world itself but by reference to other words. This is rather like trying to define or explain a word without reference to other words—it simply is not possible. It looks as though we are then forced to conclude that there is no objective way of assessing which account of the world is true or closer to the truth because every account has to be adjudged by other accounts, not by comparison to the world itself. And from this 'relativist' conclusion we may conclude that every account of the world, every definition of a weed, every version of identity is as good as any other. The relativist's dilemma is usually taken to mean that an anarchic free for all exists with no mechanism for establishing truth from falsehood, morality from immorality, weeds from plants, or true identities from false. In some ways this is an accurate (I hesitate to use the word 'true'!) conclusion: there is no objective way to be absolutely and permanently sure of the truth. On the other hand, this does not necessarily mean that any morality is as good as any other or that we must abandon attempts to analyse the world. On the moral problem it simply means that we need to agree a form of morality that we can all live with—and this includes agreeing what to do about those people who refuse to accept this agreement. On the analytic problem the issue is surely not that every account of the world is as good as any other because some accounts are taken to be more reliable and robust than others and thus the issue is: what makes successful accounts successful? For our purposes this means that we do not have to agree, for example, that British versions of the Anglo-Zulu wars are more objective than Zulu or third-party versions, but we might want to investigate why British versions appear to be more *persuasive*. And rather than worrying about whether the British mutineers were 'really' revolutionaries, we might consider why and how one side attempted to persuade the population that this was the case.

It is also important to remember *how* identities are forged not just why they are forged. For instance, the mutineers represented themselves—and were vilified in

12   INTRODUCTION: THE ARTS OF LEADERSHIP

the press—for flying the 'red flag' from their masts. Thus we should be alert to the way symbols are deployed, perhaps never more so than in Hitler's Nazi parades, but more conventionally in school and corporate uniforms, in company songs, in clothing, and in corporate images. Indeed, A.P. Cohen (1985) has suggested that the symbolic construction of a community is especially relevant where the apparent equality of community has to transcend the inequalities that exist in collective hierarchies. In short, the greater the difference between individuals in a community, the more the symbolic element is likely to be deployed to persuade people that the differences are less relevant than the similarities.

The emergence of the 'true' identity of a character in a play is often constructed through a particular revelation: one's origins are revealed to lie in a 'handbag' or one's true father is revealed as the individual whom you previously murdered and whose wife you married, and so on. In practice, however, the social constitution of identity is more akin to a labour of Sisyphus than Odysseus' quest: there is no 'homecoming' awaiting the completion of the tasks, there is only another task; there is no single final truth, only different interpretations that construct, rather than reflect, the phenomenon. The struggle is to persuade others that your own version of their identity is true, and it is also a struggle to convince them that they have not been convinced—in effect, that it is not through argument that their identity exists, but through revelation of the 'truth'. Thus, for example, whether the mutineers in England were loyal sailors, merely industrial 'strikers' seeking the resolution of legitimate grievances, or whether they were political firebrands seeking to import the heady ideas of the French Revolution, is not something that can be revealed by looking closely at them, but is something that was—and still is—fought over. Their identity is not essentially embodied by their actions and words; it is constructed by themselves and those around and after them. Relatedly, whether the Zulus were bloodthirsty 'savages' bent on expanding their beastly empire, or whether precisely the same description fits better on the shoulders of the British army fighting them, is something that, again, was and remains contested. And whether Nightingale was a heroine and 'her' soldiers were forgotten lambs, or whether she was an interfering busybody and her soldiers were the scum of the earth, has yet to be agreed by all and sundry. More significantly for us, it may well be that whichever leader can most successfully 'construct'—as opposed to 'tap'—the identity of his or her followers in a way that generates maximum effort may also be the most successful leader. For Branson, the youthful, customer-focused, and entrepreneurial Virgin identity remains a critical component of his success; for Laker, the identity or branding was not so much a youthful 'alternative' to the staid corporations but appeared more like a cheap, and second-class, substitute.

To some extent leaders seem to forge not just a community or a common ideology but a parallel practice. For example, many military leaders take personal risks in an attempt to galvanize their troops to do the same. But leaders do not need to resemble their followers to remain as successful leaders. For example, many leaders purposefully adopt clothes or styles of speech that differentiate

INTRODUCTION: THE ARTS OF LEADERSHIP   13

them from their followers. Even some of the most long-lived leadership systems have not necessarily been rooted in a physical or social alignment between followers and leaders: 'The late British Empire, for example, has not been ruled by an "English" dynasty since the early eleventh century; after that a motley parade of Normans (Plantagenets), Welsh (Tudors), Scots (Stuarts), Dutch (House of Orange) and Germans (Hanoverians) have squatted on the imperial throne' (Anderson1991: 83). Of course, where thought beneficial, the various 'British' ruling families have asserted either that they are descendants of an unbroken ancestral line since whenever, or insisted that they are truly British. But what, precisely, does this mean anyway?[2]

To sum up, the constructivist approach does not necessarily deny the importance of leadership. However, it does assert that an epistemological question mark hangs over all issues, human and non-human, and, particularly for us, the issue of—and literally the invention of—identity. And for this reason we may regard the construction of identity both as a critical element and task of leadership and as one that is appropriately captured by the image of the philosopher's study, for it is in philosophical endeavours that one's identity is considered and constructed and it is through philosophy that we begin to answer that slippery question: *who* are we? But there is more to leadership than answering this question, for, having constructed an answer, we are then forced to consider the *what* question: *what* do we want to be and do?

The What Question: Strategic Vision and the Invention of Leadership

Leadership is an invention. I do not mean that this implies leadership is a trick or is unnecessary or false in some sense—although it might be any or all of these at times; rather, I mean that leadership is primarily rooted in, and a product of, the imagination. Imagination is the 'faculty or action of producing mental images of what is not present or has not been experienced' (*Collins English Dictionary* 1979). To imagine 'what is not present' is to concern oneself both with what may be and what was but is no longer. It is to look at the *what*—the content of the vision—but also to consider *where* this will be achieved, *when* it will be achieved, and *why* it should be achieved. In other words, this aspect of the imagination can look backwards as well as forwards; leaders may rekindle the activities of their followers by recalling some golden age of the past, quite possibly mythical—or imagined—but which nevertheless mobilizes people to move from one situation to a different one. To imagine 'what has not been experienced' is to relay to one's followers the hope of a better future, or again, quite possibly to remind them that a preferable state of affairs did once exist but that such a state has not been experienced by the current generation. In this sense the imagination of the leader is very much locked into notions of utopia—imaginary other worlds that are literally 'no place' at the present but may be in the future. From Plato's *Republic* to More's original *Utopia*, utopian thought has attempted to transcend the present rigidities and construct a better future. And, although many have criticized

14 INTRODUCTION: THE ARTS OF LEADERSHIP

utopian thought on the grounds that it is impossibly naïve, there are good reasons to suggest it has a kernel of critical importance to leadership; for, if leaders cannot imagine a preferable alternative to the status quo, why should followers follow them? Thus, if we ensure that utopias must be capable of realization—that is, concrete rather than merely abstract—then we can utilize the creative potential of the imagination and not suffer from it or suffer from its absence (see Bloch 1986 and Grint 1995: 90–123).

Most leaders do not actually do a great deal—in the sense that they usually lead the making of parts on the assembly line by sitting at a machine, or they usually lead an army by being at the front, or they usually lead a political party by speaking on the doorstep to voters. Instead, the role of the leader tends to be one where the imagination, not the body, is required to act. They have to dream up new strategies to expand the business, they have to devise plans for the defence of a nation, and they have to imagine a way for their party to take or retain power. Many people in positions of leadership do none of these things for the community they lead. They imagine little and do little, or they imagine ways to siphon off riches from the community to their own bank account, or they imagine ways to remain in power no matter what the consequences may be for the community. These may be poor leaders as far as the community is concerned, but they are still leaders.

The imagination is also crucial in the construction of what may be the most important element of leadership: the community narrative or myth. Again, I do not mean 'myth' in the sense of a false story but rather myth in the sense of a narrative that roots a community in the past, explains its present, and conjures up a preferred future. A leader without a persuasive account of the past, present, and future is unlikely to remain a leader for long. Even overtly corrupt and tyrannical leaders cannot survive on their own; they too must persuade their coterie of gorillas and gangsters that life under them is preferable to life under an imaginary alternative.

The level of leadership is less relevant than the process. A supervisor on the shop floor, a trade-union shop steward, a corporal with a section of soldiers, and a locally elected politician all face the same form of problems: who are we, how did we get here, where do we want to go to, why should we go there, and what do we need to do to get there? These are all problems of the imagination in the first place.

The imagination of followers is also relevant because they have to interpret events, gestures, speeches, texts, and so on to mean something similar to that which the leader implies. There cannot be a way of *ensuring* that followers interpret a leader's actions or words in precisely the same way that the leader intends, but there are methods for trying to limit the discrepancy between the two and it is this discrepancy, this gap of the imagination, upon which leaders need to concentrate.

Naturally, there will be followers who cannot or will not close this gap of imagination to join the community and facilitate its goals. Here the leader may well fail in his or her attempt to mobilize the entire community, but is this critical? Not necessarily, and for several different reasons.

First, there are many examples, some of which will be covered later, where only a limited proportion of the community are ideologically mobilized in line with the leader. Indeed, a majority of followers may be disinterested in the issue, but, providing a sufficient core of people is mobilized, they can persuade or coerce the rest into undertaking the action necessary to achieve the goal. For example, the soldiers at the front may have little idea why they are fighting, but, providing their immediate officers are willing to share the risks of injury, and providing there are sufficient coercive systems to deter desertion and mutiny, they may well be prepared to risk their own lives for a cause that does not interest them. Similarly, shop-floor or office workers may simply disbelieve the vision and mission statements of their employers and take no interest in what the firm is trying to achieve, but, providing the line managers are true believers, the goal may still be achieved (see Abercrombie *et al.* 1980). In this case the imagination of the front-line officers must be mobilized by the top leadership, but it may not be necessary to fire the imagination of all and sundry. In short, a critical mass of subordinate leaders may need 'to believe' but the mass need only obey.

Secondly, self-interest may generate the necessary response on the part of followers without mirroring the interests of the leaders. For instance, office-cleaners may have no real interest in providing the cleanliness that their boss says the cleaning company guarantees—but, if the cleaners' jobs are suddenly on the line then they may make the effort, not because they are concerned for the customer or their boss but for self-interest. But even here the leader must get inside the head of the follower to ascertain what will persuade the follower to undertake the necessary action.

However, even though we may have established that gaps between the imagination of the leader, manifest in the strategic vision, and the action of the followers in pursuit of that vision can be transcended, it is still the case that the most successful leaders appear to be those whose inventiveness is rooted in, rather than separate from, the imagination and lived experience of their followers. By that I mean that leaders are most likely to be followed when their strategic vision is not simply clear but also resonates with the desires of the followers; in effect, that the strategic vision operates within the *Zeitgeist*—literally the time spirit of an age. This is probably best represented by the likes of Horatio Nelson, whose vision of destroying the French fleet coincided with and mirrored the threat felt by many of the British population of a French invasion. Similarly, Hitler's rabid incantations against the shame of Versailles and the November 'stab in the back' resonated with the resentment of many ordinary Germans against the cause and effects of the defeat in the First World War. Furthermore, where the strategic visions of a community or organization become aligned with the personal agenda of the leader—as they were in both the previous cases—then we have the potential for a very seductive message: followers should sacrifice themselves to the requirements of the leader, not because this will fulfil the leader's private ambitions but because it will further the social needs of the collective.

16 INTRODUCTION: THE ARTS OF LEADERSHIP

To summarize, the role of invention is so significant that we should perhaps attempt to formalize its role in metaphorical terms. In this sense, not only is leadership an art in general; it is a particular form of the arts, in effect, fine art. Since the fine arts include painting, drawing, and sculpture, we might suggest that this art is most appropriately considered as the one responsible for constructing the strategic vision of an organization—that is, its future destination, its current direction, and its past deployment. It is, in effect, the world of the artist's studio, for here the fine artist/leader must draw or paint or sculpt the future. Moreover, leadership in this context must engage in drawing for the future by drawing on the past and in each case the imaginative use of the paintbrush distinguishes the powerful from the indifferent vision. Furthermore, where the fine artist/leader manages to construct a vision that superimposes his or her own agenda onto the collective agenda—without the superimposition being crudely self-evident—the imaginative vision can be crucial in explaining the success or failure of a leader. But there is more to leadership than constructing an identity and imagining the future—that is, answering the *who* and the *what* questions. To achieve the *what*, leaders need to consider the *how* as well.

The How Question: Organizational Tactics and the Indeterminacy of Leadership

In Shakespeare's *Henry V*, the King is certainly active in envisioning for his troops a memorable victory on the basis of a glorious past. And one of the reasons why Agincourt is regarded as a great English victory is because it was achieved against considerable odds; indeed, a simple stacking-up of the resources on both sides in any objective sense would have *determined* that the English must lose to the French. They did not, and this indeterminacy of leadership, this inability to predict the outcome of events on the basis of objectively analysing the resources available to each side, is a second critical weakness in conventional approaches to leadership.

Indeterminacy concerns the political gap between theory and practice—that is, between the issuing of orders/requests and achieving appropriate action. The orders/requests may appear perfectly logical to the leader but not necessarily to the followers, and even if they do appear logical that is not a sufficient reason to expect them to be carried out. I may understand that completing my task is essential for the success of the organization, but if that also means losing my job once the task is completed then I have a logical reason for not completing the task that is contrary to the logical reasoning of the organizations. In short, the logic of the leader is seldom sufficient to persuade followers to follow.

The suggestion that a gap exists between theory and practice, between dream and reality, and between what you want and what you get is, of course, hardly new. In Shakespeare's *Othello*, Iago is the antagonist to Othello, and political contest between individuals remains the very essence of many narratives, fictional or not. The assumption that political conflicts are an inevitable component of all organizations—and therefore that leaders should take cognizance of their inevitability—is something that many writers seem to have understood—but not many leaders. The assumption that technology is shot through with the same problem is something that few writers have even discussed.

For Clausewitz (1976), for instance, an army commander naturally and normally commanded unswerving obedience from his, or very occasionally her, troops. There was occasionally some 'friction' in any military machine, through the breakdown of weapons, supplies, weather, or even the troops themselves, but these were abnormal issues that could be resolved through the appropriate application of corrective techniques.

For Marx, the corrosion or friction between what workers were paid to do and what they did, between labour power (theory) and labour (practice), ensured that workers' discretion remained an essential element in the so-called labour process, and remains a central element in the 'labour-process' approach to this day (see Marx 1954 and Grint 1998a). Littler (1982), for example, calls this the 'central indeterminacy of capital', while Boreham (1983) applies a related notion of indeterminacy to the professions.

Adopting the original Greek word, *agon*, meaning contest,[3] Foucault suggests that conventional power relations can be classified as 'agonism', a permanent struggle between two sides in which neither side dominates.[4] Further, Foucault (1980: 39) insists that power is not a property but a relationship. That is, power is not something that you can hold or have, but, rather, is a relationship between people: 'it is exercised *within* the social body, rather than above it.' This 'capillary power', then, works through us rather than upon us: we are both held in place by—and responsible for holding in place—power. Another French writer, Latour (1986), has suggested that between the 'principle' of power, or its 'ostensive existence', and the 'practice' of power, or its 'performative existence', lies this same gap. This gap also generates the distinction between power as a *cause* of subordinate action and power as a *consequence* of subordinate action: followers can almost always refuse to carry out the leader's requirements—and suffer the consequences—so whether a leader has power over his or her followers depends upon the action of the followers more than the order of the leader (see Grint 1995). This is critical because it implies that networks of power are the foundations of success. That is to say, only a sufficiently extensive network is strong enough to deter subordinates from resisting superordinates and widening the gap between theory and practice, orders and actions, demands and results. The gap is also one that Strauss (1978) talks of as facilitating 'the negotiated order' of organizational existence.

When we move from the problem of accounting for people's inability to do what they are supposed to do, to the problem of accounting for the equivalent issue in non-human phenomena, such as machines—usually an essential element of any kind of leadership—the same kind of debate recurs. Hence, what a machine is, what it will do, and what its effects will be tend to be more or less indeterminate, the upshot of specific readings of the machine rather than the direct result of the essence of an unmediated or self-explanatory technology. A technology's capacity and capability are never transparently obvious and necessarily require some form of interpretation; technology does not speak for itself but has to be spoken for. Thus our apprehension of technical capacity is the upshot of our interpreting or being persuaded that the technology will do what, for example, its producers say it will do. The crucial role of interpretation and persuasion suggests we need to attend closely to the process of interpretation rather than assuming that we are persuaded by the effectiveness of the technology. Again, this does not mean that any interpretation is as good as any other. Rather, the point is to analyse why some accounts seem more persuasive than others. Very often the most powerful accounts are those rooted in the strongest and most heterogeneous networks.

In sum, all of these writers recount a similar problem: between the order and the execution, between the leader's wishes and the followers' actions, there is a form of political corrosion that undermines leadership, not as an occasional, unusual, or atypical event, but as a systematically recurrent problem. This does not mean that there is no relationship between what leaders want and what actually happens, but it does mean that subordinates may comply with leaders' requests for their own reasons and in pursuit of their own interests. It is this that undermines the direct link between the request and the act; the leader and the led.

Even if we can ensure that followers do what leaders want them to do it may still not secure the wishes of the leader, because the resources available may be inadequate. Conventionally, of course, success tends to be associated with accumulating sufficient power and resources to bludgeon the opposition, competitor, or enemy into submission. For example, when the Nazis entered Poland, the contest was grossly unequal and Hitler simply used his manifestly greater power to destroy the Polish armed forces. In business, this kind of success through dominating the market is achieved by monopolistic firms such that consumers have little choice but to buy the products of the monopoly producer. Beyond the military and business we might consider here how a small number of very rich football clubs dominate the leagues of their country with their extensive purchasing power that buys in the best available players. In effect, their sporting success is premised upon their financial and physical domination of the opposition.

The sporting arena is a useful way of thinking about the different forms of organizational tactics, especially if we adopt the idea of the Martial Arts and its requisite site: the dojo. And at an individual level this approach is captured in karate's traditional reliance upon the development of sufficiently overpowering strength and technique to deliver a single strike to a pressure point of an opponent that will effectively terminate an attack.[5] But not many of us are blessed with the physical strength or technical skill to dominate all others, nor are we leaders of organizations that are resource rich while all others are resource poor. Very often we may find that the competition is just as well equipped and resourced and skilful as we are. Under these circumstances, a 'battle' of attrition is likely, manifest in the trench warfare of the First World War, or the battle for market control

INTRODUCTION:THE ARTS OF LEADERSHIP   19

by Coca-Cola or Pepsi, or the struggle between two relatively equal political parties that vie for electoral office. In these conditions the victor may well be the side with the marginally superior resources or tenacity or stamina or just better luck, but the tactical aim remains the same—to eliminate or undermine the opponent.

And what happens if we are significantly weaker than the opposition? Well at least two possibilities remain open—beyond submission or retreat—though it is important to note that leadership is critical here too, for the inability to recognize an impending defeat and a determination to struggle on when the costs are unnecessarily high is surely the sign of poor leadership. In other words, that submission or defeat ought to be regarded as a pro-active decision not something forced upon the weaker side if damage limitation is something leaders are concerned with.

Neutralization of the opposition's resources is one such possibility beyond defeat or failure. Here the other's resources are not resisted but rather avoided. Aikido tends to rest upon this tactic of neutralization—the intention is to neutralize the attacker and prevent further attack. There is no first strike and the aim is to return the attacker to a position of stability where no further aggression will occur. It is inherently a reactive system designed solely for personal protection and promotes a version of moral action intended to minimize damage to an attacker. But if we consider aikido as a metaphor for organizational tactics rather than simply a personal self-defence system we can see how applicable it can be in markedly different areas. For example, in business Swatch managed to survive the onslaught of cheaper Asian products by neutralizing the primary resources of the producers—their cheap labour. By redesigning the Swatch product, the company reduced the proportion of costs taken up by labour down to 10 per cent—a point at which quality and fashion aspects became the main selling point, not the costs of the watch.[6] In political terms perhaps a good example of a neutralizing principle in action would be Hitler's acquisition of power. In theory the political opposition in the guise of the Social Democratic Party and the trade unions could have made Hitler's rule untenable—but this was premised upon his *illegitimate* seizure of power, and when Hitler took control legally all their power and resources were neutralized. In short, the determinate power of Hitler's internal opponents was rendered indeterminate.

But it is also possible to consider indeterminacy in which it is not just that the weaker side wins but that the weaker side's victory is premised upon using the strength of the stronger against itself. Take the Battle of Cannae, for example, where Hannibal's smaller and less cohesive Cathaginian army defeated the larger and more cohesive Roman force. To explain this we have to turn to the notion of resource inversion. A conventional assessment would suggest a relatively simple Roman victory, because the Romans had more troops and fought in a way that every Roman soldier would have been familiar with. Hannibal's only hope of success in an open battlefield was to avoid a head-on conventional clash and seek a way of using the greater Roman strength to undermine itself. Whether by luck or stratagem, this is what Hannibal did, as is revealed in Fig. 1.4. In phase (1) 80,000 Roman infantry attacked Hannibal's 45,000 troops, while the latter's

20   INTRODUCTION:THE ARTS OF LEADERSHIP

6,500 heavy cavalry on his left under Hasdrubal attacked the Roman cavalry. On Hannibal's right his 4,000 Numidian light cavalry met the Roman cavalry attack. In phase (2) the Carthaginian infantry, which were more numerous in the centre, bowed under the Roman assault, but the wings, composed of African troops, remained firm as the centre, composed of Spanish and Celtic troops, gave ground. Meanwhile both Roman cavalry wings were driven from the battlefield. In phase (3) the Carthaginian heavy cavalry returned to attack the Roman infantry from the rear and the African infantry extended their positions around the flanks of the Romans to complete the encirclement in (4) and (5). In phase 6 a small number of Romans fought their way out of the circle to safety but the rest were caught. About 2,500 Romans surrendered but around 49,000 Romans were killed.

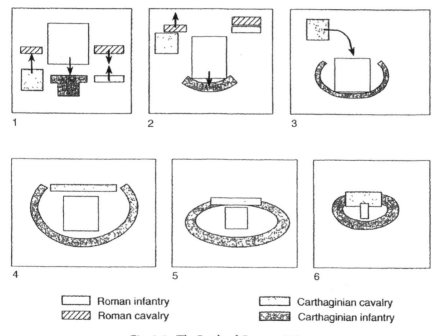

☐ Roman infantry	▭ Carthaginian cavalry
▨ Roman cavalry	▨ Carthaginian infantry

Fig. 1.4. The Battle of Cannae, 216BC

The critical question here concerns the principle by which Hannibal pulled off the victory. Since he could not match the Romans in strength he could have avoided a battle, but this would not have secured him the victory he needed. Instead, he used the Roman strengths—their propensity to fight in solid formation and to depend upon a well-armoured infantry advance—to his advantage. Had the Romans not been so successful in this battle tactic previously they would not have retained it, but that they did enabled Hannibal to make use of their

INTRODUCTION: THE ARTS OF LEADERSHIP 21

resources to his own advantage. In short, Hannibal enticed the Romans into a trap that only their own strength made possible.

The Trojan Horse has a similar explanation. The Greeks had spent twelve years attempting to break down or through the walls of Troy but to no avail. As is well known, ultimately they devised a stratagem that involved them leaving the city and apparently sailing away leaving only a wooden horse, within which were left several Greek soldiers. Once the horse was dragged inside the city, the hidden Greeks managed to open the city gates and let in the now-returned Greek army. Thus the pitching of Greek force against Trojan walls simply failed because the latter were too strong. But, knowing that the Trojans were confident in their defences, the Greeks used that resource against them: if an entire Greek army could not enter the city, then what harm could this strange wooden statue do? So, when the Greeks inverted the strength of the Trojans, the Greeks succeeded.

At Agincourt the strength of the French army lay in its heavily armoured cavalry and the English could not hope to match them in a traditional contest. Instead, the desire of the French cavalry to close with and eliminate the English led the former to attack in a narrow area that rapidly filled with French dead, cut down by English arrows, to the extent that the size of the French attack made manœuvre impossible amidst the growing body of dead.

Wars abound with similar examples: the impenetrable French Maginot Line that could not be breached by the German army was not breached by it, because the Germans went round it through Belgium. But the consequence of the Maginot Line was that France generated a level of overconfidence in its defences wholly out of keeping with the situation in 1940. The fall of the 'impregnable fortress' of Singapore to the Japanese is a cognate story. The principle of using the opposition's force against it was also clearly demonstrated when the Allies led the Germans to believe that the Pas de Calais was the site of the invasion. This encouraged the Germans to mass their armour around the area, thereby freeing up Normandy for the real invasion. In effect, the strength of German armour was used against itself.

But we do not need to remain in the military world to see the significance of this resource inversion. Take Dell computers, for example. When Michael Dell first began considering the idea, he faced the giants of IBM, Apple, Compaq, and DEC, all of which had a large slice of the market and delivered through conventional shops. There was little hope of Dell meeting this competition head-on because he had no network of shops to sell through and little hope of developing a traditional distribution channel. However, by choosing to market his computers through direct mail he not only avoided a direct clash with the giants—which he probably would not have won—but he ensured that the giants remained stuck with distribution channels that proved increasingly inefficient. In short, the more they used their traditional strengths against him, the more Dell benefited. By March 1999 Dell, then the world's fastest-growing computer manufacturer, and IBM, then the world's biggest computer manufacturer, signed the world's largest information-technology agreement, a $16 billion dollar deal, to develop the next

22   INTRODUCTION: THE ARTS OF LEADERSHIP

generation of computer technology (Finch 1999). By September 1999 Dell (with 20 per cent of the market) had overtaken Compaq (with 15 per cent) to become the UK's biggest PC seller (IBM had 6 per cent of the UK market) (Doward 1999).

Similarly, Avis-Rent-a-Car developed a whole customer care service and a cultural tradition based on being the *second* largest rental company and therefore having to work much harder to retain its customers than the premier rental company.

It is, then, this resource inversion that appears to explain some of the more remarkable examples of leadership when the resource imbalance is considerable, when the determinate is reversed. Here, the closest martial art is probably something like T'ai Chi, a 'soft' martial art where the aim is to use an opponent's strength to defeat him or her rather than attempting to stop him or her head-on, as in much of karate, or neutralize his or her efforts to continue the attack, as in Aikido. Now that we have established *who* we are, *what* the vision is, and *how* we can overcome opponents, we have still to consider that group without whom there are no leaders: the followers—for *why* should they follow a leader?

The Why Question: Persuasive Communication and the Irony of Leadership

One of the most interesting scenarios in everyday life is the purchase—by which I mean the mechanism and skills with which sales representatives induce us to part with our hard-earned money for the dubious benefits of a timeshare, or a new car, or whatever. Sales representatives do not sell on the basis of the benefits to themselves, in terms of commission or bonus or shifting old stock and so on, and we would be wary of any such approach. Yet the irony is that so often leaders at all levels assume that they can persuade their subordinates to change on the basis of the leader's problems, or rationale, or advantages. So, for example, leaders regularly demand belt-tightening efficiencies or sacrifices on the basis of their own budgetary problems or the needs of the shareholders—and such leaders are just as regularly surprised when their subordinates appear unimpressed by such impeccable business logic or corporate needs. What is so often missing from business leadership, ironically in the circumstances of the context, is any attempt to *persuade* followers to follow, to *sell* them the future.

This brings us to a further element of irony, in which not only must a leader fire the imagination of the followers in their own identity, induce them to seek their future destination, and develop the organizational tactics to get them there, but he or she must also ensure that, within that imaginary alternative, that victory, that sales success, that production target, or whatever, the followers are sufficiently motivated to get there. That motivation is partly constructed through the envisioning of an identity, a strategic vision, and set of organizational tactics that enhance the chances of success and reduce the risks of failure, but it is primarily achieved through the fourth form of leadership art: the performing arts. In this we can include the theatrical performances that leaders must engage in if they are to achieve the necessary mobilization of followers and it is also derived from the

INTRODUCTION:THE ARTS OF LEADERSHIP   23

skills of rhetoric and the skills of negotiation. Thus having a persuasive message, delivering it effectively, and deploying negotiating skills to achieve movement are also critical elements of leadership. But again, although science and rational argument can be used to support these practices, they are fundamentally rooted in emotional and symbolic grammars, not the language of science. At a very basic level this can be demonstrated by trying to capture the persuasive effects of Martin Luther King's 'Dream Speech' by simply repeating it word for word—it simply does not move people, though clearly the original did. Thus the irony of leadership includes an acknowledgement that persuasive communication is the bedrock of achieving change, but relying on rational logic to move followers seldom works. For example, it may well be that managers and workers will agree with the rational logic that suggests the company must remain efficient and effective—but when that same logic also requires the dismissal of those same people somehow the logic fails to work. Thus, just as a play comes alive only if the script is regarded as good, the actors as persuasive, and the sets appropriate for the context, and the audience are engaged to *believe* in the production, so leaders can be successful only if their followers come to believe in the collective identity, the strategic vision, and the organizational tactics of the leader. For that to happen the skills of the performing arts are crucial. Leadership, therefore, is more a performance than a routine; it is the world of the theatre and it has to be continuously 'brought off' rather than occasionally acted out.

Theatres are about communication—communicating the plot, the characters, the atmosphere, the interpretation, and so on—and it is clear that Hitler relied heavily upon his theatrical rhetoric to construct and recruit to the identity of the new Germany. Theatre is overwhelmingly a rhetorical communication but is not solely rhetorical. That is to say, the focus is usually upon the words and the way that the words persuade the audience to accept the stage and its narrative as 'real', but that 'reality' has to be brought off in the imagination of the audience. As the chorus/narrator in Shakespeare's *Henry V* suggests at the beginning of the play:

> But pardon, gentles
> The flat unraised spirit that hath dar'd
> On this unworthy scaffold to bring forth
> So great an object: can this cockpit hold
> The varsty fields of France? . . .
> On your imaginary forces work.

A performative approach to communication seems a long way from the earliest academic business research where 'how to win friends and influence people' was the order of the day, but actually the two are not that far apart—nor are they especially distant from the initial assumptions and analyses of rhetoric in ancient Greek society. In all three cases the critical issue was how to persuade someone of something. Much of the writing in the field of communication is still locked into the persuasive issue but often premised on quite different axioms from those considered here. In the main, most business research still seems rooted in what has been called the 'transmission' or 'conduit' model, in which the crucial point of communication is to ensure that the message from the origin to the destination, usually from (active) superordinate to (passive) subordinate, is transmitted or carried in as undistorted a fashion as possible. This essentially means that all kinds of organizational problems can be explained away through 'communication failures'—that is, because of distorted or misperceived messages. Hence the solution is to clarify communications as much as possible, to simplify and repeat messages because the subordinates have not understood. That the subordinates have understood the message perfectly well (for example, 'you are our greatest asset'), but may construe it as a blatant lie, is seldom part of this approach.

A second way of considering communication is as a lens or filter, in which the information flying around an organization is of such a great quantity that some form of quality filtering is necessary to make sense of it all (Putnam *et al.* 1996). In this case the filtering may be by the individual receiving the message or it may occur at a higher level in the hierarchy. At its most obvious, this occurs through censorship during war; at its least obvious we may never know whether the communication has been censored. In the latter case this runs into what Marx called the 'dominant ideology', where distorted communications appear undistorted because they reflect what is taken for granted as 'common sense'.

A third way of considering leadership is as a performance. A performance is not just the uttering of words from a script, though these are obviously important. A performance involves the script, the props, the players, the audience, the interpretations, the context, the shared cultures, and so on and so forth. Reading the text of Shakespeare's *Henry V* may give you some idea about leadership, but it is not the same as watching a performance of the play itself. The equivalent for leaders would be to assume that reading this or any other book on leadership will provide you with all you need to know about leadership; it probably will not. Leadership is something to be experienced rather than simply read. Of course, it helps if we know the plot of *Henry V*, and, if we are familiar with the lines and their apparent meanings, then this can enhance our appreciation of the play as it is performed; but the text and the performance are not identical.

However, the error of reducing the performance to the text should not be taken to mean that a clear and significant difference exists between rhetoric and reality. On the contrary, it is only through language, only through rhetoric, that we can experience, nay imagine, what reality really is. For example, to take Machiavelli's point again, since few of us ever met or knew Princess Diana (or any other figurehead or leader for that matter) we can only know her through various forms of language: we are persuaded by TV programmes, or the radio, or the newspapers or magazines, that she was a particular kind of person. These interpretations differ, so we must choose between them or accept that the confusion is an inevitable reflection of the complexity of the case. Either way, our knowledge of the 'reality' is one constituted by the language of others, which we, in turn, interpret.

Sometimes a particular speech by a leader is held to be responsible for a radical change of direction in a community. The Peruvian rebel José de San Martín

INTRODUCTION:THE ARTS OF LEADERSHIP 25

allegedly achieved this in 1821 by declaring: 'In future the aboriginees shall not be called Indians or natives; they are the children and citizens of Peru and they shall be known as Peruvians' (quoted in Anderson 1991: 193). Similarly, Lincoln's Gettysburg address is regarded by Wills (1994) as another such case where the core of the nation's identity is ruptured and remade through the 272 words that he uses at the memorial service to the dead. But, as we shall see later, the meaning of the words is deeply embedded in the past, present, and future of the USA. It is not simply a series of sentences that anyone can read at any time and expect to reproduce the same experience; it was a performance not merely a speech act. Moreover, the irony is that 'mere' words are as responsible for the 'effects' of the American Civil War as the bullets and cannonballs.

The significance of persuasive rhetoric echoes Foucault's (1998) argument about the relationship between power and knowledge in discourse. Since, for Foucault, power is implicitly encased by knowledge, and vice versa, we cannot secure a true representation of the world that is untainted by power relations. Discourse, then, is not so much a reflection of material reality but a construction of it, a particular way of representing the world through language and practice. As Gergen (1992) argues, the modernist assessment construes 'truth' and language in a reflective relation, such that language acts as a slave to the 'truth'; the more objective the empirical measure of 'reality', the closer is language to the 'truth'. Against this, more sceptical currents prioritize the status of language and representation more generally: what counts as true and false is not determined by the essence of the phenomena themselves, because such phenomena are brought into existence only through representation. In short, the 'truth' is determined by the power of the discourse. In Foucault's (1980: 13) terms: 'Truth isn't outside power . . . each society has its regime of truth, its "general politics" of truth.'

The importance of this issue becomes clear when we try and 'discover' the truth about a leader such as Nightingale. None of the people reading this book will have met her, so we have to rely on the words and accounts, including pictures, artefacts, and so on of others. Even those who fought in the Crimea when Nightingale was there may not have met her personally and few of those that did would have known exactly what she was like or thought or felt. So how does the leadership of someone like Nightingale work? Certainly not through riveting speeches, since, by all accounts, she avoided public speaking wherever possible. But, if we consider Nightingale's leadership as rooted in a 'performance', then we may get a better grip on it. For example, her past 'performances' and doing of good deeds before the Crimea would have played some part—but note again that only a few people would have witnessed these—so others' accounts of these (and her own) would have locked the past into a rhetorically replayable present. Her personal risk taking is alleged to have mobilized her nurses and followers to great personal sacrifice. But few of the soldiers in hospital would have been able to verify this with their own eyes, so again they would have had to rely on the verbal accounts of others to know what happened. Nightingale's leadership reputation would also have been generated through her development of hospital

26   INTRODUCTION: THE ARTS OF LEADERSHIP

organization, but only her fellow nurses would have been personally privy to these, so, again, her reputation would have had to have been transmitted—by word and print—to others for it to have assumed significance. In effect, therefore, Nightingale's leadership *performance* is inevitably reproduced, expanded, distorted, and reconstructed through rhetoric of one form or another. We need not reduce performance to rhetoric to acknowledge that the reproduction of performance is essentially a rhetorically grounded device.

Similarly, General Patton had a reputation for theatrical leadership, but we should be careful about attributing his actions to a particular cause. For example, Patton was renowned for taking inordinate personal risks, yet, ironically, he was an extremely fatalistic individual who believed himself destined to command a great army across Europe; thus any dangers before this great act were regarded by him as insignificant. On the other hand, Patton was constantly aware that fear stalked every soldier, himself included, and to prove to himself that he was unafraid he would take extreme risks—not because he was brave but to prove to himself that he was not a coward. Whether such actions were interpreted by his subordinates and superiors as bravery, stupidity, or anything else depended more upon their state of mind than his. Hence his performances were not objectively good or bad or brave or stupid but simply performances that were adjudged by others—once communicated—to be one thing or another.

In Patton's case it could be said that his successes were forged. Again I take this to mean two different but related things: forged in the sense of false and forged in the sense of beaten into shape. For example, Patton's success with the illusionary FUSAG (First US Army Group) on D-Day persuaded the Germans that he was about to invade the Pas de Calais with a much larger force than had just landed in Normandy—but this was a blatant 'forgery' because there was no FUSAG. At a different level one might want to question the claims of many leaders to have instigated or led successful change programmes when the 'real' cause of success lay elsewhere. On the other hand, the 'forging' of Patton's Third Army, which did so much damage to the Germans after D-Day, was, allegedly, a direct result of his vigorous—not to say zealous—disciplinary approach to war: his military successes were 'forged' in the heat of battle—or so we are told, since few, if any, of us would have been there.

Patton, like Henry Ford, was a strong believer in reincarnation and certain that he had also fought at Gettysburg, but Gettysburg is remembered not just as the site of major battle in the American Civil War, but as a turning point in the history of that nation. The change of direction, strangely enough, was retrospective and rhetorical—though one might be forgiven for not assuming this if one had heard Lincoln's own assumption of the power of his speech: 'The world will little note, nor long remember what we say here, but it can never forget what they did here.' Seldom can a speaker have been so completely wrong yet achieve precisely what he intended: to bring a nation (back) to life by breathing new words into its shredded lungs. When Lincoln sought to reduce the significance of his speech, in favour of raising the significance of the Union dead, at Gettysburg on

19 November 1863 during the American Civil War, he reproduced a common subordination of the word to the deed. For Mao Tse-Tung the equivalent was to pronounce, in his *Problems of War and Strategy,* that 'political power grows out of the barrel of a gun'. Jonathan Swift, however, in his *Ode to . . . Sancroft,* had a rather different view: for him, language was itself a weapon, for he could unleash 'the artillery of words' to great effect. For others it is represented by the children's phrase:

> Sticks and stones may break my bones
> But words will never hurt me.

Contrast Stephen Spender's retort in the *Express* that:

> My parents kept me from children who were rough
> Who threw words like stones and who wore torn clothes.

And for those of us well past childhood (in age if not sense), it may be the more common retort that 'actions speak louder than words' that rings in our ears— though Ralph Waldo Emerson's *The Poet* thought that 'words are also actions, and actions are a kind of words'. This is why persuasive communications are so important to leadership, for without a persuasive *why* there is little to mobilize followers further than you can push them.

Philosophical, Fine, Martial, and Performing: Leadership Arts

To summarize, therefore, I am suggesting that leadership might better be considered as an art rather than a science, or, more specifically, as an ensemble of arts. Under this approach we might consider how four particular arts mirror four of the central features of leadership: the invention of an identity, the formulation of a strategic vision, the construction of organizational tactics, and the deployment of persuasive mechanisms to ensure followers actually follow. In sum, leadership is critically concerned with establishing and coordinating the relationships between four things: the *who,* the *what,* the *how* and the *why:*

- *Who* are you?—An identity.
- *What* does the organization want to achieve?—A strategic vision.
- *How* will they achieve this?—Organizational tactics.
- *Why* should followers want to embody the identity, pursue the strategic vision, and adopt the organizational tactics?—Persuasive communication.

Science may help the leader and the organization achieve these but fundamentally they are all subjective issues and are better considered as various arts.

- *Identity* is constructed out of the amorphous baggage of myth and the contested resources of history; it is not a reflection of the world but a construction of it. It is rooted in the philosopher's stone not the scientist's microscope.

28 INTRODUCTION: THE ARTS OF LEADERSHIP

- *Strategic visions* are designed through the imagination not the experiment, they are the equivalent of the fine arts not physics, for they involve imagination rather than experimentation, they are paintings not photographs.
- *Organizational tactics* are rather better envisaged as martial arts than mathematics, for here the leader must evaluate the organizational forms and manœuvres suitable for the competition and must take account of the likely indeterminacy of outcome.
- *Persuasive communication* can certainly be supplemented by scientific knowledge, but fundamentally this is the world of the performing arts, the theatre of rhetorical skill, of negotiating skills, and of inducing the audience to believe in the world you paint with words and props.

Fig. 1.5 summarizes the four areas of concern.

Notes

1. Two cases will suffice to demonstrate the point. In August 1964 President Lyndon Johnson authorized air attacks on North Vietnam after 'unprovoked' torpedo attacks upon two US destroyers. There is now considerable doubt as to the veracity of the official claims (Lennon 1999). In June 1994 an RAF Chinook helicopter carrying British military security officers crashed on the Mull of Kintyre killing all twenty-nine passengers and crew after what was officially described as 'pilot error'. Again, there are now doubts as to the veracity of the official report (Millar 1999).
2. See also Colley (1999) for a succinct critique of the 'special relationship' between the USA and the UK.
3. From which we have derived the terms agonist, where one muscle is opposed by another, agony, antagonist, and protagonist.
4. Such domination for Foucault did not imply a power relationship at all (Foucault 1983: 208–26).
5. George A. Dillman (1992) has long regarded pressure-point karate as the most legitimate inheritance from the martial arts.
6. See the original interview with Nicolas Hayek by William Taylor in the *Harvard Business Review* (Mar.–Apr. 1993: 99–110), and a subsequent analysis by Pino (1999).

References

Abercrombie, N., Hill, S., and Turner, B. S. (1980), *The Dominant Ideology Thesis* (London: Tavistock).

Anderson, B. (1991), *Imagined Communities: Reflections on the Origin and Spread of Nationalism* (London: Verso).

Barth, F. (1969) (ed.), *Ethnic Groups and Boundaries* (Oslo: Universitetsforlaget).
Acceleration through Science Education (CASE) Project (King's College, London).

Bloch, E. (1986), *The Principle of Hope* (Oxford: Oxford University Press).

Boreham, P. (1983), 'Indetermination: Professional Knowledge, Organization and Control', *Sociological Review*, 31/4: 693–718.

Clausewitz, C. Von. (1976), *On War* (Princeton: Princeton University Press).

Cohen, A. P. (1985), *The Symbolic Construction of Community* (London: Tavistock).

Colley, L. (1994), *Britons: Forging the Nation 1707–1837* (London: Pimlico).

Cooley, C. H. (1922), *Human Nature and the Social Order* (New York: Scribners).

Douglas, M. (1966), *Purity and Danger* (London: Routledge & Kegan Paul).

Doward, J. (1999), 'Dell Vaults to No. 1 in PCs', *Guardian*, 15 Aug.

Elias, N. (1989), *Studien über die Deutschen* (Frankfurt: Suhrkamp).

Finch, J. (1999), 'Dell and IBM Sign $16bn Pact', *Guardian*, 6 Mar.

Foucault, M. (1980), *Power/Knowledge* (Brighton: Harvester).

Gergen, K. J. (1992), 'Organization Theory in the Postmodern Era', in M. Reed and M. Hughes (eds.), *Rethinking Organization: New Directions in Organization Theory and Analysis* (London: Sage).

Grint, K. (1995), *Management: A Sociological Introduction* (Cambridge: Polity Press).

—— (1998a), *The Sociology of Work*, 2nd edn. (Cambridge: Polity Press).

—— and Woolgar, S. (1997), *The Machine at Work* (Cambridge: Polity Press).

Jabri, V. (1996), *Discourses on Violence: Conflict Analysis Reconsidered* (Manchester: Manchester University Press).

James, S. (1999), *The Ancient Celts: Ancient People or Modern Invention?* (London: British Museum Press).

Jenkins, R. (1996), *Social Identities* (London: Routledge).

Keitner, C. (1997), 'Power and Identity in Nationalist Conflicts', *Oxford International Review*, 8/2: 11–18.

Latour, B. (1986), 'The Powers of Association', in J. Law (ed.), *Power, Action and Belief* (London: Routledge).

Lewis, H. B. (1971), *Shame and Guilt in Neurosis* (New York: International Universities Press).

Littler, C. (1982), *The Development of the Labour Process in Britain, Japan and the USA* (London: Heinemann).

REFERENCES

Machiavelli, N. (1981), *The Prince* (Harmondsworth: Penguin).

Malcolm, N. (1999), *Kosovo: A Short History* (London: Papermac).

Marx, K. (1954), *Capital*, i (London: Lawrence & Wishart).

Putnam, L. L., Phillips, N., and Chapman, P. (1996), 'Metaphors of Communication in Organization', in S. R. Clegg, C. Hardy, and W. R. Nord (eds.), *Handbook of Organizational Studies* (London: Sage).

Sadowski, Y. (1998), 'What Really Makes the World Go to War', *Guardian*, 1 Aug.

Sahlins, P. (1989), *Boundaries: The Making of France and Spain in the Pyrenees* (Berkeley and Los Angeles: University of California Press).

Scheff, T. (1994), 'A Theory of Ethnic Nationalism', in C. Calhoun (ed.), *Social Theory and the Politics of Identity* (Oxford: Blackwell).

Strauss, A. (1978), *Negotiations: Varieties, Processes, Contexts and Social Order* (London: Jossey-Bass).

Wills, G. (1992), *Lincoln at Gettysburg: The Words that Remade America* (New York: Touchstone).

Willis, J., and Turnock, R. (1998), 'The Veil of Tears', *Guardian*, 17 Aug.

[25]

Beyond Goffman: Some Notes on Life and Theatre as Art

Iain L. Mangham

School of Management, University of Bath, United Kingdom

This paper discusses two events: a scene from a performance of 'Waiting for Godot' and an incident from a team development meeting for a group of senior managers. The focus is upon the nature of the experiences of the respective audiences not upon the instrumental value of the performances. Drawing upon the work of Heidegger and Shklovsky in particular, the author comments, compares and contrasts the two events. Particular emphasis is given to the notion of art as an "unconcealment" and upon the notions of imaginative and present truth.

Dramaturgy, as a perspective on social life, has existed for several hundred years. The notion that social life resembles theatre was a cliché as early as the sixteenth century. Jacques' use of it in Shakespeare's *As You Like It* is but a confirmation of what passed for an everyday analogy then:

All the world's a stage
And all the men and women merely players:
They have their exits and their entrances:
And one man in his time plays many parts.

Today the metaphor continues to be commonplace. We speak without reflection about "making a scene", "playing our parts", "knowing our roles", "putting on a show", "hogging the limelight", "taking a bow", "missing our cues", and so on. For most of us most of the time, the terms we use have lost any direct link with the theatre. For a few literary critics, however, and a generation of sociologists and social psychologists, the link between the way we conduct ourselves as human beings and the language of theatre and drama is more explicit.

The literary critic Kenneth Burke developed the so-called dramatistic perspective on social life in his book *Permanence and Change* (1935; see also *A Grammar of Motives*, 1945; *A Rhetoric of Motives*, 1955) in which he argued that human beings express themselves and relate to each other in much the same way as actors do when playing roles on a stage. His work was made more accessible to social scientists and further developed by Hugh Duncan some thirty or so years later (H.D. Duncan, 1953, 1963, 1968), but it was the publication of *The Presentation of Self in Everyday Life* (1959) by Erving Goffman that brought the metaphor into mainstream sociology and social psychology.

32 *I.L. Mangham*

Goffman's early books (1961a, 1961b, 1963a, 1963b, 1967) examined the ways in which a social actor reads a situation and constructs his/her behaviour so as to make an impression upon other social actors. As he puts it, life itself is a "dramatically enacted thing . . . It does take deep skill, long training, and a psychological capacity to become a good stage actor, but this fact should not blind us to another one: that almost anyone can quickly learn a script well enough to give a charitable audience some sense of realness in what is being contrived before them." (Mangham and Overington, 1987: 204).

Goffman's work spawned a host of studies all more or less informed by the notion of theatre as dissembling. To these followers of Goffman (and more particularly to his detractors), social actors are for the most part seen as duplicitous, deceitful and fraudulent beings who hide their purposes from others as they act; beings who use props, costumes, gestures, words, settings to manage and manipulate the behaviour of others. It is a partial, limited and damaging use of the metaphor, but not a surprising use given that it was initiated by someone who shows no evidence of having attended a theatrical performance and is promoted by dozens of others who rejoice in a similar ignorance.

These notes depart from the mainstream of dramaturgical analysis and focus upon theatre as art. It is in this sense that I claim it is *beyond* Goffman: "Outside the limit or sphere of, past; out of the grasp or reach of" – Oxford English Dictionary. It is an attempt to capture a little of what the theatre is about and to use that essence to illuminate the discussion of behaviour in organizations. It is informed by a lifetime of interest in the arts, particularly in the theatre, far too many years sitting in rooms with managers and some acquaintance with the literatures which pertain to both activities.

I will begin with a couple of events.

The scene is a School Hall in Mexborough, Yorkshire, England. It is a cold February night and an audience of some three hundred people is watching the closing moments of *Waiting for Godot* as performed by a semi-professional group of actors.

Estragon: You say we have to come back tomorrow?
Vladimir: Yes.
Estragon: Then we can bring a good bit of rope.
Vladimir: Yes.

Silence

Estragon: Didi.
Viadimir: Yes.
Estragon: I can't go on like this.
Vladimir: That's what you think.
Estragon: If we parted? That might be better for us.
Vladimir: We'll hang ourselves tomorrow. (*Pause*) Unless Godot comes.
Estragon: And if he comes?
Vladimir: We'll be saved.
   (*Vladimir takes off his hat, peers inside it, feels about inside it, shakes it, knocks on the crown, puts it on again.*)
Estragon: Well? Shall we go?
Vladimir: Pull on your trousers.

Estragon:	What?
Vladimir:	Pull on your trousers.
Estragon:	You want me to pull off my trousers?
Vladimir:	Pull ON your trousers.
Estragon:	(*realizing his trousers are down*). True. (*He pulls up his trousers.*)
Vladmir: ·	Well? Shall we go?
Estragon:	Yes, let's go.
	They do not move

CURTAIN

Silence. No one applauds. Backstage, tears are coursing down the faces of both actors and crew. It seems inappropriate, somehow out of proportion, to open the curtains and take a bow. The performance appears to have torn something apart, a disjuncture has occurred, time has been put out of joint; there is something almost tangible, physical, corporeal visceral about the moment – an opening, a field of space, a shape into which meanings swarm awaiting realization. A low rumbling noise gradually swells and turns into – applause. The curtains go back, the actors walk forward. The show is rounded off.

The scene is a hotel room in Chester. It is a cold February night and ten senior managers are gathered around a table having eaten and drunk a great deal. Ostensibly they are here for a strategy meeting scheduled for the next day; occasionally these so-called away days are used to *deal with* difficulties between members of the group. More often than not, this *dealing with* consists of joking, scapegoating and other attempts to cut the victims *down to size*. On this occasion, Graham, the manager of a business unit, has raised some issues about the role that Eric, the managing director, and Steve, the personnel director, are playing in his business. Several attempts have been made to cut him down to size:

Eric:	(*to the waiter*) And we'll need some more brandy. Bring another bottle. Right. Where were we before we were so rudely interrupted? Ah, yes. The question of commitment, Graham?
Graham:	I was not talking about commitment, I was talking about Personnel's right to shift people around without consultation.
Eric:	But the rest of us *were* talking about commitment, Graham.
Colin:	My people are committed to plan, Graham, are yours?
Graham:	You might have been happy to join in, Colin, for reasons best known to yourself, but *I* was not talking about commitment, *I* was talking about poaching my people.
Roger:	But your people are not committed, I've heard them say it themselves.
Graham:	Roger, I do not give a toss what you claim to have heard. I am not talking about plans or commitment! I am talking about poaching!
Tony:	(*drunkenly*) He's right! He's right! That's what we started talking about. That's what the boy started on about. I distinctly remember.
Roger:	You're too pissed to remember anything . . .
Eric:	Get it off your chest. Tell us what the issue is and then we'll talk about commitment.

34   *I.L. Mangham*

Graham: Eric, I've told you what I think the issue is and I don't want to talk about
             commitment, as you keep calling it, now or later. Either I am running my
             unit or I am not. I deeply resent Steve telling me that he is moving one of
             my better – no, my *best* man – and giving him to Roger.
Steve: It wasn't like that, Graham, and you know it. I talked to you about it . . .
Graham: You talked to me about it AFTER . . . AFTER you had decided – with Eric
             no doubt and probably Roger – what you were going to do. He is my man,
             in my unit, working for me.
Eric: And for the good of the team as a whole, we decided that we needed his
             contribution elsewhere .
Graham: Cant! Sheer bloody unadulterated cant! "For the good the team." What
             bloody team? This lot? Us? Look at us! Senior managers in a public
             company, pissed as newts, debating nonsense – *Commitment, the good of
             the team! Working together, contributing to the company*. It's all wind!
             Bloody hypocrisy. Tripe. We make bloody biscuits and crisps, and snacks
             and pizzas. What's all this talk of commitment? It's not life or death, is
             it? It's no big deal. Biscuits, crisps, toffee bars, stuff everyone can do
             without. What is all this crap about *commitment* and *team spirit*? We are
             not supposed to be a bloody religious order. We are not on some crusade
             to save the world! *Commitment*, for God's sake. Who cares if we make a
             few more Nut Surprises? Sell a few more Dream Delights? A handful of
             shareholders, that's who cares? We have to ask ourselves what all this is
             about. What is the point of pouring huge amounts of energy into making
             more and more things that are of no use to anyone? Dream Delights, for
             God's sake! What's it all come down to? What's it all about? We throw
             ourselves into this nonsense as if it mattered. As if we were working to free
             the world from cholera or something. We are riding a monster. Production,
             profit, grind it out. Push it on. Where is it all leading? I'll tell you where –
             bloody nowhere! It is not progress making more and more biscuits, more
             and more crisps, the biggest pizza in the world. We go on about being
             committed as though a few thousand quid either way will make a
             difference. Right, if you want to know, I am not *committed*, as you put it. I
             do not spend every waking hour thinking about Nut Surprises or Dream
             Delights. I do not *want* to spend my life thinking about Nut Surprises or
             Dream Delights. I question the sanity of anyone who does. I don't want to
             be in the office at seven in the morning and leave nine or ten at night. I
             do not want to spend time here. Now. Listening to this twaddle about
             commitment. Arguing about who works for whom. You are welcome to
             my staff, Roger – all of them. I'd rather be at home. What do you want
             from me? Blood? I work to live, not the other way round. And so do most
             of the rest of you – if you don't, you are mad. I work hard not because I
             am *committed*. I work to support my wife and family. There is life beyond
             this company, and I am sick of pretending otherwise. You can have me from
             nine to five, beyond that I am my own man . . .

> *Silence. No one moves. No one catches anyone else's eye. Something has been put asunder, a disjuncture has occurred; one senses a space, a void, a crack opening up, a rush of stale air being expelled; something starkly, rudely present. The door opens and the waiter enters . . .*

It may be appropriate to read through the events once more. It would not be appropriate to seek to *understand* what they mean nor – God forbid – to attempt to deconstruct them. Please experience them again.

I will return to the passages shortly. My purpose in placing them where I have in this text was to give you the opportunity of responding to them free from the direct influence of anything which follows. It was also an attempt to induce in you the posture of a spectator. More of this later. I will eschew the kind of analysis that I have attempted elsewhere (Mangham, 1986). From such a perspective, it would be possible to interpret *Waiting for Godot* as a play about authority (or the absence of it). One could look at the interactions of the two main characters as if they were manifestations of individual attempts at securing power and status. One could offer a similar analysis of the interactions at Chester. It is, after all, obvious that Graham is the subject of an attempt to make him conform and equally obvious that he responds by asserting his own position. My focus here is different. It is more concerned with the impact of the experiences. I will proceed by making a few assertions about the nature of art and theatre and will continue by relating these observations to some general comments about behaviour in organizations and about the events at Mexborough and Chester in particular.

Let me be clear. I am interested in the experience, not its value. Much of the discussion about the nature of a spectator's response to incidents such as that which occurred at Chester focus upon the value of the experience. Perhaps the most famous example of the former is Aristotle's view of tragedy. Having taken on Goffman in my opening paragraphs, let me offend a few others by asserting that Aristotle also has it wrong (although he no doubt was an avid theatregoer). It will be recalled that Aristotle identified a couple of emotions as being at the heart of tragedy: pity (for the pain others are feeling) and fear (there but for the grace of God go I). His view was that by arousing pity and fear, tragedy achieves a purification or clarification – a catharsis – of our emotions. From this perspective, what the audience to *Waiting for Godot* achieved was a sense of calm after a powerful experience of both pity and fear. By extension, what the managers arrived at in Chester was a sense of calm after having experienced a similar sense of pity and fear during Graham's curtain speech. I am not going to indulge in a protracted discussion as to whether or not either event was a tragedy, a tragi-comedy, a farce or whatever; the only point I wish to make is that Aristotle (and so many of his followers) in talking about catharsis has reduced the impact of art to that of medicine. The cure for pity and fear? Two tickets for *Oedipus Rex*. A guaranteed homeopathic remedy. As Malcolm Budd (1995) notes, by locating the benefit to be derived from art in its after-effects, Aristotle's perspective assigns only "an instrumental, not an intrinsic, value to the experience". Further, it fails "to locate a distinctive pleasure *in* the experience of the tragic emotions: the pleasure it identifies is pleasure in the freedom from the (overcharged) emotions of pity and fear."

(1995: 111) I am not happy with the emphasis upon pleasure, but I agree with what I take to be the sentiment: art is about the intensity of the experience, not the relief from it.

Some comments drawn from Martin Heidegger's essay on the origins of the work of art may help to illustrate my drift:

"It is the same with the sculpture of the god, a votive offering of the victor in the athletic games. It is not a portrait whose purpose is to make it easier to realize how the god looks; rather, it is a work that lets the god himself be present and thus *is* the god himself. The same holds for the linguistic work. In the tragedy nothing is staged or displayed theatrically, but the battle of the new gods against the old is being fought. The lingusitic work, originating in the speech of the people, does not refer to this battle; it transforms the people's saying so that now every living word fights the battle and puts up for decision what is holy and what unholy, what great and what small, what brave and what cowardly, what lofty and what flighty, what master and what slave." (Heidegger, edited D.F. Krell, 1993: 168/169, italics in the original)

Heidegger's notion of the god being brought forth, made present, is similar to anthropological observations on ritual:

"Every ritual has the character of happening now, at this very moment. The time of the event that the ritual commemorates or re-enacts is made present, 're-presented', so to speak, however far back it may been in ordinary reckoning. Christ's passion, death and resurrection are not simply remembered during the services of Holy Week: they really happen then before the eyes of the faithful." (Eliade, 1970: 392)

Maybe Heidegger would not go quite as literal as this, but he certainly appears to hold that what we witness in a theatre is a *presentation* of the truth, the essence of the god appears before us. What occurs in the ritual and on the stage is not simply a reference to an event elsewhere, there and then, but a celebration, a realisation of an essence here and now.

The notion of an essence (a 'work', in Heidegger's terminology) being 'brought forth' is important to Heidegger's discussion of the origin and nature of art. In effect he is picking up on one of the meanings of mimesis. Since Plato and Aristotle, the importance of the concept of mimesis as 'imitation' or 'representation' has been stressed in philosophy and aesthetics. Scholars now are increasingly recognizing the importance of the related meaning of the term as performative as, indeed, standing for a 'bringing forth' and 'monstration', a presentation rather than a representation. (Bogu and Spariosu, 1994: vii)

Heidegger's discussion of Van Gogh's painting of the peasant shoes illustrates this point. We recognize the forms in the picture as shoes, but that, he claims, does not mean that such a recognition exhausts the meaning of the painting. Indeed everything about the picture draws us into it and prevents us from referring elsewhere. As Heidegger puts it, "The artwork lets us know what shoes are in truth." Not, as he points out, by a simple description of a pair of shoes; not by any report of the making of shoes and not by the observation of the actual use of shoes ". . . but only by bringing ourselves before Van Gogh's painting. This painting spoke. In the nearness of the work we were suddenly somewhere else than we usually tend to be" (Heidegger, 1993: 161). In this state the painting reveals something to us that until this moment had been concealed. "The establishing of truth in the work is the bringing forth of a being such as never was before and will never come to be again." (ibid: 187)

It is not a matter of the shoes having been painted by Van Gogh as opposed to Joe Bloggs: "It is not the *N.N. fecit* that is to be made known. Rather the simple *factum est* is to be held forth into the open region by the work: namely this, that unconcealment of a being has happened here and that as this happening it happens here for the first time; or, that such a work *is* at all rather than is not." (ibid: 190)

The notion that the work *is* is unusual and one of the features that marks it out as a work of art. A hammer is created but its essence "disappears in usefulness" (ibid: 191). As Heidegger puts it, "In general, of everything present to us, we can note that it *is*, but this also, if it is noted at all, is noted only soon to fall into oblivion, as is the wont of everything commonplace" (ibid: 190). In a work of art, however, its *isness* proclaims itself. "The event of its being created does not simply reverberate through the work; rather, the work casts before itself the eventful fact that the work is as this work, and it has constantly this fact about itself. The more essentially the work opens itself, the more luminous becomes the uniqueness of the fact that it is rather than is not. The more essentially this thrust comes into the open region, the more strange and solitary the work becomes. In the bringing forth of the work there lies this offering 'that it be'" (ibid: 190–191).

Heidegger is adamant that it is not a matter of representation. "But above all, the work did not, as might seem at first, serve merely for a better visualizing of what a piece of equipment is. Rather the equipmentality of equipment [the essence of shoeness, at it were] first expressly comes to the fore through the work and only in the work." For Heidegger, in the presence of Van Gogh's painting, in the different kind of "here" we experience from where we "usually tend to be", we apprehend that the painting "is the disclosure of what the equipment, the pair of shoes, is in truth" (ibid: 161, material in brackets my own).

Art, for Heidegger is a mode of knowing. "For Greek thought the essence of knowing consists in *aletheia*, that is, in the revealing of beings. It supports and guides all comportment toward beings. *Techne*, as knowledge experienced in the Greek manner, is bringing forth of beings in that it *brings forth* what is present as such *out* of concealment and specifically into the unconcealment of its appearance." (1993: 184) Art lies in the bringing forth of truth: "*Art then is a becoming and happening of truth*" (ibid: 196, italics in the original).

Enough of Heidegger for the moment. I would like to hang on to three of his observations as we proceed: first, the notion that art/truth is a matter of bringing forth, presenting an essence, an unconcealment; second, that this unconcealment manifests itself as a createdness, an establishing, a thatisness, a reverberation that proclaims itself to be unique; and thirdly, that in order to apprehend the bringing forth we must allow ourselves to be present, we must achieve a nearness to the poem, play, painting or whatever.

Let me return to the passages with which I began this piece. I take it that many would agree that *Waiting for Godot* could be seen as a matter of presenting an essence, an example of art revealing a truth which reverberates through its every moment.

As presented in Mexborough, the tramps hung around on the edge of the stage (leaving an empty central position from which nobody offers direction) inquiring about the absent but awaited authority – Godot – unable to depict him or, for that matter, much else clearly and unequivocally. Waiting. Passing the time in pursuits which start up, falter and die:

Estragon:	That's the idea, let's abuse each other.
	(They turn, move apart, turn again and face each other)
Vladimir:	Moron!
Estragon:	Vermin!
Vladimir:	Abortion!
Estragon:	Morpion!
Vladimir:	Sewer-rat!
Estragon:	Curate!
Vladimir:	Cretin!
Estragon:	*(with finality)* Critic!

Trivial rites, as Bruce Wilshire calls them in a powerful analysis of the play (Wilshire, 1982: 73–79); burlesque routines which take on great importance as surrogate structures of significance and continuity. The point seems to be, Wilshire argues, and the Mexborough experience confirms, that "the authority whose view of them, and certification of them, the tramps must incorporate and make their own if they are to be vitally alive is absent in such a way that his felt presence in the world cannot sustain them, at least not beyond merely waiting for him." (ibid: 76) He is experienced by us all, on stage and off, as a gaping absence. There is nothing for any of us to do but to wait.

Vladimir and Estragon reveal an emotional emptiness, appear as deserted husks of beings, insubtantial wraiths, trying and, for the most part, failing to make contact with each other. And, mockingly, they draw attention to us:

Vladimir:	Where are all these corpses from?
Estragon:	These skeletons.
Vladimir:	Tell me that.
Estragon:	True.
Vladimir:	We must have thought a little.
Estragon:	At the very beginning.
Vladimir:	A charnel-house! A charnel house!
Estragon:	You don't have to look.
Vladimir:	You can't help looking.

The play is suffused by an inability to take action and ends in it:

Vladimir:	Well, shall we go?
Estragon:	Yes, let's go.

They do not move

The silence at the end of the performance at Mexborough was the silence, perhaps, of an audience which had discovered a truth, had experienced an unconcealment. The question of the meaningfulness of the world (our world) is put at issue in *Waiting for Godot* and it is deeply disturbing. The emptiness of our existence is brought forth before us. It emerges from the text, it is made flesh before us; we are present, dreadfully near to the work as it unfolds. For a moment we stagger a little. There is nothing to be said.

We wonder, in Wilshire's marvellous phrase, whether the production can be sealed off or if its "content will soak through, as blood would through a bandage." (ibid: 80) But then, like the tramps, we recover and continue:

Estragon: So long as one knows.
Vladimir: One can bide one's time.
Estragon: One knows what to expect.
Vladimir: No further need to worry.
Estragon: Simply wait.
Vladimir: We're used to it.

The incident at Chester has, I believe, similar characteristics. There is an unconcealing, a space is opened up, there is a createdness; a truth is glimpsed and, perhaps, apprehended. Something is disclosed. Each one around that table falls silent. Graham's peroration reduces us to silence. Perhaps, just perhaps, the silence reveals the quiet struggle that we must each undertake if we are to render the world that we have just experienced meaningful again. Meanings swarm in. A world where the market should not rule. A world where the routines of planning and budgets are declared to be of no value; a world in which cornflakes, dogfood, crisps, nutcrunches are not seen to be of consequence; a world in which own brands, shelf position, discounts is regarded as so much gibberish; a naked, brazen challenge to a world knee deep in empty crisp packets, where well-educated, well-heeled individuals pursue their own ends at the expense of the environment; a calling into question of a world where some have wealth and many starve; a world where the predominance of economic perspectives on social life is impugned. Is it too much to suggest that, momentarily, in a massive, sapping body blow, Graham calls into question the entire structure of sales and numbers, cash and targets, drive and ambition? Perhaps as each of the managers reels back we glimpse the emptiness of it all?

"Art", claims Victor Shklovsky, "exists that one may recover the sensation of life; it exists to make one feel things, to make the stone *stony*. The purpose of art is to impart the sensation of things as they are perceived and not as they are known. The technique of art is to make objects 'unfamiliar', to make forms difficult, to increase the difficulty and length of perception because the process of perception is an aesthetic end in itself and must be prolonged. *Art is a way of experiencing the artfulness of an object; the object is not important.*" (Shklovsky, 1965: 12, italics in the original)

From Shklovsky's point of view, *Waiting for Godot* is art and the incident at Chester is not. I do not wish to quarrel with such an interpretation. In no sense did any of us around the table in Chester regard the outburst as an aesthetic end in itself, something to be prolonged as a means of experiencing the artfulness of the object. Most of us, however, did experience it as a matter of consequence and feeling – intense feeling; most of us experienced the direct stoniness of the soliloquy; and most of us sensed that our world taken for granted had been jolted, turned upside down, rendered unfamiliar. All of us were near enough to the event to experience these aspects of it. Some of us were nearer; near enough to experience the sensation of things as Graham perceived them. And we cannot unexperience that.

At this point let me borrow an idea from David Cole (1975). We live, he claims, between two kinds of truth, neither of which is entirely satisfactory. *Imaginative truth* satisfies "our longing for coherence, but it is only an envisioning, cannot *be there*" (ibid: 3), and *present truth*, that which *can* be there, seeable and graspable, but which lacks the coherence of the imaginative form. He quotes Sartre: ". . . the real and the imaginary cannot coexist by their very nature . . . To prefer the imaginary . . . is not only an escape from the content of the real (poverty, frustrated love, failure of one's enterprise, etc.), but from the form of the real itself, its character of *presence*." (ibid: 5)

The possibility of synthesizing the two kinds of truth he regards as problematic and cites both Wordsworth and Rilke as those who may have had moments when, in the words of the latter,

"the external thing itself – tower, mountain, bridge – already possessed the unheard of, unsurpassable intensity of those inner equivalents by means of which it might have been represented. Everywhere appearance and vision came, as it were, together in the object, in every one of them a whole inner world was exhibited."

Perhaps that night in Chester, appearance and vision, *imaginative* and *present* truth, were made manifest in one of their rare conjunctions. If so, the link with theatre and theatre alone would be clear. Theatre, Cole claims, provides an opportunity of experiencing imaginative truth as present truth. "In theatre, imaginative events take on for a moment the presentness of physical events; in theatre, physical events take on for a moment the perfection of imaginative form." (ibid: 6) Were I to have the skill to render the present truth of the incident at Chester in imaginative and theatrical terms, both could be offered to an audience primarily but not exclusively through the presence of the actor – at once a role-possessed body and an embodied role. All of the arts, as Heidegger is aware, make present; "theatre alone *makes presence*" (ibid: 6).

And now, of course, the cat is out of the bag. The examples with which I began this piece cannot be anything other than a poor reflection of the evenings in Mexborough and Chester. I am attempting to talk about imaginative truth, present truth and unconcealment, disclosing, but I am, perforce, doing it in a literal and unimaginative fashion. I have not the techne, the words or the artifice, to bring the truth of these events to your attention; I cannot draw you in and render what I am about stony. The presences of the events are absent and cannot be recreated other than in the theatre and, for the happenings at Chester, perhaps not even there. I hope, however, that I have suggested enough about theatre, art and some forms of interaction to stimulate further exploration of the metaphor beyond its more popular and, now, somewhat tired manifestations.

References

Bogu, R. and Spariosu, M.I. (1994) *The Play of Self*. New York: State University of New York Press.
Budd, M. (1995) *Values of Art: Pictures, Poetry and Music*. Harmondsworth: Penguin.
Burke, K. (1935) *Permanence and Change: An Anatomy of Purpose*. New York: Bobbs Merrill.
Burke, K. (1945) *A Grammar of Motives*. New York: Bobbs Merrill.
Burke, K. (1955) *A Rhetoric of Motives*. New York: Bobbs Merrill.

Cole, D. (1975) *The Theatrical Event: A Mythos, a Vocabulary, a Perspective.* Middletown: Wesleyan University Press.

Duncan, H. Dalziel (1953) *Language and Literature in Society.* Chicago: University of Chicago Press.

Duncan, H. Dalziel (1963) *Communication and Social Order.* New Jersey: Bedminster Press.

Duncan, H. Dalziel (1968) *Symbols in Society.* New York: Oxford University Press.

Eliade, M. (1970) *Patterns in Comparative Religion* (trans. R. Sheed). London: Harper.

Goffman, E. (1959) *The Presentation of Self in Everyday Life,* Garden City. New Jersey: Doubleday Anchor.

Goffman, E. (1961a) *Asylums: Essays on the Social Situations of Mental Patients and Other Inmates,* Garden City. New Jersey: Anchor.

Goffman, E. (1961b) *Encounters.* Indianapolis: Bobbs Merrill.

Goffman, E. (1963a) *Stigma,* Englewood Cliffs. New Jersey: Prentice Hall.

Goffman, E. (1963b) *Behaviour in Public Places.* New York: Free Press.

Goffman, E. (1967) *Interaction Ritual,* Garden City. New Jersey: Anchor Books.

Heidegger, M. (1993) The Origin of the Work of Arts. In *Basic Writings: Martin Heidegger, second edition,* edited by David Farrell Krell. London: Routledge.

Mangham, I.L. (1986) *Power and Performance in Organizations.* Oxford: Blackwell.

Mangham, I.L. and Overington, M.A. (1987) *Organizations as Theatre: A Social Psychology of Dramatic Appearances.* Chichester: John Wiley.

Shklovsky, V. (1965) Art as Technique. In L.T. Lemon and M.J. Reis Lincoln (eds and trans.) *Russian Formalist Criticism: Four Essays.* Omaha: University of Nebraska Press.

Wilshire, B. (1982) *Role Playing and Identity: The Limits of Theatre as Metaphor.* Bloomington: University of Indiana Press.

[26]

PLANNING ON THE LEFT SIDE, MANAGING ON THE RIGHT

Henry Mintzberg

The article reprinted here preceded the last by more than a decade and took me into a somewhat different although perhaps more fundamental issue: the relationship between analysis and intuition, as manifested in the long and sometimes strained relationship between "staff" and "line," with special reference to planners and managers. The first two articles of this book grew out of years of research and contemplation; this third one developed rather spontaneously. In the summer of 1975, on a small farm in the Perigord region of France, I read Robert Ornstein's *The Psychology of Consciousness,* a popular account of the findings on the two hemispheres of the human brain. Although attention to these findings had become faddish at the time, to me they provided a basis for much of what I had been finding in my own research.

There is a lovely irony in the fact that intuition was in some sense brought back to life by the biologists. You see, intuition should really be a psychological concept. But most psychologists, in order to be perceived as good scientists, have long slighted it, when not ignoring it altogether. After all, if intuition is a thought process inaccessible to the *conscious* mind, how could they use *scientific* methods to describe it? Then along came people like Roger Sperry—real scientists, who cut tissue with knives and the like—and they were the ones to rediscover intuition, in a sense hiding all along in the mute right hemisphere of the human brain!

In reading Ornstein's book, I came to realize that I had really been celebrating intuition in my own research, uncovering it in all kinds of odd and clandestine places. This was at odds with the mainline management literature—applied no less than academic—that emphasized, almost to the point of obsession, the role of analysis in organizations, especially under so-called professional management. The title hit me first, then I wrote the article. (Usually it has been the other

44   On Management

way around.) My writing almost always goes through many drafts
before the editors get their hands on it and propose further changes.
"Planning on the Left Side and Managing on the Right" appeared
in the *Harvard Business Review* in 1976 almost as I first put it down
on that small farm in the Perigord.

In the folklore of the Middle East, the story is told about a man
named Nasrudin, who was searching for something on the ground. A
friend came by and asked: "What have you lost, Nasrudin?"

"My key," said Nasrudin.

So the friend went down on his knees too, and they both looked for
it. After a time, the friend asked: "Where exactly did you drop it?"

"In my house," answered Nasrudin.

"Then why are you looking here, Nasrudin?"

"There is more light here than inside my own house."

This little story has some timeless, mysterious appeal which has much
to do with what follows. But let me leave that aside for a moment
while I pose some questions—also simple yet mysterious—that have
long puzzled me.

  • First: Why are some people so smart and so dull at the same
time, so capable of mastering certain mental activities yet so incapable
of mastering others? Why is it that some of the most creative thinkers
cannot comprehend a balance sheet, and that some accountants have
no sense of product design? Why do some brilliant management scientists have no ability to handle organizational politics, while some of
the most politically adept individuals seem unable to understand the
simplest elements of management science?

  • Second: Why do people sometimes express such surprise when
they read or learn the obvious, something they already must have
known? Why is a manager so delighted, for example, when he or
she reads a new article on decision-making, every part of which must
be patently obvious to him or her even though never before seen in
print?

  • Third: Why is there such a discrepancy in organizations, at
least at the top levels, between formal planning on the one hand and
informal managing on the other? Why have none of the techniques
of planning and analysis really had much effect on how top managers
function?

I intend below to weave answers to those three questions around the
theme of the specialization of the hemispheres of the human brain. Later

I shall use my own research to draw out some implications of this for management, returning to our story of Nasrudin.

THE TWO HEMISPHERES OF THE HUMAN BRAIN

Let us first try to answer the three questions by looking at what is known about the hemispheres of the human brain.

QUESTION ONE

Scientists—in particular, neurologists, biologists, and psychologists—have known for a long time that the brain has two distinct hemispheres. They have known, further, that the left hemisphere controls movements on the body's right side while the right hemisphere controls movements on the left. What some have discovered more recently, however, is that the two hemispheres are specialized in more fundamental ways.

In the left hemisphere of most people's brains (lefthanders largely excepted), the mode of operation appears to be largely linear, information being processed sequentially, one bit after another, in an ordered way. Perhaps the most obvious linear faculty is language. In sharp contrast, the right hemisphere appears to be specialized for simultaneous processing; that is, it seems to operate in a more holistic, relational way. Perhaps its most obvious faculty is comprehension of visual images.

Although relatively few specific mental activities have yet been associated with one hemisphere or the other, research has provided some important clues. For example, an article in *The New York Times* cited research which suggests that emotion may be a right-hemispheric function.[1] This notion is based on the finding that victims of right-hemispheric strokes are often comparatively untroubled about their incapacity, while those with strokes of the left hemisphere often suffer profound mental anguish.

What does this specialization of the brain mean for the way people function? Speech, being linear, is a left-hemispheric activity, but other forms of human communication, such as gesturing, are relational and visual rather than sequential and verbal so tend to be associated with the right hemisphere. Imagine what would happen if the two sides of a human brain were detached so that, for example, in reading stimuli, words would be separate from gestures. In other words, in the same person, two separate brains—one specialized for verbal communication, and the other for gestures—would react to the same stimulus.

46 On Management

This, in fact, describes how the main breakthrough in the research on the human brain took place. In trying to treat certain cases of epilepsy, neurosurgeons found that by severing the corpus callosum, which joins the two hemispheres of the brain, they could ''split the brain,'' isolating the epilepsy. A number of experiments run on these ''split-brain'' patients produced some fascinating results.

In one experiment, doctors showed a woman epileptic's right hemisphere a photograph of a nude woman. (This is done by showing it to the left half of each eye.) The patient said she saw nothing, but almost simultaneously blushed and seemed confused and uncomfortable. Her ''conscious'' left hemisphere, including her verbal apparatus, was aware only that something had happened to her body, but not what had caused the emotional response. Only her ''unconscious'' right hemisphere knew. Here neurosurgeons observed a clear split between the two independent consciousnesses that are normally in communication and collaboration.[2]

Scientists have found further that some common human tasks activate one side of the brain while leaving the other largely at rest. For example, learning a mathematical proof might evoke activity in the left hemisphere of the brain, while viewing a piece of sculpture or assessing a political opponent might evoke activity in the right.

So now we seem to have the answer to the first question. An individual may be smart and dull at the same time simply because one side of his or her brain is more developed than the other. Some people—perhaps most lawyers, accountants, planners—may have better developed left-hemispheric thinking processes, while others—perhaps, artists, athletes, politicians—may have better developed right-hemispheric processes. Thus an artist may be incapable of expressing certain feelings in words, while a lawyer may have no facility for painting. Or a politician may not be able to learn mathematics, while a management scientist may be constantly manipulated in political situations.

QUESTION TWO

A number of word opposites have been proposed to distinguish the two hemispheric modes of ''consciousness,'' for example: explicit versus implicit; verbal versus spatial; argument versus experience; intellectual versus intuitive; and analytic versus gestalt.

I should interject at this point that these words, as well as much of the evidence for these conclusions, can be found in the remarkable book entitled *The Psychology of Consciousness* by Robert Ornstein, a research

Planning on the Left Side, Managing on the Right   47

psychologist in California. Ornstein uses the story of Nasrudin to further the points he is making. Specifically, he refers to the linear left hemisphere as synonymous with lightness, with thought processes that we know in an explicit sense. We can *articulate* them. He associates the right hemisphere with darkness, with thought processes that are mysterious to us, at least "us" in the Western world.

Ornstein also points out how the "esoteric psychologies" of the East (Zen, Yoga, Sufism, and so on) have focused on right-hemispheric consciousness (for example, altering pulse rate through meditation). In sharp contrast, Western psychology has been concerned almost exclusively with left-hemispheric consciousness, with logical thought. Ornstein suggests that we might find an important key to human consciousness in the right hemisphere, in what to us in the West has been the darkness.

Now, reflect on this for a moment. (Should I say meditate?) There is a set of thought processes—linear, sequential, analytical—that scientists as well as the rest of us know a good deal about. And there is another set—simultaneous, relational, holistic—that we know little about. More importantly, here we do not "know" what we "know" or more exactly, our left hemispheres do not seem able to articulate explicitly what our right hemispheres know implicitly.

So here, seemingly, is the answer to the second question as well. The feeling of revelation about learning the obvious can be explained with the suggestion that the "obvious" knowledge was implicit, apparently restricted to the right hemisphere. The left hemisphere never "knew." Thus it seems to be a revelation to the left hemisphere when it learns explicitly what the right hemisphere knew all along implicitly.

Now the third question—the discrepancy between planning and managing—remains.

QUESTION THREE

By now, it should be obvious where my discussion is leading (at least, to the reader's right hemisphere and, now that I write it, perhaps to the reader's left hemisphere as well). It may be that management researchers have been looking for the key to management in the lightness of logical analysis whereas perhaps it has always been lost in the darkness of intuition.

Specifically, I propose that there may be a fundamental difference between formal planning and informal managing, a difference akin to

48   On Management

that between the two hemispheres of the human brain. The techniques of planning and analysis are sequential and systematic; above all, articulated. Planners and management scientists are expected to proceed in their work through a series of logical, ordered steps, each one involving explicit analysis. (The argument that the successful application of these techniques requires considerable intuition does not really change my point. The occurrence of intuition simply means that the analyst is departing from his or her science.)

Formal planning, then, seems to use processes akin to those identified with the brain's left hemisphere. Furthermore, planners and management scientists seem to revel in a systematic, well-ordered world, and many show little appreciation for the more relational, holistic processes.

What about managing? More exactly, what about the processes used by top managers? (Let me emphasize here that I am focusing this discussion at the senior levels of organizations, where I believe the dichotomy between planning and managing is most pronounced.) Managers plan in some ways, too (that is, they think ahead), and they engage in their share of logical analysis. But I believe there is more than that to the effective managing of an organization. I hypothesize, therefore, that *the important processes of managing an organization rely to a considerable extent on the faculties identified with the brain's right hemisphere.* Effective managers seem to revel in ambiguity, in complex, mysterious systems with relatively little order.

If true, this hypothesis would answer the third question about the discrepancy between planning and managing. It would help to explain why each of the new analytic techniques of planning and analysis has, one after the other, had so little success at the senior levels. PPBS, strategic planning, "management" information systems, and models of the firm—all have been greeted with great enthusiasm, then, in many instances, a few years later quietly ushered out the back door.

MANAGING FROM THE RIGHT HEMISPHERE

Because research has so far told us little about the right hemisphere, I cannot support with evidence my claim that a key to managing lies there. I can only present to the reader a "feel" for the situation, not a reading of concrete data. A number of findings from my own research on senior management processes do, however, suggest that they possess characteristics of right-hemispheric thinking.

Planning on the Left Side, Managing on the Right 49

One fact recurs repeatedly in all of this research. The key managerial processes are enormously complex and mysterious (to me as a researcher, as well as to the managers who carry them out), drawing on the vaguest of information and using the least articulated of mental processes. These processes seem to be more relational and holistic than ordered and sequential, more intuitive than intellectual; they seem, in other words, to be most characteristic of right-hemispheric activity.

Here are some general findings:

1. The five chief executives I observed strongly favored the oral media of communication, especially meetings, over the written forms, namely reading and writing. Of course oral communication is linear, too, but it is more than that. Managers seem to favor it for two fundamental reasons that suggest a relational mode of operation.

First, oral communication enables the manager to "read" facial expressions, tones of voice, and gestures. As I mentioned earlier, these stimuli seem to be associated with the right hemisphere of the brain. Second, and perhaps more important, oral communication enables the manager to engage in the "real-time" exchange of information. Managers' concentration on the oral media, therefore, suggests that they desire relational, simultaneous methods of acquiring information, rather than the ordered and sequential ones.

2. In addition to noting the media managers use, it is interesting to look at the content of managers' information, and at what they do with it. The evidence here is that a great deal of the managers' inputs are soft and speculative—impressions and feelings about other people, hearsay, gossip, and so on. Furthermore, the very analytical inputs—reports, documents, and hard data in general—seem to be of relatively little interest to many managers.

What can managers do with this soft, speculative information? They "synthesize" rather than "analyze" it, I should think. (How do you analyze the mood of a friend or the grimace someone makes in response to a suggestion?) A great deal of this information helps the manager understand implicitly his or her organization and its environment, to "see the big picture." This very expression, so common in management, implies a relational, holistic use of information.

A number of words managers commonly use suggest this kind of mental process. For example, the word "hunch" seems to refer to the results of using the implicit models that managers develop subconsciously in their brains. "I don't know why, but I have a hunch that if we do

50   On Management

x, then they will respond with y.'' Managers also use the word "intuition"
to refer to thought processes that work but are unknown to them. This
seems to be a word that the verbal intellect has given to the mysterious
thought processes. Maybe ''a person has good intuition'' simply means
that person has good implicit models in his or her right hemisphere.

3. Another consequence of the oral nature of the managers' information
is of interest here. Managers tend to be the best-informed members of
their organization, but they have difficulty disseminating their information
to their subordinates. Therefore, when managers overloaded with work
find a new task that needs doing, they face a dilemma: They must either
delegate the task without the background information or simply do the
task themselves, neither of which is satisfactory.

When I first encountered this "dilemma of delegation," I described
it in terms of time and of the nature of the manager's information:
Because so much of a manager's information is oral (and stored in his
or her head), the dissemination of it consumes much time. But now
the split-brain research suggests a second, perhaps more significant, reason
for the dilemma of delegation. The manager may simply be incapable
of disseminating some relevant information because it is inaccessible to
his or her consciousness.

4. Earlier in this article I wrote that managers revel in ambiguity, in
complex, mysterious systems without much order. Let us look at evidence
of this. What I have discussed so far about the managers' use of information suggests that their work is geared to action, not reflection. We see
further evidence for this in the pace of their work (''Breaks are rare.
It's one damn thing after another.''); the brevity of their activities (half
of the chief executives' activities I observed were completed in less
than nine minutes); the variety of their activities (these chief executives
had no evident patterns in their workdays); the active preference for
interruption in their work (stopping meetings, leaving their doors open);
and the lack of routine in their work (few regularly scheduled contacts,
and hardly any issues related to general planning).

Clearly, the manager does not operate in a systematic, orderly, and
intellectual way, puffing on a pipe in a mountain retreat, as problems
are analyzed. Rather, the manager deals with issues in the context of
daily activities—one hand on the telephone, the other shaking hands
with a departing guest. The manager is involved, plugged in; the mode
of operating is relational, simultaneous, experiential, that is, encompass-
ing all the characteristics associated with the right hemisphere.

Planning on the Left Side, Managing on the Right 51

5. If the most important managerial roles of the ten described in my research were to be isolated, leader, liaison, and disturbance handler would certainly be among them. Yet these are the roles least understood. *Leader* describes how the manager deals with his or her own subordinates. It is ironic that despite an immense amount of research, managers and researchers still know virtually nothing about the essence of leadership, about why some people follow and others lead. Leadership remains a mysterious chemistry; catchall words such as *charisma* proclaim our ignorance.

In the *liaison* role, the manager builds up a network of outside contacts, which serve as his or her personal information system. Again, the activities of this role remain almost completely outside the realm of articulated knowledge. And as a *disturbance handler* the manager handles problems and crises in his or her organization. Here again, despite an extensive literature on analytical decision-making, virtually nothing is written about decision-making under pressure. These activities remain outside the realm of management science, inside only the realm of intuition and experience.

6. Let us turn now to our research on strategic decision-making processes.[3] Two aspects of this—the *diagnosis* of decision situations and the *design* of custom-made solutions—stand out in that almost nothing is known about them. Yet these two stand out for another reason as well: They seem to be the most important aspects. In particular, diagnosis seems to be *the* crucial step in strategic decision-making, for it is here that the whole course of decision-making is set. It is a surprising fact, therefore, that diagnosis goes virtually without mention in the literature of planning or management science, most of which deals with the formal evaluation of given alternatives. The question becomes, *where* and *how* does diagnosis take place? Apparently in the darkness of judgment and intuition.

7. Another point that emerges from studying strategic decision-making processes is the existence and profound influence of a set of dynamic factors. Strategic decision-making processes are stopped by interruptions, delayed and speeded up by timing responses, and forced repeatedly to branch and cycle. Yet it is these dynamic factors that the ordered, sequential techniques of analysis are least able to handle. Thus, despite their importance, the dynamic factors go virtually without mention in the literature of management science.

Let us look at timing, for example. It is evident that timing is crucial in virtually everything the manager does. No manager takes action without

52   On Management

considering the effects of moving more or less quickly, of seizing initiatives or of delaying to avoid complications. Yet in one review of the
literature of management, the authors found fewer than ten books in
183 that refer directly to the subject of timing.[4] Essentially, managers
are left on their own to deal with dynamic factors, which involve simultaneous, relational modes of thinking.

8. When managers do have to make serious choices from among
options, how do they in fact make them? Three fundamental modes of
selection can be distinguished—analysis, judgment, and bargaining. The
first involves the systematic evaluation of options in terms of their consequences on stated organizational goals; the second is a process in the
mind of a single decision-maker; and the third involves negotiations
between different people.

One of the most surprising facts about how managers made the strategic
decisions we studied is that so few reported using explicit analysis.
There was considerable bargaining, but in general the selection mode
most commonly used was judgment. Typically, the options and all kinds
of data associated with them entered the mind of a manager, and somehow
a choice later came out. *How* was never explained. *How* is never explained
in any of the literature either.

9. Finally, we turn to our research on strategy-making in organizations.
This process does not turn out to be the regular, continuous, systematic
process depicted in so much of the planning literature. It is most often
an irregular, discontinuous process, proceeding in fits and starts. There
are periods of stability in strategy development, but also there are periods
of flux, of groping, and of global change. To my mind, "strategy"
represents the mediating force between a dynamic environment and a
stable operating system. Strategy is the organization's "conception" of
how to deal with its environment for a time.

Now, the environment does not change in any set pattern. And even
if it did, the human brain would be unlikely to perceive it that way.
People tend to underreact to mild stimuli and overreact to strong ones.
It stands to reason, therefore, that strategies that mediate between environments and organizations cannot change in regular patterns.

How does strategic planning account for these fits and starts? The
fact is that it does not. So again, the burden to cope falls on the manager,
specifically on his or her mental processes—intuitional and experiential—
that can deal with the irregular inputs from the environment.

10. Where do new strategies come from? This is not the place to
probe into that complex question. But research does make one thing

clear. Formal, analytical processes that generally go under the label of planning are not likely to produce innovative strategies so much as "main-line" ones common to organizations in a given industry.[5] Innovative strategies seem to result from informal processes—vague, interactive, and above all oriented to the synthesis of disparate elements. No management process is more demanding of holistic, relational thinking than the creation of an integrated strategy to deal with a complex, intertwined environment. How can analysis, under the label strategic planning, possibly produce such a strategy?

Another famous old story has relevance here. It is the one about the blind men trying to identify an elephant by touch. One grabs the trunk and says the elephant is long and soft; another holds the leg and says it is massive and cylindrical; a third touches the skin and says it is rough and scaly. As Ornstein points out:

> Each person standing at one part of the elephant can make his own limited, analytic assessment of the situation, but we do not obtain an elephant by adding "scaly," "long and soft," "massive and cylindrical" together in any conceivable proportion. Without the development of an overall perspective, we remain lost in our individual investigations. Such a perspective is a province of another mode of knowledge, and cannot be achieved in the same way that individual parts are explored. It does not arise out of a linear sum of independent observations.[6]

What can we conclude from these findings? I must first reemphasize that everything I write about the two hemispheres of the brain falls into the realm of speculation. Researchers have yet to formally relate any management process to the functioning of the human brain.* Nevertheless, these findings do seem to support the hypothesis stated earlier: *The important policy-level processes required to manage an organization rely to a considerable extent on the faculties identified with the brain's right hemisphere.*

This conclusion does not imply that the left hemisphere is unimportant for policy-makers. Every manager engages in considerable explicit calculation when he or she acts, and much intuitive thinking must be translated into the linear order of the left hemisphere if it is to be articulated and

---

* Almost concurrently with the publication of this article, Robert Doktor was, in fact, reporting on research with senior line managers and staff analysts which uncovered physiological evidence (through EEG measurement of brainwaves) for the lateral specialization implied here. See R. Doktor, "Problem Solving Styles of Executives and Management Scientists," *TIMS Studies in the Management Sciences,* no. 8 (1978), pp. 123–34.

54   On Management

eventually put to use. The great powers that appear to be associated
with the right hemisphere are obviously useless without the faculties of
the left. The artist can create without verbalizing; the manager cannot.

Truly outstanding managers are no doubt the ones who can couple
effective processes of the right (hunch, intuition, synthesis) with effective
processes of the left (articulateness, logic, analysis). But there will be
little headway in the field of management if managers and researchers
continue, like Nasrudin, to search for the key to management in the
"lightness" of ordered analysis. Too much will stay unexplained in
the "darkness" of intuition.

IMPLICATIONS FOR THE LEFT HEMISPHERE

What does all this mean for those associated with management?

First, I would not like to suggest that planners and management scientists pack up their bags of techniques and leave organizations, or that
they take up basket-weaving or meditation in their spare time. (I haven't—
at least not yet!) It seems to me that the left hemisphere is alive and
well; the analytic community is firmly established, and indispensable,
at the operating and middle levels of most organizations. Its real problems
occur at the senior levels. Here analysis must coexist with—perhaps
even take its lead from—intuition, a fact that many analysts and planners
have been slow to accept. To my mind, organizational effectiveness
does not lie in that narrow-minded concept called "rationality"; it lies
in a blend of clear-headed logic *and* powerful intuition.

For one thing, only under certain circumstances should planners try
to plan. When an organization is in a stable environment and has no
use for an innovative strategy, then the development of formal, systematic
strategic plans (and main-line strategies) may be in order. But when
the environment is unstable or the organization needs an innovative strategy, then strategic planning may not be the best approach to strategy
making, and planners have no business pushing their organizations to
use it. Further, effective decision-making at the senior level requires
good analytical input; it is the job of the planner and management scientist
to ensure that top management gets it. Managers are very effective at
securing soft information. But they tend to underemphasize analytical
input that is often important as well. The planners and management
scientists can serve their organizations effectively by carrying out ad
hoc analyses and feeding the results to top management (need I say

Planning on the Left Side, Managing on the Right   55

orally?), ensuring that the very best of analysis is brought to bear on policy-making.

For teachers of management, if the suggestions in this article turn out to be valid, then educators had better revise drastically some of their notions about management education. Unfortunately, the revolution in that sphere over the last fifteen years—while it has brought so much of value—has virtually consecrated the modern management school to the worship of the left hemisphere.

Should educators be surprised that so many of their graduates end up in staff positions, with no intention of ever managing anything? Some of the best-known management schools have become virtual closed systems in which professors with little interest in the reality of organizational life teach inexperienced students the theories of mathematics, economics, and psychology as ends in themselves. In these management schools, management is accorded little place. There is a need for a new balance in our schools, the balance that the best of human brains can achieve, between the analytic and the intuitive.

As for managers, the first conclusion should be a call for caution. The findings of the human brain should not be taken as license to shroud activities in darkness. Artificially mystifying behavior is a favorite ploy of those seeking to protect a power base; this helps no organization and neither does trying to impose intuition on activities that can be handled effectively by analysis. But a misplaced obsession with analysis is no better, and to my mind represents a far more prevalent problem today.

A major thrust of development in our organizations, ever since Frederick Taylor began experimenting in factories late in the last century, has been to shift activities out of the realm of intuition, toward conscious analysis. That trend will continue. But managers, and those who work with them, need to be careful to distinguish that which is best handled analytically from that which must remain in the realm of intuition. That is where we shall have to continue looking for the lost keys to management.

55a   Notes

Chapter 3 Planning on the Left Side, Managing on the Right

1. Richard Restak, "The Hemispheres of the Brain Have Minds of Their Own," *New York Times*, January 25, 1976.

2. Robert Ornstein, *The Psychology of Consciousness* (San Francisco: Freeman, 1975), p. 60.

3. Henry Mintzberg, Duru Raisinghani, and André Théorêt, "The Structure of 'Unstructured' Decision Processes," *Administrative Science Quarterly*, 1976, pp. 246–75.

4. Clyde T. Hardwick and Bernard F. Landuyt, *Administrative Strategy and Decision Making*, 2d edition (Cincinnati: South Western, 1966).

5. This point is elaborated upon in Henry Mintzberg, a forthcoming book on *Strategic Planning*.

6. Ornstein, *Psychology of Consciousness*, p. 10.

[27]

The Theory Behind the Practice

GARETH MORGAN

In the foregoing chapters, I have presented a view of imaginization with practice in mind. Now, it's time to address the theoretical base.

In the following pages, I provide a reflective essay on the key ideas shaping the approach. It includes a discussion of the role played by images and metaphors in the social construction of reality and provides a more detailed discussion of the principles of imaginization as a mode of personal empowerment and an approach to change.

SOME PHILOSOPHICAL BACKGROUND

As the twentieth century has progressed, increasing attention has been devoted to understanding how language, images, and ideas shape social reality and our understanding of the world at large. Interest in this notion can be traced back to ancient Greece, but it's only in the last 80 or 90 years that the view has achieved real prominence.

It is difficult to put a finger on the turning point. The whole ferment in science and philosophy toward the end of the nineteenth century played a major part. Growing interest in electricity, electromagnetism, and the discovery of the subatomic world in science was paralleled in the humanities by the discovery of the unconscious and a growing interest in phenomenology. The everyday world, while concrete, real, and ordered on the surface, seemed to be underpinned by more complex structures and forces beyond the reach of traditional explanations.

Reality was not what it seemed to be!

The new insights were also mirrored in the world of art as strictly representational forms gave way to impressionism, cubism, and searches for the hidden structure of things. The work of Picasso stands as the most obvious example.

The ferment and change underpinning these developments shook the roots of knowledge and spun off in many directions. For example, in science, the stable worldview of Newton gave way to the relativity of Einstein, with the relativity of the physical universe becoming mirrored in a relativity of knowledge as scientists like Werner Heisenberg (1958) and Neils Bohr (1958a, 1958b) showed how even the most scientifically controlled experiments are shaped by the assumptions and views of the scientists involved. If one studied light as a particle, it revealed itself as a particle. If one studied light as a wave, it revealed itself as a wave. As Thomas Kuhn (1970) later formulated the idea, it seemed that the mind-set or "paradigm" of the scientist played a powerful role in shaping the nature of scientific knowledge. In the nineteenth century, science was seen as providing a foundation for generating objective knowledge. But, as the twentieth has progressed, it has become clear that science, despite all the claims for objectivity, is just producing a form of socially constructed knowledge and that scientific "truths" are only "true" under accompanying sets of assumptions.

Similar ideas have emerged in the humanities. Take, for example, the relationship between language and reality. The early view, expressed in Wittgenstein's (1922) "picture theory" of language, was that reality *gives us* language: that our words, images, and ideas are reflections of the world "out there." The newer view reverses this, suggesting that words, images, and ideas are not neutral reflections of reality. They are the means through which we *make* our reality. This perspective, found in the work of the later Wittgenstein (1958) and philosophers like Derrida (1978), Gadamer (1975, 1976), and Rorty (1979, 1985), emphasizes that there are no sharp distinctions between subjective and objective worlds and that language and reality are part of an integrated life-world in and through which humans and their realities are coproduced. For example, in his later work, Wittgenstein emphasized how language and action are interwoven, creating a kind of "language game" through which people engage, understand, and experience their reality, shaping their world through the constructs, actions, and processes embedded in the game itself. In his view, we live our language as part of a broader activity or "form of life." Or, as Heidegger has put it, it seems that "language speaks us as much as we speak language."

The focus on language as a means of revealing how humans construct and *make* reality has proved very insightful, because, as philosophers like Jacques Derrida have shown, its use illustrates the complex yet fragile and tentative webs of meaning on which so much social practice is based.

Take, for example, the process through which we use language to construct meaning. Words, at face value, are clear and precise. They depict an image, idea, and agreed meaning. But is the process this simple? As Derrida (1978) and his interpreters have shown (e.g., Cooper 1989), language in the form of written and social text is never self-evident. Meanings and actions are always mediated by external contexts and points of reference. *Black* only acquires significance in relation to the concept and meaning of *white*, just as *day* takes form in relation to *night*. To grasp and understand even the simplest meanings,

it seems that we have to draw on all kinds of implicit knowledge and engage in complex acts of social construction and
interpretation that are tentative, paradoxical, and always in
danger of breaking down. The worlds in which we live, it
seems, are truly extensions of ourselves and the forms of life
through which we experience and engage them.

All these ideas have been enormously influential, laying the
basis for a general social-constructionist view that, whatever
the characteristics of the "objective" world, they are *always*
known and experienced subjectively. Humans play an active
role in *constructing, making,* and *enacting* their realities (Berger
and Luckmann 1966; Gadamer 1975, 1976; Gergen 1982, 1985;
Weick 1979). But this view itself raises fascinating paradoxes,
for, while humans can in principle be seen as active agents in
perceiving, constructing, and acting on their worlds, they do
so in circumstances that are not of their own choosing. For
example, as philosophers like Michel Foucault (1973, 1980)
have shown, there are all kinds of power relations embedded
in the language, routines, and discourses that shape everyday
life. People's views of reality are influenced by conscious and
unconscious social constructions associated with language,
history, class, culture, and gender experience. Often, these
exert a decisive impact, locking people into a feeling that they
are hemmed in by deterministic forces over which they have
no control. As a result, despite our ability to enact or make our
world, existing social constructions of reality often become
difficult to break, with people becoming no more than passive
"voices," reflecting and "speaking" their social contexts.

These paradoxes have brought the social-constructionist
movement to an interesting point in its development, which
can fork in at least two ways. One path leads to the view that,
whether they know it or not, humans have the potential to
make and transform themselves and their world through individual and collective enactments that can "real-ize" new images, ideas, and worldviews. The other leads to the conclusion
that, while this may be true in principle, the deep structure of
power relations lends the world a resilient logic of its own.
While the former encourages people to see and grasp the
liberating potential of new individual and collective enactments, the latter tends to dwell on the idea that, to change the

social constructions that shape our world, one has to begin by addressing underlying power relations.

IMAGINIZATION AND THE SOCIAL CONSTRUCTION OF REALITY

Imaginization, as an approach to understanding social reality and as an approach to change, belongs to the social-constructionist school of thought and follows the former path. It is underpinned by the idea that human awareness and knowledge have an unfolding transformative potential and that the images and ideas people hold of themselves and their world have a fundamental impact on how their realities unfold. Like those writers who emphasize how the social construction of reality is embedded in deeper power relations, I too believe that we act on a stage shaped by deeply ingrained assumptions and discourses, where certain groups and individuals have much greater power than others to shape the infrastructure of what we do. Knowledge of these deeper power relations can be instructive. But the image that we live in a world shaped by forces over which we have little control is generally overwhelming. It tends to create complacency and feelings of futility.

Hence, in my work, I try to strike an intermediate and positive stance. Along with educators like Paolo Freire (1970), who emphasize the liberating potential of human consciousness, I believe that people *do* make and shape their world and have the ability to do so anew. As the "power theorists" suggest, people often get trapped by the cultural beliefs and social practices through which they make their reality "real." They frequently lose sight of the ideas, attitudes, assumptions, and other social constructions that are ultimately shaping the structure and experience of their daily realities. But, despite this, they always have the potential to break into new modes of consciousness and understanding. This, I believe, can be a fundamental source of individual and social change and is the premise on which my approach to imaginization builds. I believe that change, though often difficult, begins with individuals; that, if people want to change their world, they have to start with themselves; and that individual change becomes social change when a critical mass of people begin to push in the same direction.

The basic perspective is captured in the so-called "hundredth monkey syndrome," related by Lyall Watson (1979). As the story goes, when sweet potatoes were introduced as a new food for monkeys living on an island off Japan, they got a poor reception. The potatoes were dropped in the sand and, while tasty inside, were unpleasant to eat. Then, one day, one of the monkeys was observed washing the potatoes before eating them. Gradually, the process caught on. Each day, increasing numbers began to wash their potatoes. Then, when a critical point was reached (the symbolic hundredth monkey), *all* the monkeys, including those on neighboring islands, engaged in the potato-washing procedure. Social change in human societies often has the same quality. When resonant ideas or new practices "catch on," whole fields of action can be transformed.

Imaginization, as an approach to change, seeks to mobilize the potential for understanding and transformation that rests within each and every one of us. It seeks to challenge taken-for-granted ways of thinking and, in the process, open and broaden our ability to act in new ways. While stressing the art of the possible, and of finding means of helping people to discover and shape themselves and their realities in new ways, it is sensitive to the realities of power. But it does not allow those "realities" to create a sense of immobility. Hence, throughout this book, I have tried to show how it's possible to increase individual and collective consciousness of how our realities are constructed and how we can tap our individual and collective imaginations as a source of change. While I have focused on applying the basic ideas to the field of organization and management, which is my sphere of professional interest, I believe that the basic philosophy can be applied to most aspects of daily life.

THE IMPORTANCE OF IMAGES AND METAPHORS

In terms of specific background, my interest in this social-constructionist approach to change originated in a study conducted with Gibson Burrell on how different worldviews shape how we understand organization and management (Burrell and Morgan 1979). One of the main insights emerging from this work was that social scientists, like people in everyday life, tend to get trapped by their perspectives and assumptions. As a result, they construct, understand, and interpret the social world in partial ways, creating interesting sets of insights but obliterating others as ways of seeing become ways of not seeing. It was the old story of whether light is a "wave" or a "particle." Pursuing the insights, I became interested in exploring how different theoretical perspectives could be used to broaden fields of study and to help people generate deeper understandings of the issues addressed.

This eventually led to further investigation of how social scientists working in the field of organization and management construct their theories and perspectives (Morgan 1980, 1983a) and to the role played by images and metaphors in shaping domains of study and in the social construction of reality. As I explored, I came to realize, along with other theorists, that metaphor is not just a literary or linguistic device for embellishing or decorating discourse. It's a primal means through which we forge our relationships with the world (see, for example, Brown 1977; Lakoff and Johnson 1980; Morgan 1980, 1983a, 1983b; Ortony 1979; Schön 1963, 1979; White 1978). Metaphor has a formative impact on language, on the construction and embellishment of meaning, and on the development of theory and knowledge of all kinds.

To illustrate, consider a young child who catches his first sight of the moon and says "balloon" or who, on seeing a tiger at the zoo, says "meow." The child is engaging in metaphor whereby familiar elements of experience (the balloon and cat) are used to understand the unfamiliar (the moon and tiger). This process, it seems, lies at the root of how meaning is forged: from the development of language to how we think and develop formal knowledge.

Language develops as concepts associated with one domain of meaning are extended metaphorically to another. To illustrate, consider the history of the word *organization*. It stems from the ancient Greek word *organon*, meaning a tool or instrument: "something with which one works." Gradually, the use of *organon* was extended metaphorically to describe musical instruments, surgical instruments, and body organs of animals and plants—hence the English words *organ, organize,* and *organization. To organize* came to mean putting connected "organs" into a systematic form, and the word *organization,* a collection of organs used to perform other ends. The idea of describing a group of people as "an organization" became popular in the wake of the Industrial Revolution and acquired mechanical overtones. Organizations, like machines, came to be viewed as instruments that could be rationally designed and managed, so that their human and technical "organs" behaved in a rational, predictable way.

The same process can be observed in the development of everyday knowledge and in scientific theory. Knowledge emerges and develops as a domain of extended metaphor. For Newton, the world was seen as a kind of celestial machine. Einstein's breakthrough on relativity came through imagining what it would be like to "ride on a light wave." The images thus created allowed reality to be seen in new ways and to be studied in detail through more reductive (metonymical) processes whereby the implications of the guiding image are elaborated in detail (Morgan 1983a, 1983b; White 1978).

Unfortunately, the key role played by metaphor in helping us to understand our world has become obscured. As the word *reality* signifies, people have come to believe that they are living in a domain of meaning that seems much more real and concrete than it actually is. The same is true in science. Scientific knowledge is often seen as searching for, and offering, "the Truth." If we take a close look at the process, however, we find that science is just offering an interesting and useful metaphorical perspective, an interesting and useful way of seeing and thinking about the world! This may allow one to act on the world and to produce predictable results, as in scientific experiments, but the broad context of interpretation and meaning is ultimately grounded in the linguistic and other socially constructed frameworks within which the experiments and knowledge are set.

This is a controversial and unpopular view in the scientific community because it undermines the idea that science *should* involve the generation of some kind of literal truth (e.g., Pinder and Bourgeois 1982; Tsoukas 1991). Indeed, metaphorical knowledge is often distinguished from "literal knowledge." Metaphor is seen as belonging to the realm of creative imagination. The "literal" is seen as something that is real and true, as something that has an unambiguous empirical correspondence. Yet, if we examine the very concept of *literal*, we find that it is itself a metaphor. The word plays on the image of a letter or letters and is connected with the notions of literate and literature. The connection would no doubt be much clearer if the word were spelled *letteral!* By *evoking* the idea of a "literal truth," scientists are in effect *creating* the idea that there is a nonmetaphorical realm of knowledge. But it's no more than a metaphorical idea, one through which we try to create the notion that our understanding of reality is a little more "real" than it actually may be.

All this may seem to be playing with words. But, at a deeper level, it concerns basic issues relating to the nature of knowledge. In the early eighteenth century, the Irish philosopher George Berkeley (1910a, 1910b) noted that objectivity belongs as much to the realm of the observer as to that of the object observed. This point is central to the issues being discussed here.

Knowledge as objective or literal truth places too much emphasis on the *object* of knowledge and not enough on the paradigms, perspective, assumptions, language games, and frames of reference of the observer. The challenge before us now is to achieve a better balance, by recognizing that all knowledge is the product of an interpretive process. To achieve this, we need fresh metaphors for thinking about the process through which knowledge is generated. Instead of placing emphasis on the need for "solid," "literal," "foundational," "objective Truth," we need more dynamic modes of understanding that show how knowledge results from some kind of implicit or explicit "conversation," "dialogue," "engagement," or interaction between the interests of people and the world in which they live (Bernstein 1983; Checkland 1981; Checkland and Scholes 1990; Gergen 1982; Morgan 1983a; Rorty 1979, 1985). Instead of seeing knowledge as an objective, known "thing," we need to see it as a capacity and potential that can be developed in the "knower"—hence my interest in imaginization as a process through which, metaphorically, we "read" and "write" the world of organization and management.

280   IMAGINIZATION

Imaginization, as a way of knowing and as a way of acting, seeks to advance the power of the "everyday knower" and the power of the "everyday writer" of social life!

IMAGES OF ORGANIZATION

My first attempt at exploring this process was presented in my book *Images of Organization* (1986), where I demonstrated the metaphorical basis of organization theory and showed how different perspectives could generate different insights. In essence, the book explored a series of *"what if . . . ?"* questions:
What if we think about organizations as machines?
What if we think about them as organisms?
      . . . as brains?
      . . . as cultures?
      . . . as political systems?
      . . . as psychic prisons?
      . . . as flux and transformation?
      . . . as instruments of domination?
As I developed the implications of each perspective, I showed how they created complementary and competing insights, each of which possesses inherent strengths and limitations. For example, while a "machine view" of organization focuses on organization as the relationship between structures, roles, and technology, the "culture view" shows how organization rests in shared meanings. The psychic prison metaphor shows how structures and shared meanings can become conscious and unconscious traps. The political perspective shows how these characteristics are often shaped by clashes of interest and power plays—and so on. I showed how all the different perspectives could be used to "read" the nature and significance of different aspects of organizational life as well as how the injunctions or implications of each metaphor offered specific ideas for the design and management of organizations in practice. Though the book restricted itself to using eight broad metaphorical frameworks to illustrate its message, it developed the idea that organization ultimately rests in ways of thinking and acting and that, in principle, there are no limits to number of images and metaphors that can be used to enrich this process.

My aim in all this was to show how managers and others interested in the world of organization can become more effective in understanding and shaping the realities with which they have to deal. Throughout, I was at pains to avoid asserting the supremacy of any given metaphor or theoretical perspective, because I wanted to encourage "the reader" to realize that there is no one theory, metaphor, synthesis, or perspective that is going to provide all the answers. Hence, in using the book, one is left with many insights about the nature of organization but with no single theory saying that "this is the best way of seeing or thinking about organization." Instead of trying to offer an authoritative statement on "the way organizations are," it throws the problem of interpretation right back onto each and every one of us—on "the knowers" rather than "the known." Or, as I put it in earlier chapters of this book, it obliges and encourages us to become "our own theorists," forging our own understandings and interpretations of the situations we face.

This is what distinguishes *Images of Organization* from the majority of books on organization and management. Most of these offer a specific theory for understanding and managing organizations or try to develop an integrated framework that highlights certain dimensions over others. They reduce our understanding of organization to a particular way of seeing. My approach, on the other hand, was to suggest that, because any *particular* way of seeing is limited (including the one being advocated!), the challenge is to become skilled in the "art of seeing," in the art of "understanding," in the art of "interpreting" and "reading" the situations we face.

In many respects, the approach fits what is known as a postmodern approach to understanding organizational life. The postmodernist movement has grown in strength and significance over the last few decades, suggesting that the search for universal, authoritative, "true" explanations of social reality are always problematic and incomplete because they end up elevating the priority of a particular perspective while downplaying others. As it is sometimes put, "the presence" of the ideas and insights highlighted by a particular theory or perspective always creates "an absence": the insights, ideas, and perspectives that are pushed from view. This creates a problem for anyone who wishes to interpret and explain something, particularly in science and the humanities, where explanations are expected to carry some weight and authority.

For the most part, postmodernism has only resulted in critiques of modes of writing and social processes that elevate one view over another: to disrupt what is typically viewed as "normal" and self-evident so that the problematic nature of "normality" becomes clear. This critical stance has done much to help us understand how biases and blind spots can accompany and sometimes dominate ways of seeing and how all "explanations" are only forms of rhetoric that seek to persuade people to join or accept a particular point of view (see, for example, Berman 1988; Calas and Smircich 1988; Cooper 1989; Cooper and Burrell 1988; Harvey 1989; Linstead and Grafton-Small 1992; Martin 1990; Reed and Hughes 1992).

But, in my view, there is another way in which the postmodern perspective can be developed: by recognizing that, because partiality, incompleteness, and distortion are ever present in explanations of how we see and understand the world, perhaps we need to develop ways of theorizing and explaining the world that explicitly recognize and deal with the distorting nature of knowledge.

My approach to understanding organization and management discussed in *Images of Organization* began to address this task. It is continued in the current book in my general attempt to develop the process of imaginization, as a mode of theorizing and an approach to social change that seeks to help people mobilize highly relativistic, open-ended, evolving interpretive frameworks for guiding understanding and action. The aim is to help people develop ways of seeing, thinking, and theorizing that can improve their ability to understand and manage the highly relativistic, paradoxical, and changing character of the world with which they have to deal.

The old mechanistic worldview, on which so much organization and management theory—and, indeed, science—has been based, encouraged a search for fixed theories and linear methods and techniques of understanding and practice. The postmodern worldview, which, of interest, is paralleled in aspects of the new science emphasizing the chaotic, paradoxical, and transient nature of order and disorder (see, for example, the work of writers like Gleick 1987; Hampden-Turner

1990; Jantsch 1980; Nonaka 1988; Prigogine and Stengers 1984; Quinn 1990; Smith and Berg 1987), requires an approach that allows the theory and practice of organization and management to acquire a more fluid form.

This is precisely what my approach to imaginization sets out to achieve. It develops the implications of the basic methodology offered in *Images of Organization* to create a relativistic, self-organizing approach to management and management theory capable of contributing to the challenges of the Einsteinian world in which we now find ourselves.

IMAGINIZATION AS THE ART OF CREATIVE MANAGEMENT

In terms of specifics, the current book starts where *Images* left off, inviting you to become your own theorist, using images and metaphors to engage in a continuous construction and deconstruction of meaning in your encounters with everyday reality. It offers a highly personalized method for understanding organizations using the metaphor of reading and writing organizational life as its dominant frame. Like *Images*, it treats organizational reality as a kind of "living text" that is simultaneously "written" and "read." Some of the chapters (especially 5 to 8) pay particular attention to illustrating "reading in practice," developing the themes introduced in *Images* and showing how innovative "readings" can lay the basis for innovative "writing." Others, especially Chapters 2 to 4 and 9 to 12, give specific attention to ways in which we can "author" or "write" new organizational realities through a range of processes that mobilize imaginative ways of thinking and acting. The whole book demonstrates the "become your own author-reader- theorist" theme in practice and pursues the no-limits-to-metaphor principle. It shows how traditional concepts of organization can be radically transformed through imaginative processes whereby new images and metaphors are used to create evocative and energizing patterns of shared meaning. It invites us to unleash our powers of creative thought, interpretation, and insight to broaden the possibilities for creative action.

284   IMAGINIZATION

In terms of specific practice, the process of imaginization illustrated in these chapters builds on a number of key principles. These are addressed below under three headings:

1. the interconnection between "reading" and "writing,"
2. how images can be used as "mirrors" and "windows," and
3. imaginization as personal empowerment.

The Interconnection Between "Reading" and "Writing"

At various points in this book, I have used the ideas of "reading" and "writing" as metaphors for capturing the challenge of interpreting and shaping organizational life. As noted above, this builds on the underlying metaphor of reality as a kind of living text.

At first glance, the image seems far-fetched. But, if one thinks about it, the language, images, ideas, and actions through which we write daily life parallel how a book uses words to fix and communicate meaning. Readers, whether of books or life, in turn create their own meaning; in effect, they add their own authoring to the text. In this way, the whole of life can be seen as a living "real time" process of simultaneous reading and writing, producing evolving and diverse patterns of meaning.

This metaphorical frame has provided the basis for a hermeneutic school of social theory specializing in the art of interpretation (see, for example, Boland 1989; Gadamer 1975, 1976; Hollinger 1985; Rorty 1979, 1985; Shotter 1990; Turner 1983). It recognizes that, as readers and authors of our everyday realities, we all have limited horizons, shaped by the values, assumptions, worldviews, interests, and perspectives that we possess as individuals and as members of social groups. Hence our readings and subsequent authorings tend to be partial and one sided, committing us to live realities reflecting all kinds of conscious and unconscious social constructions associated with class, gender, culture, and the daily context in which we live. The hermeneutic perspective focuses on understanding the never-ending circle of relations underlying this social construction of reality.

My theory of reading and writing organizational life builds on these core ideas, but in a loose way. My primary aim has been to develop the metaphor as a *method* for exploring the multidimensional nature of organizations, showing how the horizons generated by different metaphors can be used to create new insights and action possibilities. Richard Boland (1989) has provided an outstanding critique of my approach from this point of view. At its simplest, the approach involves developing a "diagnostic reading" and "story line," using different metaphors as frames for highlighting and ordering different aspects of the reality with which we are dealing. For illustrations, turn to the readings produced in relation to Teleserve (Chapter 5, Exhibits 5.1, 5.2), Network (Chapter 6, Exhibits 6.1, 6.3), and Stereotype (Chapter 7, Exhibits 7.1, 7.2). They illustrate how I try to remain open to multiple and evolving interpretations of a situation, picking up key cues and signals as I go along, to develop a "story line" that evaluates and integrates the various insights into an overall understanding of the situation. The evolving story lines in the above cases are reflected in the progressive development of the "readings," often captured through new images or metaphors of the moment that helped to make sense of the overall situation.

For example, in Teleserve (Chapter 5), my diagnostic reading developed from the multiple dimensions illustrated in Exhibit 5.1, to the interconnection between the political, cultural, and domination metaphors highlighted in Exhibit 5.2, to the story line that "we're engaged in a game of 'political football.' "

For any given situation, it's always possible to generate multiple authentic readings and story lines, because readings are just orderings of reality and are always shaped by the horizon of the reader and the interests to be served (Gadamer 1975, 1976; Habermas 1972). The analysis and story lines that emerge are really forms of rhetoric through which the "author-reader" produces an understanding that serves the interests and agenda that he or she brings to the situation at hand.

For example, the readings that I produced in the interventions discussed in Chapters 5 to 7 were shaped by my use of the framework developed in *Images of Organization* as an analytical tool and by my ability (or inability) to detect the nuances with which I was dealing. And the story lines that I eventually produced were influenced by the nature of the assignments and the interventionist role that I was being asked to play. For example, as I discuss at the very end of the Teleserve case (Chapter 5), the nature and outcome of this intervention would probably have been very different if the assignment had been shaped from "labor" or "gender" perspectives. These would have created different horizons, leading to different readings and to "story lines" and action strategies with different interests and aims in mind—hence the emphasis that I have placed throughout the text on how the process of imaginization can serve different and, indeed, competing interests. It depends on the perspective or horizon from which it is used!

This view on the essential relativity of imaginization links back to the point made earlier regarding "foundational" versus "conversational" approaches to knowledge. A foundational view leads one to look for authoritative, "this is the way it is!" interpretations of a situation. Imaginization, on the other hand, builds around the paradox that any given situation may have multiple dimensions and multiple meanings, which acquire significance in the context of interpretation. None of these is necessarily absolute or "true." The challenge is to recognize that as interpreters and constructors of reality we face many options and that, just like scientists studying light as waves or particles, we can't study all dimensions at the same time. Our challenge is to dialogue and converse with the situations with which we are involved, to "real-ize" meaningful knowledge, knowledge that will allow us to be edified or to act in a personally significant way. That doesn't necessarily satisfy those who are looking for an absolute meaning or "truth" in a situation. But it does capture what seems to be the nature of the human condition: that, as humans, we can only ever acquire limited, partial, *personally significant* ways of knowing the world.

Viewed in this way, we are encouraged to see the "reading" and knowledge generation process in terms of what Donald Schön (1983) has described as "reflective practice," as the product of a craft shaped by assumptions and perspectives of all kinds. Imaginization is a form of "reflective practice" encouraging us to become skilled interpreters of the situations with which we have to deal. It encourages us to develop our skills of framing and reframing, so that we can learn to see the same situation in different ways, so that we can remain open and flexible to multiple meanings, so that we can generate new insights and become comfortable with the paradox that the same situation can mean many things at the same time. It encourages us to become reflective, creative, and expansive in understanding the situations with which we have to deal. A reflective practitioner is someone who is aware of how implicit images, ideas, theories, frames, metaphors, and ideas guide and shape his or her practice and how they can be used to create new possibilities.

In this context, and in terms of my own reflective practice, it is appropriate to recognize that the concept of imaginization is itself a metaphor and, as such, has inherent strengths and limitations. In fusing the concepts of imagination and organization, it seeks to open the process of organizing to an expansive, creative mode of thinking, as opposed to the reductive mode that has dominated the development of mechanistic thought. It highlights and stresses creative possibility. But, at the same time, as critics may rush to point out, it can gloss and downplay the importance of existing power relations, a point addressed in the following pages, and may underestimate some of the deep structural rigidities in patterns of both thought and action. It thus suffers the fate of all metaphors, and indeed of all paradigms, concepts, and modes of understanding, in that it elevates the importance of certain aspects of reality over others.

In this regard, in presenting my approach to imaginization, I have tended to emphasize how new images can help to create new realities, perhaps at the expense of underestimating how new actions can also be used to create new realms of meaning. This is one of the limitations of the particular horizon that I have brought to the writing of this book. Chapter 12 stands as an exception, but much more could be said on the issue.

Images Can Provide "Mirrors" and "Windows"

At one level, the process of imaginization is about the art of framing and reframing (Schön 1963, 1979; Watzlawick, Weakland, and Fisch 1974). It uses images, metaphors, readings, and story lines to cast situations in new perspective and open possibilities for creative action. But there's another dimension to the process, involving a theory about the relationship between a system's sense of identity and its ability to change. More specifically, imaginization builds on the principle that people and organizations tend to get trapped by the images that they hold of themselves and that genuine change requires an ability to see and challenge these self-images in some way. The previous chapters have demonstrated the process, showing how images and metaphors can be used as "mirrors" through which people and groups can see themselves and their situations in fresh light, creating an opportunity for reflection and change.

I like to talk about the process as one involving "mirrors" and "windows." If one can look in the mirror and see oneself in a new way, the mirror can become a "window," because it allows one to see the rest of the world with a fresh perspective. Or, in terms of the imagery introduced earlier, it opens new "horizons," creating opportunities for new actions.

Hence, in the Teleserve case (Chapter 5), I used the image of "political football" to help the human resource management team *see themselves* in a new light so that they could reflect on the need for a new direction. In Network (Chapter 6) and Nursing Services (Chapter 8), I used the method of getting staff to describe the current organization and its problems through animal imagery so that they could see and express their problems and situations in an unconventional way. In Chapters 2 to 4, I tried to create similar leverage on the way we think about management styles, organization structures, and approaches to change.

The aim throughout is to disrupt normal ways of seeing so that people can ask constructive questions about what they are seeing and what they should do. I find the use of metaphor particularly powerful in this activity, because it creates distance and space from conventional ways of thinking: space in which people can feel free to think and act creatively. This is vital in trying to unlock new understandings or a new sense of identity, because one cannot create the new in terms of the old.

Several aspects of the process through which I generate and use metaphorical imagery seem particularly important in this regard.

The Theory Behind the Practice   **289**

1. Metaphor always involves a sense of paradox and the absurd, because, as illustrated in Exhibit A.1, it invites the users to think about themselves or their situations in ways that are patently false.

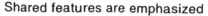

Shared features are emphasized

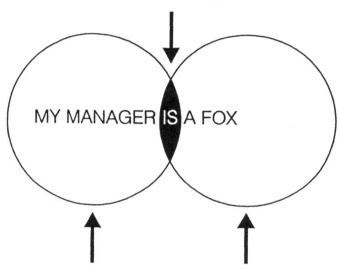

MY MANAGER IS A FOX

Differences are downplayed

The "injunction of the metaphor" is to:
  See the fox-like aspects of the manager: his cunning, guile, craftiness, smooth image.

But:

  Ignore that he doesn't have a black pointed nose, fur, four legs, or tail!

EXHIBIT A.1 The Nature of Metaphor

"My manager is a fox."
"I'm a strategic termite."
"We're a spider-plant organization."
"We're playing political football."
"We're on the Yellow Brick Road."

Metaphor works by playing on a pattern of similarity and difference. Its user seeks to evoke the similarities while downplaying the differences. It involves the generation of a "constructive falsehood" that helps to break the bounds of normal discourse. This plays a crucial role in creating space for change.

2. Metaphor requires its users to *find* and *create* meaning. They have to *find* the similarities between the manager and the fox, to *find* the relevance of the spider plant, to *find* the precise way in which an image can create relevant insights. This helps to create distance and space from conventional understandings and also helps to create *ownership* of the insights. There is nothing self-evident in the meaning of metaphor; meaning has to be created by those involved. Meaning is thus immediate and personal, not distant or abstract.

3. Metaphors only have an impact when they "ring true," "hit a chord," and "resonate" around fundamental insights. One cannot force a metaphor to work, because the process soon becomes an empty ritual where everyone realizes there is little substance. The process thus has a self-regulating quality; there has to be a resonance and authenticity to create energy and involvement. When different people generate different metaphors that have a great deal in common (for example, Charlotte's spiders or the dandelion seeds and supernova in Network, Chapter 6), one knows that one is dealing with highly resonant insights.

4. Metaphors that are generated by the participants in a change project are often more powerful than those generated from outside, because they are directly owned and have immediate meaning. The facilitator of a process can, however, play a powerful role in finding resonant metaphors for capturing insights that others may not see or for recovering and synthesizing key insights that have gotten lost from view. In either case, resonance is key. The metaphor must energize and "take hold."

5. When metaphors are introduced from the outside, it's crucial that people be encouraged to find and elaborate meaning for themselves. When the implications of a metaphor are

laid out in detail, its evocative power is often lost. Metaphors invite a conversational style where meaning and significance emerge through dialogue; resonant meaning cannot be imposed, it has to be evoked.

6. The tentative nature of metaphorical insights means that they cannot be taken too seriously or made too concrete. This has the advantage of helping to create open modes of understanding that have a capacity to self-organize and evolve as one goes along.

When used with these principles in mind, metaphorical images can provide powerful tools for helping people look at themselves and their situations in new ways and, as a result, see and act in the world somewhat differently. The process operates by creating a tension between existing and potential understandings, creating space for the new to emerge. As I have illustrated in several chapters, however, new images do not result in new actions, unless there is an appropriate degree of shared understanding and a will to act on the insights thus generated.

This, I believe, defines an important frontier for development. People writing on the theory of change (e.g., Argyris and Schön 1974; Watzlawick et al. 1974) have made important distinctions between superficial change where the context remains invariant (called single-loop learning or first order change) and change where the context is also transformed (called double-loop learning or second order change). This has important implications for the practice of imaginization, because it highlights how one may be able to generate hundreds of new insights without substantial impact. The challenge of imaginization is to create insights that allow one to reframe contexts substantially rather than superficially. It's the old problem of rearranging the deck chairs on the Titanic! Superficially, one can create the impression of making a lot of changes; but, at base level, nothing of significance may have really changed.

This issue brings us back to the point made earlier about the role of imaginization in transforming horizons. Horizons define contexts. The challenge of imaginization is to help people see and understand the horizons that shape their context, to appreciate their limits, and to open up other horizons when necessary. Or, to change the metaphor, again, the challenge is to open new windows on the world, to create new ways of seeing that can lay the basis for new ways of acting.

Imaginization as Personal Empowerment

Large-scale transformation and change tend to occur when developments acquire the critical mass represented by the "hundredth monkey." But the process usually begins at a more modest level, with individuals or small groups of people taking the initiative.

This, I believe, is where imaginization has to begin.

Imaginization starts with ourselves and, in its broadest sense, invites us to assume our personal power in rethinking and reshaping the world around us. Against the background of the rigidities and resilience of old organizational structures and mind-sets, and the immense social problems that the universe now faces, this may seem like a call to spit into the wind. But, if modern theories of chaos and self-organization have anything to say, a lot of spitting can make a difference. It's a question of critical mass.

We have all probably experienced situations where individuals or groups have tried to imaginize and act on a new reality only to find the process reversed by those exercising power over their lives. We have all probably experienced situations where the gulfs and divides between rival stakeholders are so deep that those involved would rather continue occupying entrenched battle lines than find a shared way forward. We have all read stories of *successful* individuals, communities, and organizations that suffer dramatic reversals in fortune, perhaps being more or less eliminated overnight as the result of uncontrollable changes in the world economy. These are some of the harsh, all-too-real aspects of the socioeconomic context with which we have to deal. They point to what is happening in the infrastructure of the "Titanic," and at times it may seem overwhelming.

Yet, if we dwell on the enormity of the problems, our powerlessness soon becomes a self-fulfilling prophesy. For everyone, at every level, can see themselves as being hemmed in by processes and situations over which they feel they have no control. Employees often feel constrained by the perspectives, biases, and interests of their managers. The managers, in turn, feel constrained by "the culture" of the organization and the expectations that they feel *their* managers are imposing. These more senior managers, in turn, feel hemmed in by the dictates of HQ, stock analysts reports, and general corporate policy. Even the chief executive or chairman of the board can point to her powerlessness as she sees forces of global change buffeting and reshaping the economic context with which she has to deal. If we pursue the logic of this kind of thinking, we quickly find that no one seems to have any real power to do anything of any real significance.

But we do!

And that's why I bring the core challenge of imaginization right down to the issue of personal empowerment.

There are, no doubt, deep structures of power shaping the structure and logic of the global economy. We are, no doubt, caught up in all kinds of sedimented patterns of culture, ideology, and social practice that inhibit capacities for change. The power of macro global forces do encourage a sense of inevitability and powerlessness when it comes to having a significant impact on our world. Indeed, even the leaders of major countries sometimes feel that they have no power to shape things and have no option but to swim with the prevailing tide.

That's why we have to bring it all back down to the level of the individual and individual capacities for change—for change is an individual affair! Individuals can form groups, and groups can become social movements. But the process begins and ends with the commitments and actions of individuals. Certainly, it makes a big difference if one is the head of a large corporation as opposed to the average man or woman in the street. But it is the individual involved who has to move.

That's why I present imaginization as an attitude of mind that encourages people to become their own personal theorists, playing an active role in "writing" the realities that they would like to realize. I believe that our innate imaginizing capacities can serve us well in tackling some of the major social and organizational problems of the current time. We are reaching the end of a line of development associated with the mechanistic thinking of the industrial age and are in need of an alternative. We need new metaphors that can help us *remake* ourselves, our society, and our relations with planet Earth.

In short, we need to imaginize as never before!

THE THEORY BEHIND THE PRACTICE

Most of the detailed references relating to the ideas presented in this appendix are provided directly in the text. For convenience, some of the general references are reproduced below, together with other citations that will be helpful to readers interested in pursuing the general ideas.

On the debate about the social construction of reality, and the socially constructed nature of knowledge, see Berger and Luckmann (1966), Bernstein (1983), Burrell and Morgan (1979), Kuhn (1970), Morgan (1983), and Weick (1979).

On the relationship between knowledge and power, see Dreyfus and Rainbow (1982), Flax (1990), Foucault (1973, 1980), Freire (1970), Habermas (1972), and Rainbow (1984).

On the hermeneutic approach to social analysis, see Boland (1989), Gadamer (1975, 1976), and Rorty (1979, 1985). Boland (1989) provides a particularly clear exposition of basic principles.

On the role of images and metaphors in the social construction of reality, see Lakoff and Johnson (1980), Morgan (1983b), Ortony (1979), and White (1978).

On the links between knowledge, dialogue, and conversation, and the connection between knowledge and human interests, see Bernstein (1983), Bohr (1958a, 1958b), Heisenberg (1958, 1971), Morgan (1983), and Rorty (1979, 1985).

On the role of "reflective practice" and the art of framing and reframing, see Schön (1983) and Watzlawick et al. (1974).

On the relationship between understandings and actions in shaping reality, see Weick (1979).

On the postmodern approach to social theory and its relevance for organization and management theory, see Berman (1988), Calas and Smircich (1988), Cooper (1989), Cooper and Burrell (1988), Harvey (1989), Linstead and Grafton-Small (1992), Martin (1990), and Reed and Hughes (1992).

On the new science, cybernetics, and emerging theories of chaos and self-organization and their implications for management, see Gleick (1987), Jantsch (1980), Nonaka (1988), Prigogine and Stengers (1984), Stacey (1992), and Zimmerman (1992).

On the role of self-identity in processes of change, see Morgan (1986: 249-246), which links this issue, and by implication the idea of mirroring discussed in Appendix A, with writings on the theory of autopoiesis (Maturana and Varela 1980; Smith 1984; Varela, Maturana, and Uribe 1974). This theory seeks to explain how systems are able to produce and reproduce themselves and acquire enduring structure over time. The theory is very abstract and has been developed primarily to understand biological and cognitive systems. Its main proponents disclaim any direct relevance for understanding social systems. But, despite this, I find myself intrigued with one of the key autopoietic ideas: that the *identity* of a system is its most important product. This is an interesting notion, because most applications of systems theory emphasize how social systems like organizations are guided by goals and objectives and that relationships with the environment are shaped and structured to achieve these ends. The theory of autopoiesis seems to suggest otherwise: that systems structure their relationships with the environment to sustain a sense of identity, that they enact their environments as extensions of themselves. This has important implications, suggesting that, if you wish to change a system, it may be more important to work on its sense of identity than on the goals it is trying to achieve. If one can affect a system's basic sense of identity, one creates a potential for the system to reorganize its understanding of its environment. If you only try to change goals and objectives, the system's understanding of the environment may remain unchanged. These are some of the basic ideas underpinning the mirroring methodology discussed in Appendix A.

Bibliography

Argyris C. and D. Schön. *Theory in Practice*. Reading, MA: Addison-Wesley, 1974.

Berger P. and T. Luckmann. *The Social Construction of Reality*. Garden City, NY: Doubleday, 1966.

Berkeley, G. *A Treatise Concerning the Principles of Human Knowledge*. New York: Everyman (reprint), 1910a.

Berkeley, G. *A New Theory of Vision*. New York: Everyman (reprint), 1910b.

Berman, A. *From the New Criticism to Deconstruction*. Urbana: University of Illinois Press, 1988.

Bernstein, R. J. *Beyond Objectivism and Relativism: Science, Hermeneutics and Praxis*. Philadelphia: University of Pennsylvania Press, 1983.

Bohr, N. *Atomic Theory and the Description of Nature*. Cambridge, UK: Cambridge University Press, 1958a.

Bohr, N. *Atomic Theory and Human Knowledge*. New York: John Wiley, 1958b.

Boland, R. J. "Beyond the Objectivist and the Subjectivist: Learning to Read Accounting as Text." *Accounting, Organizations and Society*, 14: 591-604, 1989.

Brown, R. H. *A Poetic for Society*. New York: Cambridge University Press, 1977.

Burrell, G. and G. Morgan. *Sociological Paradigms and Organizational Analysis*. London: Heinemann, 1979.

Calas, M. and L. Smircich. "Reading Leadership as a Form of Cultural Analysis," in J. G. Hunt, R. D. Belliga, H. P. Dachler, and C. A. Schriesheim (eds.), *Emerging Leadership Vistas*, 201-226. Lexington, MA: Lexington, 1988.

Checkland, P. *Systems Thinking, Systems Practice*. Chichester, UK: John Wiley, 1981.

Checkland, P. and J. Scholes. *Soft Systems Methodology in Action*. Chichester, UK: John Wiley, 1990.

Cooper, R. "Modernism, Postmodernism, and Organizational Analysis 3: The Contribution of Jacques Derrida." *Organization Studies*, 10/4: 479-502, 1989.

Cooper, R. and G. Burrell. "Modernism, Postmodernism and Organizational Analysis: An Introduction." *Organization Studies*, 9: 91-112, 1988.

Derrida, J. *Writing and Difference.* Chicago: University of Chicago Press, 1978.

Foucault, M. *The Order of Things: The Archeology of the Human Sciences.* New York: Vintage, 1973.

Foucault, M. *Power/Knowledge,* C. Gordon (ed.). Brighton, UK: Harvester, 1980.

Freire, P. *Pedagogy of the Oppressed.* New York: Seabury, 1970.

Gadamer, H. G. *Truth and Method.* New York: Seabury, 1975.

Gadamer, H. G. *Philosophical Hermeneutics.* Berkeley: University of California Press, 1976.

Gergen, K. J. *Toward Transformation in Social Knowledge.* New York: Springer-Verlag, 1982.

Gergen, K. J. "The Social Constructionist Movement in Modern Psychology." *American Psychologist,* 40/3: 266-275, 1985.

Gleick, J. *Chaos.* New York: Viking, 1987.

Habermas, J. *Knowledge and Human Interests.* London: Heinemann, 1972.

Hampden-Turner, C. *Charting the Corporate Mind.* New York: Free Press, 1990.

Harvey, D. *The Condition of Postmodernity.* Oxford, UK: Basil Blackwell, 1989.

Heisenberg, W. *Physics and Philosophy.* New York: Harper, 1958.

Hollinger, R. (ed.). *Hermeneutics and Practice.* Notre Dame: University of Notre Dame Press, 1985.

Jantsch, E. *The Self Organizing Universe.* Oxford, UK: Pergamon, 1980.

Kuhn, T. S. *The Structure of Scientific Revolution.* Chicago: University of Chicago Press, 1970.

Lakoff, G. and M. Johnson. *Metaphors We Live By.* Chicago: University of Chicago Press, 1980.

Linstead, S. and R. Grafton-Small. "On Reading Organizational Culture." *Organization Studies,* 13: 331-356, 1992.

Martin, J. "Deconstructing Organizational Taboos: The Suppression of Gender Conflict in Organizations." *Organization Science,* 1: 339-359, 1990.

Morgan, G. "Paradigms, Metaphors and Puzzle-Solving in Organization Theory." *Administrative Science Quarterly,* 25: 605-622, 1980.

Morgan, G. (ed.). *Beyond Method: Strategies for Social Research.* Beverly Hills, CA: Sage, 1983a.

Morgan, G. "More on Metaphor: Why We Cannot Control Tropes in Administrative Science." *Administrative Science Quarterly,* 28: 601-607, 1983b.

Nonaka, I. "Creating Organizational Order out of Chaos: Self Renewal in Japanese Firms." *California Management Review,* Spring: 57-73, 1988.

Ortony, A. (ed.). *Metaphor and Thought.* Cambridge, MA: Cambridge University Press, 1979.

Pinder, C. C. and V. W. Bourgeois. "Controlling Tropes in Administrative Science." *Administrative Science Quarterly,* 27: 641-652, 1982.

Bibliography **294**d

Prigogine, I. and I. Stengers. *Order out of Chaos*. New York: Bantam, 1984.

Quinn, R. E. *Beyond Rational Management: Mastering the Paradoxes and Competing Demands of High Performance*. San Francisco: Jossey-Bass, 1990.

Reed, M. and M. Hughes (eds.). *Rethinking Organization*. London: Sage, 1992.

Rorty, R. *Philosophy and the Mirror of Nature*. Princeton, NJ: Princeton University Press, 1979.

Rorty, R. *Consequences of Pragmatism*. Minneapolis: University of Minneapolis Press, 1985.

Schön, D. A. *Invention and the Evolution of Ideas*. London: Tavistock, 1963.

Schön, D. A. "Generative Metaphor: A Perspective on Problem Setting in Social Policy," in A. Ortony (ed.), *Metaphor and Thought*, 254-283. Cambridge, MA: Cambridge University Press, 1979.

Schön, D. A. *The Reflective Practitioner*. New York: Basic Books, 1983.

Shotter, J. "The Manager as Author." A paper prepared for the Conference on Social-Organizational Theory, St. Gallen, Switzerland, August 1990.

Smircich, L. "Studying Organizations as Cultures," in G. Morgan (ed.), *Beyond Method*, 160-172. Beverly Hills, CA: Sage, 1983.

Smith, K. K. and D. N. Berg. *Paradoxes of Group Life*. San Francisco: Jossey-Bass, 1987.

Tsoukas, H. "The Missing Link: A Transformational View of Metaphors in Organizational Science." *Academy of Management Review*, 16: 566-585, 1991.

Turner, S. "Studying Organization Through Levi-Strauss's Structuralism," in G. Morgan (ed.), *Beyond Method*. Beverly Hills, CA: Sage, 1983.

Watson, L. *Lifetide*. New York: Simon & Schuster, 1979.

Watzlawick, P., J. Weakland, and R. Fisch. *Change: Principles of Problem Formation and Problem Resolution*. New York: Norton, 1974.

White, H. *The Tropics of Discourse*. Baltimore: Johns Hopkins University Press, 1978.

Wittgenstein, L. *Tractatus Logico-Philosophicus*. London: Routledge & Kegan Paul, 1922.

Wittgenstein, L. *Philosophical Investigations*. Oxford, UK: Basil Blackwell, 1958.

[28]

Foresight

Alfred North Whitehead

SECTION I. By the phrase Historical Foresight, I mean something quite different from the accurate exercise of Scientific Induction. Science is concerned with generalities. The generalities apply, but they do not determine the course of history apart from some anchorage in fact. There might have been many alternative courses of history conditioned by the same laws. Perhaps, if we knew enough of the laws, then we should understand that the development of the future from the past is completely determined by the details of the past and by these scientific laws which condition all generation. Unfortunately our knowledge of scientific laws is woefully defective, and our knowledge of the relevant facts of the present and the past is scanty in the extreme. Thus as the result of all our science, we are ignorant of that remote epoch when there will be a second collision between the sun and a passing star, we are ignorant of the future of life on the earth, we are ignorant of the future of mankind, we are ignorant of the course of history a year hence, we are ignorant of most of the domestic details of our lives tomorrow, we are even ignorant of the term that has been set to our own existence.

This catalogue of ignorances at once reminds us that our state is not that of blank absence of knowledge. Our ignorance is suffused with Foresight. Also the basis of our defect in foresight is our scant knowledge of the relevant detailed facts in past and present which are required for the application of the scientific laws. Where the circumstances are comparatively simple, as in Astronomy, we know that the facts and the astronomical laws provide an apparatus of great accuracy in forecast. The main difficulty in Historical Foresight is the power of collecting and selecting the facts relevant to the particular type of forecast which we wish to make. Discussions on the method of science wander off onto the topic of experiment. But experiment is nothing else than a mode of cooking the facts for the sake of exemplifying the law. Unfortunately the facts of history, even those of private individual history, are on too large a scale. They surge forward beyond control.

It is thus evident that this topic of Historical Foresight is not to be exhausted by a neat description of some definite methods. It is faced with two sources of difficulty, where science has only one. Science seeks the laws only, but Foresight requires in addition due emphasis on the relevant facts from which the future is to emerge. Of the two tasks required for Foresight, this selection amid the welter is the more difficult. Probably a neat doctrine of Foresight is impossible. But what can be done is to confine attention to one field of human activity, and to describe the type of mentality which seems requisite for the attainment of Foresight within that field. The present state of the world, and the course of the discussions in this book, suggest the field of Commercial relations. This field will therefore be chosen to illustrate the function of ideas in the provision of anticipation and purpose.

To avoid misunderstanding I must disclaim the foolish notion that it is possible for anyone, devoid of personal experience of commerce, to provide useful suggestions for its detailed conduct. There is no substitute for first-hand practice. Also the word 'commerce' is here used in the largest sense of that term, in which it includes a variety of activities. Any useful theory, capable of immediate application to specific instances, must depend on a direct knowledge of the relevant reactions of men and women composing that society, or perhaps group of nations, within which the specific business in question is to flourish. In this discussion there is no pretence of such detailed knowledge.

There remains, however, the question of the general type of mentality which in the present condition of the world will promote the general success of a commercial community. Such a type is, of course, very complex. But we are considering one unquestioned element in it, namely Foresight, and will discuss the conditions for its development and its successful exercise.

Some people are born with astounding knacks of the mind. For example, there are calculating boys who can perform intricate operations of mental arithmetic in a flash, there are also other sorts of peculiar faculties of divination; in particular there are men with a knack of shrewdness in judging circumstances within the narrow range of their immediate observation. But after all, bankers prefer that their clerks should learn arithmetic, and trained geologists are preferred to men with divining rods. In the same way, there are general conditions of training which promote the development of a wider type of foresight.

It is a great mistake to divide people into sharp classes, namely, people with such-and-such a knack and people without it. These trenchant divisions are simply foolish. Most humans are born with certain aptitudes. But these aptitudes can easily remain latent unless they are elicited into activity by fortunate circumstances. If anyone has no aptitude of a certain type, no training can elicit it. But, granted the aptitude, we can discuss the ways of training it. Foresight depends upon understanding. In practical affairs it is a habit. But the habit of foreseeing is elicited by the habit of understanding. To a large extent, understanding can be acquired by a conscious effort and it can be taught. Thus the training of Foresight is by the medium of Understanding. Foresight is the product of Insight.

SECTION II. The general topic to be understood is the entire internal functioning of human society, including its technologies, the biological and physical laws on which these technologies depend, and including the sociological reactions of humans depending on fundamental psychological principles. In fact, the general topic is sociology in the broadest sense of the term, including its auxiliary sciences. Such a width of understanding is, of course, beyond the grasp of any single human. But no part of it is entirely foreign to the provision of foresight in business. Such a complete understanding is a coöperative enterprise; and a business community maintains its success for long periods so far as its average foresight is dominated by some approach to such general understanding.

We shall comprehend better the varieties of individual understanding which go to complete this general equipment of an ideal business community, if we commence by considering the contrast between understanding and routine.

Routine is the god of every social system; it is the seventh heaven of business, the essential component in the success of every factory, the ideal of every statesman. The social machine should run like clockwork. Every crime should be followed by an arrest, every arrest by a judicial trial, every trial by a conviction, every conviction by a punishment, every punishment by a reformed character. Or, you can conceive an analogous routine concerning the making of a motor car, starting with the iron in the ore, and the coal in the mine, and ending with the car driving out of the factory and with the President of the Corporation signing the dividend warrants, and renewing his contracts with the mining Corporations. In such a routine everyone from the humblest miner to the august president is exactly trained for his special job. Every action of miner or president is the product of conditioned reflexes, according to current physiological phraseology. When the routine is perfect, understanding can be eliminated, except such minor flashes of intelligence as are required to deal with familiar accidents, such as a flooded mine, a prolonged drought, or an epidemic of influenza. A system will be the product of intelligence. But when the adequate routine is established, intelligence vanishes, and the system is maintained by a coördination of conditioned reflexes. What is then required from the humans is receptivity of special training. No one, from President to miner, need understand the system as a whole. There will be no foresight, but there will be complete success in the maintenance of the routine.

Now it is the beginning of wisdom to understand that social life is founded upon routine. Unless society is permeated, through and through, with routine, civilization vanishes. So many sociological doctrines, the products of acute intellects, are wrecked by obliviousness to this fundamental sociological truth. Society requires stability, foresight itself presupposes stability, and stability is the product of routine. But there are limits to routine, and it is for the discernment of these limits, and for the provision of the consequent action, that foresight is required.

The two extremes of complete understanding and of complete routine are never realized in human society. But of the two, routine is more fundamental than understanding, that is to say, routine modified by minor flashes of short range intelligence. Indeed the notion of complete understanding controlling action is an ideal in the clouds, grotesquely at variance with practical life. But we have under our eyes countless examples of societies entirely dominated by routine. The elaborate social organizations of insects appear to be thoroughgoing examples of routine. Such organizations achieve far-reaching, complex purposes: they involve a differentiation of classes, from cows to serfs, from serfs to workers, from workers to warriors, from warriors to janitors, and from janitors to queens. Such oganizations have regard to needs in a distant future, especially if the comparatively short space of life of the individual insects is taken into account as the unit of measurement.

These insect societies have been astoundingly successful, so far as concerns survival power. They seem to have a past extending over tens of thousands of years, perhaps of millions of years. It is the greatest of mistakes to believe that it has required the high-grade intelligence of mankind to construct an elaborate social organization. A particular instance of this error is the prevalent assumption that any social routine whose purposes are not obvious to our analysis is thereby to be condemned as foolish. We can observe insects performing elaborate routine actions whose purposes they cannot possibly understand, which yet are essential either for their own individual survival or for race-survival.

But these insect societies have one great characteristic in common. They are not progressive. It is exactly this characteristic that discriminates communities of mankind from communities of insects. Further, this great fact of progressiveness, be it from worse to better, or from better to worse, has become of greater and gerater importance in Western civilization as we come to modern times. The rate of change has increased even in my life-time. It is possible that in future ages mankind may relapse into the stage of stable societies. But such a relapse is extremely unlikely within any span of time which we need take into account.

SECTION III. The recent shortening of the time-span between notable changes in social customs is very obvious, if we examine history. Originally it depended upon some slow development of physical causes. For example, a gradual change of physical configuration such as the elevation of mountains: the time-span for such a change is of the order of a million years. Again, a gradual change of climate: the time-span for such a change is of the order of five-thousand years. Again a gradual over-population of the region occupied by some community with its consequent swarming into new territories: having regard to the huge death-rate of pre-scientific ages, the time-span for such a change was of the order of five-hundred years. Again, the sporadic inventions of new technologies, such as the chipping of flints, the invention of fire, the taming of animals, the invention of metallurgy: in the pre-scientific ages, the average time-span for such changes was, at least, of the order of five-hundred years. If we compare the technologies of civilizations west of Mesopotamia at the epochs 100 A.D., the culmination of the Roman Empire, and 1400 A.D., the close of the Middle Ages, we find practically no advance in technology. There was some gain in metallurgy, some elaboration of clockwork, the recent invention of gun powder with its influence all in the future, some advance in the art of navigation, also with its influence in the future. If we compare 1400 A.D. with 1700 A.D., there is a great advance; gunpowder, and printing, and navigation, and the technique of commerce, had produced their effect. But even then, the analogy between life in the eighteenth century and life in the great period of ancient Rome was singularly close, so that the peculiar relevance of Latin literature was felt vividly. In the fifty years between 1780 and 1830, a number of inventions came with a rush into effective operation. The age of steam power and of machinery was introduced. But for two generations, from 1830 to 1890, there was a singular uniformity in the principles of technology which were regulating the structure of society and the usages of business.

The conclusion to be drawn from this survey is a momentous one. Our sociological theories, our political philosophy, our practical maxims of business, our political economy, and our doctrines of education, are derived from an unbroken tradition of great thinkers and of practical examples, from the age of Plato in the fifth century before Christ to the end of the last century. The whole of this tradition is warped by the vicious assumption that each generation will substantially live amid the conditions governing the lives of its fathers and will transmit those conditions to mould with equal force the lives of its children. We are living in the first period of human history for which this assumption is false.

Of course in the past, there were great catastrophes: for example, plagues, floods, barbarian invasions. But, if such catastrophes were warded off, there was a stable, well-known condition of civilized life. This assumption subtly pervades the premises of political economy, and has permitted it to confine attention to a simplified edition of human nature. It is at the basis of our conception of the reliable business man, who has mastered a technique and never looks beyond his contracted horizon. It colours our political philosophy and our educational theory, with their overwhelming emphasis on past experience. The note of recurrence dominates the wisdom of the past, and still persists in many forms even where explicitly the fallacy of its modern application is admitted. The point is that in the past the time-span of important change was considerably longer than that of a single human life. Thus mankind was trained to adapt itself to fixed conditions.

Today this time-span is considerably shorter than that of human life, and accordingly our training must prepare individuals to face a novelty of conditions. But there can be no preparation for the unknown. It is at this point that we recur to the immediate topic, Foresight. We require such an understanding of the present conditions, as may give us some grasp of the novelty which is about to produce a measurable influence on the immediate future. Yet the doctrine, that routine is dominant in any society that is not collapsing, must never be lost sight of. Thus the grounds, in human nature and in the successful satisfaction of purpose, these grounds for the current routine must be understood; and at the same time the sorts of novelty just entering into social effectiveness have got to be weighed against the old routine. In this way the type of modification and the type of persistence exhibited in the immediate future may be foreseen.

SECTION IV. It is now time to give some illustrations of assertions already made. Consider our main conclusions that our traditional doctrines of sociology, of political philosophy, of the practical conduct of large business, and of political economy are largely warped and vitiated by the implicit assumption of a stable unchanging social system. With this assumption it is comparatively safe to base reasoning upon a simplified edition of human nature. For well-known stimuli working under well-known conditions produce well-known reactions. It is safe then to assume that human nature, for the purpose in hand, is adequately described in terms of some of the major reactions to some of the major stimuli. For example, we can all remember our old friend, the economic man.

The beauty of the economic man was that we knew exactly what he was after. Whatever his wants were, he knew them and his neighbours knew them. His wants were those developed in a well-defined social system. His father and grandfather had the same wants, and satisfied them in the same way. So whenever there was a shortage, everyone—including the economic man himself—knew what was short, and knew the way to satisfy the consumer. In fact, the consumer knew what he wanted to consume. This was the demand. The producer knew how to produce the required articles, hence the supply. The men who got the goods onto the spot first, at the cheapest price, made their fortunes; the other producers were eliminated. This was healthy competition. This is beautifully simple and with proper elaboration is obviously true. It expresses the dominant truth exactly so far as there are stable well-tried conditions. But when we are concerned with a social system which in important ways is changing, this simplified conception of human relations requires severe qualification.

It is, of course, common knowledge that the whole trend of political economy during the last thirty or forty years has been away from these artificial simplifications. Such sharp-cut notions as 'the economic man', 'supply and demand', 'competition', are now in process of dilution by a close study of the actual re-actions of various populations to the stimuli which are relevant to modern commerce. This exactly illustrates the main thesis. The older political economy reigned supreme for about a hundred years from the time of Adam Smith, because in its main assumptions it did apply to the general circumstances of life as led, then and for innumerable centuries in the past. These circumstances were then already passing away. But it still remained a dominant truth that in commercial relations men were dominated by well-conditioned reactions to completely familiar stimuli.

In the present age, the element of novelty which life affords is too prominent to be omitted from our calculations. A deeper knowledge of the varieties of human nature is required to determine the reaction, in its character and its strength, to those elements of novelty which each decade of years introduces into social life. The possibility of this deeper knowledge constitutes the Foresight under discussion.

Another example which concerns sociological habits, and thence busines srelations and the shifting values of property, is to be seen in the history of cities. Throughout the whole span of civilization up to the present moment, the growth of condensed aggregates of humans, which we call cities, has been an inseparable accompaniment of the growth of civilization. There are many obvious reasons, the defence of accumulated wealth behind city walls, the concentration of materials requisite for manufacture, the concentration of power in the form of human muscles and, later, in the form of available heat energy, the ease of mutual intercourse required for business relations, the pleasure arising from a concentration of æsthetic and cultural opportunities, the advantages of a concentration of governmental and other directing agencies, administrative, legal, and military.

But there are disadvantages in cities. As yet no civilization has been self-supporting. Each civilization is born, it culminates, and it decays. There is a widespread testimony that this ominous fact is due to inherent biological defects in the crowded life of cities. Now, slowly and at first faintly, an opposite tendency is showing itself. Better roads and better vehicles at first induced the wealthier classes to live on the outskirts of the cities. The urgent need for defence had also vanished. This tendency is now spreading rapidly downwards. But a new set of conditions is just showing itself. Up to the present time, throughout the eighteenth and nineteenth centuries, this new tendency placed the homes in the immediate suburbs, but concentrated manufacturing activity, business relations, government, and pleasure, in the centres of the cities. Apart from the care of children, and periods of sheer rest, the active lives were spent in the cities. In some ways, the concentration of such activities was even more emphasized, and the homes were pushed outwards even at the cost of the discomfort of commuting. But, if we examine the trend of technology during the past generation, the reasons for this concentration are largely disappearing. Still more, the reasons for the choice of sites for cities are also altering. Mechanical power can be transmitted for hundreds of miles, men can communicate almost instantaneously by telephone, the chiefs of great organizations can be transported by airplanes, the cinemas can produce plays in every village, music, speeches, and sermons can be broadcast. Almost every reason for the growth of cities, concurrently with the growth of civilization, has been profoundly modified.

What then is to be the future of cities, three hundred years hence, a hundred years hence, or even thirty years hence? I do not know. But I venture a guess: —that those who are reasonably fortunate in this foresight will make their fortunes, and that others will be ruined by mistakes in calculation.

My second point that the reasons for the choice of sites for cities have also been modified is illustrated by recent changes in my own country, England. The first effect of the new industrial age of the eighteenth and nineteenth centuries was to concentrate population round the coalfields. Thus the central portion of England on its northern edge has become one huge city, disguised under different names for its various regional parts. But the novel conditions are shifting population and manufactures to the south of England, near to the great southern ports which look towards the Mediterranean, the South Atlantic Ocean, and the Panama Canal. They are the best ports, with the easiest navigation, and with uncrowded land around them. At present the transmission of electric power is one of the major pre-occupations of the government of England.

The effect of new technologies on the sites of cities, and on transformations of cities, is one of the fundamental problems which must enter into all sociological theories, including the forecasting of business relations. We must not exaggerate the importance of these particular examples. They are just two examples selected from a whole situation which can be analysed into innumerable examples with the same moral. I mean nothing so absurd as that all industrialists should meditate on the future of cities. The topic may be quite irrelevant to the future activities of most of them. Also I am ignorant as to how much Political Economy they should study.

But we are faced with a fluid, shifting situation in the immediate future. Rigid maxims, a rule-of-thumb routine, and caste-iron particular doctrines will spell ruin. The business of the future must be controlled by a somewhat different type of men to that of previous centuries. The type is already changing, and has already changed so far as the leaders are concerned. The Business Schools of Universities are concerned with spreading this newer type throughout the nations by aiming at the production of the requisite mentality.

Section V. I will conclude this chapter by a sketch of the Business Mind of the future. In the first place it is fundamental that there be a power of conforming to routine, of supervising routine, of constructing routine, and of understanding routine both as to its internal structure and as to its external purposes. Such a power is the bedrock of all practical efficiency. But for the production of the requisite Foresight, something more is wanted. This extra endowment can only be described as a philosophic power of understanding the complex flux of the varieties of human societies: for instance, the habit of noting varieties of demands on life, of serious purposes, of frivolous amusements. Such instinctive grasp of the relevant features of social currents is of supreme importance. For example, the time-span of various types of social behaviour is of the essence of their effect on policy. A widespread type of religious interest, with its consequent modes of behaviour, has a dominant life of about a hundred years, while a fashion of dress survives any time between three months and three years. Methods of agriculture change slowly. But the scientific world seems to be on the verge of far-reaching biological discoveries. The assumption of slow changes in agriculture must therefore be scanned vigilantly. This example of time-spans can be generalized. The quantitative aspect of social changes is of the essence of business relations. Thus the habit of transforming observation of qualitative changes into quantitative estimates should be a characteristic of business mentality.

I have said enough to show that the modern commercial mentality requires many elements of discipline, scientific and sociological. But the great fact remains that details of relevant knowledge cannot be foreseen. Thus even for mere success, and apart from any question of intrinsic quality of life, an unspecialized aptitude for eliciting generalizations from particulars and for seeing the divergent illustration of generalities in diverse circumstances is required. Such a reflective power is essentially a pihlosophic habit: it is the survey of society from the standpoint of generality. This habit of general thought, undaunted by novelty, is the gift of philosophy, in the widest sense of that term.

SECTION VI. But the motive of success is not enough. It produces a short-sighted world which destroys the sources of its own prosperity. The cycles of trade depression which afflict the world warn us that business relations are infected through and through with the disease of short-sighted motives. The robber barons did not conduce to the prosperity of Europe in the Middle Ages, though some of them died prosperously in their beds. Their example is a warning to our civilization. Also we must not fall into the fallacy of thinking of the business world in abstraction from the rest of the community. The business world is one main part of the very community which is the subject-matter of our study. The behaviour of the community is largely dominated by the business mind. A great society is a society in which its men of business think greatly of their functions. Low thoughts mean low behaviour, and after a brief orgy of exploitation low behaviour means a descending standard of life. The general greatness of the community, qualitatively as well as quantitatively, is the first condition for steady prosperity, buoyant, self-sustained, and commanding credit. The Greek philosopher who laid the foundation of all our finer thoughts ended his most marvellous dialogue with the reflection that the ideal state could never arrive till philosophers are kings. Today, in an age of democracy, the kings are the plain citizens pursuing their various avocations. There can be no successful democratic society till general education conveys a philosophic outlook.

Philosophy is not a mere collection of noble sentiments. A deluge of such sentiments does more harm than good. Philosophy is at once general and concrete, critical and appreciative of direct intuition. It is not—or, at least, should not be—a ferocious debate between irritable professors. It is a survey of possibilities and their comparison with actualities. In philosophy, the fact, the theory, the alternatives, and the ideal, are weighed together. Its gifts are insight and foresight, and a sense of the worth of life, in short, that sense of importance which nerves all civilized effort. Mankind can flourish in the lower stages of life with merely barbaric flashes of thought. But when civilization culminates, the absence of a coördinating philosophy of life, spread throughout the community, spells decadence, boredom, and the slackening of effort.

Every epoch has its character determined by the way its populations re-act to the material events which they encounter. This reaction is determined by their basic beliefs—by their hopes, their fears,
their judgments of what is worth while. They may rise to the greatness of an opportunity, seizing its drama, perfecting its art, exploiting its adventure, mastering intellectually and physically the network
of relations that constitutes the very being of the epoch. On the other
hand, they may collapse before the perplexities confronting them.
How they act depends partly on their courage, partly on their intellectual grasp. Philosophy is an attempt to clarify those fundamental
beliefs which finally determine the emphasis of attention that lies at
the base of character.

Mankind is now in one of its rare moods of shifting its outlook.
The mere compulsion of tradition has lost its force. It is our business
—philosophers, students, and practical men—to re-create and
reënact a vision of the world, including those elements of reverence
and order without which society lapses into riot, and penetrated
through and through with unflinching rationality. Such a vision is
the knowledge which Plato identified with virtue. Epochs for which,
within the limits of their development, this vision has been widespread are the epochs unfading in the memory of mankind.

Our discussion has insensibly generalized itself. It has passed
beyond the topic of Commercial Relations to the function of a properly concrete philosophy in guiding the purposes of mankind.

Part VI
Spirituality in Organizations

Introduction to Part VI

Spirituality in Organizations

Jonathan Gosling

It may seem strange to link spirituality with the performance of organizations. One aspires to union with the infinite, the other to the attainment of very material and tangible outcomes. Nonetheless, working life is as much a crucible for the development of the human spirit as it may be, metaphorically, a crucifix on which this spirit is stretched and tortured.

Spiritus in Latin means 'breath', taken as the vital force, energy or immaterial substance which brings life, and with it the possibility of consciousness and self-awareness. Defined in this way, spirit is not simply a development or outgrowth of human potential; it is something outside or beyond the individual, although becoming fully human – individually or collectively – involves becoming infused or *inspired* by the 'breath' of spirit. It is important to insist that spirit, and spirituality, is supra-personal; otherwise we are left with a notion that is indistinguishable from 'imagination', 'awareness' and other similar phenomena of the human psyche. Physical and psychological activity is a precondition for spirituality, but it makes no sense to collapse these concepts. When it comes down to it, when we talk about spirituality, we are referring to *transcendence* of the boundaries of both body and soul.

Transcendence does not necessarily imply 'getting away from' individuality. It is more a matter of identifying with a broader, more inclusive selfhood. This is often named as compassion or love. Although described as unbounded and beyond all definition, transcendent love is associated with living a certain kind of life – adhering to spiritual disciplines. Thus, all the great writers on spirituality prescribe prayer, meditation and contemplation as practices which – gradually – open the individual consciousness to spirituality. These authorities also recommend abstinence from some activities that they deem likely to hinder such progress. And so 'spirituality' comprises, it seems, a paradox: it is transcendence of individual personality towards universal love and compassion; yet it requires the strengthening of personal resolve, insight and awareness in a rather comprehensive practice of self-management.

So spirituality is about managing the self in order to reach beyond selfhood. We cannot realistically expect a spiritual life without self-discipline, although self-discipline is not an end in itself; it is rendered purposeful and productive by the infusion of compassion and love. This, I think, points us to the elusive distinction between management and leadership. Leadership, by this analogy, represents the purposefulness that infuses productive management. Leadership is something which anyone can participate in, but is also a quality which comes to be attributed to some people due, perhaps, to the way in which they manage themselves and the realities they perceive.

Before introducing the essays I have selected for Part VI, let me return to the final sentence of my opening paragraph. I have put together *development* and *suffering*. It is a commonplace that we grow and learn through hardship. Sacrifice – making sacred – is deeply connected with suffering in Judeo-Christian and Islamic traditions. In Buddhism the recognition of suffering and the causes of suffering is the essential starting point on the Path. Even the most gentle of spiritual teachings requires discipline and a certain amount of self-restraint. So it is strange that much popular writing on 'spirituality' is presented as a pain-free expression of 'the human spirit' or of connectedness, community or 'self-actualization'. It is as if a spiritual life is an escape *from*, rather than a path *through*, reality. On the other hand, we are faced with mountains of books and articles that describe organizational life as if it was purely rational; as if ideals and aspirations were irrelevant; and as if 'personal objectives' are really the limit of our aspirations. So let's be clear: by 'spirituality' we do not mean wishful thinking for a life without struggle, but we do refer to a life that is enthused with ideals, hope, sensitivity and creativity – all oriented by a sense of love and transcendence.

The following definition by Rebecca Fox goes some way towards describing (if not expressing) the experience of spirituality:

> Spirituality is defined as an altered state of consciousness where an individual may experience a higher sense of self, inner feelings, inner knowledge, awareness and attainment to the world and one's place in it, knowledge of personal relationships and the relationship to the environment, or a belief in a power greater than imaginable. (Rebecca Fox, quoted in Miles and Priest, 1999, p. 455)

However, there is nothing in this definition to distinguish the 'genuine' from the delusional. This definition says what it might feel like, but doesn't tell us, with authority, what it *is*. If we are to talk about spirituality as something real and substantial, we must assert its source beyond personal experience. Maybe it is something conjured up in collective consciousness (a group spirit or a spirit of community); or perhaps it is participation in a universal Mind or a divine presence. In any case, when we combine leadership and spirituality, we are referring to kinds of relationships that stretch us beyond the ordinary – which reveal something of a supra-personal awareness and meaningfulness and connectedness.

The relationship between spiritual life and organizational performance is increasingly becoming a subject for academic, as well as business-oriented, study not only because it is clearly important to individuals, but also because so many organizations depend on the imagination, creativity, motivation and supra-material aspirations of their employees. It seems as if there is a dream worth aspiring to: the realization of human potential aligned to the value-creating activities of an organization, combining to transcend the material conditions of work and transform labour into something divine.

The essays collected in Part VI approach this topic in a number of different ways.

For many authors, the turbulence and uncertainty of modern life is best dealt with by recourse to the inherent but latent spirituality of human nature. Margaret Wheatley is a brilliant apostle of this view, which she initially proposed by linking leadership with so-called chaos theory (which reveals patterns of order and symmetry independent of human intention) in her bestselling *Leadership and the New Science* (1992/1999). More recently, she has concentrated on processes of dialogue – reminiscent of Aristotle's notion of *phronesis*, a kind of social wisdom which comes into being through conversation amongst people who care for each other and a shared community.[1] The short essay included here (Chapter 33) is a kind of summation of Wheatley's advice for how to live well. It is also published on her website (she doesn't write scholarly articles, and her books need to be read as a whole).

'"Soul Work" in Organizations' by Philip H. Mirvis (Chapter 29) is a classic in the field. Mirvis is an academic and consultant who is not afraid of his own curiosity and where it might lead him, and yet has sustained a consistent focus on the struggles to be fully human within the constraints of economically productive organizations. This essay is about how to have 'soul' in an organization – linking 'soul' to community, shared values and community spirit. He is concerned here with what one can do – not necessarily from a position at the top of a hierarchy, since in fact he concentrates more on the roles of facilitator and group (or community) member. But this essay is also about leadership, because it describes how to enable the emergence of spirit, much as I have defined it above. His core argument is as follows: '*To the extent that we acknowledge people as spiritual beings, and are at least open to an "unseen order" in the world around us, it seems to me that the drive to create wholeness must take account of people's spiritual life and its collective potential*' (p. 487). But this is not a dogmatic rant: it is a carefully crafted and well-argued account, referring to many of the established critiques of his position and to examples from organizational life.

Despite all I have said thus far, it must be admitted that religion does not have a good track record when in cahoots with established forms of state or corporate power. Many of the luminaries of Western liberal thought have argued for a clear distinction between the secular and the sacred – J.S. Mill, Karl Marx, Bertrand Russell and Karl Popper amongst them – each from rather different points of view. Instead of essays by any of these authors, I have selected a rather modest essay by Willa Bruce and John Novinson. 'Spirituality in Public Service: A Dialogue' (Chapter 30) takes the form of a debate between an advocate of spirituality in the workplace and a public-sector manager who is opposed on the grounds that, first, strong personal religious beliefs may compromise professional integrity and, second, that it is anyway a redundant notion: we can describe motivation and values well enough without resorting to 'spirituality'.

Behind much of what I have said so far lies an assumption that spirituality is a good thing in itself. But it is worth asking whether this is so – for example, does it make us happier? And what do we mean by 'a good thing' anyway? In a brilliant and comprehensive essay, Adrian Furnham tackles these questions head-on. 'Ethics at Work: Money, Spirituality, and Happiness' (Chapter 32) examines the arguments – and the evidence – that wealth is associated with happiness. He proceeds to a critical assessment of the claim that being ethical makes one happier, and provides a concise summary of Max Weber's seminal argument that the rise of capitalism is intimately connected to the value-systems encapsulated in Protestantism. He offers summaries of various alternative 'ethics' – welfare, leisure, sports, romance, 'being'

---

[1]   For those who want to return to this original text, see Aristotle's *Nichomachean Ethics*, Books 6–8. Although he describes *phronesis* as a social and intellectual virtue, Aristotle admits, in Book 10, that long and diligent practice of this kind of principled conversation opens the way to the virtue or capacity for *theoria*, which is derived from a divine or spiritual connection.

and narcissism – the last two of which offer especially rich insights into contemporary work culture and why we might experience some aspects as 'spiritual'.

This essay appeared originally in the *Handbook of Workplace Spirituality and Organizational Performance*, edited by Robert Giacalone and Carole Jurkiewicz (2002a). This eclectic collection contains 32 chapters by scholars from various fields of business and organization studies, many of which are worth reading. To my mind, Adrian Furnham's chapter provides an intellectual context that encourages critical intellectual speculation on this important topic; but the reader seeking an experimental framework and prepared to adopt rather complicated intellectual structures may want to look at the following. The opening chapter of the book cited above, by its editors, is called 'Toward a Science of Workplace Spirituality' (Giacalone and Jurkiewicz, 2002b), and attempts to construct a comprehensive model relating motivation, values and community. Another recent essay which tackles the same project is Louis W. Fry's 'Toward a Theory of Spiritual Leadership' (2003).

Leadership and spirituality are united, in many people's minds and hearts, by charisma. Charismatic leaders are believed by their followers to encapsulate supernatural or divine qualities and powers. One can see obvious links to more recent notions of 'transformational leaders', but I have chosen to stay with the original notion of charisma because of the quality of critical writing about the subject. If we can get to grips with this, the more popular and familiar works on transformational and transactional leadership become easily understandable. Conger's and Kanungo's many essays (1987, 1992, 1994) on charisma have set the pace for contemporary studies of charisma in business organizations. Their first essay (1987) sets out the theoretical ground; subsequent work elaborates this with a research methodology and instrument; and numerous other essays and papers elaborate the theme. All these are commendable essays but, for the present collection, I have selected an essay by Robert Tucker which sets out the fundamental concepts. 'The Theory of Charismatic Leadership' (Chapter 31) provides a readable assessment of Weber's ideas and applies them to the fascinating examples of Hitler and Lenin. Each is considered in their economic and social context, with reference to the ideologies and beliefs which enthused their followers at the time. The final section on succession ensures a balanced view of whether charisma rests in the leader or in the beliefs of followers; by the end of this essay I hope the reader will be encouraged to read more on the topic.

What have I left out of this selection? Much too much! I have included nothing from the great religious traditions, although much can be gleaned from them on leadership, both directly and indirectly. All five essays in Part VI are by Westerners, thus excluding insights from the great Chinese authorities – from Confucius to Mao, from the commentaries on the Hindu epics and from the contemporary analyses of collective spirit and tacit knowledge in Japan. Nor have I included the writings of great leaders who themselves linked their power to their spiritual lives – Marcus Aurelius and the Stoics in particular, but also Justinian and later neo-Platonists. And, perhaps unforgivably, I have omitted any mention of the role of religious fervour in contemporary leadership – the Christian fundamentalism underpinning American political power, the Islamic enthusiasm mobilizing much of the Middle East, North Africa and South-east Asia, and so-called new-age cults around the world. But I hope I have offered a small collection which points to a number of relevant and interesting directions for the appreciative study of leadership and spirituality.

References

Aristotle (2004), *The Nicomachean Ethics*, London: Penguin.

Conger, J.A. and Kanungo, R.N. (1987), 'Toward a Behavioural Theory of Charismatic Leadership in Organisational Settings', *Academy of Management Review*, **12**(4), pp. 637–47.

Conger, J.A. and Kanungo, R.N. (1992), 'Perceived Behavioral Attributes of Charismatic Leadership', *Canadian Journal of Behavioral Science*, **24**, pp. 86–102.

Conger, J.A. and Kanungo, R.N. (1994), 'Charismatic Leadership in Organizations: Perceived Behavioral Attributes and their Measurement', *Journal of Organizational Behavior*, **15**, pp. 439–52.

Fox, R. (1999), 'Enhancing Spiritual Experience in Adventure Programmes', in J.C. Miles and S. Priest (eds), *Adventure Programming*, State College, PA: Venture Publishing.

Fry, Louis W. (2003), 'Toward a Theory of Spiritual Leadership', *Leadership Quarterly*, **14**(6), December, pp. 693–727.

Giacalone, Robert A. and Jurkiewicz, Carole L. (eds) (2002a), *Handbook of Workplace Spirituality and Organizational Performance*, Armonk, NY: M.E. Sharpe.

Giacalone, Robert A. and Jurkiewicz, Carole L. (2002b). 'Toward a Science of Workplace Spirituality', in Robert A. Giacalone and Carole L. Jurkiewicz (eds), *Handbook of Workplace Spirituality and Organizational Performance*, Armonk, NY: M.E. Sharpe, Ch. 1.

Miles, J.C. and Priest, S. (1999), *Adventure Programming*, State College, PA: Venture Publishing.

Wheatley, Margaret J. (1999), *Leadership and the New Science: Discovering Order in a Chaotic World* (rev. edn), San Francisco, CA: Berrett-Koehler. First published in 1992.

[29]

"Soul Work" in Organizations

Philip H. Mirvis

The Cedars—PO Box 265, 1601 Olney-Sandy Spring Road, Sandy Spring, Maryland 20860

I came to my first community building workshop in the late 1980s rather skeptical about the whole idea. The previous five years I'd spent researching a book on cynicism in American life: people's inclinations to act primarily out of self-interest and to view other's motives with mistrust and suspicion (Kanter and Mirvis 1989). Data told part of my story: Over twentysome years pollsters showed Americans losing faith in government, business, and most every institution. My own surveys found them doubting their neighbors and the goodness of human nature.

The other part of the story was my own. As a teen in the 1960s, I had been fired by ideals of making a better world. But in the death of the Kennedys and King was a little bit of me. The bloodless body counts in Vietnam, the lies in Watergate, followed by two decades of high-level shenanigans and cover-ups, had doused me with disillusionment about the workings of the nation-state. Ongoing urban flight and decay, the break up of so many families, the breakdown of most civic institutions, and the onset of mass downsizing, free agent management, and such in business had dimmed my hopes of creating community on a more everyday plane. All of this, plus the "swim with the sharks" ethic of the 1980s, made me somewhat edgy about getting together with strangers to "break bread."

Still, I was agreeable when a good friend of mine, a business executive and civic leader, invited me to join him at the workshop. He thought it might deepen my work in companies where I help people give voice to their values and organize around their vision of effectiveness and well-being (Mirvis 1996). This is good work, in theory, but often constrained in practice by people's doubts and fears, their inability to communicate openly with one another, and by short-term profit pressures that allow their companies to rationalize incivility in the name of the "bottom line."

The workshop was being run by the Foundation for Community Encouragement (FCE) and its founder, M. Scott Peck. Peck (1978, 1987, 1993) is a prophet to legions who have read his multi-year bestseller about spiritual awakening *The Road Less Traveled*. He is also an activist and organizer; following publication of *The Different Drum*, he put his moneys and energy into

forming FCE, whose volunteer leaders teach principles of community building and peacemaking in large group workshops and consult with organizations—religious, civic, and commercial—that want to operate as a community.

To prepare myself for the plunge, I skimmed Peck's writings and was taken with his model of the "stages" of community making, particularly the notion that "emptiness" precedes the creation of *true* community. From my experiences in training groups, as well as with some task forces and teams in organizations, this sort of breakthrough typically follows a struggle over leadership or control of the agenda (c.f. Slater 1966). The "storming" gives way as a group examines and works through power issues and thence *organizes* itself, a phase of group development called "norming" (Tuckman 1965). Peck proposes a different method of working this through: Emptying entails vulnerability and requires active surrender of one's leadership, goals, issues, and, interestingly, collective appeals to organization. Build community, he counsels, and then set your agenda. Sounded interesting.

By comparison, Peck's "spiritual" slant, wherein he equates messages from the unconscious with grace and likens the experience of community to a miracle, seemed rather woolly and more than a touch messianic. I conjured up images of people meditating, chanting, or, worst yet, thanking everyone for sharing. Not to belabor, I arrived at my first workshop with plenty of preconceptions and, as the saying goes, lots of baggage. Turned out to be handbags in comparison; the 100 or so others in attendance were carrying steamer trunks.

At Quaker meeting, members take about 45 minutes or so to "empty" themselves—of everyday thoughts and feelings as well as their most profound pleasures and pains—to make room for the "inner light." Evidently they have it down because we spent over a day at that workshop unburdening ourselves. After a brief proto-typical spell in what Peck calls "pseudo-community," wherein a few people told the group about themselves or what they hoped to find in the workshop, we entered a period of chaos. Here, in traditional group dynamics theory, power struggles begin and, in psycho-

PHILIP H. MIRVIS *Crossroads*

dynamic terms, the bowels metaphorically come into play (Bennis and Shephard 1956). We instead operated like a "recovery" group and heard tales from alcoholics, abused spouses, workaholics, spouse abusers, children who had loved parents who did everything but love them, all amidst lots of weeping. Hey, I thought mashing my teeth, can we lighten up? "Any joy here?" I eventually asked. "Yes," said one, "and now let us get back to work."

Welcome to witnessing. And letting it in and sitting with it. New stuff for action-oriented, ready-for-a-power-struggle me. Always quick to conceptualize, my mind was mush. Furthermore, the group seemed shapeless and wasn't taking any direction. So this was emptying. Naming this phase gave me some comfort. Then I recalled the Zen Buddhist teaching to the effect that understanding a ritual is no substitute for participating in it. I paid attention, and my ears opened . . . .

One man's story about growing up with an alcoholic parent jarred me. My mom was an alcoholic, but the family was slow to grasp it and not very skilled at working with it. Neither was mom. Then a tale of job failure caught my attention. Not my story, but I knew the anger and self-doubt in the voice. Finally, I talked about "going native" in my studies of cynicism and how my wariness was preventing me from being "fully present." Nothing heavy. Why was I tearful?

Consciousness—of the self and other—are two cornerstones on which to build community. Be aware of yourself and what moves you, Peck advises, and what inhibits you and causes you to crawl into a shell. But such self-awareness comes from gaining consciousness of the "other": from seeing others fully, listening to their stories, and comprehending their lives and circumstances. This is, at root, the stuff of personality formation, whereby children differentiate themselves from the world around them, and thence the architecture of relationships, wherein our separate selves come together (Fromm 1956, Klein 1959). The connection to community is in *seeing ourselves in the other and the other in ourselves*. Meanwhile, projection, stereotyping, intellectualization, over-identification—all the so-called defense mechanisms (see Freud 1965) that inhibit this connection and reinforce self-reference—were coming to life in my mind and to light in the workshop. So this is what I had to let go of . . . .

I began afresh really tuning in to people's stories. And paying deeper attention to myself in doing so. The range of my receptors increased and new ones switched on. Stimuli were coming through via my head and heart and even my hands. Slowly then surely my past

life was being accessed in fast forward. Others' stories were triggering trace memories and forgotten emotions. There was my mom, and my family, and my friends in my mind's eye, and my own pains. And I was connecting to those of the others in the workshop.

Now these kinds of emotions and experiences are common among attendees of twelve-step programs and self-help groups where empathy, understanding, and ultimately connection emerge from "relating" to another's life story and sharing your own (c.f. Buber 1965, 1970). In such forums, however, people share a common addiction or affliction. Here the sources of hurt, rejection, or disappointment in one's self were many and varied. What did we have in common? Only what Peck calls a universal "fear of disarming ourselves."

Then someone commented about predilections to be "pain junkies," not directed at anyone specific but to the group as a whole. We chewed over the idea of healthy versus unhealthy pain and what constituted "legitimate" suffering in a "broken world." And we also began to exchange puns and laugh. Happy moments pulsed through from my past, too. This, I guess, marked our movement into a new phase of group development.

Over the next day, the group looked less to Peck and the workshop facilitators as role models or targets for disaffection. A collective letting go of these expectations gradually gave the group a rhythm and together we forged the means to manage ourselves. People were saying the right thing, to each other and to the group as a whole. They were also group guardians, reaching out to the silent who wanted to speak, and letting the talkative know when the group could gain most from their silence.

"Group consciousness" is a third cornerstone of community. It requires paying attention to the parts *and* the whole (c.f. Bateson 1972). Our workshop group was gaining a new and fluid organization as we attended to our collective dynamics and shared responsibility for building relationships. Now I'd experienced this simultaneous awareness of the forest-and-trees in other group encounters and lived it in out-of-doors workshops when helping teammates across a stream or up a mountain. This capacity to "see the system" while operating within it seems to develop when groups immerse themselves deeply and repetitively into their experience, much as in therapy (Smith and Berg 1987). This proved a comforting explanation at the time; it put psycho-logic to my feelings of communion.

Late in the workshop I was resting on the floor, close to Peck's feet. Suddenly, "religious" images dammed (or damned) up in my psyche began bursting forth. I imagined myself as the apostle Paul being thrown from

PHILIP H. MIRVIS *Crossroads*

his horse as a phrase circled the air above me: "Many are called, but few are chosen." The spell was broken when a voice inside me boomed: "Who does the choosing?" I suddenly wondered: God? Me?

Years of religious baggage were lifted for my inspection: overly-friendly priests and too-distant nuns, fear of hellfire and guilt over disappointing Jesus. Peck reminds that spirituality is *not* the same as religion, but here the naming did not provide much comfort. Neither did the recognition that people's identities and anxieties outside of a system have a way of creeping into their experiences within it (c.f. Alderfer 1966). Still, I wasn't troubled, hepped up, or even hung up by the recollections, nor was I crafting fine distinctions between my rejection of God "out there" and willingness to apprehend God "within." I was just, well, peaceful.

Now I know about the power of suggestion, and how this can all be explained in the male psychodynamics of transference: me a little guy in the big hands of God the Father cum Scott Peck. And I'm not talking about being born again. But *something* was happening. And not only to me. People around me sounded thoughtful and poetic. We together were in sync and working well. Suppressed conflicts were surfaced. And many of our manifest disagreements were rapidly resolved. The group seemed to be blessed . . . .

The final cornerstone of community is to organize in harmony with what William James (1902) calls the "unseen order of things." People who work with groups and organizations without otherworldly reference simply call it alignment (Harrison 1983). But, aligned toward what? Mission, vision, values: these were my prior referent points in working with organizations. Love? You see that in business, too, and surely in relationships. But aligned with the Spirit? A metaphor, I reasoned, of *these* people in *this* setting.

Three months later my mom died: lung failure following exploratory surgery that diagnosed her as having a difficult-to-treat cancer. In the course of a few days after the surgery, she was resuscitated once and got to say her goodbyes to me and my brother and sisters. And we to her. We also spent our time sorting out the meaning of her living will with doctors and medical ethicists and, even more so, sorting things out among ourselves. We worked through hyper-rationality, estrangement, anger, sorrow, and exhaustion. And we did it well.

Now to what extent events and circumstances are dictated by chance or law is a source of profound speculation among philosophers and theologians, scientists and lay people. On this matter, Peck is a believer in serendipity. His is a universe where the dice roll in cycles both vicious and virtuous. On this subject, I can only say that I was unusually prepared to be with my mother at her death bed, and to reach out to my family, in a manner most serendipitous.

Community Defined

So far, I've used the term "community" without defining it. It may help to say what it does *not* mean in this discussion. For example, community does not refer here to a physical place, like a neighborhood, workplace, or gathering spot. Nor does it connote necessarily a social space, or affiliation, such as a political party, family, or reference group. As a starting point, see in the root word "common" notions of sharing, mutual obligation, and commitment that link people together (Bellah et al. 1985, McMillan and Chavis 1986). This yields, insofar as a person is concerned, what Seymour Sarason (1974) terms "the psychological sense of community" and encompasses the emotive experience of feeling chose to others, being connected to them by reciprocity or empathy, and even of living at least some of your life with and through them.

But what of a community's collective character? Ties that bind, such as shared values, congruent interests, cohering rituals, and a common purpose are sociological indicators. To this, those who study ongoing communities add concepts like caring, support, mutual aid, and trust (c.f. Kanter 1972, Bellah et al. 1991, Wuthnow 1991, Putnam 1992). But are Communitarians, Unitarians, or Rotarians any more communal than, say, Libertarians, Branch Davidians, or Wall Street traders in these regards? Much depends, in Peck's formulation, on the degree of consciousness and intention that motivates their collectivity.

This brings up the component of "unity" in community. Contemporary sociologists speak of this as the "solidarity" people experience with community members or their collective sense of "we-ness" (Etzioni 1993). Charles Horton Cooley (1922), a forebear of today's community-minded sociologists, characterized it as the "fusion of personalities into a larger whole." Peck espouses this same holistic concept but configures it in a "group mind." This speaks to the need for community members to consciously embrace unity and to inquire deeply and periodically into their reasons for doing so. He questions, for example, the "blind trust" sometimes found in cults and mindless followership that can mark bands of "true believers." Peck also believes that the *exclusivity* found in groups that are caring, supportive, and helpful to their own kind but unresponsive and even hostile to others counterfeits their claims to community.

The objection here is that those who would unite on the basis of like minds, a similar heritage, or a common enemy may be side-stepping the struggle essential to fusing with "unlike" others (c.f. Friedman 1983). True community, in Peck's terms, is born of *inclusiveness* and comes into being as a group *transcends* differences. John Gardner (1995) terms this "wholeness incorporating diversity." In this light, community is understood as a "process," rather than a psychological state or sociological condition. Thus it can be experienced in a weekend workshop among strangers as well as in the daily life and doings of ongoing groups, organizations, and other intentional communities.

Behind Community Building Experience

A group from 50 to 75 meet to participate in one of FCE's community building workshops. The first session begins with a reading of the "Rabbi's Gift," an apocryphal story of a 12th century monastery restored after a wise, old rabbi advises that one of the monks, but unknown which one, is the "messiah." Then silent reflection. What follows is a group's unique wending through the stages pseudo-community, chaos, and emptiness described earlier. The creation of community is itself emergent, not itself predictable, programmable, or reducible to precise formula, nor a function simply of the collective effort of high-minded people with good intentions. In the community building experience, however, Peck and FCE leaders assert that the process cycles and deepens through frank and intimate communication.

Their counsel: Be open, inquire deeply, be realistic and authentic, and bring things to light mindful of the moment. These timeless truisms about how to talk, listen, and be with others were refined by human relations researchers decades ago and are taught today by management educators, school teachers, the clergy, and healers of all types, usually through experiential exercises. What FCE adds is the Quaker-like injunction that people be "moved to speak": to wait to be moved before speaking and, importantly, to speak when so moved. This takes skill at listening to one's inner self and courage to speak from the heart.

There is, broadly, something new in how we think about and construct communication exercises that is by no means unique to FCE. The "dialogues" studied at MIT (Isaacs 1993), the "appreciative" inquiries at Case Western Reserve (Cooperrider 1990), and the "socio-

therapy" groups of Patrick DeMare et al. (1991), to name but a few examples, all incorporate traditional human relations techniques and experiences but derive from a different set of assumptions about group development and social organization.

For instance, drawing from the tenets of humanistic psychology in the 1950s and 1960s, many human relations trainers stress the importance of dealing directly with "here and now"behavior and regard interpersonal feedback as key to the "helping" relationship (c.f. Bradford et al. 1964). Indeed, to heighten self-awareness in sensitivity training, people are encouraged to "mirror" their reactions to other's behavior and, in some circles, to offer interpretations. By comparison, participants in community-building workshops are advised to speak to the "group as a whole" and urged to self-reflect, and be aware of their filtering and judgments, all in service of emptying oneself of what gets in the way of truly hearing another person. The idea, as expressed by William Isaacs (1994) with reference to dialogue groups, is that by "observing the observer" and "listening to your listening," self-awareness of thoughts, feelings, and experiences, past and present, seep gently into consciousness.

In turn, the notion of offering Rogerian-type counseling in a group—to help people see themselves more clearly through questioning or clarifying—is discouraged. In FCE's lingo, this equates to "fixing," a worthy aspiration that has to be emptied in order to experience oneself and others more fully. On this point, it is worth noting that Peck, an MD and psychotherapist by training, in no way equates community building with group therapy. Nor does he see it as an especially fertile medium for personal growth. The focus in FCE workshops is on collective development and interpretive comments, if offered at all, are aimed at the group as a whole (c.f. Bion 1961).

Still, there are obvious parallels between the dynamics in therapy or encounter groups and in community building workshops. Community building groups, for example, are just as apt to express dependency on leaders, to engage in fight-and-flight, to form pairing relationships, and to manifest the myriad unconscious conflicts that surface in other kinds of group encounters. But the intent is not to "work through" these dynamics by confronting them directly. Rather, the group serves as a "container" to hold differences and conflicts up for ongoing exploration. This keeps "hot" conversation "cooled" sufficiently that people can see the "whole" of the group mind. This facilitates development of group consciousness by counteracting tendencies toward "splitting" in group dynamics whereby people identify with "good part" of their group and reject the "bad part." This container resides in what some call the "quantum universe"(Wilbur 1984, Talbot 1986). From the study of particle physics, it is believed that observation of a particle influences the quantum field around it, meaning literally that observing affects the observed (Capra 1976, 1982). David Bohm (1986), the physicist whose theories stimulated development of the dialogue process, generalized the point to human communication and gatherings. By simultaneously self-scanning and inquiring with a group, in his view, people create a connective field between observer and observed. By "holding" this field, in turn, a group can "contain"both energy and matter, and investigate more fully what it is producing. And in uncovering this "tacit infrastructure," some theorists believe, lay the possibility of creating new collective dynamics.

Here is where FCE's principles apply. At the start of a workshop, aspirations are set to welcome and affirm diversity, deal with difficult issues, bridge differences with integrity, and relate with love and respect. In this sense, community building advances by the "positive values = positive action" equation that guides groups involved in appreciative inquiries. At the same time, FCE leaders are admonished that they cannot "lead"a group to community. They may be "moved" to empty themselves of feelings, or to commune with a co-leader, and these may serve as a stimulus and example to a group that has had enough of fighting or fleeing and is ready to examine some new behavior. Leaders, and anyone else present, are also free to call a group into silence, slow discussion down, or offer up thoughts for contemplation, the sorts of things that lend themselves to what Bohm (1989) describes as "superconductivity" in a group: where the electrons, or in this case the elements of the conversation, move as a "whole"rather than as separate parts.

It is plausible to think of the heightened group consciousness in community building workshops in the psychodynamic terms of bisociation: people reclaiming "split off" ideas, feelings, and subgroups and reconstituting the group-as-a-whole. But what of the spiritual connection with the "unseen order of things?" Testimonials abound about the creative breakthroughs that groups experience in Outward Bound programs, when engaged in sports and the arts, in meditation and therapy, and in other mediums where the experience of wholeness translates into creative insight or action or both. These are labelled "flow" experiences (Csikszentmihalyi 1990) and attributed to the harmonious co-evolution of mental and material forces (c.f. Bateson 1979).

Several variants of the "new science" speak to this dynamic. The order to be found in chaos, for instance, revolves around an aptly named "strange attractor;" Margaret Wheatley (1993), among others, suggests that its human equivalent is *meaning*. Theories of transpersonal psychology are, so to speak, on the same wave length. But, to Peck, Willis Harman, founder of the World Business Academy, and others like them, such notions of an implicate order come from the field of inquiry known as "spiritual science" where, it is presumed, mind and matter co-evolve and interpenetrate

As novel and scientific-sounding as these ideas might seem, they can be found in ancient Buddhist tracts and other tenets of "eastern" thought and in many indigenous peoples' ways of understanding the world. They have also reached the west over the centuries in novels, poetry, and arts, in the words of mystics and deeds of heretics. In testimony to its timelessness, it is customary to say that this kind of knowledge is inspired or revealed, rather than invented or discovered. Perhaps the source is a muse, or a spirit, or some other "unseen" force?

In an evocative essay, Diana Whitney (1995) describes spirit variously as energy, as meaning, and as epistemology. Her illustrations come from Native American traditions, Chinese medicine, the myths of the new science, and the musings of organizational scientists trying to make sense of the forces that impinge on themselves and those they study. In many cultures, she notes, spirit is also sacred. This moves us from the realms of philosophy and metaphor to matters of faith. It is clear enough that the world's great religions, as well as more personal or idiosyncratic ones, offer different ways of apprehending and expressing their revealed truths. Yet the comparative study of religions suggests that all have, at their core, a near universal means of accessing spiritual knowledge. It is this that Willis Harman (1988) calls their "perennial wisdom."

Peck and FCE are adamant that community building is *not* religion and that its rules are by no means sacred. Religion is about answers, so they say, spirituality is about questions. Yet the experience of making community is described as transcendent: a term that means literally to "climb over"or, more colloquially, to achieve a "peak experience" or find one's"higher self" (c.f. Maslow 1954, 1968). William James, speaking of the common core of relevation, says we find "MORE" of that quality "which is operative in the universe outside of (ourselves)."

Sit easy with James' capitalization and the mountaintop imagery: Buddhism teaches that we can find "more"

PHILIP H. MIRVIS   *Crossroads*

when approaching everyday tasks like sweeping the floor, washing the dishes, and working in the work-a-day world whenever we are especially "mindful" (Hahn 1990, 1993). The paradox here is that emptiness may be essential to mindfulness and vice versa. Whether it is this embrasure of yin and yang, or of paradox broadly, or simply, as physician Bernie Siegel (1986) put it, a miracle, it seems to me that what dialogue groups, appreciative inquiries, and community building workshops offer, in much the same way as do tribal kivas and Quaker meetings, is that near-universal *medium for accessing spiritual knowledge and becoming our better selves.*

Spirit in Organization Life

However we characterize the experience of community and its spiritual dimensions, it is plain enough that vast numbers of people, from all walks of life, are searching for new relationships, attachments, and "something more" in their individual and collective lives. That this yearning is being felt in the workplace is not surprising. People are spending more of their time working and number among closest friends their coworkers (Schor 1991). Lacking continuity and connection in so many other settings, many naturally look to their organization as a communal center.

The problem is that organizations seem far less hospitable to community making than in the recent past. From post-WWII to the early 1980s, the American workplace, corporate and governmental, was a relatively stable and secure setting in which to develop a career, make friends, give and get social support, and participate in purposeful activities larger than one's self. Today's workplace, marked by multiple changes in ownership and large-scale layoffs, more internal movement and individual job hopping, and increasing numbers of people on temporary assignment or working part-time, is riven instead by fear, pressure, and impermanence. What are the prospects, then, of making community and finding spirit amidst these spoils?

They seem to be growing: Over 100 employees of the World Bank gather together at 1:00 pm every Wednesday and discuss the potential of "soul consciousness" in their organization (*Business Week* 1995); Boeing has had poet David Whyte (1994) stir 500 or so of its top managers with recitations from his volume on "the preservation of the soul in corporate America;" and Tom Chappel, CEO of a health products company and proponent of running a prayerful business, is in demand on the lecture circuit. These are but a few

examples of how people are searching for and finding community at work today (c.f. Cox 1993).

It's easy enough to dismiss "soul work" in business as marginal and gatherings of this sort as "feel good" palliatives. A closer look, however, reveals many different ways in which community and spirituality are making their way into organization life and have something to offer, to both practice and theory.

Leading from Within

One place to locate this new emphasis is in contemporary models of leadership and leadership development. It wasn't too long ago that "situational leadership" was in vogue and executives were advised to make their leadership style "contingent" on the situation. By comparison, Robert Greenleaf's (1993) notion of "servant leadership," Max Depree's (1989) accounts of "artful" practice, Stephen Covey's (1990) "principle-centered" approach, and Abraham Maslow's (1965) prescient writings on "eupsychian" management all speak, in one way or another, to a leader's inner sources of inspiration and outward embodiment of ideals. Why this emphasis on leading from within? In his account of "leading minds" throughout history, Howard Gardner (1995) makes the observation that "it is the particular burden of the leader to help individuals determine their personal, social, and moral identities." Leaders accomplish this, he finds, by relating "identity stories" about their life struggles and how they resolved their own identity issues. Note, in support of this point, how many autobiographies of business executives have been published these past several years not to mention a few volumes of their business-related poetry.

Shell Oil has incorporated this general thrust into its leadership development agenda. As part of its "Leaders Developing Leaders" program, Jerome Adams, head of Shell's Learning Center, has had the top 200 executives record their life histories and career experiences to identify sources of personal passion and meaning. The executives, guided by myself and community artist Maggie Sherman, also fashioned a plaster cast of their face and decorated it with symbols of their life journey and leadership transformation in Shell. The decorated masks, and stories behind them, were shared with colleagues and today appear in offices throughout the corporation. Interestingly, Shell's top ten executives helped to "prime the pump" by telling their own identity stories and participating in mask making. In turn, the 200 shared their masks and stories in a subsequent program aimed at middle management.

PHILIP H. MIRVIS *Crossroads*

It should be remembered that McGregor's (1960) influential writings of thirty-five years ago urged managers to probe their own "Theory X versus Y" assumptions. Thereafter, a science of self-assessment emerged, exemplified by Schon's (1983) studies of "reflective practitioners," Agryris's (1982, 1985) approach to uncovering motives behind actions (right/left hand columns), and a myriad of self-scoring personality tests, type indicators, and competency evaluations. Nowadays, however, development-minded leaders are returning to simpler and more timeless approaches—prayer, meditation, journaling, and spiritual retreats—methods traditionally classified under "care for the soul" (c.f. Moore 1991). Furthermore, in lieu of power lunches, executives are attending prayer breakfasts, such as the one hosted by the First Tuesday Club in Boston that typically includes the CEOs of Digital, Gillette, the Bank of Boston, and Raytheon, along with the heads of smaller outfits. Finally, my impression is that many more leaders, at every level in organizations, are joining support groups, involving themselves in mentoring relationships, and going to conferences where they engage in "inner work" and contemplate the meaning of what they do with fellow searchers.

Meaning in Work

Work itself is also being rediscovered as a source of spiritual growth and connection to others. Recall laments about the "blue-collar blues" or "white-collar woes?" Thirty years of study has shown that the components of fulfilling work—producing a "whole" product or service, and finding variety, autonomy, and challenge in tasks—can be modeled, measured, and translated into work fit for human capabilities. As a result, many job designs once based on scientific management principles are being enriched and close supervision is giving way to self-managing teams. But does intellectually enriched work truly satisfy the heart and make the human spirit soar?

Studies of artisans and craftspersons, inventors, wordsmiths, and other creative types, not to mention scientists, athletes, and musicians, find them immersed in their tasks, carried away or elevated to new heights, envisioning a creation in its fullness (Koestler 1964, Arieti 1976). For a time, scholars attributed these experiences to something "intrinsic" to work, as though it were present without the worker and absent context (Herzberg et al. 1959). Now, this is understood in a web of relationships: in the interplay of person and material, and in a larger context that makes it more or less meaningful (c.f. Mirvis 1980).

Perhaps these "relational" qualities of work are easiest to find among people who care for people. Doctors, for instance, diagnose, cut, and drug but their "laying on of hands" is vital to curing. In the same way, the treatment of mental illnesses centers on the relationship between therapist and patient. To generalize the point, some scholars contend that empathy, support, and caregiving are the prime ingredients of truly meaningful work (Kahn 1993, Fletcher 1996).

On this matter, research by Michael Learner (1996) finds that what middle-class blue- and white-collar workers bemoan most is the absence of love and care in the workplace and any connection between their jobs and larger purpose in life. What are organizations doing today to help people meet their meaning needs in the workplace? There are a growing number of firms whose statements of vision, mission, or purpose lift up the value of work products and services and speak directly to employees' dignity and self-worth. In the best of cases, employees at all levels have had the chance to shape or affirm these visions or craft one for their own work areas.

On a communal scale, companies are holding community building workshops, dialogues, and appreciative inquiries, as well as countless team-building programs that offer a regimen of human relations training, time and space for reflection, and maybe a ropes course, river raft, or some other "opening up" experience. The close bonds forged are well documented along with gains in team performance (Beinecke 1994). Interestingly, social service is increasingly a part of team building in companies like Ameritech, Ford Motor Company, and General Electric. Noel Tichy has designed a variety of such "service learning" experiences wherein employees help to rebuild inner-city housing, assist in clinics and orphanages, or counsel those in need. What's it all about?

It is, according to Tichy, a means to get people in touch deeply with themselves, their teammates, and the human condition around them. Naturally, there is some crabbing about the "relevance" of such experiences and the "transfer of training" back to the workplace. Anita Roddick (1990), founder of the Body Shop and innovator in this regard, counters that one can "find the spirit in the world through (social) service." She adds a pragmatic point: "You educate people by their passions . . . . You want them to feel that they are doing something important, that they're not a lone voice . . . . I'd never get that kind of motivation if we were just selling shampoo or body lotion." Beyond its benefits to the business, it is the social significance of

PHILIP H. MIRVIS *Crossroads*

this kind of work that connects people's employment to their larger purpose in life.

Goodness in Groups

Scholarly papers on work groups usually begin with a discussion of the Hawthorne studies and commentary on how productive norms developed in the bank wiring room once management showed its human face (c.f. Cartwright 1951, Hackman and Suttle 1977). As an alternative, Charles Hampden-Turner's (1971) analysis focuses on people's liberation from mindless rules, dawning consciousness of their powers and responsibilities, followed by consensual commitment to look out for one another and do the job right. In his view, the women in the bank wiring room became a "self-managing" work group.

The broader Hawthorne studies have become a parable for organizational scientists over the years, reinterpreted by every generation to affirm their view of how the world works. Some contend that it was changes in the lighting that led to increased productivity; others point to management's empowerment of workers; still others to the feminine impulse to bond and work together. My question: Could the struggle with chaos and emptying of resentments, fears, and learned limits have helped to unleash collective creativity in the bank wiring room? And could, perhaps, we be referring to "something more" when we talk about the "Hawthorne" effect?

It is the researcher's job to parse out variables and identify their unique contribution to collective life. I remember well my own eye opening about our field's peculiarly anti-social psychology when administering a questionnaire to production workers at a plant in Bolivar, Tennessee in the mid-1970s. They had formed into work teams, with the assistance of Michael Maccoby, and busied themselves learning problem-solving skills. The workers also set up a "school" to teach each other how to read, improve the yield of their gardens, balance checkbooks, handle problems with their kids, and deal with other chores at the intersection of work and life. Our questionnaire measured concepts like social distance, participation in decisions, communication patterns, conflict resolution, and such. Maccoby asked me which questions measured group "spirit?" I was at a loss to answer.

The "Principles of Community" developed at Carlisle Motors, a multi-location auto dealership in west Florida, asks employees to "relate with love and respect" and to be "open to Spirit." Several community building workshops among staff are credited with "breaking down the walls" between the sales force and

back office and with humanizing working relationships throughout the auto dealership. Taking its principles to market, the dealership has adopted a "fair and simple" approach to auto pricing, that eliminates "haggling" and the disadvantages incurred therein by women and minorities in new and used car purchases. Buyers can also return their cars with "money back" to sales people who now work on salary rather than commission. Profits-per-car are down, but volume has soared. According to Scott Wilkerson, CEO, this is simply a matter of "living the principles." I would hypothesize further that as people relate to each other with love and respect, and strive to be open to Spirit, their aspirations to produce "something more" at work are awakened.

Company as Community

The distinction between company and community blurs in firms like the Body Shop, Ben & Jerry's and other so-called "companies with a conscience" that have a dual bottom line: doing good and doing well. Over the past several years, the case has been made that such firms can juxtapose social responsibility alongside the profit motive and still achieve commercial success (c.f. Scott and Rothman 1992, Ray and Rinzler 1993). What is interesting for the present purpose is the impact on employees. Employees at Ben & Jerry's register extraordinary high ratings of job meaning, camaraderie with coworkers, and trust in management in their biennial survey. Interestingly, however, neither material rewards nor these psychosocial factors are the prime predictors of job satisfaction and commitment to the organization. Rather it is pride in and support for the firm's "social mission" that best differentiates between the most- and least-fulfilled employee. This social mission is reflected in the firm's products and marketing and is brought to life in countless acts of social service undertaken by Ben & Jerry's employees. One result, regularly recorded on surveys and in group discussions, is that many employees have, in effect, "found themselves" through their employment in the company. In addition, many report that they have had their "consciousness raised" as a result of their involvement in social and political issues and several attest to having "learned compassion" through their social service work in the company.

The theme of company = community is also being expressed today in the myriad of good works being undertaken within firms today to advance social welfare and justice. Studies find that companies that are leaders in employee training, work enrichment, and progressive human resource management take the lead

PHILIP H. MIRVIS   *Crossroads*

in valuing workforce diversity and promoting work/family balance as well (c.f. Mirvis 1993a). At one time, schools, families, and other community institutions provided leadership and the necessary supports in these regards. Nowadays, the best-managed companies are taking on these communal responsibilities. Furthermore, they are often doing so through employee task forces and committees, literally taking on a communal governance structure to do the human community's business.

This reminds that there is a *process* side to running a business like a community: Robert Bellah and colleagues (1991) contend that constant attention to purpose, marked by inquiry into what is going on and face-to-face participation by people in decisions, are earmarks of the "civil" organization. Communal processes are being introduced into companies in the form of search conferences, town meetings, and the like (c.f. Schindler-Rainman and Lippitt 1980, Wiesbord 1992, Bunker and Alban 1992). Carrying this further, a "soul committee" was formed at Lotus Development Corporation to revitalize the software maker's originating spirit in light of ongoing layoffs and competitive market pressures. Digital Equipment undertook a variation of the theme (Greenfield 1996). And top executives at Shell Oil join together to explore "leadership as being" and regularly host dialogues throughout the company where personal values are compared with corporate directions. This process, which has people dig into their hearts and bring what they find into communal conversation, is very much a part of the "work" in these organizations (c.f. Gozdz 1996, Shaffer and Anundsen 1993).

Describing the Indescribable

I have seen Richard Hackman at a loss for words. He was leading a seminar at the Kennedy School at Harvard about his research at People Express airlines. Talking through a model of the developmental stages of high performance organizations, he opined that *something* had led People Express to move swiftly and fluidly through the typical crises encountered by start-up businesses that center on leadership and competition among subgroups in the organization. There were lots of hypotheses about how market and organizational dynamics might have "sped up" the developmental process but, when pressed, Hackman talked about *indescribable* processes and moods in the company that seemed to create an alignment of energy and yield timely decisions and actions. What is more, he con-

fessed, he felt himself "caught up" in these and no longer had an objective view of how the company worked.

I've had my own problems trying to talk about community in business without sounding silly or sliding into cynicism. At another FCE gathering, following two days of building community, we discussed applications of the experience to the management of business. I began with all sorts of caveats and cautions about the inhuman aspects of human relations training and how T-groups and other social technologies had proved faddish and ineffective as means of organization change. Still, with all the interest in corporate culture, and with managers growing comfortable with the idea of organizing around vision and values, and, especially, with working people thirsting for community at work, it seemed to me that it was worth exploring how we might build community in companies.

"Bullshit," a leading management writer and advisor in attendance shouted, cutting through it all. I lacked realism and was pie-eyed to think that community building had anything to do with the central mission of business: to make money. Worse, conducting workshops in business would be akin to preparing "lambs for the slaughter." So there I was, facing the stereotypical nay-sayer and the whole of the military-industrial complex. My initial retorts were scarcely civil. Then, suddenly, I saw my own shadow and called for a moment of silence and reflection.

Self-reference in a social system is difficult to describe. But in the group, to use Peck's terms, we seemed to recycle through chaos to emptying to civil community in that quiet time and space. I do remember hearing birds in the distance. The discussion picked up again, but it was no longer between two male buffaloes cum management experts. Others chimed in. Defensiveness gave way to heartfelt statements and listening. We two supposed experts never really found common ground. (What do you expect, miracles?) But the group discussion was elevated and more than a few left the gathering bound-and-determined to move organizational behavior in their companies in some new directions.

For God and Company?

To an extent, Ben & Jerry's and the Body Shop, like Levi Strauss, Hershey, Corning Glass, and many other "values-led" businesses reflect their founder's personal values. There are also examples of companies whose principles explicitly express their leader's spiritual grounding. For instance, many of Digital Equipment's

PHILIP H. MIRVIS *Crossroads*

egalitarian policies can be traced to founder Ken Olsen's religious beliefs; the same is true of Cummins Engine whose longtime chairman J. Irwin Miller is a proponent of "ethical culture." And Max Depree, former head of Herman Miller, not only writes about the moral and spiritual sources of leadership, he also welcomes countless visitors who come to benchmark his company's communal practices and culture.

One executive who is unabashed about using "God language" is C. William Pollard, Chairman of Service-Master, whose corporate objectives, carved in a marble wall at headquarters, begin with the aspiration "To honor God in all we do." Pollard contends that this gives employees a "reason for being and doing." He asserts that faith in God gives leaders a moral compass and is not shy about debating stockholders on, say, the relationship between God and profits. He also encourages employees to discuss "what's right and what's wrong" in decisions they make on their jobs. The intent is summed up in one of ServiceMaster's leadership principles: "We have all been created in God's image, and the results of our leadership will be measured beyond the workplace. The story will be told in the changed lives of people."

Is Pollard unique? As a person, of course. So is the head of Mary Kay Cosmetics who attributes her company's success to the principles of "God first, family second, and career third, giving women a chance to keep their lives in proper perspective." Yet a recent *Forbes* survey of *Fortune* 500 executives finds that over two-thirds regularly worship at church or synagogue. Is ServiceMaster's pledge of service to God without precedent? The Atlanta-based Fellowship of Companies for Christ numbers over 500 firms around the U.S. while the California-based Full Gospel Fellowship sponsors 3,000 chapters in nearly 100 countries.

The foregoing raises troubling questions about who has access to these leadership networks and to what extent nonbelievers are at a disadvantage in these companies or even welcome at all? Certainly the CEOs cited above are all Christians and the associations of like-minded business people primarily involve Boston Catholics and Congregationalists, Midwestern Lutherans and Methodists, Bible Belt Baptists, and born-agains on the west coast. In turn, there have been many cases where employees have suffered discrimination in hiring, promotion, or access to important social circles because they did not subscribe to the religious tenets of the leaders of their enterprise.

Pollard (1996) speaks to this directly in his book *The Soul of the Firm* and points to a top leadership team

composed of Christians, Muslims and Jews. As to other misuses of spirituality in organization, my colleagues in FCE urge me to "trust the process." I do so, but with caveats and cautions.

Caveats and Cautions

There are good reasons to be careful when doing community building in the business world. Obviously the culture and climate in many organizations are antithetical to community building and openness to the Spirit. That said, proselytize about religion or using spiritual beliefs to exclude others undermines the requirement for inclusiveness. Still some organization members regard conversations of the sort found in community building workshops to be invasive of their privacy and feel a subtle coercion to reveal something about their own private lives. Furthermore, others view "loose talk" about spirituality, soul, and other things sacred as inappropriate in a secular setting. It is crucial, therefore, to *secure people's informed consent* before subjecting them to this kind of experience and to ensure that they can opt out without prejudice or harm (Mirvis 1993b). It is also worth noting that all manner of corporate consultants, helpers, and healers are out there peddling their own variant of community building and spiritual enrichment. The upshot? Buyer beware.

There is also potential danger when community takes hold in a business. The indescribable feelings that Hackman reported can also be called indoctrination. Pundits have gone so far as to say that People Express practiced "Kool Aid Management," likening its demise to Rev. Jim Jones' cult in Guyana that ended in enforced mass suicide. By all accounts, the airline's employees willingly embraced its management principles, including the high-minded aspiration of "making a better world." Nonetheless, critics assert that this sort of testimony is itself evidence of the pervasiveness of corporate mind control (see *Time* 1986, Bennet 1986, Prokesch 1986).

The introduction of spirituality into the mix raises the stakes. There are, for example, documented cases of companies that proselytize employees with specific religious doctrine (Nash 1996). And cases of corporate programs wherein employees, exposed to "New Age" ideas about consciousness and the cosmos, felt their own brand of faith compromised (*Newsweek* 1987). Thus the tendency in public education, as well as in most private venues, has been to erect a wall between, say, church and state, faith and reason, the spiritual and secular. Needless to say, this makes thoughts and

ORGANIZATION SCIENCE/Vol. 8, No. 2, March-April 1997

PHILIP H. MIRVIS *Crossroads*

feelings about the spirit "undiscussable" in most organizations.

At the same time, human resource specialists,
whether incorporating workforce diversity or reaching
out to employees in their fullness, stress the importance of engaging the "whole" person at work (Kahn
1992, Hall and Mirvis 1996). The idea of "seeing" a
system-as-a-whole is taking hold in corporate plants,
offices, and boardrooms. *To the extent that we acknowledge people as spiritual beings, and are at least open to an
"unseen order" in the world around us, it seems to me that
the drive to create wholeness must take account of people's
spiritual life and its collective potential.* Certainly there
are voices making the case for open discussion of faith,
gods, spirituality, and religion in public schools and
civic forums (c.f. Carter 1994). How can we not, they
argue, if we are to tend to our community? I would
make the same case for businesses that strive to be
communities.

Yet I've also argued that if companies turn into
"total communities" there is some risk that people will
become "lost" in the oceanic mood and lose sight of
the world beyond the boundaries of their firm. Why
worry about preschool education when your company
provides for your children's needs? Why make community with your neighbors when you are called to do so
at work? Why even go to church when your company's
spiritual gatherings have a lot more sizzle? On this
count, I am heartened by Carlisle Motors reaching out
to its customers, by Ben & Jerry's setting up ice cream
"partnershops" with community groups, by the Body
Shop's attentiveness to the animal and natural environment, and by many other examples of companies who
find "something more" to do with the community impulse that just taking care of their own. As organization scientists, we can turn a cold, objective eye on this
search for spirituality and quest for community in
business and see it as a monster sure to get us in the
end. Why then are growing numbers of organizational
scientists welcoming it?

Spirituality and Community in Organization Science

Some of the reasons are because our own institutions
and belief systems are breaking down, connection and
meaning have become more elusive for many of us, and
we are part and parcel of the larger postmodern social
process that surrounds us (c.f. Habermas 1971, Etzioni
1988, Hawley 1993). As evidence of our field's search
for something more, consider the ferment in organiza-

tion sciences occasioned by feminism, multiculturalism,
and environomentalism. This search has led scholars to
form into subgroups of women, people of color, and
environmentalists within the Academy of Management,
to join a society to advance socioeconomics, to advocate for the "politics of meaning," and go "on line" in
many and varied "electronic communities."

In addition, many practitioners—line managers, human resource specialists, consultants, and workers at
every level in companies—are bringing matters of faith
and spirit into public discourse. I counted more than
30 conferences that addressed spirituality and business
through their whole program or in segments in 1996.
Add to this all the rage around "learning organizations" where it is presumed that heightened consciousness—of the self, others, and the system as a
whole—undergirds a learning community (Kofman and
Senge 1993). Furthermore, Senge (1990) himself hints
at the spiritual foundations of this in his appendix on a
uboric "sixth discipline."

But can organization scientists consider seriously the
idea that companies can be organized along the lines
of an "unseen order" or, what theologian H. Richard
Niebuhr (1963) calls, in words that appeal to my ears,
the "universal community... whose boundaries cannot
be drawn in space, in time, or extent of interaction,
short of a whole in which we live and move and have
our being." In his deeper reflections, Gregory Bateson
(1979) posits that social systems are gifted with wisdom. Some who go deep within themselves believe that
we humans have "tacit" knowledge of universal community and can co-create a new order in our collective
lives in line with it (c.f. Polanyi 1969, Chopra 1989).
This is the utopian aspiration for business outlined by
Harman and Hormann (1990) in *Creative Work*. They
make the point that the "central project" of laborers
and leaders in the Middle Ages was construction of
great churches in honor of their god. It shifted as god
moved from the center of the universe and earthly
science and material pursuits defined who we are and
why we work. Today they wonder if a new central
project for civilization might emerge from our new
consciousness and new appreciation of what is the
center of our existence. Peck (1993) hopes so in concluding *A World Waiting to be Born*: "Utopia may not
be impossible to achieve after all."

Where to go with all of this? One option is to take
the concept of community-in-organizations seriously
and inquire into it (c.f. Rothschild-Whitt 1979). Surely
it is worthwhile for postmodern scholars to deconstruct
this concept and assess whose interests are served by

PHILIP H. MIRVIS   *Crossroads*

organizations introducing spirituality into their modus operandi. At the same time, it would also be useful to work together with colleagues in theology, utopian studies, and the spiritual sciences to understand how their disciplines understand these things and think about them in the business world. Such inquiry could yield more popular books like *Jesus, CEO* (Jones 1995) and works like *Spirit at Work* (Conger et al. 1994) that combine ideas from the organizational sciences with those of several spiritual traditions.

Field research also beckons: consider studying the cultures of ServiceMaster and Hewlett Packard. Both have strong, entrepreneurial cultures and transmit values through storytelling about their founders and heroes; yet one emphasizes faith in God and the other stresses perseverance and cooperation. Or simply take a closer look at faculty meetings where Meryl Louis (1994) finds, at least in one case, the principles of community at work.

Second, there is the exploration of your own voice on these matters. To this point, the best writing on the subject at hand comes from Parker Palmer, Max DePree, John Gardner, and M. Scott Peck: all practitioners in the best sense of the word. William Torbert, Jean Bartunek, Peter Vail, and Mary Ann Hazen are among the few organizational scientists who have spoken directly to matters of community and spirit over the course of their scholarly careers. I can envision, however, an outpouring of ideas and creative dialogue as we plumb our own depths and consider seriously what it would mean to be organized in line with "universal community."

Finally, we can do our collective work in new ways. Consider some examples:

• A conference on "Working with Spirituality in Organizations" in Scotland in 1990 (Snell et al. 1991);

• An Academy of Management symposia on "Organizations as Spiritual Settings" in 1991 (Journal of Organization Change Management 1994);

• A gathering of practitioners and scholars in Massachusetts in 1993 to discuss spirituality and leadership (leading to Conger et al. 1994);

• A conference on "Global Organizational Change," sponsored by the Academy of Management and Case Western Reserve, that intermixed talks on theory and strategy with sacred readings and tribal dancing.

Even as our interest in all of this increases, a new community of business people and scholars is taking shape. Its members meet at gatherings like Bretton Woods and successor sites, join the World Business Academy, an offshoot of the Institute of Noetic Sciences, participate in FCE programs and conferences,

and put their energies into reforming the curricula taught to management students or start "alternative" business schools. In turn, new voices emerge in volumes like *Community in Business* (Gozdz 1996) and familiar ones take on an unfamiliar but pleasing tone, as in Bolman and Deal's (1995) *Leading with Soul* and Quinn's (1996) *Deep Change*.

Who knows where this will take us? Likely as not, to a place we know but have never been before.

References

Alderfer, C. P. (1966), "An Intergroup Perspective on Group Dynamics," in J. Lorsch (Ed.), *Handbook of Organizational Behavior*, Englewood Cliffs, NJ: Prentice-Hall.

Argyris, C. (1982), *Reasoning, Learning, and Action*, San Francisco, CA: Jossey-Bass.

—— (1985), *Strategy, Change, and Defensive Routines*, Cambridge, MA: Ballinger.

Arieti, S. (1976), *Creativity*, New York: Basic Books.

Bateson, G. (1972), *Steps to an Ecology of the Mind*, New York: Chandler.

—— (1979), *Mind and Nature: A Necessary Unity*, New York: Dutton.

Beinecke, R. H. (1994), "Assessing the Economic Impact of Personal Development Programs," in F. Heuberger and L. Nash (Eds.), *The Fatal Embrace? Assessing Holistic Trends in Human Resources Programs*, New Brunswick, NJ: Transaction.

Bellah, R., R. Madsden, W. Sullivan, A. Swinder and S. Tipton (1985), *Habits of the Heart*, New York: Harper & Row.

——, ——, ——, —— and —— (1991), *The Good Society*, New York: Knopf.

Bennet, A. (1986), "Airline's Ills Point out Weaknesses of Its Unorthodox Management Style," *Wall Street Journal*, August 11.

Bennis, W. G. and H. A. Shephard (1956), "A Theory of Group Development," *Human Relations*, 9, 415–437.

Bion, W. R. (1961), *Experiences in Groups*, London, UK: Tavistock Publications.

Bohm, D. (1986), *Wholeness and the Implicate Order*, London, UK: Ark.

—— (1989), *On Dialogue*, David Bohm Seminars, Ojai, Ca.

Bolman, L. and T. Deal (1995), *Leading with Soul*, San Francisco, CA: Jossey-Bass.

Bradford, L. P., J. R. Gibb and K. W. Benne (Eds.) (1964), *T-Group Theory and Laboratory Method*, New York: Wiley.

Buber, M. (1965), *Between Man and Man*, New York: McMillan.

—— (1970), *I and Thou*, New York: Scribner.

Bunker, B. B. and B. T. Alban (Eds.) (1992), "Large Group Interventions," *Journal of Applied Behavioral Science*, 28, 4.

Business Week (1995), "Companies Hit the Road Less Traveled," June 5.

Capra, F. (1976), *The Tao of Physics*, New York: Bantam.

—— (1982), *Turning Point: Science, Society, and the Rising Culture*, New York: Bantam.

Carter, S. L. (1994), *The Culture of Disbelief*, New York: Basic Books.

Cartwright, D. (1951), "Achieving Change in People: Some Applications of Group Dynamics Theory," *Human Relations*, 4, 4, 381–392.

PHILIP H. MIRVIS *Crossroads*

Chopra, D. (1989), *Quantum Healing*, New York: Bantam Books.

Conger, J. & Associates (1994), *Spirit at Work*, San Francisco, CA: Jossey-Bass.

Cooley, C. H. (1922), *Human Nature and the Social Order*, New York: Scribner's.

Cooperrider, D. (1990), "Positive Image, Positive Action," in S. Srivastva and Associates (Eds.), *Appreciative Management and Leadership*, San Francisco, CA: Jossey-Bass.

Covey, S. (1990), *Principle-Centered Leadership*, New York: Summit.

Cox, M. (1993), "Business Books Emphasize the Spiritual," *Wall Street Journal*, December 14.

Csikszentmihalyi, M. (1990), *Flow: The Psychology of Optimal Experience*, New York: Harper & Row.

De Mare, P., R. Piper and S. Thompson (1991), *Koinonia: From Hate Through Dialogue to Culture in the Large Group*, London, UK: Karnac.

Depree, M. (1989), *Leadership Is an Art*, New York: Doubleday.

Etzioni, A. (1988), *The Moral Dimension*, New York: Free Press.

____ (1993), *The Spirit of Community*, New York: Touchstone.

Fletcher, J. (1996), "A Relational Approach to the Protean Worker," in D. T. Hall and Associates (Eds.), *The Career is Dead—Long Live the Career*, San Francisco, CA: Jossey-Bass.

Freud, S. (1965), *New Introductory Lectures on Psychoanalysis*, in J. Strachey (Ed.), New York: Norton.

Friedman, M. (1983), *The Confrontation of Otherness: In Family, Community and Society*, New York: Pilgrim Press.

Fromm, E. (1956), *The Art of Loving*, New York: Harper & Row.

Gardner, H. (1995), *Leading Minds*, New York: HarperCollins.

Gardner, J. (1995), *Building Community*, Washington, DC: Independent Sector.

Gozdz, K. (Ed.) (1996), *Community Building in Business*, San Francisco, CA: New Leaders Press.

Greenfield, H. (1996), "Corporate Community," in K. Gozdz (Ed.), *Community Building in Business*, San Francisco, CA: New Leaders Press.

Greenleaf, R. (1993), "The Leader as Servant," in C. Whitmyer (Ed.), *In the Company of Others*, New York: Putnam.

Griffin, E. (1993), *The Reflective Executive: A Spirituality of Business and Enterprise*, New York: Cross Roads.

Habermas, J. (1971), *Knowledge and Human Interests*, Boston, MA: Beacon Press.

Hackman, J. R. and J. L. Suttle (1977), *Improving Life at Work*, Santa Monica, CA: Goodyear.

Hahn, Thich Nhat (1990), *The Miracle of Mindfulness*, Berkeley, CA: Parallax Press.

____ (1993), "Awareness: The Consciousness of Community," in C. Whitmyer (Ed.), *In the Company of Others*, New York: Putnam.

Hall, D. T. and P. H. Mirvis (1996), "The New Protean Career: Psychological Success and the Path with a Heart," in D. T. Hall and Associates (Eds.), *The Career is Dead—Long Live the Career*, San Francisco, CA: Jossey-Bass.

Hampden-Turner, C. (1971), *Radical Man*, New York: Doubleday.

Harman, W. (1988), *Global Mind Change*, New York: Warner.

____ and J. Hormann (1990), *Creative Work*, Indianapolis, IN: Knowledge Systems, Inc.

Harrison, R. (1983), "Strategies for a New Age," *Human Resource Management*, 22, 209–235.

Hawley, J. (1993), *Reawakening the Spirit in Work: The Power of Dharmic Management*, San Francisco, CA: Berrett-Koehler.

Herzberg, F. B., B. Mausner and B. Synderman (1959), *The Motivation to Work*, New York: Wiley.

Isaacs, W. N. (1993), "Dialogue: The Power of Collective Thinking," *The Systems Thinker*, 4, 3.

____ (1994), "Dialogue, Collective Thinking, and Organizational Learning," *Organizational Dynamics*.

James, W. (1902), *The Varieties of Religious Experience*.

Jones, L. B. (1995), *Jesus, CEO*, New York: Hyperion.

Journal of Organizational Change Management (1994) 7.

Kahn, W. A. (1992), "To Be Fully There: Psychological Presence at Work," *Human Relations*, 45, 4, 321–349.

____ (1993), "Caring for the Caregiver: Patterns of Organizational Caregiving," *Administrative Science Quarterly*, 38, 4, 539–563.

Kanter, D. L. and P. H. Mirvis (1989), *The Cynical Americans*, San Francisco, CA: Jossey-Bass.

Kanter, R. M. (1972), *Commitment and Community: Communes and Utopias in Sociological Perspective*, Cambridge, MA: Harvard University Press.

Klein, M. (1959), "Our Adult World and Its Roots in Infancy," *Human Relations*, 12, 291–303.

Koestler, A. (1964), *The Act of Creation*, New York: Macmillan.

Kofman, F. and P. Senge (1993), "Communities of Commitment: The Heart of the Learning Organization," *Organization Dynamics*, Fall.

Learner, M. (1996), *The Politics of Meaning*, Reading, MA: Addison-Wesley.

Louis, M. R. (1994), "In the Manner of Friends: Learning from Quaker Practice for Organizational Renewal," *Journal of Organizational Change Management*, 7, 1, 42–60.

Maslow, A. H. (1954), *Motivation and Personality*, New York: Harper.

____ (1965), *Eupsychian Management*, Homewood, IL: Irwin/Dorsey.

____ (1968), *Toward a Psychology of Being*, New York: Van Nostrand.

McGregor, D. (1960), *The Human Side of Enterprise*, Englewood-Cliffs, NJ: Prentice-Hall.

McMillan, D. W. and D. M. Chavis (1986), "Sense of Community: A Definition and Theory," *Journal of Community Psychology*, 14, 6–23.

Mirvis, P. H. (1980), "The Art of Assessing the Quality of Work Life," in E. Lawler, D. Nadler, and C. Camman (Eds.), *Organizational Assessment*, New York: Wiley Interscience.

____ (Ed.) (1993a), *Building the Competitive Workforce*, New York: Wiley.

____ (1993b), "Human Development or Depersonalization: The Company of Total Community," in F. Heuberger and L. Nash (Eds.), *The Fatal Embrace?* New Brunswick, NJ: Transaction.

____ (1996), "Midlife as a Consultant," in P. J Frost and M. S. Taylor (Eds.), *Rhythms of an Academic's Life*, Beverly Hills, CA: Sage.

Moore, T. (1991), *Care of the Soul: A Guide of Cultivating Depth and Sacredness in Everyday Life*, New York: Harper-Collins.

Nash, Laura (1996), Professor at Boston University, working on a book on "Christian-based" organizations.

PHILIP H. MIRVIS   *Crossroads*

Newsweek (1987), "Corporate Mind Control," May 4.

Niebuhr, H. R. (1963), *The Responsible Self*, New York: Harper and Row.

Peck, M. S. (1978), *The Road Less Traveled*, New York: Simon and Schuster.

____ (1987), *The Different Drum*, New York: Simon and Schuster.

____ (1993), *A World Waiting to Be Born*, New York: Bantam.

Polanyi, M. (1969), *Knowing and Being*, in Marjorie Grene (Ed.), Chicago, IL: University of Chicago Press.

Pollard, C. W. (1996), *The Soul of the Firm*, New York: HarperBusiness.

Prokesch, S. (1986), "Behind People Express's Fall: An Offbeat Managerial Style," *New York Times*, September 23.

Putnam, R. D. (1992), *Making Democracy Work*, Princeton, NJ: Princeton University Press.

Quinn, R. E. (1996), *Deep Change*, San Francisco, CA: Jossey-Bass.

Ray, M. and A. Rinzler (1993), *The New Paradigm in Business*, New York: Tarcher/Perigee.

Roddick, A. (1990), *Body and Soul: Profits with Principles*, New York, Crown.

Rothschild-Whitt, J. (1979), "The Collectivist Organization: An Alternative to Rational-bureaucratic Models," *American Sociological Review*, 44, 509–527.

Sarason, S. (1974), *The Psychological Sense of Community*, San Francisco, CA: Jossey-Bass.

Schindler-Rainman, E. and R. Lippitt (1980), *Building the Collaborative Community: Mobilizing Citizens for Action*, University of California Extension.

Schon, D. (1983), *The Reflective Practitioner*, New York: Basic Books.

Schor, J. B. (1991), *The Overworked American*, New York: Basic Books.

Scott, M. and H. Rothman (1992), *Companies with a Conscience*, New York: Birch Lane Press.

Senge, P. (1990), *The Fifth Discipline*, New York: Doubleday.

Shaffer, C. R. and K. Anundsen (1993), *Creating Community Anywhere*, New York: Tarcher/Putnam.

Siegel, B. S. (1986), *Love, Medicine & Miracles*, New York: Harper & Row.

Slater, P. E. (1966), *Microcosm*, New York: Wiley Interscience.

Smith, K. and D. N. Berg (1987), *Paradoxes of Group Life*, San Francisco, CA: Jossey Bass.

Snell, R., J. Davies, T. Boydell and M. Leary (Ed.) (1991), "Joining Forces," *Management Education and Development*, 22, 3.

Talbot, M. (1986), *Beyond the Quantum*, New York: Bantam Books.

Time (1986), "People Express," January 13.

Tuckman, B. W. (1965), "Developmental Sequences in Small Groups," *Psychological Bulletin*, 54, 229–249.

Wheatley, M. J. (1993), *Leadership and the New Science: Learning about Organization from an Orderly Universe*, San Francisco, CA: Berrett-Koehler Publishers, Inc.

Whitney, D. (1995), "Spirituality as a Global Organizing Potential," Paper delivered at conference on The Organizational Dimensions of Global Change, Cleveland, OH: Case Western Reserve University.

Whyte, D. (1994), *The Heart Aroused*, New York: Doubleday.

Wiesbord, M. (1992), *Discovering Common Ground*, San Francisco, CA: Barret-Koehler.

Wilbur, K. (1984), *Quantum Questions*, Boston, MA: Shambala.

Wuthnow, R. (1991), *Acts of Compassion: Caring for Others and Helping Ourselves*, Princeton, NJ: Princeton University Press.

[30]

Spirituality in Public Service: A Dialogue

Willa Bruce
John Novinson

Willa Bruce, an academic, wrote a short essay on spirituality in public administration. John Novinson, a village manager, read the essay and responded to Willa Bruce. Their dialogue is reprinted here. Editor

John

When I read your essay, I was far from comfortable with the idea that spirituality is a missing ingredient in public service. You anticipate some of my feelings when you discuss the reluctance of some to even entertain the idea. I even find it difficult to begin framing questions. Perhaps the first problem is the abstract nature of the suggestion.

Each time I try to operationalize the concept, I run into unpleasant options. For example, we, like many communities, are looking at ways to revitalize our central business area. As a relatively advantaged community, the motivation has more to do with a sense of place and aesthetic concerns for the advocates of change while those opposed are concerned about the right of individual property owners to control their own destiny.

As staff we are focused on a value: providing a process and services that ends with both sides willing and ready to say they were treated fairly.

As such, we try hard to put aside many other values and judgements that interfere with the primary goal.

I wonder how providing a safe haven for "spirituality" might affect an already difficult environment. Can you help me better understand your idea by relating it to this example or some other tangible circumstance?

John

Willa

Hi John,

Yes, spirituality is an abstract concept—much easier to talk about than to operationalize I expect. So, before tackling how one might apply spirituality to the dilemma you posed, let me see if I can make the notion of spirituality at work more concrete.

When I talk about spirituality, I'm defining it as a "search for meaning and values, which includes some sense of the transcendent." That is, some force or life energy beyond ourselves that is often identified with religions, but which may be simply a sense of interconnectedness with others and a desire to make meaning and live out one's own values about good and wrong. Elements of spirituality that I think can empower us in the government workplace are:

1. A call to integrity—that is, a self expectation that one will make an effort to discern right from wrong, act on the discernment of right, and say openly that one is acting on one's own understanding of right. It sounds to me like you do that, when you say that you want the resolution of what will happen to your downtown area to result in both sides feeling they were treated fairly.

2. Relationships—that is a recognition that people are intricately connected to one another and that each action has a ripple effect. When you refer to you and

your staff as "we" you are expressing a sense of relationship. Your concern over how citizens with opposing views might feel about the outcome of the downtown dilemma says to me that you're concerned about relationships. If you weren't, you'd just say something like, "I don't care what anyone thinks, I've decided based on my expertise that X or Y is the best decision, and that's what I'll do."

3. Love—the kind of love that emerges from spirituality is what the Greeks called "philio" or brotherly love and "agape" charity. Love in the workplace calls us to do unto others as we'd hope they do for us. Your concern for an outcome of fairness suggests to me that you yourself value fairness and want to ensure that it exists for others. I expect you have other values as well that guide your sense of what is "right." Spiritual persons simply make decisions and act based on their sense of how others should be treated. That may be easier for someone in positions such as yours and mine where we have some measure of discretion and authority in our jobs. It may be more difficult for someone in a position where he or she is expected to implement a decision, rather than make it. I do think, however, that if one cannot act out of love and integrity on the job, one ought to reconsider one's place of employment.

4. Search for meaning—A search for meaning involves seeing the "big picture." It tries to make sense of sometimes senseless happenings and wrongful acts. It requires that one ask what problems need new solutions; it asks how issues are interconnected and what unspiritual thoughts are contributing to problems. It requires an expectation that meaning may come from diverse places and that others may make different meanings from the same situation.

When you wonder how providing a safe haven for spirituality might affect an already difficult environment, I think you are searching for meaning and trying to make sense of a tough situation. Searching for meaning enables us to link our outer work with our inner work. Inner work is what we do to promote self-development and growth.

I guess if I were to summarize all this, I'd say that spirituality at work means simply living out one's own deep values. In the public sector we've often been expected to attempt to separate facts from values and deal with the facts alone. Spiritual persons recognize that "facts" are tempered by perceptions, biases, and world-views. Spiritual persons have the courage to speak from their own deeply held values and to listen to and respect the values of others, even when they are in conflict.

I don't think spirituality will solve our problems. I think it will change the way problems are perceived, and change the way we deal with one another.

Now to your specific question—how might spirituality affect an already difficult environment?

Difficult environments occur whether or not one is spiritual. Spiritual persons deal with them differently. They look for shared values, celebrate the diversity and interconnectedness of the people involved and their differing world-views, and they treat the persons involved with the kind of charity and love they hope for themselves. They try to make meaning out of the difficulty, asking such questions as, "What can I learn from this?" "How can I help?" "Who else can help?" "Who will be hurt and who will be helped by this or that decision?" Spiritual persons remain true to their own deeply held convictions, so that others can look at them and say, "you always know where they will stand."

Spiritual persons are more likely to put difficult issues in perspective. They may ask questions such as, "What can I learn from this?"

"What is God (however transcendence is perceived) trying to teach me?" "How can I use what I'm learning here, to prevent or solve this same difficulty in the future?"

Spiritual persons are more likely to deal with one another out of love (brotherly love/charity). They are more likely to be patient, respectful, and empowering.

However, spiritual persons are as human as everyone else. They are not perfect, and bad things happen to them, too. The main reason to be spiritual, I think, is that spirituality offers hope.

I hope this sparks some more of your thoughts.

Willa

John

Hello Willa:

It is difficult to be "uncomfortable" with a definition of spirituality when it is crafted in so appealing and compelling a manner. Yet I find that the application of individual spiritual values does not always manifest itself in a benign and supportive manner. I cannot "define out" spiritual convictions that there may be inferior and superior races cultures and motives. I do not know how I can distinguish between the application of deeply held beliefs that may conflict with our fundamental mission. How do I deal with an employee who's spiritual values are in conflict with our mission?

Why is spirituality superior to professionalism, fairness, and respect when it comes to public service?

Let's return to the sample problem. In our redevelopment area, there is a property owner who resists change. Emotional attachement to the property prevents the owner from considering any sale or change to it. It is a key location and the leadership of the community believes that the welfare of the community is injured if this blighted property is not included in the redevelopment.

Let's say that we have encouraged employees to incorporate their spirituality into their work and that a key member of our team is deeply committed to this philosophy and even 100 percent consistent with your ideal. How is that person going to function in this situation? Will he or she empathize so strongly with the passionate resistance of the property owner that he or she will be compelled toward conflict with the rest of the team? Will it be more difficult to deal with confidential information that conflicts with such values? Will intense empathy give incorrect impressions of the community's determination? Will this lead to a larger problem because the owner is encouraged?

Now, we tend to value a team that sees problems and works toward solutions. We are comfortable with looking for win/win solutions but if one view point is "right" because it is consistent with deeply held values of spiritual significance and the other is "wrong" because it is in opposition to those values, I can see everything getting a little more difficult for everyone.

This may seem like an argument for the Pontius Pilate school of management. Maybe it is. But, the issues get tougher without some dispassionate distancing. I am a "professional" manager. I recall Max Weber being an advocate of separating policy and administration. That requires some toning down of passions. Good administrators need a fairly large range of tolerance when it comes to policies, especially in a multi-cultural, diverse democracy.

Professionalism does not require indifference and it does not exclude empathy. It does make the commitment to the organization and the task at hand primary. It often requires a good sense of the opportunities for compromise. Even the best spiritual values can aggravate problem solving.

And the best values do not necessarily present themselves. History tells us that truly terrible spiritual values can find their way into too much of life. One does not need to look too long or far to find a "spiritually" motivated inquisition. Consider the Taliban in Afghanistan and the spiritually motivated militias here in America.

Well, I have violated my own determination to keep this short.

I look forward to hearing from you.

John

Willa

Hi John!

I would not want to create discomfort. I do want, however, to generate thinking about spirituality and the public service.

You and I appear to view spirituality through different lenses. Your worry that the "application of spiritual values does not always manifest itself in a benign and supportive manner" sounds to me like you think of spirituality as the icing on a cake—not necessary, not always nice.

To me spirituality is a part of the cake, itself. Cakes are made of flour, baking powder, butter, eggs, sugar, milk, and salt. All are inexplicably intertwined and necessary for full flavor. Spirituality is like the salt in the cake. One could have cake without it, but the cake would taste flat, not quite cake, but not bread either.

> I cannot "define out" spiritual convictions that there may be inferior and superior races cultures and motives.

I cannot define away convictions about inferiority and superiority either. I do not, however, see such convictions as spiritual. They are doctrinaire and separatist. Spirituality is interconnected and inclusive. While some religious traditions argue for their own superiority, these are intellectual biases not spiritual convictions. Elements of spirituality are:

1) interconnectedness, 2) integrity, 3) love, 4) search for meaning, and 5) sense of the transcendent. Each of these elements can be found in the spiritual wisdom of most sacred scriptures.

These elements of spirituality call everyone into relationship, not into divisiveness. Differences of culture and motives become secondary and enriching.

> I do not know how I can distinguish between the application of deeply held beliefs that may conflict with our fundamental mission. How do I deal with an employee who's spiritual values are in conflict with our mission?

Depends on what your mission is. If its focus is on the growth and development of your city or of specific areas in it, I'd have a hard time seeing how spirituality might conflict with that. Spiritual persons might approach accomplishing the mission differently. More about this when I respond to your sample problem below.

The only place I can see spiritual values conflicting with the mission would be if the mission was inherently corrupt. A ready example is always the Nazi regime during WWII. A great deal of documentation exists to suggest that good people did horrible things because they followed orders rather than their conscience. Suppose those who believed in love, interconnectedness, integrity, meaning, and transcendence had just said "No."

> Why is spirituality superior to professionalism, fairness, and respect when it comes to public service?

It isn't. I don't claim that there's a hierarchy of values with spirituality at the top of the list. If we stick with the cake metaphor, it's easy to see that there's not a hierarchy of ingredients in a cake. Neither milk nor flour nor sugar are superior—they're all necessary. Alone, each tastes pretty awful. Stirred together with a little salt and baked, they are transformed.

> Let's return to the sample problem. In our redevelopment area, there is a property owner who resists change. He/She will not consider any sale or change in his/her property for emotional attachment reasons. The property occupies a key location and the leadership of the community

believes that the welfare of the community is
injured if this blighted property is not included in
the redevelopment.

What we have here is an economic development problem, not a spiritual one and I cannot presume to speak
for all spiritual persons in my response to it. So, I'll simply tell you how I'd handle it. I'll try to make it a spiritual
response. It will certainly come out of my own values,
which push me to affirm the dignity and worth of each
person involved in a dilemma and to work for a win-win
solution. It's been my experience that complex problems
rarely have only one solution I don't think there is "one
best way" to deal with this one.

A small town with which I am familiar had a similar
problem recently. In the heart of downtown was a building that housed a long-time family business. The building accidentally caught on fire and burned to the ground.
The family wanted to rebuild. The public officials,
including the manager, wanted the area for a parking lot.
A lot of rhetoric, infused with a lot of emotion, went into
the debate over the now and future use of this land.
While the debate still raged, with hurtful words hurled
from both sides, the problem was "solved" by the city.
The city council condemned the building, claimed eminent domain, and early one morning, while it was still
dark, a city bulldozer leveled it.

That was certainly one solution. It was not the only
one. In my opinion it was far from the best, and I think
a spiritual person would have handled the situation differently.

Values that are apparent to me in the town's solution
are efficiency, legal rights of the city, and economic development. I cannot help but wonder what the decision
would have been had the values been interconnectedness
with the building owners, heritage of the town, caring,
responsiveness, and, yes, economic development.

What would I have done as the city manager? I would
have initiated a discernment process in which all those
concerned could freely, in a nonjudgmental forum,
express their views and be heard. I'd encourage a collective cost-benefit analysis which included the "rational"
data of the city and the personal concerns of the building
owner. I would have worked for solution which involved
the building owners, saved their pride, yet ultimately
moved the city ahead. One way to do this is described in
Beyond Majority Rule by Michael Sheeran, S.J. (Philadelphia: Philadelphia yearly meeting, 1983). It offers a
quaker approach to decision making in controversial situations.

The key to this type of solution generation is mutual
respect and a commitment to trying to understand the
other's position. Leonard Swidler offers ten rules for
interideological dialogue that can further guide the discussion ("The Dialogue Decalogue: Ground Rules for
Interreligious, Intercultural Dialogue" (in L. Bade, *Envisioning a Global Ethic*. Philadelphia: Global Dialogue
Institute, 1997).

Would the solution after all this be any different?
Maybe, maybe not. The difference would be in the
decrease in frustration and increase in acceptance of the
solution by all participants. A basic tenet of leadership is
that "people accept what they help to create."

What has this approach to do with spirituality? It recognizes the interconnectedness of all participants in the
situation, it offers a way to approach the situation with
love and integrity. It encourages participants to make
personal meaning of the decision, to look for a redeeming
grander purpose beyond a decision about one or a few
buildings, and through it all to see God's hand at work
improving lives.

To be a spiritual person means to know and live
according to the knowledge that God is present to us in
grace as the principle of personal, interpersonal, and
social transformation. Being open to the spirit is to
accept who one is and who one is called to become, then
direct one's life accordingly—that is what it means to live
with integrity.

Let's say that we have encouraged employees to
incorporate their spirituality into their work and
that a key member of our team is deeply committed to this philosophy and even 100 percent consistent with your ideal....

I don't really think you need to encourage employees
to incorporate their spirituality into their work. I think
that persons who have spiritual values already do. I think
you just need to recognize that and be open to including
values as a part of policy decisions. In public administration, we've long talked about the fact-value debate. I
really don't think facts exist in isolation from values.
Indeed, when people disagree over what actions should
be taken, the disagreement is likely rooted in a values perspective and spiritual values are a part of that perspective.

How is that person going to function in this situation?

I don't know. If we eliminate spirituality from the person's calculus, can you predict how a person unknown to
you will act? People are so marvelously complex, they're
full of surprises!

However, I do believe that a truly spiritual person (i.e.
one committed to interconnections, integrity, love, search
for meaning, and sense of the transcendent) will speak
out against clearly evil acts. I also suspect that spiritual
persons are predictable. If you think about your staff
right now, you can probably name who will consistently
take the side of the under-dog, take the time to express
caring when times are tough, and generally come down
on the side of overall fairness and responsiveness.

You may even know who takes the time to pray.

Will they empathize so strongly with the passionate resistance of the property owner that they will

be compelled toward conflict with the rest of the team? Will they find it more difficult to deal with confidential information that conflicts with their values? Can they empathize so much that they will give incorrect impressions of the community's determination? Will this lead to a larger problem because the owner is encouraged?

Spiritual persons are persons of integrity. This means they live out their values and "practice what they preach." I think you're asking several questions here:
Will a spiritual person identify with property owners over city administration?
I'd say no more than a nonspiritual person might.
Will a spiritual person be able to hold information in confidence?
I'd certainly hope so!
Will a spiritual person put the wants of individual citizens above those of the community?
No more than a nonspiritual person.
I think the difference between spiritual persons and nonspiritual will be that spiritual persons are more likely to attempt to make meaning of the issues and the decisions and see them in a greater context.
Let me use a personal, nonwork related example. A few weeks ago, a man driving a huge blazer hit the back-end of my car while I was at a gas station, pumping fuel into my gas tank. He hit my car hard enough to dent the bumper and knock me into my car door. I was furious, but not hurt. I asked him why he hit my car. He responded, "because you were in my way."
A nonspiritual person would have been as furious and probably shouted the same obscenities I did. A nonspiritual person would have also written down his license plate number and called and reported it to the police as I did. The difference comes next. As a person trying to be spiritual, I prayed for the man and tried to search for what I could learn about myself and humankind from the incident. I am working at forgiving him.
I think this incident shows that the same events happen to the spiritual and nonspiritual alike. The difference is in how the event is handled.
Seems to me that the major issue in your questions is one of trust. I think what you're really saying is "can I trust a spiritual person to be a good/trustworthy/dependable person who is committed to the city, to fellow workers, to me?"
I hope so.
However, I have met people who claim they have the "truth" in terms of religion and spirituality, and that that somehow gives them claim to greater knowledge than any of the rest of us. I call that "faux spirituality." The great spiritual traditions share a common awe of mystery and a common search for wisdom. They are about making one's self and the world a better place, but not about denigrating nor harming others.

Now, we tend to value a team that sees prob-

lems and works toward solutions.

Me Too!

We are comfortable with looking for win/win solutions but if one view point is "right" because it is consistent with deeply held values of spiritual significance and the other is "wrong" because it is in opposition to those values, I can see everything getting a little more difficult for everyone.

By now you know that I believe that spirituality is not about "wrong" and "right." It is about interconnectedness, integrity, love, search for meaning, and sense of the transcendent. It is about living one's values wherever one is, but it is not about imposing those values on others.
I think you express very well the fears that many have whenever one talks about spirituality. It often arises out of religious convictions and often religious zealots try to convert others to their way of thinking. I think I can best respond at this point by quoting Mclaughlin and Davidson in their 1994 book called *Spiritual Politics* (p. 164-65): "Historically, great abuses occurred when christianity became a state religion. That is why in the early days of our nation, our founding fathers legislated freedom of religion and no establishment of a state religion. But was it their intention to relegate spiritual values solely to the religious sphere and exclude spiritual and moral considerations—and the sacred dimension of life—from public affairs? This seems highly unlikely since many of them evidenced a profound belief and faith in a higher power."

This may seem like an argument for the Pontius Pilate school of management. Maybe it is. But, the issues get tougher without some dispassionate distancing.

I do not think you are "washing your hands" of the issue. On the contrary, your efforts to raise important issues enrich my own thinking and will be a real asset to the thinking of others!

I am a "professional" manager. I recall Max Weber being an advocate of separating policy and administration.

Me too. But this begs the question. Both politicians and administrators can be spiritual. A very recent gallup poll (reported in 1997) found that 95 percent of Americans believe in some form of higher power and that more than ever before we are seeking spiritual help for tough decisions.

That requires some toning down of passions. Good administrators need a fairly large range of tolerance when it comes to policies especially in multi-cultural, diverse democracy.

Professionalism does not require indifference and it does not exclude empathy. It does make the commitment to the organization and the task at hand primary. It often requires a good sense of the opportunities for compromise. Even the best spiritual values can aggravate problem solving.

As I understand this, you're saying that professional administrators must commit themselves totally to the employing agency or level of government.

I, too, believe that professional administrators are fiduciaries of the public trust. They must be responsive to regime values (Rohr) and they must hold the values of the american people: accountability, efficiency, responsiveness, and responsibility (Klingner and Nalbandian). I argue that all of this is necessary, but insufficient, for it ignores the innate spirituality of humankind. I claim that it's time to quit pretending that people do not have a spiritual dimension and that an open acknowledgment of that part of humankind will enrich and empower the public service.

And the best values do not necessarily present themselves. History tells us that truly terrible spiritual values can find their way into too much of life. One does not need to look too long or far to find a "spiritually" motivated inquisition. Consider the Taliban in Afghanistan and the spiritually motivated militias here in America.

This seems to me more self-serving power than spirituality. The Taliban are an ethnic group and many good Moslems in Afghanistan claim that they're interpreting the laws of the Koran in a biased way based on their ethnic heritage. This seems like an attempt to assert authority, not a manifestation of spirituality. Similarly, American militias who claim religious justification, are using a very narrow interpretation of the Bible. These are ideological movements that use the trappings of a very narrow religiosity to justify themselves. This is not spirituality in the sense of interconnectedness, love, integrity, search for meaning, and sense of the transcendent.

In Christian scripture, Jesus said, "by their fruits, you shall know them.... A good tree cannot bear bad fruit, nor can a rotten tree bear good fruit" (Mt. 7: 16-18). And St. Paul described the fruits of the spirit as "love, joy, peace, patience, kindness, generosity, faithfulness, gentleness, self-control" (Gal: 5: 22-23).

Well, I have violated my own determination to keep this short. We may produce an editor's

nightmare at this rate. Perhaps it is well that we have laid out our basic positions. From here perhaps we can limit ourselves to something more concise.

As you can see, conciseness is not one of my strengths. I do believe, however, our task is to sort this out, however long it takes. The editor's task is to cut and summarize.

I look forward to hearing from you.

Willa

John

Hi Willa:

I was interested in the way you were able to dissect a piece that was written as a whole.

At this point, I am still a little confused. In your essay you say that spirituality should be an "issue for the public service." Later, in our dialogue, you say that we "do not need to encourage employees to incorporate their spirituality into their work."

In the essay you assert that we do not often talk of spirituality. You also assert that the "public service needs to be animated by spirituality." That sounds a lot like encouraging. I do not know how we can talk more about anything in a neutral or positive way without de facto encouraging it.

I do not believe an issue like spirituality can be discussed and "animate" the public service within the comfortable confines of your definitions. I believe it is a "loaded term" that will be defined by the user. Rather, I see animating the public service with spirituality as a slippery slope that will just as likely lead in negative as positive directions.

I also have a problem with how this is really different from what goes on in many organizations every day. Especially if we define away any aspect of spirituality that conflicts with a benign application of individual values. There are more direct routes to the kind of participative processes you characterize. We can get there by discussing what works best, how we can meet the needs of various constituencies, win/win, alternative dispute resolution and other techniques that are likely to get to the same result without the definitional issues.

I certainly agree that the spiritually motivated employees will bring their values to the work place. A wise employer, public or private will allow the free expression of those ideas. Those organizations will be more successful to the extent that they provide open environments for expression while they strive to accomplish their goals. That will happen without the perception that we "need to animate the public service" with spirituality if the employer is simply committed to the free expression of ideas. Spiritually motivated ideas will get the same hearing that more "profane" concepts receive.

If the aim of your essay was to encourage conversations about spirituality in the public service, you have succeeded. This is such a conversation. It is also the right forum. Not the workplace and especially not the public workplace.

John

Willa

Hi John,

In response to your comments, I'll say very little (rare for me).

Yes, I did, indeed want to get conversation started about spirituality and the public service and that has now begun to happen, thanks to your willingness to get involved. And, *PAR* is the right forum for public dialog. I never did think that public employees, while at work, should sit about discussing spirituality.

We're operating on two different levels here: one is the level of public dialog and debate, the other is the practical, everyday arena. I think we all need to be talking about spirituality *and* acting spiritually. I also think that most of us are responsible employees who have the wisdom to discern when and where conversations take place. People are searching and people want to support and be supported. A 1997 survey reported in *Self* magazine, found that of the nearly 2,100 respondents, 70 percent described themselves as "spiritual" and another 27 per-

cent said they were "somewhat spiritual." While that may mean that only spiritually inclined persons replied to the survey, it's existence and appearance indicate a growing openness and awareness of spiritual issues. I'm seeing a hunger for lived spirituality in the work place.

I'd like to leave our dialog with the suggestion that you and any interested readers take a look at *Self* magazine, December, 1997, and some of the following books: Jeffrey Salkin, *Taking God to Work*; John Hauhgey, *Converting 9 to 5: A Spirituality of Daily Work*; Alan Briskin, *The Stirring of Soul in The Workplace*; Steven Carter, *Integrity*; and, of course, George H. Frederickson, *The Spirit of Public Administration*.

Thanks for all your effort. Your insights and questions have assisted my own thinking.

Willa Bruce

John

Hi Willa

One thought. Beware survey results like those that you have quoted. A vast majority of our citizens describe themselves as "environmentalists" in survey after survey. Yet the same individuals rather routinely report that they will object to modifying their own behaviors that threaten the environment. They want to save the earth but not enough to car-pool.

John

[31]

The Theory of Charismatic Leadership

ROBERT C. TUCKER

I

IN A recent survey of Max Weber's political ideas, Karl Loewen-stein observes that the concepts of "charisma" and the "charismatic leader" have had the greatest impact upon the thinking of our time. Unquestionably, many Western social scientists have been influenced by the Weberian idea of the leader who enjoys his authority not through enacted position or traditional dignity, but owing to gifts of grace (charisma) "by virtue of which he is set apart from other men and treated as endowed with supernatural, superhuman, or at least specifically exceptional powers or quali-ties."[1] Few aspects of Weber's political sociology have been so much discussed in the recent literature of political science, and interest in the subject is still growing. Yet no scholarly consensus seems to have formed, or even to be in process of formation, on the scientific worth and precise application of the concept of charismatic leadership.

Some writers are impressed with its power or potentiality as a tool for analyzing certain leadership situations of the historical past and present; others are skeptical and doubt whether the idea of charismatic leadership has much place in political science. Loewenstein himself belongs to the latter group. Noting that the idea comes from the religious realm and that Weber undertook to transfer it to politics, he contends that the world of religion re-

While working on the subject of this essay, I greatly benefited from the op-portunity to discuss a number of the problems involved with Dr. Ann Ruth Willner, a fellow associate at the Center for International Studies of Princeton University, and to consult her own writings on charisma referred to below.

ROBERT C. TUCKER

mains the fundamental locus of charisma. Hence the category applies chiefly to the pre-Cartesian West and, in our time, to those parts of Asia and Africa that have not yet broken away from the "magico-religious ambiance"; and it ceases to have relevance in our age of technological mass democracy.[2] Carl Friedrich, another critic, argues for a restrictive interpretation of charisma. He points out that in Rudolph Sohm's *Kirchenrecht* (1892), from which Weber derived the term and idea of charisma, charismatic leadership was understood as leadership based upon a transcendent call by a divine being in which both the person called and his followers believe; and Friedrich feels that such leadership should properly be conceived as grounded in a faith in God or gods. He objects to Weber's broadening of the category to include secular and non-transcendent types of callings, inspirational leadership of the demagogic type, and so forth. "Hitlers," he asserts, "represent a very different kind of leadership than the founders or even the inspired supporters of a religion." Even psychologically speaking, they fall in different categories, since the totalitarian leaders are typically preoccupied with power, especially organizational power, while the founders of religions are not.[3] Among other, less sweeping criticisms, two closely related ones are especially noteworthy. First, it is pointed out that on the basis of Weber's various formulations—some of which are rather nebulous —it is not easy to distinguish between leaders who really are charismatic and leaders who are not. And secondly, critics have observed that Weber provided no clear statement or catalogue of the personal qualities in charismatic leaders which give rise to the special emotional bond with their followers that charisma implies. In short, the theory of charismatic leadership, as Weber himself expounded it, leaves us in some doubt as to which leaders are charismatic and what makes them so.[4]

Let me begin by placing myself squarely upon Weber's side in the issue regarding the usefulness of the concept of charismatic leadership. I believe that this concept meets a vital theoretical need. Indeed, it is virtually indispensable, particularly for the student of revolutionary movements of various kinds, Communist ones included. Moreover, it was not, in my view, an error on Weber's part but a very great merit to take this category out of the historical world of religion and apply it to political life. For the realms of politics and religion interpenetrate in many ways. Nor does the concept of charisma, despite its mystical component,

70

The Theory of Charismatic Leadership

cease to have relevance to political life in an age of technological mass democracy. The secularization of society does not so much mean the disappearance of religion as it does the weakening of the hold of religion *in its traditional forms,* along with the displacement of religious emotion into other areas, particularly the political. Millenarian political movements have dotted the Western social landscape from the eighteenth century and so far show little sign of disappearing in the highly secularized industrial society of the present century. Societies far removed from what Loewenstein calls the "magico-religious ambiance" may still experience the pervasive influence of a modern political religion. Moreover, modern communications media make possible the *projection* of a charismatic leader of such a movement to a far greater number of people than ever before. And to insist, as Friedrich does, that charisma can properly appear only in the setting of a belief in a divine being ("God or gods") is arbitrarily to equate the realm of religion with a particular set of theologies. The psychological argument with which he supports this thesis is also a shaky one. On the one hand, founders of religions have not invariably been indifferent to considerations of power. On the other hand, it is difficult to generalize concerning the motivations of "totalitarian leaders." While a preoccupation with organizational power is characteristic, there is little evidence that these men seek power simply for power's sake; they appear, on the basis of our still inadequate knowledge of them, to be persons of great psychological complexity in all cases.

But after we have rejected the extreme positions of those critics who would severely restrict the applicability of the concept of charisma or deny its continued relevance in the modern age, we still have to reckon with the arguments about the concept's unclarity and the difficulty of applying it in practice. Here the critics are on stronger ground. Weber's principal statements on charisma appear in the context of his tripartite division of the forms of legitimate authority into traditional, rational-legal, and charismatic. Although a typology of the grounds of legitimate authority is a perfectly valid scholarly objective, it is not necessarily the best framework for developing a theory of charismatic leadership. For this reason, among others, Weber's pertinent writings, though strewn with invaluable insights, present no adequate treatment of charisma as a phenomenon in the realm of political leadership. Above all, they do not make the concept of charismatic

71

ROBERT C. TUCKER

leadership sufficiently operational to serve as a guide for further research. The aim of the present essay is to help remedy this deficiency.

Since my approach to the problem differs from the one most characteristic of contemporary writings in the social sciences concerning charisma, it may be useful to preface the essay with a short comment on its origin and relation to the scholarly literature. As shown by the work of writers like Edward Shils, David Apter, and Dorothy and Ann Ruth Willner, Western social scientists have tended in the recent past to approach the phenomenon of charisma in the context of a study of modernization and political development in ex-colonial "new states." The result is a functional theory of charisma according to which charismatic leadership is essentially a fulcrum of the transition from colonial-ruled traditional society to politically independent modern society; and the Weberian typology is, in effect, historicized into a sequence that runs from traditional through charismatic to rational-legal forms of authority.[5] In contrast, I approached the phenomenon of charisma through a study of revolutionary movements, Russia's in particular.

In connection with a work in progress on Stalin and Russian Communism, it became necessary to re-examine the role of Lenin as founder and supreme leader of the Bolshevik revolutionary movement. In the course of this effort, Weber's notion of charisma proved a highly useful tool of analysis of the remarkable personal authority that Lenin exercised over the Bolsheviks from the inception of the movement at the turn of the century to his death. Also, however, the application of the general concept to a concrete historical case, one on which we happen to have quite detailed factual knowledge, suggested some adaptations of Weber's formulation, some ways in which the idea of the charismatic leader might be restated for theoretical purposes. Afterwards, it seemed worthwhile to generalize these results and take preliminary soundings on the applicability of the modified concept to some other historical cases. The outcome is a reformulation of the theory of charismatic leadership from a perspective other than that of political development and modernization, although there is nothing in the reformulated theory that would keep it from being applied to charismatic leadership of "new states." The perspective also differs somewhat from that of Weber himself, but preserves his underlying view that charisma is a phenomenon of universalistic significance whose *political* manifestations, however important

72

The Theory of Charismatic Leadership

from the standpoint of political scientists, are only one of its manifold dimensions.

II

An exposition of the concept of charisma can proceed in either of two ways. One is to bring together all that Weber himself wrote on the subject and systematize this material. Here the aim would be to present a general interpretation of Weber's thinking; and fidelity to his meaning and position would be the chief test of success. The alternative procedure—which is the one to be followed here—is to take Weber's principal pertinent thoughts as a point of departure for an independent reformulation of the concept of charismatic leadership. In doing this, one's aim is not essentially to be exegetic, but rather to develop the theory of charisma into a more workable tool of understanding and research. Accordingly, the outcome may not be a faithful reflection in all ways of Weber's thinking. Certain of his thoughts may be neglected, others may be much more heavily emphasized than they were in his writings, and still others, which were not present in Weber, may be added. Here the result should be evaluated as a contribution not to the history of ideas, but to the needs of scholarship in the field of leadership.

Weber uses "charisma" in a value-neutral manner: To be a charismatic leader is not necessarily to be an admirable individual. In Weber's own expression, the manic seizure and rage of the nordic beserker or the demagogic talents of a Cleon are just as much "charisma" as the qualities of a Napoleon, Jesus, Pericles.[6] Among the examples cited are founders of religions, prophets, warrior heroes, shamans, and great demagogues, such as the leader of the Bavarian leftist rising in 1918, Kurt Eisner. Owing to their extraordinary qualities, or what are perceived to be such, these leaders inspire followings among which their superior authority is freely accepted. Oftentimes, the relationship of the followers to the charismatic leader is that of disciples to a master, and in any event he is revered by them. They do not follow him out of fear or monetary inducement, but out of love, passionate devotion, enthusiasm. They are not as a rule concerned with career, promotion, salary, or benefice. The charismatic following is a nonbureaucratic group. In Weber's words, the disciples or followers tend to live primarily in a communistic relationship with their leader on means which have been provided by voluntary gift.[7]

ROBERT C. TUCKER

In describing the charismatic authority-relation, Weber stresses at times the obedience that the followers render to the leader, and some commentators have highlighted this theme. We are thus invited, or at least permitted, to infer that in a genuine case of charismatic leadership, it would be virtually inconceivable for a follower to contradict or disagree with the leader or to question his infallibility in any way. It is necessary, however, to enter a caveat here. Weber's thinking on charisma was much influenced by the examples with which he was familiar from the settings of traditional religion, where absolute obedience would of course be characteristic of the charismatic as well as other types of authority-relation. But if charisma is, in principle, a universalistic phenomenon, as we are assuming along with Weber, then we should be more prepared than he was to recognize that codes of conduct in the relations between charismatic leaders and their followers will in certain respects vary according to the political culture. What is specific to the charismatic response is not absolute obedience toward the leader, but simply the fact that by virtue of extraordinary qualities he exercises a kind of "domination" (as Weber puts it) over the followers. Followers can be under the spell of a leader and can accept him as supremely authoritative without necessarily agreeing with him on all occasions or refraining from argument with him. In the highly argumentative atmosphere of a modern radical party, for example, a leader can be both charismatic and contested on specific points, as Lenin often was by his close followers. Indeed, he can even manifest some of his charisma in the inspired way in which he conquers dissent by the sheer power of his political discourse. Immense persuasiveness in argument may, in other words, be one of the extraordinary qualities by virtue of which a leader acquires charisma in his followers' eyes. We should not, therefore, envisage the charismatic authority-relation as one that necessarily involves automatic acquiescence of the followers in the leader's views or excludes the possibility of their disagreeing with him on occasion and up to a point. All the more so since as an innovator the charismatic leader tends at times to break with established ways of thinking and acting, and thus to take positions which diverge from his followers' expectations and consequently raise disturbed questions in their minds. Needless to add, there will always be some among the followers who would never dream of taking issue with him, even on the most trivial points.

74

The Theory of Charismatic Leadership

It is presumably necessary to possess extraordinary qualities in order to be widely perceived over a period of time as the bearer of them. Yet Weber stresses the response of the followers as the crucial test of charisma. To *be* a charismatic leader is essentially to be *perceived* as such: "It is recognition on the part of those subject to authority which is decisive for the validity of charisma."[8] Furthermore, such recognition of charisma on the part of the followers must be reinforced from time to time by the leader's demonstration of charismatic powers. He must furnish "signs" or "proof" of the exceptional abilities or qualities for the sake of which his followers render him their personal devotion; if he fails to do so over a long period, his charismatic authority may disappear. As Weber puts it:

By its very nature, the existence of charismatic authority is specifically unstable. The holder may forego his charisma; he may feel "forsaken by his God," as Jesus did on the cross; he may prove to his followers that "virtue is gone out of him." It is then that his mission is extinguished, and hope waits and searches for a new holder of charisma.[9]

One other theme that Weber stresses in his treatment of charisma is its innovative and even revolutionary character. Charisma, he says, is alien to the world of everyday routine; it calls for new ways of life and thought. Whatever the particular social setting (religion, politics, and so forth), charismatic leadership rejects old rules and issues a demand for change. It preaches or creates *new* obligations. It addresses itself to followers or potential followers in the spirit of the saying: "It is written . . . , but I say unto you . . . ." In contrast and opposition to bureaucratic authority, which respects rational rules, and to traditional authority, which is bound to precedents handed down from the past, charismatic authority, within the sphere of its claims, "repudiates the past, and is in this sense a specifically revolutionary force."[10]

From this summary it is evident that charismatic leadership, in Weber's view, typically appears in the setting of a social *movement* of some kind or creates such a movement. The charismatic leader is not simply any leader who is idolized and freely followed for his extraordinary leadership qualities, but one who demonstrates such qualities in the process of summoning people to join in a movement for change and in leading such a movement. This is, I believe, a point of central importance for any endeavor to systematize the theory of charisma. And it is one to which Weber himself, although he uses the phrase "charismatic move-

ROBERT C. TUCKER

ment" on occasion, does not give due emphasis. To remedy this,
let us postulate that charismatic leadership inherently tends to
become the center of a charismatic movement—that is, a charismatically led movement for change. To speak of charismatic
leaders, then, is to speak of charismatic movements; the two
phenomena are inseparable.

Although not all movements for change are charismatic, those
that are cover a broad spectrum, ranging from small coterie-move-
ments to genuine mass movements and from those with little
organization to those with elaborate organization. They appear in
diverse forms of society—democratic and authoritarian, Western
and non-Western, highly developed and under-developed economically. And they cross ideological lines. As Robert Michels showed
in *Political Parties,* marked charismatic tendencies appeared in
various West European socialist movements of the later nineteenth
century, the leaders of which became objects of a "cult of
veneration among the masses." Ferdinand Lassalle, for example,
was received "like a god" when he toured the Rhineland in 1864.[11]
In the twentieth century, some Communist movements, starting
with Russian Communism under Lenin, have been charismatic.
We also find charismatic leadership in many of the fascist movements and in nationalist movements of such widely varying
character and locale as the Indian independence movement and
the Black Muslims of America.

It would appear that charismatic movements arise in different
ways. On the one hand, the movement can be charismatic from
the outset—that is, inspired and brought into being by the charismatic leader-personality who heads it. The July 26 Cuban revolutionary movement created by Castro and German National Socialism under Hitler may be cases in point. Alternatively, the
movement simply as a movement for change may be in existence
before the rise of the charismatic leadership and then undergo
transformation into a charismatic one. A non-charismatic Russian
Marxist revolutionary movement was in existence, for example,
before the appearance in its leadership of Lenin, a charismatic
leader-personality. As this instance shows, however, when a movement for change exists before the appearance of charismatic
leadership, a schism may result. Instead of homogeneously undergoing metamorphosis into a charismatic movement, it divides into
those who reject and those who accept the charismatic leader.
Thus, Bolshevism arose as Lenin's charismatic following *within*

The Theory of Charismatic Leadership

the Russian Marxist revolutionary movement. In time, it split off from the Mensheviks and took shape as an independent movement claiming to be the sole authentic voice of Russian Marxism.

A charismatic movement's growth may be represented in a series of concentric circles. The initial phase is the formation of a charismatic following—a group of persons who cluster around the charismatic personality and accept his authority. The little Bolshevik colony in Geneva at the beginning of the century, which formed the historical core of Lenin's charismatic following, is a good example. The relation of the Geneva Bolsheviks to Lenin was that of disciples to the master, his authority in all things revolutionary was acknowledged, and his mission to lead the revolutionary movement was taken for granted.[12] As a charismatic following grows, attracting new members in larger and larger numbers, it achieves the status of a movement. It also develops an organization, which in the case of a modern-day revolutionary movement is likely to be a party organization. The growth curve of the movement may fluctuate, periods of growth being followed by periods of decline. Under propitious conditions, the movement may turn into a mass movement with tens of thousands of followers. And if it is a political movement, a further critical growth-point is reached at the time when it acquires (if it does acquire) political power. Once in power, the movement becomes a movement-regime with enormous resources of influence. The entire citizenry of the country concerned as well as others abroad now enter into a vastly enlarged potential charismatic following. Finally, a charismatic movement, particularly one that comes to power in a major nation, may become international in scope, radiating across national boundaries and enlisting new followers everywhere. For example, the world Communist movement that came into existence under Russian Communist auspices after 1917 was, in one of its several aspects, an international charismatic movement of followers of Lenin.

Emphasis upon the charismatic movement as the typical habitat or creation of charismatic leaders has important methodological implications for the study of such leadership. It means that when we study a case—or possible case—of charismatic leadership, we should always go back to the beginnings of the given leader-personality's emergence as a leader, rather than start with the status achieved at the zenith of his career. We should look for indications of a charismatic following or movement (which may,

77

ROBERT C. TUCKER

as in Lenin's case, be a movement within a movement) very early in the career and in any event before power is achieved. The test of whether or not a charismatic movement takes shape before the leader's advent to power is not, of course, infallible, for there presumably are certain instances in which circumstances (for example, military status) have militated against the growth of a charismatic movement in the early period. Thus, a career officer like Nasser of Egypt might have been a potential charismatic leader without, at an earlier time, having been able to become the center of a movement. But even in such instances, one would expect to find signs of the early formation of at least a small charismatic following with the given figure's milieu.

All this has a bearing upon the problem of identifying charisma. Since scholars usually show a special interest in leaders' careers in power, there has been a certain tendency both to search for examples of charismatic leadership among leaders in power and to study the charismatic leader-follower relation primarily as manifested then. When we concentrate attention upon that stage, however, we run greater risk of error in identifying a given leader as charismatic; for power is a source of phenomena that resemble the effects of charisma without actually being such. It brings prestige and, especially in modern technological conditions, possibilities of artificial inducement or simulation of mass adulation of a leader. Examples that immediately come to mind are the personality cults of Stalin in Russia and Nkrumah in Ghana, neither of whom—as later became clear—were hero-worshiped by their citizens in the way that some foreign visitors believed on the basis of what they saw and heard in the two countries when the two leaders were in power.

To sum up the foregoing, a leader need not achieve power—national or other—in order to qualify as charismatic. What is decisive is whether or not he attracts a charismatic following and shows a marked tendency to become the center of a charismatic movement as defined above. To minimize the risk of error in classifying a given leader as charismatic, it is of great importance, therefore, to study his impact upon those around him *before* he achieves office. We may lay it down as a general rule that when a leader-personality is genuinely charismatic, his charisma will begin to manifest itself before he becomes politically powerful. For the student of charisma, then, the pre-power stage of a leader's career is of critical significance. Unless there is evidence of the sponta-

78

The Theory of Charismatic Leadership

neous formation of at least a small charismatic following on a purely voluntary basis, the likelihood of a given figure being a charismatic leader-personality is quite small. Needless to add, none of this is meant to imply that the charismatic leader-follower relation ought not to be studied in later stages of political careers. It merely argues for a genetic approach to the phenomenon in concrete cases.

In what forms does the evidence of early charisma appear? In the cases of contemporary figures—Castro, for example—it may be possible to investigate the responses of others to them at the formative stages of their careers by interviewing erstwhile associates who speak from personal experience and observation. But in most cases of interest to us, we are likely to be dependent to a great extent upon written materials as sources of evidence. The value of the biographical and general historical literature on major figures is limited because biographers and historians, with few exceptions, have not approached the study of these figures with the concept of charismatic leadership in mind, and so have not always been attuned to evidence of it in their researches. On the other hand, for this very reason what evidence we do find of charisma in such general secondary sources is often of considerable value. Memoir literature and letters of those who were closely associated with the given figure early in his career are likely, however, to be of greatest importance in many instances. Certain problems of the critical use of such sources naturally arise, in part from the tendency of some memoirs to project, consciously or unconsciously, upon the past a charismatic response that either was not experienced at the earlier time or was not experienced to such a degree. To minimize the chance of being misled by retrospective exaggeration of charismatic response, it is important to search out any available historical witnesses whose bias, if any, would be against such exaggeration, and who set down their memories under conditions of complete freedom of self-expression. Consider, for example, the following memoir of Lenin by a Russian Marxist who worked closely with him on the newspaper *Iskra* at the turn of the century when Lenin, at thirty, was emerging as one of the leaders of the movement:

No one could so fire others with their plans, no one could so impose his will and conquer by force of his personality as this seemingly so ordinary and somewhat coarse man who lacked any obvious sources of charm. . . . Neither Plekhanov nor Martov nor anyone else possessed the secret

79

ROBERT C. TUCKER

radiating from Lenin of positively hypnotic effect upon people—I would even say, domination of them. Plekhanov was treated with deference, Martov was loved, but Lenin alone was followed unhesitatingly as the only indisputable leader. For only Lenin represented that rare phenomenon, especially rare in Russia, of a man of iron will and indomitable energy who combines fanatical faith in the movement, the cause, with no less faith in himself. If the French king, Louis XIV, could say, *L'Etat c'est moi*, Lenin, without putting it into words, always had the feeling, *Le Partie c'est moi;* he had the feeling that in him the will of the movement was concentrated in one man. And he acted accordingly. I recall that Lenin's sense of mission to be the leader at one time made an impression upon me also.[18]

The value of this statement as evidence that Lenin was a charismatic political personality is obviously enhanced because it comes from A. N. Potresov, who long before writing it had become one of the leaders of Russian Menshevism and a political enemy of Lenin. Also noteworthy is the place of writing and original publication of the memoir: Germany, 1927.

III

Why does charismatic leadership emerge in the setting of movements for change, and what is the explanation of the passionate devotion that the charismatic leader of such a movement typically receives from his followers? In answering these two closely related questions, we must focus attention first upon the followers and their needs. Here again we find that Weber himself has made the crucial point although without giving it adequate emphasis and elaboration. He tells us that charismatic leaders have been the natural leaders "in time of psychic, physical, economic, ethical, religious, political distress," and, elsewhere, that charisma inspires its followers with "a devotion born of distress and enthusiasm."[14] In short, the key to the charismatic response of the followers to the leader lies in the *distress* that the followers experience.

Why movements for change arise and spread at times of widespread distress in society is obvious. The further connection between distress in its many forms and responsiveness to charisma in leaders of movements for change is only slightly less manifest. Briefly, the charismatic leader is one in whom, by virtue of unusual personal qualities, the promise or hope of salvation—deliverance from distress—appears to be embodied. He is a leader who convincingly offers himself to a group of people in distress as one peculiarly qualified to lead them out of their predicament. He is in essence a

The Theory of Charismatic Leadership

savior, or one who is so perceived by his followers. *Charismatic leadership is specifically salvationist or messianic in nature.* Herein lies its distinctiveness in relation to such broader and more neb- ulous categories as "inspired leadership" or "heroic leadership." Furthermore, this fundamental characteristic of charismatic leader- ship helps to explain the special emotional intensity of the charis- matic response, and also why the sustaining of charisma requires the leader to furnish periodical "proof" of the powers that he claims. The followers respond to the charismatic leader with pas- sionate loyalty because the salvation, or promise of it, that he ap- pears to embody represents the fulfillment of urgently felt needs; their faith in his extraordinary capacities is kept alive (or not, as the case may be) by the periodical demonstration that he gives (if he does) of powers of efficacious leadership on the road to the sal- vationist goal. These may be, for example, miracle-working powers if the movement is religiously salvationist, or revolution-making powers if it is a charismatically led revolutionary movement, or war-making powers if it is a movement seeking to effect change by military means.

Of course, not all movements for change arising in society are charismatic or become so. In many societies at many times, there are non-charismatic movements of reform dedicated to the im- provement of conditions underlying the dissatisfactions normally experienced by many people. Charismatic movements are likely to appear alongside these others when prevailing widespread dissatis- faction deepens to the point of becoming genuine "distress" (suf- fering or acute malaise that conceivably could be alleviated); and when extraordinary leader-personalities come forward with appeals of salvationist character, persuasively proclaiming the possibility of overcoming the situation of distress, pointing to ways of doing so, and offering their own leadership along this path to those who are willing to follow. At such a time, numbers of those in distress will usually rally to the salvationist appeal, and charismatic movements for change are born.

The first determinant of charismatic response is situational; the state of acute distress predisposes people to perceive as extraordi- narily qualified and to follow with enthusiastic loyalty a leadership offering salvation from distress. This being so, we must reckon with the possibility of at least a low level of charismatic response to leaders who, for one or another reason, would not fulfill, or would fulfill only imperfectly, the second of the two conditions just laid

ROBERT C. TUCKER

down. Examples are not far to seek. Thus, in the state of threatened national existence experienced by the people of Britain in 1940, when their island lay open to German invasion, there was no doubt some charismatic response to the war leadership of Sir Winston Churchill, who personified the will never to surrender and the determination to fight on to victory; and yet Sir Winston, as both pre-war and postwar history shows, was not a notable example of the charismatic leader-personality. Again, when Franklin D. Roosevelt became President in a crisis-stricken U.S.A. in 1933, exuding confidence and proclaiming that there was nothing to fear but fear itself, he evoked from many Americans a charismatic response that for the most part subsided when the acute national emergency was overcome. We might use the term "situational charisma" to refer to instances where a leader-personality of non-messianic tendency evokes a charismatic response simply because he offers, in a time of acute distress, leadership that is perceived as a source and means of salvation from distress.[15]

The foregoing considerations suggest strongly that when the situational determinant of charismatic response is present, the presence or absence of a genuinely charismatic leader-personality may be a critical historical variable. If we ask, for example, why the distress of German society in 1933 should have led to the triumph of National Socialism whereas the distress of British society in 1931 led simply to a rather emotional general election, the presence of Adolf Hitler on the German scene and the absence of a correspondingly charismatic leader-figure on the British scene may go a considerable distance toward providing the answer, although it would have to be added that the German distress was deeper and broader, and the general state of emergency more acute, than in the British case. Again, so great was the importance of the personal charismatic leadership of Lenin in leading the Bolsheviks to power in the Russian Revolution that even Trotsky, who was not given to exaggerating the role of personality in history, observed in later years that without Lenin there probably would have been no October Revolution in Russia.[16]

Distress occurs in such a wide variety of forms that it seems hardly feasible for a theorist of charismatic leadership to catalogue them. They range from the physical and material distress caused by persecution, catastrophes (for example, famine, drought), and extreme economic hardship to such diverse forms of psychic or emotional distress as the feelings of oppression in peoples ruled by

The Theory of Charismatic Leadership

foreigners, the radical alienation from the existing order experienced by revolutionaries, or the intolerable anxieties that have motivated many followers of religious millenarian movements in the past and political millenarian movements in the modern age. Although distress in one form or another is more or less endemic in social history, it is at times of crisis, of extremely serious and widespread distress, that charismatic movements for change develop in profusion as would-be messiahs attract followers *en masse*. For example, pretenders to the role of messiah arose among European Jewry during the massacres from the eleventh to the fourteenth centuries, and each time there resulted a wave of millenarian enthusiasm, often expressing itself in a mass migration towards Palestine.[17] It seems likely, moreover, that charismatic movements attain their greatest force at times of confluence of multiple forms of distress in society. Thus, German National Socialism, as a charismatic movement led by Hitler, acquired a mass following at a time when several forms of distress were rampant in German society: wholesale unemployment and poverty in the great depression, economic troubles and status anxiety in the lower-middle class, and injured national feelings resulting from defeat in World War I and the terms of the Versailles treaty.

Deeper and more systematic analysis of the phenomenon of distress—in particular, its psychological varieties—is an obvious requisite for further development of the theory of charismatic leadership. Erik H. Erikson has suggested[18] that there are certain historical conditions, such as the waning of religion, in which people in large numbers become "charisma-hungry." Pursuing the point further, he distinguished three forms of distress to which a charismatic leader may minister: "fear," as in the fear of the medieval European Jews for their lives or the obscure, subliminal fear of nuclear destruction in contemporary Western man; "anxiety," especially as experienced by persons in an "identity-vacuum" or the condition of not knowing just who or what they are; and "existential dread," or the distress that people experience under conditions in which rituals of their existence have broken down. Correspondingly, a charismatic leader is one who offers people salvation in the form of safety, or identity, or rituals, or some combination of these, saying to them in effect: "I will make you safe," or "I will give you an identity," or "I will give you rituals." In the case of Gandhi, for example, the people of India were given a new collective identity.

ROBERT C. TUCKER

Erikson's observations are highly relevant to the "functional" theory of charisma mentioned earlier, for they help illuminate the charismatic role of some leaders of "new states" in the process of transition to independent nationhood and modernity. Anxiety and existential dread, in the senses just defined, are two forms of psychic distress that may, for obvious reasons, be both widespread and acute in societies at this stage of historical development. On the one hand, people for whom the fundamental ambiance of life has always been the village community may be plunged into the anxiety of an identity-vacuum as life becomes urban- and nation-oriented in the transition period. And on the other, the process of modernization may create a great deal of existential dread by upsetting the habits and customs that have regulated life in the society since time immemorial. The leader who at such a juncture can make national identity meaningful and thereby give the people of his country a sense of belonging to a new and greater community, and who at the same time can help them find their way to a new life-style, a new ritualization of existence, will certainly acquire great charisma in the eyes of very many. By the same token, however, he is likely to arouse fanatical hatred on the part of those who remain devotees of the old order of things in the society. Here, by the way, we touch upon what is probably a universal feature of the charismatic leader: his capacity to inspire hatred as well as loyalty and love. Precisely as an exponent of change, the leader who evokes a positive charismatic response from some is likely to evoke a negative one (we might speak of this as "counter-charisma") from others. The same leader who is charismatic in the eyes of people in distress, for whom salvation lies in change, will be counter-charismatic in the eyes of those who see in change not salvation but ruination. Lenin, for example, became a shining hero for many Russian peasants during the revolutionary period, and a veritable antichrist in the eyes of others for whom the old Russian ways remained dear.

A charismatic movement does not necessarily turn into a mass movement. If, for example, a particular social group experiences extreme distress at a time when the general distress level in the society is relatively low, a charismatic movement of great vigor but small size may emerge. Such might be the pattern in a society with an oppressed racial or ethnic minority. Alternatively, and depending upon the character of the charismatic movement in question, events may transform the situation by creating mass misery and thereby greatly augmenting the movement's following. A

The Theory of Charismatic Leadership

case in point is the career of Russian Communism before and during World War I. Before 1914, Lenin's charismatic following was quite small and limited almost exclusively to members of the radical intelligentsia. By 1917, however, the war had produced such misery among masses of Russians—particularly workers, soldiers, and peasants—that substantial numbers of them became responsive to Lenin's revolutionary charisma. After the October Revolution, the charismatic following of Lenin, while it included many individuals in the population at large, remained concentrated in the Communist Party. And because he had, through his personal leadership of the Revolution, given stunning "proof" of revolution-making powers, he was quite literally idolized by many of the followers. Characteristic testimony on this score comes from Walter Duranty, who reported at the time of Lenin's death:

I have seen Lenin speak to his followers. A small, busy, thick-set man under blinding lights, greeted by applause like thunder. I turned around and their faces were shining, like men who looked on God. Lenin was like that, whether you think he was a damnable Antichrist or a once-in-a-thousand-years' prophet. That is a matter of opinion, but when five thousand faces can light up and shine at the sight of him, as they did, and I saw it, then I say he was no ordinary individual.[19]

To sum up, charismatic movements for change arise and spread at times when painful forms of distress are prevalent in a society or in some particular stratum of a society. The unique personal authority of the leader and the rapturous response of many of the followers grow out of their feeling that he, by virtue of his special powers as a leader, embodies the movement's salvational promise, hence that which may be of supreme significance to them. Since he ministers to their most pressing need—the need to believe in the real possibility of escape from an oppressive life-predicament—they not only follow him voluntarily and without thought of material recompense, but tend to revere him and surround him with that spontaneous cult of personality which appears to be one of the symptomatic marks of the charismatic leader-follower relationship.

This explains why we cannot rightly view the phenomenon of charisma as belonging primarily to the historical past. Wherever and whenever human beings in serious numbers live in desperation or despair or similar states, charismatic leaders and movements are likely to appear. Depending upon such factors as the quality of the leadership and the depth and breadth of the existential disquiet to which it appeals, these movements will sometimes prove of

ROBERT C. TUCKER

little consequence and sometimes of great. Finally, there is no evident basis for believing that humanity is about to enter a new age of general content in which charismatic movements will grow more and more anachronistic. On the contrary, at a time when chronic famines may be approaching in various countries in which population burgeons while food supply does not, and when man in the more affluent industrialized parts of the world lives not only with the terrors and anxieties of the nuclear era but also, increasingly, with the deep ennui and distress of unrelatedness that life can breed in mass technological society, the outlook is rather for new messiahs and movements led by them.

IV

We have so far considered the charismatic response from the followers' standpoint, seeing it as the readiness of persons in distress to accept with enthusiasm the authority of a leader in whom the hope of salvation appears to be embodied. Now the question arises as to the nature of the extraordinary qualities that cause a leader to be regarded as a potential savior. This question has not received systematic treatment in the existing literature on charisma and can only be resolved on the basis of numerous future case studies in depth of actual charismatic movements and their leaders.[20] Such studies should make the requisite generalizations possible. Meanwhile, a few preliminary general observations may be hazarded.

Charismatic qualification may, on the one hand, consist in extraordinary powers of vision and the communication of vision, especially when this vision relates to the possibility and ways of overcoming distressful conditions. Alternatively, it may consist in unusual powers of practical leadership of people along the way to such a goal. In the one case, the charismatic leader appears as prophet; in the other, as activist. But there is no hard-and-fast separation between these two basic charismatic leader-roles. In practice, the difference is one of prevailing tendency. If, for example, one were to take Marx and Lenin as illustrations of the prophetic and activist types respectively, it would have to be added by way of qualification that Marx was an organizer of revolutionary movements as well as Communism's great prophet, and that Lenin, whose charismatic powers showed themselves chiefly in

86

The Theory of Charismatic Leadership

the field of practical leadership, was likewise an ideologue of Communist revolution and something of a visionary. Gandhi, too, was a social visionary although he demonstrated his extraordinary leadership powers primarily in the teaching and practice of nonviolence as a practical method of changing men and conditions. Finally, there appear to be some leaders who defy classification according to this dichotomy because they not only combine both kinds of charismatic qualifications, but fulfill both roles in their respective movements. Hitler, who was at once the principal ideologue and inspirer of National Socialism and its *Fuehrer* to the end, might be mentioned as an example.

Although charismatic leaders may vary in type, there appear to be certain qualities common to them as a class. Notable among these is a peculiar sense of mission, comprising a belief both in the movement and in themselves as the chosen instrument to lead the movement to its destination. The charismatic leader typically radiates a buoyant confidence in the rightness and goodness of the aims that he proclaims for the movement, in the practical possibility of attaining these aims, and in his own special calling and capacity to provide the requisite leadership. Needless to say, in the lives of most of these leaders—even those who do achieve success—there are moments of discouragement and despair when they and their cause seem fated to fail. But it is not characteristic of them to display such feelings in public. Rather, they show a stubborn self-confidence and faith in the movement's prospects of victory and success. This, indeed, may be the quality that most of all underlies their charisma and explains the extreme devotion and loyalty that they inspire in their followers; for people in need of deliverance from one or another form of distress, being in very many instances anxiety-ridden, easily respond with great emotional fervor to a leader who can kindle or strengthen in them a faith in the possibility of deliverance.

This belief in the movement and sense of personal mission to lead it is a common element, for example, in the varied biographies of three of the most strikingly successful charismatic leaders of the first half of the twentieth century—Lenin, Hitler, and Mussolini. Potresov's above-cited memoir illustrates much direct testimony to the compelling quality of Lenin's revolutionary faith—his *tseleustremlennost'* or "goal-fixation" as some have called it—and his self-assured belief in his own mission to lead the revolutionary cause. When he put out his powerful tract *What Is to Be Done?* shortly

87

ROBERT C. TUCKER

after the turn of the century, there was a widespread mood of discouragement in the Russian Marxist milieu. His actual and literary personality injected into this milieu new confidence in Russian revolution as a historically imminent prospect, something that a small group of determined revolutionaries could seriously hope to spark and lead by their collective efforts under Lenin's guidance. Numbers of Russian Marxists gravitated into his orbit, and Bolshevism emerged as a Lenin-centered charismatic movement within Russian Marxism.

Whereas Lenin's charismatic appeal was concentrated for a long while within the Bolshevik Party, both Hitler and Mussolini comparatively early in their careers found mass followings in their distress-filled nations. In both these cases, moreover, the man's boundless faith in himself, or appearance of it, seems to have been a key to the charismatic response by large numbers of people. Describing the reactions of many Germans to Hitler at the beginning of the 1930's, Hadley Cantril, for example, concludes:

The message of Hitler, his own obvious belief in the righteousness of his program, his sincerity, and his faith in himself made an indelible impression on those who heard him. In a period of doubt and uncertainty, here was a speaker who did not argue the pros and cons of policies but who was fanatically self-confident.[21]

And in an appraisal of Mussolini's impact upon people in the Italy of 1922, Laura Fermi emphasizes his "ability to impersonate, at the most timely moment, the superman and the savior to whom as he had said himself, 'nothing is impossible.'" She explains:

In 1922, to a population that had lost sight of its aims and will, that lacked faith in itself and was affected by a mass inferiority complex, that suffered from both real and imaginary ills, the idea of a savior capable of bringing well-being to all by the sheer force of his will was not only appealing, it was a last hope. And Mussolini, savior and superman, promised law and order, a full appreciation of victory and its worth, an Italy cured of poverty, restored to its dignity, resuming its place among the great nations of Europe, and governed by youth and youthful energy.[22]

I do not mean to suggest that a charismatic leader acquires charisma exclusively because of his inspirational sense of mission and belief in the movement, or even that his personality *per se*, independently of the content of his message, is sufficient explanation for his impact upon his followers. We cannot properly say of char-

The Theory of Charismatic Leadership

ismatic leaders that "the medium is the message," although it is a large part of it. They offer to followers and potential followers not simply and solely their extraordinary selves as instruments of leadership, but also a formula or set of formulas for salvation. They address themselves in one way or another to the predicaments that render masses of people potentially responsive to the appeal of a movement for change and offer some diagnosis of these predicaments. Indeed, they characteristically strive to *accentuate* the sense of being in a desperate predicament, as if following the motto of the young Marx who wrote: "The Germans must not be given a minute for self-deception and resignation. The real oppression must be made still more oppressive by adding to it the consciousness of oppression; the shame still more shameful by publicizing it."[23] And they propound certain ideas, ranging from the most nebulous to the most definite and concrete, as a way out of the predicament.

Thus, Marx, having diagnosed the sufferings of the working class as a necessary outcome of the capitalist mode of production, advocated the class struggle leading to proletarian revolution and Communism as the formula for man's salvation—for the transcending of human alienation in all its forms. Lenin, addressing himself at the turn of the century to the predicament of Russian Marxism *as a revolutionary movement,* provided a complex formula for what was to be done both to cure this movement of its ills (such as the "economist" heresy) and to make Russian revolution a certainty: create a militant organization of revolutionaries as a proselytizing nucleus of a future nationwide resistance movement of the discontented and disaffected of Russia against the Tsarist order. The charismatic response of numbers of Russian radicals to the Lenin of *What Is to Be Done?* was partly a consequence of the cogency of this revolutionary formula to their minds. The infinite fertility of his tactical imagination, his astonishing capacity to devise formulas for the movement's policy at every turn and in every predicament, was undoubtedly one of the sources of the spell that he exerted upon the Bolsheviks. But the impact of a charismatic leader's formulas for salvation (in this instance, salvation by Communist revolution) cannot, in the final analysis, be divorced from that of his personality. Lenin's formulas derived much of their cogency from the immense assurance with which he usually propounded and defended them in party councils, and from his great personal powers of persuasion. Thus, a Bolshevik known for his reserve and self-control reminisced as follows about the effect that Lenin's speeches

89

ROBERT C. TUCKER

had upon him when he first heard him speak, at the Bolshevik conference in Tammerfors in 1906:

I was captivated by that irresistible force of logic in them which, although somewhat terse, gained a firm hold on his audience, gradually
electrified it, and then, as one might say, completely overpowered it. I
remember that many of the delegates said: "The logic of Lenin's speeches
is like a mighty tentacle which twines all round you and holds you as in
a vice and from whose grip you are powerless to tear yourself away:
You must either surrender or resign yourself to utter defeat."[24]

Special mention should be made of one sort of salvational formula that has played an exceedingly important part in social movements of past and present, charismatic ones included. This formula
traces the ills plaguing a people, or race, or mankind as a whole to
a great and deadly conspiracy the destruction of which, it is held,
will solve everything. Franz Neumann distinguished five main variants of such a "conspiracy theory of history" in the postmedieval
West: the Jesuit conspiracy, the Freemason conspiracy, the Communist conspiracy, the Capitalist conspiracy, and the Jewish conspiracy. And he found anti-conspiracy gospels associated with
"affective leader-identifications," or what we have here been calling
the charismatic response of followers to a leader:

Just as the masses hope for their deliverance from distress through
absolute oneness with a person, so they ascribe their distress to certain
persons who brought this distress into the world through a conspiracy. . . . Hatred, resentment, dread, created by great upheavals, are
concentrated on certain persons who are denounced as devilish con-
spirators.[25]

We may restate the point in terms of the theory of charismatic
leadership by saying that some leaders of the charismatic type
have attracted followers with formulas that derive from conspiracy
doctrines. Offering both a diagnosis of the distress that people are
experiencing in times of anxiety and a gospel of salvation through
struggle against and ultimate elimination of the purported conspiracy and its bearers, these conspiracy doctrines encourage the
followers of a movement to restructure their thinking and their
lives in apparently more meaningful and satisfying ways and
thereby give the would-be messiah charismatic authority in their
eyes. And here again we find that formula and personality are
mutually reinforcing. The leader's personality becomes more salient
and magnetic for many because of its identification with the conspiracy doctrine, and the latter, however fantastic it may be, be-

90

The Theory of Charismatic Leadership

comes more believable because of the leader's paranoid earnestness, the obsessive conviction with which he portrays the conspiracy and inveighs against it. To a generation that remembers Hitler and *Mein Kampf,* lengthy illustrations of the point are unnecessary. Examples closer to home are to be found in the recent history of movements on the radical right in America.

V

In conclusion, a few comments on the problem of what happens to charismatic movements when their founding leaders pass on. Weber treated this problem under the heading of "routinization" and "depersonalization" of charisma. He elaborated these themes in complex ways that I shall not attempt to summarize here in any detail. Suffice it to say that charisma, according to Weber, characteristically undergoes transformation from an extraordinary and purely personal relationship into an established authority structure that is no longer necessarily dependent upon personal charismatic qualification in the incumbent leader. Thus, it is transmitted from leader to leader according to established rules of succession, such as designation by the charismatic leader of his own successor or, alternatively, designation of a successor by the charismatic followers of the leader (as in the selection of a new Pope). In the process of depersonalization, charisma evolves into hereditary or "familial" charisma with its locus in a royal family, for example, or into institutional charisma attached to an office like the priesthood.[26]

Although it is useful and suggestive at many points, Weber's discussion of "routinization" and "depersonalization" of charisma is also, unfortunately, rather confusing and open to serious objections. How can something that has been defined as antiroutine and personal in its essence be routinized and depersonalized? As Carl Friedrich has pointed out, it makes little sense for Weber to speak of "routinized" charisma, since "routine and charisma are contradictory terms, if the initial specification of the term 'charisma' is taken at all seriously."[27] Hence Weber might have stood on firmer ground if he had couched this part of his theory of charismatic leadership—as, indeed, he tended to do in places—not in terms of the routinizing of charisma, but rather in terms of its transformation into other forms of authority.

On the other hand, it is not my intention to argue that charisma, by its very nature, ceases to exist with the death or departure of

ROBERT C. TUCKER

the original leader in whom it inheres as a personal quality. On the contrary, it appears to be a phenomenon that can and often does live on after the charismatic individual is gone. But the form in which it characteristically lives on is the cult of the departed leader —something to which Weber gives little consideration in his theory of routinization. Thus, the charisma of the founder of a religious movement survives, insofar as it survives at all, primarily in the cult of the founder, the revering of his memory by the followers who live after. It is the same with the founders of charismatic political and ideological movements. Thus, Marx and Engels underwent, as Robert Michels expressed it, a "socialist canonization" in movements that carried on in their names. And Lenin, who had strongly disapproved of the manifestations of Lenin-worship that appeared in the Russian Communist movement in his later lifetime and had more or less succeeded in suppressing them, became on the morrow of his death the object of a great public Lenin cult that expressed not only certain pragmatic needs of the Communist movement, but also, and first of all, the feelings of very many of its members.

But insofar as the charisma of a successful charismatic leader survives in the form of a cult of the dead leader, it does not cease to be personal in quality; it remains his even in death. The cult, in other words, may be a special form of "routinization" of his charisma, but is not a "depersonalization" of it. This conclusion, however, has an immediate and obvious bearing upon the Weberian idea that charisma is transmitted to the original leader's successors according to established rules of succession. Not only does the cult tend to conserve the original leader's charisma and keep it in his own name; it may, as a result, actually *militate against* the transmission of his charisma to a successor, and it may do this even though the practical interests of the movement make transmission desirable. It is not at all evident, therefore, that the successors of a charismatic leader at the head of a movement that outlives him will themselves be leaders of charismatic quality. And insofar as they are, it is not by virtue of succeeding to the dead leader's charisma, but by virtue of what they themselves are and how the followers perceive them.

REFERENCES

1. Max Weber, *Theory of Social and Economic Organization* (New York, 1947), p. 358.

92

The Theory of Charismatic Leadership

2. Karl Loewenstein, *Max Weber's Political Ideas in the Perspective of Our Time* (Amherst, 1966), pp. 79, 90. For Loewenstein's remarks on the influence of Weber's theory of charisma, see *ibid.*, p. 74.

3. Carl J. Friedrich, "Political Leadership and Charismatic Power," *The Journal of Politics*, Vol. 23, No. 2 (February, 1961), pp. 14-16. On the etymological and theological background, see E. San Juan, Jr., "Orientations of Max Weber's Concept of Charisma," *The Centennial Review*, Vol. 11, No. 2 (Spring, 1967), pp. 270-85.

4. For examples of these two criticisms, see in particular K. J. Ratnam, "Charisma and Political Leadership," *Political Studies*, Vol. 12, No. 3 (1964), pp. 344, 354.

5. See, in particular, David Apter, *Ghana in Transition* (New York, 1963), esp. pp. 320-30, and Ann Ruth Willner and Dorothy Willner, "The Rise and Role of Charismatic Leaders," *The Annals of the American Academy of Political and Social Science*, Vol. 358 (March, 1965), pp. 77-88. The Willners write: "Charismatic leadership seems to flourish today particularly in the newer states that were formerly under colonial rule" (p. 80). The article does not *define* charisma in the setting of the "newer" states, however, but follows Weber in giving the concept a universalitic definition.

6. Max Weber, "The Three Types of Legitimate Rule," *Berkeley Publications in Society and Institutions*, Vol. 4, No. 1 (Summer, 1958), p. 7.

7. Weber, *Theory of Social and Economic Organization*, pp. 359-61.

8. *Ibid.*, p. 359.

9. *From Max Weber: Essays in Sociology*, trans. H. H. Gerth and C. Mills (New York, 1946), p. 248.

10. Weber, *The Theory of Social and Economic Organization*, p. 362. As Reinhard Bendix puts it: "The charismatic leader is always a radical who challenges established practice by going to 'the root of the matter.'" (*Max Weber: An Intellectual Portrait*, p. 300.)

11. Robert Michels, *Political Parties* (New York, 1959), pp. 64-67.

12. N. Valentinov, *Vstrechi s Leninym* (New York, 1953), pp. 71-75.

13. A. N. Potresov, *Posmerty sbornik proizvedenii* (Paris, 1937), p. 301.

14. *From Max Weber*, pp. 245, 249. In their introductory essay in this volume, Gerth and Mills speak of charismatic leaders as "self-appointed leaders who are followed by those who are in distress and who need to follow the leader because they believe him to be extraordinarily qualified" (*ibid.*, p. 52).

15. I am indebted to Ann Ruth Willner for the phrase "situational charisma," as well as for data on American charismatic response to Roosevelt at the outset of his Presidency. On these and other points, see her important

ROBERT C. TUCKER

forthcoming study *The Theory and Strategies of Charismatic Leadership,* which views the phenomenon of charisma in the universalistic terms of reference set by Weber.

16. Leon Trotsky, *Trotsky's Diary in Exile: 1935* (New York, 1963), p. 46.

17. Norman Cohn, "Medieval Millenarism: Its Bearing on the Comparative Study of Millenarian Movements," ed. Sylvia Thrupp, *Millenial Dreams in Action, Essays in Comparative Study. Comparative Studies in Society and History,* Supplement 2 (The Hague, 1962), p. 32.

18. Oral remarks at the Tuxedo conference on Leadership (October, 1967), in discussion of the present paper.

19. Walter Duranty, *Duranty Reports Russia* (New York, 1934), p. 170.

20. For a first attempt at a systematic catalogue of qualities characteristic of a large number of charismatic leaders, see the aforementioned forthcoming study by Ann Ruth Willner.

21. Hadley Cantril, *The Psychology of Social Movements* (New York, 1963), p. 235.

22. Laura Fermi, *Mussolini* (Chicago, 1966), pp. 214-15.

23. Karl Marx, "Zur Kritik der Hegelschen Rechtsphilosofie: Einleitung," Karl Marx-Friedrich Engels, *Werke,* Vol. 1 (Berlin, 1957), p. 381.

24. J. V. Stalin, "Lenin," in *Works* (Moscow, 1953), p. 57.

25. Franz Neumann, "Anxiety and Politics," in *The Democratic and the Authoritarian State: Essays in Political and Legal Theory* (Glencoe, 1957), p. 279.

26. For Weber's extended discussions of routinization, see particularly *Theory of Social and Economic Organization,* pp. 364-71, and "The Three Types of Legitimate Rule," pp. 8-10. See also Bendix, *Max Weber,* pp. 308-28.

27. Carl J. Friedrich, *Man and His Government: An Empirical Theory of Politics* (New York, 1964), p. 172.

94

[32]

ETHICS AT WORK

Money, Spirituality, and Happiness

Adrian Furnham

Work is often dedicated to material advancement and productivity. Work is a social activity; spirituality often a personal endeavor. Work has mainly extrinsic rewards; spirituality mainly intrinsic rewards. But spirituality is not just about business ethics and morality: it extends much further than that and has often been associated with a particular faith and religious condition. However, it is possible to have secular spirituality of the sort of people who feel spirituality in nature or even in poetry. The arts, particularly music, can have both short-term and enduring effects on the spiritual outlook of individuals.

The concept of spirituality at work has returned to capture the imagination of many in the West. It is clear that this is a very old concept and it remains a socio-historical question why its demise and reappearance occurs. Some argue that it is due to downsizing, globalization, and greater work insecurity.

In Great Britain there was a great deal of surprise at the outpouring of the public grief over the death of Diana, Princess of Wales. Social commentators, church leaders as well as academics attempt to explain the acute and chronic grief reaction of so many, as well as many public manifestations of private mourning. Britain was considered a post-Christian, postmodern, secular society famous for its skepticism and stoicism. Yet this event alerted people to the fact that there are powerful wells of spirituality in the nation that one only really sees in times of personal and national crisis.

This response can also be seen during times of economic crisis: when a company goes out of business or lays off staff. As well as anger there is often a remarkable spiritual change in the management and employees, often to their own surprise. Moreover, increasing talk about the work-life balance is couched in the language of spirituality. The contrast is between the material and the spiritual; stress-inducer and stress-releasor; short-term and long-term; meaningless and meaningful work; less important, more important to the job holder. An increasing interest in workplace spirituality may be seen as a reaction to the demands of the modern workplace, which insists on the total commitment of individuals but without addressing some of their fundamental needs.

More recently for social scientists the concept of spirituality at work has surfaced in the concept of spiritual intelligence: the idea that spirituality is an ability as well as a preference. It is considered an individual difference factor that predicts how people behave in the workplace and elsewhere.

258   CONCEPTUALIZING WORKPLACE SPIRITUALITY

SPIRITUAL INTELLIGENCE

Emmons (2000) believes the core of the concept of spiritual intelligence is fourfold: the capacity for transcendence; the ability to enter into heightened spiritual states of consciousness; the ability to invest everyday activities, events, and relationships with a sense of the sacred or divine; and an ability to utilize spiritual resonance to solve problems in everyday living. Mayer (2000) preferred the term *spiritual consciousness*, which involves (1) attending to the unity of the world and transcending one's existence; (2) consciously entering into heightened spiritual states; (3) attending to the sacred in everyday activities, events, and relationships; (4) structuring consciousness so that problems in living are seen in the context of life's ultimate concerns; and (5) desiring to act, and, consequently, acting in virtuous ways (to show forgiveness, to express gratitude, to be humble, to display compassion).

Gardner (1999) has written about existential, as opposed to spiritual, intelligence, though there is clearly overlap between the two concepts. He agues that it is "a concern with 'ultimate issues' (and) seems the most unambiguously cognitive strand of the spiritual" (60). It is the "capacity to locate oneself with respect to such existential features of the human condition as the significance of life, the meaning of death, the ultimate fate of the physical and the psychological worlds, and such profound experiences as love of another person or total immersion in a work of art."

For Gardner (1999) existential intelligence is a cognitive ability acquired through learning and personal experience. He notes in a very personal section of his book that he is frightened and intrigued by spiritual individuals—fearing both the strangeness of their ideas but also fascinated by the power of charismatic leaders over hapless followers. He points out the effects of music on himself: ". . . lose track of mundane concerns, alter my perceptions of space and time, and occasionally, feel in touch with issues of cosmic import. . . . I feel enriched, ennobled and humbled by the encounter" (65).

From the ability perspective, spiritual or existential intelligence is being sensitive to spiritual issues. Presumably people are normally distributed on this ability so that people may score from very low to very high ability. The intriguing question of course is where that intelligence comes from: that is, its genetic/biological versus environmental determinants. Equally interesting is the attitudinal, cognitive, and behavioral correlates of spiritual intelligence. Are people with more spiritual intelligence happier at work, more money conscious, more stressed by work adversity? These remain important empirical questions for those who conceive of spirituality in this way.

WORK SPIRITUALITY

A cursory "surfing of the Web" indicates a proliferation of Web sites, newsletters, and conferences all on the topic. However, it is very apparent that the concept has multiple meanings. These include: Acting with honesty and integrity in all aspects of work; treating employees, suppliers, shareholders, and customers in a responsible, caring way; having social, environmental, and ecological responsibility by serving the "wider social community"; holding religious study groups and/or prayer/meditation meetings at work; and being able to discuss values without the dogmatism and overstructuring of organized religion.

Certainly there is a range of values that seems to fall under the umbrella of spirituality: accountability, caring, cooperativeness, honesty, integrity, justice, respect, service, and trustworthiness. Spirituality is a means, not an end. It encourages questions like: Are our business decisions based exclusively on profit? Are employees required to sacrifice private/family time to be successful? Are we self-centered and forgetting the principles of service to others in the wider community? But also, do employees get a sense of wonder at work? Do they have a sense of community?

Another theme rediscovered within the rubric of workplace spirituality is the concept of vocation: to work consciously and to celebrate all aspects of work's purpose. Indeed the word *vocation* has always had both secular and spiritual significance: it can mean both a divine call to religious life and also the work in which a person is regularly employed. It implies that the fit is right between person and organization, that they suit each other in terms of preferences, values, and lifestyles.

Sceptics and cynics of the workplace spirituality concept have such concerns as the imposition of religious concepts or ethics of a particular religious group on everyone. Others are concerned by the superficiality and trivialization of religious and spiritual belief. Some are worried about cost, time wasting, and the potential harassment of the "nonspiritual." It has been suggested that the movement is in fact led by the baby-boomer generation who is now postmaterialist and much more aware of its mortality. But it does seem to have "struck a nerve." Further there has been considerable multidisciplinary academic interest, and this book is testament to that.

A focus on workplace spirituality makes the workplace somewhere to express and fulfill one's deeper purpose. Work is an integral part of life and one does not disengage heart or brain at the factory door or office. People bring to work their attitudes, beliefs, and values about both material and spiritual affairs. Even within more formal religious beliefs, historically there has not been a clear distinction between work and nonwork. One does not suspend faith and values on entering the workplace. Personal ethics and values are relevant in nearly all aspects of work: from the very choice of vocation itself to the treatment of colleagues and customers.

MONEY AND HAPPINESS

Does happiness come with being financially well-off? When asked what would improve the quality of our lives, for most people the first answer would be "More money." Yet researchers in the area have showed only a modest correlation between income and happiness. Money and happiness is akin to the issue of materialism and spirituality. Can material goods (e.g., art) increase spiritual experiences? If so, when and how? To many people these are either antithetical or unrelated concepts. There is, however, a relatively recent and often counterintuitive literature on the relationship between money and happiness.

The central issue for researchers is whether increasing personal and national wealth lead to increasing happiness and contentment. Longitudinal data collected over seventy years in the West shows first a linear rise in personal income (such that it doubles every thirty years) but second a flat, horizontal line for self-reported happiness/well-being suggests little or no difference over time (Myers 1992). The results seem to suggest that, at least after a certain point, there is no relationship between personal wealth and happiness.

However, aggregated data such as this may easily obscure important differences between individuals, between organizations, and between countries. At the individual difference level there is considerably accumulating evidence that happiness is related to stable, biologically based personality traits (extraversion and stability). This suggests that happiness is stable over the lifetime in part because people with particular personality profiles seek out and change situations to fit their personality. A more intriguing and salient question is whether there are similar links between personality and spirituality; are certain people more prone to spirituality and others not? This raises the interesting possibility of personality as an intervening or moderating variable. Is it possible that personality is related both to spirituality and happiness and that the observed rela-

260   CONCEPTUALIZING WORKPLACE SPIRITUALITY

tionship between the two is simply epiphenomenal? Also it is possible that people with particular "spirituality-prone" profiles seek out particular work settings (while avoiding others) with other like-minded people and experience strong spirituality there.

Personality and differential psychologists emphasize the important role of traits as causal factors. However organizational and work psychologists are equally happy to focus on work group, company, and organizational differences as possible causes of different levels of both (or either) happiness and spirituality. Organizations differ widely in structure, process, and product as well as culture, mission, and vision. Over the last twenty years organizations were encouraged to focus on the philosophic nature of their business and consider their vision and mission. In many instances these were expressed in almost spiritual terminology. While certain cynics saw these as little more than "advertorials" for the business (Anderson 2000), others saw these as expressing the beliefs and values of many who worked in the business. Further, they had the effect of attracting particular people to the business. For many they came to be seen as an acknowledgment of at least the nonmaterial nature of the business.

Certainly those interested in corporate culture have noted dramatic differences between organizations in what they do, believe, and value (Furnham and Gunter 1993). Because corporate culture is an implicit but powerful force, it can have an effect on the manifestations or suppression of spirituality in the workplace. Some organizations seem happy to acknowledge the spiritual dimension to life while others find it faintly embarrassing.

At the third level—namely cultural/national—there are also interesting differences. Some cultures seem more spiritual than others, though, of course, the spirituality is manifested quite differently. History, geography, language, and religion as well as economic development all have a part to play in the quality and quantity of spirituality in a culture. Countries differ most obviously in their wealth, which has been linked to a national feeling of well-being. However it is never clear in cross-cultural correlational studies whether wealth leads to happiness, vice versa, or the relationship (or lack of it) is moderated by a third variable.

In a review, Diener (1984) summarizes the data thus: "There is an overwhelming amount of evidence that shows a positive relationship between income and SWB (subjective well-being) within countries. . . . This relationship exists even when other variables such as education are controlled. . . . Although the effect of income is often small when other factors are controlled, these other factors may be ones through which income could produce its effects . . ." (571).

There are also consistent national differences in happiness. Inglehart (1990) reported an extensive study with representative samples of 170,000 people in sixteen nations. Results indicated that first, there are genuine national differences. For example, the Danes, Swiss, Irish, and Dutch feel happier and more satisfied with life than do French, Greeks, Italians, and West Germans. Second, the nations' well-being differences correlate modestly with national affluence, but the link between national affluence and well-being is not consistent. In fact there is no clear statistical relationship or trend. For instance, for the French, the average income was almost doubled the Irish, but the Irish were happier.

However, there is more than one fact that makes the nations differ in self-reported happiness. For instance, the most prosperous nations have enjoyed stable democratic governments, and there is a strong link between a history of democracy and national well-being. Moreover, countries that have both democracy and a free press also tend to have happier people. Further, the freedom in choosing type of jobs, the workplace, and one's own lifestyle, which are associated with democracy, may also be the contributors of individual SWB.

From another point of view, within any country are the richest the happiest? Some surveys have shown that here again, there is a modest link between SWB and being financially well-off.

Those who live in affluent countries yet have low incomes, clearly live with less joy and more stress than do those who live with the comfort and security of higher incomes (Easterlin 1995).

In a cross-cultural study, Diener and Suh (1999) surveyed forty-one nations and found that there are substantial differences between nations in reported SBW. People in wealthier nations tend to report greater SWB than people in poor nations. However the causal factors relating wealth to well-being are not yet understood. The wealth of nations strongly correlates with human rights, equality between people, the fulfillment of basic biological needs, and individualism. Another variable that also correlated with higher SWB in nations is political stability and a related variable, interpersonal trust. Unfortunately, because of the high intercorrelations of predictor variables and the relatively small sample sizes of nations, the various potential national factors that cause SWB could not be disentangled. For example, Diener, Diener, and Diener (1995) reported that income correlated with human rights and with the equality within nations .80 and .84, respectively. Besides, individualism is a cultural variable that correlates across nations with both higher reported SWB and higher suicide rates. With sample sizes of nations that rarely exceed forty in number, the effects of such overlapping variables cannot be statistically disentangled and larger samples and longitudinal designs are needed to ascertain the causal influence on SWB of the variables that tend to occur together with the national affluence.

In a longitudinal study, intended to test the most fundamental idea in economics that money makes people happy, Gardner and Oswald (2001) examined approximately 9,000 randomly chosen people. Results showed that those in the panel who receive windfalls (by winning lottery money or receiving an inheritance) have higher mental well-being in the following year. Specifically, a windfall of £50,000 ($75,000) is associated with a rise in well-being of between 0.1 and 0.3 standard deviations.

In another study, Kasser and Sheldon (2000) examined the connection between feelings of insecurity and materialistic behavior by experimentally inducing feelings of insecurity. Results showed that participants exposed to death (by writing short essays about death) became greedier and consumed more resources in a forest-management game. They conclude, ". . . people's tendencies toward materialism and consumption stem in part from a source unlikely to disappear: the fear of death. It remains to be seen whether psychological research can discover effective ways of helping people find more adaptive and beneficial means of coping with their insecurities. . ." (351).

In a review of family and economic well-being, White and Rogers (2000) found that women showed stronger income growth than men in the decade, and two-earner households became increasingly associated with advantage. In particular, they reviewed four dimensions of family outcomes: family formation, divorce, marital quality, and child well-being. The review supports the expectation that both men's and women's economic advantage is associated with more marriage, less divorce, more marital happiness, and greater child well-being.

But having more than enough provides little additional boost to SWB. One plausible reason is that low income is a strong predictor of negative affect but not positive affect. Since positive and negative affect, contrary to common belief, are found to be fairly independent (Bradburn 1969), the scales designed to measure happiness or SWB (normally contain positive affect but not negative affect) do not readily detect the causes (predictors) of negative affect, thus fail to obtain substantial associations between income and SWB. However, as the best predictor of happiness or SWB is the balance of positive and negative affect as Bradburn and many other researchers have indicated, both the causes of positive and negative affect should be examined before a conclusion as to what are the causes of full human functioning can be drawn.

Theoretically speaking, it might be true that human needs can be arranged on different levels, like the famous hierarchy formulated by the founder of humanistic psychology, Abraham Maslow

262   CONCEPTUALIZING WORKPLACE SPIRITUALITY

(1954). It states that human beings have a set of different kinds of needs, which starts at the biological level such as food, water, and air followed by security needs such as shelter, clothes, and basic belongings; next is the love needs (family, children); then the esteem needs (self-esteem and the esteem from others); and finally the highest needs: the needs for self-actualization (self-fulfilling, develop one's potential, etc.). Once the lower level of needs is gratified, a higher one would become more urgent. From this point of view, it is likely that the lower levels of needs such as the biological and security needs are mainly associated with negative affect and mental illness, and the deprivation of these needs would lead to the presence of negative affect and mental distress; whereas the higher levels of needs such as self-actualization and esteem needs are more strongly associated with positive affect and mental health such as happiness or SWB, and satisfying these needs would lead to the presence of positive affect and psychological well-being. No doubt the deprivation of biological needs would cause the extinction of the life of any living being, and the lack of the security needs, such as low income, would lead to various psychological as well as physical dysfunction such as stress-related illness and emotional disorder, which is in line with the previous findings. On the other hand, various studies have shown that self-esteem is one of the most powerful predictors of happiness and SWB. Moreover, the well-established happiness measure, the Oxford Happiness Inventory (Argyle, Martin, and Crossland 1989), which has psychometrically sound properties, contains one principal factor, named satisfaction from achievement (Furnham and Brewin 1990).

The strongest predictors of happiness are found to be personality traits such as stability and extraversion (e.g., Argyle and Lu 1990; Brebner, Donaldson, Kirby, and Ward 1995; Francis 1999; Furnham and Brewin 1990; Furnham and Cheng 1999), agreeableness (Furnham and Cheng 1997), and high self-esteem (Campbell 1981; Campbell, Converse, and Rodgers 1976; Furnham and Cheng 2000; Rosenberg 1965), which account for more than two-thirds of the variance of psychological well-being and mental health.

However, there is much evidence for the moderate association between wealth and happiness (Brickman, Coates, and Janoff-Bulman 1978; Csikszentmihalyi 1999; Eysenck 1990). There are many sound theoretical reasons why this may be so (Furnham and Argyle 1998): these include adaptation level theory (one soon adapts to wealth at any level), social comparison theory (one's comparison group changes, so that one never feels rich), and the marginal declining utility of money. Yet the idea that money brings happiness remains pervasive.

Those interested in spirituality at work are not necessarily antimaterialists (or anticapitalists). However, many would not be surprised by the psychological data that finds no relationship between income and happiness. For many, they already know that it is nonmaterial things like social support, empathy, and integrity at home and work that lead to real and continuing happiness.

It could be that how people actually perceive their money is important to individual happiness. Thus, there may be a spiritual-material dimension with the former or sacred-profane. For the economist money is almost profane: it is not treated irreverently or disregarded but it is commonplace and not special. It has no spiritual significance. However, money can be sacred—it is feared, revered, and worshiped. Belk and Wallendorf (1990) point out that it is the myth, mystery, and ritual associated with the acquisition and use of money that defines its sacredness and spirituality.

For all religions, certain persons, places, things, times, and social groups are collectively defined as sacred and spiritual. Sacred things are extraordinary, totally unique, set apart from, and opposed to, the profane world. Sacred objects and people can have powers of good or evil. "Gifts, vacation travel, souvenirs, family photographs, pets, collections, heirlooms, homes, art, antiques and objects associated with famous people can be regarded as existing in the realm of the sacred by many people" (Belk and Wallendorf 1990, 39). They are safeguarded and considered special and of spiritual value. Art and other collections become for many people sacred personal icons. Equally, heirlooms serve as mystical and fragile connections to those who are deceased. They can have more than "sentimental value" and some believe that a neglected or damaged heirloom could unleash bad luck or evil forces.

Unlike sacred objects, profane objects are interchangeable. They are valued primarily for their mundane use value. Sacred objects often lack functional use and cannot, through exchange, be converted into profane objects. Further, exchange of sacred objects for money violates their sacred status, because it brings them into inappropriate contact with the profane realm.

Money can be too sterile and ordinary to be used on special occasions. In Western societies money cannot buy brides, expiation from crimes, or (ideally) political offices. The Judeo-Christian ethic is paradoxical on money. People with money acquired honestly may be seen as superior, even virtuous, and removing the desire to accumulate money is condemned. Believers are called on to be altruistic, ascetic, and selfless, while simultaneously being hard-working, acquisitional, and, frankly, capitalistic. The sacred and profane can get easily mixed up (Furnham 1995).

Belk and Wallendorf (1990) also believed that the sacred meaning of money is gender and class linked. They argue that women think of money in terms of the things into which it can be converted, while men think of it in terms of the power its possession implies. The money women deal with is profane (unless used for personal pleasure, in which case it is evil), while some of the use of money by men is sacred. Similarly, in working-class homes men traditionally gave over their wages to their wife for the management of profane household needs with a small allowance given back for individual personal pleasures, most of which were far from sacred. Yet in a middle-class house, men typically gave, and indeed sometimes still give, their wife an allowance (being a small part of their income) for collective household expenditure.

Money (an income) obtained from work that is not a source of intrinsic delight is ultimately profane, but an income derived from one's passion can be sacred. An artist can do commercial work for profane money and the work of the soul for sacred money. From ancient Greece to twentieth-century Europe, the business of making money is tainted. It is the activity of the nouveau riche, not honorable "old money." Thus, volunteer work is sacred, while the identical job that is paid is profane. The idea of paying somebody to be a mother or home-keeper may be preposterous for some because it renders the sacred duty profane. But the acts of prostitutes transform a sacred act into a formal business exchange. Some crafts people and artists do sell their services but at a "modest," almost not going-rate, price because their aim is not to accumulate wealth but to make a reasonable income and not become burdened by their work.

Belk (1991) considered the sacred uses of money. A sacred use—for example, a gift—can be "desacralized" if a person is too concerned with price. Sacralizing mechanisms usually involve the purchase of gifts and souvenirs, donations to charity, as well as the purchase of a previously sacralized object. The aim is to transform money into objects with special significance or meaning. Money-as-sacrifice and money-as-gift are clearly more sacred than money-as-commodity. Charity giving is a sacred gift only when it involves personal sacrifice and not when there is personal gain through publicity or tax relief. Money used to redeem and restore special objects (e.g., rare works of art, religious objects) also renders it sacred.

Thus, to retain all money for personal use is considered antisocial, selfish, miserly, and evil. To transform sacred money (a gift) into profane money (by selling it) is considered especially evil. Many people refuse to turn certain objects into money, preferring to give them away. Money violates the sacredness of objects and commodifies them. Equally, people refuse money when offered by those who have been voluntarily helped. The "good Samaritans" thereby assign their assistance to the area of the gift rather than a profane exchange. Thus, a gift of help may be reciprocated by another gift.

The argument is thus: the dominant view of money concentrates on its profane meaning. It is a utilitarian view that sees money transactions as impersonal and devoid of sacred money. But it becomes clear when considering the illogical behavior of collectors, gift-givers, and charity donors that money can and does have sacred meanings, both good and evil. Further, it is these sacred meanings that so powerfully influence our attitudes to money.

ETHICS AT WORK

The idea that religious/spiritual values may be important at work goes back a long way. Perhaps the most well known theory of the effect of spirituality at work is referred to as the Protestant Work Ethic (Furnham 1995). It embodied the idea that work is not merely an economic activity but a spiritual end in, and of, itself.

The Protestant Ethic and the Spirit of Capitalism was published, in German, nearly 100 years ago by Max Weber as a two-part article in the 1904–1905 issue of the journal *Archive für Sozialwissenschaft und Sozialpolitik.* Some fifteen years later it was revised and published as a single volume with rebuttals to criticism of the earlier work. It was the revised edition that was first translated into English by Talcott Parson in 1930.

For Weber the central problem was explaining the fact that people pursue wealth and material gain (the achievement of profit) for its own sake, not because of necessity. The aim of obtaining, accumulating, and storing money/capital is an end in itself, not a means to an end. Weber located the answer to this problem in Puritan asceticism and spirituality and the concept of calling for the individual to fulfill his or her duty in this (rather than the other) world. Weber maintained that Puritans felt obliged to be regarded as chosen by God to perform good works. Success in a calling (occupational rewards) thus came to be seen as a sign of being the elect. Puritans thus sought to achieve salvation through economic activity.

There were four elements in Weber's scheme:

1. "The Doctrine of Calling," according to which the believer is called by God to work for His glory, and hence work itself was virtuous and had to be excellently and honestly done. However, this aspect is least central to Weber's argument and serves merely as an introduction to the PWE concept itself.
2. A second theme was "The Doctrine of Predestination," which suggested that signs of God's grace, such as occupational success, could be seen in this life, and hence successful people could see themselves as among the elect. Because one has only limited time to grasp God and make sure of one's election by attaining that quiet self-confidence of salvation that is the fruit of true faith and of proving one's regeneration in the conduct of one's daily life, then every moment spent in idleness, leisure, gambling, or hedonism is worthy of moral condemnation and is a sign of imperfect grace.
3. Strong asceticism is another crucial cornerstone of the theory that stressed saving, investment, the systematic use of the amassing of capital and the reduction of expenditure on vices and luxuries.
4. Finally, "The Doctrine of Sanctification," which, by rejecting the mystical sacramental system of Catholicism, stressed rational control over all aspects of life. Rationalization was a common theme in Weber's work, and he argued that in Calvinism each individual had to make his or her own moral decisions and that all actions had to be considered in terms of their ethical consequences.

Weber explained the origin of capitalism by arguing that the acquisitive motive was transformed from personal eccentricity into a moral order, which destroyed reliance on traditional forms of economic satisfaction and replaced it with the rational calculus of returns coming from the investment of given amounts of capital and labor.

Hampden-Turner (1981) has attempted to summarize and contrast PWE beliefs and what he calls Anglo-Catholic organicism (see Table 17.1). Relying heavily on the work of Koestler, among others, Hampden-Turner (1981) argued that PWE beliefs have informed scientific epistemology. He notes: "It is my contention that modern doctrines of scientism and behaviorism, so far from having escaped from religion, 'superstition,' and a priori beliefs, are steeped in Calvanistic ideology, having borrowed even its most objectionable characteristic, a devastating lack of self-awareness" (36).

There are relatively few clear statements on the actual constituents of the PWE. Innumerable writers have tried to define or elucidate the components of the PWE. Oates (1971) noted:

> The so-called Protestant Work Ethic can be summarized as follows: a universal taboo is placed on idleness, and industriousness is considered a religious ideal; waste is a vice, and frugality a virtue; complacency and failure are outlawed, and ambition and success are taken as sure signs of God's favour; the universal sign of sin is poverty, and the crowning sign of God's favour is wealth. (84)

Cherrington (1980) listed eight attributes of the PWE. The broader meaning of the work ethic typically refers to one or more of the following beliefs:

1. People have a normal and religious obligation to fill their lives with heavy physical toil. For some, this means that hard work, effort, and drudgery are to be valued for their own sake; physical pleasures and enjoyments are to be shunned; and an ascetic existence of methodical rigor is the only acceptable way to live.
2. Men and women are expected to spend long hours at work, with little or no time for personal recreation and leisure.
3. A worker should have a dependable attendance record, with low absenteeism and tardiness.
4. Workers should be highly productive and produce a large quantity of goods or service.
5. Workers should take pride in their work and do their jobs well.
6. Employees should have feelings of commitment and loyalty to their profession, their company, and their work group.
7. Workers should be achievement-orientated and constantly strive for promotions and advancement. High-status jobs with prestige and the respect of others are important indicators of a "good" person.
8. People should acquire wealth through honest labor and retain it through thrift and wise investments. Frugality is desirable; extravagance and waste should be avoided. (20)

Ditz (1980), in an interesting essay on the PWE and the market economy, has described the PWE idea of profit making as a calling, "the sacramentalization of acquisition." He explains in lay economic terms how the PWE beliefs and spirituality affected the market economy (what Marx called capitalism) over the last few hundred years. Ditz (1980) believed that various features

266   CONCEPTUALIZING WORKPLACE SPIRITUALITY

Table 17.1

Anglo-Catholic Organicism Versus the Protestant Work Ethic

Anglo-Catholic organicism	*Puritan atomistic individualism:*
The person is part of an organic hierarchy, a great chain of being, rooted in kinship, feudal loyalties, neighborhood, animals, and land.	The person is alone, a saintly outcast from corrupt feudalism but can enter holy leagues or covenants with other upright persons.
Communal mediated relationships	*Private direct relationships*
Salvation is in communal faith, with access to God mediated by kings, bishops, judges, and lords.	Salvation is a private matter between God and His agents on earth, who have direct access to His will.
Intercessionist God	*Delegating God*
God is ever-present, interceding in human affairs in miraculous and supernatural ways.	God is distant and delegates His power to chosen human instruments and the laws of nature.
Salvation through communion	*Salvation through work*
Man is saved less by his own efforts than by faith and partaking of the passion, mercy, forgiveness, and indulgence of the crucified God in the family of believers.	God is the taskmaster to His earthly agents, a state of grace they can demonstrate but not alter. Interpersonal emotions are indulgences of a corrupt order.
God experienced with many senses	*The Word read, heard, enacted*
God is experienced as mystery in many dimensions, inritual, community, sacrament, awe, asceticism, and participation, by way of Mary and the saints.	God gives ambiguous instructions to man's reason by way of His objective words. Mystery, magic, and speculation are vain, when compared with active obedience.
Other worldliness	*This worldliness*
In this vale of tears the greatest respect belongs to those who prepare us for the world to come.	God's kingdom will be founded in this world by the saints doing the work to which God calls them.
Human personality cultivated	*Personality submerged in work*
Virtue is personified by self-cultivation, courtliness, wit, charm, and the flamboyant manners of the cavalier.	Virtue is achieved by self-effacement, and becoming the mere agent of God's objective order (e.g., the Roundhead).

would inevitably lead to a decline in the PWE. These included: the waning of religious faith and with it the moral justifications for the market economy; the fact that excessive individualism loosened kinship and ethnic community ties, so leading to a weakening of the overall social structure; the emergence of unionism, monopolies, and other anti-PWE ethics; hedonism replacing asceticism; institutional minimal risk taking replacing individual risk taking; indifference and disrespect for rationality and the "calculating" professions; desacramentalization of property, erosion of property rights, and indifference to crimes of property; taxation and inflation causing a waning of consumer sovereignty; an increase in egalitarianism that inhibits innovation, entrepreneurship, and risk taking.

Debate about the work ethic has continued for a century. The spiritual values of the Puritans, the Protestants, and others have been examined in detail. Indeed it probably represents the best study of spirituality at work.

ALTERNATIVE ETHICS

Scholars, in their attempt to define and delineate the work ethic have suggested the existence of many other ethics, some of which coexisted with the work ethic (Furnham 1995). Maccoby and Terzi (1981) found that the term *PWE* was being used very loosely and actually contained few overlapping ethics including the *Puritan ethic* supporting a highly individualistic character, oriented to self-discipline, saving, and deferred rewards and antagonistic to sensuous culture; the *craft ethic* emphasizing pride in work, self-reliance, independence, modernization, mobility, and thrift; the *entrepreneurial ethic*, which emphasized merchandising not manufacture, the organization and control of craftsmen, growth, and zeal to succeed; and the *career ethic* that emphasizes meritocracy, talent, and hard work within organizations leading to success and promotion.

There are alternatives to the work ethic, each with its own distinctive values and type of emphasis on spirituality. These alternatives have been espoused by different groups at different times, often in reaction to other dominant ethics. The following are briefly described and an attempt is made to be comprehensive, at least from a Western perspective.

We shall consider seven work-related ethics that are all forms of ethics. They have very different ideas about the part of work, money, and spirituality in the workplace.

The Wealth Ethic

Kelvin and Jarrett (1985) dismiss the PWE thesis as a wholly false account of the past (in fact a myth) whose function is more to inspire the present than explain the past. They are adamant that the PWE is an explanatory concept of our time, invented to explain the past. But Kelvin and Jarrett (1985) are not content to dismiss the PWE as a historically incorrect self-fulfilling prophecy. They suggest that what has been incorrectly historically perceived as the work ethic was in fact the wealth ethic.

> When one looks at the situation from the very historical perspective that ostensibly gave rise to it, explanations in terms of the Protestant Ethic emerge as little more than an invention of twentieth-century social science, with unwarranted pretensions to an ancient lineage. The "ethic" which has truly been predominant and pervasive is not a work ethic but, for want of a better term, a wealth ethic. Wealth is (quite correctly) perceived as the basis of economic independence: that is the key issue, and has been so for centuries. The "ethic" is to make or to have sufficient wealth not to have to depend on others; work is only one means to that end, and certainly not the only one universally most esteemed: not in any class. Provided that one has money enough to be independent, there is no great moral obligation to work, certainly not in the sense of gainful, productive employment. (Kelvin and Jarrett 1985, 104)

268   CONCEPTUALIZING WORKPLACE SPIRITUALITY

Work is normative and not an ethic and that moral significance does not attach to work, but to not living off others. In other words, not only are Kelvin and Jarrett (1985) disputing the historical, or indeed current, existence of the PWE, they believe that the essence of the PWE is the accumulation of wealth in order to ensure independence and, to a lesser extent, freedom and leisure. Work is only one, and presumably a moderately unpleasant or at least effortful, way of accumulating wealth.

For Kelvin and Jarrett (1985) all people gain numerous satisfactions from work, as well as money and things that money enables them to have and to do. The wealth ethic adherent then condemns the unemployed not for being idle, but for being poor. Spirituality that derives from this perspective is aimed at acquiring wealth honestly because of its obvious and manifest benefits.

The Welfare Ethic

Furnham and Rose (1987) have argued that the rise of the welfare state, particularly in Western Europe, has seen the emergence of what may be called the welfare ethic. This belief system is based on the idea of a cunning claimant of welfare, who believes that because welfare is so easy to obtain (and to some extent one's right), one should enjoy the good life (without work) by living off payments received from the welfare system. People who do this have become known somewhat pejoratively as "super-scroungers." The "laxness, excessive generosity, inefficiency and vulnerability to exploitation of the welfare system" (Golding and Middleton 1983, 109) makes it open to less-than-honest people. There has been quite a lot of research on attitudes toward social security claimants (Furnham 1985) that, in fact, suggests that many people not on welfare payments believe those who are, are both idle and dishonest. Although there is considerable research to show that this view is misplaced, there is anecdotal evidence of people who thrive on welfare and exploit the welfare ethic.

However, Taylor-Gooby (1983) has pointed out that whereas people are in favor of some aspects of welfare they are against others. More importantly perhaps, Taylor-Gooby (1983) found evidence for various values associated with welfare payments. These include a reduction in self-help; a more integrated, caring society; an increased tax burden; a reduction in the work ethic; and a reduction in the family ethic. Still, spirituality associated with the welfare ethic often stresses interdependence and the necessity of mutual support.

The Leisure Ethic

Many writers have talked about the new leisure ethic that states that "to leisure" is by far the greatest virtue, namely to develop one's potential in discretionary time. Although it is not entirely clear what this new ethic stands for, some empirical work has to be done in this field. Thus Buchholz (1976) attempted to measure what he termed the leisure ethic, which regards work as a means to personal fulfillment through primarily its provision of the means to pursue leisure activities. According to Buchholz (1976), the leisure ethic is defined thus:

> Work has no meaning in itself, but only finds meaning in leisure. Jobs cannot be made meaningful or fulfilling, but work is a human necessity to produce goods and services and enable one to earn the money to buy them. Human fulfillment is found in leisure activities where one has a choice regarding the use of his time, and can find pleasure in pursuing activities of interest to him personally. This is where a person can be creative and involved.

Thus the less hours [time] one can spend working and the more leisure time one has available, the better. (1180)

Studies using the leisure ethic have found it to be related to occupational status (high status people endorse it less than low status), age (leisure ethic beliefs decline with age), and nationality (Americans endorse it more than Scots [Dickson and Buchholz 1977]). The leisure ethic has also been shown to be significantly negatively correlated with general conservative beliefs, the PWE, and measures of job involvement (Furnham 1984a). The leisure ethic may be seen as the positive opposite of the work ethic. People who do not endorse the PWE may or may not endorse the leisure ethic, but it is unlikely that people endorse both the PWE and the leisure ethic. The leisure ethic spirituality emphasizes that it is through leisure rather than work that one recreates, refreshes, and renews oneself. Thus, the more work approaches the idea of leisure, the better.

The Sports Ethic

Ritzer, Kammeyer, and Yelman (1982) have implied that the norms that govern sport are not dissimilar from those of the PWE. Sport is thought of in many countries as an important and healthy socialization experience for young people, and it is assumed that they learn many important lessons.

Sporting norms have "become a conservative force functioning to maintain and reinforce certain of the traditional American values, beliefs and practices while countering others" (Ritzer et al. 1982, 18). These include sportsmanship, competition, success, universalism (open to all and evaluated according to performance), diligence, self-discipline, and teamwork.

However, as it is quite apparent, some of these values are in conflict. Individualism conflicts with teamwork, self-discipline with accepting orders. Nevertheless, the outward portrayal of the sporting ethic, which may be seen in lockers and slogans, in postsuccess sporting speeches, and in sports commentators, is remarkably similar to that of the PWE. No doubt the above are largely the values espoused by sports-oriented organizations.

Some sports stress more of a spiritual component than others. Thus, some sports like mountaineering and orienteering find the former panentheism in nature. Fast, highly competitive sports like squash have little spiritual component though nearly all team sports put strong emphasis on team spirit and cooperation that is often expressed in spiritual terms.

The Narcissistic Ethic

Many commentators on contemporary culture have attempted to discern trends and patterns that trace the waxing and waning of movements, ethics, or cults. Lasch (1985) argued that the dominant current American culture of competitive individualism has changed into the pursuit of happiness and a narcissistic preoccupation with self.

Lasch (1985) argued that PWE values no longer excite enthusiasm or command respect for a variety of reasons: inflation erodes investments/savings; the society is now fearfully, rather than confidently, future-oriented; self-preservation has become self-improvement; moral codes have changed. But this change has been graduated over the centuries. The Puritan gave way to the Yankee, who secularized the PWE and stressed self-improvement (instead of socially useful work) that consisted of the cultivation of reason, wisdom, and insight as well as money. Wealth was valued because it allowed for a program of self-improvement and was one of the necessary preconditions of moral and intellectual advancement. The nineteenth century saw the rise of the "cult

270   CONCEPTUALIZING WORKPLACE SPIRITUALITY

of compulsive industry" that was obsessed with the "art of money-getting," as all values would be expressed or operationalized in money terms. Further, there became more emphasis on competition.

The spirit and spirituality of self-improvement, according to Lasch (1985), was debased into self-culture—the care and training of the mind and body through reading great books and healthy living. Self-help books taught self-confidence, initiative, and other qualities of success. "The management of interpersonal relations came to be seen as the essence of self advancement. . . . Young men were told that they had to sell themselves in order to succeed" (58). The new prophets of positive thinking discarded the moral overtones of Protestantism that were attached to the pursuit of wealth, save that it contributed to the total human good. The pursuit of economic success now accepted the need to exploit and intimidate others and to ostentatiously show the winning image of success.

The new ethic meant that people preferred admiration, envy, and the excitement of celebration, to being respected and esteemed. People were less interested in how people acquired success—defined by riches, fame, and power—than in that they had "made it." Success had to be ratified and verified by publicity. The quest for a good public image leads to a confusion of successful completion of the task with rhetoric that is aimed to impress or persuade others. Thus impressions overshadow achievements and the images and symbols of success are more important than the actual achievements.

For Lasch (1985) the cult or ethic of narcissism has a number of quite distinct features:

- The waning of the sense of historical time. The idea that things are coming to an end means that people have a very limited time perspective, neither confidently forward nor romantically backward. The narcissist lives only in, and for, the present.
- The therapeutic sensibility. Narcissists seek therapy for personal well-being, health and psychic security. The rise in the human potential movement and the decline in self-help tradition has made people dependent on experts and organizations to validate self-esteem and develop competence. Therapists are used excessively to help develop composure, meaning, and health.
- From politics to self-examination. Political theories, issues, and conflicts have been trivialized. The debate has moved from the veridical nature of political propositions to the personal and autobiographical factors that lead proponents to make such suppositions.
- Confession and anti-confession. Writers and others attempt single self-disclosure, rather than critical reflection, to gain insight into the psycho-historical forces that lead to personal development. But these confessions are paradoxical and do not lead to greater, but lesser, insights into the inner life. People disclose not to provide an objective account of reality, but to seduce others to give attention, acclaim, or sympathy and, by doing so, foster the perpetual, faltering sense of self.
- The void within. Without psychological peace, meaning, or commitment, people experience an inner emptiness that they try to avoid by living vicariously through the lives of others, or seeking spiritual masters.
- The progressive critique of privatism. Self-absorption, which dreams of fame, avoidance of failure, and quests for spiritual panacea means that people define social problems as personal ones. The cult suggests a limited investment in life and friendship, avoidance of dependence, and living for the moment.

In fact it could be argued that current interest in spirituality is a direct reaction to the self-obsessed, narcissistic ethic.

The Romantic Ethic

Campbell (1987) proposed that a cultural, anti-Puritan force—the romantic ethic—was responsible for the rise of the modern consumer ethic. He attempted to identify an autonomous, imaginative, pleasure-seeking force—the romantic ethic—which created and justified consumer hedonism at the onset of the Industrial Revolution. He argued that one should distinguish between traditional and modern hedonism—the former concerned with sensory experience and discrete, standardized pleasures while the latter is envisaged as a potential quality in all experience.

Campbell (1987) attempted to explain the high growth of consumerism in the middle classes, supposedly ascetic, puritanical bearers of the PWE. He argued that, after the seventeenth century, Calvinist Christianity changed to allow emotional sentimentalism. Concern with aesthetics was inherited from the aristocratic ethic, and taste became a sign of moral and spiritual worth. Taste allowed people to take genuine pleasure in the beautiful and respond with tears to the pitiable. In this romantic movement pleasure becomes the crucial means of recognizing that ideal truth and beauty that imagination reveals and that become the means by which art encourages moral enlightenment. The romantics assured that people could be morally improved through the provision of cultural products that yielded pleasure and that helped people dream about a more perfect world.

It is also suggested that both individuals and society have a compatible "purito"-romantic personality system when the values of puritan-utilitarianism and romantic sentimentalism occur compatibly, but are conveniently compartmentalized in time and space, allowing both to exist. He quotes evidence as wide-ranging as Victorian sentimentalism and utilitarianism, as well as lifestyle of the bourgeois individual that passes from youthful romanticism to adult bureaucracy. It is further suggested that Puritanism is primarily socialized into males and romanticism into females; hence the stress on science for males, arts for females.

The Being Ethic

Many religious and philosophic systems have distinguished between two strong opposing beliefs or "ways of existence." First there is the having model of modern industrialist societies, which concentrates on material possession and power. The second is the being model of many postmodern groups, which puts greater stress on shared experience and the affirmation of living. There are many ways to contrast these two approaches: acquisitiveness versus existence, pleasure versus joy.

Fromm (1980) argued persuasively for the being model. This may be best illustrated in his description of "the new man," which is in a sense a blueprint for the being model. This model is summarized in Table 17.2.

Though he recognized the theme in many other Western and Eastern writers, Fromm (1980) has exposed this new ethic of being. The argument is predicated on the assumption that the materialistic way of having has failed. Economic and technical progress that at any rate has remained restricted to richer nations is not conducive to well-being. This ethic is based on two erroneous principles: that the aim of life is to maximize pleasure and happiness; and that egoism, selfishness, and greed lead to harmony and peace. Though rather crudely stated, these two assumptions of the way of having are thought to have the seeds of destruction within them.

Thus one needs a new ethic—that of being. Whereas the having mode is characterized by possessing and owning, for which the dictum is I am equal to what I have and what I consume, the being mode is characterized not by greed, envy, and aggressiveness but love, joy, and ascendancy

Table 17.2

The New Man and the Philosophy of Being According to Fromm

1. Willingness to give up all forms of having, in order to fully be.

2. Security, sense of identity, and confidence based on faith in what one is, on one's need for relatedness, interest, love, solidarity with the world around one, instead of on one's desire to have, to possess, to control the world, and thus become the slave of one's possessions.

3. Acceptance of the fact that nobody and nothing outside oneself give meaning to life, but that this radical independence and no-thingness can become the condition for the fullest activity devoted to caring and sharing.

4. Being fully present where one is.

5. Joy that comes from giving and sharing, not from hoarding and exploiting.

6. Love and respect for life in all its manifestations, in the knowledge that not things, power, all that is dead, but life and everything that pertains to its growth are sacred.

7. Trying to reduce greed, hate, and illusions as much as one is capable.

8. Living without worshipping idols and without illusions, because one has reached a state that does not require illusions.

9. Developing one's capacity for love, together with one's capacity for critical, unsentimental thought.

10. Shedding one's narcissism and accepting the tragic limitations inherent in human existence.

11. Making the full growth of oneself and of one's fellow beings the supreme goal of living.

12. Knowing that to reach this goal, discipline and respect for reality are necessary. Knowing also, that no growth is healthy that does not occur in a structure, but knowing, too, the difference between structure as an attribute of life and "order" as an attribute of no-life, of the dead.

13. Developing one's imagination, not as an escape from intolerable circumstances but as the anticipation of real possibilities, as a means to do away with intolerable circumstances.

14. Not deceiving others, but also not being deceived by others; one may be called innocent, not naïve.

15. Knowing oneself, not only the self one knows, but also the self one does not know—even though one has a slumbering knowledge of what one does not know.

16. Sensing one's oneness with all life, hence giving up the aim of conquering nature, subduing it, exploiting it, raping it, destroying it, but trying, rather, to understand and cooperate with nature.

17. Freedom that is not arbitrariness but the possibility to be oneself, not as a bundle of greedy desires, but as a delicately balanced structure that at any moment is confronted with the alternative of growth or decay, life or death.

18. Knowing that evil and destructiveness are necessary consequences of failure to grow.

19. Knowing that only a few have reached perfection in all these qualities, but being without the ambition to "reach the goal," in the knowledge that such ambition is only another form of greed, of having.

20. Happiness, in the process of ever-growing aliveness, whatever the further point is that fate permits one to reach, for living as fully as one can is so satisfactory that the concern for what one might or might not attain has little chance to develop.

Source: Fromm 1980.

over our material values. Perhaps because it is difficult to elucidate the concept of having—which is rejected and described in straw-man terms—it is described in detail and it is for the reader to infer that the opposite is desirable.

Fromm (1980) reports a change in the PWE character described as authoritarian, obsessive, and hoarding, to what he calls a marketing character. This character type is based on experiencing oneself as a commodity and one's value as exchange value.

Success depends largely on how they get their "personality" across, how nice a "package" they are; whether they are "cheerful," "sound," "aggressive," "reliable," "ambitious"; further-more, what their family background is, what clubs they belong to, and whether they know the "right" people. The type of personality required depends to some degree on the special field in which a person may choose to work. A stockbroker, a salesperson, a secretary, a railroad execu-tive, a college professor, or a hotel manager each offers a much different kind of personality that, regardless of their differences, must fulfill one condition: to be in demand. What shapes one's attitudes toward oneself is the fact that skill and equipment for performing a given task are not sufficient; one must win in competition with many others in order to have success. But since success depends largely on how one sells one's personality, one experiences oneself as a com-modity or, rather, simultaneously as the seller and the commodity to be sold. A person is not concerned with his or her life and happiness, but with becoming saleable.

Fromm (1980) goes on to describe the new type, occasionally loosely distinguishing his contempt for it, and indeed its connection with the PWE. This new ethic of being is spelled out in a number of points such as: Security, sense of identity, and confidence based on faith in what one is, in one's need for relatedness, interest, love, solidarity with the world around one instead of one's desire to have, to possess, to control the world, and thus become a slave of one's possessions.

This new ethic of being is in accordance with many other spiritual and religious teachings. It is pantheistic, amaterialist, and humanist. Directly opposed to PWE values on some accounts, it is tangential at others. Certainly there is nothing new in this ethic and it is uncertain how widely it is held.

CONCLUSION

Table 17.3 shows the emphases of the different ethics.

In this chapter it has been suggested that there are many different spiritual beliefs in the work-place. There is, in a sense, nothing new about the idea of workplace spirituality as beliefs about and experiences at work, leisure, and money are all integrated and certainly set out specifically in all of the world's major religions as well as ethical systems. Special attention was paid to the topic of money in the workplace and the curious lack of relationship between money and happiness in aggregated figures. It was suggested that money carries different meanings for different individu-als and that if this is taken into consideration, maybe the relationship would become clearer. It was suggested one could distinguish between the spiritual/sacred and materialistic/profane atti-tude to money, possessions. and work. However, almost no empirical work has been done in this area.

To some extent spirituality stands in contrast to materialism. However, it must be acknowl-edged that there may be various (superficially) different forms of both spirituality and material-ism. To be anti- or amaterialist, however, does not necessarily imply the presence of a spiritual approach. The two phenomena may be unrelated one to another.

In a related vein, the study of business ethics shows that there are contrasting positions to

Table 17.3

Comparing the Eight Ethics and Their Emphasis on Seven Factors

Ethic		Emphasis on					
	Work	Success	Development	Money	Happiness	Spirituality	Competitiveness
Work	++	+++	+	++		+	++
Wealth	-	++		+++			+++
Welfare	--			+	+		
Leisure					+	+	
Sports	++	+++	++	++	++		-
Narcissistic		+++	+++	+	+++		+++
Romantic		+	++		+++	++	+
Being	+		+++		+++	++	--

Scale: +++ ++ + strong positive emphasis; - - - - - strong negative emphasis.

recommendations of how one should behave at work. There is no agreed standard. Indeed if one looks at the work ethic it is clear there are many alternative ethics as proposed and followed by different groups. Some of these ethics are clearly spiritual (e.g., the being ethic) while others are not (e.g., the wealth ethic). Each represents a way of understanding the role of work in one's life and the most appropriate conduct in the workplace. These alternative ethics may be related: thus, there is an overlap between the wealth and narcissistic ethic and between the welfare and leisure ethic, though each is conceptually distinct. Some would see the role of spirituality at work much more clearly than others, particularly whose who endorse the romantic and being ethic.

REFERENCES

Anderson, D. (2000). *Good Companies Don't Have Missions.* London: Social Affairs Unit.

Argyle, M. (1987). *The Psychology of Happiness.* London: Routledge.

Argyle, M., and L. Lu. (1990). "The Happiness of Extraverts." *Personality and Individual Differences* 11: 1011–1017.

Argyle, M.; M. Martin; and J. Crossland. (1989). "Happiness As a Function of Personality and Social Encounters." In *Recent Advances in Social Psychology: An International Perspective*, ed. J.P. Forgas, and J.M. Innes. North Holland: Elsevier.

Belk, R. (1991). "The Ineluctable Mysteries of Possessions." *Journal of Social Behavior and Personality* 6: 17–55.

Belk, R., and M. Wallendorf. (1990). "The Sacred Meaning of Money." *Journal of Economic Psychology* 11: 35–67.

Bradburn, N.M. (1969). *The Structure of Psychological Well-being.* Chicago: Aldine.

Brebner, J., J. Donaldson, N. Kirby, and L. Ward. (1995). "Relationships Between Personality and Happiness." *Personality and Individual Differences* 19: 251–258.

Brickman, P.; D. Coates; and R. Janoff-Bulman. (1978). "Lottery Winners and Accident Victims: Is Happiness Relative?" *Journal of Personality and Social Psychology* 36: 917–927.

Buchholz, R. (1976). "Measurement of Beliefs." *Human Relations* 29: 1177–1198.

Campbell, A. (1981). *The Sense of Well-being in America: Recent Patterns and Trends.* New York: McGraw-Hill.

Campbell, A.; P.E. Converse; and W.L. Rodgers. (1976). *The Quality of American Life.* New York: Sage.

Campbell, C. (1987). "The Romantic Ethic and the Spirit of Modern Consumerism." Oxford: Blackwell.

Cherrington, D. (1980). *The Work Ethic: Working Values and Values That Work.* New York: AMACOM.

Csikszentmihalyi, M. (1999). "If We Are So Rich, Why Aren't We Happy?" *American Psychologist* 54: 821–827.

Dickson, J., and R. Buchholz. (1977). "Differences in Beliefs About Work Between Managers and Blue-Collar Workers." *Journal of Management Studies* 16: 235–251.

Diener, E. (1984). "Subjective Well-being." *Psychological Bulletin* 95: 542–575.

Diener, E., and E.M. Suh. (1999). "National Differences in Subjective Well-Being." In *Well-Being: The Foundations of Hedonic Psychology*, ed. D. Kahneman and E. Diener. New York: Russell Sage Foundation, 434–450.

Diener, E.; M. Diener; and C. Diener. (1995). "Factors Predicting the Subjective Well-being of Nations." *Journal of Personality and Social Psychology* 69: 851–864.

Ditz, G. (1980). "The Protestant Ethic and the Market Economy." *Kyklos* 33: 623–657.

Easterlin, R.A. (1995). "Will Raising the Incomes of All Increase the Happiness of All?" *Journal of Economic Behavior and Organization* 27: 35–47.

Emmons, R. (2000). "Spirituality and Intelligence: Problems and Prospects." *International Journal for the Psychology of Religion* 10: 57–64.

Eysenck, M. (1990). *Happiness, Facts and Myths.* London: Erlbaum.

Francis, L. (1999). "Happiness Is a Thing Called Stable Extraversion." *Personality and Individual Differences* 26: 5–11.

Fromm, E. (1980). *To Have or to Be.* London: Abacus.

Furnham, A. (1984a). "The Protestant Work Ethic, Voting Behaviour, and Attitudes to the Trade Unions." *Political Studies* 32: 420–436.

———. (1984b). "Many Sides of the Coin: The Psychology of Money Usage." _Personality and Individual Differences_ 5: 501–509.

———. (1985). "The Determinants of Attitudes Towards Social Security Benefits." _British Journal of Social Psychology_ 25: 19–27.

———. (1995). _The Protestant Work Ethic._ London: Routledge.

Furnham, A., and M. Argyle. (1998). _The Psychology of Money._ London: Routledge.

Furnham, A., and C. Brewin. (1990). "Personality and Happiness." _Personality and Individual Differences_ 11: 1093–1096.

Furnham, A., and H. Cheng. (1997). "Personality and Happiness." _Psychological Reports_ 80: 761–762.

———. (1999). "Personality As Predictors of Mental Health and Happiness in the East and West." _Personality and Individual Differences_ 27: 395–403.

———. (2000). "Lay Theories of Happiness." _Journal of Happiness Studies_ 1: 227–246.

Furnham, A., and B. Gunter. (1993). _Corporate Assessment: Auditing a Company's Personality._ London: Routledge.

Furnham, A., and M. Rose. (1987). "Alternative Ethics: The Relationship Between the Wealth, Work and Leisure Ethic." _Human Relations_ 40: 561–574.

Gardner, H. (1999). _Intelligence Reframed._ New York: Basic Books.

Gardner, J., and A. Oswald. (2001). "Does Money Buy Happiness? A Longitudinal Study Using Data on Windfalls." Unpublished manuscript, University of Warwick, UK.

Golding, P., and S. Middleton. (1983). _Images of Welfare._ Oxford: Martin Robertson.

Hampden-Turner, C. (1981). _Maps of the Mind._ New York: Collier Books.

Inglehart, R. (1990). _Culture Shift in Advanced Industrial Society._ Princeton, NJ: Princeton University Press.

Kasser, T., and K.M. Sheldon. (2000). "Materialism, Mortality Salience, and Consumption Behaviour." _Psychological Science_ 11: 348–351.

Kelvin, P., and J. Jarrett. (1985). _Unemployment: Its Social Psychological Effects._ Cambridge: Cambridge University Press.

Lasch, C. (1985). _The Culture of Narcissism._ Glasgow: Collins.

Maccoby, M., and R. Terzi. (1981). "What Happened to the Work Ethic?" In _The Work Ethic in Business_, ed. W. Hoffman and T. Wyly. Cambridge, MA: Oelgeschlager, Gunn & Hain.

Maslow, A.H. (1954). _Motivation and Personality._ New York: Harper and Row.

Mayer, J. (2000). "Spiritual Intelligence or Spiritual Consciousness." _International Journal for the Psychology of Religion_ 10: 47–56.

Myers, D. (1992). _The Pursuit of Happiness._ New York: Avon Books.

Oates, W. (1971). _Confessions of a Workaholic: The Facts About Work Addiction._ New York: World Publishing.

Ritzer, G.; C. Kammeyer; and N. Yelman. (1982). _Sociology: Experiencing a Changing Society._ Boston: Allyn and Bacon.

Rosenberg, M. (1965). _Society and the Adolescent Self-image._ Princeton, NJ: Princeton University Press.

Taylor-Gooby, P. (1983). "Legitimation Deficit, Public Opinion and the Welfare State." _Sociology_ 17: 165–184.

White, L., and S.J. Rogers. (2000). "Economic Circumstances and Family Outcomes: A Review of the 1990s." _Journal of Marriage and the Family_ 62: 1035–1151.

[33]

Leadership in Turbulent Times Is Spiritual

Margaret J. Wheatley

As our world grows more chaotic and unpredictable, leaders are asked questions for which their professional training did not prepare them.

> *How do I plan when I don't know what will happen next?*
> *How do I maintain my values when worldly temptations abound?*
> *Do I have a purpose to my life?*
> *Where can I find meaning in my life?*
> *Where can I find the courage and faith to stay the course?*

Humans have sought answers to these questions for as long as we've been around. It is a fundamental human characteristic to look at the circumstances of one's life and ask, "Why?" No matter how poor or desperate we are, we always need to assign a reason to *why* things are as they are. Every culture has its rituals and spiritual practices to answer this fundamental quest.

As our age has become more chaotic and complex, we've turned for answers to the contemporary god worshipped by Western culture, science. We've asked science to explain how to deal with chaos, catastrophes, and life's unpredictability. We want science to teach us how to prevent the sudden events that suddenly destroy lives and futures. We want science not just to explain chaos but to give us tools for controlling it. We want science to stop us from aging and dying and to get us out of all life's challenges.

But of course, this god of science can only fail us. Chaos can't be controlled; the unpredictable can't be predicted. Instead, we are being called to encounter life as it is: uncontrollable, unpredictable, messy, surprising, erratic. One of my own spiritual teachers commented, "The reason we don't like life is that it behaves like life."

I know that leaders today are faced with enormous challenges, most of them not of their own doing. As times grow more chaotic, as people question the meaning (and meaninglessness) of this life, people are clamoring for their leaders to save and rescue them. Historically, people often given away their freedom and allow dictatorship when confronted with uncertainty. People press their leaders to do anything to end the uncertainty, to make things better, to create stability. Even leaders who would never want to become dictators, those devoted to servant leadership, walk into this trap. They want to help, so they exert more control over the disorder. They try to create safety, to insulate people from the realities of change. They try to give answers to dilemmas that have no answers. No leader can achieve this, and it drains energy out of those who try.

Leadership through command and control is doomed to fail. No one can create sufficient stability and equilibrium for people to feel secure and safe. Instead, as leaders we must help people move into a relationship with uncertainty and chaos. Spiritual teachers have been doing this for millennia. Therefore, I believe that the times have led leaders to a spiritual threshold. We must enter the domain of spiritual traditions if we are to succeed as good leaders in these difficult times.

Why Leadership Is Spiritual Work

I believe that several principles describe the essential work for leaders in this era. I label this as "spiritual" work because each principle has been the focus of spiritual inquiry for centuries; these perspectives are found in nearly all spiritual traditions. It is in these traditions that we can find our answers.

Life Is Uncertain

How can we understand that change is just the way it is? In Buddhist thought, the source of true happiness comes from understanding this fact. Instead of holding on to any one thing or form, we expect that it will change. Good things, bad things—they come and go in this ever-changing world we live in. With this perspective it's easier to move on rather than cling desperately to old practices. But generally, we cling to what feels familiar until it no longer works for us. As a leader, it doesn't help to get angry when people cling to old ways. It's much more helpful to encourage people to reflect on their personal life experiences, to notice that they've changed many times in their life. People do know how to change. They also may notice that, at those times when they've let go and surrendered to uncertainty, they haven't died.

Life never stops teaching us about change. As leaders, hopefully we can be patient guides and coaches so that people discover their own experience with life's true nature.

Life Is Cyclical
Poet David Whyte has noted, "If you think life is always improving, you're going to miss half of it." Life is cyclical—we pass through different moods; we live through seasons; we have times of rich harvests and times of bleak winter. Life uses cycles to create newness. We move from the old to the new only if we let go.

Instead of fleeing from the fearful place of chaos or trying to rescue people from it, leaders can help people stay with the chaos, help them walk through it together, and look for the new insights and capacities that always emerge.

In Christian traditions, times of chaos have been called "dark nights of the soul." In our present culture, we call these "clinical depressions." I prefer the spiritual framing. In the dark night, we feel devoid of meaning, totally alone, abandoned by God. (Christian mystics believe that God consciously gives us these dark nights.) These dark times are the conditions for rebirth, for a new and stronger self to emerge. You probably have walked through many dark nights, and I encourage you to think how you changed, what new capacities you possessed when you emerged back into the light.

Meaning Is What Motivates People

Nothing motivates us humans more than meaning. I've seen many disillusioned and depressed staff groups develop high levels of energy and insight when they were asked to think about the meaning of their work. Consultant Kathy Danne-miller always asked groups to think about how the world would change because of the work they were doing. In such brutal times as these, when good work gets destroyed by events and decisions far beyond our influence, when we're so overwhelmed with tasks that we have no time to reflect, it is very important that the leader create time for people to remember *why* they're doing this work. What were we hoping to accomplish when we started this? Who are we serving by doing this work?

I have always been astonished by the deep meaning people ascribe to their work. Most people want their work to serve a greater good, to help other people. It doesn't matter what the work is; we'd rather be doing it in service to other people. In certain professions, such as health care, education, and non-profits, or whenever we feel "called" to our work, it is easier to remember the meaning of it. But we seldom have time to pause for a moment and remember the initial idealism and desire to serve that led us into our profession. However, our energy and rededication are only found there, in our ideals.

Service Brings Us Joy

Over the years, I've interviewed people who participated in disaster relief. I've always been astonished to notice that no matter how tragic and terrible the disaster, they always spoke of that experience with joy. They've led me to realize that there is nothing equal to helping other people. In service, we discover profound happiness. We all witnessed this in the days after September 11. As one survivor stated: "We didn't save ourselves. We tried to save each other."

The joy and meaning of service is found in every spiritual tradition. It has been expressed very simply in an ancient Buddhist teaching. "All happiness in the world comes from serving others; all sorrow in the world comes from acting selfishly."

Courage Comes from Our Hearts

Where do we find the courage to be leaders today? The etymology of the word *courage* gives the answer. *Courage* comes from the old French word for heart, *coeur*. When we are deeply affected, when our hearts respond to an issue or person, courage pours out from our open hearts. Please note that *courage* does not come from the root word for *analysis* or for *strategic planning*. We have to be engaged at the heart level in order to be courageous champions. As much as we may fear emotions at work, leaders need to be willing to let their hearts open and to tell stories that open other people's hearts.

We Are Interconnected with All Life

Every spiritual tradition speaks about oneness. So does new science. As leaders, we act on this truth when we're willing to notice how a decision might affect others, when we try and think systemically, when we're willing to look down the road and notice how, at this moment, we might be affecting future generations. Any act that takes us past the immediate moment, and past our self-protective ways, acknowledges that there's more to life than just us.

I learned a wonderfully simple way to think about our actions from a woman minister. She told how any time she makes a decision, she asks herself, "Is this decision going to bring people together? Will it weave a stronger web? Or will it create further disintegration and separation?" I like to ask another question as well: "In what I am about to do, am I turning toward others or turning away? Am I moving closer, or am I retreating from them?"

We Can Rely on Human Goodness

This is the first value of The Berkana Institute, the leadership foundation I cofounded in 1992. As Berkana does its work in the world, we rely on the great generosity and caring of humans. We know that there's more than enough human badness in the world, but the prevalence of badness only pushes us to rely even more on human goodness.

In your own leadership, what qualities of people do you rely on? I believe in these dark times that we can rely only on the hope, resiliency, and love that is found in the human spirit. Many people through history have suffered terribly, and many continue to suffer right now. Those we remember and admire— Helen Keller, Nelson Mandela, Ann Frank, war veterans, Holocaust survivors, genocide victims, cancer survivors—demonstrate what is best about us. We love to hear their stories because they illuminate what is good about being human. Vaclev Havel, the president of the Czech Republic, says that hope is not a result of the condition of our lives. It is fundamental to being human. (The state motto of South Carolina is similar: "If I breathe, I hope.")

We Need Peace of Mind

All spiritual traditions teach us ways to find peace of mind and acceptance. In the research on mind–body health, cultivating peace is a prerequisite for health. And who do we like to be around? Do we seek out angry or peaceful people? Do we find relief in noise or in quiet? As leaders, we need to find ways to help people work from a place of inner peace, even in the midst of turmoil. Frantic activity and fear only take us deeper into chaos. I've observed the power of starting a meeting with two minutes of silent contemplation. Or, when the meeting gets heated, of asking people to stop talking and just be silent for a minute. It's amazing how differently people come back into the fray if we've had those moments to pause.

Few of us want to work as frantically as we do; most of us hate meetings where tempers boil over. Brief moments of quiet can work wonders—silence is truly the pause that refreshes. Educator Parker Palmer tells of his initial discomfort at working in a Quaker organization, where they observed five minutes of contemplative silence before the start of every meeting. At one meeting, when there was a particularly contentious issue on the agenda, he was relieved to hear the leader announce that because of this serious issue, today they would not spend the first five minutes in silence. But then, to his dismay, he heard her announce, "Instead, we'll be silent for twenty minutes."

Attending to Your Personal Spiritual Health

I'd like to offer a few simple practices that I have found to be essential to maintain a sense of focus and peace as a leader.

Start the Day Off Peacefully

I've raised a large family, so I laugh as I state this. But I've learned that I can't expect to find peace at work. However peaceful I am as I leave my home, that's probably my peak peaceful experience of the day. So I have a strong motivation to find peace before I begin work. There are many ways to cultivate peace at the start of your day. You can drive to work in silence or listen to a particularly soothing piece of music. You can reflect on a spiritual phrase or parable. You can take a few minutes to just sit, either meditating or focusing on a lovely object. You can look for something beautiful outside your window. As your day grows crazier, it helps to know what peace feels like. Sometimes you can even recall that feeling in the midst of very great turmoil.

Learn to Be Mindful

Anytime you can keep yourself from instantly reacting, anytime you can pause for just a second, you are practicing mindfulness. Instead of letting your reactions and thoughts lead you, you step back and realize you can choose your reaction. Instead of being angry, you hesitate for a moment and realize you have other responses available. Instead of saying something hurtful, you pause and give yourself more options.

Slow Things Down

If you can't slow down a group or meeting, you can at least slow down yourself. I've learned to notice how I'm sitting. If I find myself leaning forward, moving aggressively into the discussion or argument, I force myself to sit back in the chair, even for just a moment. If I find my temper rising, I slow down and take just one deep breath. These are small things, but they yield big results.

Create Personal Measures

We all would prefer to be better people. We don't like to be angry or fearful or to be creating more problems for other people. But how can we know that we're succeeding in becoming people we respect? What are our personal measures? Some people create a measure such as telling fewer lies, or speaking the truth to people more often. Some notice when they are more patient or angry less often. I also use the question of "Am I turning toward or away?" as a personal measure of good behavior.

Expect Surprise

We're old enough now to know that life will keep interrupting our plans and surprising us at every turn of the way. It helps to notice this wisdom that we've been forced to acquire. Surprise is less traumatic once we accept it as a fact of life.

Practice Gratefulness

Most of us have been taught this, but how often do you take time, daily, to count your blessings? The wonder of this process is that as we take this daily inventory, we grow in gratefulness. We start to notice more and more—

people who helped us, grace that appeared, little miracles that saved us from danger. The daily practice of gratefulness truly changes us in wonderful ways. When you develop the practice of expressing your gratefulness to colleagues, your relationships improve dramatically.

I believe that, because you are human, you've already experienced the powers, fears, and joys that I've described. It is more important to access your own wisdom than to seek advice from anyone else. Life is a consistent teacher. It always teaches the same lessons. Change is just the way it is. Peace is not dependent on circumstances. We are motivated by meaning. We want to express our love through service. And when we believe that, as leaders, we are playing our part in something more purposeful than our small egos can ever explain, we become leaders who are peaceful, courageous, and wise.

Name Index